The New Imperial Histories Reader

In recent years, imperial history has experienced a newfound vigour, dynamism and diversity. There has been an explosion of new work in the field, which has been driven into even greater prominence by contemporary world events. However, this resurgence has brought with it disputes between those who are labelled as exponents of a 'new imperial history' and those who can, by default, be termed old imperial historians.

This collection not only gathers together some of the most important, influential and controversial work which has come to be labelled 'new imperial history', but also presents key examples of innovative recent writing across the broader fields of imperial and colonial studies. Stephen Howe's Introduction suggests a new view of the state of the subject and its possible future directions. The first group of articles seeks to 'explain' the new imperial history and examine some of the key intellectual battles in the area. The chapters which follow explore some of the major themes that have been influential in new imperial history, including ecology, the body, feminism, sexuality and religion, and influences from other disciplines, such as psychology and anthropology.

The collection includes the work of George Balandier, Antoinette Burton, Dipesh Chakrabarty, Frederick Cooper, Nicholas Dirks, Richard Gott, Bernard Cohn, Ashis Nandy, Alan Lester, Carl Bridge and Kent Fedorowich, Philip S. Zachernuk, Ann Laura Stoler, Kathleen Wilson, Richard H. Grove, Nancy J. Jacobs, Tony Ballantyne, Jonathon Glassman, Jonathan Hyslop, John M. MacKenzie, Wendy Webster, Andrew S. Thompson, Paul Gilroy, Bill Schwarz, Joan Dayan, Deborah A. Thomas, E.S. Atieno Odhiambo, Selim Deringil, Laurent Dubois, Anthony Pagden and Partha Chatterjee.

This book is the perfect companion for any student interested in empires and global history.

Stephen Howe is Professor of the History and Cultures of Colonialism at the University of Bristol. His previous books include *Afrocentrism* (1998) and *Empire: A Very Short Introduction* (2002). He is also co-editor of the *Journal of Imperial and Commonwealth History*.

Routledge Readers in History

The New
Imperial Histories
Reader

Edited by

Stephen Howe

Routledge
Taylor & Francis Group

LONDON AND NEW YORK

First published 2010 by Routledge
2 Park Square, Milton Park, Abingdon, Oxon OX14 4RN

Simultaneously published in the USA and Canada
by Routledge
270 Madison Ave, New York NY 10016

Routledge is an imprint of the Taylor & Francis Group, an informa business

Typeset in Perpetua and Bell Gothic by
Florence Production Ltd, Stoodleigh, Devon
Printed and bound in Great Britain by
TJ International, Padstow, Cornwall

British Library Cataloguing in Publication Data
A catalogue record for this book is available from the British Library

Library of Congress Cataloging in Publication Data
   New imperial histories reader/edited by Stephen Howe
      p. cm.
      "Simultaneously published in the USA and Canada"—T.p. verso
      Includes bibliographical references
   1. Imperialism – History.   2. Colonies – History.   3. Postcolonialism –
   History.   4. Europe – Colonies – History.   5. History, Modern.
   I. Howe, Stephen, 1958–.
   JV105.N49 2009
   325'.309–dc22   2009016791

ISBN10: 0–415–42457–7 (hbk)
ISBN10: 0–415–42458–5 (pbk)

ISBN13: 978–0–415–42457–8 (hbk)
ISBN13: 978–0–415–42458–5 (pbk)

Contents

Acknowledgements

We are grateful to all of those who have granted us permission to reproduce the extracts listed below. While every effort has been made to trace and acknowledge ownership of copyright material used in this volume, the publishers will be glad to make suitable arrangements with any copyright holders whom it has not been possible to contact.

1 George Balandier, 'The Colonial Situation: A Theoretical Approach' in *Social Change and the Colonial Situation*, ed. I. Wallerstein, © 1951 Presses Universitaires de France. Reproduced with permission of John Wiley & Sons, Inc.

2 Antoinette Burton, 'Rules of Thumb: British History and "Imperial Culture" in Nineteenth- and Twentieth-century Britain' *Women's History Review* 3,4 (1994). Reproduced by kind permission of the author and Taylor & Francis (http://tandf.co.uk/journals).

3 Dipesh Chakrabarty, 'Provincializing Europe: Postcoloniality and the Critique of History' *Cultural Studies* 6,3, 1992. Reproduced by kind permission of the author and Taylor & Francis (http://tandf.co.uk/journals).

4 Frederick Cooper, 'Postcolonial Studies and the Study of History' in *Postcolonial Studies and Beyond* (Ania Loomba *et al.* eds), pp.401–22. Copyright, 2005, Duke University Press. All rights reserved. Used by permission of the publisher.

5 'Coda: The Burden of the Past', Dirks, Nicholas B. *Castes of Mind: Colonialism and the Making of Modern India*. © 2001 Princeton University Press. Reprinted by permission of Princeton University Press.

6 Richard Gott, 'Shoot Them to Be Sure'. This article first appeared in *The London Review of Books* 25 April 2002. www.lrb.co.uk. Reproduced by permission of *The London Review of Books*.

7 Cohn, Bernard, *Colonialism and Its Forms of Knowledge. The British in India.* © 1996 Princeton University Press. Reprinted by permission of Princeton University Press.

8 Ashis Nandy, *The Intimate Enemy: Loss and Recovery of Self Under Colonialism* (Delhi, 1983) – from Part 1: The Psychology of Colonialism: Sex, Age and Ideology in British India. Reproduced by permission of Oxford University Press India, New Delhi.

9 Extracts from the 'Introduction' and 'Concluding Remarks' from *Imperial Networks: Creating Identities in Nineteenth-century South Africa and Britain*, Alan Lester, Copyright © 2001 Alan Lester. Reproduced by permission of the author and Taylor & Francis Books UK.

10 Carl Bridge and Kent Fedorowich, 'Mapping the British World' from Bridge and Fedorowich eds. *The British World: Diaspora, Culture and Identity* (London, 2003). Reproduced by permission of Taylor & Francis Books UK.

11 Philip S. Zachernuk *Colonial Subjects: An African intelligentsia and Atlantic Ideas*, pp.28–46. © 2000. University of Virginia Press. Reproduced with permission.

12 *Carnal Knowledge and Imperial Power: Race and the Intimate in Colonial Rule* (paper) by Ann Laura Stoler. Copyright 2002 Regents of the University of California. Published by the University of California Press. Reproduced by kind permission of the author and publisher.

13 Kathleen Wilson, 'Thinking Back: Gender Misrecognition and Polynesian Subversions Aboard the Cook Voyages' from K. Wilson ed. *The New Imperial History: Culture, Modernity and Identity, 1660–1836*, 2004, Copyright © Cambridge University Press 2004, reprinted with permission of the author and publisher.

14 Richard H. Grove, 'Conclusions', *Green Imperialism: Colonial Expansion, Tropical Island Edens, and the Origins of Environmentalism, 1660–1860*, 1995, Copyright © Cambridge University Press 1995, reprinted with permission of the author and publisher.

15 Nancy J. Jacobs, 'Retrospectives on Socio-Environmental History and Socio-Environmental Justice', *Environment, Power, and Injustice: A South African History*, 2003, Copyright © Nancy J. Jacobs 2003, published by Cambridge University Press, reprinted with permission of the author and publisher.

16 Dr Tony Ballantyne, *Orientalism and Race: Aryanism in the British Empire*, published 2001 by Palgrave, Copyright © Tony Ballantyne 2002, reproduced by permission of the author and Palgrave Macmillan.

17 Jonathon Glassman, 'Slower Than a Massacre: The Multiple Sources of Racial Thought in Colonial Africa' *American Historical Review* 109,3, 2004, pp.720–54. Reproduced by kind permission of the author and the American Historical Association.

18 Jonathan Hyslop, 'The Imperial Working Class Makes Itself "White": White Labourism in Britain, Australia, and South Africa before the First World War,' *Journal of Historical Sociology* 12, 1999, pp.398–421. © 1999 Blackwell Publishing. Reproduced with permission of Blackwell Publishing.

19 John M. MacKenzie 'The Persistence of Empire in Metropolitan Culture' from *British Culture and the End of Empire*, by Stuart Ward (ed.), 2001, Manchester University Press, Manchester, UK.

20 Wendy Webster, 'There'll Always be an England: Representations of Colonial Wars and Immigration, 1948–1968' *Journal of British Studies* 40,3, 2001. © 2001 The North American Conference on British Studies. Reproduced by permission of the author and University of Chicago Press.

21 Andrew S. Thompson, 'The Language of Imperialism and the Meanings of Empire' *Journal of British Studies* 36,2, 1997. © 1997 The North American Conference on British Studies. Reproduced by permission of the author and University of Chicago Press.

22 Paul Gilroy, *After Empire: Melancholia or Convivial Culture?* © 2004 (Routledge, London). Reproduced by permission of the author and Taylor & Francis Books UK.

22 Paul Gilroy, *Post-Colonial Melancholia* (Columbia University Press, 2004). Reproduced by kind permission of the author and publisher.

23 Bill Schwarz, 'Claudia Jones and the *West Indian Gazette*: Reflections on the Emergence of Post-colonial Britain' *20th Century British History* 14,3 (2003). Copyright © 2003 by the Oxford University Press. By permission of the author and Oxford University Press.

24 Joan Dayan, 'Haiti, History, and the Gods' in Prakash, Gyan, *After Colonialism*. Copyright © 1995 Princeton University Press. Reprinted by permission of Princeton University Press.

25 Deborah A. Thomas, 'Modern Blackness: "What We Are and What We Hope to Be"' *Small Axe*, 6,2, pp.25–48. Copyright, 2002, Small Axe, Inc. All rights reserved. Used by permission of the current publisher, Duke University Press.

26 E.S. Atieno Odhiambo, 'Re-introducing the "People Without History": African Historiographies' (unpublished paper). Reproduced by kind permission of the author.

27 Selim Deringil, '"They Live in a State of Nomadism and Savagery": The Late Ottoman Empire and the Post-Colonial Debate' *Comparative Studies in Society and History*, 2003. Copyright © Society for Comparative Study in Society and History, published by Cambridge University Press. Reproduced by permission of the author and publisher.

28 Laurent Dubois, 'La République Métissée: Citizenship, Colonialism, and the Borders of French History' *Cultural Studies* 14,1 (2000). Reproduced by kind permission of the author and Taylor & Francis (http://tandf.co.uk/journals).

29 Anthony Pagden, 'Imperialism, Liberalism and the Quest for Perpetual Peace' *Daedalus*, 134,2 (Spring, 2005), pp. 46–57. © 2005 by the American Academy of Arts and Sciences. Reproduced by permission of the author, the journal and the publisher, MIT Press Journals.

30 Partha Chatterjee, 'Empire After Globalisation' *Economic and Political Weekly* 11 September 2004. Reproduced by kind permission of the author.

Introduction

New Imperial Histories

STEPHEN HOWE

IMPERIAL HISTORY IS experiencing a newfound vigour, dynamism, diversity and even fashionability. New journals are founded, conferences and online discussion lists proliferate, as do popular books and television documentaries as well as more heavyweight academic productions. There is a striking variety as well as sheer volume of new work in the field. In North America especially, a turn to imperial history is widely seen as the way for British Studies, and perhaps the study of other European countries that were once empire-owners, to escape institutional decline and marginalisation.[1]

All this represents a remarkable reversal of long-standing trends. For decades, imperial history was seen as fusty, hidebound, backward-looking — and it appeared to many that studying empires necessarily meant being in favour of or nostalgic for them. Studying formerly colonised countries or regions, their peoples and cultures, was 'in'; and this usually meant doing so within national or regional frameworks, and often (especially in the 1960s and 1970s) taking anticolonial nationalism as one's main object of study. Studying empires as such — which, it was felt, most often meant studying (and identifying or sympathising with) imperialists, and doing so via the procedures of top-down, old-fashioned political, diplomatic or strategic history — was 'out'.[2]

The turning of that tide, and the new atmosphere of optimism and dynamism in imperial history, is surely good news to anyone interested in the field. Meanwhile the number of those who *are* interested has obviously also shot up, as ideas and arguments about empire, especially the notion of American empire, have been driven into ever greater prominence by contemporary world events. But there has also been a rather disconcerting downside to all of this. Historians of empire have appeared to become embroiled in a slow-burning civil war, between those who proclaim themselves or are labelled as exponents of a 'new imperial history' and those who, by default, must presumably be termed old imperial historians.[3]

The label 'new imperial history' has most often been deployed by students of the nineteenth and twentieth centuries; though the phrase has also been used in reference to the 'First British Empire', to the eighteenth century and before.[4] Initially, it focused mainly on studies of the British Empire – although some recent work on the French, Spanish, German and other empires' histories has elective affinities to it, and such work is now rapidly swelling in quantity. Increasingly, too, in the very recent past, writing on ideas of American 'empire' and of 'the colonial present' has exhibited many shared interests, influences and emphases with the 'new (British) imperial history'.

The idea of a new imperial history has, however, been used in very varying ways. To some, it means first and foremost cultural, as opposed to political or economic, histories of empire. Others intend the term mainly to refer to ecological history.[5] Others again mean primarily histories informed by feminism and gender studies, or by literary theories of colonial discourse and postcoloniality. 'New imperial history' has involved a very wide range of new or renewed themes and topics of investigation. As well as those already mentioned, we might note particularly the way in which imperial and colonial histories of the body have proliferated in the past few years, partly as an aspect of the feminist-inspired history of gender and sexuality (and latterly of gay and queer studies), partly under the influence of Michel Foucault's successive, suggestive but often speculative writings on the topic.[6] The role of religion in both colonialist and anticolonialist beliefs and mobilisations has also drawn revived attention.

Despite such diversity, most of those who have used the tag seemingly have a shared core understanding – albeit often an inexplicit one – of what they mean by it.[7] This embraces all or most of the currents mentioned above, and more. They mean approaches to imperial history centred on ideas of culture and, often, of discourse; ones with strong attention to gender relations and/or to racial imaginings; ones which emphasise the impact of colonialism's cultures on metropole as well as on the colonised, and tend also to urge its continuing effects after the end of formal colonial rule. They pose questions – or make assumptions – about the relationships among knowledge, identity and power, including a high degree of explicit self-consciousness about the positioning of the historians themselves. And this extends, often, to a strong insistence on the desired, or expected, political or ethical effects of the scholars' own work. Antoinette Burton, perhaps the most insistent evangelist for the idea of a new imperial history, urges that: 'The stakes . . . are incredibly high, for the practice of history no less than for contemporary politics.'[8]

Much of this new work proclaims itself to be interdisciplinary in focus, in stark contrast to most older imperial historiography, combining history, literary criticism, cultural studies, ethnography and human geography; and drawing on ideas from philosophy, linguistics and psychoanalysis.[9] And there has been a sharp critique of nation-centred historical models, with sometimes a suggestion that notions of imperial cultures as global networks should be put in their place. British history – or that of other former colonial powers – could form the centre of a worldwide web of interconnecting stories; but in tracing those connections, the centre itself would be decentred.[10]

A particular set of shared influences and theoretical resources is widely acknowledged. The most obvious come from feminist theory, and from cultural and literary studies: above all, of course, Edward Said's work. The 'political turn' in criticism, of which the rise of colonial cultural studies has been perhaps the most vigorous manifestation, has here coincided and interacted with the linguistic turn in historiography. Foucauldian, discourse-analytical, postmodernist and poststructuralist ideas are widely invoked, albeit often at second or third hand. Indeed, it is often claimed that there is a particularly intimate relationship among postcoloniality, postmodernism and poststructuralism. This can even be posed, in some recent work, as a self-evident association. The impact of the Indian Subaltern Studies school – or rather, of a particular understanding and appropriation of that work – has also been important. So in some quarters has an influence from anthropology: perhaps especially from Bernard Cohn's pioneering work on British India, represented in this volume, but also from Clifford Geertz's wide-ranging studies and from the more recent historical and cultural anthropologies of scholars such as Arjun Appadurai, Talal Asad, Jean and John Comaroff, and James Clifford.

We might immediately note what is not included as 'new imperial history' by some at least of those who use the label; what a distinctive selection is being made from the range of recent work in the field. The small explosion of new writing on colonialism in political theory, from people as diverse as Barbara Arneil, Bhikhu Parekh or David Armitage, for instance, seems to be excluded. The neglect of economic history has been so often noted that one need not belabour that complaint again here; but there is thus far also startlingly little attention to legal or military institutions, or indeed to the state itself as such. Elsewhere, too, influences are notably and sometimes disconcertingly selective. No reader of Edward Said will need convincing of the point that 'travelling theories' often, perhaps inevitably, become distorted and in a sense disarmed during their migrations.[11] That certainly seems to be the case in some recent appropriations of Indian, African, Middle Eastern and other postcolonial debates by those who proclaim affiliation to a new imperial history. It is also intriguing that, so far, another usage of the phrase 'new imperial history' seems to have developed almost entirely separately from that centred on the western European and especially British empires' histories. This is the body of new writing on Russian, Soviet and post-Soviet history centred around the journal *Ab Imperio*.

As that implies, what intends, or proclaims, itself to be an integrative, barrier-dissolving body of work has sometimes instead seemed to produce new schisms and antagonisms. The idea of the new imperial history has already occasioned a remarkable number of negative polemics: often extremely heated ones, with strong political and/or ethical overtones. From the 'old historians' side of the disputes, much work in the 'new' is – in line with the general epistemological-cum-political cleavage already noted – seen as, quite simply, not being properly historical at all. There are, though, also serious and genuine historiographical issues at stake, and debates far more substantive and interesting than mere name-calling. Writing about imperial history is more varied and exciting than ever before, whatever the shortcomings of some particular currents within this broad stream. Important, innovative work is emerging in 'traditional' circles devoted to diplomatic, high-political or military history, as well as 'newer' feminist or ecological ones. Indeed, the rhetorics of temporality, of oldness and newness, may obstruct rather than further genuinely innovative endeavours, both scholarly and political. Equally, the singularity of a supposed 'new imperial history' is perhaps misleading and unhelpful. We should pluralise it and speak instead of fresh, creative histories of imperialism.

This collection of essays, articles and excerpts from books thus aims *both* to gather together some of the most important, influential and controversial work which has come to be labelled 'new imperial history', *and* to include notable examples of recent writing which either pursues issues neglected by most of that work or indeed challenges the 'old/new' dichotomy. It seeks to embrace, and to balance, all of the following:

- 'manifestoes' for a new imperial history;
- polemical articles debating the state and future of the field;
- examples of work from, or drawing on, the various intellectual disciplines outside history itself, which have greatly influenced these developments;
- a selection of particularly influential substantive investigations, including ones relating to colonial experiences other than the British;
- a handful of examples of recent work *not* ordinarily seen as 'new imperial history', but embodying very different − but perhaps, potentially, in part complementary − kinds of innovation;
- one or two indications of how recent trends in historical and related studies of colonialism and postcoloniality have influenced, or related to, ideas about present-day global politics.

Debate over what imperial history is, has been, could be or should be has thus become, in recent years, unprecedentedly lively, multifaceted and sometimes acrimonious. In the remainder of this Introduction, I attempt to sketch some of the main lines of those debates, as I see them. It should be noted, however, that many of my conclusions are negative; in the sense that I emphasise how deeply *divided* students of these questions have been. These divisions, as I shall seek to show in broad outline, have had several different dimensions − which have also intermingled in complex and sometimes unhelpful ways. They include methodological and epistemological disputes, inter- and intra-disciplinary ones (especially those between 'traditional' historians and social scientists on the one hand, colonial and postcolonial cultural theorists on the other) and directly political ones. I shall organise my comments on these developments under no fewer than twelve summary headings. Each of them involves an issue which has manifested itself in quite sharp recent disputes among analysts of empire, but may also suggest new opportunities and directions for the subject.

Languages

First, the most basic issues of terminology have been found problematic. 'Empire', 'imperial' and 'imperialist' are terms with complex and contested histories: one is even tempted to think of them as *essentially* contested concepts in the philosophers' sense. In the political discourse of the twentieth century's second half, they were almost always used pejoratively. Almost nobody, and no state, was willing to adopt them as self-descriptions. Only the most hostile critics of United States foreign policy, for instance, described it as either imperial or imperialist, or called America an empire. Today, however, the notion of an American empire is employed from a far wider range of viewpoints. It is, of course, still favoured by many negative critics of the phenomena concerned. But it is now used also by those who seemingly intend it in a neutral, analytical or descriptive way, and − in a more striking change − by strong supporters of a globally activist or interventionist policy.

This has been accompanied by ever more vigorous debates over the relevance or otherwise to present-day US power of 'lessons from history', whether the earlier history of the USA and its international role themselves, or those of older imperial systems.

'Colonialism', initially a more precise term, has also been put to ever wider and more problematic uses.[12] Early usages of 'colony', 'colonist' and 'colonial' denoted settlements of farmers or cultivators: hence, by extension, agricultural settlers in a new place and, from that, places outside Europe to which European migrants moved in significant numbers. For over three hundred years, until some point in the nineteenth century, 'colony' in English meant as Moses Finley points out 'a plantation of men [sic], a place to which men emigrated'.[13] Its root was the Latin *colere*, to cultivate or farm (an etymology it shares with 'culture', which should delight the colonial discourse theorists). Thus, as the term was ordinarily used before the twentieth century, only conquered territories of white settlement – Australia, the South African Cape, the mainland Americas – were 'colonies'. South and Southeast Asia or European possessions in most of Africa were not. During the late nineteenth and early twentieth centuries, the term was extended to embrace all areas subject to formal political rule and control by other (usually European) states. This is still the most common usage; thus making 'colonialism' a subset of the term 'imperialism', which is used also to denote informal modes of domination or influence. There are evident problems with this definition, of which I shall for the moment note just two. First, it leaves open the question of numerous borderline cases – sometimes literally as well as metaphorically so. When is the expansion of a polity over directly neighbouring territories to be described as colonialist? Also, does there have to be a clear pre-existing claim to sovereignty, at least of a *de facto* kind, which the intruders have overridden, before an occupation can be called colonial? Second, given the usual association of the colonial idea with European (or 'white') rule over non-Europeans, which if any circumstances where neither or both conquerors and conquered are European should be called colonial? For example – an example which involves both problems – was the substitution of Indian for Portuguese sovereignty over Goa in 1961 a decolonisation, a change of colonial rulers, or what?

Theories

Second, a significant part of the importance, the appeal, but also in some quarters the contentiousness of 'new imperial history' lies in the part certain theoretical influences have played in its formation. In the study of empire, there have been comparatively few big ideas and, by comparison with many other spheres both of historical and of social scientific research, relatively little theory-building. One need only think of how much debate still revolves around the century-old theories of J.A. Hobson, or the fifty-year-old ones of Ronald Robinson and Jack Gallagher. The most widely influential 'new wave' of the past few decades, Saidian cultural analysis, has been spurned or scorned by at least as many students of empires as have embraced it: here, as we shall see, lies one of the main lines of division between 'old' and 'new' imperial histories. Very few historians have been at all attracted by Michael Hardt and Antonio Negri's eloquent and suggestive but also impressionistic or even internally inconsistent arguments, or think that these offer fruitful 'leads' for historical research.[14] Yet this relative dearth of theoretical elaboration co-exists with a remarkable effervescence of controversy and – especially, perhaps, since the 1980s – with influences coming from numerous academic disciplines, milieux and indeed theoretical traditions. Empire, its aftermaths and enduring significance have not only been the concerns of historians and political or International Relations analysts. In recent years, they have become major preoccupations among cultural and literary critics and theorists. In some other fields too – political theory, economics and 'development studies', anthropology, human geography and more – they have generated a rapidly growing and often highly contentious literature in the past few decades. These new approaches often come carrying a weighty conceptual and political baggage, including, crucially, the influence of postmodernism and poststructuralism. If theory-building *within* imperial history as such has been sparse, the impact *on* it of various kinds of theory drawn from elsewhere has been ever more substantial and contentious.

The second sphere of debate I wish to highlight, therefore, involves epistemological disputes of the most fundamental kind. Most imperial historians have tended to be empiricists, if not positivists. Distaste for grand theory is deeply ingrained. They have been especially uncomfortable, if not hostile, towards anything that smacks of post-structuralism, postmodernism, deconstruction or relativism. And they have tended to associate use of colonial and postcolonial cultural theories with all those unwelcome tendencies and even with a total disregard for historical specificity and accuracy.

The influences most sharply at issue are those around textualism and the linguistic turn in historical and social studies. As Luise White reminds us, texts, including those modern historians and cultural critics produce, compete by claiming truth. Looking at how texts compete, at what they compete over, and what is at stake in their competition, can tell us a lot, not least about contemporary ideologies and power relations.[15] Many postcolonial critics, however, go on to suggest – in what one is tempted by now to call identikit-Foucauldian style – that all such claims are necessarily and equivalently also exercises in power, all articulating similarly equivalent truths. As we shall see, positions taken for or against such a theoretical stance have very often been associated with *political*, and even ethical, attitudes towards empire, its legacies and its apparent revival.

That stance has seemed especially popular within what has become known as colonial discourse analysis or sometimes, now, simply 'postcolonialism'. Such theories have also sometimes exhibited a tendency to see colonial power as an all-embracing, transhistorical force, controlling and transforming every aspect of colonised societies. The writings and attitudes of those involved with empire are seen as constituting a system, a network, a discourse in the sense made famous by Michel Foucault; though the notion of 'colonialism as a system' goes at least as far back as Sartre.[16] It inextricably combines the produc-tion of knowledge with the exercise of power. It deals in stereotypes and polar antitheses. It has both justificatory and repressive functions. And, perhaps above all, it *is* a singular 'it': colonial discourse and by extension the categories in which it deals (the coloniser, the colonised, the subject people, etc.) can meaningfully be discussed in unitary terms.

In part, the difficulties and schisms here have a disciplinary origin: in dispute over whether (or sometimes, one fears, the presumption that) the tools and techniques of literary criticism are interchangeable with those of historical, social and economic analysis. The few individual colonial texts and incidents discussed in some cultural analyses of empire are often used not even as 'symptoms' of wider social phenomena (a problematic enough procedure in itself, which has been the general besetting sin of what has been called 'new historicism' in literary studies), but as perfunctory pegs on which to hang sweeping assertions about a generalised colonial situation. Claims initially made about the forms and reception of specific literary texts are thus illegitimately generalised into claims about the historical and political situations from which such texts derive. The texts are characteristically assumed to express a shared colonial, or anticolonial, mentality. This is in many instances associated with what may be called a culturalist bias: indeed a cultural reductionism which is mirror-image of the economic reductionism typical of some parts of the Marxist tradition. Despite the debts to Marxism proclaimed by many exponents of colonial cultural studies, there is rarely any apparent interest in the economics of colonial or postcolonial relations – and where passing references are made to these, they are often by way of ill-understood claims derived from dependency theory.[17] Conversely, of course, many analysts of imperial economic, military, social or political history lie open to the charge of neglecting the force of culture.

Power, knowledge and interest

A third and closely linked problem thus lies in the relative lack, still, of interaction between political, economic and strategic studies of global power on the one hand, and work by literary and cultural studies scholars interested in the cultures and discourses of imperialism, on the other. These spheres of research have operated largely in an atmosphere of mutual indifference or even antagonism – and although here too a growing body of recent work (some of it 'showcased' in this selection) seeks to close the gaps, for some they remain very wide. The post-1980s wave of cultural histories of colonialism and nationalism developed in large part out of literary studies, and has continued to bear the marks of its origin. It has also diverged sharply from much earlier work on related issues in its fundamental 'take' on the nature of imperial power.

     One could over-simply say that one camp sees the crucial relationships for analysing colonial and indeed postcolonial histories as being those between knowledge and power, whereas the other views them as being those between *interest* and power. The focus on a knowledge-power nexus derives, of course, above all from Foucault and, more directly, from Said's *Orientalism* and Bernard Cohn's essays on colonialism's 'forms of knowledge'.[18] This involves not merely a stress on the centrality, power and purposefulness of colonial discourses (or ideologies: those two concepts are, disconcertingly often, used as synonyms) but on colonialism's capacity in a strong sense to create that which it claimed to find in colonised societies. Arguments doubting this, ones seeing colonial knowledge either as essentially neutral 'information' or as being created by colonised as well as colonising subjects, ones denying that Orientalism in Said's sense was a coherent system of thought, ones stressing the weakness of colonial power and the degree of agency retained by the colonised, all amount (in Nicholas Dirks' terms) to an abject 'disavowal of colonial power and prejudice' or, yet more starkly, to 'blam[ing] the victim again'.[19] We shall return to such charges and their implications a little further on.

Colonialism, as classically conceived, is very specifically a political phenomenon, a matter of the state. In my view, any coherent analysis or even definition of it must bear this constantly in mind, retaining the recognition that its core is a juridical relation between a state and a territory; one in which the colonising state took (or at least proclaimed) complete power over the government of the territory which it had annexed. This clearly distinguishes colonial polities from those which have internal self-government, such as British Dominions, and from formally sovereign states subject to various forms and degrees of influence or control from outside (though the latter, by the definitions we have adopted, may well be instances of *imperialism*).

Some 'new imperial historians' silently abandon this focus, and inexplicitly substitute at best a notion of a colonialism of civil society, at worst a purely discursive conception of colonial power. The former focuses on interest groups, religious bodies, educational institutions and so on, while too often failing to specify the relationship of their projects to colonial state power. Insofar as it is at all theoretically explicit, other than about its relations to earlier *literary* theory, it takes much of its inspiration from the later Foucault, with his rejection of attention to the state as privileged source or instance of power. Much post-structuralist theory, of course, goes further, spurning not only the state but society as an object of analysis. Here colonial discourse analysis connects with the 'linguistic turn' in social and historical studies more generally in its rejection of social explanation and very often of totalising explanation *tout court*. Or rather, its ostensible rejection; for, in fact, very sweeping kinds of general claim are characteristic of some writers in the genre. Not least among these is the all-pervasive, all-determining power accorded to 'colonialism' itself. At the extreme, as for Timothy Mitchell, it seems that colonialism is modernity and vice versa: 'Colonising refers not simply to the establishing of a European presence but also to the spread of a political order that inscribes in the social world a new conception of space, new forms of personhood, and a new means of manufacturing the experience of the real.'[20]

There are tendencies in some of this for things which should be hypotheses to become instead founding assumptions for certain 'new imperial historians'. Thus, for instance, some influential recent work proceeds simply by assuming that colonial expansion was both ubiquitously constitutive of metropolitan British culture, and equally crucially dependent on it – that culture was (and is) necessarily colonialist and colonialism cultural. Those few earlier historians and theorists who are judged to have shown some partial recognition of this are faintly praised. Those who fail that test are damned not only for insularity or economic determinism, but for simply not taking empire or race seriously enough, being indulgent or over-charitable towards the historical record of British power, indeed for being morally complicit in the continuing effects of that power's multiple abuses.

Colonialism and capitalism

A fourth great interpretive schism in historical debate might be encapsulated under the heading: 'Histories of capitalism, or of colonialism?' For some 'second generation' Subaltern Studies authors, in particular (Dipesh Chakrabarty or Gyan Prakash, for example) a crucial failing of Eurocentric historiography, even or especially in its Marxist forms, has been to write global history as the story of capitalism's, and hence modernity's, inexorable universalisation.[21] This failing among Marxists is derided as reliance on a singular 'modes of production narrative', and certainly issues of empire play a surprisingly small part in the work of many major Marxist historians. For some among these critics, colonialism instead of capitalism becomes *the* great trans-historical organising concept. An emerging body of writing on 'alternative' or 'multiple' modernities mounts a somewhat similar line of critique, albeit in a very different idiom and, perhaps, in more nuanced form.

To subsume colonialism and its crimes within a homogenising, teleological 'modes-of production narrative', supposedly typical of orthodox Marxism, also – in critics' eyes – leads one to obscure, as Prakash had put it: 'How and why this logic of capital distinguishes between brown and white people in the latter's favour'.[22] This again, it is claimed, not only misrepresents but systematically downplays, even erases, the whole question of colonialism. Nicholas Dirks similarly argues that to place the concept of capitalism, rather than that of colonialism, at the heart of one's historical story is an essentially apologetic move.[23]

What is the point of this accusation? It lies above all, I think, in many contemporary critics' conviction that those thus criticised see emphasis on colonialism as a, let alone *the*, great force in contemporary history as dangerous. There is – and this is a trope which Dirks, Prakash, Mrinalini Sinha and others have recently employed – a *fear* of engaging properly with colonial power and its continuing effects. This in its turn is for directly contemporary and political reasons. As Dirks has elsewhere put it:

> Accounts of the problems of third-world states . . . that ignore the role of the imperial past clearly serve to justify the imperial present, even when the point is not made explicit. The resurgence of interest in imperial history has been accompanied by a kinder and gentler view of the European role in Empire, on occasion scripted with specific lessons for the present.[24]

On that view, critique of positions associated with a school of imperial history is, at the most fundamental level, *really* all about engaging with imperialism's legacies, and still more with imperialism's revival, today. Historians' arguments which are ostensibly about nineteenth-century Calcutta or Calabar are 'really' all about twenty-first-century Fallujah or Ramallah. But all this is, surely, *too* present-minded, too inclined to reduce questions of scholarship entirely to ones of politics and prejudice. It is a little tempting, in reaction, to see some of these harsh antagonisms as more matters of style than of substance. They relate to what Geoff Eley and Keith Nield accurately referred to as a disturbingly widespread current stylistic trend: 'its sometimes peremptory, exhortatory timbre, its apocalyptic and apodictic tone. Historians *must* do this, they *cannot ignore* that, they had better get their general act together.'[25] Sanjay Subrahmanyam – to whom I am indebted – has suggested that the interpretive schisms over imperial history should not be taken so seriously as I have been inclined to do; they are mere family quarrels.[26] Yet I feel this bends the stick too far the other way again: if the image is at all apt, then in my view the 'family' in question is large, quarrelsome, and perhaps quite dysfunctional; while some members seem not to talk to one another at all. By bringing together writing by some even of the most distantly-related members of the 'family', this collection hopes in some small way to further the still necessary conversation.

Ideologies

A fifth kind of interpretive cleavage is that over the role of ideas, ideals and ideology in imperial expansion and rule. On one side lie those, perhaps again especially in literary and cultural theory, who very frequently assume that European colonialism was a wholly willed phenomenon. On the other, are those who stress the extent to which colonial rule in general, and the British Empire in particular, was a patchwork quilt, an enormously varied set of forms of rule and domination, largely the product of improvisation and full of internal contradictions and strains, rather than a deliberately constructed global system. Ideologies of empire, on this latter view, were far more often *ex post facto* rationalisations for acts of expansion undertaken for a very wide range of reasons, opportunistically driven by crisis, or by the availability of new means of domination (technological and other), not by the ideology itself.

Most famously and influentially, Jack Gallagher and Ronald Robinson – in works which continue to shape a vast body of research – argued that Britain's preferred mode of expansion was always *informal*, the direct annexation of overseas territory being a last resort, and one undertaken not in response to pressure from public opinion or economic interests, but by a policy-making élite: the famous 'official mind'. This élite's actions, notably the Scramble for Africa, were driven by crises on the periphery, and by desire to protect British control of India, the nucleus of empire. Neither the supposed needs of industrial or finance capital, nor any significant or elaborated imperialist ideology, played much of a role.[27] This view, in its turn, has been subjected to multiple criticisms, some of which have centred on its allegedly exculpatory effects, which are said to deny or downplay the culpability of imperialists along with their purposefulness and intentionality.[28]

Spaces and places

A sixth major issue and focus for debate lies in recent British and European work about the impact of empires on metropoles.[29] The central focus has naturally been on the histories of discourse, ideology and mentality. But there has also been – as a notable part of a wider trend, what is sometimes rather grandly called the spatial turn in the human sciences – a strong interest in the making and remaking of space and place, the 'imperialising' of, and physical traces of empire in, landscapes and (especially) cityscapes. There has been a small flood of recent books and articles on both physical and imaginative makings of 'imperial cities' and 'colonial space'. What kinds of relationships between 'home' and 'colony' operated, for instance, across Britain's modern history? Some answers have been sought in the relations of localism and globalism, in complex 'mappings' of real and imaginative landscapes: those of memory, of power, of exile, of loss and death. To a somewhat lesser but rapidly increasing extent, similar questions are being posed by historians of France, Germany, Belgium and other European former imperial powers – and indeed those of Russia and America.[30]

How though, by what criteria of judgement, can we decide what features of British culture are 'imperial'? It has proved difficult to formulate such criteria and set limits, despite the mass of recent historical work in the field, and despite the seemingly elaborately organised, sometimes officially sponsored nature of the putatively relevant British cultural production. Assessment of the historical place of empire in British life is still marked by stark polarity between silent assumptions about its utter marginality and vociferous ones about its centrality or ubiquity – and the current and forthcoming work in this field of which I am aware, like that by Bernard Porter, Bill Schwarz and Andrew Thompson, appears unlikely to close the gap.[31] In some quarters (perhaps especially, and intriguingly, among some US-based students of British imperialism) there is a danger of over-compensating for previous neglect of the interpenetration of domestic and imperial, failing to recognise that in many spheres of British life and thought, there really were powerful kinds of insulation between them. It almost inevitably, if dispiritingly, follows that Porter's forceful recent 'counter-attack' against such claims of empire's significance for Britain and Britishness has drawn ferocious criticism.[32]

Nations or networks?

My seventh sphere of contention is that over appropriate levels and units of analysis. As we have seen, the British 'new imperial history' has often criticised nation-centred historical models, and suggested that imperial cultures or social formations be seen as interactive global networks. Some others – including some who would in this over-polarised debate be characterised as 'old' historians, such as A.G. Hopkins – also urge that important trends in the contemporary world both give the history of Empire a renewed relevance, and enable new perspectives on it. If the great historiographical shift of the twentieth century's second half was from Imperial to national history, there are strong grounds for this now to be reversed.[33]

Yet the resistances against such a move will be substantial: not only among those committed, whether on scholarly or political grounds, to narratives of a national past in Britain, Ireland and other European states, but from their counterparts in many former colonies too. Australian historian Ann Curthoys puts it only half-jokingly: 'We've just started making national histories, and you want us to stop already?'[34] But perhaps the opposition will be most formidable of all in the American historical profession, or the country's wider public culture. Given US historical traditions, the writing of trans-national, postnational or non-national histories, though surely necessitated in some sense by sustained analysis of America's global role, will prove even harder than it has seemed for historians of Britain's empire. Among the latter it is still more gestured towards than undertaken. Increasingly, scholars have revived or worked with such notions as 'the imperial social formation', 'the British diaspora', 'Greater Britain', even 'The British World' or 'Anglobalization', but all are more suggestive than exhaustive – and some may be already rather oversold.

Ideas about 'race' are central to these. 'Global Britishness' was not only found among those of British descent. One found non-white groups in – and sometimes even outside – the empire styling themselves as British, perhaps most notably in the Anglophone Caribbean. Conversely, contest over and rejection of the label British by important groups within the United Kingdom has been a central development of recent decades, amounting in some eyes to a 'break-up of Britain' as the natural culminating stage of the end of empire. The key questions here thus revolve around how far or in what ways – if, indeed, at all – notions of themselves as 'being imperial' enter into, or even become in some strong sense constitutive of, collective identities among both colonisers and colonised, their relationship to ideas about 'race' and ethnicity – and of course, though I am shamefacedly conscious of adding this in utterly tokenistic style, ideas about gender. If relationships to ideas of Britishness among a wide range of people in different parts of the empire, for instance, were complex, contested and rapidly changing (as clearly they were), and if they often included 'feeling British' in some sense and among other things, then evidently it follows that the alienness of colonial rule was also a complex and variable thing.[35] This is so also in a different sense where (unlike the British or indeed any modern European-imperial case) the ruling élites of empires were themselves ethnically diverse, as with the later Roman empire or the Ottoman one.

Collaboration

Eighth, the whole idea of colonial 'collaboration' is intensely contested. A crucial argument in much modern scholarship on European empire – perhaps especially that rather loosely identified by critics as a conservative 'Cambridge school' of imperial historiography – is that colonialism depended crucially on collaboration. Collaborative bargains were not only inherent in the imperial relationship, but the nature of these bargains determined the character, and the longevity, of colonial rule. Again, ideas and ideology had little to do with it. Conversely, the social bases of anticolonial nationalism lay in a web of particularistic relationships which linked locality, province and nation. Nationalist politics in India was crucially formed by local patron-client networks, by the ways in which resources were fought over or bargained for, and thus by the very structures of the Raj, as the biggest controller of such resources. All this implies great scepticism about the claims of Congress, either to represent a unified national will or to be driven by high principles of national liberation.

There is, then, a contest over the historical legitimacy or integrity of anticolonial nationalism. The view thus sketched is, in critics' eyes, in itself colonialist, according the colonised no will of their own, no meaningful role other than collaboration, no politics other than that structured by the imperial system itself. In a somewhat different, more overtly present-minded and indeed more strident vein, some current writers – the best-known, perhaps most extreme case in the Anglophone world would be Niall Ferguson – see those who resist imperial power, past and present, as typically doing so in the name of deeply unattractive, inward- or backward-looking ideologies, and the postcolonial states they created a disaster for most poor countries. The continuation or renewal of some form of imperial governance might be better than independence for many. That last claim in its turn rests, of course, on the viability, both as historical reconstruction and as present programme, of a model of 'liberal empire' such as that which Ferguson sketches.[36]

Here too the ideas and influence of Robinson and Gallagher are seminal, with those of Gallagher's Trinity, Cambridge colleague and close collaborator Anil Seal, and a number of younger scholars – mostly their research students – including Gordon Johnson, David Washbrook and Chris Bayly, who came to be seen as pursuing and elaborating the shared programme and common perspectives. In some eyes, however, this Indian 'Cambridge school' approach was merely the subcontinental application of a set of wider arguments, proposed in the 1950s and early 1960s by Gallagher together with Robinson, and made more systematic in Ronald Robinson's later essays on collaboration.[37]

A handful of key propositions can, I think, be deduced from this considerable body of work. (Let us leave aside for the moment the question of how many of these claims, at least in the stark form presented here, were actually adhered to by all, many, or even any of the members of the alleged school.)

- That colonialism depended crucially on collaboration.
- That anticolonial nationalism was a loose, indeed strikingly fragile alliance of local and sectional interests.
- That – a near-inevitable consequence of the former two claims – conflict between colonial rulers and nationalists was neither a fundamental clash of principled aspirations, nor the main dynamic of late-imperial social or political change, but a limited and superficial affair, often mere shadow boxing.

Among many critiques of this line of argument, most important and influential have been those from historians associated with Subaltern Studies. Their project defined itself against two historiographical enemies: what founder Ranajit Guha in a manifesto-like introduction to its first volume called 'colonialist or neo-colonialist elitism and bourgeois-nationalist elitism'. The former, he said, was mainly a British product, though with Indian imitators. It saw the making of the Indian nation crudely in terms of stimulus and response: British rulers, policies, institutions and culture as stimulus, nationalism as reaction.[38] Thereafter, increasingly fierce critiques of 'Cambridge school' history have proliferated across the writings of Subaltern Studies authors. Guha himself, in the sixth volume, described David Washbrook as neocolonial history's best current exemplar – 'the old colonialist argument rejuvenated'.[39] Partha Chatterjee, in *The Nation and its Fragments*, says Washbrook's purpose is to 'erase colonialism out of existence'. Chatterjee's critique of the 'revisionist' approach, which in his view downplays or denies the impact of colonialism, identifies Washbrook, with Bayly, as the foremost exemplars of this deplorable trend.[40] Vinay Lal suggested that 'Gallagher and Robinson posited a *reluctant* imperialism; their Empire, moreover, had nothing to do with power'. Their disciples offer merely a 'refurbished and seemingly more subtle' form of the 'trite and comical' colonialist narrative. Guha's characterisation of the Cambridge approach as a simplistic stimulus-response model was given a yet sharper edge by Lal: 'Imperialist stimulus, nationalist response: the scientist in the laboratory, the rat in the cage: here is the story of Indian nationalism, that sordid tale.'[41]

Resistance

My ninth theme is in a sense a mirror-image of the disputes over concepts of collaboration: it concerns the question of anticolonial resistance. Much of the most contentious argument over interpretations of colonialism, colonial discourse and postcoloniality has centred on these issues. Among cultural theorists, there have been three main phases to these debates.

First came the narratives of anticolonial nationalism, invoking heroic successions of rebels and resisters whose efforts culminated in the *telos* of the postcolonial nation-state and its reawakened 'national' culture. Second, in Said's *Orientalism* and much of the writing which this inspired, there was an overwhelming focus on the discourses of colonial power/knowledge, with little if any attention to the counter-discourses of the colonised or to anticolonial opposition in general. In the hands of theorists more rigidly poststructuralist than Said, this sometimes involved extreme, explicit claims about the inevitable silence of the colonial subaltern (as by Gayatri Chakravorty Spivak), or assumptions about the capacity of the coloniser entirely to (re)model or (re)make colonised cultures and societies.[42] Third, in partial reaction against this and taking inspiration from Fanon, Guha and others as well as, often, from Foucault's later work, came a renewed focus on resistance; but one in which definitions of resistance itself were massively extended. Not only overt protest or armed insurrection, but a myriad forms of refusal, flight, evasion, deceit, passivity – even, in some versions, all language-acts by the colonised – are defined as instances of anticolonial defiance.[43] This third current has sometimes been associated with an aggressive antihistoricism and often antirationalism, identifying the celebration of resistance with a critique of 'Western logocentrism' and an elaboration of oppositional, deconstructive mythographies.[44]

Violence – and genocide?

My tenth theme is perhaps the most emotive and contentious of all. This is the role of violence, repression and atrocity in empire, and in its representations and memories. In Britain right now, some politicians urge that it is time to 'stop apologising' for the imperial past and instead celebrate its positive achievements and the abiding virtues of Britishness: speeches by the then Chancellor Gordon Brown are the most striking cases in point. Countering this, critics press for renewed attention to past British colonial atrocities, drawing above all on two recent and very important books on 1950s Kenya, which reveal patterns of abuse and massacre far wider than previously acknowledged.[45] Belgium is, since the opening of the 'Memory of Congo' exhibition at the Tervuren Africa Museum on 3 February 2005, confronting a brutal imperial past more fully than ever before.[46] Yet still, the texts accompanying the exhibition remained defensive if not evasive on the dark side of Belgium's colonial record – and the speech by minister Karel De Gucht at its opening was an almost defiant defence of that record.[47] Australia is embroiled in its own 'history wars' following Keith Windschuttle's provocative case that, contrary to the orthodoxies of the historical profession, stories of widespread massacre – let alone genocide – of Aboriginals by white settlers are largely fabricated.[48] In all those places and many more, repeatedly and inescapably, the historical arguments are linked with images of Guantanamo Bay and Abu Ghraib. Arguments over the relationship between empire and violence – including stark claims that colonialism is inherently bound up with extreme, pervasive, structural and even genocidal violence, whose most famous early proponents were the French-Antillean thinkers Frantz Fanon and Aimé Cesaire – have today a vigorous new lease of life. Some historians suggest that most episodes of genocide and mass murder in world history have been associated with empire-building: and in a particularly thought-provoking and disturbing twist, Michael Mann has recently argued that 'democratic' colonisers are the most likely to be genocidal.[49]

Modernity and archaism

Eleven: one particular aspect of debates over the historical salience and transformative force of European (and, again, especially British) expansion has been especially vigorous. Should colonial rule be viewed primarily in terms of modernisation or of archaism? The notion of 'colonial modernity' – even, as we saw in the case of Timothy Mitchell's work, colonialism *as* modernity – has been very widely invoked, especially among recent cultural historians of empire.[50] The idea of colonialism as a modernising, state-building, centralising, developmentalist and secularising force has been deployed too by those (again most forcefully if not stridently, Niall Ferguson) urging a positive appraisal both of the British imperial record and of American 'empire' today.[51] Yet on the other hand some British historians, such as David Cannadine, stress instead the traditionalist and even archaising features of British imperial ideology. And many students of British India urge, such as Maria Misra, that the British actually promoted the 'traditionalisation' of India, undermining many indigenous impulses towards modernisation.[52]

But there is also a more structural problem with the 'modernising' picture. The notion of the colonial relationship coming from a rationalistic, homogenising drive by the expansionary power simply does not fit what we know of the British – or indeed any other colonialist – state in the nineteenth and earlier twentieth centuries. These were in many ways premodern, precapitalist states; their ruling orders (and perhaps especially those fractions of the governing class most heavily involved in colonial expansion) largely aristocratic, only minimally subject to bourgeois rationality or fettered by popular democracy.[53] One does not have wholly to buy Joseph Schumpeter's view that imperialism was both utterly irrational and the product of feudal-military rather than capitalist elites, to recognise that the picture of a rationalistic capitalist imperialism painted by Edward Said or Dipesh Chakrabarty – and the ideologically opposed but oddly congruent Fergusonian construct of a 'liberal empire' – is strikingly one-sided, if not entirely misleading.[54]

What's the point?

Twelfth and finally, we might simply ask: what is a scholarly, or indeed a politically engaged, focus on empire or colonialism *for*? Previous generations of historians inhabited a time and a worldview in which the alternatives to empire seemed not only readily apparent and attractive, but to be on the road to global victory. Anticolonial nationalism, postcolonial 'nation-building', new global solidarities of the formerly oppressed combined to produce an optimistic, progressivist, even triumphalist metahistorical narrative of what Samir Amin has dubbed the 'Bandung Era'.[55]

That moment, clearly, is not ours, and those alternatives to empire are not ones that command widespread faith or even hope, at least in the forms that they did during the moment of decolonisation. It is perhaps 'no accident' (as old-fashioned Marxists used to say when they couldn't puzzle out the precise connection) that studies of anticolonial resistance have so often recently focused on the utopian, the irrational and the superstitious.[56] David Scott has insistently and powerfully posed the question: as the narratives of postcolonial nationalism recede, what is *the problem* of empire for us? What were those of the anticolonial nationalist generation, and their historians, seeking to overcome, and how does it relate to anything that we now are seeking to overcome?[57] Nationalist histories, Scott suggests (drawing of course on Hayden White), were typically emplotted as romance. Today, they must be rewritten as tragedy. Should the multiple histories of empire, and of *opposition* to empire, the attempts to escape from alien rule, be recast as part of a new, tragic metanarrative?

Conclusions

A longish list of themes and disputes over imperial history has been sketched here. Although I have put some of my own prejudices on display, I have on the whole not 'adjudicated' these disputes. The lack of closure is deliberate. Embracing analytical diversity, even eclecticism, is not just a matter of avoiding the polemical excesses noted above, which have marked an over-simple division between 'new' and 'old' imperial histories. It may also aptly reflect the multiplicity of forms of empire itself: not merely variation across time, but the coexistence of very different kinds of empire within the same system, at the same time. Even where empires, especially imperial ideologies, display close family resemblances, this has sometimes reflected conscious imitation more than structural congruity. It is tempting, indeed, to urge a definitive abandonment of the singular term 'empire' – which tends, even when its users are stressing and tracing differences, to imply that these are variations on a single essence – and to follow those who insistently and compellingly pluralise 'modernities' by doing the same for empires and imperialisms.[58]

There's a risk here that in urging that many of the divisions are unnecessary, that some apparently rival trends of thought could actually be complementary, one can sound merely exhortatory, crying rather emptily 'Why can't we all just get along?' But we can surely try to overcome the unprofitable barriers erected between cultural and politico-economic analyses of empires, between the ultra-empiricist and the over-theoreticist, between 'old' and 'new'. We can also attempt to dismantle or evade the still more troublesome barriers – strikingly often following the same contours as the first – which too readily and aggressively associate particular historical methods, approaches or judgements with determinate politico-ethical stances towards the historically varied forms of empire, expansion and colonial rule. The future lies not with a 'new imperial history', but with new histories of empires and imperialisms: some of which are, in truth, not entirely novel but rather renewals of the old.

Notes

1   Peter Stansky *et al.*, *NACBS Report on the State and Future of British Studies in North America* (North American Conference of British Studies, 1999).

2   See for instance the fascinating memoirs of one of the most important pioneer Africanist historians, Jan Vansina, in which repeatedly 'imperial historians' are identified, not only as hidebound but as the 'enemy' of the Africanist enterprise: *Living with Africa* (Madison, WI, 1994).

3   The 'old' imperial history is frequently seen as best represented today by David Cannadine, *Ornamentalism: How the British Saw their Empire* (London, 2001); and Wm. Roger Louis (ed.), *The Oxford History of the British Empire* (5 vols. Oxford, 1998/9) – with the former seen as a microcosm of the latter. For such claims, see for instance Tony Ballantyne, 'Introduction: Debating Empire' and Modhavi Kale, 'OHBEhave! The Mini-Me Version', both in *Journal of Colonialism and Colonial History*, 2002, vol. 3(1).

4   Kathleen Wilson (ed.) *The New Imperial History: Culture, Modernity and Identity, 1660–1836* (Cambridge, 2004).

5   Indeed, ecological history is perhaps second only to the histories of gender and sexuality in the quantity of new work it has generated in colonial and postcolonial studies. It is here, too, that some of the most innovative research has been conducted, and the most genuinely ground-breaking books published. This is unsurprising in that, more generally, the historical study of ecologies is perhaps the most genuinely novel of all the enterprises for which the notion of 'new histories' has been invoked.

6   Pioneering works included Mrinalini Sinha, *Colonial Masculinity: The 'Manly Englishman' and the 'Effeminate Bengali' in the Late Nineteenth Century* (Manchester, 1995) and Timothy Burke, *Lifebuoy Men, Lux Women: Commodification, Consumption and Cleanliness in Modern Zimbabwe* (Durham, NC, 1996). A major recent collection is Tony Ballantyne and Antoinette Burton (eds), *Bodies in Contact: Rethinking Colonial Encounters in World History* (Durham, NC, 2005).

7   See for instance Kathleen Wilson (ed.) op. cit; Antoinette Burton (ed.) *After the Imperial Turn: Thinking With and Through the Nation* (Durham, NC and London, 2003); Mrinalini Sinha, 'Britain and the Empire: Toward a New Agenda for Imperial History', *Radical History Review* 72 (1998); and numerous manifesto-like articles by Burton, including 'Who Needs the Nation?' *Journal of Historical Sociology,* 1997, vol. 10(3) and 'Thinking Beyond the Boundaries', *Social History*, 2001, vol. 26(1).

8   Burton, 'Déjà Vu All Over Again', in the special issue of the *Journal of Colonialism and Colonial History*, 2002, vol. 3(1) devoted to David Cannadine's *Ornamentalism*.

9   A particularly influential early example of the last is Ashis Nandy's *The Intimate Enemy: Loss and Recovery of Self Under Colonialism* (Delhi, 1983), excerpted in Chapter 8 below.

10 See for instance the contributions by Alan Lester and Tony Ballantyne below. A significant, partly separate but conceptually related body of new historical writing has revived the concept of the 'British World', as exampled in Carl Bridge and Kent Fedorowich's chapter here; while various 'Oceanic' histories, notably Atlantic (including 'Black Atlantic') have also brought fresh insights to the history of empires. Among many relevant works, one might single out J.H. Elliott's monumental *Empires of the Atlantic World* (New Haven and London, 2006).

11 See Said's essays 'Travelling Theory' in *The World, the Text, and the Critic* (London, 1984) and 'Travelling Theory Reconsidered', in *Reflections on Exile and Other Essays* (Cambridge, MA, 2000).

12 Perhaps the most lucid and probing investigation of these issues is now Frederick Cooper, *Colonialism in Question: Theory, Knowledge, History* (Berkeley, CA, 2005).

13 Moses Finley (1976): 'Colonies – An Attempt at a Typology', *Transactions of the Royal Historical Society*, 5th Series, vol. 26. p. 171. Ann Laura Stoler and Carole McGranahan have recently urged the importance of 'retracing' some of these older meanings: 'Introduction: Refiguring Imperial Terrains' in ibidem and Peter C. Perdue (eds). *Imperial Formations and their Discontents* (Santa Fe, 2007).

14 Michael Hardt and Antonio Negri, *Empire* (Cambridge, MA, 2000) and *Multitude* (New York, 2004). See for instance the critical remarks by Partha Chatterjee in Chapter 30 below.

15 *The Assassination of Herbert Chitepo* (Bloomington, IN, 2003) 3.

16   And perhaps *the* first exposition of an analytical standpoint seeing colonialism as a 'total social fact' is in Georges Balandier's 1951 essay, which is included below as the opening selection in this book.

17   See also the different but in some respects converging lines of criticism set out in Frederick Cooper's chapter here.

18   Cohn, *An Anthropologist Among the Historians and Other Essays* (Delhi, 1987); *Colonialism and its Forms of Knowledge. The British in India* (Princeton, 1996).

19   For a particularly sharp attack on such lines, see Dirks, *Castes of Mind: Colonialism and the Making of Modern India* (Princeton and Oxford, 2001) esp. 303–15, excerpted as Chapter 5 below. A similar critique is repeated in his *The Scandal of Empire* (Cambridge, MA, 2006).

20   Mitchell, *Colonising Egypt* (Berkeley 1988; cited from 1991 pb. 2nd edn), p. ix.

21   See for instance Prakash 'Writing Post-Orientalist Histories of the Third World: Perspectives from Indian Historiography', *Comparative Studies in Society and History*, 1990, vol. 32(2), idem. 'Colonialism, Capitalism and the Discourse of Freedom', *International Review of Social History*, 1996, vol. 41, Supplement; Chakrabarty, 'Postcoloniality and the Artifice of History: Who Speaks for "Indian" Pasts?' *Representations*, 1992, vol. 37; 'The Death of History? Historical Consciousness and the Culture of Late Capitalism', *Public Culture*, 1992, vol. 4(2); 'Provincializing Europe: Postcoloniality and the Critique of History', *Cultural Studies*, 1992, vol. 6(3).

22   'Can the "Subaltern" Ride? A Reply to O'Hanlon and Washbrook', *Comparative Studies in Society and History*, 1992, 34(1), 177.

23   Dirks, *Castes of Mind* op. cit. See pp. 92–105 below.

24   'Colonial and Postcolonial Histories: Comparative Reflections on the Legacies of Empire', *UN Human Development Report Occasional Paper*, 2004, p. 27.

25   'Starting Over: The Present, the Postmodern and the Moment of Social History', *Social History* 1995, 20(3), 355.

26   Personal communication.

27   Robinson and Gallagher, 'The Imperialism of Free Trade', *Economic History Review*, 2nd Series, 1953, vol. VI(1); ibidem with Alice Denny, *Africa and the Victorians: The Official Mind of Imperialism* (London, 1961); and see Wm. Roger Louis (ed.) *Imperialism: The Robinson and Gallagher Controversy* (New York, 1976).

28   Among the earliest such attacks was Arnold Temu and Bonaventure Swai, *Historians and Africanist History: A Critique* (London, 1981).

29   See the contributions by John Mackenzie, Wendy Webster, Andrew Thompson, Paul Gilroy, Bill Schwarz and Laurent Dubois in this volume.

30   See for instance Ulrich van der Heyden and Joachim Zeller (eds) *Kolonialmetropole Berlin: eine Spurensuche* (Berlin, 2002).

31   See amidst a rapidly swelling literature – John Mackenzie 'The Persistence of Empire in Metropolitan Culture' in Stuart Ward (ed.) *British Culture and the End of Empire* (Manchester, 2001); Wendy Webster, 'There'll Always Be an England: Representations of Colonial Wars and Immigration, 1948–1968,' *Journal of British Studies*, 2001, 40(3) (both included here); Bill Schwarz *Memories of Empire* (3 vols, Oxford, forthcoming); Paul Gilroy, *After Empire: Melancholia or Convivial Culture?* (London, 2004); Bernard Porter, *The Absent-minded Imperialists: The Empire in English Society and Culture,* c. *1800–1940* (Oxford, 2004); Andrew Thompson, 'The Language of Imperialism and the Meanings of Empire', *Journal of British Studies*, 1997, 36(2) – part of which appears here below – and his wider-ranging work on the domestic consequences of empire: *Empire Strikes Back* (London, 2005). Another important recent collection is Catherine Hall and Sonya Rose (eds) *At Home with the Empire: Metropolitan Cultures and the Imperial World* (Cambridge, 2006).

32   E.g. Antoinette Burton's review of Porter, *Absent-Minded Imperialists*, *Victorian Studies*, 2006, 47(4). Bernard Porter responds trenchantly to his critics in 'Further Thoughts on Imperial Absent-Mindedness', *Journal of Imperial and Commonwealth History*, 36(1).

33   Hopkins, 'Back to the Future: From National History to Imperial History', *Past and Present*, 1999, vol. 164.

34   The title of her contribution to Burton (ed.) *After the Imperial Turn*, op. cit.

35   I try to explore some aspects of this in 'C.L.R. James: Visions of History, Visions of Britain', in Bill Schwarz (ed.) *West Indian Intellectuals* (Manchester, 2003) and 'Britishness and Multiculturalism', in Rene Cuperus, Karl Duffek and Johannes Kandel (eds) *The Challenge of Diversity: European Social Democracy Facing Migration, Integration and Multiculturalism* (Berlin, Amsterdam and Vienna, 2004). See also P.S. Zachernuk, *Colonial Subjects: An African Intelligentsia and Atlantic Ideas* (Charlottesville and London, 2000) – part of which appears in this volume – and Peter Limb, 'Early ANC Leaders and the British World: Ambiguities and Identities', *Historia*, 2002, 47(1).

36   Niall Ferguson, *Empire: How Britain Made the Modern World* (London, 2003) and *Colossus: The Rise and Fall of the American Empire* (London, 2004) – in both cases I cite the British editions, which have intriguingly different titles from the US ones.

37   Full citation is impossible here; but see especially Gallagher, Gordon Johnson and Anil Seal (eds) *Locality, Province and Nation: Essays on Indian Politics* (Cambridge, 1977); and among Robinson's later essays 'Imperial Theory and the Question of Imperialism after Empire', in Robert F. Holland and Gowher Rizvi (eds), *Perspectives on Imperialism and Decolonization* (London, 1984); 'The Excentric Idea of Imperialism, with or without Empire', in Wolfgang J. Mommsen and Jurgen Osterhammel (eds) *Imperialism and After: Continuities and Discontinuities* (London, 1986); 'Non-European Foundations of European Imperialism: Sketch for a Theory of Collaboration', in Roger Owen and Bob Sutcliffe (eds) *Studies in the Theory of Imperialism* (London, 1972). An important recent reformulation of such arguments is in Colin Newbury, *Patrons, Clients, and Empire: Chieftaincy and Over-rule in Asia, Africa, and the Pacific* (Oxford, 2003).

38   Guha, 'On Some Aspects of the Historiography of Colonial India', in Guha (ed.) *Subaltern Studies 1* (Delhi, 1982) 1.

39   Guha 'Dominance without Hegemony and its History', in Guha (ed.) *Subaltern Studies VI* (Delhi, 1989) 292, 294.

40   *The Nation & Its Fragments: Colonial & Postcolonial Histories* (Princeton, 1993) 33.

41   Vinay Lal, *The History of History: Politics and Scholarship in Modern India* (Delhi, 2003) 195, 199; see also Lal, 'Imperial Nostalgia', *Economic and Political Weekly*, 17–24 July 1993, 28(29–30).

42   Gayatri Chakravorty Spivak, 'Can the Subaltern Speak? Speculations on Widow Sacrifice', in Cary Nelson and Lawrence Grossberg (eds) *Marxism and the Interpretation of Culture* (London, 1988).

43   The most influential works here – and ones free of the irrationalism noted below – are perhaps those of James C. Scott, including *The Moral Economy of the Peasant* (New Haven, 1976); 'Protest and Profanation: Agrarian Revolt and the Little Tradition', *Theory and Society*, 1977, 4(1); *Weapons of the Weak: Everyday Forms of Peasant Resistance* (New Haven, 1985).

44   See Frederick Cooper, 'Conflict and Connection: Rethinking Colonial African History', *American Historical Review*, 1994, 99(5) for a thoughtful critique of the over-inflated, vague concepts of resistance in postcolonial studies.

45   David Anderson, *Histories of the Hanged: Britain's Dirty War in Kenya and the End of the Empire* (London, 2005); Caroline Elkins, *Britain's Gulag: The Brutal End of Empire in Kenya* (London, 2005). A.W.B. Simpson, *Human Rights and the End of Empire: Britain and the Genesis of the European Convention* (Oxford University Press, 2001) includes substantial discussion of abuses in late colonial wars, while for an earlier colonial period Richard Price, *Making Empire: Colonial Encounters and the Creation of Imperial Rule in Nineteenth-Century Africa* (Cambridge, 2008), stresses both the violence of the imperial impact and the extent to which this was 'hidden' from metropolitan Britain.

46   Jean-Luc Vellut (dir.) *La Memoire du Congo, Le Temps Coloniale* (Tervuren, 2005) and the Museum's website: africamuseum.be.

47   diplomatie.be/en/press/speechdetails.asp?TEXTID=30931.

48   See Keith Windschuttle, *The Fabrication of Aboriginal History: Volume One, Van Diemen's Land, 1803–1847* (Sydney, 2002); Robert Manne (ed.) *Whitewash: On Keith Windschuttle's Fabrication of Aboriginal History* (Melbourne, 2003); Roger Milliss, *Waterloo Creek: The Australia Day Massacre of 1838, George Gipps and the British Conquest of New South Wales* (Sydney, 1992), *Aboriginal History*, 2001. 25, Special section: '"Genocide"? Australian Aboriginal History in International Perspective'; Henry Reynolds, *An Indelible Stain? The Question of Genocide in Australia's History* (Ringwood, Vic., 2001); Stuart MacIntyre and Anna Clarke, *The History Wars* (Melbourne, 2003).

49   Michael Mann, *The Dark Side of Democracy: Explaining Ethnic Cleansing* (Cambridge, 2004). See also, amidst a large literature on colonialism, identity, modernity and genocide, Vinay Lal, 'Genocide, Barbaric Others, and the Violence of Categories: A Response to Omer Bartov', *American Historical Review*, 1998, 103(4); Ben Kiernan, 'Myth, Nationalism and Genocide', *Journal of Genocide Research*, 2001, 3(2); Amin Maalouf, *In the Name of Identity: Violence and the Need to Belong* (New York, 2002) and Patrick Wolfe, *Settler Colonialism and the Transformation of Anthropology: The Politics and Poetics of an Ethnographic Event* (London and New York, 1999).

50   Such a view could, with little exaggeration, be called the 'common sense' of colonial and postcolonial cultural studies. A particularly widely cited general picture is Ashis Nandy, *The Intimate Enemy*. Among the most detailed, and nuanced, local studies is Jean and John Comaroff, *Of Revelation and Revolution: Christianity, Colonialism and Consciousness in South Africa* (2 vols, Chicago, 1991 and 1997).

51   Stanley Kurtz, 'Democratic Imperialism: A Blueprint', *Policy Review*, 2003, April–May, 118; Robert Cooper, 'The next empire', *Prospect*, October 2001; Ferguson, *Empire* and *Colossus*, op. cit.

52   Maria Misra, 'Lessons of Empire: Britain and India', *SAIS Review*, 2003, 23(2), 133.

53   cf. Arno J. Mayer, *The Persistence of the Old Regime: Europe to the Great War* (London, 1981); Perry Anderson, *English Questions* (London, 1992).

54   Schumpeter, *Imperialism and Social Classes* (Cleveland, 1955).

55   Amin, *Re-Reading the Postwar Period: An Intellectual Itinerary* (New York, 1994).

56   For instance Clifton Crais, *The Politics of Evil: Magic, State Power, and the Political Imagination in South Africa* (Cambridge, 2002); Luise White, *Speaking with Vampires: Rumor and History in Colonial Africa* (Berkeley, CA, 2000).

57   Scott's *Refashioning Futures* (Princeton, NJ, 1999) and *Conscripts of Modernity* (Durham, NC, 2005) are important meditations on what it means to rethink colonialism, anticolonialism and postcoloniality 'after Bandung'.

58   A useful recent addition to the argument is Alan Lester, *Imperial Networks: Creating Identities in Nineteenth-century South Africa and Britain* (London, 2001), which identifies three key – and conflicting – kinds of British colonial discourse: governmentality, humanitarianism and settler colonialism. Part of its argument is included as Chapter 9 here.

PART 1

Promoting and explaining 'new imperial history'

Chapter 1

George Balandier

THE COLONIAL SITUATION:
A THEORETICAL APPROACH

Georges Balandier, born in 1920, is among France's most distinguished
anthropologists. This essay, written as a young man in 1951, was in many
ways astonishingly ahead of its intellectual time. To a remarkable degree,
it anticipated many of the themes which were – over ensuing decades
and in some cases not until the 1990s and since – to become major
preoccupations of colonial studies and of the 'new imperial history'.
Perhaps above all, it goes to the heart of the too-little posed question:
'What's so special about colonialism anyway?' It is thus a fitting 'opener'
for this collection, as well as much deserving to be brought to the
attention of a new generation of readers in English.

Stephen Howe

ONE OF THE MOST STRIKING EVENTS in the recent history of
mankind is the expansion throughout the entire world of most European peoples.
It has brought about the subjugation and, in some instances, the disappearance of virtually
every people regarded as backward, archaic, or primitive. The colonial movement of the
nineteenth century was the most important in magnitude, the most fraught with
consequences, resulting from this European expansion. It overturned in a brutal manner
the history of the peoples it subjugated. Colonialism, in establishing itself, imposed on
subject peoples a very special type of situation. We cannot ignore this fact. It not only
conditioned the reactions of 'dependent' peoples, but is still responsible for certain
reactions of peoples recently emancipated.

The *colonial situation* poses problems for a conquered people – who respond to these
problems to the degree that a certain latitude is granted to them – problems for the
administration representing the so-called protective power (which also defends that power's

local interests), problems for the newly-created state on which still rests the burden of colonial liabilities. Whether currently present or in process of liquidation, this situation involves specific problems, which must arrest the attention of a sociologist. The postwar period has clearly indicated the urgency and importance of the colonial problem in its totality. It has been characterized by difficult attempts at reconquest, by the granting of independence to some, and by more or less conditional concessions to others. It has announced a technical phase in colonialism in the wake of a political-administrative phase.

It was only a few years ago that a rough but significant estimate noted the fact that colonial territories covered at that time one-third of the world's surface and that seven hundred million individuals out of a total population of some two billion were subject peoples.[1] Until very recently the greater part of the world's population, not belonging to the white race (if we exclude China and Japan), knew only a status of dependency on one or another of the European colonial powers. These subject peoples, distributed throughout Asia, Africa, and Oceania, all belonged to cultures designated 'backward' or 'pre-industrial.' They constituted the field of research within which anthropologists or ethnologists carried on – and still carry on – their investigations. And the scientific knowledge that we have of colonial peoples is due in large part to the efforts of these scholarly investigators. Such studies, in principle, could not (or should not) ignore such an important fact as colonialism, a phenomenon which has imposed, for a century or more, a certain type of evolution on subjugated populations. It seemed impossible not to take into account certain concrete situations in which the recent history of these peoples evolved. And yet it is only now and then that anthropologists have taken into consideration this specific context inherent in the *colonial situation*. (We have substantiating evidence to present in a study presently in preparation.) On the one hand, we find researchers obsessed with the pursuit of the ethnologically pure, with the unaltered fact miraculously preserved in its primitive state, or else investigators entirely absorbed with theoretical speculations regarding the destiny of civilizations or the origins of society. And, on the other hand, we find researchers engaged in numerous practical investigations of very limited scope, satisfied with a comfortable empiricism scarcely surpassing the level of using a technique. Between the two extremes the distance is great – it leads from the confines of a so-called 'cultural' anthropology to the confines of one described as 'applied' anthropology. In one case, the colonial situation is rejected as being a disturbing factor or is seen as only one of the causes of cultural change. In the other case, the colonial situation is viewed only in certain aspects – those immediately and obviously relating to the problem under investigation – and never appears as a force acting in terms of its own totality. Yet any *present-day* study of colonial societies striving for an understanding of current realities and not a reconstitution of a purely historical nature, a study aiming at a comprehension of conditions as they are, not sacrificing facts for the convenience of some dogmatic schematization, can only be accomplished by taking into account this complex we have called the *colonial situation*. It is precisely this situation that we wish to describe. But first it is necessary to sketch the essential outlines of this system of reference that we have invoked.

Among recent studies undertaken in France, only those of O. Mannoni assign an important role to the notion of colonial situation.[2] But as Mannoni was intent on treating the subject from a purely psychological or psychoanalytical point of view, he offers only an imprecise definition of the phenomenon we refer to. He presents it as 'a situation of incomprehension,' as 'a misunderstanding,' and, accordingly, he analyzes the psychological attitudes that characterize the 'colonizer' and the 'colonized,' attitudes that permit an understanding of the relationship maintained on both sides.[3] This is not enough, and Mannoni seems to recognize the fact when he cautions against 'under-estimating the (capital) importance of economic relationships.' Moreover, he concedes having selected a rather ill-defined aspect of the colonial situation. We, for our part, assume an opposite position from his. We are biased in favor of dealing with the question as a whole, believing there is something deceitful in examining only one of the many facts implied in this situation.

Such a situation as that created by the colonial expansion of European states during the last century can be examined from different points of view. Each one constitutes an individual approach to the subject, a separate analysis with a different orientation depending on whether the point of view is that of a colonial historian, an economist, a politician and administrator, a sociologist preoccupied with the relationships of foreign cultures, a psychologist concerned with a study of race relations, etc. And if one is to hazard an over-all view of the problem, it seems indispensable to discover what can be gleaned from each of these individual specialties.

The historian examines the various periods of colonization with respect to the colonial power. He enables us to grasp the changes that occur in the existing relationships between that power and its territorial dependencies. He shows us how the isolation of colonial peoples was shattered by a caprice of history over which these peoples had had no control. He evokes the ideologies which, at different times, have been used to justify colonialism and have created the 'role' adopted by the colonial power, and he reveals the discrepancies separating facts from theories. He analyzes the administrative and economic systems which have guaranteed 'colonial peace' and permitted an economic profit (for the metropole) from the colonial enterprise. In short, the historian makes us understand how, in the course of time, the colonial power implanted itself in the heart of its colonial societies. Acting in this manner he furnishes the sociologist with his first and indispensable frame of reference. He reminds the sociologist that the history of a colonial people has developed as a result of a foreign presence, while at the same time he elucidates the different aspects of the latter's role and influence.

Most historians have insisted on the fact that the pacification, the organization, and the development of colonial territories were carried out 'with respect to the interests of the western powers and not with local interests in mind . . . by assigning (the needs) of native producers to a position of secondary importance.'[4] They have shown how, in less than a century, the European absorption of Asia, Africa, and Oceania 'transformed the shape of human society through force and the imposition of reforms, often bold reforms.' They have shown how such upheavals were made necessary by 'colonial imperialism' (which is merely one manifestation of economic imperialism).[5] They have reminded us that economic exploitation is based on the seizure of political power – the two characteristic features of colonialism.[6] Thus historians enable us to see to what extent a colonial society is an instrumentality of the colonial power. We can observe this instrumental function in the politics practised by the European power, which consists in compromising the native aristocracy by tempting it with inducements calculated to appeal to its self-interest: 'Enlist the ruling class in our cause,' said Lyautey;[7] reduce the native chiefs to the role of 'mere creatures,' said R. Kennedy; and the evidence is even more obvious in the policies pursued in transplanting populations and in the recruitment of workers, all based exclusively on the economic interests of the colonial power.[8] By reminding us of certain 'bold' measures – population transfers and the policy of 'reserves,' the transformation of traditional laws, and questioning the ownership of resources, policies requiring a certain level of productivity, etc., the historian draws our attention to the fact that 'colonialism was literally at times an act of social surgery.'[9] And this observation, more or less valid, according to the peoples and areas under consideration, is of great interest to a sociologist studying colonial societies. It indicates to him that these societies are, in varying degrees, in a state of latent crisis, that they are involved to some extent in a kind of social pathology. It is valuable evidence of the special features of the sociology of colonial peoples and suggests the practical and theoretical results one may expect from such a discipline. We shall have occasion to note its importance elsewhere in our analysis.

But after having noted this external pressure applied to colonial societies, the historian points out the various kinds of reactions that have resulted. The reactions of Far Eastern peoples, the Arab world, and Black Africa have often been the subject of comparative studies. In general terms we learn of the opposition of 'closed societies' in the Far East, despite outward appearances of westernization; the tense relations with Islamic society which refuses to abandon a notion of superiority and maintains 'a competitive spirit that can be veiled and silent but nevertheless remains at the heart of the problem'; the 'openness' of the black world which is explained by 'the African readiness to imitate,' by a lack of 'confidence in the depths and resources of its own past.'[10] And in a rather special case, the history of Africa, the colonial continent *par excellence*, reveals important differences in ways of resisting the ascendancy of European nations within the very heart of Black Africa. After having exposed the importance of 'the external factor' with respect to transformations affecting colonial societies, the history of colonialism confronts us with an 'internal factor' inherent in social structures and subjugated societies. At this point the history of colonialism touches on territory familiar to the anthropologist. But in offering a picture of the varied responses to the colonial situation, history shows us how much that situation can reveal to us. Colonialism appears as a trial, a kind of test imposed on certain societies or, if we may call it such, as a crude sociological experiment. An analysis of colonial societies cannot overlook these specific conditions. As certain anthropologists have perceived,[11] they reveal not only the processes of adaptation or rejection, the new guideposts set up for a society whose traditional models have been destroyed (the 'patterns' of Anglo-American authors), but they also disclose 'the points of resistance' among colonial peoples, the fundamental structure and behavior of such a people. They touch society's bedrock. Such information offers unmistakable theoretical interest (if we consider the colonial situation as a fact calling for scientific observation, independent of any moral judgments it may provoke), and it has a truly practical importance: it shows the fundamental premises in terms of which each problem must be conceived.

The historian reveals the way in which the colonial system was established and transformed. He describes, according to differing circumstances, the various political, juridical, and administrative aspects of the system. He also enables us to take due note of the ideologies used to justify colonialism.[12] Numerous studies emphasize the gap that has existed between announced principles and actual practices, between 'the civilizing mission' (*la mission civilisatrice* — a phrase used with particular emphasis under Napoleon III — and the desired 'utility' that Eugene Etienne, the 'colonialist of Oran' defined in 1894 as 'the sum total of profits and advantages accruing to the metropole' from any colonial enterprise).[13] H. Brunschwig calls attention, in his history of French colonization, to the long series of misunderstandings (nay, outright lies) that stand out so conspicuously. L. Joubert reminds us of 'the gulf that separated facts from theories following the formal declarations of responsibility for civilizing the subject peoples; the rupture between these alleged objectives and their application, if not the blatant hypocrisy which, in the name of humanitarian principles, condoned exploitation pure and simple . . .'[14] The colonial situation thus appears to have assumed an essentially spurious character. It sought continually to justify itself by means of pseudo-reasons. In his study entitled 'The Colonial Crisis and the Future,' R. Kennedy shows how each characteristic of 'colonialism' – the *color line*, political dependency, economic dependency, virtually non-existent 'social' benefits, the lack of contact between natives and 'the dominant caste' – is predicated on 'a series of rationalizations'; for example, the superiority of the white race; the inability of the native population to govern itself correctly; the despotism of traditional chiefs; the temptation for present leaders to form 'a dictatorial clique'; native inability to develop their own natural resources; the feeble financial resources of colonial peoples; the need to maintain national prestige, etc.[15] In the light of such evidence, the sociologist understands the extent to which a European colonial power, motivated by a dubious doctrine whose historical development can be traced, condemned to resort to deceit and hypocrisy, and wedded to a fixed image of the native population, acted upon colonial societies in terms of these concepts. We have called attention elsewhere to the importance of this fact.[16] No valid sociological study of colonial peoples is possible which ignores this attention given to ideologies and to the more or less stereotyped behavior they produced.

The historian reminds us that contemporary colonial societies are the product of a dual history. Thus in the case of Africa, the one history is entirely African: 'these societies, so stable, so seemingly immobile, all resulted, or almost all, from the variable combinations of diverse peoples who were thrown together, clashed with one another, or were superimposed on each other by historical events'[17] – a history that 'brought together (in a relationship of domination or assimilation) homogeneous, social forms';[18] while on the other hand, the other history, largely conditioned by European domination, 'brought into contact social forms that were radically heterogeneous' and presented a picture of 'disintegration.' 'Three forces,' says Ch.-A. Julien, 'have disintegrated Africa: governmental administration, missionaries, and the new economy.'[19] Any current study of these societies can be made only by viewing them in terms of this dual history.

It is customary to recall that colonialism, broadly speaking, has involved the interplay of three closely inter-related forces – an historical association, as R. Montagne has pointed out by observing that 'the effort to spread the Christian gospel has been tied historically to European expansion in the commercial, political, or military spheres.'[20] The economic, governmental, and missionary objectives have been experienced by subject peoples as closely associated activities,[21] and it is in terms of these factors that anthropologists have usually analyzed 'social changes.' But in an effort to describe modern European colonialism and to explain its appearance, certain historians have been inclined to place the greatest emphasis on one of these aspects – the economic factor. 'Colonial imperialism is but one form of economic imperialism,' Ch.-A. Julien has written in an article on this subject.[22] At this point, history impinges on another point of view that is indispensable for understanding the colonial situation.

The propaganda for political expansion based its arguments, in part, on economic arguments. In 1874, P. Leroy Beaulieu argued France's need to become a colonial power. J. Ferry wrote in 1890: 'Colonial policy is the child of industrial policy . . . colonialism is an international manifestation of the eternal laws of competition . . .'[23] It was economic reasons that colonial powers invoked to justify their presence – the resources that were developed and the equipment built were regarded as property as of right – and economic advantages were the last to be surrendered even after more or less genuine agreements for political independence had been arrived at. Even before the studies of Marxist writers appeared, certain analyses devoted to 'imperialism' revealed its economic characteristics.[24] Lenin was the first Marxist to offer a systematic theory in his famous work: *Imperialism: the Highest Stage of Capitalism*. Ch.-A. Julien stressed its central thesis by recalling that 'colonial policies are the offspring of monopoly, of the exportation of capital and the quest for spheres of economic influence.'[25] Whether it involves colonization or an economic protectorate, a Marxist discovers one and the same reality, one that is linked to capitalism and must disappear with it. The close ties that exist between capitalism and colonial expansion have prompted certain non-Marxist authors to compare the 'colonial question' with the 'social question' and to observe, like J. Guitton, 'that they are not fundamentally different because the *metropole-colony* relationship is in no sense different from the *capital-labor* relationship, or the relationship Hegel has termed *master-servant*.'[26] Note the possible identification of 'colonial peoples' with the 'proletariat.' 'In both cases,' P. Reuter writes, 'we are dealing with a population that produces all the wealth but does not share in its political or economic advantages and constitutes an oppressed class.'[27]

For a Marxist there is no doubt whatsoever about this common identity. Politically, it justifies the combined action of the proletariat and the colonial peoples. Stalin devoted a number of studies to the colonial question and, after having shown that 'Leninism . . . destroyed the wall separating Whites from Blacks, Europeans from Asiatics, the "civilized" from the "non-civilized" slaves of imperialism,' he recalled that 'the October Revolution inaugurated a new era, the era of colonial revolutions in the oppressed countries of the world, in alliance with the proletariat and under the direction of the proletariat.'[28] The colonial peoples themselves stress the economic aspect of their condition more than its political aspect. An African journalist from the Gold Coast writes on this subject:

> Nations whose economic power is preponderant are precisely those whose political influence predominates . . . As of now the authorities have made no effort at all to encourage native populations in their colonies to reach an economic level commensurate with their political advancement.[29]

Without envisaging the colonial situation exclusively in terms of its economic manifestations, a sociologist who tries to understand and interpret colonial societies must recognize the importance of such demonstrable facts. They will remind him that the structures of these societies are not explained simply in terms of contacts between a technically advanced civilization and a primitive, nontechnical society. They will indicate that between the colonial power and the colonized population certain relationships exist which connote tension and conflict. (We have already referred to the instrumental nature of relationships in the colonial society.) This observation would have proved useful to the theoretical views of Malinowski. When the famed anthropologist established the doctrine of 'a practical anthropology,' he declared that a 'wise' control of the forces for change 'can guarantee a normal and stable development,'[30] and this misunderstanding of the extremely antagonistic nature of the situation led him, according to one commentator, to pose the problems 'in the most naive terms.'[31]

The economic aspect of the colonial situation has been expressed in general terms by certain anthropologists or geographers who have specialized in tropical countries. R. Kennedy (in a previously mentioned study) has indicated its principal characteristics:[32]

the quest for raw materials by colonial powers for utilization in the metropolitan industrial complex – a fact that explains the inferior (if not in fact nonexistent)[33] industrial equipment in colonial territories; large-scale exploitation and import – export trade are entirely within the hands of 'societies' which reap all the profits for themselves;[34] the 'distance' separating the Europeans from the colonial peoples (the latter essentially reduced to the role of peasants, laborers, and domestics), explaining the native's difficulty 'in raising himself economically'; and finally, the economic stagnation of the indigenous masses.

Among French-language studies, those dealing with Indo-China are particularly valuable (indeed, they are the only ones which have real depth). That they are the work of geographers such as Charles Robequain and P. Gourou[35] is quite indicative of the current disregard for the present that has characterized French ethnology. 'Peasants' represent 90 to 95% of the Indo-Chinese population, and these studies are essentially concerned with the peasantry. Aside from the importance attached first of all to available technical means (which were not improved, or only slightly improved, by the colonial power) emphasis is placed on the loss of property holdings,[36] on 'property dispossession' producing an uprooted and proletarian population. And we find, as a concomitant trend, the establishment of a bourgeoisie (essentially agrarian in origin) born 'like the proletariat, from contact with western civilization and from a weakening of traditional values.' The growth of this class results almost always 'from exploitation of the rice fields and the system of money-lending associated therewith.'[37] The observations dealing with business (native businesses are broken up into many small and unimportant enterprises, while big businesses and export trade are in the hands of Europeans or foreigners – Chinese and Indians) and the observations concerning industry (a stagnation of local industry, a lack of any industrial processing, and a negligible growth of the work force – since 1890 the average annual increase in the work force was only 2,500 according to Charles Robequain – and the low level of skilled workmen) all substantiate the general picture presented by R. Kennedy. It is on the basis of such facts that P. Naville could give a precise and strictly Marxist interpretation of the economic and political conditions of the Vietnamese revolution.[38]

Studies relating to Africa, especially Central and South Africa, disclose the same kinds of facts. These studies are primarily by Anglo-American anthropologists rightly concerned with 'practical anthropology.' The situation created in South Africa by a European minority is well known: territorial segregation imposed by the Native Land Act of 1913 (*native areas* comprise only 12% of the entire territory of the Union of South Africa); social segregation legalized by the Colour Bar Act of 1926 which restricts black workers to jobs requiring manual labor only; the disproportionately small share of national income enjoyed by the Negroes (representing 69 per cent of the population, they receive only 20 per cent of the national income, whereas the Whites, who make up 21 per cent of the population, receive 74 per cent of the income); the racial bases and racist premises of economic and political structures; the profound contradictions in a policy that establishes segregation (the Whites fearing to be overrun by the Blacks) while at the same time it must 'sound the call for native workers,'[39] thus provoking a rural exodus resulting in 'proletarization' and 'de-tribalization' of the indigenous population. The special situation in South Africa, still in some ways almost a caricature of these conditions, shows the extent to which economic, political, and racial questions are closely interrelated.[40] And it shows, too, how these questions cannot be ignored by anyone undertaking a study of present-day conditions in the Union of South Africa. It is in the light of these facts that we reaffirm the compelling need to consider the *colonial situation* as a single complex, as a totality.

Anglo-American anthropologists have assigned an important role to economic facts considered as one of the principal 'forces' responsible for 'culture-change.' In her celebrated work, *Reaction to Conquest*, Monica Hunter examines the transformations that occurred in Pondo society (in South Africa) in terms first of the economic factor and then of the political factor ('which, historically speaking, has an economic origin, whatever non-Marxists may say about it'). But these studies, already quite numerous on the question of Africa alone,[41] are conducted solely along economic lines, analyzing the 'primitive' social organization and economy with regard to the dislocations brought about by a 'modern' economy and the problems created by the latter. They fail to relate these to the colonial economy, the colonial situation. They fail to convey the notion of reciprocity of outlooks existing between the colonial population, on the one hand, and the colonial power, on the other. The studies inspired by Malinowski are conspicuous for these shortcomings, since they reveal only the results of 'contact' between 'institutions' of the same nature, and scarcely go beyond a simple description of certain transformations and the enumeration of certain problems. This explains why they are concerned primarily with rural questions, with changes affecting the village and 'the family,' with rural depopulation. In this field, they have outlined significant patterns of 'culture-change': destruction of the extended family, predominance of economic values, the emancipation of the younger generation, the establishment of a monetary economy which upsets personal relationships, the threat to traditional hierarchies (wealth and rank no longer always being closely associated), etc. Certain special research fields – such as that relating to living standards[42] – have been developed, but important facts – such as the new social groupings resulting from the dislocation of traditional groupings, the appearance of social classes, the nature and role of the proletariat, etc. – are touched on only in very general terms, and the conflicts they imply are rarely analyzed.[43]

Yet it is precisely these aspects of the problem that are given highest priority in studies inspired by the condition of crisis that exists in colonial societies and by the political and administrative implications deriving from this crisis. In this area of study, the declarations made by a Marxist observer find common ground with those of the highly placed colonial administrator. Each, for different reasons, draws attention to the degradation of the peasantry, to the constant increase of a colonial proletariat, and to the antagonisms arising therefrom. With respect to French North Africa and French Black Africa, we call the reader's attention to two general studies that complement or reinforce each other, one by geographer J. Dresch and the other by High Commissioner R. Delavignette.[44] The movement of dispossession on the one hand ('730,000 rural families are totally deprived of land and must be regarded as indigent,' J. Dresch writes), of 'uprooting' the peasantry, and the correlative increase in the proletarian population, measured by the accelerated growth of urban centers, are analyzed within the framework of local conditions. Elsewhere the accent is on those characteristics peculiar to the colonial proletarian:

> The natives of North Africa are becoming proletarians, but unskilled proletarians, colonial proletarians, judged equally good and equally unfit for any kind of employment, servants of an elementary and speculative economy, threatened by crises alternately produced by droughts and the uncertainty of sources of raw materials.
>
> (J. Dresch)

The proletariat 'is the vehicle for racism; imbuing the class struggle with a fierce degree of violence by linking it with a racial struggle,' and, in the face of this threat, there is a mounting temptation on the part of 'certain Europeans' to keep the peasantry as long as possible in 'a primitive state (which they think) is one of tranquility' (R. Delavignette). Such observations indicate to what extent the colonial population, in its urban as well as its rural aspects, together with the colonial power, form a system, a whole. There is a need for any study dealing with one of these elements to take cognizance of the whole. Such observations also draw attention to the antagonisms existing in the very heart of this situation as a result of a stratification by classes that is achieved at the expense of traditional social structures, and to the conflicts that can be explained only within the framework of the colonial situation. In other portions of these studies we find that the concept of 'crisis' is at the very root of these preoccupations ('a crisis that strikes a dislocated society and, little by little, destroys it,' to quote J. Dresch). These observations enable us to discover — by singling out and even perhaps exaggerating the situation — this pathological aspect of colonial societies to which we have called attention.

Elsewhere in these same studies considerable attention is given to the role of the judicial and administrative apparatus charged with maintaining this domination. One critic, after having denounced its 'arbitrariness,' talks of the actions of an organization 'that has separated peoples of the same ethnic origin and the same social structure and has thrown together dissimilar ethnic groups of different social structures . . .' The arbitrary nature of the colonial boundaries and administrative divisions, between and within colonies, results in — or aims at — fragmenting important ethnic groups, breaking up political units of any significance, and artificially juxtaposing incompatible or antagonistic ethnic groups.[45] Certain recent actions on the part of colonial peoples can be explained as a reaction to such conditions as, for instance, the manifestation of a desire to restore former social groupings. In the case of Black West Africa alone, we can point out: the demands for unification among the Ewe (divided between French and British Togoland); the attempts to establish tribal federalism in the South Camerouns; the more or less explicit desire for regrouping evidenced by the African churches — known by the name of Kimbangism — occurring in the Ba-Kongo country (in the Belgian Congo and in the French Congo).

The maintenance or creation of this type of 'balkanization,' with its attendant rivalries or hostilities among ethnic groups, treated as pawns of administrative policies, have imposed on these groups, within the framework of the colonial situation, a particular history which no sociological analysis can afford to ignore. And a recent study dealing with the Malagasies indicates how this desire to weaken an ethnic group (for fear of encountering a national consciousness) is often accompanied by the desire to destroy the group's historical record (for fear of providing a basis for 'pride in being a malagasy and thus justifying a sense of nationalism,' as the author puts it).[46] We again come upon the already mentioned question of ideologies. The effort to pervert a people's history affects their collective memory, provoking an inevitable backlash, and thus we see the possible importance of such facts in any effort to understand colonial peoples.

If we set forth in a very schematic fashion the various social groupings brought together by the colonial situation, classifying them, starting with the colonial power (the dominant group) and ending with the colonial population (the subject group), we find:

(a)   the colonial power, not including foreigners of the white race;
(b)   white 'foreigners';

(c)   the 'coloured' – to use the English expression which is defined broadly;
(d)   the colonized population, namely, all those whom the British call 'the natives.'

We find a distinction and a hierarchy based, first of all, on criteria of race and nationality, implying as a sort of postulate the excellence of the white race, and more especially, of that fraction which is the colonial power (its supremacy is given as a fact of history, established by nature).

Of course, this is only a rough outline which needs to be filled in. R. Delavignette has devoted a chapter of his book to a study of colonial society[47] (that is, its European component). He recalls certain characteristics that define it: a society 'of European origins, oriented to the homeland,' constituting a numerical minority, middle-class in character, given to the 'notion of heroic superiority' (a doctrine partially explained by the greater percentage of males – and, for the most part, young men, especially numerous during the early stages of colonization). Above all we are dealing with a society whose function it is to achieve political, economic, and spiritual domination. In the words of R. Delavignette, this society tends to instill in its members 'the feudal spirit.' The important fact is that this dominant group constitutes a numerical minority to a very large degree; there is a great imbalance between the mass of the 'colonizers' and the mass of those 'colonized.' And there is a more or less persistent fear of seeing the hierarchy re-established on the sole basis of the size of the masses. This fear is revived in times of crisis and explains seemingly inexplicable reactions such as the 'events' in Madagascar. And L. Wirth offers an oversimplified judgment when he declares, with respect to colonial situations, that 'the dominant group can maintain its superior situation simply by utilizing its military and administrative machinery.' So great is the disproportion between civilizations![48] He underestimates thus a number of important aspects – the means by which the European population renders itself untouchable:

(a)   keeping contacts at a bare minimum (segregation);
(b)   offering the European as the model for emulation, while effectively blocking any means to that end (assimilation is held out as the basis for equality – because it is known full well that assimilation is either impossible of attainment or is restricted to a very limited few);
(c)   maintaining ideologies justifying the position of the dominant group;
(d)   employing political tactics designed to preserve the imbalance in favor of the colonial power (and its European homeland);
(e)   more or less deliberately transferring to certain groups the attitudes and feelings provoked by political and economic domination: thus, for example, to the Lebanese-Syrians in French West Africa (where they represent about one-fourth of the population designated administratively as 'European and assimilated') or regularly to the Indians and 'Coloured' in the Union of South Africa (at the time of the troubles in 1947, 1948, and 1949, the Africans attacked only Asians).

To the extent that the distance between cultures is less, the relative size of the groups plays a greater role. Force alone no longer suffices to maintain control, and more indirect methods are resorted to – the element of 'misunderstanding' comes into play (a fact that struck H. Brunschwig in his historical analysis and Mannoni in his psychoanalytical one). These indirect methods are used most frequently, depending on individual circumstances, racial or religious differences of an antagonistic nature (as in India during the heyday of British colonialism). It must be remembered that the European colonial society is not perfectly homogeneous. It has its 'factions,' its 'clans' (the 'administrators,' the 'private sector,' the 'military,' and the 'missionaries,' according to the terminology used in French territories). These groups are more or less self-contained, more or less competitive (antagonism between the administration and the missions, or between the administration and the commercial sector occurs frequently). Each group practices its own native policies (indeed, to such an extent, that certain English anthropologists have regarded each one of them as 'an agent' provoking 'cultural change'). They cause widely varied reactions. In other respects the European colonial society is essentially a closed one, more or less remote from the colonized population. But a policy of domination and prestige demands that it be closed and aloof, a situation that does not facilitate mutual understanding and appreciation, a situation that allows (or encourages) the easy recourse to 'stereotypes.' Isolated in the 'colony,' this society has also partially severed its connections with the homeland. R. Delavignette has made due note of this fact in writing about 'the colonials': 'Europeans in the colony, they become colonials at home . . . they seek to channel their energies into a jealous sort of particularism . . .'[49]

Among the groups discriminated against by those in control, colored people (mixed breeds and colored foreigners) are held in the lowest esteem. For what amounts to an essentially racial reason, the colored man is rejected both by the colonial power and by the colonial peoples themselves. He has few contacts with either. His isolation becomes even greater (by means of discriminatory measures), reducing him to the role of an 'exotic' community, as he achieves greater economic importance. The Indian problem in South Africa is thus explained by the fact that certain Indians 'have become too rich and are surreptitiously acquiring positions held by the Whites.' Here we see clearly an overlapping of facts of a racial nature and facts of an economic nature. In the case of half-breeds (metis), the isolation is even more absolute because of their racial impurity – 'a racial compromise.' Only in rare instances do they succeed in regrouping and forming a viable society. The case of the 'Bastards of Rehoboth' in former German Southwest Africa is especially famous. And a very strict isolation was imposed on this group. As A. Siegfried has noted with regard to the 'Cape coloured,' these half-breeds are forced 'into the hands of a black race with which they do not want to be identified.' They aim at becoming assimilated by the colonial society which remains closed to them (more or less, according to local circumstances), or which grants them a special status[50] conferring a legal recognition of their particular position. If they are 'a racial compromise,' they are in no sense 'a social compromise.' One can scarcely regard them as being a liaison between the colonial power and the colonized population. Their political alliance with the elite of a colonial society was never durable. Thus, for example, the Conference of Non-Europeans, created in 1927 in South Africa, which tried to unite in a common endeavor Coloureds, Indians, and Bantus, produced no effective results and was short-lived. The 'Coloureds' are more in conflict than in agreement with the colonized population, because of their improved economic and social condition and because of the racial factor. They cannot pretend thus to leadership of the colonial peoples.

The colonial population presents two salient characteristics: its overwhelming numerical superiority,[51] and the rigid control to which it is subjected. While a numerical majority, it is nevertheless a sociological minority. In the words of R. Maunier, 'colonialism is a fact of power': it involves the loss of autonomy and 'a legal or *de facto* trusteeship.'[52] Each sector of the controlling society has as its function to maintain the domination of the colonial power in some specific domain (political, economic, and, almost always, spiritual). This domination by the European power is an absolute one owing to the absence of any advanced technology or material power other than sheer numbers. It finds its *de facto* expression in practices which, while not codified into laws, incur sharp and immediate disapproval if they are not respected, whereas other practices are given legal sanction. As we have already mentioned several times, colonial domination is based on an ideology, on a system of pseudo-justifications and rationalizations. It has a racist foundation, more or less acknowledged, more or less obvious. A colonial people is subjected to the pressures of every group comprising the colony. All exert their pre-eminence in some area with the result that a colonial people is made to feel all the more keenly its subordinate status. The agencies of the colonial power regard the colony itself as essentially a productive source of wealth (whereas the colonial people keep only a very small part of that wealth despite their greater numbers). This fact conditions in part the relations it maintains with the other groups (who derive from the colony their economic advantages). These relations, however, are not simple. They are not merely the relationship of the exploiter to the exploited, of the dominant to the dominated. They are not that simple because of the lack of unity among colonial peoples themselves and, above all, because of the extremely heterogeneous character of the culture (or rather, the cultures) which are to be found in the society.

The colonial population is divided ethnically. The divisions are rooted in the society's own history but are utilized by the colonial power (we recall the utility of that old principle: 'Divide and rule'), and these divisions are complicated by the arbitrary colonial 'divisions' and by administrative 'splitting up' of tribes within the colony. These ethnic divisions not only orient the relations of each ethnic group with the colonial power (for example, the peoples who acted as 'intermediaries' during the period of African slave trade and the establishment of trading settlements (*comptoirs*) tried to transfer their role from the economic to the political plane and became 'militant' minorities), but these divisions likewise orient their attitude with respect to the culture introduced by the colonial power (some ethnic groups are more 'assimilationist' or more 'traditionalist' than certain neighboring groups, a reaction, in part at least, to the attitudes adopted by the latter). The colonial population is spiritually divided. Spiritual divisions may have preceded European colonization and be associated notably with the waves of Islamic conquest. But we are familiar with the tactics adopted by European colonial powers. The strategy of English domination in India is well known. In many places colonialism brought about religious confusion by opposing Christianity to traditional religions, while Christian churches presented differences among themselves. We mention in this connection an African of Brazzaville who recalled 'this state of affairs whose only effect is to create a lamentable confusion in the individual's moral and psychological development' and who added: 'The Black African, whoever he is, has the rudiments of a religion. To deprive him of them by introducing atheism or a confusion of religious doctrines can only result in completely unhinging him.'[53] The author almost went so far as to ask the 'colonizer' to impose unity! This serves to illustrate the extent to which these new divisions, added to the old ones, have had the most painful effects on certain groups. But colonization has brought other divisions we may designate as social in nature, products of administrative and economic action and of educational policies: the separation of city dwellers from rural groups,[54] the separation of proletariat from bourgeoisie, of the 'elites' (or '*evolués*' – groups who have *evolved*, according to the usual expression) from the masses of the population,[55] and that between generations. We have touched on all these factors and indicated their importance in various parts of our analysis. Each of these fragmented groups participates differently in the world society. The contact between races and civilizations, which colonization has brought about, has neither the same meaning nor the same consequences for any one of them. The contact must be studied in the light of this diversity (for which it is partly responsible in the first place, but which is now in turn partly influenced by the very conditions it helped bring about).

Most studies dealing with present-day colonial societies stress the state of crisis affecting them and 'the arduous and complex problems' they pose. To a greater or lesser degree, they are regarded as sick societies,[56] which is true to the extent that the colonial power opposes any genuine solutions. For it is an apparent fact that, among colonial peoples, the quest for norms coincides with the quest for autonomy. And this fact imposes on the sociologist an analytical method that is in some measure clinical. We have indicated, in the previously mentioned study, how an approach to the question of colonial societies, concentrating on their specific crises, constitutes 'an unexcelled standpoint for analysis,' 'the only point at which one can grasp *the evolution of indigenous social structures placed in the colonial situation.*'[57] Such crises force re-examination of the society as a whole, its institutions as well as its component groups and symbols; the social dislocations provide opportunities for the analyst to penetrate and explore from within, and not merely arrive at some abstract notions of the phenomena arising from the contact between a colonial power and a colonial people. The analyst will be better able to understand the latter in its traditional forms by discovering certain systems and weaknesses (as we shall indicate in the case of the Fang of Gabon, a people among whom the colonial situation encouraged certain ruptures already inherent in its previous social structure), or certain unshakeable structures and collective representations (thus, for example, a study of the religious crisis and of 'Negro churches' characteristic of Bantu Africa would reveal what remains of traditional religions despite all the other pressures brought to bear – the irreducible element). Each crisis, affecting the global society as a whole, constitutes a point of insight into that society and the relationships it implies.[58] Looking at such crises permits that concrete and comprehensive approach already recommended by Marcel Mauss. And to complete the illustration just given, we recall a recent thesis devoted to 'the Negro churches' and the activities of Bantu prophets (in South Africa) in which the author, B.G.M. Sundkler, shows that the problems posed are not only of a religious nature, but raise the question of Bantu reactions as a whole to White domination, and that the study of these 'churches' leads to a study of all the social problems characterizing the Union of South Africa.[59]

At first glance these crises are noteworthy for the radical changes in, or the outright disappearance of, certain institutions and certain groups. But a sociological analysis cannot limit itself to these aspects of the social picture – its institutional or structural forms – and merely note the changes and disappearances, locating new social structures and describing them. It is indispensable to go beyond these considerations and to reach for 'the forms of sociability,' to borrow the expression of Georges Gurvitch.[60] For it seems quite apparent that certain 'ways of forming links,' certain social ties persist, even when the structures within which they operate are radically altered or destroyed, while at the same time new ties appear as a result of the colonial situation and the social conjunctures it creates. These social ties can co-exist and impart to the innovations conceived by the colonial society those characteristics that are both traditionalist and modernist, that peculiar state of ambiguity noted by several observers.

We have frequently alluded to the importance of race relations, the racial basis for social groupings, to the racial coloration of political and economic facts (current literature confuses or associates racism and colonialism) in the framework of the colonial situation. And various authors insist on the interracial nature of 'human relationships in overseas territories,' on the fact that, beneath 'the political or economic causes still dividing the white race and the colored peoples, there is almost always a racial motive.' These authors insist that the society remains 'interracial', even when national independence is acquired.[61] We have several times indicated that colonial anthropologists have paid little attention to these racial facts and problems and given little room to them in their research projects. This is explained by the greater attention given to cultures rather than to societies and can be attributed to the more or less conscious desire on the part of these anthropologists to avoid questioning the very foundations (and ideology) of the society to which they belong, the society of the colonial power.[62]

We have just considered certain facts which Anglo-American writers place under the headings of 'the clash of civilizations' or 'the clash of races,' but we have shown that, in the case of colonial peoples, these 'clashes' (or 'contacts') occur under very special circumstances. To these collective circumstances we have given the name *colonial situation*. The latter may be defined by singling out and retaining the most general and most obvious of these conditions:

(1)   the domination imposed by a foreign minority, racially (or ethnically) and culturally different, acting in the name of a racial (or ethnic) and cultural superiority dogmatically affirmed, and imposing itself on an indigenous population constituting a numerical majority but inferior to the dominant group from a material point of view;

(2)   this domination linking radically different civilizations into some form of relationship;

(3)   a mechanized, industrialized society with a powerful economy, a fast tempo of life, and a Christian background, imposing itself on a non-industrialized, 'backward' society in which the pace of living is much slower and religious institutions are most definitely 'non-Christian';

(4)   the fundamentally antagonistic character of the relationship between these two societies resulting from the subservient role to which the colonial people are subjected as 'instruments' of the colonial power;

(5)   the need, in maintaining this domination, not only to resort to 'force,' but also to a system of pseudo-justifications and stereotyped behaviors, etc. But this enumeration by itself is inadequate.

With the help of the particular 'views' offered by each discipline, we have preferred to grasp the colonial situation as a whole, and as a system. We have set forth the elements in terms of which any specific situation can be described and understood and have shown how these elements are interrelated, with the result that any analysis of a part is necessarily distorted. This oneness raises doubts about the reality of the 'groups' comprising 'the global society' (the colony) as collective representations peculiar to each of these groups. This sense of totality is felt at all levels of social reality. But owing to the heterogeneous character of the groups, of the cultural 'models,' of the various representations confronting each other, and owing to the changes that occur in the system responsible for maintaining artificially the conditions of domination and subordination, the colonial situation becomes greatly modified, and at a rapid pace. This fact requires that the situation be studied in an historical manner, that the dates be specified.

It is rather significant that many anthropologists, operating within the structure of a colonial society and preoccupied with its current aspects and problems, have avoided (unconsciously, in most cases) describing the concrete situation applicable to such a society. Out of a more or less conscious fear of having to take into consideration a specific kind of 'system' and society: the society of the colonial power to which they themselves belong. They have dealt with less compromising systems – 'western civilization' and 'primitive cultures,' or else have confined themselves to limited problems for which they have proposed solutions of a limited nature. And it is because of a refusal to accept this attitude, which they regard as inevitable and profitable only to the colonial power, that certain anthropologists decline to treat their discipline as 'an applied' science.[63] We are confronted here with a fact that belongs in the framework of critical judgment in the domain of human sciences and one which suggests the extensive critical preparation, incumbent upon anyone who contemplates offering an analysis of colonial societies.

We have frequently noted the somewhat pathological character of colonial societies, the *crises* marking the stages of the so-called process of 'evolution' – crises that do not correspond to necessary phases of this process, yet which have nevertheless specific characteristics in relation to the type of colonial society under consideration and the nature of the colonial society (the Islamized Africans do not react like 'animist' Africans or pseudo-Christians; African societies of the same type do not react in the same manner to 'the French presence' and 'the British presence', etc.). By focusing clearly on those facts that characterize a society subjected to colonial domination, and on those facts that characterize the colonial situation in its particular aspects, these 'crises' enable a sociologist to achieve a comprehensive analysis, since they constitute the only points from which one can grasp, in a global sense, the transformations occurring among a colonial people under the influence and actions of the colonial power. They are conducive to reaching overall views, an awareness of essential ties and relationships. They allow one to avoid fragmentary analyses (changes in the economic life, in the political life, etc.), which are both incomplete and artificial and can only lead to an academic sort of description and classification. We have already indicated that these 'crises' constitute so many vantage points from which to view not only the phenomena of contact, but also the colonized society in all its traditional aspects. We must add that they also permit in this manner an analysis which takes into account, simultaneously, 'the external milieu' and 'the internal milieu' – and takes them into account in terms of existing conditions and relationships, in terms of actual life experiences.

We may be criticized for having resorted, in a more or less explicit manner, to the dangerous notion of the pathological and be asked to define the criteria characteristic of colonial crises. Our answer is to refer the critic to all the passages in this study which set forth the antagonistic aspects of relations between a colonial people and a colonial power, between a native culture and an imported culture – relationships between domination and subjection, to the heterogeneous nature of societies and cultures in contact with each other – and in which the critic will find a suggestion as to the way in which these conflicts are felt by the individuals involved. The history of colonial societies reveals periods during which conflicts are merely latent, when a temporary equilibrium or adjustment has been achieved, and periods during which conflicts rise to the surface and are apparent on one level or the other, according to circumstances (religious, political, and economic). But conflicts expose at the same time the totality of relationships between colonial peoples and colonial powers and between the cultures of each of them (as we have reminded the reader in the case of Negro churches in Bantu Africa), moments when the antagonism and the gulf between a colonial people and a colonial power are at their maximum and are experienced by the colonial rulers as a challenge to established order, but by the colonial peoples as an effort to regain their autonomy. At each of these moments, which can be clearly delineated throughout the history of a colonial people, the latter present an unmistakable state of crisis, and it is precisely at such moments we can study the colonial society in terms of the concrete colonial situation.

Notes

1   R. Kennedy, 'The Colonial Crisis and the Future,' in R. Linton (ed.) *The Science of Man in the World Crisis*, 1945, 307.
2   O. Mannoni, *Psychologie de la Colonisation*, Éditions du Seuil, 1950. This author did not however originate the expression which is found with different connotations in previous works, notably in studies by the American sociologist, L. Wirth, devoted to the 'typology of minorities.'
3   We refer the reader to our summary of O. Mannoni's work published in the *Cahiers Internationaux de Sociologie*, 1950, IX, 183–6.
4   L. Joubert, 'Le Fait colonial et ses prolongements,' *Le Monde non Chrétien*, 1950, vol. 15.
5   Ch.-A. Julien, 'Impérialisme économique et impéralisme colonial,' in *Fin de l'ère coloniale* (Paris, 1948).
6   cf. R. Kennedy, op. cit., 308–9, and R. Grousset, 'Colonisations,' in *Fin de l'ère coloniale*.
7   Quotation appears in the excellent book by H. Brunschwig, *La Colonisation francaise* (Calman-Lévy, 1949).
8   For example, the displacements carried out on behalf of the Office du Niger, which gave rise to the most heated controversy; see P. Herrart's pamphlet, *Le Chancre du Niger*, with a preface by André Gide, Gallimard, 1939.
9   E. Chancele, 'La Question coloniale,' *Critique*, 1949, no. 35.
10   cf. L. Joubert, op. cit., part II.
11   cf. L.P. Mair, 'The Study of Culture Contact as a Practical Problem,' *Africa*, 1934, VII(4).
12   cf. J. Harmand, *Domination et Colonisation*, Flammarion, 1910, as a 'classic' example of a juridical type of justification.
13   Quoted from H. Brunschwig, op. cit., 64.
14   ibid., 265.
15   R. Kennedy, op. cit., 312–18.
16   G. Balandier, 'Aspects *d'évolution* sociale chez les Fang du Gabon,' *Cahiers Internationaux de Sociologie*, 1950, IX, 82.
17   R. Montagne, 'Le Bilan de l'oeuvre européenne au-déla des mers,' in *Peuples d'Outre-Mer et Civilisation Occidentale*, Semaines Sociales de France, 1948.
18   G. Balandier, op. cit., 78.
19   Ch.-A. Julien, *Histoire de l'Afrique*, Collection *Que sais-je?*, Presses Universitaires de France, 1944, 123.
20   R. Montagne, op. cit., 49.
21   cf. especially Pham Nhuam, 'Appel,' in *Que pensent les étudiants coloniaux*, Le Semeur, December 1947, January 1948.
22   Ch.-A. Julien, 'Impérialisme économique et impérialisme colonial,' op. cit., 25.

23   P. Leroy-Beaulieu, *De la colonization chez les peoples modernes*, 1874, 1st edn, J. Ferry, preface to *Le Tonkin et la Mère-Patrie*, 1890.

24   cf. A. Conant, *The Economic Basis of Imperialism*, 1898, and J.A. Hobson, *Imperialism, A Study*, 1902 (whose worth was recognized by Lenin), both works quoted by Ch.-A. Julien, op. cit.

25   Ch.-A. Julien, op. cit., 29. cf. on the subject of Africa, S.H. Frankel, *Capital Investments in Africa*, 1936.

26   J. Guitton, 'Crises et valeurs permanentes de la Civilisation occidentales,' in *Peuples d'Outre-Mer et Civilisation Occidentale*, 61.

27   P. Reuter, 'Deux formes actuelles de l'Impérialisme colonial: protectorat économique et pénétration communiste,' in *Peuples d'Outre-Mer et Civilisation Occidentale*, 142.

28   J. Stalin, *Le Marxisme et la question nationale et coloniale*, éd. francaise, *Éditions Sociales*, 1949, 179, 247.

29   *The African Morning Post*, June 2, 1945, quoted in Univers, 'L'Avenir de la colonisation,' October 1945.

30   B. Malinowski, *The Dynamics of Culture Change* (Yale University Press, 1945).

31   cf. the excellent analysis of M. Gluckman, 'Malinowski's "Functional" Analysis of Social Change,' *Africa*, April 2, 1947, XVII.

32   R. Kennedy, op. cit., 309–11.

33   cf. L. Durand-Reville, 'Le Problème de l'industrialisation des territoires d'Outre-Mer,' *Le Monde non Chrétien*, 13, January–March 1959, where this aspect is suggested and in which the author, a member of the French parliament from Gabon, sets forth the changes made necessary by the last war as well as present-day needs.

34   For facts concerning French Africa, we refer the reader to the excellent studies of the geographer, Jean Dresch.

35   cf. especially Ch. Robequain, *L'Évolution economique de l'Indochine francaise* (Paris, 1940) and P. Gourou, *L'Utilisation du sol en Indochine francaise and Les Pays Tropicaux* (Paris, 1948).

36   For a comprehensive study of this phenomenon, see *Land Tenure in the Colonies*, V. Liversage, 1945; quoted by P. Naville, *La Guerre du Vietnam* (Paris, 1949).

37   cf. Ch. Robequain, op. cit.

38   P. Naville, op. cit. (Paris, 1949); cf. especially, 'La Politique francaise en Cochinchine,' 'La Bourgeoisie cochinchinoise,' 'Les Paysans annamites et la Révolution,' 'Le Développement de la classe ouvrière et de l'industrie.'

39   J. Borde, 'Le Problème ethnique dans l'Union Sud-Africaine,' *Cahiers d'Outre-Mer*, 1950, no. 12; an excellent over-all view and bibliography.

40   cf. W.G. Ballinger, *Race and Economics in South Africa*, 1934.

41   For South Africa, we mention I. Schapera, M. Hunter; for East Africa, L.P. Mair, Audrey Richards, M. Read, M. Gluckman; for West Africa, M. Fortes, D. Forde, K.L. Little. We regard their works as the most important.

42   cf. M. Read, *Native Standards of Living and African Culture-Change* (London, 1938).

43   K.L. Little, 'Social Change and Social Class in the Sierra-Leone Protectorate,' *American Journal of Sociology*, July 1948, 54. An important study.

44   J. Dresch, 'La Prolétarisation des masses indigènes en Afrique du Nord,' in *Fin de l'ere coloniale*, op. cit., 57–69, and R. Delavignette, 'Les Problèmes du travail: Paysannerie et Proletariat,' in *Peuples d'Outre-Mer et Civilisation Occidentale*, 273–91.

45   G. D'Arboussier, 'Les Problèmes de la culture,' *Afrique Noire*, special edition of Europe, May–June 1949.

46   O. Hatzfeld, 'Les Peuples heureux ont une histoire. Étude malgache,' *Cahiers du monde non Chrétien*, 1950, 16.

47   *Les Vrais chefs de l'Empire*, a new edition under the title *Service Africain*, 1946; ch. II, 'La Societe coloniale.' (Translated as *Freedom and Authority in French West Africa*, 1950.)

48   op. cit., 353.

49   op. cit., 41.

50   cf. A. Siegfried, *Afrique du Sud*, Armand Colin, 1949, 75. Also, *Handbook on Race Relations in South Africa*, E. Hellmann, 1949 and J. Borde, op. cit., 339–40.

51   For Black Africa alone, R. Delavignette gave, in 1939, the following proportions in respect to the population designated as European: the Union of South Africa (25.0%), former German Southwest Africa (10.0%), Rhodesia (4.5%), Angola (1.0%), Kenya (0.5%), Belgian Congo (0.2%), French West Africa and French Equatorial Africa (0.1%); op. cit., p. 36. Concerning the latter territories, since 1945 the increase in European population has been important.

52   cf. R. Maunier, *Sociologie Coloniale*, 19, 30, 33.

53   J.-R. Ayouné, 'Occidentalisme et Africanisme' in *Renaissances*, special edn, October 1944, 204.

54   We call attention to Brazzaville where the African population rose from 3,800 inhabitants in 1912 to 75,000 in 1950; that is more than one-tenth of the population of the Central Congo.

55   cf. Dr. L. Aujoulat, 'Élites et masses en pays d'Outre-Mer' in *Peuples d'Outre-Mer et Civilisation Occidentale*, op. cit., 233–72.

56   cf. L. Achille, 'Rapports humains en Pays d'Outre-Mer' in *Peuples d'Outre-Mer et Civilisation Occidentale*, op. cit.

57   G. Balandier, 'Aspects de L'Évolution sociale chez les Fang du Gabon; I. Les implications de la situation coloniale,' op. cit.

58   Monica Hunter had come close to making this observation. She wrote: 'The study of culture contact makes very clear that society is a unity, and when one aspect is modified, the whole is affected'; *Reaction to Conquest*, 552. She was content simply to make this observation and did not seek to explore its implications or discover its consequences in a methodical manner.

59   B.G.M. Sundkler, *Bantu Prophets in South Africa* (London, 1948).

60   cf. *La Vocation Actuelle de la Sociologie*, in particular, 98–108. The definition of sociology and its essential distinctions are set forth. Chapters III and IV are devoted to microsociology, whose true founder is Georges Gurvitch.

61   cf. L. Achille, op. cit., 211–15.

62   A carefully reasoned and concise critical analysis was given by M. Leiris in a lecture entitled 'l'Ethnographe devant le colonialisme' in 1950, later published in *Les Temps Modernes*.

63   cf. F.M. Keesing, 'Applied Anthropology in Colonial Administration,' in R. Linton (ed.) op. cit.

Chapter 2

Antoinette Burton

RULES OF THUMB: BRITISH HISTORY AND 'IMPERIAL CULTURE' IN NINETEENTH- AND TWENTIETH-CENTURY BRITAIN[1]

In the work of Antoinette Burton, and perhaps especially in several successive programmatic essays she has produced, one finds almost all the dominant themes of the 'new imperial history' brought together. Indeed one might aptly think of those essays as 'manifestoes' for that intellectual current. Here, in one of the earliest and most influential of them, she especially argues for the dissolving of barriers between British 'imperial' and 'domestic' history.

Stephen Howe

I cannot help thinking that in discussions of this kind, a great deal of misapprehension arises from the popular use of maps on a small scale. As with such maps you are able to put a thumb on India and a finger on Russia, some persons at once think that the political situation is alarming and that India must be looked to. If the noble Lord would use a larger map – say one on the scale of the Ordinance Map of England – he would find that the distance between Russia and British India is not to be measured by the finger and thumb, but by a rule.

(Lord Salisbury, 1877)

H ISTORIANS HAVE ALWAYS BEEN concerned with maps and mapping and British historians are certainly no exception. Because history-writing in the West has been instrumental to the building of nation-states, historiography itself has become an institutionalized expression, not just of national identity but of the geographical reach of national power as well. In the British context – where the very use of the term

'British' denotes the coercive power of the English state to create a Greater Britain out of itself and the Celtic fringe – doing modern British history has implicitly meant accounting for what constituted Britain territorially and, not coincidentally, elaborating the territorial extent of British influence.[2] While this preoccupation with geographical parameters may be attributed to Britain's insularity, it was also, from the mid-nineteenth century onward, a consequence of British imperial conquest and of the sense of historical mission, which both motivated and sustained it. J.R. Seeley's *The Expansion of England* (1883) not only gave imperial history its 'institutional life . . . [and] respectability, it helped to guarantee that the boundaries between the history of Great Britain and that of Greater Britain were clearly drawn.'[3] For in spite of the fact that empire was believed to be 'a determining fact in the life of both the metropolis and its dependencies', for almost a century the history of empire was treated as if it occurred on another planet, far away from England's 'green and pleasant lands', disconnected in time and space from 'the Mother Country' – that saccharine, stolid and basically static imperial referent. It was not routinely the purview of conventional British historians, but remained the territory of self-styled 'imperial historians', the *burra sahibs* of the British historical establishment. It was often examined and interpreted from the vantage point of established university chairs in 'imperial history', giving armchair imperialism a whole new meaning. Imperial history has historically been a kind of national subfield, albeit an important one, into which scholars who are not of the British Isles, and even some who are, wander at their peril.[4] A.P. Thornton likened American students of Victorian imperialism to 'tourists in an unfamiliar terrain', adding that 'their academic forbears would as willingly have become Mexican citizens as have written books on the British Empire'.[5]

Until recently in historical terms then, the rule of thumb in British history has been to map a set of quite differently imagined communities: 'home' on the one hand and 'empire' on the other. 'Home' itself was of course as falsely unitary as 'empire', with England as the symbolic center and Wales, Scotland, and Ireland its 'internal others'.[6] It is a testament to the power of a common racial heritage – and to the forces which invent it – that in nineteenth-century and early twentieth-century Britain, the domestic under classes and white ethnic minorities who were prominent in the colonial enterprise could and did become the imperial 'over classes' by virtue of their essential Britishness.[7] Home and empire have nonetheless traditionally been constituted as separate and distinct spheres: one the source of Britishness/progress/civilization, the other precisely that: the other side of the world, the 'dark continent', the as-of-yet undomesticated space of cultural backwardness. For all Britain's claims to be the 'mother country', there was no doubt among contemporaries or, for that matter, generations of imperial historians after Seeley, about where the 'heart of darkness' lay on the map of Greater Britain. Staging Britain and its empire as dichotomous rather than as dialectic spaces was itself a technology of imperial rule – one of many 'grandiloquent displays' – which called upon Britons and others to recognize and hence to legitimate Britain's role as a world-imperial power.[8]

Generations of historians of the Victorian Empire have more typically than not maintained these artificial distinctions, focusing on the geopolitical hows and whys of European imperial formations rather than on the domestic socio-political forces which enabled Britain's imperial projects in India, Africa, and throughout the white settler colonies or, more subversively, on the extent to which neither society was purely, homogeneously either 'home' or 'empire'. Historians of conventionally domestic British history have been, for their part, remarkably insular, so much so that 'British historians have largely failed to ask what empire has done to us'.[9] Cecil Rhodes's conviction that the working classes' support for empire at home prevented civil war is an important clue to the centrality of empire to domestic social attitudes and domestic political ideologies, but his was an observation not much heeded by his contemporaries writing imperial history. The first modern imperial historians (J.R. Seeley, E.A. Freeman, Lord Acton) were more concerned with articulating the historical racial connections between Anglo-Saxons, Teutons, and Greeks in order to promote Britain's imperial greatness to the world than with examining popular manifestations of that racialism in their own historical present.[10] History from the bottom up had yet to be invented and in the meantime, imperial history like 'domestic' historiography operated not just from the top down, but from the center outward. The Anglo-centricity of the combined enterprise can hardly be in doubt. As J.G.A. Pocock observed over a decade ago, it is largely as 'English history' that the history of Britain and its settler colonies was and to some extent still is 'historically intelligible'.[11]

That practitioners of imperial history have been ultimately concerned with the imperial nation at home, there can be equally little doubt. Understanding how a small metropolitan state like Britain grew into a global empire was instrumental for sustaining those quintessentially Victorian myths of cultural and racial superiority which, after 1900 and especially after 1945, did not seem as historically guaranteed or as unshakable as they once had.[12] But even when the security of the nation was a motive force behind the production of imperial history, it did not necessarily entail working to understand or to historicize the interactions between metropole and empire. This was ironic, since much of the business of colonial India was run from Whitehall, while the office of the secretary for India was known as 'India in England'.[13] Failure to think and to write dialectically also tended to foreclose the role of the colonial dependencies in the historical development of British imperial power. Although the colonies-as-agent approach did find expression in the later work of Robinson and Gallagher, tracing its particular trajectories was a task claimed largely by colonial nationalists.[14] As Partha Chatterjee and others have insisted, interpretations of colonial agency have proven to be as influenced by Western Imperial paradigms as traditional 'imperial history', though in significantly different ways.[15] And, in keeping with Whig-historical notions of progress, the movement of ideas, culture, and 'improvement' was presumed to flow in one direction: from home to away. P.J. Marshall rightly reminds us that British models – from utilitarianism to the welfare state – have historically been projected on to the empire, much as Lord Salisbury advised that the Ordnance map of England be used to assess the true scope of territorial possession and any external threat to it.[16] Historiographical practice down to the 1950s neatly replicated the orientalist frame out of which it distantly originated, so that the Otherness of empire became the natural possession of British national identity at the site of academic institutionalization, as well as at other institutional sites throughout the culture. All of which has led Salman Rushdie to remark, with his usual flippant accuracy, that 'the trouble with the English is that their history happened overseas, so they don't know what it means'.[17]

Rushdie is correct in at least one important respect: empire still occupies a basically marginal place on the map of traditional British history. This is perhaps paradoxical, especially in light of the flurry of Raj memorabilia – the making of *A Passage to India*, the production of *The Raj Quartet* by British television, the re-release of *Lawrence of Arabia* – which the 1980s witnessed, and which has been so effectively critiqued by Indian scholars and others who insist on its function as nostalgia and its uncritical reproduction of Victorian racialism, orientalism, and convictions of cultural superiority.[18] It may also seem an odd claim to make, in light of the volume of scholarship currently being produced on race and imperialism in the North American academy – a trend of which the conference in Cincinnati, from whence this collection emerged, is self-consciously a part. But Rushdie's observation misses an important point. For what both popular cultural productions and some of the recent scholarship (especially when it is concerned with European Imperialist ideologies) have failed to recognize is that empire was not a phenomenon 'out there'. The consequences of empire – its attendant enterprises (like the slave trade), its socio-cultural appendages (foreign missions, zenana teacher training societies) and most importantly, its colonial subjects – were everywhere in European culture at home. Empire was not a singular place, but a set of geographical and cultural spaces. To borrow from Gyan Prakash's definition of the Third World, empire can be understood as 'a variety of shifting positions which have been discursively articulated'.[19] Its history, therefore, is neither a distant cousin to that of Britain proper, nor a discrete dimension of the British historical experience. It is an integral part of 'British' social, political, and cultural history because empire itself was the product of British national institutions, and because 'domestic' British culture was so thoroughly influenced by its apparently external empire. We can and perhaps should speak, as Helen Callaway does in her study of colonial Nigeria, of 'imperial culture' at home.[20] For if, as Shula Marks has argued, it is impossible to understand histories of Britain or historical notions of Britishness 'outside of the imperial and postimperial experience', it is equally impossible to conceptualize the map of Great Britain without appreciating that the cultural effects of imperialism have historically been inscribed on it.[21]

There is much recent historical work, which suggests that the nature and extent of imperial culture in the British Isles require the attention of British historians, whether their 'field' is Great or Greater Britain. Bernard Semmel's *Imperialism and Social Reform* was a breakthrough in 1960, insisting, as Disraeli, the Webbs and other less well-known Victorians had, on the connections between domestic social reform and imperial ideologies, especially after 1895.[22] While they echo many of the concerns raised by Semmel, John Mackenzie's *Propaganda and Empire* (1984) and *Imperialism and Popular Culture* (1986) have taken a different methodological tack, arguing for the notion of imperialism as a core ideology that could mediate class differences and thus worked to produce a unifying imperial British identity.[23] By enumerating the ways in which empire and its signifiers were produced and manipulated at home – in music halls, on biscuit tins, through film and other avenues of popular culture – Mackenzie and his collaborators point to the artificiality of empire conceived of as exclusively 'over there', and effectively refute the notion, so central to traditional imperial history, that 'the man in the street cares more about the Australian cricket matches' than about imperial affairs.[24] Indeed, the British culture of sport, as C.L.R. James clearly understood, has provided one of the most revealing arenas for analyses of imperial ideologies and practices during particular historical moments, down to and including the present day.[25]

Historical work on white women active in the imperial enterprise has helped break down another kind of separate spherism inherent in traditional imperial history, by demolishing the assumptions that empire was no place for a white woman, and was acquired 'in a fit of absence of wives' – both convictions which were practically axiomatic among a certain generation of imperial historians. Jane Hunter's *The Gospel of Gentility* (1984), Claudia Knapman's *White Women in Fiji* (1986), and Helen Callaway's *Gender,*

Culture and Empire (1987) are each concerned with demonstrating that empire was not an exclusively white masculine space and that the export of both Victorian gender ideology and European women impacted European communities and indigenous populations in colonial societies. As critics have pointed out, such attempts to re-map the colonial landscape can observe their own rules of thumb, privileging gender over race privilege and at times failing to understand the cooperation of race, class, and gender systems in the production of culturally imperial ideologies and practices.[26] They can also, by centralizing the experience of white women, marginalize Third World women (again) right off the proverbial map – thus 're-enacting their historical disenfranchisement' and illustrating that Western feminist/women's studies discourses are no more exempt from the political impact of the locations which produce, without finally determining, them than those of traditional imperial historians have been.[27]

Although it remains peripheral to the production of conventional British history, the influence of both empire at home and of gender on empire is beginning to be acknowledged and written into the historiography of Britain 'at home'. Suvendrini Perera has argued that the very form of 'the English novel' was constituted with reference to imperial ideologies, while Jenny Sharpe demonstrates that 'the colonial scene' shaped apprehensions of the sexual politics of empire in ways that were fundamental to the constitution of that 'domestic' genre.[28] Using other kinds of historical evidence, Catherine Hall, Leonore Davidoff, and Mary Poovey have examined the links between gender, race, and class in part by foregrounding the imperial context in which domestic gender ideologies have been articulated – so that empire is not simply the backdrop but an active agent in the construction of cultural and especially social reform discourses.[29] For Poovey, in particular, race and empire played a crucial role in the ideological work of gender in mid-Victorian England.[30] Clare Midgley's *Women Against Slavery: the British campaigns, 1780–1870* continues in this direction, re-materializing the ways in which anti-slavery politics shaped both high politics and feminist discourses in Victorian Britain.[31] Susan Pedersen's study of the sexual politics of colonial policy-making by feminists in the twentieth century, and the essays in Michael Roper and John Tosh's edited collection *Manful Assertions*, are two more excellent examples of the ways in which British historians are working to understand the impact of imperialism on both dominant and oppositional discourses and to shed a longstanding cultural amnesia about the impact of whiteness on English/British history and in turn on its historiography.[32]

The ramifications of this for traditional political history in Britain are enormous, since taken together these scholarly analyses demonstrate how thoroughly political subjectivity was dependent on the exercise of authority over 'Others', thus revealing more concretely the ways in which empire was fundamental, if not central, to the histories of Western democratic, humanitarian, and liberal traditions. What scholars of British literary traditions take for granted, British historians seem loathe fully to countenance – namely that, in the words of Gayatri Spivak, it is not possible to read modern British literature or history 'without remembering that imperialism, understood as England's social mission, was a crucial part of the representation of England to the English'.[33] And, we might add, to British, European, and colonial native audiences as well. For even if we acknowledge, as for example Nigel Leask insists in his recent book on British Romantic writers and the East, that such representations were directed at a European audience and hence were 'saturated by the nationalist and proto-nationalist claims of rival European states', we are still obliged to engage the premise that 'national culture was as much a product of imperial expansion as imperialism was an . . . exportation of that culture'.[34] There will be disagreement over the relationships between 'national' culture and 'imperial' culture and about the role of historians and cultural critics in perpetuating misapprehensions about the dynamics of their interaction. As Gauri Viswanathan has suggested, the stakes are high since the political culture of entire historiographical traditions are invested in not just the marginalization of colonialism, but also in the ways in which its relation to metropolitan cultural formations has been under-examined and, above all, under-theorized.[35]

For all their innovativeness, these new cartographies are problematic as well. The danger here is to continue to polarize: to view home as the original Mother to which empire was 'beamed back', and to conceptualize empire as a 'dark continent' which European women (the Western cultural Other) actually did miraculously 'penetrate' and 'uplift'. Even Freda Harcourt, whose important and often-overlooked essay on the linkages which Disraeli self-consciously forged between the political reform of 1866 to 1868 (which created a host of new national/political subjects at home) and Britain's almost simultaneous involvement in the war in Abyssinia (which provided 'a conspicuous site where British imperial strength could be . . . paraded' before the newly enfranchised, thus generating their commitment to an imperial nation), tends toward reifying the very same polarities of empire versus home which Victorians themselves seemed determined to articulate.[36] In reality, there was so much movement 'back' and 'forth' between Britain and its imperial possessions, the imperial culture cannot be located exclusively either in the metropole or in the colonies. The fact that E.M. Forster wrote *A Passage to India* in Weybridge is an ironic reminder of the proximity of empire to home, and of how little fixity the distant parts of empire had.[37] Judith R. Walkowitz's recent study of narratives of sexual danger in Victorian London also underscores the portability of imperial referents: the division of the capital into East and West occurred along racial, if not imperial, lines and mapped an urban space where ostensibly domestic Others were not without their imperial signifiers.[38] But even the term 'imperial culture' (with its implicitly hegemonic whiteness) is at risk, since British culture at home was shaped, and had been at least since the fifteenth century, by non-white populations living in Britain – the result of slavery and of early modern imperial expansion. Peter Fryer's work on black Britons, Rozina Visram's work on Indians throughout the British Isles, Bhikhu Parekh's collection on immigrant intellectuals – these histories, and many others, do more than re-affirm the fact that multicultural diversity has always been at the heart of self-styled Anglo-Saxon culture.[39] They require that we reject the traditional binaries of home/empire, Britain/the colonies, in order to account for the geographic dispersal of 'imperial' culture and 'colonial' power relations. In the wake of 1492/1992, it is particularly urgent that we understand modern British imperialism in particular and European colonialism in general, not just as acts of conquest but as a significant new phase in the history of intercultural discovery, negotiation, and contest.

This is not to obscure the violence with which European conquistadors 'explored' their new world: for it is undeniable that 'at its most powerful, colonialism is a process of radical dispossession'.[40] Nor is it my intention to erase the exercise of imperial power to which all colonial subjects could finally be subject. Jamaicans and Trinidadians did not voluntarily 'discover' the cities and seaports of the metropole, and the conditions under which they negotiated the dominant culture in Britain were not completely of their own making. Even for someone such as C.L.R. James, who claimed to feel British 'not merely in historical facts but in the instinctive responses', living in Britain always felt like being transplanted as a hot-house flower.[41] And yet residence in Britain certainly meant living in the 'Empire' for men and women like James, even as many of them came to make of it their 'home' and, by doing so, to contest and transform what constituted Britain and Britishness.[42] As Thomas Holt's recent book, *The Problem of Freedom: Race, Labor, and Politics in Jamaica and Britain, 1832–1938* bears out, the very term 'British Isles' meant more than simply England, Ireland, Scotland, and Wales from the vantage point of black Britons for whom the Caribbean was also 'home' – an insight which suggests once again how multivalent and politically powerful the geographical referents in 'British' history remain in the construction of national identities.[43] These historical circumstances (to which I have done little more than allude, despite the volume of historical work which testifies to them) point to the heterogeneity of 'imperial' experiences and the multiplicity of 'colonial' spaces which were among the historical consequences of British imperialism. Needless to say, it is the historical condition of postcolonialism that makes an appreciation of them possible. Those who wish to map histories of 'Britain' cannot therefore continue to anchor their work either at home or in the Empire, but must seriously consider situating it in the multiple eurocolonial locations produced by the historical projects of imperialism. To borrow from Anna Davin, it is imperative to develop a more expansive sense of 'where', as well as of 'when' and of 'how', while doing British history.[44]

To achieve this, historians of Britain must heed C.A. Bayly's admonition that traditional imperial history, traditional 'British' history, and especially nationalist histories, all belong in the same field of debate.[45] To these I would add women's histories and feminist histories as well. British imperial expansion and its ideological practices must be understood in the context of the most far-reaching discursive fields possible – fields in which imperialist attitudes at home and anti-imperial movements in the colonies played influential, and interdependent, roles. The rise of Liberal Unionism, typically seen as part of the 'English-Irish question', occurred if not in conjunction with the institutionalization of Indian nationalism, then certainly in relation to it. British women's movements and domestic opposition to them were equally enmeshed in imperial discourses and the nationalist ideologies which animated them.[46] Colonialized men and women simultaneously borrowed and rejected the terms of both Western feminism and colonial nationalisms as they sought to fashion their own political subjectivities.[47] And the activities of the British Committee of the Indian National Congress, as well as a variety of Indian and African statesmen, male and female students and intellectuals who travelled and worked in Britain from the mid-Victorian period forward, place much of what has been considered 'colonial' politics and culture 'at home'. These kinds of interrelationships add legitimacy to Edward Said's claim that 'no country on earth is made up of homogeneous natives; each has its immigrants, its internal 'Others', and each society . . . is a hybrid.[48] The geopolitical effects of this hybridization should not be underestimated. Gandhi's experiences in South Africa and in London – two differently imperial/colonial locations – shaped his nationalism, his political strategies and with them, the whole direction of the British Empire.[49]

Such emigrations and the variety of colonial/imperial identities they created disrupt the kind of historiographical boundary-keeping which I have been describing. And as if Gandhi's attitudes toward Indian women were not enough proof of the need for continued attention to the historical operations of gender in national and imperial histories, his admiration for some British suffrage women, acquired during one of his visits to Britain, suggests how his 'nationalist' views were partly shaped by his experience of 'imperial women'.[50] British feminists' associations with Indian nationalists, with the campaign to repeal the Contagious Diseases Acts in India after 1886 and with Indian feminists in India and Britain, point in turn to the impact which colonial nationalism had on the cause of female emancipation in the West – a cause which, at least in the United Kingdom, took the Empire as its proper sphere of action.[51] Historians of Britain clearly cannot afford to see either imperialism, colonial responses, or women as marginal to their concerns. Because of what we know to be the interlocking operations of race, gender, and class systems in the constitution of Englishness, Britishness, and 'Otherness', we need to structure analyses of these cultural paradigms into our understanding of what constituted Britain in the nineteenth and twentieth centuries. Attention to the 'intermixture' which characterized Britain and the world, particularly in the nineteenth century and after, may endanger the production of 'national' histories, but not without first revealing the ways in which those histories have been unfaithful to the fragmentary bases out of which, like modern nations themselves, they have been consolidated.[52]

Although reading practices are rarely examined or talked about as constitutive of historiographical production, they are, as every practising historian knows, fundamental to the construction of methodologies, fields of historical research and analytical/theoretical positions.[53] The historiographical divide which I have described in the British tradition can and should be remedied by a shift in reading habits, particularly among practitioners and teachers of conventionally 'domestic' Victorian history. In this respect Kumkum Sangari and Sudesh Vaid's collection *Recasting Women: Essays in Colonial History* is a must-read for British historians, precisely because its contributors take as 'the social' the wide spectrum of colonial/imperial relations. It has much to tell us about the ways in which gender was used to define dominant ideologies in India and in Britain, and the conversations it has generated suggest how both colonizer and colonized relied on notions of Indian tradition as a strategy for political and cultural containment.[54] Mrinalini Sinha's work on the Ilbert Bill controversy, Janaki Nair's research on Englishwomen's representations of the zenana, Barbara Ramusack's essays on twentieth-century British women involved in Indian campaigns involving women, and Catherine Candy's study of Margaret Cousins are recommended reading for historians of modern Britain because they demonstrate some of the ways in which imperial and colonial discourses meshed and clashed and, most significantly, how they spilled over traditional imperial/colonial boundaries.[55] My own work and that of Vron Ware and others on 'imperial feminism' indicates that British feminists, Indian nationalists, and Indian feminists shared a set of discourses which orbited around many of the same assumptions. When conflicts occurred among them, it was not always along an imperial/colonial axis; relationships could also be fragmented or cemented around gender, class/caste, or the terms of political self-determination. In this political/cultural diaspora, Britain was no more or less the center of empire than India was, geographically speaking. Though the dominant discourses of the time may have invented these polarities, and certain historically specific generations of British/imperial historians reproduced them, we need not accept them as signifiers of historical truth. Re-materializing 'imperial culture' in fact not only radically decenters the narrative of traditional British history, it continuously destabilizes the binaries that have underwritten it as well.[56] Ideological encounters did not occur between East and West, or between 'the mother country' and her 'colonial sons'. They were dispersed through the various mappings of imperial power, colonial resistance, and political collaboration, which individuals, groups, and institutions themselves proliferated in the pre and postcolonial period and beyond. To be a 'British' historian in the late twentieth century requires doing more than simply acknowledging the importance of such cartographies; it means continually interrogating the ways in which they structure the very ground of one's historical research, reading, and teaching. It means, in short, transforming the very foundations of what has traditionally been 'British' history. And it means, finally, taking seriously the ways in which feminist and postcolonialist histories themselves have made possible and indeed, as Sangari and Vaid have recently argued, continue to make imperative such critical re-mappings.[57]

To argue that Britain itself has become a foundational concept, a totalizing unitary subject of historical practice, is not, as some will surely argue, simply to taint pure British history with critical theory – whether postmodern or feminist or both. Rather, this maneuver throws into question the sacral character with which many British historians have invested Britain itself. The point is not necessarily to do away with foundations. By critiquing the ways in which 'Britain' has been deployed in British history, I am not suggesting that we repudiate it, but that we problematize it by revealing its fundamentally politicized nature, particularly when it comes to the subjects of women/feminism and colonialism. The task is, as Judith Butler has recently written, 'to interrogate what the theoretical move that establishes foundations authorizes, and what precisely it excludes or forecloses'.[58] Our own re-mappings are, needless to say, subject to the same interrogations, because they cannot but be as historically and politically contingent as the cartographies which have come before.

I am, in keeping with this concern, acutely aware of the fact that the alternative cartography I propose is rooted, as Chandra Mohanty has written about her own mappings, 'in my own discontinuous locations'.[59] I foreground my whiteness, my gender, and my class position inside the North American academy not as any kind of disclaimer, but as a recognition of my own accountability and the ways in which it is shaped, without being fully determined, by the situations I occupy. I understand too that our perspectives as historians are shaped, again without being ultimately dictated, by the way we become 'professionalized' and by the way the discipline of history is institutionalized in Western university settings. The nation-state may no longer be an appropriate unit of historical analysis,[60] but historians in North America are still trained largely in accordance with its boundaries, not to mention at the heart of many of its nation-building structures (Anglo-American graduate programs, national libraries and archives, multi-national corporate publishing houses). I am equally concerned about being mistaken for someone endorsing what Dipesh Chakrabarty has recently called the 'artifice of History' [capital H] – by which he means the tendency to read every history produced in the academy as if it were a history of Europe, even when it is properly 'about' China, India, or Africa.[61] Nor, finally, do I wish to be confused with those who have a romantic longing for 'home' and therefore want to extend its reach by domesticating all the spaces of, in this case, 'imperial' culture. How 'India', 'Britain', 'home', and 'empire' are configured is a set of historically specific processes of interest to many of us engaged with the politics of history-writing in the West, articulating as they do not just historical realities but the contingency of all historiographical productions. We are vigilant against investing any of these places with essentialized meanings, hopefully because we understand them as discursive terrains which shift and change shape depending on their – and our – historical specificity.[62] This is more than just a throw-away line or a one-off 'de-colonizing' gesture. As Jane Haggis reminds us, our voices as historians are a part of the colonial/imperial relationships which we seek to describe, and we must not neglect to map our own shifting locations as we set about re-imagining specific historical traditions.[63]

What brings together these heretofore discontinuous 'fields' of history is not spatial connectedness, or even disconnectedness. Lord Salisbury's comments reveal how that kind of approach is in itself a product of imperial mappings and, as I have suggested here, of historiographical over-mappings as well. It is rather the fact that they share a temporal – and hence an historical – space, a coincidence of place in time, which warrants our attention and our intervention. Recognizing this, and reconstituting British history accordingly, requires that we rethink what Ann Stoler has identified as 'colonial categories . . . [and] the boundaries of rule'.[64] We must also confront and reject the postEnlightenment conviction which still underlies much of the practice of Western history-writing today: namely that 'the time of European modernity . . . [is] the time of the globe', that the West is the future which its Others will eventually encounter.[65] Until we dis-embed our own historical practices from that unwritten assumption we will continue to stage what Johannes Fabian calls 'the scandal of domination', and to map home and empire, Britain and the colonies, as territories separated in time and space whose distances can only be measured by the traditional rules of thumb.[66]

Notes

1   This paper has benefited from the support and criticism of Paul Arroyo, Catherine Candy, Gary Daily, Chandra de Silva, Darlene Hantzis, Mike Kugler, Philippa Levine, Arvid Perez, Barbara Ramusack, Deborah Rossum, Sudipta Sen, Nyan Shah, Susan Thorne, and Jocelyn Zivin. Special thanks to Barbara Ramusack and Kali Israel for their commitment to organizing the Cincinnati conference on 'Feminism, Imperialism and race: India and Britain', which provided the critical spaces within which this paper developed.

2   For a useful discussion of the problems inherent in the historiography of the 'United Kingdom' see K. Robbins 'Core and periphery in modern British history', *Proceedings of the British Academy*, 1984, 52, 275–97.

3   D.K. Fieldhouse (1984) 'Can humpty-dumpty be put together again? Imperial history in the 1980s', *Journal of Imperial and Commonwealth History*, 13(2), 9–10.

4   For a set of discussions on doing Irish history as colonial history, see T. Eagleton, F. Jameson, and E. Said (1990) *Nationalism, Colonialism and Literature* (Minneapolis: University of Minnesota Press).

5   A.P. Thornton (1959/1985) *The Imperial Idea and its Enemies: a Study in British Power*, X (New York: St. Martin's Press). Himself a Scot, Thornton headed departments at Toronto and at the University of the West Indies, thus plotting his own particular imperial/colonial trajectories. See N. Mansergh (1986) 'A.P. Thornton: realism tempered by wit', in G. Martel (ed.) *Studies in British Imperial History: Essays in Honour of A.P. Thornton*, 1–7 (New York: St. Martin's Press).

6   M. Hechter (1975) *Internal Colonialism: the Celtic Fringe in British National Development* (Berkeley: University of California Press); R. Colls and P. Dodd (eds) (1986) *Englishness: Politics and Culture* (London: Croom Helm).

7   J. Mackenzie (1984) *Propaganda and Empire: the Manipulation of British Public Opinion, 1880–1960*, 254 (Manchester: Manchester University Press).

8   History was by no means the only stage for such apprehensions of imperial power. See J.S. Bratton *et al.* (1991) *Acts of Supremacy: the British Empire and the Stage, 1790–1930* (Manchester: Manchester University Press) and B.S. Cohn (1983) 'Representing authority in Victorian India', in E. Hobsbawn and T. Ranger (eds) *The Invention of Tradition*, 165–210 (Cambridge: Cambridge University Press).

9   S. Marks 'History, the nation and empire: sniping from the periphery', *History Workshop Journal*, 1990, 29, 117. See also C. Hall (1992) *White, Male and Middle-class: Explorations in*

Feminism and History, 20 (New York: Routledge). Even some, such as Douglas Lorimer, who have recognized the important of domestic discourses on race, have down-played its imperial significances. See his (1987) *Colour, Class and the Victorians: English Attitudes Toward the Negro in Mid-nineteenth Century Britain* (Leicester: Leicester University Press).

10   H.A. McDougall (1982) *Racial Myth in English History: Trojans, Teutons and Anglo-Saxons*, 89–116 (Montreal: Harvest House).

11   J.G.A. Pocock 'The limits and divisions of British history: in search of the unknown subject', *American Historical Review*, 1982, 87, 314.

12   J. Darwin (1991) *The End of the British Empire: the Historical Debate* (Oxford: Basil Blackwell).

13   A.P. Kaminsky (1986) *The India Office, 1880–1910*, ch. 1 (New York: Greenwood Press).

14   For an overview of Robinson and Gallagher's contributions to imperial historiography, see W.R. Louis, Jr. (ed.) (1976) *Imperialism: the Robinson and Gallagher Controversy* (New York: Franklin Watts).

15   P. Chatterjee (1986) *Nationalist Thought and the Colonial World: a Derivative Discourse?* (London: Zed Books); G. Prakash 'Writing postorientalist histories of the third world: perspectives from Indian historiography', *Comparative Studies in Society and History*, 1990, 32, 383–408.

16   J. Marshall 'Empire and authority in the later eighteenth century', *Journal of Imperial and Commonwealth History*, 1987, 15, 105.

17   Quoted in H.K. Bhabha (1990) 'Dissemination: time, narrative, and the margins of the modern state', in Bhabha (ed.) *Nation and Narration*, 317 (New York: Routledge).

18   J. Liddle and R. Joshi 'Gender and colonialism: women's organisations under the raj', *Women's Studies International Forum*, 1985, 8, 521–9; N. Chaudhuri and M. Strobel (eds) (1992) *Western Women and Imperialism: Complicity and Resistance*, 1–2 (Bloomington: Indiana University Press).

19   G. Prakash, 'Writing postorientalist histories', 384. Jane Haggis calls it 'a dialectic complexity of "meetings" between two social formations'. See her (1990) 'The feminist research process – defining a topic', in Liz Stanley (ed.) *Feminist Praxis: Research, Theory and Epistemology in Feminist Sociology*, 73 (London: Routledge).

20   H. Callaway (1987) *Gender, Culture and Empire: European Women in Colonial Nigeria,* 5 (London: Macmillan).

21   S. Marks, 'History, the nation and empire', 113. See also L. Stanley 'British feminist histories: an editorial introduction', *Women's Studies International Forum*, 1990, 13, 3–7.

22   B. Semmel (1960) *Imperialism and Social Reform: English Social-imperial Thought 1895–1914* (New York: Anchor Books).

23   J. Mackenzie, *Propaganda*, 1–10; and J. Mackenzie (1986) *Imperialism and Popular Culture* (Manchester: Manchester University Press).

24   Arthur Godley, Under Secretary of State for India from 1883–1910, quoted in A. Kaminsky, *The India Office*, 174.

25   Walvin and J.A. Mangan (eds) (1987) *Manliness and Morality: Middle Class Masculinity in Britain and America 1800–1940* (New York: St Martin's Press); J.A. Mangan (1986) *The Games Ethic and Imperialism* (London: Viking); B. Stoddart 'Sport, cultural imperialism, and colonial response in the British empire', *Comparative Studies in Society and History*, 1988, 30, 649–73.

26   J. Haggis 'Gendering colonialism or colonizing gender? Recent women's studies approaches to white women and the history of British colonialism', *Women's Studies International Forum*, 1990, 13, 105–15.

27   A. Levy (1991) *Other Women: the Writing of Class, Race, and Gender, 1832–1898*, 5 (Princeton: Princeton University Press); C.T. Mohanty 'Feminist encounters: locating the politics of experience', *Copyright*, 1987, 1, 32. See also K. Jayawardena (1986) *Feminism and Nationalism in the Third World* (London: Zed Books) and M. Strobel (1991) *European Women and the Second British Empire* (Bloomington: Indiana University Press).

28   S. Perera (1991) *Reaches of Empire: the English Novel from Edgworth to Dickens* (New York: Columbia University Press); J. Sharpe (1993) *Allegories of Empire: the Figure of Woman in the Colonial Text* (Minneapolis: University of Minnesota Press).

29   L. Davidoff and C. Hall (1987) *Family Fortunes: Men and Women of the English Middle-class, 1780–1850* (Chicago: University of Chicago Press); C. Hall 'The economy of intellectual prestige: Thomas Carlyle, John Stuart Mill and the case of Governor Eyre', *Cultural Critique*, 1989, 12, 167–96.

30   M. Poovey (1988) *Uneven Developments: the Ideological Work of Gender in Mid-Victorian Britain* (Chicago: University of Chicago Press). See also J. Rowbotham (1989) *Good Girls Make Good Wives: Guidance for Girls in Victorian fiction* (Oxford: Basil Blackwell). She devotes an entire chapter to the imperial dimension of girls' fiction because by the middle of the nineteenth century the British empire was already a part of the consciousness of middle-class society, featuring in its cultural artifacts from art to literature and considered by that class to involve all levels of society, 180.

31   C. Midgley (1992) *Women Against Slavery: the British Campaigns, 1780–1870* (London: Routledge).

32   S. Pedersen 'National bodies, unspeakable acts: the sexual politics of colonial policy-making', *The Journal of Modern History*, 1991, 63, 647–80; J. Roper and M. Tosh (eds) (1991) *Manful Assertions: Masculinities in Britain Since 1800* (New York: Routledge). The use of the term 'amnesia' as it relates to these issues is Catherine Hall's. See her *White, Male and Middle-class*, especially ch. 1, 'Feminism and feminist history'.

33   G. Spivak (1989) 'Three women's texts and a critique of imperialism', in C. Belsey and J. Moore (eds) *The Feminist Reader: Essays in the Politics of Literary Criticism*, 175 (New York: Basil Blackwell).

34   Leask (1992) *British Romantic Writers and the East*, 103, 86 (Cambridge: Cambridge University Press).

35   G. Viswanathan 'Raymond Williams and British colonialism', *The Yale Journal of Criticism*, 1991, 4(2) 47–66. I am grateful to Mrinalini Sinha for pressing me to recognize the ways in which the relationships between 'national' and 'imperial' culture are themselves contested in postcolonial studies.

36   It had become a commonplace observation in 1866 that Britain's center of gravity had moved to Calcutta. What Disraeli wished to do was to reflect back into Europe the strength that Britain drew from India, and the policy that he pressed Derby to adopt in 1866 was designed for this purpose. F. Harcourt 'Disraeli's Imperialism 1866–1868: a question of timing', *The Historical Journal*, 1980, 23, 97. I am grateful to Susan Thorne for bringing this essay to my attention.

37   In a similar vein, Paul Rich points out how the Martian invasion of the English countryside in H.G. Wells' *The War of the Worlds* brought the colonial experience home. 'The Quest for Englishness', in G. Marsden (ed.) (1900) *Victorian Values: Personalities and Perspectives in Nineteenth-Century Society* (London: Longman).

38   Although empire, and especially 'imperial anxieties', tend to function more as an unelaborated backdrop than as cultural agents in her book, and the ramifications of London as an 'Imperial City' are underdeveloped from my point of view, *City of Dreadful Delight* raises some important questions about how the map of empire was inscribed onto London itself. J.R. Walkowitz (1992) *City of Dreadful Delight: Narratives of Sexual Danger in late-Victorian London* 17–19, 25–6, 42–8 (Chicago: University of Chicago Press). See also T.C. Davis (1991) *Actresses as Working Women: Their Social Identity in Victorian Culture* (New York: Routledge), especially ch. 5, 'The geography of sex in society and theatre'.

39   P. Fryer (1984) *Staying Power: the History of Black People in Britain* (London: Pluto Press); R. Visram (1986) *Ayahs, Lascars and Princes: Indians in Britain 1700–1947* (London: Pluto Press); B. Parekh (ed.) (1974) *Colour, Culture and Consciousness: Immigrant Intellectuals in Britain* (London: George Allen & Unwin).

40   S. Deane, 'Introduction' to *Nationalism, Colonialism and Literature*, 10.

41   Quoted in D.J. Rossum (1991) 'A vision of black Englishness: the black press in England and the construction of black identity', paper delivered at the joint meeting of the North American and Pacific Coast Conference on British Studies, Santa Clara University, and provided courtesy of the author.

42   L. Tabili (1991) 'A place of refuge: black workers and black settlements in interwar Britain', paper delivered at the joint meeting of the North American and Pacific Coast Conference on British Studies, Santa Clara University, and provided courtesy of the author.

43   I am grateful to Catherine Candy for sharing this insight with me in correspondence. See also T.C. Holt (1992) *The Problem of Freedom: Race, Labor and Politics in Jamaica and Britain, 1832–1938* (Baltimore: Johns Hopkins University Press) and M.R. Trouillot 'Discourses of rule and the acknowledgement of the peasantry in Dominica, WI, 1838–1928', *American Ethnologist*, 1989, 16, 704–18.

44   A. Davin 'Standing on Virginia Woolf's doorstep', *History Workshop Journal*, 1991, 31, 73.

45   C.A. Bayly (1989) *Imperial Meridian: the British empire and the world*, p. 11 (London: Longman). The term 'field' is itself imperially marked, and when invoking it we might remember, with Vivian Twostar, that the terms we use are part of the vocabulary of the colonizer. 'Discovery. Possession. How different was I from the construct I fabricated?', in Louise Erdrich and Michael Dorris (1991) *The Crown of Columbus*, 269 (New York: Harper Paperbacks).

46   A. Burton 'The feminist quest for identity: British imperial suffragism and 'global sisterhood', 1900–1915, *Journal of Women's History*, 1991, 3(2), 46–81; V. Ware (1992) *Beyond the Pale: White Women, Racism and History* (London: Verso); B. Harrison (1978) *Separate Spheres: the Opposition to Women's Suffrage in Britain* (New York: Holmes & Meier).

47   K. Jayawardena, *Feminism and Nationalism*; A.M. Cromwell (1986) *An African Victorian Feminist: the Life and Times of Adelaide Smith Casely Hayford* (London: Frank Cass); H. Shaarawi (1986) *Harem Years: the Memoirs of an Egyptian Feminist*, translated and introduced by M. Badran (New York: The Feminist Press); R.S. Hossain (1988) *Sultana's Dreams and Selections from the Secluded Ones*, ed. and trans. by Roushan Jahan (New York: The Feminist Press); M. Badran and M. Cooke (eds) (1990) *Opening the Gates: a Century of Arab Feminist Writing* (Bloomington: Indiana University Press); G. Forbes (1979) 'Votes for women: the demand for women's franchise in India, 1971–1937', in V. Mazumdar (ed.) *Symbols of Power: Studies of the Political Status of Women in India*, 11–23 (Bombay); M. Badran 'Dual liberation: feminism and nationalism in Egypt, 1870s–1925', *Feminist Issues*, 1988, 8, 15–34.

48   E.W. Said 'Identity, authority and freedom: the potentate and the traveler', *Transition*, 1991, 54, 12. I am grateful to Sherifa Zuhur for sharing this essay with me.

49   S. Hay 'The making of a late-Victorian Hindu: M.K. Gandhi in London, 1888–1891', *Victorian Studies*, 1989, 33, 74–98; M.K. Gandhi (1957) *An Autobiography: the Story of My Experiments with Truth*, 113–17 (Boston: Beacon Press).

50   M. Kishwar 'Gandhi on women', *Race and Class*, 1986, 28, 43–61; G. Forbes (1988) 'The politics of respectability: Indian women and the Indian national congress', in D.A. Low (ed.) *The Indian National Congress: Centenary Hindsights*, 54–97 (Delhi: Oxford University Press); J. Hunt (1976) 'Suffragettes and satyagraha: Gandhi and the British women's suffrage movement', paper presented to the Annual Meeting of the American Academy of Religion in St Louis, Missouri (available in the Fawcett Library, London).

51   A. Burton, 'The feminist quest', 46–81; B.N. Ramusack (1992) 'Cultural missionaries, maternal imperialists, feminist allies: British women activists in India, 1865–1945', in Chaudhuri and Strobel (eds) *Western Women*, 118–36.

52   For a debate on the fate of national histories in the era of internationalism, see I. Tyrrell and M. McGerr 'American Historical Review Forum', *American Historical Review*, 1991, 96, 1031–72. I. Tyrrell's book (1991) *Woman's World, Woman's Empire: the Women's Christian Temperance Union in International Perspective, 1880–1930* (Chapel Hill: University of North Carolina Press) is an interesting example of international history in practice.

53   L. Stanley, *Feminist Praxis*, 64.

54   K. Sangari and S. Vaid (eds) (1989) *Recasting Women's Essays in Colonial History* (New Delhi: Kali for Women); R. Radhakrishnan (1992) 'Nationalism, gender and the narrative of identity', in A. Parker, M. Russo, D. Sommer, and P. Yaeger (eds) *Nationalisms and Sexualities*, 77–95 (New York: Routledge).

55   M. Sinha (1992) 'Chathams, Pitts and Gladstones in Petticoats: the politics of gender and race in the Ilbert Bill controversy, 1883–1884', and Ramusack (1992) 'Cultural missionaries',

both in Chaudhuri and Strobel (eds) *Western Women,* 98–118 and 118–36, respectively. See also B.N. Ramusack 'Embattled advocates: the debate over birth control in India, 1920–40', *Journal of Women's History,* 1990, 1, 34–64; J. Nair 'Uncovering the zenana: visions of Indian women in Englishwomen's writings, 1813–1940', *Journal of Women's History,* 1990, 2, 8–36; C. Candy (1991) 'Mother India and the ideal "femaculine": an Irish orientalist feminist in India', paper presented at the Annual Meetings of the American Historical Association, Chicago, provided courtesy of the author.

56   This is an extrapolation of Sara Suleri's claim that: 'the story of the colonial encounter is itself a radically decentering narrative' . . . See her (1992) *The Rhetoric of English India,* 2 (Chicago: University of Chicago Press).

57   This literature is rich in both theoretical innovation and evidentiary sources. In thinking about new ways to conceptualize imperial culture I have been particularly influenced by the concept of diaspora, used primarily though not exclusively by African-American historians. See for example R. Terborg-Penn, S. Harley, and A. Benton Rushing (eds) (1987) *Women in Africa and the African Diaspora* (Washington: Howard University Press).

58   J. Butler (1992) 'Contingent foundations: feminism and the question of the postmodernism', in J. Butler and J. Scott (eds) *Feminists Theorize the Political,* 7 (New York: Routledge).

59   C.T. Mohanty (1991) 'Cartographies of struggle: third world women and the politics of feminism', in C.T. Mohanty, A. Russo, and L. Torres (eds) *Third World Women and the Politics of Feminism,* 3 (Bloomington: Indiana University Press).

60   ibid., 2: E.J. Hobsbawm (1990) *Nations and Nationalism since 1780: programme, myth, reality,* 177 (Cambridge: Cambridge University Press).

61   D. Chakrabarty 'Postcoloniality and the artifice of history: who speaks for "Indian" pasts?', *Representations,* 1992, 37, 1.

62   For an excellent discussion of the problem of constituting 'home' see B. Martin and C.T. Mohanty (1986) 'Feminist politics: what's home got to do with it?', in T. de Lauretis (ed.) *Feminist Studies/Critical Studies,* 191–212 (Madison: University of Wisconsin Press). B.J. Reagon offers another powerful reflection on home in her (1990) 'Foreword: nurturing resistance', in M. O'Brien and C. Little (eds) *Reimagining America: the Arts of Social Change,* 1–8 (Philadelphia: New Society Publishers). My thanks to Darlene Hantzis and the students in 'Feminist Theories' at ISU in the fall of 1992 for sharing their insights on this essay with me.

63   J. Haggis, 'The feminist research process', in L. Stanley (ed.) *Feminist Praxis,* 77.

64   A.L. Stoler 'Rethinking colonial categories: European communities and the boundaries of rule', *Comparative Studies in History and Society,* 1989, 31, 134–61.

65   C.T. Mohanty, 'Feminist encounters', 30; Aiwha Ong 'Colonialism and modernity: feminist re-presentations of women in non-western societies', *Inscriptions,* 1988, 3/4, 79.

66   J. Fabian (1983) *Time and the Other: How Anthropology Makes its Object,* X (New York: Columbia University Press).

Chapter 3

Dipesh Chakrabarty

PROVINCIALIZING EUROPE: POSTCOLONIALITY AND THE CRITIQUE OF HISTORY[1]

Dipesh Chakrabarty, an important and prolific associate of the Indian 'Subaltern Studies' group of historians, here argues for a profound rethinking of the intellectual relationships between 'Europe' and 'the rest' of the world. The case made here is expanded in several other writings, especially his book *Provincializing Europe: Postcolonial Thought and Historical Difference* (Princeton University Press, 2000). His claims have evoked considerable debate – see for instance the essay by Frederick Cooper below.

Stephen Howe

I N THE ACADEMIC DISCOURSE OF HISTORY – that is, 'history' as a discourse produced at the institutional site of the university – 'Europe' remains the sovereign, theoretical subject of all histories, including the ones we call 'Indian', 'Chinese', 'Kenyan', etc. There is a peculiar way in which all these other histories tend to become variations on a master narrative that could be called 'the history of Europe'. In this sense, 'Indian' history itself is in a position of subalternity; one can only articulate subaltern subject-positions in the name of history.

That Europe works as a silent referent in historical knowledge itself becomes obvious in a highly ordinary way. There are at least two everyday symptoms of the subalternity of non-Western, third-world histories. Third-world historians feel a need to refer to works in European history; historians of Europe do not feel any need to reciprocate. Whether it is an Edward Thompson, a Le Roy Ladurie, a George Duby, a Carlo Ginzberg, a Lawrence Stone, a Robert Darnton, or a Natalie Davis – to take but a few names at random from our contemporary world – the 'greats' and the models of the historian's enterprise are always at least culturally 'European'. 'They' produce their work in relative ignorance of, say, non-Western histories and this does not seem to affect the quality of their work.

This is a gesture, however, that 'we' cannot return. We cannot even afford an equality or symmetry of ignorance at this level without taking the risk of appearing 'old-fashioned' or 'outdated'.

This problem of asymmetric ignorance is not simply a matter of 'cultural cringe' (to let my Australian self speak) on our part or of cultural arrogance on the part of the European historian. These problems exist but can be relatively easily addressed. Nor do I mean to take anything from the achievements of the historians I mentioned. Our footnotes bear rich testimony to the insights we have derived from their knowledge and creativity. The dominance of 'Europe' as the subject of all histories is a part of a much more profound theoretical condition under which historical knowledge is produced in the third world. This condition ordinarily expresses itself in a paradoxical manner. It is this paradox that I shall describe as the second everyday symptom of our subalternity, and it refers to the very nature of social-science pronouncements themselves.

For generations now, philosophers and thinkers shaping the nature of social science have produced theories embracing the entirety of humanity. As we well know, these statements have been produced in relative, and sometimes absolute, ignorance of the majority of humankind, that is, those living in non-Western cultures. This in itself is not paradoxical for the more self-conscious of European philosophers have always sought theoretically to justify this stance. The everyday paradox of third-world social science is that we find these theories, in spite of their inherent ignorance of 'us', eminently useful in understanding our societies. What allowed the modern European sages to develop such clairvoyance with regard to societies of which they were empirically ignorant? Why cannot we, once again, return the gaze?

There is an answer to this question in the writings of philosophers who have read into European history an entelechy of universal reason, if we regard such philosophy as the self-consciousness of social science. Only 'Europe', the argument would appear to be, is theoretically (i.e., categorically, at the level of the fundamental categories that shape historical thinking) knowable; all other histories are matters of empirical research that fleshes out a theoretical skeleton that is substantially 'Europe'.

Such an epistemological proposition underlies Marx's use of categories such as 'bourgeois' and 'pre-bourgeois' or 'capital' and 'pre-capital'. The prefix 'pre' here signifies a relationship that is both chronological and theoretical. The coming of the bourgeois or capitalist society, Marx argues in the *Grundrisse* and elsewhere, gives rise for the first time to a history that can be apprehended through a philosophical and universal category, 'capital'. History becomes, for the first time, theoretically knowable. All past histories are now to be known (theoretically, that is) from the vantage point of this category, that is, in terms of their differences from it.[2] To continue with Marx's words:

> Even the most abstract categories, despite their validity – precisely because of their abstractness – for all epochs, are nevertheless themselves a product of historical relations. Bourgeois society is the most developed and the most complex historic organisation of production. The categories which express its relations, the comprehension of its structure, thereby also allow insights into the structure and the relations of production of all the vanished social formations out of whose ruins and elements it built itself up, whose partly still unconquered remnants are carried along within it, whose mere nuances have developed significance within it, etc. . . . The intimations of higher development among

the subordinate animal species . . . can be understood only after the higher development is already known. The bourgeois economy thus supplies the key to the ancient.

(Marx, 1973: 105).

For 'capital' or 'bourgeois', I submit, read 'Europe'.

Marx's methodological/epistemological statements have not always successfully resisted historicist readings. There has always remained enough ambiguity in these statements to make possible the emergence of 'Marxist' historical narratives. These narratives turn around the theme of 'historical transition'. Most modern third-world histories are written within problematics posed by this transition narrative of which the overriding (if often implicit) themes are those of development, modernization and capitalism. This tendency can be located in our own work in the Subaltern Studies project (Guha and Spivak, 1988). My book on working-class history struggles with the problem (Chakrabarty, 1989). Sumit Sarkar's (another colleague in the Subaltern Studies project) *Modern India*, justifiably regarded as one of the best textbooks on Indian history written primarily for Indian universities, opens with the following sentences:

> The sixty years or so that lie between the foundation of the Indian National Congress in 1885 and the achievement of independence in August 1947 witnessed perhaps the greatest transition in our country's long history. A transition, which in many ways remains grievously incomplete, and it is with this central ambiguity that it seems most convenient to begin our survey.
>
> (Sarkar, 1985a: 1).

What kind of a transition was it that remained 'grievously incomplete'? Sarkar hints at the possibility of there having been several, by naming three: so many of the aspirations aroused in the course of the national struggle remained unfulfilled – the Gandhian dream of the peasant coming into his own in Ram-rajya {the rule of the legendary and the ideal god-king Ram}, as much as the left's ideals of social revolution. And as the history of independent India and Pakistan (and Bangladesh) was repeatedly to reveal, even the problems of a complete bourgeois transformation and successful capitalist development were not fully solved by the transfer of power of 1947 (Sarkar, 1985a: 4).

Neither the peasant's dream of a mythical and just kingdom, nor the left's ideal of a social(ist) revolution, nor a 'complete bourgeois transformation' – it is within these three absences, these 'grievously incomplete' scenarios, that Sarkar locates the story of modern India. The tendency to read Indian history in terms of a lack, an absence, or incompleteness that translates into 'inadequacy' is obvious in these excerpts. As a trope, however, it is an ancient one, going back to the hoary beginnings of colonial rule in India. The British conquered and represented the diversity of 'Indian' pasts through a homogenizing narrative of transition from a 'medieval' period to 'modernity'.

In the nineteenth and twentieth centuries, generations of elite Indian nationalists found their subject-positions, as nationalists, within this transition-narrative that, at various times depending on one's ideology, hung the tapestry of 'Indian history' between the two poles of the homologous sets of oppositions, despotic/constitutional, medieval/modern, feudal/capitalist. Within this narrative shared between imperialist and nationalist imaginations, the 'Indian' was always a figure of lack. There was always, in other words, room in this story for characters who embodied, on behalf of the native, the theme of 'inadequacy' or 'failure'. For Rammohun Roy as for Bankimchandra Chattopadhyay, two of India's most prominent nationalist intellectuals of the nineteenth century, British rule was a necessary period of tutelage that Indians had to undergo in order to prepare precisely for what the British denied but extolled as the end of all history: citizenship and the nation-state.

In nationalist versions of this narrative, as Partha Chatterjee has shown, it was the peasants and the workers, the subaltern classes, who were given to bear the cross of 'inadequacy', for, according to this version, it was they who needed to be educated out of their ignorance, parochialism or, depending on your preference, false consciousness (Chatterjee, 1986). Even today, the Anglo-Indian word 'communalism' refers to those who allegedly fail to measure up to the 'secular' ideals of citizenship. That the British rule put the practices, institutions and the discourse of bourgeois individualism in place in the Indian soil is undeniable. Early expressions – that is, before the beginnings of nationalism – of this desire to be a 'legal subject' make it clear that to Indians in the 1830s and 1840s, to be a 'modern individual' was to become a 'European'. However, later Indian nationalists abandoned such abject desire to be 'Europeans' themselves. Nationalist thought was premised precisely on the assumed universality of the project of becoming individuals, on the assumption that 'individual rights' and abstract 'equality' were universals that could find a home anywhere in the world, that one could be both an 'Indian' and a 'citizen' at the same time. We shall soon explore some of the contradictions of this project.

Many of the public and private rituals of modern individualism became visible in India in the nineteenth century. One sees this, for instance, in the sudden flourishing in this period of the four basic genres that help express the modern self: the novel, the biography, the autobiography and history.[3] Along with these came modern industry, technology, medicine, a quasi-bourgeois (though colonial) legal system supported by a state that nationalism was to take over and make its own. The transition-narrative that I have been discussing underwrote, and was in turn underpinned by these institutions. To think this narrative was to think these institutions at the apex of which sat the modern state,[4] and to think the modern or the nation-state was to think a history whose theoretical subject was Europe. Gandhi realized this as early as 1909. Referring to the Indian nationalists' demands for more railways, modern medicine and bourgeois law, he cannily remarked in his book *Hind Swaraj* that this was to 'make India English' or, as he put it, to have 'English rule without the Englishman' (Gandhi, 1909/63: 15). This 'Europe' was of course nothing but a piece of fiction told to the colonized by the colonizer in the very process of fabricating colonial domination. Gandhi's critique of this 'Europe' is compromised on many points by his nationalism and I do not intend to fetishize his text. But I find his gesture useful in developing the problematic of non-metropolitan histories.

I shall now return to the themes of 'failure', 'lack' and 'inadequacy' that so ubiquitously characterize the speaking-subject of 'Indian' history. As in the practice of the insurgent peasants of colonial India, the first step in a critical effort must arise from a gesture of inversion (Guha, 1983: ch. 2). Let us begin from where the transition-narrative ends and read 'plenitude' and 'creativity' where this narrative has made us read 'lack' and 'inadequacy'. According to the fable of their constitution, Indians today are all 'citizens'. The constitution embraces almost a classically liberal definition of citizenship. If the modern state and the modern individual, the citizen, are but the two inseparable sides of the same phenomenon, as William Connolly argues in his interesting book *Political Theory and*

Modernity (1989), it would appear that the end of history (shades of Fukuyama!) is in sight for us in India. However, this modern individual, whose political/public life is lived in citizenship, is also supposed to have an interiorized 'private' self which pours out incessantly in diaries, letters, autobiographies, novels and, of course, in what we say to our analysts. The bourgeois individual is not born until one discovers the pleasures of privacy. But this is a very special kind of 'private' – it is, in fact, a deferred 'public', for this bourgeois private, as Habermas has reminded us, is 'always already oriented to an audience (Publikum)' (Habermas, 1989: 49). Indian public life may mimic on paper the bourgeois legal fiction of citizenship – the fiction is usually performed as a farce in India – but what about the bourgeois private and its history? Anyone who has tried to write 'French' social history with Indian material would know how impossibly difficult the task is (Sarkar, 1985b: 256–74). It is not that the form of the bourgeois private did not come with European rule. There have been, since the middle of the nineteenth century, Indian novels, diaries, letters and autobiographies, but they seldom yield pictures of an endlessly interiorized subject. Our autobiographies are remarkably 'public' (with constructions of public life that are not necessarily modern) when written by men, and tell the story of the extended family when written by women.[5] In any case, autobiographies in the confessional mode are notable for their absence. The single paragraph (out of 963 pages) that Nirad Chaudhuri spends on describing his experience of his wedding night in the second volume of his celebrated and prize-winning autobiography is as good an example as any other and is worth quoting at some length. I should explain that this was an arranged marriage (Bengal, 1932) and Chaudhuri was anxious lest his wife should not appreciate his newly acquired but unaffordably expensive hobby of buying records of Western classical music. The passage is a telling exercise in the construction of memory, for it is about what Chaudhuri 'remembers' and 'forgets' of his 'first night's experience'. He screens off intimacy with expressions such as 'I do not remember' or 'I do not know how' (not to mention the very Freudian 'making a clean breast of'), and this self-constructed veil is no doubt a part of the self that speaks:

> I was terribly uneasy [writes Chaudhuri] at the prospect of meeting as wife a girl who was a complete stranger to me, and when she was brought in and left standing before me I had nothing to say. I saw only a very shy smile on her face, and timidly she came and sat by my side on the edge of the bed. I do not know how after that both of us drifted to the pillows, to lie down side by side.

Chaudhuri adds in a footnote:

> Of course, fully dressed. We Hindus . . . consider both extremes fully clad and fully nude – to be modest, and everything in-between as grossly immodest. No decent man wants his wife to be an 'allumeuse'. Then the first words were exchanged. She took up one of my arms, felt it and said: 'You are so thin. I shall take good care of you'. I did not thank her, and I do not remember that beyond noting the words I even felt touched. The horrible suspense about European music had reawakened in my mind, and I decided to make a clean breast of it at once and look the sacrifice, if it was called for, straight in the face and begin romance on such terms as were offered to me. I asked her

timidly after a while: 'Have you listened to any European music?' She shook her head to say 'No.' Nonetheless, I took another chance and this time asked: 'Have you heard the name of a man called Beethoven?' She nodded and signified 'Yes'. I was reassured, but not wholly satisfied. So I asked yet again: 'Can you spell the name?' She said slowly: 'B,E,E,T,H,O,V,E,N.' I felt encouraged . . . and [we] dozed off.

(Chaudhuri, 1987: 350–1).

The desire to be 'modern' screams out of every sentence in the two volumes of Chaudhuri's autobiography. His legendary name now stands for the cultural history of Indo-British encounter. Yet in the 1,500-odd pages that he has written in English about his life, this is the only passage where the narrative of Chaudhuri's participation in public life and literary circles is interrupted to make room for something approaching the intimate. How do we read this text, this self-making of an Indian male who was second to no one in his ardour for the public life of the citizen, yet who seldom, if ever, reproduced in writing the other side of the modern citizen, the interiorized private self unceasingly reaching out for an audience? Public without private? Yet another instance of the 'completeness' of bourgeois transformation in India?

These questions are themselves prompted by the transition-narrative which in turn situates the modern individual at the very end of history. I do not wish to confer on Chaudhuri's autobiography a representativeness it may not have. Women's writings, as I have already said, are different, and scholars have just begun to explore the world of autobiographies in Indian history. But if one result of European imperialism in India was to introduce the modern state and the idea of the nation with their attendant discourse of 'citizenship' which, by the very idea of 'the citizen's rights' (i.e. 'the rule of law') splits the figure of the modern individual into 'public' and 'private' parts of the self (as the young Marx once pointed out in his 'On the Jewish Question'), these themes have existed – in contestation, alliance and miscegenation – with other narratives of the self and community that do not look to the state/citizen bind as the ultimate construction of sociality (Marx, 1975: 215–52). This as such will not be disputed but my point goes further. It is that these other constructions of self and community, while documentable in themselves, will never enjoy the privilege of providing the meta-narratives or teleologies (assuming that there cannot be a narrative without at least an implicit teleology) of our histories. Partly because these narratives often themselves bespeak an antihistorical consciousness, that is, they entail subject-positions and configurations of memory that challenge and undermine the subject that speaks in the name of history. 'History' is precisely the site where the struggle goes on to appropriate, on behalf of the modern (my hyper-real Europe), these other collocations of memory. To illustrate these propositions, I will now discuss a fragment of this contested history in which the modern private and the modern individual were embroiled in colonial India.[6] What I present here are the outlines, so to speak, of a chapter in the history of bourgeois domesticity in colonial Bengal. The material – in the main texts produced in Bengali between 1850 and 1920 for teaching women that very Victorian subject, 'domestic science' – relates to the Bengali Hindu middle class, the bhadralok or 'respectable people'. British rule instituted into Indian life the trichotomous ideational division on which modern political structures rest, for example, the state, civil society and the (bourgeois) family. It was therefore not surprising that ideas relating to bourgeois domesticity, privacy and individuality should come to India via British rule. However, what I want to highlight here, through the example of the bhadralok, are certain cultural operations by which the 'Indians' challenged and modified these received ideas in such a way as to put in question two fundamental tenets underlying the idea of 'modernity' – the nuclear family based on companionate marriage and the secular, historical construction of time.

As Meredith Borthwick (1984), Ghulam Murshid (1983) and other scholars have shown, the eighteenth-century European idea of 'civilization' culminated, in early nineteenth-century India, in a full-blown imperialist critique of Indian/Hindu domestic life which was now held to be inferior to what became mid-Victorian ideals of bourgeois domesticity.[7] 'The condition of women' question in nineteenth-century India was part of that critique, as were the ideas of the 'modern' individual, 'freedom', 'equality' and 'rights'. In passages remarkable for their combination of egalitarianism and orientalism, James Mill's *The History of British India* (1837) joined together the thematic of the family/ nation and a teleology of 'freedom':

> The condition of women is one of the most remarkable circumstances in the manners of nations . . . The history of uncultivated nations uniformly represents the women as in a state of abject slavery, from which they slowly emerge as civilization advances . . . As society refines upon its enjoyments, the condition of the weaker sex is gradually improved, until they associate on equal terms with the men, and occupy the place of voluntary and useful coadjutors. A state of dependence more strict and humiliating than that which is ordained for the weaker sex among the Hindus cannot be easily conceived
>
> (Mill, 1837: 309–10).

As is well known, the Indian middle classes generally felt answerable to this charge. From the early nineteenth century onwards, a movement developed in Bengal (and other regions) to reform 'women's conditions' and to give them formal education. Much of this discourse on women's education was emancipationist in that it spoke the language of 'freedom', 'equality' and 'awakening', and was strongly influenced by Ruskinian ideals and idealization of bourgeois domesticity (Borthwick, 1984). If one looks on this history as part of the history of the modern individual in India, an interesting feature emerges. It is that in this literature on women's education certain terms, after all, were much more vigorously debated than others. There was, for example, a degree of consensus over the desirability of domestic 'discipline' and 'hygiene' as practices reflective of a state of modernity, but the word 'freedom', yet another important term in the rhetoric of the modern, hardly ever acted as the register of such a social consensus. It was a passionately disputed word and we would be wrong to assume that the passions reflected a simple and straightforward battle of the sexes. The word was assimilated to the nationalist need to construct cultural boundaries that supposedly separated the 'European' from the 'Indian'. The dispute over the word was thus central to the discursive strategies through which a subject-position was created enabling the 'Indian' to speak. It is this subject-position that I want to discuss here in some detail.

What the Bengali literature on women's education played out was a battle between a nationalist construction of a cultural norm of the patriarchal, patrilocal, patrilineal, extended family and the ideal of the patriarchal, bourgeois nuclear family that was implicit in the European/imperialist/universalist discourse on the 'freedoms' of individualism, citizenship and civil society.[8] The themes of 'discipline' and 'order' were critical in shaping nationalist imaginings of aesthetics and power. 'Discipline' was seen as the key to the power of the colonial (i.e. modern) state, but it required certain procedures for redefining the self. The British were powerful, it was argued, because they were disciplined, orderly and punctual in every detail of their lives, and this was made possible by the education of 'their' women who brought the virtues of discipline into the home. The 'Indian' home, a colonial construct, now fared badly in nationalist writings on modern domesticity. To quote a Bengali text on women's education from 1877:

> The house of any civilized European is like the abode of gods. Every household object is clean, set in its proper place and decorated; nothing seems unclean or smells foul . . . it is as if [the goddess of] order [srinkhala: order, discipline; srinkbal: chains] had become manifest to please the [human] eye. In the middle of the room would be a covered table with a bouquet of flowers on it, while around it would be [a few] chairs nicely arranged [with] everything sparkling clean. But enter a house in our country and you would feel as if you had been transported there by your destiny to make you atone for all the sins of your life. [A mass of] cowdung torturing the senses . . . dust in the air, a growing heap of ashes, flies buzzing around . . . a little boy urinating into the ground and putting the mess back into his mouth . . . the whole place is dominated by a stench that seems to be running free . . . There is no order anywhere, the household objects are so unclean that they only evoke disgust.
>
> (Anon, 1877: 28–9).

This self-division of the colonial subject, the double movement of recognition by which it both knows its 'present' as the site of disorder and yet moves away from this space in desiring a discipline that can only exist in an imagined but 'historical' future, is a rehearsal, in the context of the discussion of the bourgeois domestic in colonial India, of the transition-narrative we have encountered before. A historical construction of temporality (medieval/modern, separated by historical time), in other words, is precisely the axis along which the colonial subject splits itself. Or to put it differently, this split is what is history; writing history is performing this split over and over again.

The desire for order and discipline in the domestic sphere thus may be seen as having been a correlate of the nationalist, modernizing desire for a similar discipline in the public sphere, that is for a rule of law enforced by the state. It is beyond the scope of this paper to pursue this point further, but the connection between personal discipline and discipline in public life was to reveal itself in what the nationalists wrote about domestic hygiene and public health. The connection is recognizably modernist and it is what the Indian modern shared with the European modern. What I want to attend to, however, are the differences between the two. And this is where I turn to the other important aspect of the European modern, the rhetoric of 'freedom' and 'equality'.

The argument about 'freedom' – in the texts under discussion – was waged around the question of the Victorian ideals of the companionate marriage, that is, over the question as to whether or not the wife should also be a friend to the husband. Nothing threatened the ideal of the Bengali/Indian extended family (or the exalted position of the mother-in-law within the structure) more than this idea wrapped up in notions of bourgeois privacy, that the wife was also to be a friend or, to put it differently, that the woman was now to be a modern individual. I must mention here that the modern individual, who asserts his/her individuality over the claims of the joint or extended family, almost always appears in nineteenth- and early twentieth-century Bengali literature as an embattled figure, often the subject of ridicule and scorn in the same Bengali fiction and essays that otherwise extolled the virtues of discipline and scientific rationality in personal and public lives. This irony had many expressions. The most well-known Bengali fictional character who represents this moral censure of modern individuality is Nimchand Datta in Dinabandhu Mitra's play *Sadhabar Ekaclasbi* (1866). Nimchand, who is English-educated, quotes Shakespeare, Milton or Locke at the slightest opportunity and who uses this education arrogantly to ignore his duties towards his extended family, finds his nemesis in alcohol and debauchery. This metonymic relationship between the love of 'modern'/English education (which stood for the romantic individual in nineteenth-century Bengal) and the slippery path of alcohol is suggested in the play by a conversation between Nimchand and a Bengali official of the colonial bureaucracy, a Deputy Magistrate. Nimchand's supercilious braggadocio about his command of the English language quickly and inevitably runs to the subject of drinks (synonymous, in middle-class Bengali culture of the period, with absolute decadence):

> I read English, write English, speechify in English, think in English, dream in English – mind you, it's no child's play – now tell me, my good fellow, what would you like to drink? – Claret for ladies, sherry for men and brandy for heroes.
>
> (Mitra, 1981: 138).

A similar connection between the modern, 'free', individual and selfishness was made in the literature on women's education. The construction was undisguisedly nationalist (and patriarchal). 'Freedom' was used to mark a difference between what was 'Indian' and what was 'European/English'. The ultra-free woman acted like a memsahib (European woman), selfish and shameless. As Kundamala Devi, a woman writing for a women's magazine *Bamabodhini Patrika*, said in 1870: 'Oh dear ones! If you have acquired real knowledge, then give no place in your heart to memsahib-like behaviour.'

This is not becoming in a Bengali housewife (Borthwick, 1984: 105). The idea of 'true modesty' was mobilized to build up this picture of the 'really' Bengali woman. Writing in 1920, Indira Devi dedicated her *Narir ukti* (A Woman Speaks) – interestingly enough, a defence of modern Bengali womanhood against criticisms by (predominantly) male writers – to generations of ideal Bengali women whom she thus described:

> unaffected by nature, of pleasant speech, untiring in their service [to others], oblivious of their own pleasures, [while] moved easily by the suffering of others, and capable of being content with very little.
>
> (Devi, 1920: dedication page).

This model of the 'modern' Bengali/Indian woman – educated enough to appreciate the modern regulations of the body and the state but yet 'modest' enough to be unself-assertive and unselfish – was tied to the debates on 'freedom'. 'Freedom' in the West, several authors argued, meant jathechhachar, to do as one pleased, the right to self-indulgence. In India, it was said, 'freedom' meant freedom from the ego, the capacity to serve and obey voluntarily. Notice how the terms 'freedom' and 'slavery' have changed positions in the following quote:

> To be able to subordinate oneself to others and to dharma duty/moral order/proper action], to free the soul from the slavery of the senses, are the first tasks of human freedom . . . That is why in Indian families boys and girls are subordinate to the parents, wife to the husband and to the parents-in-law, the discipline to the guru, the student to the teacher . . . the king to dharma . . . the people to the king, [and one's] dignity and prestige to [that of] the community [samaj].
>
> (Bandyopadhyaya, 1887: 30–1).[9]

There was an ironical twist to this theorizing that needs to be noted. Quite clearly, this theory of 'freedom-in-obedience' did not apply to the domestic servants who were sometimes mentioned in this literature as examples of the 'truly' unfree, the nationalist point being that (European) observers commenting on the unfree status of Indian women often missed (so some nationalists argued) this crucial distinction between the housewife and the domestic. Obviously, the servants were not yet included in the India of the nationalist imagination.

Thus the Bengali discourse on modern domesticity in a colonial period when the rise of a civil society and a quasi-modern state had already inserted the modern questions of 'public' and 'private' into middle-class Bengali lives. The received bourgeois ideas about domesticity and connections between the domestic and the national were modified here in two significant ways. One strategy, as I have sought to demonstrate, was to contrapose the cultural norm of the patriarchal extended family to the bourgeois patriarchal ideals of the companionate marriage, to oppose the new patriarchy with redefined versions of the old one(s). Thus was fought the idea of the modern private. The other strategy, equally significant, was to mobilize on behalf of the extended family, forms and figurations of collective memory that challenged, albeit ambiguously, the seemingly absolute separation of 'sacred' and 'secular' time on which the very modern ('European') idea of history was/is based (Burke, 1969). The figure of the 'truly educated', 'truly modest' and 'truly Indian' woman is invested, in this discussion of women's education, with a sacred authority by subordinating the question of domestic life to religious ideas of female auspiciousness that joined the heavenly with the mundane in a conceptualization of time which could be only antihistorical. The truly modern housewife, it was said, would be so auspicious as to mark the eternal return of the cosmic principle embodied in the goddess Lakshmi, the goddess of domestic well-being by whose grace the extended family (and clan, and hence by extending the sentiment, the nation, Bharatlakshmi) lived and prospered.

These voices, combining the contradictory themes of nationalism, of patriarchal clan-based ideology, of women's struggles against men, and opposed as the same time to friendship between husbands and wives, remind us of the deep ambivalences that marked the trajectory of the modern private and bourgeois individuality in colonial India. Yet historians manage, by manoeuvres reminiscent of the old 'dialectical' card-trick called 'negation of negation', to deny a subject-position to this voice of ambivalence. The evidence of what I have called 'the denial of the bourgeois private and of the historical subject' is acknowledged but subordinated in their accounts to the supposedly higher purpose of making Indian history look like yet another episode in the universal and (in their view, the ultimately victorious) march of citizenship, of the nation-state, of themes of human emancipation spelt out in the course of the European Enlightenment and after. It is the figure of the citizen that speaks through these histories. And so long as that happens, my hyper-real Europe will continually return to dominate the stories we tell. 'The modern' will then continue to be understood, as Meaghan Morris has so aptly put it in discussing her own Australian context 'as a known history, something which has already happened elsewhere, and which is to be reproduced, mechanically or otherwise, with a local content'. This can only leave us with a task of reproducing what Morris calls 'the project of positive unoriginality' (Morris, 1990: 10).

Yet the 'originality' – I concede that this is a bad term – the idioms through which struggles have been conducted in the Indian subcontinent, has often been in the sphere of the nonmodern. One does not have to subscribe to the ideology of clannish patriarchy, for instance, to acknowledge that the metaphor of the sanctified and patriarchal extended family was one of the most important elements in the cultural politics of Indian nationalism. In the struggle against British rule, it was frequently the use of this idiom – in songs, poetry and other forms of nationalist mobilizations – that allowed 'Indians' to fabricate a sense of community and to retrieve for themselves a subject-position from which to address the British.

Colonial Indian history is replete with instances where Indians arrogated subjecthood to themselves precisely by mobilizing, within the context of 'modern' institutions and sometimes on behalf of the modernizing project of nationalism, devices of collective memory that were both antihistorical and antimodern. This is not to deny the capacity of 'Indians' to act as subjects endowed with what we in the universities would recognize as 'a sense of history' (what Peter Burke (1969) calls 'the renaissance sense of the past') but to insist at the same time that there were also contrary trends, that in the multifarious struggles that took place in colonial India, antihistorical constructions of the past often provided very powerful forms of collective memory (Burke, 1969; Guha, 1983).

There is then this double bind through which the subject of 'Indian' history articulates itself. On the one hand, it is both the subject and the object of modernity, because it stands for an assumed unity called the 'Indian people' that is always split into two – a modernizing elite and a yet-to-be modernized peasantry. However, as such a split subject, it speaks from within a meta-narrative that celebrates the nation-state; and of this meta-narrative the theoretical subject can only be a hyper-real 'Europe', a 'Europe' constructed by the tales that both imperialism and nationalism have told the colonized. The mode of self-representation that the 'Indian' can adopt here is what Homi Bhabba (1987, also 1990) has justly called 'mimetic'. Indian history, even in the most dedicated socialist or nationalist hands, remains a mimicry of a certain 'modern' subject of 'European' history and is bound to represent a sad figure of lack and failure. The transition-narrative will always remain 'grievously incomplete'.

On the other hand, manoeuvres are made within the space of the mimetic and therefore within the project called 'Indian' history – to represent the 'difference' and the 'originality' of the 'Indian', and it is in this cause that the antihistorical devices of memory and the antihistorical 'histories' of the subaltern classes are appropriated. Thus peasant/worker constructions of 'mythical' kingdoms and 'mythical' pasts/futures find a place in texts designated 'Indian' history, precisely through a procedure that subordinates these narratives to the rules of evidence and to the secular, linear calendar that the writing of 'history' must follow. The antihistorical, antimodern subject, therefore, cannot speak itself as 'theory' within the knowledge-procedures of the university, even when these knowledge-procedures acknowledge and 'document' its existence. Much like Spivak's (1988) 'subaltern' (or the anthropologist's peasant who can only have a quoted existence in a larger statement that belongs to the anthropologists alone), this subject can only be spoken for and spoken of by the transition-narrative which will always ultimately privilege the modern (i.e. 'Europe') (see also Spivak, 1990).

So long as one operates within the discourse of 'history' produced at the institutional site of the university, it is not possible simply to walk out of the deep collusion between 'history' and the modernizing narrative(s) of citizenship, bourgeois public and private and the nation-state. 'History' as a knowledge-system is firmly embedded in institutional practices that invoke the nation-state at every step – witness the organization and politics of teaching, recruitment, promotions and publication in history departments, politics that survive the occasional brave and heroic attempts by individual historians to liberate 'history' from the meta-narrative of the nation-state. One only has to ask, for instance: Why is history a compulsory part of education of the modern person in all countries today, including those that did quite comfortably without it until as late as the eighteenth century? Why should children all over the world today have to come to terms with a subject called 'history' when we know that this compulsion is neither natural nor ancient?[10] It does not take much imagination to see that the reason for this lies in what European imperialism and third-world nationalisms have achieved together: universalize the nation-state as the most desirable form of political community. Nation-states have the capacity to enforce their truth-games, and universities, their critical distance notwithstanding, are part of the battery of institutions complicit in this process. 'Economics' and 'history' are the knowledge-forms that correspond to the two major institutions that the rise (and later universalization) of the bourgeois order has given to the world – the capitalist mode of production and the nation-state ('history' speaking to the figure of the citizen).[11] A critical historian has no choice but to negotiate this knowledge. S/he therefore needs to understand the state on its own terms, that is in terms of its self-justificatory narratives of citizenship and modernity. Since these themes will always take us back to the universalist propositions of 'modern' (European) political philosophy, a third-world historian is condemned to knowing 'Europe' as the original home of the 'modern', whereas the 'European' historian does not share a comparable predicament with regard to the pasts of the majority of human-kind. Thus the everyday subalternity of non-Western histories with which I began this paper.

Yet the understanding that 'we' all do 'European' history, with our different and often non-European archives, opens up the possibility of a politics and project of alliance between the dominant metropolitan histories and the subaltern peripheral pasts. Let us call this the project of provincializing 'Europe', the 'Europe' that modern imperialism and (third-world) nationalism have, by their collaborative venture and violence, made universal. Philosophically, this project must ground itself in a radical critique and transcendence of liberalism (i.e. of the bureaucratic constructions of citizenship, modern state and bourgeois privacy that classical political philosophy has produced), a ground that late Marx shares with certain moments in both poststructuralist thought and feminist philosophy. In particular, I am emboldened by Carole Pateman's courageous declaration – in her remarkable book *The Sexual Contract* – that the very conception of the modern individual belongs to patriarchal categories of thought (Pateman, 1988: 184).

The project of 'provincializing Europe' refers to a history which does not yet exist; I can therefore only speak of it in a programmatic manner. However, to forestall misunderstanding, I must spell out what it is not while outlining what it could be. To begin with, it does not call for a simplistic, out-of-hand rejection of modernity, liberal values, universals, science, reason, grand narratives, totalizing explanations, etc. Jameson has recently reminded us that the easy equation often made between 'a philosophical conception of totality' and 'a political practice of totalitarianism' is 'baleful' (Jameson, 1988: 354). The project of 'provincializing Europe' therefore cannot be a project of 'cultural relativism'. It cannot originate from the stance that the reason/science/universals that help define Europe as the modern are simply 'culture-specific' and therefore only belong to the European cultures. For the point is not that Enlightenment rationalism is always unreasonable in itself but rather a matter of documenting how – through what historical process – its 'reason', which was not always self-evident to everyone, has been made to look 'obvious' far beyond the ground where it originated. If a language, as has been said, is but a dialect backed up by an army, the same could be said of the narratives of 'modernity' that, almost universally today, point to a certain 'Europe' as the primary habits of the modern.

This Europe, like 'the West', is demonstrably an imaginary entity but the demonstration as such does not lesson its appeal or power. The project of 'provincializing Europe' has to include certain other additional moves:

(a)   the recognition that Europe's acquisition of the adjective 'modern' for itself is a piece of global history of which an integral part is the story of European imperialism, and

(b)   the understanding that this equating of a certain version of Europe with 'modernity' is not the work of Europeans alone; third-world nationalisms, as modernizing ideologies par excellence, have been equal partners in the process.

I do not mean to overlook the anti-imperial moments in the careers of these nationalisms; I only underscore the point that the project of 'provincializing Europe' cannot be a nationalist, nativist or an atavistic project. In unravelling the necessary entanglement of history – a disciplined and institutionally regulated form of collective memory – with the grand narratives of 'rights', 'citizenship', the nation-state, 'public' and 'private' spheres, one cannot but problematize 'India' at the same time as one dismantles 'Europe'.

The idea is to write into the history of modernity the ambivalences, contradictions, the use of force, and the tragedies and the ironies that attend it. That the rhetoric and the claims of (bourgeois) equality, citizen's rights, of self-determination through a sovereign nation-state have in many circumstances empowered marginal social groups in their struggles is undeniable. What effectively is played down, however, in histories that either implicitly celebrate the advent of the modern state and the idea of citizenship is the repression and violence that are as instrumental in the victory of the modern as is the persuasive power of its rhetorical strategies. Nowhere is this irony – the undemocratic foundations of 'democracy' – more visible than in the history of modern medicine, public health and personal hygiene, the discourses of which have been central in locating the body of the modern at the intersection of the public and the private (as defined by, and subject to negotiations with, the state). However, the triumph of this discourse has always been dependent on the mobilization, on its behalf, of effective means of physical coercion. I say 'always' because this coercion is both originary/foundational (i.e. historic) as well as pandemic and quotidian. Of foundational violence, David Arnold (1994) gives a good example in a recent essay on the history of the prison in India. The coercion of the colonial prison, Arnold shows, was integral to some of the earliest and pioneering research on the medical, dietary and demographic statistics of India, for the prison was where Indian bodies were accessible to modernizing investigators. Of the coercion that continues in the names of the nation and modernity, a recent example comes from the Indian campaign to eradicate smallpox in the 1970s. Two American doctors (one of them presumably of 'Indian' origin) who participated in the process thus describe their operations in a village of the Ho tribe in the Indian state of Bihar:

> In the middle of gentle Indian night, an intruder burst through the bamboo door of the simple adobe hut. He was a government vaccinator, under orders to break resistance against smallpox vaccination. Lakshmi Singh awoke screaming and scrambled to hide herself. Her husband leaped out of bed, grabbed an axe, and chased the intruder into the court-yard. Outside a squad of doctors and policemen quickly overpowered Mohan Singh. The instant he was pinned to the ground, a second vaccinator jabbed smallpox vaccine into his arm. Mohan Singh, a wiry 40-year-old leader of the Ho tribe, squirmed away from the needle, causing the vaccination site to bleed. The government team held him until they had injected enough vaccine . . . While the two policemen rebuffed him, the rest of the team overpowered the entire family vaccinated each in turn. Lakshmi Singh bit deep into one doctor's hand, but to no avail.
>
> (Brilliant with Brilliant, 1978: 3).

There is no escaping the idealism that accompanies this violence. The subtitle of the article in question unselfconsciously reproduces both the military and the do-gooding instincts of the enterprise. It reads: 'How an army of samaritans drove smallpox from the earth'. Histories that aim to displace a hyper-real Europe from the centre towards which all historical imagination currently gravitates will have to seek out relentlessly this connection between violence and idealism that lies at the heart of the process by which the narratives of citizenship and modernity come to find a natural home in 'history'. The task, as I see it, will be to wrestle ideas that legitimize the modern state and its attendant institutions in order to return to political philosophy – in the same way as suspect coins are returned to their owners in an Indian bazaar – its categories whose global currency can no longer be taken for granted.[12]

And, finally – since 'Europe' cannot after all be provincialized within the institutional site of the university whose knowledge-protocols will always take us back to the terrain where all contours follow that of my hyper-real Europe – the project of provincializing Europe must realize within itself its own impossibility. It therefore looks to a history that embodies this politics of despair. It will have been clear by now that this is not a call for cultural relativism or for atavistic, nativist histories. Nor is this a programme for a simple rejection of modernity which would be, in many situations, politically suicidal. I ask for a history that deliberately makes visible, within the very structure of its narrative forms, its own repressive strategies and practices, the part it plays in collusion with the narratives of citizenships in assimilating to the projects of the modern state all other possibilities of human solidarity. The politics of despair will require of such history that it lays bare to its readers such reasons why such a predicament is necessarily inescapable. A history that will attempt the impossible: look toward its own death by tracing that which resists and escapes the best human effort at translation across cultural and other semiotic systems, so that the world may once again be imagined as radically heterogeneous. This, as I have said, is impossible within the knowledge-protocols of academic history, for the globality of the academia is not independent of the globality that the European modern has created. To attempt to provincialize this 'Europe' is to see the modern as inevitably contested, to write over the given and privileged narratives of citizenship other narratives of human connections that draw sustenance from dreamt-up pasts and futures where collectivities are defined neither by the rituals of citizenship nor by the nightmare of 'tradition' that 'modernity' creates. There are, of course, no (infra)structural sites where such dreams could lodge themselves. Yet they will recur so long as the themes of citizenship and the nation-state dominate our narratives of historical transition, for these dreams are what the modern represses in order to be.

Notes

1 A larger version of this article was published in Representations 37, 1992. The author wishes to express his gratitude to Ien Ang and John Hartley for their kind and generous assistance with editing this piece.

2 See the discussion in Marx (1973: 469–512 and 1971: 593–613).

3 I am not making the claim that all of these genres necessarily emerge with bourgeois individualism. See Davis (1986, 1988). See also Lejeune (1989: 163–84).

4 See Chatterjee's (1986) chapter on Nehru.

5 For reasons of space, I shall leave this claim here unsubstantiated, although I hope to have an opportunity to discuss it in detail elsewhere. I should qualify the statement by mentioning that it in the main refers to autobiographies published between 1850 and 1910. Once women join the public sphere in the twentieth century, their self-fashioning takes on different dimensions.

6 For a more detailed treatment of what follows, see Chakrabarty. 'The Difference/deferral of a colonial modernity public debates on domesticity in British India', in David Arnold and David Hardiman (eds), Sulbaltern Studies, vol. 9 (Oxford University Press, Delhi, 1994).

7 On the history of the word 'civilization', see Febvre (1973). I owe this reference to Peter Sahlins.

8 The classic text where this assumption has been worked up into philosophy is of course Hegel's Philosophy of Right (1967: 110–22). See also Hodge (1987), During (1996), Landes (1988) and Ryan (1990).

9 For a genealogy of the terms 'slavery' and 'freedom' as used in the colonial discourse of British India, see Prakash (1990a).

10 On the close connection between imperialist ideologies and the teaching of history in colonial India, see Guha (1988).

11 Without in any way implicating them in the entirety of this argument, I may mention that there are parallels here between my statement and what Gyan Prakash (1990b) and Nicholas Dirks (1990) have argued elsewhere.

12 For an interesting and revisionist reading of Hegel in this regard, see the exchange between Charles Taylor and Partha Chatterjee in Public Culture, 1990, 3(1). My book (Chakrabarty, 1989) attempts a small beginning in this direction.

References

Anon. (1877) Streesiksha vol. 1, Calcutta.

Arnold, David (1994) 'The colonial prison: power, knowledge, and penology in nineteenth-century India', in Arnold, D. and Hardiman, D. (eds) Subaltern Studies, 8.

Bandyopadhyaya, Deenanath (1887) *Nana bishayak prabandha*, Calcutta.

Bhabha, Homi (1987) 'Of mimicry and man: the ambivalence of colonial discourse', in Michelson, Annette, *et al.* (eds), *October: The First Decade 1976–1986*, Cambridge, MA: MIT Press, 317–26.

—— (1990) (ed.) *Nation and Narration*, London: Routledge.

Borthwick, Meredith (1984) *The Changing Roles of Women in Bengal 1849–1905*, Princeton, NJ: Princeton University Press.

Brilliant, Lawrence, with Brilliant, Girija (1978) 'Death for a killer disease', *Quest*, (May/June).

Burke, Peter (1969) *The Renaissance Sense of the Past*, London: Edward Arnold.

Chakrabarty, Dipesh (1988) 'Sarir, samaj o rashtra – oupanibeshik bharate mahamari o janasangskriti', *Anustup* (annual no.) [Bengali].

—— (1989) *Rethinking Working-Class History: Bengal 1890–1940*, Princeton, NJ: Princeton University Press.

—— (1991) 'Open space/public place: garbage, modernity and India', *South Asia*, 14(1), 15–32.

—— (1994) 'The diference/deferral of a colonial modernity public debates on demosticity in British India', in David Arnold and David Hardiman (eds) vol. 8, Delhi: Oxford University Press.

Chatterjee, Partha (1986) *National Thought and the Colonial World: A Derivative Discourse?*, London: Zed Press.

Chaudhuri, Nirad C. (1987) *Thy Hand. Great Anarch! India 1921–1952*, London: Chatto & Windus.

Connolly, William E. (1989) *Political Theory and Modernity*, Oxford: Blackwell.

Davis, Natalie Zemon (1986) 'Boundaries and sense of self in sixteenth-century France', in Heller, Thomas C. *et al.* (eds), *Reconstructing Individualism: Autonomy, Individuality, and the Self in Western Thought*, Stanford: Stanford University Press, 53–63.

—— (1988) 'Fame and secrecy: Leon Modena's life as an early modern autobiography', *History and Theory*, 27, 103–18.

Devi, Indira (1920) *Narir ukti*, Calcutta [Bengali].

Dirks, Nicholas B. (1990) 'History as a sign of the modern', *Public Culture*, 2(2), 25–32.

During, Simon, 'Rousseau's Patimony: primitivism, romance and becoming other', in Francis Barker, Peter Hulme and Margaret Iversen (eds) *Colonial Discourse/Postcolonial Theory*, Manchester: Manchester University Press, 1996.

Febvre, Lucien (1973) 'Civilization: evolution of a word and a group of ideas', in Burke, Peter (ed.) *A New Kind of History: From the Writings of Febvre*, trans. K. Folca, London.

Gandhi, M.K. (1909/63) Hind Swaraj, in *Collected Works of Mahatma Gandhi*, vol. 10, Ahmedabad: Navjan Publishing Trust.

Guha, Ranajit (1983) *Elementary Aspects of Peasant Insurgency in Colonial India*, New Delhi: Oxford University Press.

—— (1988) *An Indian Historiography of India: A Nineteenth-Century Agenda and Its Implications*, Calcutta: K.P. Bagchi.

Guha, Ranajit and Spivak, Gayatry C. (eds) (1988) *Selected Subaltern Studies*, New York: Oxford University Press.

Habermas, Jurgen (1989) *The Structural Transformation of the Public Sphere: An Inquiry into a Category of Bourgeois Society*, Cambridge, MA: MIT Press.

Hegel, Friedrich (1967) *Philosophy of Right*, trans. T.M. Knox, Oxford: Oxford University Press.

Hodge, Joanna (1987) 'Women and the Hegelian state', in Ellen Kennedy and Susan Mendus, editors, *Women in Western Philosophy*, Brighton, Sussex, 127–58.

Jameson, Fredric (1988) 'Cognitive mapping', in Nelson and Grossberg (1988).

Landes, Joan B. (1988) *Women and the Public Sphere in the Age of the French Revolution*, Ithaca: Cornell University Press.

Lejeune, Philippe (1989) *On Autobiography*, trans. Katherine Leary, Minneapolis: University of Minnesota Press.

Marx, Karl (1971) *Capital: A Critique of Political Economy*, vol. 3, Moscow: Foreign Languages Publishing House.

—— 1973) *Grundrisse: Foundations of the Critique of Political Economy*, trans. Martin Nicholas, Harmondsworth: Penguin.

—— (1975) 'On the Jewish question', in his *Early Writings*, Harmondsworth: Penguin.

Mill, James (1837) *The History of British India*, vol. 1, Wilson, H.H. (ed.) London: J. Madden.

Mitra, Dinabandhu (1981) *Dinabandhu racanabali*, Gupta, Kshetra (ed.) Calcutta: Sahitya Sangsad [Bengali].

Morris, Meaghan (1990) 'Metamorphoses at Sydney Tower', *New Formations*, 11 (Summer).

Murshid, Ghulam (1983) *Reluctant Debutante: Response of Bengali Women to Modernization, 1849–1905*, Rajshahi: Rajshahi University.

Nelson, Cary and Grossberg, Lawrence (eds) (1988) *Marxism and the Interpretation of Culture*, Urbana and Chicago: University of Illinois Press.

Pateman, Carole (1988) *The Sexual Contract*, Stanford: Stanford University Press.

Prakash, Gyan (1990a) *Bonded Histories: Genealogies of Labour Servitude in Colonial India*, Cambridge: Cambridge University Press.

—— (1990b) 'Writing postorientalist histories of the Third World: perspectives from Indian historiography', *Comparative Studies in Society and History*, 32(2), 383–408.

Ryan, Mary (1990) *Women in Public: Between Banners and Ballots, 1825–1880*, Baltimore: Johns Hopkins University Press.

Sarkar, Sumit (1985a) *Modern India 1885–1947*, Delhi: Macmillan.

—— (1985b) 'Social history: predicament and possibilities', in Iqbal Khan (ed.) *Fresh Perspectives on India and Pakistan: Essays on Economics, Politics and Culture*, Oxford: Oxford University Press.

Spivak, Gayatri Chakravorty (1988) 'Can the subaltern speak?', in Nelson and Grossberg (1988) *Marxism and the Interpretation of Culture*, Urbana and Chicago: University of Illinois Press.

—— (1990), interview, *Socialist Review*, 20(3).

PART 2

Intellectual battles and exchanges

Chapter 4

Frederick Cooper

POSTCOLONIAL STUDIES AND THE STUDY OF HISTORY

Fred Cooper, a distinguished historian both of colonial Africa and of colonialism in general, here offers a wide-ranging critique of many trends and emphases in recent colonial and postcolonial studies as they have related to history. Although himself much influenced by several of these intellectual movements, he argues – as will be seen – that they have also often had considerable costs. See also his further developments of many of these themes in his book *Colonialism in Question: Theory, Knowledge, History* (University of California Press, 2005).

Stephen Howe

BY THE 1970S, THE HISTORICAL STUDY of colonial empires had become one of the deadest of dead fields within the discipline of history. Students interested in pushing the frontiers of historical research looked to Africa, Asia, or Latin America, or they sought to look at Europe and North America 'from the bottom up.' The revival of interest in the colonial world a generation later reflects the influence of literature and anthropology and, more important, wider intellectual currents that threw into question the most basic narratives and the most fundamental ways in which knowledge is configured. Historians had to face the fact that the new challenges were not simply to add an African or Asian component to a previously Europe-centered curriculum but to rethink what it meant to study a continent called Europe and to examine the position of the researcher in the production of historical scholarship.[1]

But perhaps it is now the interdisciplinary domain of postcolonial studies that needs a shot in the arm, particularly a more rigorous historical practice. Postcolonial studies has brought before a large and transcontinental public the place of colonialism in world history, yet it has tended to obscure the very history whose importance it has highlighted.

A generic colonialism located somewhere between 1492 and the 1970s – has been given the decisive role in shaping a postcolonial moment, in which intellectuals can condemn the continuation of invidious distinctions and exploitation and celebrate the proliferation of cultural hybridities and the fracturing of cultural boundaries. This essay will develop a critique of ahistorical tendencies in colonial studies and argue for approaches that give more weight to the specificity of colonial situations and the importance of struggles in colonies, in metropoles, and between the two.[2]

History, as a discipline, has itself become the object of critique. Ashis Nandy argues that history is inseparable from its imperialist origins, that it necessarily imposes the imperialist's understanding of a people's past over their own. To some scholars, history confines the zigzags of time into linear pathways, privileges state building over other forms of human connection, and tells a story of progress that inevitably leaves Africans or Asians on the side, lacking some crucial characteristic necessary to attain what is otherwise universal.[3] Such arguments constitute valid criticisms of many histories, but do they amount to an indictment of the study of history itself? In fact, the indictment of history is itself historical. To trace history to imperialism is to give power to a phenomenon that is historically located. If there is some truth in Nicholas Dirks' assertion of the 'irrevocable link between History and the Nation-State,' the evidence that the nation-state is not so universal makes for another sort of history that documents more varied sorts of political imagination.[4] The question is whether one can be satisfied with the simple *naming* of imperialism or colonialism as the dark side of universality, progress, or modernity, or whether we need to know something more about imperialism and colonialism.

Here, the virtues and the weaknesses of recent scholarship run close together. If any intervention shook up historians' complacency, it was Edward Said's *Orientalism* (1978).[5] Said showed how certain visions of Asiatic societies were deeply woven into canonical European literature. Colonization no longer resided out there, in exotic places, but in the heart of European culture. Said soon faced criticism for presenting a view of the colonized as Other so tight that no room remained for alternative constructions, including those by Arabs, Africans, or South Asians. In a subsequent book, *Culture and Imperialism*, Said tried to restore balance by emphasizing not the stark separation of European and indigenous discourses but the efforts of colonized intellectuals to work between them and to develop cross-cutting languages of liberations. Such an argument necessarily proves a historical one.

To some postcolonial theorists, the goal has been no less than to overthrow the place of reason and progress as the beacons of humanity, insisting that the claims to universality that emerged from the Enlightenment occlude the way colonialism imposed not just its exploitative power but its ability to determine the terms – democracy, liberalism, rationality – by which political life the world over would from then on be conducted. By holding this universalizing modernity against the ugly particularity of colonialism, postcolonial theorists attack head-on a metanarrative of a history that shows Europe step by step repudiating the oppressiveness of its own past and making itself into a model to the rest of the world. Some hope to persuade us to 'give up the seemingly powerful corollary *presumption* that liberalism and indeed democracy (even a purportedly radical one) have any *particular* privilege among ways of organizing the political forms of our collective lives.'[6]

Critics – and even some scholars who identify themselves with postcolonial studies – at times worry that the repudiation of Enlightenment may have gone too far and brought aid and comfort to political forces – such as the Hindu Right in India – whose rejection of liberal democratic values does not serve to enhance respect for the values of different communities. Some fear that the critique of so-called foundational concepts in Western thought, particularly those of Marxist theory, disarms social scientists of the tools they need to understand the all-too-real power of global capitalism.[7]

These arguments are not what concerns me here. My focus is the double occlusion that results from turning the centuries of European colonization overseas into a critique of the Enlightenment, democracy, or modernity. First is the occlusion of European history, for the counterpart of the charge of reducing non-Western history to the lack of what the West had is the assumption that the West actually had it itself, that the metanarrative of European progress is more relevant than the messy and uneven history of post-1789 Europe. Second is the occlusion of the history of the people who lived in what became colonies. What is lost in telling nineteenth- and twentieth-century colonialism as the story of the coming ashore 'of the terrible storm called progress' or as 'the politico-ethical project of producing subjects and governing their conduct,' or as the production of 'colonial modernities through the regulation of cultural difference' is the range of experiences and actions among people who confronted colonial rule.[8] One misses the crudeness and the excess of violence of much of nineteenth-century colonization, as well as the ways in which colonized people sought – not entirely without success – to build lives in the crevices of colonial power and to deflect, appropriate, or re-interpret the teachings and preachings thrust on them. The line of argument mentioned above may celebrate 'resistance,' but the idea that struggle actually had effects on the course of colonization is lost in the timelessness of colonial modernity. The Haitian Revolution – and especially the possibility that the Haitian Revolution actually affected the meanings of citizenship or freedom in Europe and the Americas – remains as strikingly absent in prominent postcolonial texts as in conventional narratives of European progress.[9]

For some, the occlusion is explicit, as in this formulation of Robert J.C. Young: 'The postcolonial does not privilege the colonial. It is concerned with colonial history only to the extent that history has determined the configurations of power structures of the present, to the extent that much of the world still lives in the violent disruptions of its wake, and to the extent that the anti-colonial liberation movements remain the source and inspiration of its politics.'[10] How one would be able to judge 'the extent' without studying the history is not obvious, but that is beside the point: the 'colonial' that is relevant here is the generic one, a singular colonialism, spatially undefined and temporally spread out over four centuries, whose contours are exempted from examination, yet whose power still determines the present.[11] But might not this generic colonial history produce an equally generic postcolonial present?

My argument is not with the postcolonial critic's insistence that the evils of nineteenth- and twentieth-century colonialism lie firmly within the political structures, values, and understandings of its era; colonialism should not be reduced to an atavistic holdover from the past. It is with a juxtaposition of a supposed post-Enlightenment universality and colonial particularity frozen in time, isolated from the dynamics ensuing from the tensions within any ideological formation and the tensions produced by efforts of empires to install real administrations over real people. What such an approach privileges is the stance of the critic who decodes this transhistorical phenomenon, hence the label Gyan Prakash and others have attached to their project, 'colonial critique.'[12]

Such a critique has had its value, above all, in forcing historians – such as anthropologists or other social scientists – to question their own epistemological positions and to think long and hard about how historical sources, as much as interpretations, are produced. But critique is no substitute for historical or ethnographic research, and the question is how one understands and moves beyond the limits inherent to the stance of the critic.[13] Let me turn now to a brief analysis of modes of writing that can be called ahistorical history, which purport to address the relationship of past to present but which do so without interrogating the way processes unfold over time. I will mention three modes of looking at history ahistorically: story plucking, leapfrogging legacies, and time flattening. My goal in doing so is not to dismiss certain critical strategies, but to suggest limitations that can be transcended. It is not to issue a blanket criticism of 'postcolonial studies' (a category containing much variety and debate), but to point to the insufficiency and imprecision of certain concepts and certain ways of framing issues. And it is not to defend one discipline or condemn another, for some of the most searching historical questions have been asked by literary critics or anthropologists, and historians, including some who have stimulated the study of colonial questions, have also contributed to the tendency to take colonialism out of a historical framework.[14]

First, story plucking. Here I mean extracting tidbits from different times and places and treating them as a body independent of their historical relationship, context, or countervailing tendencies. Postcolonial writers from Homi Bhabha to Walter Mignolo to Dipesh Chakrabarty write with little apparent misgivings about a phenomenon labeled colonial, appearing in many places and times.[15] Implicitly or explicitly, 'coloniality,' or its related form 'postcoloniality,' can be abstracted from context and process. The weighty-*ity* attached to the colonial implies that there exists an essence of being colonized, independent of what anybody did in a colony. One can pluck a text or a narrative from Spanish America in the sixteenth century, or from the slave colonies of the West Indies in the eighteenth century, or from a moderately prosperous twentieth-century cocoa planter in the Gold Coast, and derive a lesson that conveys a generalizable meaning. What gets lost here is that colonial power, like any other, is the object of struggle, a struggle that depends on the specific resources of those involved, and that colonizer and colonized themselves constitute far from immutable categories, categories that must be reproduced by specific institutions, institutions that themselves change historically. People did not just sit around contemplating what it meant to be colonized, and examining repressive power is not the same as assuming that it alone characterized a particular situation; the extremes of colonial violence may well reflect the limits of routinized power. Traders, peasants, religious converts, and others might seize spaces that colonial authorities could not understand or bend an institution in a new direction, or else Creole elites might replicate metropolitan institutions while attacking imperial rule. Different forms of exploitation, from compulsory production on plantations to taxation of the exports of peasants whose farms and families were largely ignored, could have very different social and cultural implications. A concept like coloniality is either so dilute that it carries little meaning, or so essentializing that it becomes deeply misleading.[16] Naming the colonial says little about how people confronted the forms of power they faced, about the social and cultural resources they brought to the confrontation, or about the dynamics of interaction and struggle.

Second, leapfrogging legacies. Here I refer to claims that something at time A caused something in time C without considering time B. Students of race in the United States have encountered a striking instance of this fallacy: the Moynihan report done during Nixon's presidency, which blamed the dislocation of African American families on the legacy of slavery. The causes of dislocation were placed in the safely distant past, skipping over anything that happened between 1863 and 1963, notably the effects of industrialization and urbanization on African Americans. Colonial legacy arguments exhibit the same flaw. African political scientist Mahmood Mamdani, in his book *Citizen and Subject: Contemporary Africa and the Legacy of Late Colonialism*, draws a direct causal connection between a colonial policy, arguably important in the 1920s and 1930s, of ruling through 'decentralized despotisms,' African chiefdoms given authority under colonial auspices, and the brittle politics of authoritarianism and ethnicity in Africa in the 1980s and 1990s.[17] Like Moynihan, Mamdani has a point at either end of his leapfrog, but he misses everything in between. His book says almost nothing about the 1950s and 1960s, and thus misses the alternative explanation for Africa's malaise: that there was indeed effective mobilization in those years that cut across ethnic divisions and urban/rural distinctions, through which Africans made strong claims to citizenship, which African politicians used against colonial regimes. But once in power, such leaders understood all too well the danger such claims represented. The explosion of citizenship in the final years of colonial rule appears nowhere in Mamdani's book, and he thus misses not only the sequence of processes in the decolonization era but the tragedy of recent African history, people's heightened sense of possibility, and the thwarting of their hopes. This book does not stand alone in finding a too-ready explanation of the postcolonial by invoking the colonial, leapfrogging over precisely the period and the processes that most need examination.[18]

Third, time flattening. This refers to an assumption that a certain essence characterizes a long period of time, passing over the conflict and change within it. This constitutes an old vice of history departments, notably in course listings that divide modern and premodern, distinctions bad enough in European history, but often extended elsewhere. Era labeling has been given a new interdisciplinary lease on life, in part through the work of Michel Foucault that locates modern governmentality in a space amorphous in time and amorphous in agency and causality, but that provides a blueprint for a wide range of scholars to attribute practices and discourses to the fact of modernity, often elided with post-Enlightenment rationalism, bourgeois equality, and liberalism.

Let me take the most persuasive version of this argument, from historian Dipesh Chakrabarty.[19] He justly criticizes versions of Indian history-colonialist, nationalist, or Marxist – that measure the colonized by how well they did at class formation and state building – where Europe supposedly led the way – and attribute their failures to certain 'lacks' on their part (of a proper working class, of a proper bourgeoisie). Chakrabarty instead calls for the 'provincialization' of Europe, its history seen as particular rather than as a universal model.

But then he proceeds to do the opposite. What he variously calls post-Enlightenment rationality, bourgeois equality, modernity, or liberalism become not provincial ideologies, but a grid of knowledge and power forcing people to see the nation-state as the only political model and obliging them to give up diverse understandings of community in favor of a one-to-one relationship of the unmarked individual and the nation-state, at best seeking 'alternatives' to a modernity decidedly singular and decidedly European.

The pleasant irony of this argument is that Europeans become the people without history, a tag formerly reserved for the victims of their colonial endeavors.[20] European history, from Denis Diderot to Jacques Derrida, is flattened into a single post-Enlightenment era. A reference to Georg Wilhelm Friedrich Hegel stands in for a European history reduced to the claim of progress.[21] The problem, of course, is that Europeans – like the people they conquered – had a history that does not fit in boxes like this. Nineteenth-century Europe was immersed in struggles within and among many parochialisms and many universalities. Secularism was more often beleaguered than triumphant, *anciens regimes* and aristocracies did not die out on the guillotine. One would not know from Chakrabarty's account how intense the struggles have been over what the Enlightenment meant and what political deductions to draw from this. The balancing of the universalized, rights-bearing individual against questions of difference, constituted, as gender historian Dena Goodman argues, a vital debate *within* Enlightenment thinking. Critiques of post-Enlightenment thinking, as David Hollinger notes, have 'evacuated' the history of 'modernism in the era 1890 to 1930, with its revolt against the positivism, rationalism, realism, and liberalism,' in order to create a stark – and profoundly ahistorical – opposition between the Enlightenment and the posts in vogue today.[22]

Instead of provincializing Europe, Chakrabarty seems to be saying that Europe cannot be provincialized. He assumes not only that the Enlightenment won a complete ideological victory after 1789 over the defenders of aristocratic, Catholic, and monarchic social orders but that modernity constituted a kind of lived experience in contrast to that of India.[23] What is lost when one takes Europe out of its history is not only how badly the tale of progress fits the political, intellectual, and cultural history of this continent but the extent to which even such constructs dismissed as bourgeois equality were not some essence of 'the West,' but products of struggle. The English citizen, for example, far from constituting an unmarked individual in direct relation to the state, emerged from a vision of community centered around the idea of a jury of one's peers.[24] The ascension of a liberal idea of a rights-bearing individual over the equally liberal idea of rights as earned by the civilized behavior of a collectivity reflected the labors not only of a Frederick Douglass but of unnamed ex-slaves, dependent laborers, and colonized peasants who revealed the limits of colonial power and defined alternative modes of living and working in the crevices of authority.[25]

One antidote to writing history as the rise of the nation-state could focus on alternative readings of European history itself. Postrevolutionary France, for example, proved a peculiar combination of so-called old colonies, especially in the Caribbean, and a European France whose boundaries and degrees of 'Frenchness' were far from clear even a century later. Precisely because Saint Domingue (later Haiti) formed part of an imperial space, the question of whether the rights of man and the citizen applied there was argued over in both Saint Domingue and Paris. The Haitian Revolution of 1791 stands alongside the French in opening questions of slavery and citizenship, of cultural difference and universal rights, to wider debate, the long-term relevance of which C.L.R. James made clear in 1938.[26] Napoleon's conquests in Europe and Egypt extended even further the fact of France as a differentiated territory, establishing a differentiation that did not neatly line up in a self-Other dichotomy.[27] That ex-slaves of African descent in the old colonies became citizens in 1848 while the large Muslim population taken in by the conquest of Algeria in 1830 were defined as subjects points to the difficulties of producing a stable theory of imperial difference. Most important, the range of distinctions within the French empire meant that people of any given status knew of the other possibilities, and just as in Haiti white planters, mulatto planters, and slaves had all used the citizenship concept to make claims, the efforts of France to define an imperial space produced a succession of claims to reconfigure citizenship, especially in moments of uncertainty such as 1848, the beginnings of the Third Republic in the 1870s, and the world wars. If one wants to rethink France from its colonies, one might even argue that France itself only became a nation-state in 1962, when it finally gave up its hold on Algeria and tried for a time to define itself as a singular citizenry in a single territory.[28]

In the colonies, meanwhile, flattening nineteenth-century history into the imposition of colonial governmentality or colonial modernity produces, to an African historian at least, something unrecognizable. Certainly, one can point to efforts of geographers, explorers, and scholarly minded colonial officials in the aftermath of conquests of the 1870s to slot African cultures into schemas of scientific knowledge, but any study of knowledge and power must also recognize the deliberate ignorance of early twentieth-century colonial states: there was no need to know the laborer whom one was going to use and discard. If advocates of so-called free labor hoped to extract a market-responsive individual from the confines of both slavery and community, colonial officials soon realized that the West Indian ex-slave or the African ex-peasant was not following the script, and rather than make individual subjects, a powerful colonial lobby advocated new forms of coerced labor and the alteration of community structures to provide collective discipline. Religious conversion and education had their proponents, who wished to colonize minds, but until the 1940s, the detractors were more centrally placed in African administrations, and British, French, and German colonial regimes spent very little money to realize whatever civilizing missions they professed. In French and British Africa, a patchwork of early colonial projects to remake the African largely gave way after World War I, in the face of the inability of regimes to impose their will, to a more custodial version of colonialism, to acceptance of working through the indigenous elites once labeled primitive and tyrannical, and to a refusal to spend metropolitan funds on 'development' until confronted with a new wave of challenges in the late 1930s and 1940s. For an African living in a colony, fluctuations or variants in colonial policy could have an enormous impact: between the forced laborer on a Mozambican sugar farm and the relatively autonomous coffee farmer in the southern Gold Coast, between the teacher trained at the Ecole William Ponty in Senegal and the Algerian victimized by land alienation and labor exploitation, a great deal hung in the balance. And the kinds of politics for which such people could be mobilized varied accordingly, in place and in time. African historians since the 1970s have shed a good deal of light on such phenomena, and the specific trajectories of struggle deserve a place in the pantheon of colonial and postcolonial studies.

Doing history historically, as these examples suggest, does more to challenge the supposedly dominant narratives of nation building and development than an approach to the past based on story plucking, leapfrogging legacies, or time flattening. Criticisms of many historians for writing everything into a linear history of human progress are often accurate and appropriate, but an understanding of different forms of temporality is not assisted by positing a Western temporality divided into premodern, modern, and postmodern epochs or by focusing on an era of modernity in which European ascendancy is juxtaposed against but unaffected by the actions and ideas of colonized populations. A more dynamic view of the exercise of power, of the limits of power, and the contestations of power constitutes a fundamentally historical endeavor, demanding methodologies both rigorous and self-aware.

Colonial studies has by and large been so intent on taking apart the narrative of Western progress that it has remained rather uncurious about exploring the implications of looking backwards in time or toward the variety of forms of state power that shared the temporal field of modernity. Scholars of early modern Europe – Peter Hulme stands out in this regard – have gone further to engage postcolonial theory than have scholars of later colonization and de-colonization to extend their own temporal bounds.[29] My co-edited book *Tensions of Empire* proves no exception to this orientation toward Western Europe in the nineteenth and twentieth centuries.[30] The focus risks reproducing Eurocentrism by all but ignoring other empires – the Ottoman, the Habsburg, the Chinese, the Japanese, and the Russian – and initiatives to compare the Soviet empire of 1917–1989 to empires of Britain and France in the twentieth century have come almost entirely from the side of scholars of the Soviet Union. Nineteen eighty-nine is not celebrated here as a milestone of decolonization: Central Asian Muslims conquered by the czars and subjected to the violent modernizing project of the Soviets are not the object of analogous moral and political attention as North African Muslims colonized by the French.

The narrowing of the range is based on certain assumptions: that these empires are different sorts of animals, that they are not really colonial and, above all, that with the exception of the Soviet case, they were not 'modern.' The latter argument is actually a bit of whig history, reading backwards the collapse of the Ottoman, Habsburg, and Russian empires in 1917–1923 into a thesis of the inevitable transition from empire to nation-state. Recent scholarship has shown that far from being beleaguered holdouts against claims to the nation, these empires produced a strong empire-centered imagination that captured the minds of many self-conscious opponents of imperial power until the time of World War I. Ottomanism constituted a compelling ideology, even among Young Turks whose national focus to a large extent postdated the demolition of the empire rather than inspired it. Likewise, the critics of Habsburg conservatism included many who saw the imperial unit as a possibility offering something to reform minded intellectuals, Jews, and others who sought a bigger field than what became national units. Yet these empires were not quaint repositories of aristocratic cosmopolitanism. If difference is the hallmark of colonialism, they articulated and reproduced difference aplenty – and did not lack for repression either, but not in the same way as Britain or France.[31] And what passes for 'modern governmentalities' in nineteenth-century Europe – cadastral surveys, the enumeration of imperial subjects – was a thousand years old in China.[32] Like the empires of nineteenth-century Western Europe, these empires had both universalizing and particularizing tendencies and illustrate a stunning range of possibilities for examining their relation.

Broadening the range of oppositional movements as well as empires should underscore the point made earlier: the dangers of the backward projection of the post-1960s world of nation-states into a nineteenth-century path of inevitability. One can fruitfully put in relation to each other the saliency of Ottomanism in the late nineteenth century, the rise of pan-Arab and pan-Slavic movements in the same era, and the long history of pan-Africanism, all of which put political affinity into a non-territorial framework. Many scholars quote the same passage from Aimé Cesaire in which he eloquently depicts the horrors of colonial rule, but not everybody remembers that his vision of decolonization was not limited to forging independent nation-states, but stressed remaking France itself to eliminate the invidious inequality among the component parts of this supranational unit and recreating a capitalist world order.[33] The possibilities that the political imagination of Cesaire opened up – and the ways in which those possibilities were constrained – require a historical analysis more attuned to different voices than the assumption of a course from empire to nation-state set at the time of the French Revolution.

My own thinking has been shaped by reading old trade union pamphlets and colonial archives from French Africa in the late 1940s, where one finds workers' organizations telling officials: you want to talk about civilizing us, but what we want to talk about is equal pay for equal work, about piped water in our neighborhood, about schools for our children.[34] Such demands in their own way proved as threatening as the efforts of a Ho Chi Minh to throw France out of Southeast Asia, for they promised to turn the very premises of postwar imperial ideology into a series of expensive demands whose refusal would be ideologically as well as politically dangerous. Multiplied by many mobilizing efforts throughout the French empire, such demands not only won concrete benefits for many people – the forty-hour week for wage workers, for example – but the fact of insisting that such measures should apply to Africans as much as anybody else profoundly affected the meaning of citizenship and social distinction. They provoked doubts in Paris about the entire doctrine of postwar French colonialism, whose insistence that Greater France was the only unit of political possibility implied that the French standard of living was a legitimate reference point for colonial social movements. Political mobilization around imperial citizenship also injected a self-confidence into social movements themselves – and above all a socially focused, activist notion of citizenship that proved threatening to postindependence regimes as well.

The efforts of trade unions, farmers' organizations, traders' organizations, and groups of teachers and students to challenge modernizing colonial regimes for both material benefits and political voice risk being lost if one privileges the Manichaean version of studying colonialism and anticolonialism.[35] But more is lost than the stories of a generation of activists in the 1940s and 1950s and the important but bounded accomplishments they achieved. The very claim of the 'victors' of the politics of the 1950s and 1960s to represent a true anticolonialism and their contempt for the more diverse politics that had made the 1950s such a volatile era provided a rationale for the labeling of challengers to the new regimes as imperialist stooges or enemies of the people and the purging of the opposition from the political spectrum. The cultivation of heroic anticolonialism became part of postcolonial repression. Rather than contrast an era of pure anticolonialism, built around iconicized heroes, against a sordid picture of postcolonial corruption and venality, one can gain a more thorough understanding of the possibilities and tragedies of decolonization by examining the political space people opened for themselves, with its limitations and their compromises, provisional victories, and powerful disappointments.[36]

To some postcolonial theorists, those Africans who insisted (or who today insist) that the real issue is water, schools, or wages did not have it right. What is 'important for the present,' writes David Scott, is 'a critical interrogation of the practices, modalities, and projects through which modernity inserted itself into and altered the lives of the colonized.' Well, yes, but what about the water pipe, the health clinic, and the farmers' cooperative? Is there not a danger that we, as scholars, project onto people who lived at a certain time and in a certain place a metahistorical perspective that crowds out the question of how people, in a particular conjuncture, phrased their demands and organized themselves?[37]

The issues raised here are not mere exercises in historical refinement. History, as such, does not offer any lessons (although historians offer plenty), but to think through a historical process is to observe the relationship of action and its consequences. That is why I keep insisting on the importance of looking at the way in which specific actions by states or political movements reconfigured concepts and possibilities. If we are to do more than lament the passing of an era of true radicalism or to assume that colonialism's opponents could only follow a script written by colonizers themselves, we need to do more careful research into social and political movements at all levels, from the people trying to put together a local cooperative to transterritorial movements of intellectuals who fought to make colonialism an anathema. We cannot read that history off a text by Fanon.

There is a danger that ahistorical history encourages an apolitical politics. To take a stance against the Enlightenment, to hold modernity responsible for racial and class hierarchy, offers little account of the responsibility of elites for their words and actions and little insight into how people facing the possibilities and constraints of particular colonial situations acted. We lose the power of their example to remind us that our own moral and political choices, made in the face of the ambivalences and complications of our present situation, will have consequences in the future. As politically attuned a writer as Chakrabarty separates his politics from his critique, conceding that the liberal order and Enlightenment ideals he criticizes may be the best means for defending the position of the subaltern.[38] A more dynamic view of history would make the separation of colonial critique in the academy from politics in South Asia less artificial.

The antislavery movement, the anticolonial movement, and the antiapartheid movement have been subjected to relentless irony, for their humanistic claims can be set off against the exclusions and hierarchies they re-inscribed and the whiggishness that narrating their history seems to imply.[39] But such movements were not simply entrapped in a framework of European beliefs; they profoundly changed what Europeans thought they believed. The Haitian Revolution, the Jamaican slave revolt of 1830, the Martinique slave revolt of 1848, the countless escapes and small acts of defiance of slaves in the southern United States – all formed part of the process that made slavery, a very normal part of very normal empires, into something first questioned and then attacked. That colonialism became the object of attack in Hanoi or Paris in the 1930s the way slavery did a century earlier reflects not the opposition of an abstracted 'colonial subject' against a colonizer, but the coming together of specific forms of struggle in a particular conjuncture. At critical moments, the intersection of locally or regionally rooted mobilizations with movements deploying a liberal-democratic ideology, with attempts at articulating a Christian universalism, with the mobilization of Islamic networks, with the linkages of anti-imperialist movements in different continents and with trade union internationalism helped to shape and reshape the terrain of contestation. Such interactive mobilizations have hardly eliminated exploitation or invidious distinction, and they have had to contend with powerful forces seeming to confine challenges to carefully bounded domains, but incremental changes and systemic shifts are nonetheless part of the history of the present.[40]

One can readily agree with Uday Mehta when he writes, 'I do not claim that liberalism *must be* imperialistic, only that the urge is *internal* to it.'[41] One could just as easily write, 'I do not claim that liberalism *must be* antiimperialist, only that the urge is *internal* to it.' As in the case of nineteenth-century English liberalism, the crucial questions about arguments for liberation and democratization today are not resolvable by epistemological critique alone, but turn on the concrete possibilities that our political, economic, and social conjuncture permits and the political choices that people make. Which liberalism? Whose Enlightenment? What kind of development? Which vision of an Islamic *umma* (community)? Whose community? Which network of connections across linguistic or cultural divisions?

If such an argument is valid, the question of how one finds evidence and constructs an argument about moments of possibility and moments of constraint proves crucial. The stance of the critic has been useful in reminding scholars in dusty archives of the impossibility of seeing themselves in a position of neutral judges outside of the history about which they write. Historians are warned of the dangers of imposing a notion of 'objective truth' without probing the truth regime that gives weight to certain evidence and denies it to others; of missing the 'temporal heterogeneity,' the diverse ways people understand time and their relation to it, and of the need to get inside religious or other forms of understanding that deviate from secular, rationalist visions of how people make choices and act.[42] But it would be unfortunate if these issues were reduced to the imposition of modern reason on a recalcitrant non-modern past; they prove fundamental to understanding *any* past. How regimes of truth are constructed in a particular context has been the subject of important analyses, and the efforts (notably among African historians since the 1960s) to build a more inclusive notion of the archive and to analyze the production of history – how the telling or writing of history is itself part of a history – have helped to make history writing a more examined and debated process.[43] A critical stance need not reproduce the modern/non-modern dichotomy it pretends to deconstruct or to which it claims to provide alternatives.

Postcolonial studies has a strong stake in not carrying the contextualization of truth claims into a dismissal of truth as just another Western conceit. The moral force of the insertion of colonialism into world history depends on the reader's conviction that the slaves on a Jamaican sugar plantation actually felt the whip and that the Toussaint-Louvertures of the colonial world and the unnamed peasants who frustrated the plans of colonial agents are more than archetypes. The colonial apologist's tale of colonialism as the bringing of schools and hospitals to hapless natives might be seen as the expression by a group with its own cultural criteria, its own regime of truth, equivalent to but different from the cultural criteria and truth regimes of other groups. If all versions are to be seen as alternative fictions, each associated with a specific identity category, then there is no basis, other than an already specified position (race, gender, ethnicity) for anybody to convince anybody of anything.[44]

The historian's insistence on referring to the archive – oral, written, whatever – pushes debate toward consideration of the time and the context in which a process occurs and makes it imaginable that a historian from, say, South Asia, might convince a reader in Great Britain to question a received truth. That the ground on which contestation takes place is not even, and that the historical or any other profession may resist the reconstitution of its canons, does not negate the importance of such debate. To foster the material and political conditions that extend the range of discussion outside of academic venues in which it has become accepted is no easy task, but the importance of extending intellectual debate derives from it being more than juxtaposition of preconstituted stances.

One of the achievements of scholars who consider themselves postcolonial is to bring the colonial question out of the colonies and into Europe and North America. Here, too, there is a danger of the power of this insight becoming diffuse, of explaining generalized difference in the cities of England via reference to an undifferentiated colonial past stretching back to Columbus. One cannot understand the Le Pen phenomenon in France without understanding Algeria, but one cannot understand Le Pen by reducing him to Algeria. The terms in which Le Pen-style xenophobia is articulated also comes out of a line of right-wing Catholicism that has been anti-Semitic and anti-Protestant, loudly proclaiming itself 'French' while at the same time opposing the republican notions of civic virtue that others consider the basis of Frenchness.[45] The problems of immigrants from ex-colonies or other regions outside of Western Europe will not be solved by juxtaposing a postcoloniality that is filled with hybridity and multiculturalism against an all-containing colonial modernity.

Tejumola Olaniyan writes that 'even the most unforgiving critics of the term [postcolonial] do not deny that a lot of relevant work is being done in its name.'[46] He is certainly correct, and the most important question is how to go about continuing the work. Stuart Hall has given historians, among others, plenty of employment when he describes the domain of postcolonial studies as 'the whole process of expansion, exploration, conquest, colonisation and imperial hegemonisation which constituted the "outer face," the constitutive outside, of European and then Western capitalist modernity after 1492.'[47] This agenda will, and should be, pursued by scholars using a variety of theoretical frameworks, in useful conversation with the conceptual critiques that postcolonial theory has encouraged. But the metaclaim that the unit in question is 'Western capitalist modernity since 1492' can easily become a shortcut of just such an examination, an evocation of a past flattened into a blunt tool useful for showing the ugly flip side of European progress, but not for building up other ways of narrating and explaining a complex history. If the kind of inquiry I am advocating is consistent with the goals of many who consider themselves postcolonial theorists, some of the concepts deployed within such a framework contribute more to the flattening than to the examination, and I have suggested that coloniality, colonial modernity, post-Enlightenment rationality, and colonial legacy are among them. Similarly, Homi Bhabha and others have brought into wide usage notions such as hybridity, aporia, and fragmentation, and they have provoked a useful debate against other theorists who see discourses in colonial spaces in more Manichaean terms, but there are risks in deploying such concepts generically and at a high level of abstraction, for they may say too little (about the different forms in which hybridity appears) or not enough (about the specific conjunctures in which hybridity or dualism gain ascendancy).[48]

Let us, in short, *really* provincialize Europe. To do that is not to invert the narrative of progress to expose its underbelly, but to examine the limits as well as the power of European domination, the unevenness and conflict within Europe itself; it is to study systems of power and representation, in interaction with each other, neither presuming the centrality of modern Europe as a reference point nor shying away from analysis of power as it actually was exercised.

Enlarging the field should not dilute the importance of European colonization in its earliest or most recent manifestations, but rather produce a more compelling account of its mechanisms and its limits, including the mechanisms and limits of modes of representation. It is worth thinking about how far one can generalize about a phenomenon called colonialism, about the degree to which different historical trajectories are linked by the shared experience of coercive and cultural subjugation. One can recognize that all colonizing systems – from Rome's universal empire to Islamic universalism to the civilizing mission of twentieth-century France – created a tension between the incorporation of conquered peoples into a singular imperial system and the maintaining lines of distinction that marked the center's unique role in the system. Such a tension, and the conflicts it provoked, was built into the institutions of empires, given their geographic dispersion, extended chains of command, incorporation of regional economic circuits, local systems of authority and patronage, and often the presence of religious or ideological affinities embodied in the values not just of a subjugated community but of an alternative version of universality. Generalization can homogenize too far (as in abstracting coloniality from the lived experience of people in colonies) and demarcation can be misleading (separating modern empires from those prior or contemporaneous to those of nineteenth-century Western Europe). But comprehensive historical analysis might help sketch out likely fields of struggle, might help to look for conjunctures where power relations were most vulnerable and to probe limits of power beneath the claims to dominance. The analytical challenge consists of both comparing and studying connections, of examining changes in the imaginable and the possible across time and space.

The analytical challenge cannot be separated from a political one, for one should neither avoid the specific trajectories of Western European expansion nor fetishize power, for that is to give up a differentiated vocabulary with which to discuss the spatial them. At the same time, one loses a great deal by using colonial as a mere metaphor for extremes of 'institutional' and cultural patternings of colonial systems. I agree with Stuart Hall that one should not shy away from using *postcolonial* in an epochal sense, for the decolonization movements of the decades after World War II did in fact remove colonization from the political repertoire, and from then onward the institutionalization and representation of transnational power had to take forms other than that of a colonial empire.[49] Once again, one can try to name or invoke a 'postcolonial moment' as if it had a distinguishing essence, or one can use the concept as the point of departure for a methodologically diverse examination of different trajectories of power, of its mechanisms and limits, as well as of the changing ways in which such forms of power were contested.[50]

We are not faced with a dichotomous choice of practising history in one way only or rejecting historical scholarship altogether, between reducing colonization to a sideshow of European progress or assuming it represented a single, coherent project; between romanticizing anticolonial movements in their moment of triumph or treating colonial history as if the actions of the colonized never changed its course; between making clear the colonial histories' continued effects today or accepting that anticolonial movements have succeeded in eliminating colonial rule as a normal part of world politics. Far from having to choose between examining the complexities of a colonial past and broadening our sense of the opportunities and constraints of the future, a critical and sensitive historical practice can help us retain our focus on the possibilities of political imagination and on the importance of accountability for the consequences of our actions.

Notes

1   Most notable is the recognition within the historical profession achieved by scholars whose work crosses the colony/metropole divide: Alice Conklin and Julia Clancy-Smith in 'French' history; Antoinette Burton, Catherine Hall, and Susan Thorne in 'British' history; Lora Wildenthal in 'German' history; and Christopher Schmidt-Nowara in 'Spanish' history, to name a few. And if my generation of historians of Africa (early 1970s) tended to think that colonial topics were not African enough, subsequent generations have if anything tilted in the opposite direction. The establishment journal *American Historical Review* has recently given colonial questions a prominent place; note also the proliferation of journals such as *Postcolonial Studies, Journal of Colonialism and Colonial History*, and *Interventions: International Journal of Postcolonial Studies*.

2   Some of the critiques and analyses suggested in this essay are developed at greater length in my *Colonialism in Question: Theory, Knowledge, History* (Berkeley, 2005).

3   Ashis Nandy, 'History's Forgotten Doubles' *History & Theory*, 1995, 34.

4   Nicholas Dirks, 'History as a Sign of the Modern,' *Public Culture,* 1990, 2(2), 25.

5   Edward W. Said, *Orientalism* (New York, 1978) and *Culture and Imperialism* (New York, 1993). For a recent reassessment of Said's contribution by historians, see Andrew Rotter, K.E. Fleming and Kathleen Biddick 'Orientalism Twenty Years On' *American Historical Review,* 2000, 105, 4.

6   David Scott, *Refashioning Futures: Criticism After Postcoloniality* (Princeton, NJ, 1999) 156.

7   For sympathetic critiques, see Gayatry Chakravorty Spivak, *A Critique of Postcolonial Reason* (Cambridge, MA, 1999) and Nicholas Dirks 'Postcolonialism and its Discontents' in *Schools of Thought: Twenty-five Years of Interpretive Social Science,* Joan W. Scott and Debra Keates (eds) (Princeton, NJ, 2001). For hostile ones, see Sumit Sarkar, 'The Fascism of the Singh Parivar.' *Economic and Political Weekly,* January 20 1993; and Arif Dirlik, 'The Postcolonial Aura' *Critical Inquiry,* 1994, 20(2).

8   Dirks, 'Postcolonialism and Its Discontents,' 246; Scott, *Refashioning Futures,* 52; Antoinette Burton (ed.), 'Introduction to Burden.' *Gender, Sexuality, and Colonial Modernities* (London, 1999), 2.

9   Thus Dipesh Chakrabarty, for whom the post-Enlightenment is a crucial category, makes no mention of the post-Enlightenment of the Haitian revolutionaries. Chakrabarty, *Provincializing Europe: Postcolonial Thought and Historical Difference* (Princeton, NY, 2000). Scott does not mention Haiti either in *Refashioning Futures.* Robert Young, *Postcolonialism: An Historical Introduction* (Oxford, 2001), cites Haiti as a slave revolt, not as a revolt that shaped debates on emancipation. It is the very 'unpost' C.L.R. James who appreciated the significance of this event: *The Black Jacobins* (London, 1938).

10   Young, *Postcolonialism,* 4.

11   For Stuart Hall, the relevant unit of analysis is 'European and then Western capitalist modernity after 1492.' Hall, 'When Was "the Postcolonial"? Thinking at the Limit,' in *The Post-Colonial Question* Iain Chambers and Lidia Curti (eds) (New York, 1996) 249.

12   Gyan Prakash, 'Subaltern Studies as Postcolonial Criticism' *American Historical Review* 1994, 99, 5.

13   Young defines postcolonialism as a stance, as an assumption of the mantle of anticolonial liberation movements in a changed situation. He posits a singular intellectual-political lineage going from Marxism to analyses of the subjective affects of colonialism. Denying any particular interest in colonial history, his postcolonialism nevertheless assumes 'a common political and moral consensus towards the history and legacy of western colonialism' (*Postcolonialism,* 5). He dismisses the historians' potential concern about the variety of colonial experiences with a rhetorical flourish: 'Postcolonial critique . . . identifies with the subject position of anti-colonial activists,' while the 'empiricist' historian presumably does not (19). The problem with defining a mode of inquiry by a stance is not merely its cavalier attitude toward human experience but that any political thinking or forms of mobilization that do not fit the singular narrative are excluded from the start. Yet Young's dismissive comments are contradicted by his often context-sensitive text, and even by his subtitle, *An Historical Introduction.*

14   Any criticism of work coming out of Subaltern Studies must acknowledge that no group has done more, by exhortation and practice, to stimulate research on colonial history. Fruitful debate is also animated by Indian historians outside the Subaltern Studies fold, such as Rajnarayan Chandavarkar, *Imperial Power and Popular Politics* (Cambridge, 1998) and Sugata Bose and Ayesha Jalal, *Modern South Asia: History, Culture, Political Economy* (London, 1998).

15   Homi K. Bhabha, 'Of Mimicry and Man: the ambivalence of colonial discourse' in *Tensions of Empire,* Frederick Cooper and Ann Laura Stoler (eds) (Berkeley, 1997); Walter Mignolo, *Local Histories/Global Designs* (Princeton, NY, 2000); Chakrabarty, *Provincializing Europe.*

16   This dilution is the basic problem with using *coloniality* to express extremes of power and extremes of differentiations – but without regard to institutions – and with treating a wide range of experiences of subordination as the consequences of a generic 'centuries of Western colonial expansion,' rather than specific trajectories, as in Ramon Grosfoguel and Chloe S. Georas, 'Coloniality of Power: and Racial Dynamics.' *Identities,* 2000, 7.

17   Mahmood Mamdani, *Citizen and Subject* (Princeton, NJ, 1996). Daniel Patrick Moynihan's report was entitled 'The Negro Family: the Case for National Action,' and the controversy it provoked can be examined in Lee Rainwater and William Yancey, *The Moynihan Report and the Politics of Controversy* (Cambridge, MA, 1967).

18   For another example of the leapfrogging fallacy, see Richard Price, *The Convict and the Colonel* (Boston, 1998). This book is constructed around the ironic juxtaposition of a violent confrontation of police and demonstrators on the French island of Martinique in 1925 and the trivializing of the memory of colonization in the period of Price's fieldwork, when the people of Martinique were caught up in the peculiarities of the tourist business and the French welfare state. By omitting the history in between, Price occludes the seriousness of political mobilization in the 1930s and 1940s, when a strong Caribbean movement pressed the French government to accord this colony the status of a French department and thereby could lay claim to French educational and social resources equivalent to those claimed by other French citizens. One would not know from Price's account that this movement succeeded in 1946, that the victims of the 1925 conflict did not die in vain, or that the noted writer/activist whose authority Price invokes in indicting French colonialism, Aimé Cesaire, was the main leader of the departmentalization movement. The missing middle contains the politics.

19   Chakrabarty, *Provincializing Europe*. If in some of his writing, Chakrabarty has engaged the difficulties of using Marxist theory in colonial situations by focusing on the specific modes in which economic, political, and social power operates; other writing goes in the opposite direction, toward abstraction and away from context. See his *Habitations of Modernity* (Chicago, 2002).

20   The allusion here is to Eric Wolf, *Europe and the People without History* (Berkeley, 1982).

21   Chakrabarty, *Provincializing Europe*, 237; Gyan Prakash, *Another Reason: Science and the Imagination of Modern India* (Princeton, NJ, 1999) 8, 118; Nicholas Dirks, *Castes of Mind: Colonialism and the Making of Modern India* (Princeton, NJ, 2001) 52.

22   Dena Goodman, 'Difference: An Enlightenment Concept'; and David Hollinger, 'The Enlightenment and the Genealogy of Cultural Conflict in the United States' in *What's Left of Enlightenment?* Keith Michael Baker and Peter Hanns (eds) (Stanford, CA, 2001).

23   Similarly, Prakash places a valuable reading of the variety of ways in which South Asians engaged in science against a singular notion of European 'reason.' Prakash, *Another Reason*.

24   Margaret Somers, 'Rights, Relationality, and Membership' *Law and Social Inquiry*, 1994, 19.

25   On the role of slaves in redefining the meanings of freedom, see Robin Blackburn, *The Overthrow of Colonial Slavery* (London, 1988); George Fredrickson, *Black Liberation* (New York, 1995), and Thomas C. Holt, *The Problem of Freedom* (Baltimore, MD, 1992).

26   James, *The Black Jacobins*. See also Laurent Dubois, *Les esclaves de la Republique* (Paris, 1998).

27   Curiously, arguments about post-Enlightenment colonialism have not led to a re-examination of Napoleon's empire. This maps poorly onto a modern/nonmodern distinction, for Napoleon combined the deployment of 'scientific' principles of geography and rationalized organization with a symbolic orientation toward Rome (and Caesar's Rome more than republican Rome); he restored slavery (abolished in 1794) and was close to some elites of the *ancien regime*. Most important was that Napoleon's France was more complicated than a 'nation' subjecting others: his conquests incorporated some territories into the departmental system and ruled others through local monarchs or elites, or else through relatives or clients, and sometimes with the support of local republican elements. An attempt to rethink part of this story was a colloquium at the University of Paris VIII-Saint Denis, held in June 2002, entitled 'Retablissement de l'esclavage dans les colonies francaises: Ruptures et continuites de la politique coloniale francaise: 1802, 1804, 1825, 1830.'

28   For the switches in direction in policy toward citizenship and nationality, see Patrick Weil, *Qu'est-ce qu'un Francais?* (Paris, 2002) and Alice Conklin, *A Mission to Civilize* (Stanford, CA, 1997).

30   Cooper and Stoler, *Tensions of Empire*.

32   R. Bin Wong, *China Transformed* (Ithaca, NY, 1997).

33   Aime Cesaire, *Discourse on Colonialism* (New York, 1972) 21. A notable effort to bring a transnational perspective to studying such questions is Paul Gilroy's, *The Black Atlantic* (London, 1993). One wishes that Africa had more of a place in his Black Atlantic.

34   Cooper, *Decolonization and African Society*.

35   Hence the argument that Ann Stoler and I made claiming that understanding Manichaean tendencies within colonial ideologies should not imply taking a Manichaean position oneself. Cooper and Stoler, 'Between Metropole and Colony: Rethinking a Research Agenda,' in *Tensions of Empire*, 1–56.

36   My argument differs from David Scott's stage theory that develops from 'anti-coloniality' to 'postcoloniality' to 'after postcoloniality.' Even more striking than Scott's willingness to reduce the politics of the 1950s to its icons is the absence in his book of consideration of a liberation movement that does not fit his anticolonial stage, the struggle in South Africa against apartheid in the 1980s and 1990s. Scott, *Refashioning Futures*, 10–14, 16, 45, 199. Achille Mbembe vividly evokes the atmosphere of politics after independence, but lets the category of the postcolonial do the work that a historical analysis would do much better. Mbembe, *On the Postcolony* (Berkeley, CA, 2001).

37   Scott, *Refashioning Futures*, 17. Modernity-bashing is by no means limited to postcolonial studies. A considerable literature criticizes 'development' by focusing on its rhetoric (with less to say about the material stakes). See Arturo Escobar, *Encountering Development* (Princeton, NY, 1995).

38   Dipesh Chakrabarty, 'Modernity and Ethnicity in India,' *Economic and Political Weekly*, 1994, 30, 52, 3374.

39   A more satisfying approach is Catherine Hall's contextualized analysis of debates among antislavery advocates, which brings out the openings as well as the closures of their different discourses. Hall, *Civilising Subjects: Metropole and Colony in the English Imagination* (London, 2002).

40   I have argued elsewhere that anticolonial movements, as well as colonialism itself, have been transnational and transcontinental and that   contrary to those who write about globalization as a phenomenon of the present – both processes have a very long history. Cooper, 'What Is the Concept of Globalization Good For?' in *Colonialism in Question*.

41   Uday Mehta, *Liberalism and Empire* (Chicago, 1999) 20; emphasis original.

42   Chakrabarty, *Provincializing Europe*, 243; see also 99–113, 237–55. Chakrabarty notes that today's historian of the European Middle Ages, not just the historian of India, uses secular reason to dissect a religious framework (110–12). But so, too, will an American scholar exploring the relationship of fundamentalist Christianity to the Republican Party under the Bush administration, and such a scholar needs both to understand the religiosity of his/her subjects *and* not be limited to interpreting politics in the administration's terms. Discussion of the problematic nature of truth claims goes back, indeed, to the Enlightenment, and becomes clear in 'modernist' texts such as Karl Mannheim's *Ideology and Utopia*.

43   Ranajit Guha, 'The Prose of Counterinsurgency' in *Selected Subaltern Studies*, Guha and G.C. Spivak (eds) (New York, 1988); and Ann Laura Stoler, 'In Cold Blood' *Representations*, 1992, 37.

44   Guarav Desai astutely uses a text written by Akiga Sai, a mission-educated, colonial-era Nigerian, to show how an African could subtly insert his views into the 'colonial library.' But Desai's comments about the need to 'nuance' truth made in relation to a story illustrating the falsity of certain representations of the truth miss the point that the power of Sai's text lies in that he has already convinced the reader that one version of the story is in fact true. Desai's comments on truth depend on a stark separation of a 'modern conception and an indigenous one, which is what Sai's text refuses. See Desai, *Subject to Colonialism: African Self-fashioning and the Colonial Library* (Durham, NC, 2001) 131–6, 144, 148. See also Chakrabarty, *Provincializing Europe*, 99–100.

46   Tejumola Olaniyan, 'On "Postcolonial" Discourse,' *Callaloo*, 1993, 16(4), 745.

47   Hall, 'When Was "the Postcolonial,"' 249.

48   Homi K. Bhabha, *The Location of Culture* (London, 1994), 2–4, 171. The view of colonialism as Manichaean, most powerfully articulated by Frantz Fanon, has been defended by, among others, Abdul Jan Mohamed, *Manichean Aesthetics* (Amherst, MA, 1983).

49   Hall, 'When Was "the Postcolonial,"' 246. This redefinition of the political repertoire provides a better way of distinguishing the postcolonial epoch than a distinction based on a binary coloniality and a hybrid postcoloniality. In arguing that *postcolonial* can be used in an epochal sense, but not in a substantive one (that postcolonial societies or polities have given characteristics), I am making the reverse argument of that which Bernard Yack makes about postmodernism: that one can identify certain patterns of postmodern thought, but that such thought does not distinguish any particular era, including the present one. Although I am not convinced of a modern-postmodern divide in intellectual terms, Yack's antiepochal argument about the postmodern is not incompatible with my or Hall's epochal argument about postcolonialism. See Bernard Yack, *The Fetishism of Modernities* (Notre Dame, IN, 1997), esp. 4–5, 19, 29. It should also be noted that it is the recent decolonizations that extinguished colonialism as a legitimate political form, not earlier ones (the independence of Haiti, the United States, or Latin American countries).

50   For an extreme instance of the former, of an evocation without grounding in any kind of historical or institutional analysis (indeed, without even curiosity about the kind of information that might support one's assertions), see Michael Hardt and Antonio Negri, *Empire* (Cambridge, MA, 2000). For a critique of the way this and other works misuse the concept of empire in relation to the present conjuncture, see Cooper, 'Empire Multiplied' *Comparative Studies in Society and History*, 2004, 46, 2.

Chapter 5

Nicholas Dirks

CODA: THE BURDEN OF THE PAST

This piece was originally published as a 'Coda' to Nicholas Dirks' controversial analysis of the history of 'caste' in India. It is a sharp, indeed fierce critique of much which Dirks finds wanting in the writing of imperial history, especially that which he associates with a conservative 'Cambridge school' approach. But it is not just a negative historiographical polemic: Dirks raises many wider issues too, including some very current political ones.

Stephen Howe

History is the work expended on material documentation (books, texts, accounts, registers, acts, buildings, institutions, laws, techniques, objects, customs, etc.) that exists, in every time and place, in every society . . . [I]n our time, history is that which transforms documents into monuments . . . in our time history aspires to the condition of archaeology, to the intrinsic description of the monument.

Michel Foucault, *Archaeology of Knowledge*

WHEREAS THE NINETEENTH CENTURY was the great century of imperial power, the most astonishing accomplishment of the twentieth century has been the struggle to consign colonial rule to the past tense. Although that struggle has been successful, it has not only been drenched in violence but it has also led to the general recognition that the effects of imperialism have by no means disappeared with the demise of formal colonial regimes of rule. Colonialism lives on in the massive disparities of wealth and control over capital between north and south, in the contradictory institutional legacies that inhabit political, juridical, educational, and economic systems, and in the differential manifestations of cultural entitlement and social capacity that characterize a world of ethnic dispute and national dislocation. Even as the colonial past was written into every aspect of the early consolidation of Western metropolitan economic and political domination, it continues to be written into the new world order – in subnational ethnic violence, in national debates over immigration and identity, in the postimperial positioning of the United States after the end of the cold war, in postnational developments around liberalization, globalization, and the late twentieth-century triumph of capitalism, and in worries that the spectre of future cataclysm resides not in communism but in other civilizations. Colonialism may be dead, yet it is everywhere to be seen.

Colonialism was fundamental to the origins of capitalism in England and the West, the rise of European and North American political domination, the acceptance of an anthropological vision that conferred cultural explanations on the colonized world, and the emergence of basic assumptions of historical thought that were enshrined by Hegel and expounded by Macaulay, Mill, Seeley, and many others.[1] In this chapter I have sought to demonstrate these larger propositions in the light of specific examples in the history of caste in India. I have also attempted to show in detail how colonialism was served by, even as it produced the conditions of possibility for, forms of knowledge that, in the wake of Said's extraordinary challenge, can be characterized under the single term of 'Orientalism.' But I have sought to go much further than Said (whose project was admittedly limited to texts of Orientalism and their relations to sites of colonial power in the West), even as I have taken seriously his claim that the Orient was produced as the 'Orient' by the historical power of Orientalism, defined both as specific bodies of scholarship and as colonial knowledge writ large. In doing so, I have acknowledged the power of colonial formations, power that was both concealed and displayed through the transformations and effects of colonial rule in India. I have attempted to demonstrate how knowledge and power were entangled in an unsteady and often unstable history of institutions, representations, legislation, policies, and rhetoric, how power was realized through the incitements of colonial modernity as well as the confusions of colonial rule. The colonized as well as the colonizer participated in power, enhanced by moments of failure as well as by the complicated logics of contradiction, displacement, and deferral, and ultimately over-determined both by the historical outcome of high imperialism and by the multiple imperatives that sustained the European commitment to it. The story is neither simple nor straightforward. Embedded in historical process, it has necessarily been changed by different historical forces at different historical moments. But it is a story that insists on, and demonstrates, the overriding significance of colonialism in the making of modern India.

This is not a story that colonialism told about itself. The British, of course, took credit for all that was good and modern in India, but they also underestimated the impact they had, even as they complained about their weakness, ignorance, and lack of real power. J.R. Seeley, who assumed the chair in modern history at Cambridge in 1869, gave a series of lectures in 1881 and 1882 that became the basis for one of the best-selling history books in England in the late nineteenth century (the book was, in fact, in print until 1956, the year of Suez). Seeley was in some ways a liberal, critical of certain aspects of colonial policy at the same that he warned against imperial complacency in India; he was respectful of Indian accomplishment even as he suggested that once Indians united the empire would fall. He was also critical of Britain's enclosed sense of itself and its history, and criticized English historians for making:

too much of the mere parliamentary wrangle and the agitations about liberty, in all which matters the eighteenth century of England was but a pale reflexion of the seventeenth. They do not perceive that in that century the history of England is not in England but in America and Asia.

But he acknowledged that this amnesia was itself a reflection of the general tenor of the earlier centuries of imperial expansion, in which England did not so much conquer its colonies as stumble into them. He wrote:

> There is something very characteristic in the indifference which we show towards this mighty phenomenon of the diffusion of our race and the expansion of our state. We seem, as it were, to have conquered and peopled half the world in a fit of absence of mind.[2]

By this now famous phrase, Seeley reiterated earlier colonial views of the eighteenth century in India, in which English traders simply filled the vacuum left by the collapse of the Mughal state:

> We shall see that nothing like that what is strictly called a conquest took place, but that certain traders inhabiting certain seaport towns in India, were induced, almost forced, in the anarchy caused by the fall of the Mogul Empire, to give themselves a military character and employ troops, that by means of these troops they acquired territory and at last almost all the territory of India, and that these traders happened to be Englishmen, and to employ a certain, though not a larger, proportion of English troops in the army.[3]

And so the story that had been sold to Parliament throughout the eighteenth century, at least until Burke called Hastings to account, is transmuted here into an authoritative history of the origins of imperial rule in India.

Seeley's history both informed and was informed by his sense of the contemporary conditions of colonial rule. He wrote:

> For we are not really conquerors of India, and we cannot rule her as conquerors; if we undertook to do so, it is not necessary to inquire whether we could succeed, for we should assuredly be ruined financially by the mere attempt.[4]

By this he meant that India was governed in the same way it was conquered, through the complicity, and lack of any unified resistance, of the governed. For Seeley the liberal (of the same liberalism as that of Mill and Macaulay), this was not because of 'some enormous superiority on the part of the English race,' but rather because of the lack of any national feeling in India:

> There is then no Indian nationality, though there are some germs out of which we can conceive an Indian nationality developing itself . . . If there could arise in India a nationality-movement similar to that which we witnessed in Italy, the English Power could not even make the resistance that was made in Italy by Austria, but must succumb at once.

Seeley acknowledged the role of the British government in suppressing the rise of national resistance, as when he noted that 'the mutiny was in a great measure put down by turning the races of India against each other.'[5]

And yet, his prediction that English power would collapse in the face of nationalist mobilization was clearly refuted during the next sixty years. Even as he was correct to observe, if only in an aside, that the British played a role in the arrested history of nationality, the fact was that British rule in India was not as fragile as Seeley thought. Colonial history was colonial fiction.

That colonial history is fiction has been a major part of the argument of this book, even as I have argued that fiction makes history happen. I have suggested this through my interrogation of the colonial archive, the histories behind and beneath the production of the kinds of primary sources that have represented colonial knowledge even as they have been used to determine and justify colonial policy. The archive has enshrined, in Foucault's sense, this raw material for subsequent historical representation. In the Indian case, the archive is both the precipitate of the history of conquest and rule and the basis on which that history has been written by colonial administrators such as Mill and Risley and by colonial historians such as Macaulay and Seeley. And it is in large part because of the uncritical acceptance of the archive as a primary source, rather than itself an historical document, that colonial power has been so good at dissembling. In the historical literature, colonial power, at least in forms that were not cast solely in economic or political terms, escaped serious interrogation outside of the specific contestations of the nationalist struggle until the new critical imperial history inaugurated by figures as various as Bernard Cohn, Edward Said, and Ranajit Guha. Despite differences within this tradition of critical history, about which I will say more below, much recent work has addressed the extraordinary role of colonial knowledge in facilitating empire and in producing the very categories used to understand the effects of empire in postcolonial societies. But it has by no means supplanted scholarship in imperial history that continues to take the sources of colonial history itself, as well as the colonial historiography of so canonic a figure as Seeley, as the basis for its own understanding of colonialism. Indeed, there has been remarkable continuity between the historical proposals of Seeley and the latter-day 'Cambridge school' of Indian historians, not to mention the recent, and massive, five-volume historical encyclopedia, *The Oxford History of the British Empire*.[6] Like the aftermath of colonialism itself, colonial history lives on.

Anil Seal laid out the basic theme of early Cambridge school historiography when he asserted that colonialism could be described as 'British rule through Indian collaboration.'[7] Early work by members of this school focused on the nationalist movement, debunking claims about the ideological motives of nationalist leaders, and arguing that Indian politics emerged as a direct reflex of administrative initiatives set in motion by colonial rule. Seal himself wrote about the relationship between English education and Indian nationalism, though his students concentrated much more on the factional affiliations and structures that characterized the often nasty and always self-interested world of Indian political struggle. The basic argument was that local elites, the very groups that had been the collaborators for British rule, turned nationalist – in the context of participation in the progressively enlarged electoral arenas of provincial and municipal politics – when they realized that more of the pie could be obtained through autonomous political institutions than through colonial ones. Nationalist ideology was shown to be hollow, even as colonial rule was viewed as completely dependent on elite complicity. Seeley's sense that British colonialism was a mere veneer was thus reborn in Seal's insistence on the logic of collaboration. The Cambridge school proved its arguments by using colonial sources – frequently police records and confidential files – that documented the spurious activities of nationalist figures in what was a large-scale colonial effort to track, contain, and debunk the very politics that sought to overthrow colonial rule.

Whereas the early work of this influential group of historians first concerned nationalism – earning thereby considerable notoriety and ire from historians in India as well as in North America and Australia – Cambridge historiography has in recent years been far more trained on the eighteenth century and questions around the transition to, rather than from, colonial rule. Christopher Bayly has now produced three weighty and important volumes that have given empirical density to an argument that, along with the work of many others, has seriously modified Seeley's characterization of the eighteenth century as one of Indian decadence. Bayly has advocated Seeley's basic view, however, that 'conquest' is the wrong way to conceive of the rise of the British presence in the subcontinent. As he wrote at the beginning of his 1983 work, *Rulers, Townsmen and Bazaars*:

> Even though the late Victorians tended to see 'native' society as a static backdrop to British exploits, Sir John Seeley in the 1880s warned his audience against the chauvinistic belief that Britain had conquered India in any simple sense. The East India Company, he said, had merely taken advantage of the disturbed conditions after the end of the Mughal empire in 1707, and that was mainly by dint of the support of important groups of Indians. This change of perspective was slow in establishing itself.[8]

Bayly's own history has emphasized continuity, Indian 'agency,' and British weakness. As he wrote in a later reflection about his own historical corpus, he stressed:

> continuities even across the ruptures created by the coming of colonial capitalism. It was the fact that even under British colonialism, Indians recruited from precolonial service and commercial communities continued to control the bulk of mercantile capital and title to land and to populate the lower ranks of the army, judiciary and police, which informed the theme of continuity in *Rulers, Townsmen and Bazaars*.[9]

Guided by Ronald Robinson's insistence on the 'non-European foundations of European imperialism,' he sought to locate the 'central mechanisms of imperialism . . . in the systems of collaboration set up in pre-industrial societies which succeeded, or failed, in meshing the incoming processes of European expansion into indigenous social politics and evolving a balance between the two.'[10] In the process of documenting this claim, Bayly both emphasized the force of Indian social and economic politics and suggested that the British only succeeded in their project of expansion, and the consolidation of colonial rule, through the desires, actions, and agency of Indians.[11]

Curiously, however, Indian agency becomes a way of suggesting that colonial rule itself was an Indian project more than it was a European one. Bayly has updated Seeley's account of passive conquest, but in using the same language as his Cambridge predecessor he seems to substitute disavowal for chauvinism. He writes that:

> The British were *sucked into* the Indian economy by the dynamic of its [India's?] political economy as much as by their own relentless drive for profit. In turn, the Company was *forced* to build an army and develop new administrative methods.[12]

Bayly notes, like Seeley before him, that the British were not entirely passive: 'The Company was able to play off one state against another and offer its own formidable services for sale in the all-India military bazaar.' But Bayly is more impressed by the fact that imperial ventures were financed by Indian capitalists, despite the fact that these capitalists were often short-lived and that indigenous capital was soon subordinated entirely 'to the vast system of British peculation and inland trade.' And he makes little of the fact that the Bengal revenues, secured by force after the Battle of Plassey, financed the army and made up for shortfalls in income from trade (mostly due to the fact that British traders skimmed off Company profits by indulging in lucrative private trade). Instead, Bayly focuses on the indigenous role in colonization and the indigenous forces of change that 'continued to flow strongly even after the fuller incorporation of the subcontinent into the capitalist world system.'[13] His position complements that of David Washbrook, who has written that 'the indigenous logic of military fiscalism and commercial expansion led on to the conjuncture which produced colonialism as much as did that logic of European history, which pushed its sailors out into sea.' Indeed, Washbrook has put the issue very clearly: 'In a certain sense, colonialism was the logical outcome of South Asia's own history of capitalist development.'[14] So much for Indian agency!

Washbrook has made the same argument as Bayly, though he has taken it further, and made it with rather more polemical fervor. The polemic is partly enhanced (and on the surface distinguished from Bayly's) by Washbrook's rhetorical endorsement of a Marxist-inspired approach to issues of class and capital, but Washbrook's delight in charging Indian capitalism with full responsibility for British colonialism undermines not only his Marxism but also his historical credibility.[15] He delineates recent research that strongly suggests the indigenous roots of capitalism in South Asia (much of it Bayly's) and then asks why, 'after a few early misunderstandings, South Asia's capitalist social classes became the most loyal supporters of the British Raj and sustained it throughout the middle and later decades of the nineteenth century.' His answer is clear. 'Subordination to the dominance of British capital and loss of control over the central institutions of the commercial and fiscal systems meant the reverse of any inability to make and accumulate "private" wealth.'[16] In short, the new magnates made out like bandits, and expressed their own interests by accumulating private wealth rather than working toward the development of India.[17] These processes allowed capitalists, 'whatever their ethnic origins,' to take 'an increasingly dominant and privileged position over producers and labourers.'[18] Indeed, many Indian capitalists, such as:

> the celebrated Brahmin bureaucrats (more properly bankers, commercial agents and landowners) of Guntur who ran the district under the British . . . [or] the six leading mirasidari families of Tanjavur who ran the Collectorate office and, between 1819 and 1835, 'acquired' land rights in about one-third of all the villages in the district . . .

not only rubbed salt 'into the wounds of the Company' but also illustrated 'which was dominant in the relation between capitalism and colonialism.'[19] These capitalists manipulated formal legal and administrative mechanisms under the Company to allow them to accumulate, and hold on to, huge hoards of wealth. This, Washbrook argues, was the basis for the great success of capitalism in India, for he notes that 'India, by the middle of the nineteenth century, must be regarded as one of the most successful of all contemporary capitalist societies.'[20] Capitalism, in this case 'Indian' capitalism, under-developed India through the logic of its own success (or, perhaps, the success of its own logic). Colonialism, in this case 'British' colonialism, was incidental.

If colonialism was indeed epiphenomenal, so superficial a cover for Indian agency in the spheres of capital and accumulation, it should perhaps be of little surprise that Bayly and Washbrook both have scoffed at assertions such as mine that colonial forms of knowledge were critical in the establishment and maintenance of colonial rule in India. For Washbrook, such work at best simply exposes the mystifications of the working of capital, reifying both colonialism, and the importance of culture, in the process. But Bayly has taken great pains to counter this 'fashion' in Indian historiography. In a chapter of the *Oxford History of the British Empire*, Bayly noted that historians began, in the wake of the force of Said's work (Cohn's influence is strangely ignored), 'to argue that Indian caste, African tribe, "Islam", or "native polity" – the basic building blocks of the subject – were inventions of the colonial power in the early nineteenth century.'[21] Bayly has called this work 'retrogressive,' not only because it ignores the great body of work in British intellectual history that has traced the complexity of imperial ideas, but because 'histories in this vein tended to deny Asians, Africans, or Polynesians agency in their own histories more thoroughly than had the nineteenth-century Imperial writers.'[22] In Bayly's recent *Empire and Information*, a book written largely to dispute work of this kind, he has given full vent to his unease 'about the assumption that the "learned" ideas of orientalism played a consistent or determining part in the process of governing and exploiting India.'[23] Bayly's book is characteristically rich with documentation and erudition, but it is riddled with internal contradictions, and strangely crippled by its insistence that knowledge is really nothing more than information.[24]

Bayly has argued that Orientalism, in Said's sense, was in any case 'hardly a coherent system of thought,' remaining, even after 1820, 'self-contradictory, fractured and contested.' Stereotypes of India as 'ruled by fanaticism and caste' were only in evidence at moments of panic, and were in any case 'a product of the weakness and blindness of the state at the fringes of its knowledge rather than a set of governing assumptions at its core.' Indeed, far from being 'the property of a domineering European government in Asia,' these ideas were a reflection of Europe's 'weakness,' and of the 'fear, bafflement and guilt of its expatriate citizens.'[25] Over and over again we are told of England's weakness, how 'Orientalist fantasy flooded into gaps left by the decline of pragmatic information,' how knowledge was based on fundamental ignorance, that stereotypes came from European experience rather than from a deliberate 'attempt to create a stereotyped Orient,' that knowledge was not only unreliable, unstable, and ambiguous, but virtually entirely dependent on Indian sources.[26] Blame the victim again! Bayly notes that 'The British understanding of Indian society – as opposed to its trades – may have been extraordinarily defective, but this was more the result of a lack of reliable informants than the consequence of orientalist stereotypes,' though elsewhere he notes that the 'social and religious values motivating' Indians were often 'mysterious to Europeans.' When Bayly asserts that colonial knowledge was 'far from being a monolith derived from the needs of power,' he is simply restating his conviction that the colonial state was weak, dazed, and confused.[27] And once again Indian agency – simultaneously decisive, unreliable, and unknowable – emerges triumphant through the flaccid superstructure of colonial rule, a tribute to the heroic Indian role in the making of the British empire.

Bayly's now cliched insistence that colonial knowledge was not a monolith, that it was unstable, contested, and in constant tension with a larger world of uncertainty and unease, fails to do the rhetorical work he intends. The scholars to whose work I have affiliated my own have all been aware of the fractious and at times precarious nature of colonial knowledge. Few scholars have taken Said's general propositions about Orientalism as a single formation of knowledge as literally as Bayly suggests, at the same time it has been widely recognized that what might in reality have been internally riven often appeared, at least to the colonized under the conditions of colonial power, as monolithic.[28] To argue this is also to argue against the self-representations of colonial authors, for whom weakness and ignorance were rhetorical as well as political conceits. It has been the argument of this book that the success of colonial discourse was in any case dependent on the contradictions and apparent openness of colonial knowledge, certainly up until the middle of the nineteenth century.[29] And yet the argument favored by Bayly, Washbrook, Frykenberg, Irschick, and others that early colonial rule was a 'dialogue' seems as misguided as Seeley's assertion that the British would pack up and leave once a nationalist movement appeared.[30] Dialogue is not an appropriate way to characterize the transactions of imperial power, even when it fails to have either the full control or knowledge that it would invariably claim as its right. And, whereas colonial hegemony continued even at its peak period during the nineteenth and early twentieth centuries to secure its power in part by such heterogeneous methods and institutions as rule by law, even David Washbrook has argued in a different context how legal institutions in the nineteenth century were steadfastly controlled by colonial interests.[31]

I have demonstrated how colonial power became both more secure and more ambitious as the century wore on. The shift from historical to ethnographic preoccupations – and the shift in turn from military conquest and soon thereafter revenue collection to concerns about political loyalty – changed the character of colonial knowledge in fundamental ways. There is no doubt that colonial domination became increasingly racialized, and stark, in the years following the suppression of the Great Rebellion. But this too is either denied, or at the least made light of, by Cambridge historiography. Indeed, the conviction that colonial conquest and rule were fragile at best and at the service of Indian agency at worst is what enables Bayly to argue that neither colonial power nor colonial knowledge was really so bad. He protests that:

> It was difficult to sustain an 'apartheid' ideology stressing ineluctable racial difference in a subcontinent where Indians continued to control – albeit under severe constraint – the vast bulk of capital and almost the whole means of agricultural production. Colonial officials, missionaries and businessmen were forced to register the voices *of* native informants in ideology and heed them in practice *even if they despised and misrepresented them*.[32]

Racism, in other words, was as epiphenomenal as colonial rule itself, hardly fundamental to the 'continuous' historical experience *of* empire over the last three centuries. Small wonder that Cambridge historiography had difficulty understanding the force of nationalist ideology.

Bayly's disavowal of colonial power and prejudice is thus the predicate for his own historiographical conferral of agency onto the colonized subjects of Indian history. Washbrook, whose sense of structure makes his own rhetorical embrace of Indian agency seem especially paradoxical, seeks to dissolve the idea of colonialism entirely in the world soup of capitalism, even though in India capitalism takes on a distinctly national flavour. Washbrook's own position becomes clearer when he argues, in a variety of polemical attacks, that the attention given to colonialism works only to mystify the class interests of multicultural adherents or fellow travellers in the American academy. Both Washbrook's polemics and Bayly's rebukes lump together all of Said's 'disciples,' an extraordinary locution that seems to include Cohn (who wrote much of his early critical work on colonialism before Said's entry to the field) and his students, as well as scholars who have been associated with Subaltern Studies.[33] Although it is true that all of these miscellaneous scholars take colonialism seriously and have been critical of Orientalism, these polemics have tended to obscure the significant differences in recent writing on colonialism.

Why, indeed, has colonialism become so bad a thing 'to think,' for so many different voices in the academy today? Bayly and Washbrook find themselves joined by a steadily growing group of historians, anthropologists, and cultural critics who view the connection between critical colonial history and postcolonial critique as a new form of academic terrorism. Indeed, colonialism has become a problem precisely because of the connections made between colonial history and postcolonial concerns, whether they focus on the status of postcolonial historical writing or on the epistemological and archival problems of reading colonial sources. Figures as different as the culturalist Marshall Sahlins and the materialist Aijaz Ahmed join forces when railing against the assertion of native agency in the writing of a different kind of contemporary history. Too much emphasis on colonialism is seen to licence everything from too much stress on the role of Europe in the history of the 'third world' to too much stress on issues of race rather than questions of class. Rosalind O'Hanlon and David Washbrook, in a recent critique of post-Orientalist fashions in the writing of Indian history, included in their sweeping denunciations not only an essay by Gyan Prakash but the historical anthropology of Cohn and his students as well as the writings of the subaltern school. They referred only once to the historical question of colonialism, to disparage the writing of James Clifford about the colonial entailments of British anthropology.[34] In this lone reference to colonial history, the authors suggest that their greatest concern about colonial history has nothing to do with India but is rather about the production of the idea of culture, now used to mystify social relations that are really about class and capital. The problem of colonialism, in other words, is located in the American academy, and has to do with the use of colonialism as a significant category of historical analysis. Historiographical attention to colonialism, rather than identifying key political dynamics behind the exercise of capitalist domination in India, is now accused of merely licensing postcolonial anxiety about cultural rather than economic matters, allowing a postcolonial elite to masquerade as the oppressed rather than the oppressors.[35] A history that focused on world capitalism would instead underscore the weight of global forces that in fact differentiate peoples on the basis of access to the means of production rather than the epiphenomenal questions of cultural (racial or national) identity. And here is where Cambridge school history masquerades as Marxist history, using networks of materialist analysis and so-called class analysis to disparage anticolonial nationalism and to deny the historical reality and lasting effects of colonialism. Surely this is not what Marx had in mind by the historical analysis of class.

Toward a postcolonial historiography

The polemics discussed above not only work to separate histories of colonialism from histories of capitalism, they also obscure the very real differences within histories of colonialism. I trust that it is clear that my emphasis on colonialism has not been meant to elide capitalism, but rather to suggest that the modern history of capitalism in India has been conducted under the auspices of the political economy of colonial rule. The salience of the historical structures of colonial rule cannot be trivialized by pointing to a handful of Indian 'capitalists' who managed to secure wealth for themselves during colonial times. Further, I have taken for granted in this chapter that colonial preoccupations with economic wealth and political power provided the conditions for cultural engagement that ultimately worked to legitimate the colonial presence in India through cultural means, even as that colonial presence became dependent on cultural technologies of rule. I have also viewed culture principally as an effect of power, insisting that contemporary assumptions about cultural difference have been largely produced out of the long history of colonial domination. In this sense I have drawn on the work of Partha Chatterjee, who has used an idea of culture to delineate the particular strategies of nationalist resistance to colonialism, and has shown how cultural difference was a situated tactic, a colonial strategy, rather than an expression of essential incommensurability. That being said, I worry that Chatterjee underplays this historical dynamic in some of his writings on the 'inner sphere' of Indian nationalism.[36] And I do not share all of the proposals of Ranajit Guha, whose resort to Sanskritic sources for indigenous political theory and historical consciousness seems to betray a general commitment to writing subaltern history against the grain in most other contexts.[37] More fundamentally, Guha's sense of the autonomy of nationalism has led him to argue that colonial rule was merely about domination rather than hegemony. This sense of the illegitimacy of colonial rule produces a different reading of the complex effects of a colonizing power that, in my reading, had such a profound impact on India precisely because of the kinds of mechanisms that produced a new form of caste in modern India. The refusal to accept the hegemonic character of colonial rule in India restricts the use of the category of hegemony too resolutely within the space of a narrowly defined civil society, rendering the national subaltern autonomous, and the difference between India and Britain as absolute.[38]

And yet Guha's insistence on the significance of racial, cultural, and political exclusions in the foundation of colonial governmentality provides the basis for my own argument about the apotheosis of the ethnographic state in late colonial India. It also allows us to see that imperial societies were useful laboratories for metropolitan experimentation – in spheres as various as cartography, epidemiology, penology, anthropology, and military science – precisely because of the way imperial concerns with legitimation always referred to metropolitan constituencies rather than colonized ones.[39] But far from being entirely separate, it was the very connection between metropole and colony that made the practices of governmentality so similar, and so mutually reinforcing. Indeed, I have suggested in this book that the formation of the metropolitan nation-state was itself as much a product of imperial expansion as of domestic consolidation, and the same is true for many of the ideological covenants of the metropolitan state, as well – from the idea of a liberal democratic government to notions of religious toleration and secularism.[40] And yet this is not to return the historical gaze entirely to Europe.[41] This book has made clear, I trust, that attention to the wide historical provenance, not to mention the deep historical force, of colonialism is neither to deny the rule of colonial difference nor to lose sight of the specific histories and subjects of colonized lands.

I have focused on caste to establish the salience of the imperial archive and the extraordinary impact of colonial rule, to the point that both the sources for the understanding of tradition and the terms of reference for tradition are implicated in colonial history. But if tradition itself has been in some fundamental sense produced through the history of the colonial modern, it is this same history that so problematizes both tradition and modernity in the context of postcolonial India. Caste can only be embraced ambivalently; although it is impossible to treat caste as the object of nostalgia, it can hardly be the marker of a satisfactory present. Inasmuch as caste is a sign of the past, it is also a vehicle for the construction of a different future. The history of the production of colonial difference does not licence all expressions of nativist fundamentalism, even when it helps to explain their rise. Similarly, the writing of the history of nationalist mobilization and resistance in colonial conditions need not celebrate the promotion of an increasingly Hindu nationalist ideology that excludes women, Muslims, and lower-caste 'others' from the inner circle of the national 'we.' Finally, a critical history of the colonial role in the production of caste does not justify the use of this critique to argue against caste just at the point when it becomes the vehicle for the mobilization of an oppositional politics.

These are only some of the reasons that the writing of colonial history in a postcolonial time is so fraught. Writing has never been a neutral activity, but the brief critique above, and the critical sensibility that has animated this book, should show at least some of the specific histories that have inflected the conditions for the writing of colonial history today. In the last fifty years we have learned anew how much it matters from where we write, to whom we write, and more generally how writing is positioned: geopolitically, sociohistorically, institutionally. The crisis of writing has been ushered in by many forces, among them decolonization, a rising chorus of new nations, the re-emergence of new kinds of colonial relationships in the unequal distribution of global wealth and operations of global capital, and the dispersal through phases of migration and relocation of once colonized peoples. Postcolonial critiques have been necessary, if contentious, features of all the new landscapes we inhabit or survey. Postcoloniality in this sense is neither some new, faddish trend nor an abandonment of the real, whether postulated in positivist or materialist language. And although postcoloniality is related to current developments in identity politics, multiculturalism, ethnonationalism, and even postmodernism, it is both far more and far less than these terms imply.

I have suggested here that postcoloniality might be used to signify those places and histories, rather than either specific identities or theories, that resist the universalization of position and perspective, even as they underscore the power of the forces of universalization. Postcoloniality might then remind us of the fact that history, culture, and modernity have always been corrupt, invariably predicated on violence and domination, the terms of conquest for colonization itself. Postcoloniality both embodies the promise of the West – a promise that flows from the enlightenment and the birth of nations – and reminds us that the promise is always flawed, the present always an impossible time and place in which to live. Postcolonial history is the epic story of seduction and betrayal, destined to repeat itself again and again, even as it seeks to put the colonial past behind, for all time. But it also teaches us that there is no going back, to a time when tradition, or identity, or civilization might be recuperated whole. To think otherwise would be to open history to other forms of seduction and betrayal. And that would leave us all without any of the lessons history might still be able to teach.

Notes

1   For a commanding summary of the outlines of the economic entailments of imperial rule in India, see Irfan Habib, *Essays in Indian History: Towards a Marxist Perception* (New Delhi: Tulika, 1995), in particular the essay, 'Colonialization of the Indian Economy, 1757–1900,' 296–335.

2   J.R. Seeley, *The Expansion of England* (1883; reprint Chicago: University of Chicago Press, 1971) 9, 12.

3   ibid., 165.

4   ibid., 185.

5   ibid., 179; 184.

6   The 'Cambridge school' was founded by Jack Gallagher, co-author with Ronald Robinson of *Africa and the Victorians: The Climax of Imperialism in the Dark Continent* (New York: St. Martin's Press, 1961), and early on joined by Anil Seal. In its early years, the late 1960s and 1970s, the school included such figures as Gordon Johnson, Francis Robinson, Christopher Baker, B.R. Tomlinson, and David Washbrook. Christopher Bayly, who was trained at Oxford by Gallagher, among others, only joined Cambridge in 1970.

7   Anil Seal, 'Imperialism and Nationalism,' in John Gallagher, Gordon Johnson, and Anil Seal (eds) *Locality, Province and Nation* (Cambridge: Cambridge University Press, 1973) 12. The theme of collaboration had first been sounded in systematic fashion in Gallagher and Robinson's *Africa and the Victorians*.

8   C.A. Bayly, *Rulers, Townsmen, and Bazaars: North India in the Age of British Expansion, 1780–1870* (Cambridge: Cambridge University Press, 1983).

9   C.A. Bayly, *Origins of Nationality in South Asia: Patriotism and Ethical Government in the Making of Modern India* (Delhi: Oxford University Press, 1998) 319.

10   The words are Robinson's: Ronald Robinson, 'Non-European Foundations of European Imperialism,' in R. Owen and B. Sutcliffe (eds) *Studies in the Theory of Imperialism* (London: Longman, 1972) 120, quoted in Bayly, *Rulers*, 2.

11   Despite Bayly's interest in the economic character of empire, he has nowhere refuted the kinds of evidence adduced by Irfan Habib, among others, to demonstrate the massive colonization, and impoverishment, of the Indian economy from the mid-eighteenth through the mid-twentieth centuries. Perhaps Bayly simply assumes that the *Cambridge Economic History of India* (edited by Dharma Kumar, with the assistance of Meghnad Desai, Cambridge, 1982) had put to rest the arguments of Dutt and his successors concerning the drain of empire and the deindustrialization of India. It seems unarguable today, however, that Britain's own economic and political prosperity was integrally connected to its imperial role in India. Wealth was extracted first with the lever of new-world bullion, then through the extortionate use of land revenue to fund the management of Indian politics and the monopolization of the Indian economy; later in the nineteenth century, relying on the opium trade with China, the British used India to bankroll both its imperial and metropolitan dominance. As Habib makes clear in his essay, 'Colonialization of the Indian Economy, 1757–1900,' the evidence to document the extraordinary economic exploitation wrought by imperial rule is still overwhelming. For a critique of the *Cambridge Economic History of India,* see Habib, 'Studying a Colonial Economy – Without Perceiving Colonialism,' in his *Essays in Indian History*, 336–66.

12   C.A. Bayly, *Indian Society and the Making of the British Empire* (Cambridge: Cambridge University Press, 1988) 46–7. Emphasis added.

13   Bayly, *Indian Society* 48, 53, 51, 203–4.

14   David Washbrook, 'Progress and Problems: South Asian Economic and Social History, c. 1720–1860,' *Modern Asian Studies*, 1988, 22(1), 74, 76.

15   Washbrook's Marxism seems only to concern class formation in Britain, and as a consequence has the effect of exculpating British 'national' responsibility for the consequences of 'world' capitalism.

16   Washbrook, 'Progress and Problems,' 84.

17   These are the very magnate classes who later entered nationalist politics, according to Washbrook. See his 'Country Politics: Madras 1880–1930,' in Jack Gallagher, Gordon Johnson, and Anil Seal (eds), *Locality Province and Nation: Essays on Indian Politics, 1870–1940* (Cambridge: Cambridge University Press, 1973), 155–211.

18   Washbrook, 'Progress and Problems,' 85.

19   ibid., 86. The main example is taken from Frykenberg, *Guntur District* 1788–1848 (Oxford: Oxford University Press, 1965). When Washbrook notes that 'the cultural blindness, internal contradictions, and more meaningful 'corruptions' of the regime made successful 'concealment' of wealth not only possible but more the rule than the exception,' he is restating Frykenberg's argument. Frykenberg called his theory of colonial Indian politics the theory of the white ant, local Indian agents being likened to white ants who, invisible to the colonial overlords, managed to consume the colonial pie from the inside out.

20   Washbrook, 'Progress and Problems,' 87.

21   C.A. Bayly 'The Second British Empire,' in R.W. Winks (ed.) *The Oxford History of the British Empire*, vol. 5, *Historiography* (Oxford: Oxford University Press, 1999) 70.

22   Robert Frykenberg has put the objection even more stridently. As he wrote in his chapter in the new *Oxford History of the British Empire*, 'At least for the moment, some historians have been listening to the siren song of anti-historical literary criticism. Theory, in the names of current fashions, has become a cloak for dogma, for denial of empirical evidence, and for scorning real events in historical understandings. By whatever name such fashions parade, whether as 'colonial discourse analysis', 'deconstruction', or whatever else such nihilist impulses might be called, fulminations of this sort cannot be accepted as genuine historical understanding.' One is tempted to ask who is fulminating, but the attribution of such labels as nihilist dogma to work such as that represented in my first book would seem libelous (even if it had appeared without the authority of the editors of the new *Oxford History*) were the charges not so absurd. Robert E. Frykenberg, 'India to 1858,' in Winks (ed.), *Historiography*, 194–213.

23   C.A. Bayly, *Empire and Information: Intelligence Gathering and Social Communication in India, 1780–1870* (Cambridge: Cambridge University Press, 1996), 370.

24   Part of the reason for this is a profound unease with 'the "knowledge is power" theme of Francis Bacon and Michel Foucault' (ibid., 324), partly because of an interest in strategic and military information rather than knowledge in the larger sense. Of course, specific information of this last kind is both at the service of larger forms of knowledge, and frequently driven by it, even as it is so literally implicated in the larger project of colonial conquest and rule. I might add that Bayly seems almost deliberately to misunderstand the thrust of new work, even as he avoids any direct comment about the work of Bernard Cohn, noting only, in a footnote, that 'his seminal article attributed too great a capacity on the part of the British to 'construct' Indian society independently of the agency of its social formations and knowledge communities' (ibid., 287n).

25   ibid., 370, 371.

26   ibid., 47, 53, 143, 149, 313.

27   ibid., 48, 46, 167.

28   E.g. see James Clifford, 'On Orientalism,' reprinted in Clifford, *The Predicament of Culture* (Cambridge: Harvard University Press, 1988) 255–76.

29   I have made this argument before, as for example in 'From Little King to Landlord: Colonial Discourse and Colonial Rule,' in Dirks (ed.) *Colonialism and Culture* (Ann Arbor: University of Michigan Press, 1992), 175–208.

30   Eugene Irschick's recent book, *Dialogue and History* (Berkeley and Los Angeles: University of California Press, 1996), has been held up as the model of a new kind of colonial history

by Bayly (see *Empire*, p. 370, and 'The Second British Empire,' 71) and Frykenberg, 'India to 1858,' 212.

31   See David Washbrook, 'Law, State and Agrarian Society in Colonial India,'*Modern Asian Studies*, 1981, 15(3), 649–721.

32   Bayly, *Empire*, 142. Emphasis added.

33   All of the authors discussed above refer to Said and his 'disciples.' The disciples are invariably guilty of far more than the master himself.

34   Rosalind O'Hanlon and David Washbrook, 'After Orientalism: Culture, Criticism, and Politics in the Third World,' *Comparative Studies in Society and History* 34 (January 1992), 141–67.

35   This, in fact, is the common charge, made by O'Hanlon and Washbrook, Aijaz Ahmed, Arif Dirlik, Neil Lazarus and H.D. Harootunian, among others. See my 'Postcolonialism and its Discontents: History, Anthropology, and Postcolonial Critique,' in Joan W. Scott and Debra Keates (eds), *Schools of Thought: Twenty-five Years of Social Science and Social Change* (Princeton: Princeton University Press).

36   See my 'The Home and the World: The Invention of Modernity in Colonial India,' in R. Rosenstone (ed.) *Revisioning History: Film and the Construction of a New Past* (Princeton: Princeton University Press, 1993), 44–63. Also see Gyan Prakash's cogent critique of Chatterjee in *Another Reason: Science and the Imagination of Modern India* (Princeton: Princeton University Press, 1999).

37   Indeed, the focus on Sanskrit texts and ideas works precisely to pose the kind of problems that Ambedkar and Periyar fought against in their own political and intellectual struggles.

38   I have used the term 'hegemony' in the colonial context to specify forms of securing consent, whether in public rhetorical arenas or private law cases, that make it clear that 'domination' as an analytic term is hardly sufficient to explain the nature of colonial law. Although I used 'hegemony' in much of my earlier writing on colonial history, I would accept that there are differences between metropolitan and colonial hegemony. Significantly, I would argue that 'hegemony' is useful precisely to counter the trope of 'collaboration.' Nevertheless, colonial effects were neither minor nor controlled solely by the colonized. I cannot accept, for example, Guha's argument that 'The advent of Europe's reason in South Asia as part of a colonial cargo also had a transformative impact, no doubt. But thanks to the indigenous society's refusal to dignify an alien rulership with hegemony, the transformation shaped up essentially as a process of Indianizing the idioms of modernity imported by the Raj.' My emphasis in this chapter, of course, has been on the colonialization of the idioms of tradition under the regime of colonial modernity. See Ranajit Guha, 'Introduction,' in his *A Subaltern Studies Reader, 1986–1995* (Minneapolis: University of Minnesota Press, 1997), p. ix–xv. Also see Ranajit Guha, *Dominance without Hegemony: History and Power in Colonial India* (Cambridge: Harvard University Press, 1997).

39   It is in this context that I would situate the contrast between colonial and metropolitan governmentality. Whereas in my view colonial governmentality shares more with metropolitan governmentality than suggested by Partha Chatterjee, the similarities are always mediated by the complexity of relations of accountability, in short, by the limits of colonial despotism. Colonial hegemony worked precisely to lessen the sense of this contrast (through the promise that British rule would confer equivalent rights to Indians once education succeeded in creating the conditions for civil society), even as that hegemony increasingly came up against the limits of its own fundamental contradictions (from the British response to the rebellion to debates over the Ilbert Bill). The nationalist movement itself struggled for years with the problem of hegemony, ultimately overturning the conditions for limited hegemony, even as it appropriated many of the terms of colonial hegemony in the formation and implementation of nationalist goals. Here see Partha Chatterjee, *Nationalist Thought and the Colonial World: A Derivative Discourse* (Minneapolis: University of Minnesota Press, 1993).

40   E.g. see Peter van der Veer, *Imperial Encounters: Religion and Modernity in India and Britain* (Princeton: Princeton University Press, 2001).

41   See Dipesh Chakrabarty, *Provincializing Europe: Postcolonial Thought and Historical Difference* (Princeton: Princeton University Press, 2000).

Chapter 6

Richard Gott

SHOOT THEM TO BE SURE

It was suggested in my Introduction that maybe the most contentious of all issues in the writing of imperial and colonial history is the role of violence and atrocity in these. It is on that theme that veteran British journalist/historian Richard Gott focuses in his critical view of the most monumental modern work in British imperial history. In his view, that project's guiding spirit and the contributions of many of its authors obscure, obfuscate or underplay the extent of that violence, indeed of massacre and genocide.

Stephen Howe

A NEW HISTORY OF THE BRITSH EMPIRE might be expected to concern itself with such issues as the construction of military dictatorship through the imposition of martial law; the violent seizure and settlement of land; the genocidal destruction of indigenous peoples (and their culture and environment); the establishment of what is now called 'institutional racism'; and the continuing coercion and induced movement of labour. The new *Oxford History of the British Empire* presents a more up-beat version typical of the age of Imperial sunset. An attempt to construct a positive memorial to Empire, these volumes engage only spasmodically with the 'postcolonial' debates of the last twenty years.

The editor-in-chief of this immense project is William Roger Louis, an American – though famously Anglophile – scholar. When he was appointed dismay was expressed in conservative newspapers at the thought that a quintessentially British historical experience was to be in the hands of some renegade colonial. In the event, he has proved a sensible choice, and perhaps an inevitable one. Without American scholarship and money, this particular millennium construction would not have seen the light of day for many years.

Louis has not produced an encyclopedia. Anyone searching for information about events in specific countries, or on the origins of current crises, would be seriously disappointed. Only Ireland gets a decent showing over the centuries – here, perhaps, the interests of the North American diaspora can be detected – and it is revealed for what it was: the model colony on whose pattern the entire Empire was based. India, too, is well catered for, but other parts of the Empire are treated more cavalierly. There is nothing about the dynamite dropped into the caves of Africans who objected to their land being seized in Rhodesia in 1896; very little about the Hut Tax War in 1898 in Sierra Leone, when two military expeditions were sent to quell enraged Africans in the hinterland; not much explanation of 19th-century Indian immigration to Ceylon and Fiji, promoted by British settlers as a means to secure cheap labour; nothing about Kashmir; and very little about the permanent dissent and disorder on the North-West Frontier with Afghanistan. Iraq and Palestine are inadequately subsumed in a chapter curiously entitled 'Britain's Informal Empire in the Middle East'.

In the first volume, on Imperial 'origins', there are ground-breaking contributions from Jane Ohlmeyer on Ireland and Scotland as 'laboratories of Empire', and from Peter Mancall on the troubled relationship between Europeans and Native Americans in the 16th and 17th centuries. The second volume, concerned principally with slavery and the American Revolution, has a sparkling chapter on Native Americans by Daniel Richter, and another on the 'black experience' of Empire by Philip Morgan. But broadly speaking, the radical historians of Empire – David Killingray, Peter Sluglett, Nicholas Tarling – have been confined to the final, historiographical volume, while the more conservative have been given the meaty chapters in the bulk of the *History*.

The purpose of the *Historiography* volume is to trace themes that were dealt with inadequately in the earlier narrative volumes, and it provides a vivid account of the way historians portrayed Empire during its final century. Discussing work in Canada, D.R. Owram describes how 'older images of the British as a benevolent ruling society have tended to give way to darker pictures of indigenous peoples displaced'. Contemporary Australian historians, we are told by Stuart Macintyre, have recovered 'a forgotten history of genocidal expropriation of Aboriginal Australians'. These are welcome contributions, yet neither writer can explain why these issues are so neglected in the earlier volumes. C.A. Bayly, the Vere Harmsworth Professor of Imperial and Naval History at Cambridge, dismisses as 'fashionable' or 'anachronistic' issues that have agitated Imperial historians for the past twenty years – famine and ecology, for example; the destruction of forests and tribal peoples.

We now recognise that the Empire was not established on virgin territory, as some of the older Imperial histories liked to suggest. Land – for tax collection, for production and for settlement – had to be wrested from indigenous peoples, who were driven away, sent into permanent exile, or exterminated. A familiar pattern in the Americas in the 17th and 18th centuries, this destruction of native peoples became more purposive in the larger Empire in the 19th, and lasted well into the 20th. Colonial governors who had fought with Wellington in the Peninsular Wars, and were subsequently rewarded with jobs, often perceived native inhabitants of the Empire as an 'enemy' to be rooted out. In New South Wales and Tasmania, in India and South Africa, in the seas off Singapore and on the Arabian mainland, these officers helped create the circumstances in which British trade and investment could flourish without the tiresome physical presence of those unwilling to recognise its obvious advantages.

The most satisfactory exposition of this aspect of Imperial control comes in a brilliant essay by D.A. Washbrook about 19th-century India. In his account, the British conquerors turned what they perceived as a tradition of 'oriental despotism' to their advantage, organising a 'military offensive against civil society':

> The Army was made highly *visible* through garrison policies which *dispersed* it widely across the country. Pacification policies were developed which treated the slightest manifestation of civil disorder as incipient revolt and punished it accordingly. Soldiers were deputed to attend many of the functions of civil government, such as revenue collection. Non-military departments of the state adopted military-style uniforms and rituals . . . Flogging came to be regarded as a highly appropriate punishment for an *ever-widening* range of 'civil' offences. Martial force – that is, torture – was also extensively used in such tasks as the collection of land revenue.

Washbrook also refers to the British search-and-destroy missions sent to Central India in 1817 to slaughter the marauding Pindari armies of Chitu, although he does not quote the remark of Colonel George Fitzclarence, an aide-de-camp to the Governor of Bengal, who underlined their real purpose. The Pindaris were 'viewed as public robbers', Fitzclarence wrote, and so 'their extirpation was aimed at, and not their defeat as an enemy entitled to the rights of war'.

Such physical extermination of native peoples is largely ignored in other contributions to the *Oxford History*. The chapter on Southern Africa in the 19th century by Christopher Saunders and Iain Smith benignly suggests that 'British troops repeatedly intervened to play a crucial role in supporting settlers who were unable on their own to displace African farmers.' No attempt is made to describe what 'intervention' or 'displacement' might have involved, nor is there any reference to the prolonged campaign to exterminate the San (Bushmen) during the first decades of the 19th century. Hundreds of thousands of acres were seized by white farmers, and hardly a single Bushman band remained by 1825. A correspondent in a frontier town in 1821, describing how he had met people involved in the 'commando' expeditions sent out against them, wrote that 'they talk of shooting Bushmen with the same feelings as if the poor creatures were wild beasts'. British officials liked to think that the extermination of the San was chiefly the work of the Dutch, and some British historians have accepted this view, but John Philip, a hawk-eyed missionary in the 1820s, knew that this wasn't so. The system 'which rendered the Dutch name so infamous', he wrote, is now being carried on 'in all its horrors' under the British Government: 'Impatient to obtain undisturbed possession of the Bushman country, and tired of the slow method of exterminating the natives by commandos of Boers . . . a plan was devised to employ the Cape regiments, and the British soldiers then on the frontiers of the colony, in this work of death.' Philip concluded that, 'the mass of evil brought upon the wretched Bushmen is greater under the English Government than under the Dutch'.

Similar attitudes were evident among the British dealing with the Aborigines and the Maoris. 'How would I civilise the Maoris?' asked Captain John Guard, a former convict whose ship was wrecked off the North Island in 1834. 'Shoot them to be sure! A musket ball for every New Zealander is the only way of civilising their country.' However, no one would learn from the *Oxford History* that the slaughter of the aborigines was often intentional. Donald Denoon and Marivic Wyndham, who write here about Australia and the Pacific in the 19th century, suggest matter-of-factly that 'indigenous peoples were decimated and outnumbered by new, expanding societies of free British migrants', but they seem to believe that this 'demographic revolution' was caused by smallpox rather than the deliberate actions of colonists. There is no mention of the use of poisoned 'damper' (maize meal laced with arsenic), nor of the simple remedies suggested by wealthy Australian ranchers such as Colonel William Cox, speaking at a public meeting in Beaufort in 1825: 'The best thing that could be done would be to shoot all the Blacks and manure the ground with their carcases, which was all the good they were fit for . . . the women and children should especially be shot as the most certain method of getting rid of the race.' It is true that smallpox had a dramatic impact on other subject peoples of the Empire, notably on Native Americans in the 17th and 18th centuries, but even its spread was not always accidental. 'Could it not be contrived to send the small pox among those disaffected tribes of Indians,' wrote General Jeffrey Amherst, the British commander in North America during the great Indian rebellion led by Pontiac in 1763, another notorious utterance that finds no place in the *Oxford History*.

The fate of the Canadian Indians, too, is largely ignored in these pages, though Ged Martin, in a chapter on Canada after 1815, admits that the 19th century was 'a disaster' for its indigenous peoples: 'They had constituted at least one-fifth of the population in 1815 but by 1911 their total members halved to just over 100,000, barely 1 per cent of Canada's total.' Martin makes no attempt to explain this extraordinary development, and omits any reference to Prince Maximilian of Wied, *who* travelled in the lands south of Lake Winnipeg in the wake of a smallpox epidemic in the 1830s. 'The prairie all around is a vast field of death,' wrote the Prince. 'The Assiniboines . . . are, in the literal sense of the expression, nearly exterminated.' Out of step with today's revisionist historians, Martin is also dismissive of Indian resistance, hinting that Louis Riel, the leader of an Indian-supported rebellion in Saskatchewan in 1885, was simply a deranged millenarian whose cause few Indians cared to join.

These volumes lack any sense of outrage at the routine horror of the Empire. The rape and plunder of Imperial campaigns, and the stench of burning villages, were not confined to the early years. Things grew steadily worse as technological advances reached distant, newly acquired colonies. The late 19th-century conquest of Africa coincided with the improvement of the machine-gun; and in the 20th century, the technique of killing at a distance was refined through aerial bombing, enabling opponents and troublemakers to be destroyed, with their families, at minimum cost and with no publicity. In Somalia, Nigeria, Iraq, the Sudan and on India's North-West Frontier, aerial bombing was to prove formidably effective as a weapon of terror. Only passing reference is made to these technological developments, and there are even attempts to downgrade their significance. Robert Kubicek argues that in numerous armed clashes between the British and local peoples between 1875 and 1907, 'both sides had modern weaponry'.

So they did, but Winston Churchill was appalled by the one-sided slaughter at the Battle of Omdurman in 1898, where the followers of the Mahdi had just two machine-guns, while Kitchener's men had fifty-five.

The coercion and movement of labour is also underplayed. When indigenous peoples refused to be enslaved, or had been exterminated, alternative sources of labour had to be found. Traditional Imperial history prefers to dwell on Britain's admirable role in the abolition of its slave trade in 1807, but disavows the role played by slavery itself in establishing the seed-corn of Imperial fortunes. In fact, for much of the time until 1833, production in the outer reaches of the Empire was dependent on slave labour imported from Africa. In a chapter on the development of the Caribbean islands, Richard Sheridan underestimates the role of slave labour. 'The New World plantation represented the capitalistic exploitation of land,' he writes, 'with a combination of African labour, European technology and management, Asiatic and American plants, European animal husbandry, and American soil and climate.' So it did, yet without African slaves and their labour, the other items on Sheridan's list would have made little impact. David Richardson is more outspoken in an essay on the economics of the slave trade. Differences may exist among historians about the amount of money the slave trade made for Britain, but he has little doubt that merchants of the British Empire, the leading shippers of slaves to America, made life hell for the Africans.

When slavery was abolished throughout the British Empire in 1833, many former slaves sought to work for themselves, and withdrew their labour from the market. Colonial governments fell back on a system of forced labour. Prisoners and ordinary citizens were recruited for road construction, part of the essential infrastructure of Empire, just as it had been in the days of Rome. Private Imperial producers were less fortunate, and had to embark on a global search for cheap labour. In one bizarre episode in the 1840s, Jamaican labour recruiters brought back from Sierra Leone the descendants of the Maroons, who had been forcibly expelled from the Caribbean after a rebellion in 1795.

Eventually, a more reliable source of labour was found in India and China: the seizure of Hong Kong in 1841 provided a conduit for the dispersal of Chinese labour around the globe, while Britain's direct control over India ensured that its impoverished peasants were always available for export. Whatever their formal status, these indentured labourers often worked under conditions comparable with those of the slaves they replaced. When Indian coolies first arrived in British Guiana, they were housed in barracks known as the 'Niggers' Yard'; those who went to the sugar estates of Mauritius were housed in the 'Camp des Noirs'. In a single, inadequate chapter about this new form of Imperial labour, David Northrup argues blandly that it was 'less a new system of slavery than an old system of free labour revived to suit Imperial needs in an industrial age'. 'Limited space,' he concludes, 'prevents consideration of the conditions of labour in the various colonies.'

One casualty of this 'limited space' is Fiji, where British annexation of the islands in 1874 led to a complete collapse of 'the will to live' for many native Fijians, a phenomenon W.H.R. Rivers, the British pioneer of psychoanalysis, compared with shell shock. So remarkable was this collapse that the Governor felt obliged to set up a commission in 1893, barely twenty years after the British takeover, to seek explanations for 'the decline of the native population'. The commissioners' report identified a number of causes, including a measles epidemic carried on a British ship, and the changes wrought in traditional society through the activities of missionaries. They also found that some people believed there to be 'a mysterious malign influence surrounding the white man, like a poisonous atmosphere, which stifles every coloured race encountering it'. Four years after British annexation, the settlers found it so difficult to persuade the Fijians to work for them that they transferred boatloads of indentured Indian workers from the Subcontinent. By 1916, when the indenture system was finally abandoned, some 50,000 Indians were living in Fiji, and by 1944, they outnumbered the native Fijians.

The issue of military control is also neglected. To ensure its survival, and to avoid imposing an intolerable burden on the British population at home, the Empire was usually defended and policed by armies recruited from among each colony's indigenous peoples.

In South Africa, the Khoi-Khoi (Hottentots) were formed into the Cape Mounted Rifles to be used against the Xhosa (Kaffirs). In Australia, Aborigines were recruited into the Corps of Native Police to be deployed against other Aborigines, usually in different parts of the country. In the Caribbean, black slaves were bought up in the marketplace to serve in the British Army during the counter-revolutionary wars of the 1790s, and the projected end of the slave trade was postponed for several years to maintain this important source of military recruits. The British Army in the Caribbean, much reduced by yellow fever, was seriously deficient in manpower as it sought to quell Carib and Maroon rebellions, and to defend the white planters against the French. In Ceylon, too, the British Governor was forced to purchase Africans from the Portuguese slave market in Goa to fight the resistance wars in Kandy. Later, in the 19th century, the black soldiers of the West Indian regiments were sent from the Caribbean to fight against the children of their forebears in West Africa, and to help police the ramparts of Empire in the Middle East. A fresh Imperial pattern was created, with locally recruited regiments dispatched around the globe. African soldiers, notably from Nigeria, were hired to fight in Ghana and Sierra Leone, and during the Second World War were sent as far away as Burma.

In India, most famously, locally recruited soldiers known as 'sepoys' came to form the backbone of Britain's Imperial forces. After 100 years of service in the conquest of India itself, the sepoys were deployed in Egypt, Indonesia, the Persian Gulf and Aden, in Ethiopia and East Africa, and in Europe during the First and Second World wars. Some of the Imperial hoplites joined up gratefully – unemployment in the Caribbean colonies meant joyful scenes at the recruiting offices in 1914 – but others were less willing, and their forced recruitment became a point of resistance. Indian sepoys mutinied often, though the prospect of 'cannonading' – being 'blown from guns' – was enough to keep many from stepping out of line. There was 'not a dry eye amongst the Europeans', it is said of one occasion in 1764, when twenty-four sepoys were killed in this way on the parade ground at Patna. A mutinous soldier would be placed in front of a cannon, his shoulders against the barrel's mouth. When the gun was fired, his severed head and arms would flyaway, while the amputated body fell to the ground. The ceremony was used for the execution of Indians following the Mutiny in 1857, and in 1872 Lambert Cowan, deputy commissioner of a town in the Punjab, ordered fifty Sikh zealots to be blown from guns. The late Philip Mason, like many old India hands, used to argue that the sepoys preferred this manner of dying. During the Mutiny, he claimed, 'there were many cases of men begging to be blown from guns or shot, a soldier's death, but not to be hanged – the death of a dog'. Eyewitnesses thought otherwise: William Butler, a missionary, argued that the sepoys objected to the dishonour done to the integrity of the body. 'The disembodied ghost' of someone executed by cannonading, he wrote, would be exposed 'to a wandering, indefinite condition in the other world, which they regard as dreadful'.

By the end of the 19th century, cannonading had been abandoned, but the machine-gun, then aerial bombing, replaced the practice as powerful disincentives to mutiny. Hugh Trenchard, who spent the first decade of the 20th century quelling rebellions in Nigeria, made ready use of the new technologies. Revelations about his early career owe much to African oral traditions resurrected by historians and exploited by novelists. Chinua Achebe, in *Things Fall Apart* (1958), describes the scene on market day in Abame when punishment was exacted for the murder of a white man who had arrived in the village 'riding an iron horse'. Three white men 'and a very large number of other men surrounded the market . . . and they began to shoot. Everyone was killed, except the old and the sick who were at home.' The event on which Achebe based his story took place in southern Nigeria, in December 1905, in the village of Ahiara. The villagers had killed Dr James Stewart, an officer who had arrived in their village on a bicycle. Major Trenchard, aged 32, was the commander of the force in charge of the subsequent massacre. The historian Johnson Asiegbu interviewed people in the area in 1978, and found that some still remembered what had happened, recalling that 'after gathering the local people for a public "palaver" or meeting, the British-led soldiers opened fire on the unsuspecting people and mowed them down by the hundreds'.

Years after this largely forgotten and unreported Nigerian massacre, Air Marshal Trenchard became 'the founder' of the Royal Air Force. In the 1920s, as Chief of Air Staff, he became a devoted advocate of the aerial bombing of rebels in Iraq, a strategy that enabled the British to control the country in the absence of Indian sepoys, who were needed back in India to quell the revolutionary uprisings following the massacre at Amritsar in 1919. Trenchard concluded his career as Commissioner of the Metropolitan Police and chairman of the United Africa Company. His biography, and the findings of oral history generally, do not find a place in the pages of the *Oxford History*.

The editor's own contributions, particularly in the section of the 20th-century volume dealing with Imperial collapse, bring his American agenda to the fore. Louis is very conscious of the question posed by Gibbon: must all empires inevitably decline? Gibbon answered in the affirmative, but Louis is at pains to argue that 'empires can revive as well as die,' anxious perhaps to reassure his readers that today's American empire need not necessarily follow the British example.

In order to stage this argument, Louis must stake his position in a well-established debate as to the date of onset of the British decline. The usual view is that the Second World War sapped Britain's economic strength and Imperial will, so that in parallel with the rise of a United States hostile to the European empires was a Gadarene rush from the Indian Subcontinent and a steady withdrawal from the remaining Imperial possessions during the twenty years to follow.

An alternative view, with which I have more sympathy, is that the impact of the First World War was far more significant. The conquest of the territories of the Middle East, in particular, extended the Empire to its widest limits and helped bring about its downfall. (People were well aware of this at the time. My uncle, Sir Penderel Moon, joined the Imperial Civil Service in the 1920s and stayed on in India to work for Nehru. When I asked him in the 1980s, late in his life, why he had chosen such a career when it must have been obvious to him that British control of India was coming to an end, he replied that all his contemporaries knew that the game was up, but they had thought it would be fun, and intellectually interesting, to preside over the Empire's final years.) Louis does not accept this view. He prefers the simpler, familiar story that the Second World War put paid to the Empire, but he does give it a slight twist. His suggestion is that in the years after 1945, far from planning to give up their Empire, the British were in fact examining ways to revive it, and hoped to do so in collaboration with the Americans. Louis's reading is that the Americans did their best to prop up Britain's Empire in the early postwar years, in spite of their ideological opposition. One of the benefits (or disbenefits) of the special Anglo-American relationship was the American decision to assist the British in retaining their status as an Imperial power at a time when other European empires were being thrown to the wolves. (The Dutch received no Marshall Aid until they had undertaken to get rid of Indonesia.)

The initial beneficiary of this American munificence was the Labour Government of Clement Attlee. Although forced by imminent bankruptcy into withdrawal from India, Palestine and Greece, Labour held grimly onto its remaining colonies in Africa and Asia, imagining their future incorporation into the Commonwealth. The subsequent Conservative Governments of Churchill and Eden were also able to sustain an Imperial rearguard action backed by American money, but the tide turned after Suez, when a younger generation of Tory politicians, recruited by Harold Macmillan, decided that an Empire kept going by the Americans was not worth the candle. Louis singles out Iain Macleod, Conservative Colonial Secretary for two crucial years at the start of the 1960s, as someone who speeded up the process of decolonisation in the teeth of tremendous political opposition.

A generation later, it is New Labour that appears more eager to take up the white man's burden again, sending latter-day gunboats to the Balkans, Sierra Leone and Afghanistan. Certain members of today's Cabinet, one feels, may have had Louis's nostalgic *History* as their bedside reading.

PART 3

Influences from anthropology and psychoanalysis

Chapter 7

Bernard Cohn

COLONIALISM AND ITS FORMS OF KNOWLEDGE: THE BRITISH IN INDIA

Historical anthropologist Bernard Cohn, whose work has focused mainly on colonial India, has been a major influence on many younger practitioners of 'critical colonial studies' and a 'new imperial history'. Here, in the Introduction to his book *Colonialism and its Forms of Knowledge*, he summarises many of his key arguments on the relationship between colonial knowledge and power.

Stephen Howe

IN THE PREMODERN STATE, in Europe as elsewhere, power was made visible through theatrical displays, in the form of processions, progresses, royal entries, coronations, funerals, and other rituals that guaranteed the well-being and continued power of the rulers over the ruled.[1] The theater of power was managed by specialists (priests and ritual preceptors, historians and bards, artists and artisans) who maintained the various forms of knowledge required.

From the eighteenth century onward, European states increasingly made their power visible not only through ritual performance and dramatic display, but through the gradual extension of 'officializing' procedures that established and extended their capacity in many areas. They took control by defining and classifying space, making separations between public and private spheres; by recording transactions such as the sale of property; by counting and classifying their populations, replacing religious institutions as the registrar of births, marriages, and deaths; and by standardizing languages and scripts. The state licensed some activities as legitimate and suppressed others as immoral or unlawful. With the growth of public education and its rituals, it fostered official beliefs in how things are and how they ought to be. The schools became the crucial civilizing institutions and sought to produce moral and productive citizens. Finally, nation states came to be seen as the natural embodiments of history, territory, and society.[2]

The establishment and maintenance of these nation states depended upon determining, codifying, controlling, and representing the past. The documentation that was involved created and normalized a vast amount of information that formed the basis of their capacity to govern. The reports and investigations of commissions, the compilation, storage, and publication of statistical data on finance, trade, health, demography, crime, education, transportation, agriculture, and industry – these created data requiring as much exegetical and hermeneutical skill to interpret as an arcane Sanskrit text.[3]

The process of state building in Great Britain, seen as a cultural project, was closely linked with its emergence as an imperial power, and India was its largest and most important colony. It is not just that the personnel who governed India were British, but the projects of state building in both countries – documentation, legitimation, classification, and bounding, and the institutions therewith – often reflected theories, experiences, and practices worked out originally in India and then applied in Great Britain, as well as vice versa. Many aspects of metropolitan documentation projects were first developed in India. For example, the Indian civil service provided some of the models for the development of the Home services. Conversely, the universities and public schools in Victorian Great Britain were the factories in which the old aristocracy was associated with the new middle class, and new governing classes for the empire were produced. These models were exported to India and the other colonies to produce loyal governing elites.[4] And the central symbol of the British state and the focus of national loyalty, the Crown, was reworked in the second half of the nineteenth century in relation to India and the rest of the empire.[5] A guiding assumption in my research on the British conquest of India in the eighteenth and nineteenth centuries has been that metropole and colony have to be seen in a unitary field of analysis. In India the British entered a new world that they tried to comprehend using their own forms of knowing and thinking. There was widespread agreement that this society, like others they were governing, could be known and represented as a series of facts. The form of these facts was taken to be self-evident, as was the idea 'that administrative power stemmed from the efficient use of these facts.'[6]

What were these 'facts' whose collection lay at the foundation of the modern nation state? To the educated Englishman of the late eighteenth and early nineteenth centuries, the world was knowable through the senses, which could record the experience of a natural world. This world was generally believed to be divinely created, knowable in an empirical fashion, and constitutive of the sciences through which would be revealed the laws of Nature that governed the world and all that was in it. In coming to India, they unknowingly and unwittingly invaded and conquered not only a territory but an epistemological space as well. The 'facts' of this space did not exactly correspond to those of the invaders. Nevertheless, the British believed they could explore and conquer this space through translation: establishing correspondence could make the unknown and the strange knowable.

The first step was evidently to learn the local languages. 'Classical' Persian, Arabic, and Sanskrit as well as the currently spoken 'vernacular' languages were understood to be the prerequisite form of knowledge for all others, and the first educational institutions that the British established in India were to teach their own officials Indian languages. The knowledge of languages was necessary to issue commands, collect taxes, maintain law and order – and to create other forms of knowledge about the people they were ruling. This knowledge was to enable the British to classify, categorize, and bound the vast social world that was India so that it could be controlled. These imperatives, elements in the larger colonial project, shaped the 'investigative modalities' devised by the British to collect the facts.

An investigative modality includes the definition of a body of information that is needed, the procedures by which appropriate knowledge is gathered, its ordering and classification, and then how it is transformed into usable forms such as published reports, statistical returns, histories, gazetteers, legal codes, and encyclopedias. Some of the investigative modalities of the colonial project are quite general, such as historiography and museology, although they might include very specific practices such as the location and description of archaeological sites. Other modalities, such as the survey and the census, were more highly defined and clearly related to administrative questions. Most investigative modalities were constructed in relation to institutions and administrative sites with fixed routines. Some were transformed into 'sciences,' such as economics, ethnology, tropical medicine, comparative law, or cartography, and their practitioners became professionals. A brief discussion of a few of these modalities will illustrate my approach.

The historiographic modality

In British India, this modality is the most complex, pervasive, and powerful, underlying a number of the other more specific modalities. History, for the British, has an ontological power in providing the assumptions about how the real social and natural worlds are constituted. History in its broadest sense was a zone of debate over the ends and means of their rulership in India. From the beginning of their large-scale acquisition of territorial control and sovereignty, the British conceived of governing India by codifying and reinstituting the ruling practices that had been developed by previous states and rulers. They sought to incorporate, as much as possible, the administrative personnel employed by previous regimes. Thus knowledge of the history and practices of Indian states was seen as the most valuable form of knowledge on which to build the colonial state.

Starting in the 1770s in Bengal, the British began to investigate, through what they called 'enquiries,' a list of specific questions to which they sought answers about how revenue was assessed and collected. Out of this grew the most extensive and continuous administrative activity of the British, which they termed the land-settlement process. Entailed in this enterprise was the collection of 'customs and local histories,' which in the British discourse related to land tenure. The process culminated in the production of settlement reports, which were produced on a district-by-district basis.

A second strand of the historiographic modality involved the ideological construction of the nature of Indian civilizations, as typified in the major historical writings of Alexander Dow, Robert Orme, Charles Grant, Mark Wilks, James Mill, and James Tod. The historiographic practices and narrative genres of these writers can obviously be subjected to critical analysis, but beyond this they can be seen to have begun the formation of a legitimizing discourse about Britain's civilizing mission in India.

A third historiographic strand involves histories of the British in India. This entails what might be thought of as 'popular' history – the study of representations, whether in England or in India, of specific events. Thus stories of the Black Hole of Calcutta, the defeat of Tipu Sultan, or the siege of Lucknow involved the creation of emblematic heroes and villains, as individuals and types, who took shape in illustrations, various popular performances, and poetry; their 'history' was made concrete through the construction of memorials and sacred spaces in India.

The observational/travel modality

The questions that arise in examining this modality are related to the creation of a repertoire of images and typifactions that determined what was significant to the European eye. It was a matter of finding themselves in a place that could be made to seem familiar by following predetermined itineraries and seeing the sights in predictable ways. Two itineraries seem to have provided the narrative structure for many of the early travel accounts, and reflect the routes that brought Europeans to India. The earlier accounts follow the seventeenth-century trade pattern that brought merchants to the west coast of India, usually to Gujarat. The traveler then proceeded down the west coast to Ceylon, and up the east coast. By the eighteenth century much of British traffic to and from England went directly to Madras or Calcutta, and in the second half of the eighteenth century through the nineteenth century, arrival in Calcutta was followed by what became the standard traveler/tourist route – by boat up the Ganges, then to Delhi and either further north into the Punjab or southwest through Rajasthan and Gujarat to Bombay, then down to Malabar, Ceylon, and up the east coast to Madras. Although the travel routes were conceived as linear and continuous, there were particular things that had to be included: the river front in Banaras, the fort at Allahabad, a visit with the Nawab of Oudh, sightseeing in Agra and Delhi. In addition, travel accounts included set pieces, such as the description of Indian holy men and their austerities, encounters with traveling entertainers, and a sati seen or heard about. Increasingly in the nineteenth century, these accounts included discussions of historical sites – Hindu, Muslim, and British.

Although the itineraries and the particular sites, social types, practices, and encounters with India and Indians that are reported show considerable consistency through a two-hundred-year period, their representation changed through time. What is observed and reported is mediated by particular socio-political contexts as well as historically specific aesthetic principles, such as the 'sublime,' the 'picturesque,' the 'romantic,' and the 'realistic.'

The survey modality

The word 'survey' in English evokes a wide range of activities: to look over or examine something; to measure land for the purpose of establishing boundaries; to inspect; and to supervise or keep a watch over persons or place. In other contexts it can mean to establish the monetary value of goods and objects. For the British in India in the late eighteenth century, it also meant a form of exploration of the natural and social landscape. The survey as an investigative modality encompasses a wide range of practices, from the mapping of India to collecting botanical specimens, to the recording of architectural and archaeological sites of historic significance, or the most minute measuring of a peasant's fields.

Although the mapping and establishment of routes were part of the mercantile history of India, the beginning of a systematic survey of India can be dated to 1765, when Robert Clive assigned James Rennell, a naval officer turned surveyor, the task of making a general survey of the newly acquired Bengal territories. In the context of colonial India, the concept of the 'survey' came to cover any systematic and official investigation of the natural and social features of the Indian empire.

The result was the vast official documentation project that included the Survey of India, under the direction of George Lambton, which eventually covered India with an imaginary grid on which the government could locate any site in India. Upon the acquisition of each new territory, a new survey was launched, which went far beyond mapping and bounding to describe and classify the territory's zoology, geology, botany, ethnography, economic products, history, and sociology. The history of this documentation project has tended to be written in terms of the 'genius' and/or obsessions of great surveyors – James Rennall, William Lambton, Colin Mackenzie, Alexander Cunningham, and Francis Buchanan Hamilton. But this 'great man' theory of surveying can be enriched by a study of the structure of the practices by which such knowledge was compiled, the underlying theories of classification and their implications for the governing of India, and the process by which these vast amounts of knowledge were transformed into textual forms such as encyclopedias and extensive archives that were deployed by the colonial state in fixing, bounding, and settling India.

The enumerative modality

For many British officials, India was a vast collection of numbers. This mentality began in the early seventeenth century with the arrival of British merchants who compiled and transmitted lists of products, prices, customs and duties, weights and measures, and the values of various coins. A number was, for the British, a particular form of certainty to be held on to in a strange world. But when they turned to early attempts to enumerate the population of India in various localities, as part of early surveys, they found that even the simplest of enumerative projects raised problems of classification.

As part of the imperial settlement project after the repression of the Indian uprising of 1857–1858, the Government of India carried out a series of censuses which they hoped would provide a cross-sectional picture of the 'progress' of their rule. By 1881 they had worked out a set of practices that enabled them not just to list the names of what they hoped would be every person in India but also to collect basic information about age, occupation, caste, religion, literacy, place of birth, and current residence. Upwards of 500,000 people, most of whom were volunteers, were engaged in carrying out the census. The published census reports not only summarized the statistical information thus compiled but also included extensive narratives about the caste system, the religions of India, fertility and morbidity, domestic organization, and the economic structure of India. The census represents a model of the Victorian encyclopedic quest for total knowledge.

It is my hypothesis that what was entailed in the construction of the census operations was the creation of social categories by which India was ordered for administrative purposes.[7] The British assumed that the census reflected the basic sociological facts of India. This it did, but through the enumerative modality, the project also objectified social, cultural, and linguistic differences among the peoples of India. The panoptical view that the British were constructing led to the reification of India as polity in which conflict, from the point of view of the rulers, could only be controlled by the strong hand of the British.

The museological modality

For many Europeans India was a vast museum, its countryside filled with ruins, its people representing past ages – biblical, classical, and feudal; it was a source of collectibles and curiosities to fill European museums, botanical gardens, zoos, and country houses.

Until the 1860s the generation and transmission of knowledge of the antiquities of India – its art, architecture, scripts, and textual traditions – were largely left to individuals and scholarly societies, and were the by-products of other investigative modalities. In the late eighteenth century artists who traveled in India in pursuit of commissions and patronage, such as the Daniells brothers, William Hodges, and George Chinnery, sketched and painted not only landscapes and portraits of opulent princes and British officials but also created a visual record of the monuments of past dynasties. There was a large market in Great Britain for illustrated books, portfolios, prints, and drawings of oriental scenes and depictions of the people of India.

As a by-product of the revenue surveys and the settlement proceedings, many archaeological sites were identified and mapped. The first large-scale excavation of an Indian archaeological site was directed by Colin Mackenzie who, in addition to his official duties, carried on a twenty-year project in south India which involved the collection of archaeological specimens, texts, manuscripts, and oral histories. James Fergusson, who had gone to India as an indigo planter, traveled widely in India in 1837–1842, and wrote a series of accounts of its art and architecture, which established a hegemonic history and evaluation of Indian art and architecture. He was active in the planning of the Crystal Palace exhibition, and became the 'official' connoisseur of India's artistic achievements.

An army engineer, Alexander Cunningham, who had developed an interest in Indian archaeology, successfully lobbied Lord Canning in 1859 to establish the Archaeological Survey of India, of which he was to become the first director. The primary concern of the ASI was to record important sites on the basis of topographical research. In addition, the Survey became responsible for the preservation of historical sites, and began to develop on-site museums as well as to build a national collection of archaeological specimens. The first large-scale museum in India was built in Calcutta in the 1840s by private initiative, under the aegis of the Asiatic Society of Bengal. The museum developed into the India Museum, which is the largest general museum in India today with large collections and displays of archaeological, natural historical, and ethnographic specimens.

Representations of India bulked large in the international exhibitions and world's fairs of the second half of the nineteenth century, which in turn provided the basis of private and public collections of India arts and crafts, paintings, and antiquities. The power to define the nature of the past and establish priorities in the creation of a monumental record of a civilization, and to propound canons of taste, are among the most significant instrumentalities of rulership.

The surveillance modality

The British appear in the nineteenth century to have felt most comfortable surveying India from above and at a distance – from a horse, an elephant, a boat, a carriage, or a train. They were uncomfortable in the narrow confines of a city street, a bazaar, a *mela* – anywhere they were surrounded by their Indian subjects. In their narratives of their lives and travels in India, few Indians are named other than royalty and personal servants. Indians who came under the imperial gaze were frequently made to appear in dress and demeanor as players in the British-constructed theater of power, their roles signaled by prescribed dress, their parts authored by varied forms of knowledge codified by rulers who sought to determine how loyal Indian subjects were to act in the scenes that the rulers had constructed. Everyone – rulers and ruled – had proper roles to play in the colonial sociological theater.

There were, however, groups and categories of people whose practices threatened the prescribed sociological order. These were people who appeared by their nature to wander beyond the boundaries of settled civil society: sannyasis, sadhus, fakirs, dacoits, goondas, thags, pastoralists, herders, and entertainers. The British constructed special instrumentalities to control those defined as beyond civil bounds, and carried out special investigations to provide the criteria by which whole groups would be stigmatized as criminal.

Starting in the late eighteenth century, certain clans, castes, and villages were accused of practicing female infanticide, a crime that was difficult to prove in British courts, in which only an individual and not a group could be proven guilty. Female infanticide became a 'statistical crime' for which corporal punishment could be administered. In 1835 a Thagi and Dacoity Department was created to investigate and punish gang robberies and murders. The first task was to devise means for gathering information on the practices of those the government accused of committing a ritual form of murder, particularly of travelers. This involved primarily the use of informers who turned state's evidence, and acted not only as witnesses but also as informants on the 'culture' of the Thags. The work of the Thagi and Dacoity Department led to the formation of an archive of criminal ethnography and the designation of increasing numbers of people as members of 'criminal tribes and castes.'

The British in India (like the police in urbanizing western Europe) faced a problem identifying those who were suspected of antisocial, political, and criminal activities that the state sought to control or eliminate. The ideal was to create a systematic means of recording and classifying a set of permanent features that distinguished an individual. Although photography offered some possibilities for recording a physiognomy, India's large scale required a schema by which one could recover each of thousands from among potentially millions of images. Toward this end, in Paris in the late nineteenth century, Alphonse Bertillon, prefect of police, devised an anthropometric system that was believed to have the potential of providing the descriptive as well as classificatory power to identify individuals accurately.

At much the same time as Bertillon was carrying out his investigations, William Herschel, a civil servant in India, was experimenting with the use of fingerprints to individualize documents, as a means of preventing fraud and forgery. Herschel continued his explorations even after he left India and later Sir Francis Galton, in cooperation with Herschel and a number of Indian police officers, devised a system of classification that made possible fingerprinting as a means of identifying individuals.

Investigative modalities in the postcolonial world

Both historians and anthropologists – though the latter might not have labeled themselves as such – were always directly involved in the colonial situation. The origins of anthropology as a distinctive form of knowledge lay, in fact, in the internal and external colonies of the Europeans. Throughout the colonial period, some anthropologists argued, in a highly ambivalent fashion, that they had a particular role to play in mediating between the colonial subjects and rulers. In the colonial history of India, there were explicit efforts made to construct an 'official ethnography' at the moment that anthropology was beginning to be defined as a distinctive form of knowledge. Anthropologists developed practices through which they sought to erase the colonial influence by describing what they took to be authentic indigenous cultures. Their epistemological universe, however, was part of the European world of social theories and classifacatory schema that were formed, in part, by state projects to reshape the lives of their subjects at home and abroad.

Since the early twentieth century, there have been internal professional discussions among anthropologists about their responsibilities for their chosen subjects, who were frequently defined as 'native' or 'tribal' or 'wild men,' in relation to state policies and practices which sought to control them. With the end of political colonialism, anthropologists have translated their colonial past into history, and into a site for the critical and epistemological exploration of their own construction of knowledge.

Notes

1   Some of the material in this chapter has appeared in 'Beyond the Fringe: The Nation State, Colonialism, and the Technologies of Power,' by Bernard S. Cohn and Nicholas B. Dirks, in *Journal of Historical Sociology*, 2 June 1988, 1, 224–9.

2   Benedict Anderson has established the parallel growth of 'imagined communities,' based upon mystical notions of the common origins of nations, of shared blood, descent from mythical heroes, or membership in nations which have fathers and mothers, whose male descendants are constituted as 'brothers.' *Imagined Communities* (London, 1983). In their book *The Great Arch*, Peter Corrigan and Derek Sayer (Oxford, 1985) described and analyzed how the British state was constructed as a repertoire of rituals and routines of rule that legitimized the state's powers to control its subjects' activities.

3   It is ironic that the twentieth century, which has seen so many radical breaks with the past, has been marked by the production of innumerable new histories. With the establishment of each 'new' nation out of the old European colonial order, each has to be equipped with an official history of its precolonial past and its freedom struggle.

4   J.R. Mangan, *The Games Ethic and Imperialism* (Middlesex, 1985); Richard Symonds, *Oxford and Empire* (New York, 1986).

5   Bernard Cohn, 'Representing Authority in Victorian England,' and David Cannadine, 'The Context, Performance and Meaning of Ritual: The British Monarchy and the Invention of Tradition,' both in Eric Hobsbawm and Terence Ranger (eds) *The Invention of Traditions* (Cambridge, 1983).

6   Anthony D. Smith, *The Revival of the Modern World* (Cambridge, 1981) 153–4.

7   See Bernard S. Cohn, 'The Census, Social Structure and Objectification in South Asia,' first published in the 1960s, frequently reprinted, including Bernard Cohn, *An Anthropologist Among the Historians and Other Essays* (Delhi, 1990) 224–54.

Chapter 8

Ashis Nandy

THE PSYCHOLOGY OF COLONIALISM: SEX, AGE AND IDEOLOGY IN BRITISH INDIA

Ashis Nandy has been a staggeringly prolific and wide-ranging author for several decades, engaging with history, philosophy, religion, politics, psychology, cricket and more. Still maybe his most influential and debated work, though, is the little book on the psychology of empire, *The Intimate Enemy*, from which these extracts come.

Stephen Howe

Imperialism was a sentiment rather than a policy; its foundations were moral rather than intellectual.

D. C. Somervell[1]

IT IS BECOMING INCREASINGLY OBVIOUS that colonialism as we have come to know it during the last two hundred years cannot be identified with only economic gain and political power. In Manchuria, Japan consistently lost money and for many years colonial Indochina, Algeria and Angola, instead of increasing the political power of France and Portugal, sapped it. This did not make Manchuria, Indochina, Algeria or Angola less of a colony. Nor did it disprove that economic gain and political power are important *motives* for creating a colonial situation. It only showed that colonialism could be characterized by the search for economic and political advantage without concomitant *real* economic or political gains, and sometimes even with economic or political losses.[2]

This essay argues that the first differentia of colonialism is a state of mind in the colonizers and the colonized, a colonial consciousness which includes the sometimes unrealizable wish to make economic and political profits from the colonies, but other elements too. The political economy of colonization is of course important, but the crudity and inanity of colonialism are principally expressed in the sphere of psychology and, to the extent the variables used to describe the states of mind under colonialism have themselves become politicized since the entry of modern colonialism on the world scene, in the sphere of political psychology. The following pages will explore some of these psychological contours of colonialism in the rulers and the ruled and try to define colonialism as a shared culture which may not always begin with the establishment of alien rule in a society and end with the departure of the alien rulers from the colony. The example I shall use will be that of India, where a colonial political economy began to operate seventy-five years before the full-blown ideology of British imperialism became dominant, and where thirty-five years after the formal ending of the Raj, the ideology of colonialism is still triumphant in many sectors of life.

Such disjunctions between politics and culture became possible because it is only partly true that a colonial situation produces a theory of imperialism to justify itself. Colonialism is also a psychological state rooted in earlier forms of social consciousness in both the colonizers and the colonized. It represents a certain cultural continuity and carries a certain cultural baggage.

First, it includes codes which both the rulers and the ruled can share. The main function of these codes is to alter the original cultural priorities on both sides and bring to the centre of the colonial culture subcultures previously recessive or subordinate in the two confronting cultures. Concurrently, the codes remove from the centre of each of the cultures subcultures previously salient in them. It is these fresh priorities which explain why some of the most impressive colonial systems have been built by societies ideologically committed to open political systems, liberalism and intellectual pluralism. That this split parallels a basic contradiction within the modern scientific-rational world view which, while trying to remain rational within its confines, has consistently refused to be rational *vis-à-vis* other traditions of knowledge after acquiring world dominance, is only the other side of the same explanation.[3] It also explains why colonialism never seems to end with formal political freedom. As a state of mind, colonialism is an indigenous process released by external forces. Its sources lie deep in the minds of the rulers and the ruled. Perhaps that which begins in the minds of men must also end in the minds of men.

Second, the culture of colonialism presumes a particular style of managing dissent. Obviously, a colonial system perpetuates itself by inducing the colonized, through socio-economic and psychological rewards and punishments, to accept new social norms and cognitive categories. But these outer incentives and disincentives are invariably noticed and challenged; they become the overt indicators of oppression and dominance. More dangerous and permanent are the inner rewards and punishments, the secondary psychological gains and losses from suffering and submission under colonialism. They are almost always unconscious and almost always ignored. Particularly strong is the inner resistance to recognizing the ultimate violence which colonialism does to its victims, namely that it creates a culture in which the ruled are constantly tempted to fight their rulers within the psychological limits set by the latter. It is not an accident that the specific variants of the concepts with which many anti-colonial movements in our times have worked have often been the products of the imperial culture itself and, even in opposition, these movements have paid homage to their respective cultural origins. I have in mind not only the overt Apollonian codes of Western liberalism that have often motivated the elites of the colonized societies but also their covert Dionysian counterparts in the concepts of statecraft, everyday politics, effective political methods and utopias which have guided revolutionary movements against colonialism.

The rest of this chapter examines, in the context of these two processes and as illustrations, how the colonial ideology in British India was built on the cultural meanings of two fundamental categories of institutional discrimination in Britain, sex and age, and how these meanings confronted their traditional Indian counterparts and their new incarnations in Gandhi.

The homology between sexual and political dominance which Western colonialism invariably used – in Asia, Africa and Latin America – was not an accidental by-product of colonial history. It had its correlates in other situations of oppression with which the West was involved, the American experience with slavery being the best documented of them. The homology, drawing support from the denial of psychological bisexuality in men in large areas of Western culture, beautifully legitimized Europe's postmedieval models of dominance, exploitation and cruelty as natural and valid. Colonialism, too, was congruent with the existing Western sexual stereotypes and the philosophy of life which they represented. It produced a cultural consensus in which political and socio-economic dominance symbolized the dominance of men and masculinity over women and femininity.

During the early years of British rule in India, roughly between 1757 and 1830, when the British middle classes were not dominant in the ruling culture and the rulers came mainly from a feudal background, the homology between sexual and political dominance was not central to the colonial culture.[4] Most rulers and subjects had not yet internalized the idea of colonial rule as a manly or husbandly or lordly prerogative. I am not speaking here of the micro-politics of colonialism but of its macro-politics. Individual racialists and sadists were there aplenty among the British in India. But while British rule had already been established, British culture in India was still not politically dominant, and race-based evolutionism was still inconspicuous in the ruling culture. Most Britons in India lived like Indians at home and in the office, wore Indian dress, and observed Indian customs and religious practices. A large number of them married Indian women, offered *puja* to Indian gods and goddesses, and lived in fear and awe of the magical powers of the Brahmans. The first two governor-generals, renowned for their rapaciousness, were also known for their commitment to things Indian. Under them, the traditional Indian lifestyle dominated the culture of British-Indian politics. Even the British Indian Army occasionally had to pay respect to Indian gods and goddesses and there was at least one instance when the army made money from the revenues of a temple. Finally, missionary activity in British India was banned, Indian laws dominated the courts and the system of education was Indian.[5]

In Britain, too, the idea of empire was suspect till as late as the 1830s. Visitors to colonies such as India often found the British authority there 'faintly comical'.[6] The gentlemen of the East India Company had not actually intended to govern India but to make money there,[7] which of course they did with predictable ruthlessness. But once the two sides in the British-Indian culture of politics, following the flowering of the middle-class British evangelical spirit, began to ascribe cultural meanings to the British domination, colonialism proper can be said to have begun.[8] Particularly, once the British rulers and the exposed sections of Indians internalized the colonial role definitions and began to speak, with reformist fervour, the language of the homology between sexual and political stratarchies, the battle for the minds of men was to a great extent won by the Raj.

Crucial to this cultural co-optation was the process psychoanalysis calls identification with the aggressor. In an oppressive situation, the process became the flip side of the theory of progress, an ontogenetic legitimacy for an ego defence often used by a normal child in an environment of childhood dependency to confront inescapable dominance by physically more powerful adults enjoying total legitimacy. In the colonial culture, identification with the aggressor bound the rulers and the ruled in an unbreakable dyadic relationship. The Raj saw Indians as crypto-barbarians who needed to further civilize themselves. It saw British rule as an agent of progress and as a mission. Many Indians in turn saw their salvation in becoming more like the British, in friendship or in enmity. They may not have fully shared the British idea of the martial races – the hyper-masculine, manifestly courageous, superbly loyal Indian castes and subcultures mirroring the British middle-class sexual stereotypes – but they did resurrect the ideology of the martial races latent in the traditional Indian concept of statecraft and gave the idea a new centrality. Many nineteenth-century Indian movements of social, religious and political reform – and many literary and art movements as well – tried to make Ksatriyahood the 'true' interface between the rulers and ruled as a new, nearly exclusive indicator of authentic Indianness. The origins and functions of this new stress on Ksatriyahood is best evidenced by the fact that, contrary to the beliefs of those carrying the psychological baggage of colonialism, the search for martial Indianness underwrote one of the most powerful collaborationist strands within the Indian society, represented by a majority of the feudal princelings in India and some of the most impotent forms of protest against colonialism (such as the immensely courageous but ineffective terrorism of Bengal, Maharashtta and Panjab led by semi-Westernized, middle-class, urban youth).

The change in consciousness that took place can be briefly stated in terms of three concepts which became central to colonial India: *purusatva* (the essence of masculinity), *naritva* (the essence of femininity) and *klibatva* (the essence of hermaphroditism). The polarity defined by the antonymous *purusatva* and *naritva* was gradually supplanted, in the colonial culture of politics, by the antonyms of *purusatva* and *klibatva*; femininity-in-masculinity was now perceived as the final negation of a man's political identity, a pathology more dangerous than femininity itself. Like some other cultures, including some strands of pre-modern Christianity, India too had its myths about good and bad androgynes and its ideas about valuable and despicable androgyny. Now there was an attempt to lump together all forms of androgyny and counterpoise them against undifferentiated masculinity. Rabindranath Tagore's (1861–1941) novel *Car Adhyay* brilliantly captures the pain which was involved in this change. The inner conflicts of the hero of the novel are modelled on the moral and political dilemmas of an actual revolutionary nationalist, who also happened to be a Catholic theologian and a Vedantist, Brahmabandhav Upadhyay (1861–1907). Tagore's moving preface to the first edition of the novel, removed from subsequent editions because it affronted many Indians, sensed the personal tragedy of a revolutionary friend who, to fight the suffering of his people, had to move away from his own ideas *svabhava* and *svadharma*. It is remarkable that twenty-seven years before *Car Adhyay*, Tagore had dealt with the same process of cultural change in his novel *Gora*, probably modelled on the same real-life figure and with a compatible political message.[9]

Many pre-Gandhian protest movements were co-opted by this cultural change. They sought to redeem the Indians' masculinity by defeating the British, often fighting against hopeless odds, to free the former once and for all from the historical memory of their own humiliating defeat in violent power-play and 'tough politics'. This gave a second-order legitimacy to what in the dominant culture of the colony had already become the final differentiae of manliness: aggression, achievement, control, competition and power.[10]

(I am ignoring for the moment the structural changes which gradually came to parallel this consciousness. Kenneth Ballhatchet has recently described the distant intimacy between British soldiers and administrators, on the one hand, and Indian women, on the other, which was officially promoted and in fact systematically institutionalized.[11] I am also ignoring the parallel process, reflected in the latent recognition by a number of writers,[12] that the white women in India were generally more exclusive and racist because they unconsciously saw themselves as the sexual competitors of Indian men, with whom their men had established an unconscious homo-eroticized bonding. It was this bonding which the 'passive resisters' and 'non-co-operators' exploited, not merely the liberal political institutions. They were helped in this by the split that had emerged in the Victorian culture between two ideals of masculinity. To draw upon Ballhatchet and others, the lower classes were expected to act out their manliness by demonstrating their sexual prowess; the upper classes were expected to affirm their masculinity through sexual distance, abstinence and self-control. The former was compatible with the style of rulership of Spanish, Portuguese and, to a lesser extent, French colonialism in Latin America and Africa; the latter was compatible with, of all things, one strand in the traditional Indian concept of manliness. The Brahman in his cerebral, self-denying asceticism was the traditional masculine counterpoint to the more violent, 'virile', active Ksatriya, the latter representing – however odd this may seem to the modern consciousness – the feminine principle in the cosmos. This is how traditional India imposed limits on Ksatriyahood as a way of life. (To avoid confusion, I am avoiding here the languages in which hyper-masculinity includes withdrawal from sexuality or positive androgyny.)

In such a culture, colonialism was not seen as an absolute evil. For the subjects, it was a product of one's own emasculation and defeat in legitimate power politics. For the rulers, colonial exploitation was an incidental and regrettable by-product of a philosophy of life that was in harmony with superior forms of political and economic organization. This was the consensus the rulers of India sought, consciously or unconsciously. They could not successfully rule a continent-sized polity while believing themselves to be moral cripples. They had to build bulwarks against a possible sense of guilt produced by a disjunction between their actions and what were till then, in terms of important norms of their own culture, 'true' values. On the other hand, their subjects could not collaborate on a long-term basis unless they had some acceptance of the ideology of the system, either as players or as counterplayers. This is the only way they could preserve a minimum of self-esteem in a situation of unavoidable injustice.

When such a cultural consensus grows, the main threat to the colonizers is bound to become the latent fear that the colonized will reject the consensus and, instead of trying to redeem their 'masculinity' by becoming the counterplayers of the rulers according to the established rules, will discover an alternative frame of reference within which the oppressed do not seem weak, degraded and distorted men, trying to break the monopoly of the rulers on a fixed quantity of machismo. If this happens, the colonizers begin to live with the fear that the subjects might begin to see their rulers as morally and culturally inferior, and feed this information back to the rulers.[13] Colonialism minus a civilizational mission is no colonialism at all. It handicaps the colonizer much more than it handicaps the colonized.

I now come to the subsidiary homology between childhood and the state of being colonized which a modern colonial system almost invariably uses.[14] Colonizers, as we have known them in the last two centuries, came from complex societies with heterogeneous cultural and ethical traditions. As already noted, it is by underplaying some aspects of their culture and overplaying others that they built the legitimacy for colonialism.[15] For instance, it is impossible to build a hard, this-worldly sense of mission on the tradition to which St. Francis of Assisi belonged: one perforce has to go back to St. Augustine and Ignatius Loyola to do so. It is not possible to find legitimacy for the colonial theory of progress in the tradition of Johannes Eckhart, John Ruskin and Leo Tolstoy, based as it is on the rejection of the ideas of an omnipotent high technology, of hyper-competitive, achievement-oriented, over-organized private enterprise, and of aggressively proselytizing religious creeds operating on the basis of what Erik Erikson calls pseudo-species. One must find that legitimacy in utilitarians such as Jeremy Bentham and James Mill, in the socialist thinkers conceptualizing colonialism as a necessary step to progress and as a remedy for feudalism, and in those generally trying to fit the colonial experience within the mould of a doctrine of progress.

Childhood innocence serving as the prototype of primitive communism was one of Marx's main contributions to the theory of progress, which he conceptualized as a movement from prehistory to history and from infantile or low-level communism to adult communism. India to him always remained a country of 'small semi-barbarian, semi-civilized communities', which 'restricted the human mind within the smallest possible compass; making it the unresisting tool of superstition' and where the peasants lived their 'undignified, stagnant and vegetative life'. 'These little communities', Marx argued, 'brought about a brutalising worship of nature exhibiting its degradation in the fact that man, the sovereign of nature, fell down on his knees in the adoration of Kanuman [sic], monkey, and Sabbala, the cow.' It followed, according to Marx, that 'whatever may have been the crime of England she was the unconscious tool of history'.[16] Such a view was bound to contribute handsomely – even if inadvertently – to the racist world view and ethnocentrism that underlay colonialism.[17] A similar, though less influential, cultural role was played by some of Freud's early disciples who went out to 'primitive' societies to pursue the homology between primitivism and infantility.[18] They, too, were working out the cultural and psychological implications of the biological principle 'ontogeny recapitulates phylogeny', and that of the ideology of 'normal', fully socialized, male adulthood. Only, unlike the utilitarians and the Marxists, they did not clearly identify primitivism and infantility with disvalues such as structural simplicity and 'static history'.[19]

There was blood-curdling shadow-boxing among the competing Western schools of social philosophy, including the various versions of Western Christianity. But there can be no doubt about which sub-tradition in Europe was the stronger. There was an almost complete consensus among the sensitive European intellectuals that colonialism was an evil, albeit a necessary one. It was the age of optimism in Europe. Not only the arch-conservatives and the apologists of colonialism were convinced that one day their cultural mission would be complete and the barbarians would become civilized; even the radical critics of Western society were convinced that colonialism was a necessary stage of maturation for some societies. They differed from the imperialists, only in that they did not expect the colonized to love, or be grateful to the colonizers for introducing their subjects to the modern world.[20] Thus, in the eyes of the European civilization, the colonizers were not a group of self-seeking, rapacious, ethnocentric vandals and self-chosen carriers of a cultural pathology, but ill-intentioned, flawed instruments of history, who unconsciously worked for the upliftment of the underprivileged of the world.

The growth of this ideology paralleled a major cultural reconstruction that took place in the West during the first phase of colonialism, the phase in which colonialism was becoming consolidated as an important cultural process and a way of life for the Spanish and the Portuguese. Philippe Aries argues that the modern concept of childhood is a product of seventeenth-century Europe.[21] Before then the child was seen as a smaller version of the adult; now the child became – this Aries does not fully recognize – an inferior version of the adult and had to be educated through the newly-expanded period of childhood.

A parallel and contemporary development in Europe was the emergence of the modern concept of womanhood, underwritten by the changing concept of Christian godhead which, under the influence of Protestantism, became more masculine.[22]

The new concept of childhood bore a direct relationship to the doctrine of progress now regnant in the West. Childhood now no longer seemed only a happy, blissful prototype of beatific angels, as it had in the peasant cultures of Europe only a century earlier. It increasingly looked like a blank slate on which adults must write their moral codes – an inferior version of maturity, less productive and ethical, and badly contaminated by the playful, irresponsible and spontaneous aspects of human nature. Concurrently, probably propelled by what many Weberians have identified as the prime mover behind the modernization of West Europe, the Protestant Ethic: it became the responsibility of the adult to 'save' the child from a state of unrepentant, reprobate sinfulness through proper socialization, and help the child grow towards a Calvinist ideal of adulthood and maturity. Exploitation of children in the name of putting them to productive work, which took place in the early days of the Industrial Revolution in Britain, was a natural corollary of such a concept of childhood.[23]

Colonialism dutifully picked up these ideas of growth and development and drew a new parallel between primitivism and childhood. Thus, the theory of social progress was telescoped not merely into the individual's life cycle in Europe but also into the area of cultural differences in the colonies.[24] What was childlikeness of the child and childishness of immature adults now also became the lovable and unlovable savagery of primitives and the primitivism of subject societies.

One element in the legitimization of colonialism through reconstruing the human life cycle has not been touched upon. Not that it was unimportant in the colonial culture; but it was, I suspect, specific to India and China and, to that extent, less generally applicable to modern colonialism. I shall briefly say something about it now.

Modern Europe had delegitimized not merely femininity and childhood but also old age.[25] Judaeo-Christianity always had an element which saw aging as a natural unfolding and result of man's essential sinfulness. The decomposition of the human body was seen as only an indicator of the evil in the one degenerating: according to the old South European saying, till youth a person looked the way god made him; after that he looked the way he really was. With increasing stress on the reprobate nature of man, it was this postulate which came to the fore in Europe's new ideology of male adulthood, completing the picture of a world where only the adult male reflected a reasonable approximation of a perfect human being.

The elderly (representing wisdom and the negation of 'pure' intellect) were now increasingly seen as socially irrelevant because of their low physical power and because their social productivity and cultural role could not be easily quantified. I need hardly add that, given the nature of available technology, the ideological changes neatly fitted the emerging principles of 'productive' work and 'performance' as they were monetized and enshrined in new political and social institutions.

This part of the ideology of male-adulthood too was exported to the colonies in a few chosen cases. Kiernan does refer to the ideological problem of British colonialism in India which could not easily grapple with the fact that India had a civilization, howsoever strange by European standards. Newly discovered Africa, with its strong emphasis on the folk, the oral and the rural, could be more easily written off as savage. It was more difficult to do so for India and China, which the European Orientalists and even the first generation rulers had studied and, sometimes, venerated. And, everything said, there were the traditions of four thousand years of civic living, a well-developed *literati* tradition (in spite of all its stress on oral cultures), and alternative traditions of philosophy, art and science which often attracted the best minds of Europe. The fact that India's past was living (unlike, say, pre-Islamic Egypt) complicated the situation. Some explanation had to be given for her political and cultural 'degradation'.

The colonial ideology handled the problem in two mutually inconsistent ways. First, it postulated a clear disjunction between India's past and its present. The civilized India was in the bygone past; now it was dead and 'museumized'. The present India, the argument went, was only nominally related to its history; it was India only to the extent it was a senile, decrepit version of her once-youthful, creative self. As a popular myth would have it, Max Miller, for all his pioneering work in Indology and love for India, forbade his students to visit India; to him, the India that was living was not the true India and the India that was true had to be but dead.

Second and paradoxically, the colonial culture postulated that India's later degradation was not due to colonial rule – which, if anything, had improved Indian culture by fighting against its irrational, oppressive, retrogressive elements – but due to aspects of the traditional Indian culture which in spite of some good points carried the seeds of India's later cultural downfall. Like a sinful man, Indian culture was living through a particularly debilitating senility. The very fact that Hinduism did not have in its concept of *papa* the strong inner-directed connotations of the Christian, postreformation concept of sin was itself seen as one of the main proofs of India's fatal cultural flaw. Even a man such as Albert Schweitzer did not remain uncontaminated by this ideology; he made it a central plank of his interpretation of Hinduism.[26] Thus, in this argument, there was a postulate of continuity but it applied more to sinfuless than to virtues; for an explanation of India's virtues one had to fall back upon her contacts with the modern world.[27,28]

Notes

1   *English Thought in the Nineteenth Century* (New York: Longman Green, 1929) 186.
2   I am for the moment ignoring the fact that the colonial societies in our times lost out in the game of political and economic power in the First World itself.
3   On this other contradiction see Paul Feyerabend, *Science in a Free Society* (London: NLB, 1978). In the context of India and China this point emerges clearly from Claude Alvares' *Homo Faber: Technology and Culture in India, China and the West, 1500–1972* (New Delhi: Allied Publishers, 1979). See also Ashis Nandy, 'Science, Authoritarianism and Culture: On the Scope and Limits of Isolation outside the Clinic', M.N. Roy Memorial Lecture, 1980, *Seminar*, May 1981 (261); and Shiv Viswanathan, 'Science and the Sense of Other', paper written for the colloquium on New Ideologies for Science and Technology, Lokayan Project 1982, Delhi, mimeographed.

4   Frantz Fanon was one of the first to point out the psychological dominance of the European
middle-class culture in the colonies. See his *Black Skin, White Masks*, translated by G.L.
Markman (New York: Grove, 1967); also Gustav Jahoda, *White Man* (London: Oxford
University Press, 1961) 102, 123. Quoted in Renate Zahar, *Frantz Fanon: Colonialism arid
Alienation* (New York: Monthly Review Press, 1974) 45n. James Morris *Heaven's Command:
An Imperial Progress*, (London: Faber & Faber, 1973, 38) says, in the context of India: 'By 1835
one detects a certain smugness among the islanders, and this superior tone of voice came not
as it would later come, from an arrogant Right, but from a highly moralistic Left. The middle
classes, newly enfranchised, were emerging into power: and it was the middle classes who
would eventually prove, later in Victoria's reign, the most passionate imperialists of all.'

It is in the context of this correlation between middle-class culture and the spirit of
imperialism that one must make sense of psychologist J.D. Unwin's reported proposition:
'only a sexually restrained society . . . would continue to expand' (*Heaven's Command*,
30). The political culture of British India was however a product of the dialectic between
British feudalism and British middle-class culture. I have avoided the details of this dialectic
here.

5   E.g. Harihar Sheth, *Pracin Kalikaair Paricay* (Calcutta: Orient Books, 1982), new edn; Binoy
Ghose, *Kalkaai Culture* (Calcutta: Bihar Sahitya Bhavan, 1953); Morris, *Heaven's Command*,
75–6.

6   Morris, *Heaven's Command*, 20, 24. Morris sums up as follows: 'All in all the British were
not thinking in imperial terms. They were rich. They were victorious. They were admired.
They were not yet short of markets for their industries. They were strategically invulnerable,
and they were preoccupied with domestic issues. When the queen was crowned . . . we
may be sure she thought little of her possessions beyond the seas. She was the island queen
. . . Even the Welsh, the Scots and the Irish were unfamiliar to her then, when the world
called her kingdom simply 'England' . . . No, in 1837 England seemed to need no empire,
and the British people as a whole were not much interested in the colonies. How can one
be expected to show an interest in a country like Canada, demanded Lord Melbourne the
Prime Minister, where a salmon would not rise to a fly,' 25–6, 30.

7   Morris, *Heaven's Command*, 71–2.

8   After the Sepoy Mutiny of 1857, however, the 'universalism' which had powered the early
British reformers of Indian society had to give way to a second phase of 'tolerance' of Indian
culture due to the fears of a second mutiny. But this new cultural relativism clearly drew
a line between Indian culture seen as infantile and immoral and the culture of the British
public school products: austere, courageous, self-controlled, 'adult men'. Lewis D. Wurgaft,
'Another Look at Prospero and Caliban: Magic and Magical Thinking in British India',
mimeographed, 5–6. Wurgaft bases his analysis partly on Francis Hutchins, *The Illusion of
Permanence, British Imperialism in India* (Princeton: Princeton University Press, 1967). This
shift to tolerance however did not change the basic relationship between the colonized. As
in Albert Memmi's Africa, the 'good' and the 'bad' colonizers were but two different cogs
performing equally important functions in the same machine. See Memmi's *The Colonizer
and the Colonized*, translated by Howard Greenfeld (New York: Beacon, 1957); also Wurgaft,
'Another Look at Prospero and Caliban' 12–13. C. Northcote Parkinson in his *East and West*
(New York: Mentor, 1965), 216, sums it up neatly: 'It was the knowledgeable, efficient,
and polite Europeans who did the serious damage.'

The whole process was part of a larger picture, which involved the rejection of Europe's
pre-modern conceptualization of the East and re-incorporation of the East into European
consciousness according to the needs of colonialism. It is interesting that for European
philosophers of the eighteenth century, to men such as Voltaire for example, China, perhaps,
was the most advanced culture of the world. By the nineteenth century the Chinese had
become, for the European literati, primitives.

9   Rabindranath Tagore, 'Car Adhyay', *Racanavali* (Calcutta: West Bengal Government, 1961),
875–923; 'Gora', *Racanavali*, 1–350. On Brahmabandhav Upadhyay, see the brief article

by Smaran Acharya, 'Upadhyay Brahmabandhav: Rabindra-Upanyaser Vitarkita Nayak', *Desk*, 20 March 1982, 49(20), 27–32. On Tagore's response to the criticisms of his position on extremist politics in *Car Adhyay*, see his 'Kaifyat' (1935), reproduced in Shuddhasatva Bosu, *Rabindranather Car Adhyay* (Calcutta: Bharati Prakasani, 1979) 7–10. Bosu also provides an interesting, politically relevant, analysis of the novel.

I am grateful to Ram Chandra Gandhi for pointing out to me that even Vivekanimda, whose masculine Hinduism was a clear denial of the androgyny of his guru Rantakrishna Paramahamsa, himself became painfully aware of the cultural changes his Hinduism represented towards the end of his brief life. On Indian traditions of androgyny and myths about androgynes, see Wendy D. O'Flaherty, *Sexual Metaphors and Animal Symbols in Indian Mythology* (Delhi: Motilal Banarsidass, 1980) and *Women, Androgynes and Other Mythical Beasts* (Chicago: University of Chicago, 1980).

10   This in spite of the fact that many of these characteristics were traditionally associated with femininity in India. See on this subject my 'Woman Versus Womanliness in India: An Essay in Political and Social Psychology', *Psychoanalytic Review*, 1978, 63(2), 301–15. Also in *At the Edge of Psychology: Essays in Politics and Culture* (New Delhi: Oxford University Press, 1980), 32–46. Thus, we find the well-meaning M.C. Mallik saying in his *Orient and Occident: A Comparative Study* (London, 1913) 183, quoted in Parkinson, *East and West*, 210: 'Europeans even of a friendly type lament the want of manliness in Indian nature and conduct. It would be strange if after so many centuries of coercion by religious, spiritual and political teachers, and of demoralizing social conditions, any manliness should survive, especially as when any sign of it is displayed by individuals, it is discouraged by parents, teachers, spiritual guides and political rulers as impertinence and disloyalty . . .' It is a minor tragedy of contemporary India that one of its finest products, Satyajit Ray, expresses the same consciousness in a more sophisticated way in his movie *Shatranj Ke Khilari*. Ray's ambivalence towards the dancing, singing poet-king who loses out to British statecraft based on *realpolitik* represents a sophisticated version of Mallik's awareness. See on this my review of the movie in 'Beyond Oriental Despotism: Politics and Femininity in Satyajit Ray', *Sunday*, Annual No. 1981, 56–8.

11   Kenneth Ballhatchet, *Race, Sex and Class Under the Raj* (London: Weidenfeld and Nicholson, 1980). I have spelt out the relationship between Ballhatchet's work and the argument of this essay in my review of it in the *Journal of Commonwealth and Comparative Politics*, 1982, 20(2), 29–30.

12   This latent recognition comes close to being manifest in E.M. Forster, who was himself a homosexual. See his *A Passage to India* (London: Arnold 1967).

13   I have briefly dealt with this in my 'Oppression and Human Liberation: Towards a Third World Utopia', in *The Politics of Awareness: Traditions, Tyranny and Utopias*; see an earlier version in *Alternatives*, 1978/9, 4(2), 165–80. On this theme, see the sensitive writing of Memmi: *The Colonizer and the Colonized*. One of the best examples of the absence or erosion of civilizational mission in the colonizers is the Manchu conquest of China. The small group of conquerors became integrated in Chinese society over one or two generations and what was colonialism quickly became a variant of internal oppression. The more recent Japanese conquest of parts of China, too, failed to produce a theory of civilizational mission, though there were some efforts to do so. It is interesting that one of the main themes in these efforts was the stress on Japan's greater modernization and on her 'responsibility' to modernize other Asian societies. The modern West's contribution to Japanese society has been more wide-ranging than many believe!

The British conquest of India during its first phase showed all the signs of being similarly integrated into Indian society. What probably stopped the integration was mainly the digging of the Suez Canal, which allowed the British to have stronger links with their cultural base than they previously had, and the entry into the Indian scene of British women, which, combined with the Indian caste system and the cultural self-confidence of large parts of Indian society, ensured endogamy.

14   My over-all theoretical understanding of this homology is in 'Reconstructing Childhood: A Critique of the Ideology of Adulthood', in *The Politics of Awareness: Traditions, Tyranny and Utopias*. A briefer version in *Resurgence*, May 1982, and in *The Times of India*, 2, 3 and 4 February 1982. In the context of India, see a discussion of such a relationship in Bruce Mazlish, *James and John Mill: Father and Son in the Nineteenth Century* (New York: Basic Books, 1975), particularly ch. 6, 116–45. For a brief introduction to the over-all picture of the assimilation of new worlds by the West (which set the context for the homology among childhood, primitivism and colonial subjugation to emerge) see Michael T. Ryan, 'Assimilating New Worlds in the Sixteenth and Seventeenth Centuries', *Comparative Studies in Society and History*, 1981, 23(4), 519–38. Ryan mentions 'the tendency to compare – if not confuse – ancients with exotics', as also its relationship with the existing body of demonological theory in Europe.

15   Memmi, in *The Colonizer and the Colonized*, has graphically described the process through which the new entrant is broken into the ruling culture of the colonizer.

16   Karl Marx, 'The British Rule in India' (1853), in Karl Marx and F. Engels, *Articles on Britain* (Moscow: Progress Publishers, 1971), 166–72; see esp. 171–2.

17   These imageries provided the psychological basis of the theory of the Asiatic mode of production. I am grateful to Giri Deshingkar for pointing out to me that the Communist Party of China tried to escape this Marxian double-bind by passing an official resolution in 1927 that China was not an Asiatic society. Such are the pulls of scientific social sciences.

18   That another view of primitivism is possible, more or less within the same framework, is shown by the political use of Freud's concept of the polymorphous perverse infant in a contemporary Marxist, Herbert Marcuse, in *Eros and Civilization* (London: Sphere, 1969). Before him Wilhelm Reich in psychoanalysis, D.H. Lawrence in literature and Salvador Dali in art had explored the creative possibilities *of* primitivism within a meta-Freudian framework.

19   See on this theme, O. Mannoni, 'Psychoanalysis and the Decolonization of Mankind', in J. Miller (ed.), *Freud* (London: Weidenfeld and Nicholson, 1972) 86–95.

20   On the sense of betrayal which British colonialists had because of the 'ungratefulness' of Indians, seen as a cultural feature, see Wurgaft, 'Another Look at Prospero and Caliban'. Wurgaft obviously borrows from O. Mannoni, *Prospero and Caliban: The Psychology of Colonization*, trans. Pamela Powes (New York: Frederick A. Praeger, 1964) 2nd edn.

21   Philippe Aries, *Centuries of Childhood: A Social History of Family Life*, trans. Robert Baldick (New York: Knopf, 1962). For a different point of view, see Lloyd de Mause 'The Evolution of Childhood', in de Mause (ed.), *The History of Childhood* (New York: The Psychohistory Press, 1974) 1–73.

22   Nandy, 'Woman Versus Womanliness'.

23   See Nandy, 'Reconstructing Childhood'.

24   V.G. Kiernan says in the context of Africa in his *The Lords of Human Kind: European Attitudes to the Outside World in the Imperial Age* (Harmondsworth: Penguin, 1972) 243: 'The notion of the African as a minor, endorsed at times even by Livingstone, took very strong hold. Spaniards and Boers had questioned whether natives had souls: modern Europeans cared less about that but doubted whether they had minds, or minds capable of adult growth. A theory came to be fashionable that mental growth in the African ceased early, that childhood was never left behind.'

25   See a brief statement of the problem in its interrelatedness with colonial encounters in my 'The Politics of Life Cycle', *Mazingira*.

26   Albert Schweitzer, *Hindu Thought and its Development* (New York: Beacon, 1959).

27   The examples I shall use will be mainly from Bengal, not merely because the Bengali culture best illustrated – and dramatized – the colonial predicament in India's political, cultural and creative life, but also because it was in Bengal that the Western intrusion was the deepest and the colonial presence the longest.

28   'Meghnadvadh Kavya', 1861, Kshetra Gupta (ed.) *Madhusudan Racanavali*, vols. 1 & 2 (Calcutta: Sahitya Samsad, 1965) 35–117.

PART 4

Imperial cultures as global networks

Chapter 9

Alan Lester

IMPERIAL NETWORKS: CREATING IDENTITIES IN NINETEENTH-CENTURY SOUTH AFRICA AND BRITAIN

A key concept much used in recent 'new imperial history' writing is, as explained in the Introduction, that of the imperial network. If any one scholar can claim to be 'the' pioneer of the idea, it is Alan Lester. In these extracts from his book of that title, which centres on the South African Cape, he explains its global ramifications.

Stephen Howe

I WANT TO SUGGEST THAT BRITISH COLONIAL discourses were made and remade, rather than simply transferred or imposed, through the 'geographies of connection' between Britain and settler colonies such as the Cape in particular.[1] Colonial and metropolitan sites were connected most obviously through material flows of capital, commodities and labour. By the late eighteenth century, British material culture was already located within intensively developed circuits connecting Western Europe, Africa, Asia and South America.[2] As Susan Thorne has pointed out:

> The extraordinary scale of British imperial expansion at the end of the nineteenth century has obscured the magnitude of Britain's colonial involvement at the eighteenth century's turn . . . By 1820, the British Empire had already absorbed almost a quarter of the world's population, most 'of whom were incorporated between the Seven Years War, which began in 1756, and the Napoleonic Wars, which ended in 1815.[3]

The nodal points holding this expanded imperial web and its extra-imperial trading partners together were ports and, the means of transmission between them, ships. Within these ships, Indian calicoes moved to Africa to purchase slaves, Tahitian breadfruit was taken to the Caribbean to feed those slaves, Caribbean molasses was transported to New England where it was made into rum for trade with Native Americans, and tea, coffee, chocolate, tobacco, sugar, rice and potatoes converged, from sites dispersed across the globe, on the British metropole. Although they were incomplete and subject to disjunctures and delay, the construction of such material networks by the early nineteenth century had created 'a new set of relationships which changed what was grown, made and consumed in each part of the world'.[4]

However, colonial and metropolitan sites were articulated discursively as well as materially, and through the same kinds of network infrastructure that serviced a global commerce. While each different site within the imperial network had 'its own possibilities and conditions of knowledge' these differentiated knowledges were connected by the communicative circuits of empire, and could thus be mutually affecting.[5] British ships carried information between colonial sites, in the form of newspapers, dispatches and letters, as well as produce and personnel, enabling far-flung colonies and the metropole to participate 'in a coordinated metasystem of meaning and action'.[6] Reinforced later in the nineteenth century by the telegraph, such technologies allowed representations of indigenous peoples in one part of the world to act as precedents, guiding imageries of subsequently colonised peoples elsewhere.[7] Indeed, as Bayly argues, precisely because of the development of an imperial network, 'the period 1760–1860 was a critical one in the epistemological and economic creation of "indigenous peoples" as a series of comparable categories across the globe'.[8]

While their relative significance oscillated within metropolitan imaginations according to multiple local contingencies, the major components of the early nineteenth-century empire of settlement – India, British North America, the West Indies, the Australian colonies, New Zealand and the Cape – became the most significant locales for the production of such imageries. Images of the empire's racial Others travelled from these colonies during the early nineteenth century in the form of settler newspapers and letters, as well as in official dispatches and travellers' reports. Parliamentary commissions, with their interrogations of colonial and metropolitan witnesses, their minutes of evidence collated from various colonies and their comprehensive reports on matters ranging from slavery to trading transactions and evangelicalism, were a particularly significant mechanism by which news of social relations in these settler colonies arrived at the centre of the empire. From there, the news was frequently disseminated outwards again, via the colonial press, to other colonial sites. The Colonial Office's permanent under-secretary, Herman Merrivale, noted in 1841 that in building an empire of settlement, the British had constructed 'channels of intercommunication' throughout the world.[9]

A number of analysts, both postcolonial and materialist in orientation, have now begun to recover the complex ways in which 'knowledge' traversed these imperial circuits of information, impacting upon both Britain and each of its colonies.[10] Among historians of South Africa in particular, Shula Marks has pointed out that by the nineteenth century 'daily life in [the British Isles] – from diet to industrial discipline, from sexual mores to notions of governance – had been permeated by experiences of empire', generated in the colonies as well as the metropole.[11] As far as governance is concerned, Ann Stoler has shown that a consideration of colonial and metropolitan affairs within the same terms of reference, meant that the very 'inclusions and exclusions built into [metropolitan] . . . notions of citizenship, sovereignty and participation' were influenced by colonial social boundaries.[12] Catherine Hall has also emphasised that continual communication allowed nineteenth-century elites in the British imperial 'centres' and in its 'peripheries' to engage in debate about the proper status and treatment of their respective subordinates. She has thus advocated the recognition of power relations embedded in cultural exchanges that 'criss-crossed the globe'.[13]

I share the 'founding premise' of Stoler and Cooper, that 'social transformations are a product of both global patterns and local struggles'.[14] In particular I highlight the significance that settlers, missionaries and officials on the eastern Cape frontier consciously attached to their participation within British imperial discursive networks. I also indicate some of the ways in which their activities, reinforced by similar activities in other settler colonies, impacted upon metropolitan representations and practices.

Acutely aware that marginalisation from imperial discursive networks could lead to the loss of access to political support and material resources, and that most Britons could only imagine what their colonial environments were like, each of the colonial groups studied in this book strove continually to fashion circuits of communication with vital metropolitan interests, and thus to shape British understandings of the Cape's places and peoples. Furthermore, each colonial interest had a vital stake in maintaining correspondence with other, similar interests elsewhere in the colonial 'peripheries'.

Imperial networks and colonial discourse

The utterances of some of the key personalities who figure in this account – Governors Somerset, D'Urban, Smith and Grey, humanitarian missionary director Philip, and settler spokesman Godlonton, for instance – were situated within systems of thought that traversed a diverse and dynamic, but interconnected imperial terrain. In the 1830s, Philip reproduced a discourse of humanitarian concern that had been constructed through connections with the bourgeois reform movement in Britain, but also with abolitionists in the West Indies and with early utilitarians in India. Somerset had previously considered himself the epitome of an aristocratic governing culture that held colonies and metropole together within an ordered and properly hierarchical system of rule. By virtue of their personal experience in other colonies, their alignments with other imperial officials and their correspondence with the Colonial Office, D'Urban and Smith in turn contributed to, and learned from, reformulated discourses of government incorporating Britain, Australia, New Zealand, India and Canada. And vocal eastern Cape settlers such as Godlonton both communicated with and devised strategy alongside counterparts engaged in the redefinition of Britishness, the material production of commodities and the control of black labourers in the West Indies, New Zealand and Australia.

In the nineteenth century then, the eastern Cape was one among other imperial sites in which contests were being waged over relationships between the propertied and propertyless, whites and blacks, and men and women. It was connected to each of these sites, both materially and discursively. During moments of imperial crisis in particular, colonial representations of the Xhosa were considered in the light of Australian settlers' images of the Aborigine, New Zealand colonists' constructions of the Maori, Indian officials' notions of the 'Hindoo', West Indian planters' portrayals of former slaves and, not least, British bourgeois ideas of the labouring classes and other domestic 'subaltern' groups. As far as most colonial Britons were concerned, this mutual consideration of the empire's subordinated peoples in itself helped generate a collective consciousness of being part of a British diaspora.

In the 1830s, a consideration of metropolitan and colonial conditions within a single frame of reference had held out positive agendas for reform at both kinds of site. The newly ascendant and reforming propertied classes in Britain could conceive of rosy prospects for the inner salvation of slaves and indigenes in the colonies on the one hand, and of the lower classes in Britain on the other. From the mid-nineteenth century, however, the same intersection of colonial and metropolitan concerns created the basis for a more reactionary dominant imperial discourse. The entrenched propertied classes 'at home' now agreed more forcefully with settler capitalists in places such as the Cape that there were certain natural distinctions between social groups, defined by race, class and gender – distinctions that rendered their own political dominance and their own economic privilege a requirement that had to be defended by force if necessary.[15]

Paradoxically, it was the resistance encountered by those pursuing settler and governmental projects in the colonies that consolidated their own particular racial imageries within metropolitan discourses. The mid-nineteenth-century dominance of settler representations was contingent partly upon humanitarianism's internal contradictions, the progressive disillusionment of its colonial proponents, and changes in the nature of bourgeois liberalism in the metropole. But active settler political representations also played their part in reformulating dominant imperial discourse. Through metropolitan intermediaries such as Carlyle and Arnold, settlers pointed out the humanitarians' hypocrisy; they continually publicised their failure to transform the 'character' of indigenous peoples, and they successfully associated resistance to the British civilising mission with resistance to civilisation *per se*.

Settler representations, based on inherent difference rather than universalism, were successful partly because they seemed more robust and coherent within the very terms of humanitarian ontology, itself based, of course, on the notion that European, and especially British, civilisation was civilisation by any definition. The premise of a universal human nature, allowing global assimilation into a Christian brotherhood, was always going to be contradicted within such an ethnocentric framework of assumption, when freed slaves followed other agendas and when indigenous peoples fought tenaciously to preserve their difference. Far from being conceptually undermined by resistance to British power, however, settlers' constructions of irremediable racial difference were strengthened by it. As Catherine Hall writes, for liberals of the mid-nineteenth century, even abolitionism could be seen as 'a dream necessarily unfulfilled, since the full measure of the difference between the races had not been recognised' by its proponents.[16]

If the arguments of this book concerning the operation of imperial networks are to be better substantiated, more research needs to be conducted on the forging of British and other colonial discourses in a variety of imperial locales. First, empirical work is needed on the ways that representations from other colonial peripheries were conveyed and reinterpreted in various media, and refracted through the prisms of class and gender in the metropolis, as well as vice versa. Studies of such interactions across the spaces of empire are required especially for the critical mid-nineteenth century, when colonial settler and metropolitan bourgeois discourses intersected so potently. Only with the proliferation of such empirically grounded studies can Anne McClintock's appealing notion of imperial power emerging 'from a constellation of processes' and 'taking haphazard shape from myriad encounters with alternative forms of authority, knowledge and power', be fleshed out.[17]

The pursuit of such a research agenda also depends upon a more 'grounded' notion of colonial discourse than that which informs many foundational postcolonial texts. Certainly, in the writing of this chapter, I have found it unhelpful to imagine a single, ahistorical and aspatial colonial discourse, regardless of how internally fractured and ambivalent that discourse may be.[18] Rather, I have been led to conceive of multiple, intersecting, and often competing discourses of colonialism.[19] Such a conception, I would argue, allows for accounts of colonialism, and indeed of postcolonialism, that are more politically, spatially and temporally sensitive. It also helps make it possible to avoid some of the more obfuscatory, abstract statements that are often generated by postcolonial critics – statements that have done so much to alienate materially orientated (and other) historians.[20]

Tensions within colonial culture were the outcome of contestation between contingent constellations of colonial and metropolitan interests, each of which was competing to establish the dominance of its own representations, its own particular discourse. These constellations have certainly been conceptualised in theoretical terms, but their contingencies have necessarily been tracked empirically. Furthermore, I have posited that the power of the particular discourses that these constellations of interest generated 'derive[d] not so much from the abstract ideas they represent[ed] as from their material basis in institutions and practices that [made] up the . . . political realm'.[21] Finally, instead of using rather vacuous spatial metaphors such as 'thirdspace', which are currently popular with a number of postcolonial theorists, I have tried in this account to address the 'actual' spaces across which colonial discourses operated.[22]

While one of my main aims has been to generate a more differentiated and spatialised conception of British colonial discourses, however, I hope also to have demonstrated the limits of these discourses. The proponents of various colonial projects may have struggled for a realisable dominance in the shaping of colonial and metropolitan understandings and actions, but as numerous postcolonial and more traditional scholars have emphasised, they were by no means automatically capable of shaping the practices and imaginations of the colonised.[23] The mid-nineteenth-century development of a revised dominant discourse of empire, even one that sanctioned the Xhosa's, among others', dispossession and forceful subjection to a gamut of hegemonically inclined colonial devices, did not necessarily translate into the fulfilment of colonial programmes. The conversion of colonial discourse into material life was always a frustratingly incomplete project.

In common with colonised peoples elsewhere, I hope to have shown that most Xhosa were capable, as Gayan Prakash puts it, of shifting 'the terrain of engagement by occupying and carving out positions placed in between the powerful command of authority and the powerless silence of the victim'.[24] Each and every response, and each and every pro-active measure taken by Xhosa subjects, complicated colonial visions and further inflected colonial discourses. Whether or not they actually fought against British colonialism, collectively the Xhosa ensured that its nature failed to conform to any of the scenarios held out by various colonial interests. After the 1850s, British colonists', missionaries' and officials' endeavours entrapped more Xhosa than ever before in the cultural and discursive webs forged by imperialism, but they never resulted in the total abandonment of those practices and those 'patterns of discourse alive for many centuries' which had circulated in precolonial Xhosaland.[25] Given this resilience, as John Comaroff writes, the colonial state, and indeed I would add British colonialism as a whole, 'was always an aspiration, a work in progress, an intention, a phantasm-to-be-made-real. Rarely was it ever a fully actualised accomplishment.'[26]

Notes

1   T. Keegan, *Colonial South Africa and the Origins of the Racial Order* (London, 1996); Bank, *Liberals and Their Enemies*; C. Crais, *White Supremacy and Black Resistance in Pre-industrial South Africa* (Cambridge, 1992); R. Ross, *Status and Respectability in the Cape Colony, 1750–1870: A Tragedy of Manners* (Cambridge, 1999). The phrasing here is derived from Miles Ogborn's discussion of modernity in his *Spaces of Modernity: London's Geographies, 1680–1780* (New York and London, 1998) 19. For a South African study which takes as its central theme the cultural and political connections between the Cape and Britain, see E. Elbourne, 'To Colonize the Mind: Evangelical Missionaries in Britain and the Eastern Cape, 1790–1837', unpublished DPhil Thesis (University of Oxford, 1991).

2   C.A. Bayly, 'The British and Indigenous Peoples, 1760–1860: Power, Perception and Identity', in M. Daunton and R. Halpern (eds) *Empire and Others: British Encounters with Indigenous Peoples, 1600–1850* (London, 1999) 21. See also H.V. Bowen, 'British Conceptions of Global Empire, 1756–83', *Journal of Imperial and Commonwealth History*, 1998, 26(3), 1–27.

3   S. Thorne, 'The Conversion of Englishmen and the Conversion of the World Inseparable: Missionary Imperialism and the Language of Class In Early Industrial Britain', in F. Cooper and A.L. Stoler, *Tensions of Empire: Colonial Cultures in a Bourgeois World* (Berkeley, 1997) 254.

4   M. Ogborn, 'Historical Geographies of Globalisation, 1500–1800', in B. Graham and C. Nash (eds) *Modern Historical Geographies* (London, 1999) 43. For suggestive comments on the ways in which language, economy, religion and material forms, such as the plantation, also transgressed previously insurmountable spatial boundaries during the eighteenth century, see S. Feierman, 'Africa in History: The End of Universal Narratives', in G. Prakash (ed.) *After Colonialism: Imperial Histories and Postcolonial Predicaments* (Princeton NJ, 1995) 42–3.

5   E. Said, *Culture and Imperialism* (London, 1993) 60.

6   Feierman, 'Africa in History', 53.

7   Thus English representations of Irish and Scots were templates for images of 'savage' and 'wild' Others, even during the earliest period of English colonisation in the Americas; P.D. Morgan, 'Encounters Between British and "Indigenous" Peoples, c. 1500–c. 1800' in Daunton and Halpern, *Empire and Others*, 56–8.

8   C.A. Bayly, 'The British and Indigenous Peoples, 1760–1860: Power, Perception and Identity', in Daunton and Halpern, *Empire and Others*, 21.

9   R. Hyam, *Britain's Imperial Century, 1815–1914: A Study of Empire and Expansion*, 2nd edn (Basingstoke, 1993) 280.

10   Mary Louise Pratt was among the first postcolonial analysts to criticise the tendency 'to see European culture emanating out to the colonial periphery from a self-generating center' – a tendency which 'has obscured the constant movement of people and ideas in the other direction': M.L. Pratt *Imperial Eyes: Travel Writing and Transculturation* (London, 1992) 90.

11   S. Marks, 'History, the Nation and Empire: Sniping From the Periphery', *History Workshop Journal*, 1990, 29, 115.

12   A. Stoler and F. Cooper, 'Between Metropole and Colony: Rethinking a Research Agenda', in Cooper and Stoler, *Tensions of Empire*, 3. See also A.I. Stoler, 'Rethinking Colonial Categories: European Communities and the Boundaries of Rule' in *Comparative Studies in Society and History*, 1989, 1(13), 134–61; *Race and the Education of Desire: Foucault's History of Sexuality and the Colonial Order of Things* (Durham, NC, 1995).

13   C. Hall, 'Histories, Empires and the Post-Colonial Moment', in I. Chambers and I. Curti (eds) *The Post-Colonial Question; Common Skies, Divided Horizon* (London and New York, 1996), 76; C. Hall, *White, Male and Middle Class: Explorations in Feminism and History* (Cambridge, 1992). See also L. Colley, 'Britishness and Otherness: An Argument', *Journal of British Studies*, 1992, 31, 309–29.

14   Stoler and Cooper, 'Between Metropole and Colony', 14. A framework of analysis founded on the notion of an imperial network may help us to transcend some of the debates in which imperial historians have occasionally become bogged down. First, it brings metropole and colony into a single frame. This enables it to overcome what D.K. Fieldhouse has described as the Humpty-Dumpty syndrome in British imperial history – that is, the way in which studies of metropolitan and peripheral experiences have become disarticulated: D.K. Fieldhouse, 'Can Humpty-Dumpty Be Put Back Together Again? Imperial History in the 1980s', *Journal of Imperial and Commonwealth History*, 1984, 12(2), 9–23. See also G. Martin, 'Was There a British Empire?', *Historical Journal*, 1972, xv(3), 562–9. Second, as well as re-articulating the metropolitan and colonial circuits of empire, the concept of an imperial network enables connections between different 'core' and 'peripheral' regions to be envisaged. It thus addresses the central problem for the imperial historian identified by Feierman: 'how to capture all different levels at the same time, how to do justice to the local, the regional, and the international in a single description or a single framework of analysis': Feierman, 'Africa in History', 53. Finally, it suggests, if not a resolution, then at least a side-stepping of the issue of competing models of imperial expansion, such as those of Robinson and Gallagher's 'official mind', or Cain and Hopkins' 'gentlemanly capitalism'. The concept of a network of multiple and 'located' colonial projects, intersecting and colliding contingently through particular circuits of empire, may enable us to avoid the contest between prescriptive models altogether. See R. Robinson and J. Gallagher, *Africa and the Victorians: The Official Mind of Imperialism*, 2nd edn (London, 1981); P. Cain and A.G. Hopkins, *Imperialism: Innovation and Expansion, 1688–1914* (London, 1993). For a discussion of these and other models of imperial history 'that allow insufficient space for peoples that defy national concentration . . . armies that evade defeat . . . entire societies that inhibit the formation of power centres': cited in T. Richards, *The Imperial Archive: Knowledge and the Fantasy of Empire* (London and New York, 1993).

15   See Stoler, *Race and the Education of Desire*, op. cit.

16   C. Hall, 'From Greenland's Icy Mountains . . . to Afric's Golden Sand: Ethnicity, Race and Nation in Mid-Nineteenth-Century England', *Gender and History*, 1993, 5(2), 227.

17   A. McClintock, *Imperial Leather: Race Gender and Sexuality in the Colonial Contest* (London and New York, 1995) 16. For an imperial historian's recent analysis of these 'myriad encounters', which approaches, but does not quite approximate, the concept of an imperial network described here, see J. Darwin, 'Imperialism and the Victorians: The Dynamics of Territorial Expansion', *English Historical Review*, June 1997, 614–42.

18   Homi Bhabha seems to ascribe ambivalence within a singular, if fractured, colonial discourse to the contradictions inherent in a rather universal colonising pysche: H. Bhabha, *The Location of Culture* (London and New York, 1994). But, as Sara Mills has argued, 'in focusing attention on the colonial psyche, we risk ignoring the political and economic bases on which those psyches were constructed': S. Mills, 'Gender and Colonial Space', *Gender, Place and Culture*, 1996, 3(2) 126.

19   In clarifying my own use of the term discourse, I have found it useful to turn to critiques of one of the founding texts of postcolonialism, Edward Said's *Orientalism: Western Conceptions of the Orient* (London, 1995) (originally 1978). Although Said defined what he meant by 'Orientalism' in a number of ways, he actually seems to use the term to describe 'an enormous system or inter-textual network of rules and procedures which regulate anything that may be thought, written or imagined about the Orient': L. Gandhi, *Postcolonial Theory: A Critical Introduction* (Edinburgh, 1998) 76–7. It is this all encompassing use of the concept of discourse which has attracted most criticism from historians (see C.A. Breckenridge and P. van der Veer, 'Orientalism and the Postcolonial Predicament', in C.A. Breckenridge and P. van der Veer (eds) *Orientalism and the Postcolonial Predicament* (Philadelphia, 1993) 5–6, and J. MacKenzie, *Orientalism: History, Theory and the Arts* (Manchester and New York, 1995) esp. xv. However, rather than rejecting Said's overall premise about the power of cultural representation, I would suggest that these critiques highlight the imperative for more

complicated, spatially differentiated and precise uses of the term 'discourse', such as those deployed in F. Cooper and A.L. Stoler (eds) *Tensions of Empire*; J. Duncan, *The City as Text: The Politics of Landscape Interpretation in the Kandyan Kingdom* (Cambridge, 1990) and N. Thomas, *Colonialism's Culture: Anthropology, Travel and Government* (Cambridge, 1994).

20   See D. Kennedy, 'Imperial History and Post-Colonial Theory', *Journal of Imperial and Commonwealth History*, 1996, 24(3), 345–63.

21   T.J. Barnes and J.S. Duncan, 'Introduction' in T.J. Barnes and J.S. Duncan (eds) *Writing Worlds: Discourse, Text and Metaphor in the Representation of Landscape* (London, 1992) 9. Such a conception has the effect of recognising the power of individual agency by assuming that people are capable of appropriating elements of certain discourses and rejecting others.

22   See J. Jacobs, *Edge of Empire: Postcolonialism and the City* (London and New York, 1996) 3–5.

23   See Bhabha, *The Location of Culture*, among others.

24   G. Prakash, 'Introduction: After Colonialism', in Prakash, *After Colonialism*, 9.

25   D. Ludden, 'India's Development Regime', in N.B. Dirks (ed.) *Colonialism and Culture* (Ann Arbor, 1992) 265.

26   J.L. Comaroff, 'Reflections on the Colonial State, in South Africa and Elsewhere: Factions, Fragments, Facts and Fictions', *Social Identities*, 1998, 4(3), 341.

Chapter 10

Carl Bridge and Kent Fedorowich

MAPPING THE BRITISH WORLD

The concept of 'the British World' has been much employed and debated in recent years – though some of that debate has been over how the concept can be defined, and indeed whether it is even useful. Part of its popularity has come from the way it seeks to bring the colonies of British settlement, often neglected in other 'new' imperial and colonial histories, fully back in to the picture. Here an attempt is made to set out what the 'British World' is or was, and what historians are and might be doing with it.

Stephen Howe

Father, Mother, and Me, Sister and Auntie say:
All the people like us are 'We', And every one else is 'They'.
Rudyard Kipling, 'We and They' (1926).[1]

FOR TWO GENERATIONS THE MAJOR THRUST of Imperial Historians has been to develop an understanding of the processes behind the acquisition, administration and exploitation of the non-white empire and its subsequent decolonisation. This is reflected in the balance of the new five-volume *Oxford History of the British Empire*, where the colonies of white settlement are given a supporting rather than a central role.[2] There have been three monumental documentary series over the last 35 years – *The Transfer of Power in India and Burma* and the *British Documents on the End of Empire Project* – but there is none on the changing relations with the old Dominions.[3] Of the 30-odd monographs of the 'Cambridge Commonwealth Series' only a quarter concentrate specifically on the new Britains of Canada, Australia, New Zealand and South Africa, while in the 50-plus volumes of John M. MacKenzie's 'Studies in Imperialism' series only a handful do so. This was not always the case. The nine-volume *Cambridge History of the British Empire*, first conceived in the 1920s, was dedicated overwhelmingly to the 'white' Dominions, as was the now much ignored *Survey of British Commonwealth Affairs* series whose five volumes appeared between 1937 and 1974.[4] Before that, they were the theme of the great nineteenth-century foundation works of imperial history written by Sir Charles Dilke and Sir John Seeley, which were concerned with 'Greater Britain' and the 'Expansion of England'.[5]

The dominant explanatory concepts of the Robinson and Gallagher school – 'informal empire', the 'official mind' and 'collaboration' – are of limited use when applied to the colonies of white settlement, particularly once they had become self-governing Dominions and ultimately constitutional co-equals.[6] Even the useful concepts of 'metropole' and 'periphery', first broached by David Fieldhouse, failed to comprehend adequately the dynamic that there was a multiplicity of metropoles and peripheries in the core British world. Think of the emerging importance of cities such as Melbourne, Auckland and Toronto, which barely rate a mention in his work.[7] Next was the concept of 'gentlemanly capitalism', introduced in 1980 by P.J. Cain and A.G. Hopkins, which had the virtue of acknowledging the importance of the settler colonies. However, it was narrowly elitist in focus and economically deterministic. It also downplayed the crucial human dimension of empire.[8] These were errors to which the once very fashionable Marxist historians of the empire were also prone. In his Ford Lectures of 1974, an older and wiser Gallagher called for a broadening of the analytical field to include domestic, colonial and international dimensions in all their complexity.[9] A similar note was echoed by Fieldhouse 10 years later when he lamented that imperial history was threatened with fragmentation as a result of the popularity of area studies which was driving the discipline into distinct but constricting national and regional foci.[10] Similarly, a more reflective Hopkins has sounded the tocsin warning us that we must look 'back to the future' and re-integrate the imperial dimension into national histories.[11] Recent Saidian social approaches[12] exploiting the notion of the colonial 'other' have virtually nothing to say about the encounters millions of British migrants had with earlier generations of people who were curiously very much like themselves but also quite different. These were James Belich's 'neo-Britons' – those the Toronto *Globe* in 1901 called 'the Britons of Greater Britain'.[13] The gauntlet is being picked up by a wider international community of scholars from various traditions who have convened at two conferences on 'The British World: Diaspora, Culture and Identity' in London and Cape Town in 1998 and 2002, some of the fruits of which are gathered in this volume.[14]

For too long imperial historians have lived in a self-imposed ghetto into which many influences from outside have barely penetrated. On the other hand, for their part British historians have remained too England-centric and have not properly taken up J.G.A. Pocock's 1974 challenge to integrate the rest of the peoples of the home islands and of the British overseas into their accounts.[15] The intense debate sparked by domestic British historians such as Linda Colley on what it is to be 'British'[16] may have caused a wry smile on the faces of Australian and Canadian 'national' historians who have been dealing in the history of identity formation for decades. But it was a wake-up call both to historians of Britain and to historians of the empire. The delineation of Britishness as understood across the old Dominions is a relatively new avenue of enquiry. The adjective 'British', however, seems first to have gained popular currency in eighteenth-century North America where colonists of mixed English, Welsh, Scottish and Irish origin needed a common term to describe their heritage,[17] the central symbol of which was their common allegiance to the British Crown. Despite these straws in the wind, the idea of examining the British Empire as a phenomenon of British migration and mass settlement – as a key element in the development of 'Britishness' – has yet to be properly taken up. In 1999 Pocock could still beseech us to remember that, 'There was a British world, both European and oceanic, in the nineteenth and twentieth centuries: it had a history', which remained to be written.[18]

The writing is now in progress. The British world was a phenomenon of mass migration from the British Isles. Its core was the 'neo-Britains' where migrants found they could transfer into societies with familiar cultural values. As trans-oceanic and trans-continental travel and communications improved, so this world became more intricately inter-connected and self-defining, reaching its apogee in the period from the 1880s to the 1950s. Membership of this world did not preclude, indeed it encouraged, economic competition, political conflict and contested identities, which in turn attempted to forge an overarching consensus. In other words, being British anywhere meant exercising full civil rights within a liberal, pluralistic polity, or at least aspiring to that status. 'Whiteness' was a dominant element. Nevertheless, this world was not exclusively white. People from many ethnic backgrounds (both white and non-white) eagerly adopted British identity and were accepted to varying degrees as part of the British world, within the white Dominions, elsewhere in the empire, and to some extent even outside it. It was characteristic of this complex entity that it contained within itself the means of its own disintegration even as it continued to evolve. Arguably, the commonality of values is still present. Historians of the British world are beginning to map its contours, using among other means, the three key vectors of diaspora, culture and identity. A new, but strangely familiar, face of empire is emerging.

What is needed then, to begin with, is a fresh look at the British 'diaspora', or more accurately in most cases the British 'dispersal', for most migrants were not cast out from Britain but left voluntarily in order to better their lots.[19] This included the Irish. In a stimulating re-examination of Irish migration to the British Empire, Andy Bielenberg argues that the Irish were eager participants in British colonial expansion overseas. For example, between 1630 and 1775 the net migration from Ireland to British North America and the West Indies was an estimated 165,000 souls; 40,000 of whom comprised the largest flow of white migration to the West Indies between the mid-seventeenth and early eighteenth centuries.[20] The re-integration of the Irish into the 'British' imperial project is as interesting as it is controversial, for clearly the Irish were not always passive victims in this colonising process.[21]

With the loss of the 13 American colonies in 1783 and the birth of the second British Empire, migration from the United Kingdom remained crucial in buttressing a scattered and beleaguered British community in what remained of Britain's North American possessions. It is estimated that 22.6 million people left the British Isles between 1815 and 1914. This flood of mostly voluntary British migrants dwarfs the estimated 1.4 million Europeans who migrated to the New World between 1500 and 1783.[22] True, the United States remained the main beneficiary of this flow of settlers from all parts of the British Isles throughout the nineteenth century – estimated at 62 per cent.[23] Nonetheless, there are some interesting trends that demonstrate how important British migration was in reinforcing the sense of Britishness in the colonies of white settlement. Half a million Irish (mostly Protestant) moved to British North America between 1815 and 1845, to be followed by a third of a million more after the Great Famine. In fact, between 1815 and 1865, Irish emigrants outnumbered the combined total of English, Scottish and Welsh arrivals.[24] When New Zealand was opened up to largely English migrants between 1839 and 1850, access to information about the new colony was crucial to prospective emigrants. Eager to make an informed judgement, information flows concerning the availability of land, climatic conditions and job prospects helped to sustain the growing tide of migrants to imperial destinations throughout the nineteenth and twentieth centuries.[25]

Canada remained the favoured destination for British migrants until about 1870. The termination of transportation to the eastern Australian colonies in the 1840s and 1850s helped to reduce some of the negative publicity previously associated with free migration there. Gold strikes in the Antipodes in the 1850s and 1860s were a huge positive stimulus to increased voluntary migration. But it was the opening of the Suez Canal in 1869, combined with bigger steam-propelled ships, which shortened journey times and allowed these far-flung communities to compete for more British migrants. These changes, coupled with aggressive state-subsidised migration programmes sponsored particularly by New Zealand, Queensland and South Australia in the 1870s and 1880s, gave an increasing number of adventurous Britons from the home islands the opportunity to migrate further afield but yet remain within the British world. Emboldened by self-government and growing in political and economic confidence, Australia, Canada and New Zealand at the turn of the twentieth century were more assertive in attracting growing numbers from Britain's 'surplus' population. For the decade 1900 to 1909, an estimated 1,670,198 migrants left Britain. In 1913 alone, the staggering number of 389,394 British migrants headed overseas, an increasing proportion for destinations within the British Empire.[26]

These trends, which continued after 1918 and were strengthened by the Empire Settlement Act of 1922, saw 1,811,553 Britons migrate overseas during the decade 1920–1929. The 'constructive' imperialism in the 1920s, the bedrock of which was a state-assisted migration policy involving Britain and three of its Dominions (the exception was South Africa), confounds the myth that it was only the introduction of strict immigration quotas by the United States that made the Dominions more attractive to British migrants. As Stephen Constantine has so ably demonstrated, there were more explicit reasons for the material rise in the proportions choosing imperial destinations, 'a lift from barely one-third in the later nineteenth century to around four-fifths' by 1949.[27] Between 1946 and 1963 this proportion rose to five-sixths and some 1,034,000 migrated to the old Dominions.[28] Thus the British 'diaspora' or 'dispersal' focused primarily on the United States prior to 1900, but then shifted ever more decisively to the 'white' Dominions providing the foundation of a 'Third British Empire' as the twentieth century progressed.

In the neo-Britains these migrants helped to construct a wider British identity and culture – a broader Britishness some of which was exported back 'Home'. Examples can be found readily in political culture. Peter Marshall has called for a study of the ideas about the ordering of society, which were developed in the empire and beamed back to Britain, to complement existing work on the projection *of* political and administrative models onto the empire.[29] Nowadays forgotten or never known, these were in fact many and significant. In the 1840s, Canada, not Britain, was first to define responsible government. By the 1850s, five of the six Australian colonies had developed the secret ballot, more than 10 years before it was introduced in the United Kingdom. In 1893, New Zealand women were the first in the empire to gain the vote, a generation before their sisters in Britain. The schools in the Australian colony of Victoria were 'secular, compulsory and free' well before their counterparts back home. Universal manhood suffrage was established in Australia and New Zealand 50 years before it was in the United Kingdom.

These new Britannias, or better Britains, had no established church, they controlled migration and wage policies, resorted to state intervention for the provision of utilities, and adopted simplified land title arrangements. The colonies of settlement often put into practice what the reformers in Britain itself merely talked about. Even imperial preferences (the Fielding Tariff of 1897) and Empire Day (1899) were Canadian innovations. Many of the central principles of modern British democracy were experimented with in the colonies of settlement and shipped back to the United Kingdom. The 'unofficial mind' of the British Canadians, British Australians and British New Zealanders was what counted in this process, not the thinking of increasingly marginalised British officials. As a result, the 'rights of freeborn Englishmen' attained higher levels of democratic development in the neoBritains than in their country of origin.

The rise of colonial national identities did not contradict or undermine imperial Britishness. One person might have a number of concurrent identities. Just as in Britain one could be a Liverpudlian, Lancastrian, Englishman and Briton, so in New Zealand one might be an Aucklander, North Islander, New Zealander and Briton.[30] Beyond the core of the ethnic British diaspora there was the possibility of adopted Britishness. For instance, Aboriginal peoples, Afrikaners, French Canadians, Jews, Cape Coloureds, Hong Kong and Singapore Chinese, and West Indians all laid claim to British values and institutions.[31] Some did so with unseemly haste, such as the Transvaal lawyers Daniel Oosthuizen and A.L. Reitz, who described themselves as 'British' in the roll of the Southern Mounted Rifles as early as 1911.[32] Even those who contested the established order, such as Irish Catholics, did so using British means and methods: trade unions, law courts, free press and speech, and the political process.[33] In principle, the system was colour and class blind, and often, though by no means always, it was in practice. For instance, Australia's first native-born governor-general, Sir Isaac Isaacs (1931–1936), was a Jew, as was its first Army commander in the Great War, Sir John Monash. The great exception, of course, was the restriction of non-white immigration into the Dominions by such means as language or dictation tests (the 'Natal formula'), quotas, capitation taxes, and health and sanitation regulations.[34]

The cultural glue which held together this British world consisted not only of sentiment and shared institutional values but also of a plethora of networks. These ranged from the obvious family and community connections to business, religious, educational, scientific and professional associations, to trades unions, and to itinerant workers of all kinds: transported convicts, miners, seamen, indentured labourers, domestic servants, travelling players, soldiers and administrators. The extent and influence of these networks – globalisation from below, or at least from lower down than the commanding heights – has barely been explored let alone mapped.[35] A promising start has been made, however, with humanitarian and administrative networks between the 1820s and 1840s;[36] with scientists in South Africa in the early twentieth century;[37] with elements of the professional middle class such as engineers, civil servants and accountants;[38] with philanthropic agencies, such as the Red Cross;[39] and with women's organisations such as the Victoria League, the Guild of Loyal Women of South Africa, and the Canadian Imperial Order Daughters of the Empire.[40] Press barons, railway and shipping magnates, captains of industry – 'ungentlemanly capitalists' to a man, such as the Canadians, Sir Samuel Cunard and Lord Beaverbrook, and the Australian Essington Lewis (chairman of Broken Hill Proprietary) – were local Rhodeses born in the empire. They made careers which to one extent or another spanned it and depended on it. No 'prefabricated' white colonist 'collaborators' these, they were principal participants in the British world. Robinsonian collaboration is irrelevant not only for the Rhodeses, but also for almost everybody else in the British world. Collaboration is about 'us' and 'them', but the British world was emphatically about 'we'.

We need to understand what our generation sees as a paradox, that this British world was bound more tightly together even as it threatened to come apart. Steam navigation, rail and eventually air travel made connections easier.[41] Trans-oceanic cables, overland telegraph and then telephone and wireless technology rendered communications more efficient.[42] The empire of the airwaves brought London ever closer as an imperial metropole and, if only occasionally, brought overseas imperial cities (in themselves regional metropoles) closer to London.[43] The potential strength inherent in these connections was not lost on Lord Burnham, owner of the London *Daily Telegraph*, when he declared in 1920 that 'The British world is a world of its own, and it is a world of many homes.'[44]

The crises of war and depression brought the British world together even as they sowed the seeds of its eventual unravelling. There is more than a little truth in G.K. Chesterton's observation that the countries of the empire (by which he meant essentially the Dominions) were like passengers on a London omnibus. They did not talk to each other unless there was an accident (such as the Great War) but then they pulled together in the common cause.[45] At the beginning of the twentieth century, in a dress rehearsal for what was to come, Australia, Canada and New Zealand raised 31,500 men for the imperial forces fighting the Boers in South Africa.[46] In the First World War the old Dominions provided 1.3 million troops and India 953,000 to Britain's 6.1 million; in the second, the respective figures were 2.5 million, 2 million and about 6 million. Moreover, it is insufficiently realised that in the Second World War the British Commonwealth had more men in the fighting line than the Americans at all stages before the summer of 1944. Further, Britain would have starved but for the great dominion granaries in both wars.[47] The significance of the British world's contribution is indisputable, but in what ways it variously contributed and on what terms would reward further research. Also what should we make of the remark made by a 'prominent American' with regard to the old Commonwealth family members that 'they all write home to mother often enough, but not to one another'.[48] To answer these questions we need to know much more about the networks that bound together the British world beyond the mother country.

It is important to understand that though there is, and was, much overlap between them, the British world is a broader and more fluid concept than the British Empire or British Commonwealth, and that it casts a longer shadow. Britishness outside Britain persists well beyond the demise of the British Empire. Also, Charles Dilke, Winston Churchill and others included the United States in their Greater Britain (or English-speaking union of peoples) and certainly, in terms of shared values and aims, the Americans at some crucial or convenient junctures have identified themselves as honorary 'Britons', as in the two world wars.[49] Other places not painted red on the map had their British communities, most noticeably in South America, but also in places such as Shanghai.[50] The British world was a consensual association that included much of the formal and informal empire. The much more familiar empire of compulsion and subordination had limited relevance in this context.

Co-operation, equality and autonomy rather than coercion became the watchwords in Anglo-Dominion relations after 1918. Granted, some Dominions pursued these goals and asserted their claims with greater alacrity than others. Canada, South Africa and the Irish Free State, the fifth and newest Dominion (created in December 1921), were quicker off the mark than their seemingly more contented Antipodean cousins.[51] Despite resistance from some of the more reactionary sections of the British political establishment (such as Lord Curzon who tried unsuccessfully to orchestrate a common imperial foreign policy) these elements were forced begrudgingly to accept the Dominions' quest for full nationhood. Still, at exactly this time, as John Darwin has correctly argued, the concept emerged of a new world-system – a Third British Empire – which focused almost exclusively on Britain's relations with its 'old' Dominions. This also involved a parallel awakening of a 'Britannic' identity, which proved increasingly attractive to a growing number of politicians across the empire. Although the Dominion Idea was shaken by the Great War and Great Depression, Darwin posits that during the inter-war period there was 'a shared belief among British communities around the world in the supreme attractiveness of their institutions, ethos, literary culture, and forms of civility [which] remained extraordinarily pervasive'.[52] The balance of the British world was, however, shifting.

The changing relative importance of the various metropoles can be assessed roughly by looking at when the British world's population and economy beyond Britain came to be of any significance relative to Britain's own. The combined population of the 'old' Dominions was a quarter of Britain's in 1901, just under half in 1931 and just under four-fifths in 1961; while their combined GDP was less than half Britain's in 1901, approaching two-thirds in 1931 and nearing parity in 1961.[53] In the councils of Empire Commonwealth, Britain was the first amongst an increasingly powerful and restless set of equals.

A symptom of this growing strength was the undermining of a previously self-confident 'Britannic' identity. This can be demonstrated by examining the collapse of the concept of imperial citizenship. For generations, Australians, Canadians, New Zealanders and (some) South Africans saw no need to define a separate citizenship. They had always been British subjects by definition. In 1935 the Irish Free State was the first Dominion to assert and define its own citizenship when it passed the Irish Nationality and Citizenship Act which classified all non-Irish subjects, including British, as aliens. This was seen as an anomaly within the newly emerging Commonwealth and Whitehall seemingly paid little attention to this petulant piece of legislation. The legal doctrine of the 'indivisibility of subjecthood' remained intact.[54] The real revolution began in 1946 when Canada introduced its own Citizenship Act, under which Canadians remained British subjects but only by dint of being Canadian citizens first. 'Indivisibility of subjecthood', which had long helped to underpin the British world, was now irrevocably severed. Australia, New Zealand and South Africa followed suit in 1948/49.[55] London's response was the British Nationality Act of 1948 that introduced a complex formula involving six categories of citizenship. This Act was not, as some have argued, a deliberate attempt to 'racialise' future British immigration policy; rather, it was meant to maintain the essence of the pre-1946 arrangements, including the right of all British subjects to enter Britain. In other words, it kept the door open for subsequent waves of non-white migration into Britain in the 1950s.[56] Conversely, long-standing restrictions on non-white migration into Canada, Australia and New Zealand were liberalised in the 1960s. South Africa was another story.

Another indication of the undermining was the rapid turnaround in the connotations of the term 'British' in official discourse. In 1939 Australia's Prime Minister, R.G. Menzies, spoke of the 'entire British world' standing up to Nazi Germany, and his successors John Curtin and Ben Chifley habitually used the odd but telling phrase, 'the British-speaking race'.[57] However, there was no doubting that the Dominions were in this war on their own terms and for their own reasons. Vincent Harlow, the Rhodes Professor of Imperial

History in the University of London, who had been seconded to the Ministry of Information, warned the BBC against broadcasting that the Dominions were fighting to defend the mother country as 'they look upon the war as their concern as much as ours'. During the war the BBC ruled that for broadcasting purposes the term 'British troops' cover[ed] troops from all parts of the Empire' and that when referring solely to troops from the home islands the correct term was 'United Kingdom troops', though this clumsy usage never really took hold.[58] Twenty years later, in June 1961, British Prime Minister Harold Macmillan instructed the civil service in the United Kingdom to replace the term 'United Kingdom Government' in official papers with the term 'British Government'. He argued that 'British' was no longer an appropriate adjective to use to describe Canadians, Australians and other erstwhile overseas Britons.[59]

The term dominion fell out of official use in 1949, though it persisted in popular parlance for some years.[60] The process of de-dominionisation – not to be confused with independent behaviour – was in most cases a more drawn out affair.[61] Legal and symbolic ties were eroded over several decades. The exceptions were Ireland and South Africa, which left the Commonwealth in 1948 and 1961, respectively. Canada abolished Privy Council appeals in 1949. Australia began the process in 1968 and concluded it in 1986. New Zealand has only announced the intention to do so. In 1952, Canada styled the monarch the Queen of Canada. Twenty-one years later, Elizabeth II was styled Queen of Australia. In 1965, the senior Dominion replaced its old flag, the union jack, with a new one featuring a maple leaf. It patriated its constitution in 1982. Imperial honours were abandoned in Australia in 1975 and in New Zealand in 1996; Canada had done it in the 1920s. Australia's High Court finally pronounced that Britain was legally a 'foreign' country in 1999! Nonetheless, the Crown remains a central part of the constitutions of Australia, Canada and New Zealand.[62]

Menzies, in his final years as Australia's prime minister, and a proud 'old Commonwealth' man, regretted the birth of the new Commonwealth in the early 1960s. He saw only a 'cluster of republics' which were 'more spiritually akin to Moscow than to London'. For Menzies, the end of the 'Crown Commonwealth' (those countries which acknowledged the British monarch as their head of state) finished the 'intimate association' which had prevailed before 1948 and still clung on until the matter was finalised by South Africa's leaving in 1961. Thereafter the new Commonwealth became, in Menzies' words, 'much looser' than the old, an 'association' which 'for most of its members' was now only 'functional and occasional'. This old 'intimate association' was not merely sentimental. Wayne Reynolds has shown recently that the old firm of Australia, Canada, South Africa and New Zealand co-operated closely to help Britain develop a Commonwealth atomic bomb in the early 1950s. The Suez crisis of 1956 and its aftermath, however, meant that this 'Fourth British Empire' fell to pieces almost as soon as it was started. Thereafter, to use Robert Holland's term, Britain sought its 'nuclear apotheosis' by other, non-Commonwealth means. And the Commonwealth, under its new secretariat from 1965, in David McIntyre's term, 'de-Britannicized'.[63]

The British world was a term its inhabitants used to describe their real and imagined common origins, culture and identity. Its maximum strength was reached in the generation prior to the Great War and was probably sustained until the 1950s. Its civic and governmental institutions were moulded in the long nineteenth century and successfully defended in two world wars. It was held together not just by ties of trade, finance and defence, but also by intricate and overlapping networks and associations of all kinds –

family, occupational, professional, educational, religious and sporting to name a few. More-over, many of these are still with us today. Scholarly constructions of empire have had little if nothing to say about this British world over the last 50 years and we are only now beginning to turn our attention to its character and dynamics. Blinded by national historiographies and mesmerised by the exotic colonial 'other' we have lost contact with what was always the heart of the imperial enterprise, the expansion of Britain and the peopling and building of the trans-oceanic British world. It is time we reacquainted ourselves with what was once considered both vitally important and self-evident.

Notes

1   *Rudyard Kipling's Verse: Inclusive Edition, 1885–1932*, 4th edn (London, 1937), 743–4. This poem was first published by Kipling in his *Debits and Credits* (London, 1926).

2   For a critique see Phillip Buckner, 'Was there a "British" Empire? *The Oxford History of the British Empire* from a Canadian Perspective', *Acadiensis*, 2002, 32, 110–28. A similar line of argument is explored by Andrew Thompson, 'Is Humpty Dumpty Together Again?', *Twentieth Century British History*, 2001, 12, 9–23. Also see Dane Kennedy's explication, 'The Boundaries of Oxford's Empire', *International History Review*, 2001, 23, 604–22. Other reviews include D.A. Low, 'Rule Britannia. Subjects and Empire. The Oxford History of the British Empire', *Modern Asian Studies*, 2002, 36, 491–503.

3   One partial exception is Frederick Madden (ed.), *Select Documents on the Constitutional History of the British Empire and Commonwealth*, vols 4 and 6 (Westport, CT, 1990 and 1993).

4   Volume one of *The Cambridge History of the British Empire* was published in 1929 with most of the subsequent volumes appearing in the 1930s. The exceptions were vols 2 and 3, which were published in 1940 and 1959, respectively. The first two volumes of the five-volume *Survey of British Commonwealth Affairs*, published in 1937 and 1942, respectively, were written by W.K. Hancock and dealt with the inter-war period, especially problems of nationality (vol. 1) and the economy (vol. 2). Vols 3 and 4 were written by Nicholas Mansergh and appeared in 1952 and 1958, respectively. They focused on problems of external policy in the 1930s and on wartime co-operation and postwar change (1939–1952). The final volume (vol. 5) was written by J.D.B. Miller and appeared in 1974. Its remit was decolonisation and the emerging Commonwealth between 1953 and 1969.

5   Sir Charles W. Dilke, *Greater Britain: A Record of Travel in English-Speaking Countries during 1866 and* 1867, 2 vols (London, 1868); Sir John R. Seeley, *The Expansion of England* (London, 1883).

6   Ronald Robinson and John Gallagher with Alice Denny, *Africa and the Victorians* (London, 1961); and Ronald Robinson, 'Non-European Foundations of European Imperialism: Sketch for a Theory of Collaboration', in Roger Owen and Bob Sutcliffe (eds), *Studies in the Theory of Imperialism* (London, 1972) 117–42.

7   David Fieldhouse, *Economics and Empire 1830–1914* (London, 1974).

8   P.I. Cain and A.G. Hopkins, *British Imperialism*, vol. 1 *Innovation and Expansion, 1688–1914* (London, 1993); vol. 2 *Crisis and Deconstruction, 1914–1990* (London, 1993). See also Raymond E. Dummett (ed.), *Gentlemanly Capitalism and British Imperialism* (London, 1999).

9   J. Gallagher, *The Decline, Revival and Fall of the British Empire: The Ford Lectures and other Essays* (Cambridge, 1982). Since then, several imperial historians have accepted the challenge. Two of the best examples are John Darwin, 'Imperialism and the Victorians: The Dynamics of Territorial Expansion', *English Historical Review*, 1997, 112, 614–42; and Andrew S. Thompson, *Imperial Britain: The Empire in British Politics c. 1880–1932* (London, 2000).

10   David Fieldhouse, 'Can Humpty-Dumpty Be Put Together Again? Imperial History in the 1980s', *Journal of Imperial and Commonwealth History*, 1984, 12, 9–23.

11   A.G. Hopkins, 'Back to the Future: From National History to Imperial History', *Past & Present*, 1999, 164, 198–243.

12   Edward W. Said, *Orientalism* (New York, 1978); and, for example, Martin Daunton and Rick Halpern (eds), *Empire and Others: British Encounters with Indigenous Peoples, 1600–1850* (London, 1999); Catherine Hall, *Civilising Subjects* (Cambridge, 2002) and Lynette Russell (ed.), *Colonial Frontiers: Indigenous-European Encounters in Settler Societies* (Manchester, 2001). David Cannadine, *Ornamentalism: How the British Saw their Empire* (London, 2000) promises much and adds little to the debate. An exception in the growing literature on the colonial 'other' is the stimulating work assembled by Frederick Cooper and Ann Laura Stoler (eds), *Colonial Cultures in a Bourgeois World. Between Nation and Colony: Rethinking a Research Agenda* (Berkeley, 1997).

13   James Belich, 'Neo-Britains', paper delivered to the conference on 'The British World: Diaspora, Culture and Identity', Institute of Commonwealth Studies (London, June 1998). He has recently developed this theme in his two-volume history of New Zealand, *Making Peoples. A History of the New Zealanders. From Polynesian Settlement to the End of the Nineteenth Century* (Auckland, 1996) and *Paradise Reforged: A History of the New Zealanders: From the 1880s to the Year 2000* (Auckland, 2001) by which time 'neo-Britains' had become 'better Britains'. Toronto *Globe*, 25 September 1901, cited in Phillip Buckner's chapter below. J.G.A. Pocock coined the phrase 'neo-Britains' in his 'British History: A Plea for a New Subject', *New Zealand Journal of History*, 1974, 8, 3–21.

14   Stuart Ward, 'The British World', *Australian Historical Association Bulletin*, June 2002, 94, 30–3; P.A. Buckner and Carl Bridge, 'Reinventing the British World', *Round Table*, 2002, 92, 77–88.

15   Pocock, 'British History'. Also see the revised version and debate in the *Journal of Modern History*, 1975, 47, 601–28.

16   Linda Colley, 'Britishness and Otherness: An Argument', *Journal of British Studies*, 1992, 31, 309–29; idem, *Britons: Forging the Nation, 1707–1837* (New Haven and London, 1992). For a critique of Colley's thesis, see J.C.D. Clark, 'Protestantism, Nationalism, and National Identity, 1660–1832', *Historical Journal*, 2002, 43, 249–76. Postcolonialists and political scientists have been busy defining 'Britishness' as well. See Bill Schwarz (ed.) *The Expansion of England: Race, Ethnicity and Cultural History* (London, 1996); Keith Robbins, *Great Britain: Identities, Institutions and the Idea of Britishness* (London, 1998); David McCrone, 'Unmasking Britannia: The Rise and Fall of British National Identity', *Nations and Nationalism*, 1997, 3, 579–96; Rebecca Langlands, 'Britishness or Englishness? The Historical Problem of National Identity in Britain', *Nations and Nationalism*, 1999, 5, 53–69; Ben Wellings, 'Empire-Nation: National and Imperial Discourses in England', *Nations and Nationalism*, 2002, 8, 95–109.

17   Nicholas Canny, 'The Origins of Empire: An Introduction', *Oxford History of the British Empire*, vol. 1, *The Origins of Empire* (London, 1998) 24–5.

18   J.G.A. Pocock, 'The New British History in Atlantic Perspective: An Antipodean Commentary', *American Historical Review*, 1999, 104, 490–500. Pocock's article was one of five in the AHR forum and was written largely in response to David Armitage's, 'Greater Britain: A Useful Category of Historical Analysis?', ibid., 427–45.

19   See the essay by Stephen Constantine, 'British Emigration to the Empire Commonwealth since 1880: From Overseas Settlement to Diaspora?' in Bridge and Fedorowich, *The British World*. See also Robin Cohen, *Global Diasporas: An Introduction* (London, 1997).

20   Andy Bielenberg, 'Irish Emigration to the British Empire, 1700–1914', in Andy Bielenberg (ed.), *The Irish Diaspora* (London, 2000) 215–16.

21   Hiram Morgan, 'An Unwelcome Heritage: Ireland's Role in British Empire-Building', *History of European Ideas*, 1994, 19, 619–25; Keith Jeffery (ed.), *An Irish Empire? Aspects of Ireland and the British Empire* (Manchester, 1996); C.A. Bayly, 'Ireland, India, and the Empire, 1780–1914', *Transactions of the Royal Historical Society*, 6th series, 2000, 10, 377–97; and Donald H. Akenson, *If the Irish Ran the World: Montserrat, 1630–1730* (Liverpool, 1997).

22   Marjory Harper, 'British Migration and the Peopling of the Empire', in Andrew Porter
      (ed.) *The Oxford History of the British Empire*, vol. 3, *The Nineteenth Century* (Oxford, 1999),
      75. The latter figure is cited in Phillip Buckner, 'Whatever Happened to the British Empire?',
      Journal of the Canadian Historical Association, 1993, 4, 14.

23   Buckner, 'Whatever Happened', 17; Bielenberg, *Irish Diaspora*, 224.

24   Bielenberg, *Irish Diaspora*, 218–20.

25   Paul Hudson, 'English Emigration to New Zealand, 1839–1850: Information Diffusion and
      Marketing a New World', *Economic History Review*, 2001, 54, 680–98. Our thanks to Andrew
      Thompson for this reference. For other examples of how important the diffusion of
      information was to the migration process after 1914, see Marjory Harper, *Emigration from
      Scotland between the Wars: Opportunity or Exile?* (Manchester, 1998); Michael Roe, *Australia,
      Britain and Migration, 1915–1940* (Cambridge, 1995).

26   Stephen Constantine, 'Introduction: Empire Migration and Imperial Harmony', in S.
      Constantine (ed.), *Emigrants and Empire: British Settlement in the Empire between the Wars*
      (Manchester, 1990) 2; and *idem*, 'Migrants and Settlers', in Judith M. Brown and Wm.
      Roger Louis (eds), *The Oxford History of the British Empire*, vol. IV *The Twentieth Century* (Oxford,
      1999) 165–6.

27   Constantine, 'Migrants and Settlers', 166–7.

28   B.R. Mitchell, *British Historical Statistics* (Cambridge, 1988) 83.

29   P.J. Marshall, 'Empire and Authority in the later Eighteenth Century', *Journal of Imperial
      and Commonwealth History*, 1987, 15, 105–22. See also C.A. Bayly, 'Returning the
      British to South Asian History: The Limits of Colonial Hegemony', *South Asia*, 1994, 17,
      1–25.

30   For South African constructions of multiple identities, see Saul Dubow, 'Colonial Nationalism,
      the Milner Kindergarten and the Rise of "South Africanism", 1902–1910', *History Workshop
      Journal*, 1997, 43, 53–85; *idem*, 'Imagining the New South Africa in the Era of
      Reconstruction', in David Omissi and Andrew Thompson (eds) *The Impact of the South African
      War* (Basingstoke, 2002), 76–98. Also see Miles Fairburn, *The Ideal Society and its Enemies:
      The Foundation of Modern New Zealand Society, 1850–1900* (Auckland, 1989).

31   For examples of non-white loyalty to British values, see Bill Nasson, *Abraham Esau's War: A
      Black South African at War in the Cape, 1899–1902* (Cambridge, 1991); and, for a West Indian
      example, Anne Spry Rush, 'Imperial Identity in Colonial Minds: Harold Moody and the
      League of Coloured Peoples, 1931–50', *Twentieth Century British History*, 2002, 13, 356–83.

32   See Ian van der Waag's chapter, Bridge and Fedorowich, *The British World*.

33   Mark C. McGowan, *The Waning of the Green: Catholics, the Irish, and Identity in Toronto,
      1887–1922* (Montreal and Kingston, 1999).

34   Robert A. Huttenback, *Racism and Empire: White Settlers and Colored Immigrants in the British
      Self-Governing Colonies, 1830–1910* (Ithaca, NY, 1976).

35   Stephen Constantine makes some tantalising observations about labour markets and the export
      of skilled labour in 'Migrants and Setters', 170–2, which is expanded, in part, in his chapter
      below. So, too, does Jonathan Hyslop about white trade unionism in the British Empire.
      See Jonathan Hyslop, 'The Imperial Working Class Makes Itself "White": White Labourism
      in Britain, Australia and South Africa before the First World War', *Journal of Historical
      Sociology*, 1999, 12, 398–421. Also see Logie Barrow, 'White Solidarity in 1914', in Raphael
      Samuel (ed.) *Patriotism: The Making and Unmaking of the British National Identity*, vol. I *History
      and Politics* (London, 1989) 275–87.

36   Alan Lester, *Imperial Networks: Creating Identities in Nineteenth-Century South Africa and Britain*
      (London, 2001) and idem, 'British Settler Discourse and the Circuits of Empire', *History
      Workshop Journal*, 2002, 27–48. See also Zoe Laidlaw, 'Networks, Patronage and Information
      in Colonial Governance: Britain, New South Wales and the Cape, 1826–1843', DPhil thesis
      (Oxford, 2001).

37   Saul Dubow, 'The Commonwealth of Science: The British Association in South Africa,
      1905–1929', in S. Dubow (ed.) *Science and Society in Southern Africa* (Manchester, 2000).

38   Andrew S. Thompson, *The Empire Strikes Back: Imperialism's Impact on Britain from the Mid-Nineteenth Century to the Present Day* (Longman, 2007), ch. 1 entitled, 'The Empire and British Elites'. We would like to thank the author for showing us his work in progress on this intriguing subject.

39   E.g. Melanie Oppenheimer, 'The Best P.M. for the Empire in War?: Lady Helen Munro Ferguson and the Australian Red Cross Society', *Australian Historical Studies*, 2002, 33, 108–24.

40   Eliza Reidi, 'Women, Gender, and the Promotion of Empire: The Victoria League, 1901–1914', *Historical Journal*, 2002, 45, 569–99; Elizabeth van Heyningen and Pat Merrett, 'The Healing Touch: The Guild of Loyal Women of South Africa 1900–1912', unpublished paper (2002); Katie Pickles, *Female Imperialism and National Identity: Imperial Order Daughters of the Empire* (Manchester, 2002). Also see Julia Bush, *Edwardian Ladies and Imperial Power* (London, 2000); Angela Woollacott, *To Try Her Fortune in London: Australian Women, Colonialism, and Modernity* (Oxford, 2001); and Lisa Chilton's chapter below.

41   There is a plethora of company histories but a relative dearth of studies of whole imperial networks. See, however, Gordon Pirie, *Aviation and Empire* (Manchester, forthcoming), Meredith Hooper, *Kangaroo Route* (Sydney, 1985); and David MacKenzie, *Canada and International Civil Aviation, 1932–48* (Toronto, 1989).

42   On cables, see Robert W.D. Boyce, 'Imperial Dreams and National Realities: Britain, Canada and the Struggle for a Pacific Telegraph Cable, 1879–1902', *English Historical Review*, 2000, 115, 39–70; idem, 'Canada and the Pacific Cable Controversy, 1923–8: Forgotten Source of Imperial Alienation', *Journal of Imperial and Commonwealth History*, 1998, 26, 72–92.

43   K.S. Inglis, 'London Calling: The Empire of the Air Waves', *Working Papers in Australian Studies*, no. 118, was a keynote address at the first British World Conference at the Institute of Commonwealth Studies (London, 1998).

44   Cited in Simon Potter's chapter below.

45   Quotation cited in R.G. Casey, *Double or Quit* (Melbourne, 1949) 104.

46   Ian McGibbon, *The Path to Gallipoli: Defending New Zealand, 1840–1915* (Wellington, 1991) 106–24; Carman Miller, *Painting the Map Red: Canada and the South African War, 1899–1902* (Montreal and Kingston, 1993); and Craig Wilcox, *Australia's Boer War: The War in South Africa 1899–1902* (Melbourne, 2002).

47   Jeffrey Grey, *A Military History of Australia* (Melbourne, 1999) 116; Central Statistics Office, *Fighting with Figures: A Statistical Digest of the Second World War* (London, 1995); F.W. Perry, *The Commonwealth Armies: Manpower and Organisation in Two World Wars* (Manchester, 1988); David Dilks, *Great Britain, the Commonwealth and the Wider World, 1939–45* (Hull, 1998); Avner Offer, *The First World War: An Agrarian Interpretation* (Oxford, 1989).

48   Cited in R.G. Casey, *Friends and Neighbors* (East Lansing, MI, 1955) 16.

49   Bradford Perkins, *The Great Rapprochement* (London, 1969); David Dimbleby and David Reynolds, *An Ocean Apart* (London, 1988); David Lowe, 'Percy Spender and the American Century', *The Trevor Reese Memorial Lecture 2002* (London, 2002) 31–3.

50   Robert Bickers, 'Shanghailanders: The Formation and Identity of the British Settler Community in Shanghai 1843–1937', *Past & Present*, 1998, 159, 161–211.

51   For a recent examination of the Australian case, see Carl Bridge and Bernard Attard (eds), *Between Empire and Nation: Australia's External Relations from Federation to the Second World War* (Melbourne, 2000). For the Irish case, see Donal Lowry, 'New Ireland, Old Empire and the Outside World, 1922–49: The Strange Evolution of a "Dictionary Republic"', in John M. Regan and Mike Cronin (eds) *Ireland: The Politics of Independence, 1922–49* (London, 2000) 164–216.

52   John Darwin, 'A Third British Empire? The Dominion Idea in Imperial Politics', in Brown and Louis (eds), *The Oxford History of the British Empire*, vol. 4, 64–87, esp. 85–6.

53   Calculated from relevant tables in Mitchell, *British Historical Statistics*, and in B.R. Mitchell, *International Historical Statistics: Africa and Asia* (London, 1982); and idem, *The Americas and Australasia* (London, 1983).

54   Randall Hansen, *Citizenship and Immigration in Postwar Britain: The Institutional Origins of a Multicultural Nation* (Oxford, 2000) 40.

55   ibid., 41; Nicholas Mansergh, *Survey of British Commonwealth Affairs: Problems of Wartime Co-operation and Post-War Change 1939–1952* (Oxford, 1958) 382–7.

56   Hansen, *Citizenship*, 53. Hansen refutes Paul's and Spencer's notion that the 1948 Act was the beginning of the racialisation of British immigration policy. He shows that it was not until 1962 with the introduction of the Commonwealth Immigrants Act, which introduced limited entry, that racialisation truly began. Hansen, *Citizenship*, chs 2–4; Kathleen Paul, *Whitewashing Britain: Race and Citizenship in the Post-War Era* (Ithaca NY, 1997); Ian R.G. Spencer, *British Immigration Policy since 1939: The Making of Multicultural Britain* (London, 1997).

57   Menzies' radio broadcast as reported in the *Sydney Morning Herald*, 4 September 1939, and Neville Meaney's chapter below. Menzies was still using the term 'British world' in 1959; see Stuart Ward, 'Sentiment and Self-interest: The Imperial Ideal in Anglo-Australian Commercial Culture', *Australian Historical Studies*, 2001, 32, 98.

58   Sian Nicholas' chapter in Bridge and Fedorowich, *British World*.

59   'Britain' or 'UK', memo by Secretary of State for Commonwealth Relations, Duncan Sandys, 24 March 1961, C(61)46, Cabinet Office papers, CAB 129/104, Public Record Office (PRO), London; cabinet conclusions, CC(61)19, minute 6, 28 March 1961, CAB 128/35; 'Britain' and 'British', memos to Sandys and Macmillan by the Cabinet Secretary, Sir Norman Brook, 16 June 1961, and Macmillan's personal reply M199/61, 20 June 1961, Prime Minister's Office papers, PREM 11/3652, PRO. The authors wish to thank Stuart Ward for directing us to the last source.

60   For an account, see W. David McIntyre, *British Decolonization, 1946–1997* (New York, 1998), 103–18.

61   Kosmas Tsokhas misuses the term de-dominionisation in his, 'Dedominionization: The Anglo-Australian Experience, 1939–1945', *Historical Journal*, 1994, 37, 861–83. For a better understanding, see Jim Davidson, 'The De-dominionisation of Australia', *Meanjin*, 1979, 38, 139–53.

62   Stuart Ward, *Australia and the British Embrace: The Demise of the Imperial Ideal* (Melbourne, 2001); David Goldsworthy, *Losing the Blanket: Australia and the End of Britain's Empire* (Melbourne, 2002); *Daily Telegraph*, 8 February 2003.

63   Menzies to Macmillan, 15 January 1962, cited in Goldsworthy, *Losing the Blanket*, 111; Menzies' speech, *Commonwealth* [of Australia] *Parliamentary Debates*, 16 October 1962; Wayne Reynolds, *Australia's Bid for the Atomic Bomb* (Melbourne, 2000); Robert Holland, *The Pursuit of Greatness: Britain and the World Role, 1900–1970* (London, 1991) 180; McIntyre, *British Decolonization*, 122.

Chapter 11

Philip S. Zachernuk

THE ROOTS OF COLONIAL INTELLECTUAL LIFE

If 'imperial networks' included those among people of British or other European descent, there were also vigorous, important, and still too little studied African ones. In his pioneering study, from which these excerpts come, Philip Zachernuk looks at the global influences and contacts of early West African intellectuals – including their connections with the 'British World'.

Stephen Howe

IN 1839 SOME SIXTY-SEVEN SETTLERS from Sierra Leone arrived in Badagry in search of a better future. These pioneers were Saro, people of Yoruba descent who had been enslaved in southern Nigeria, shipped overseas, liberated by the British antislavery squadron, then settled and perhaps educated in Sierra Leone. Soon followed by others from Sierra Leone as well as European missionaries, they established new communities in Lagos and its hinterland. British expeditions up the Niger in 1841 and 1854, combining exploration, trade, and missionary interests and staffed in part by Sierra Leonean returnees, soon added an eastern wing. This was anchored to a mission station in Calabar from 1846. From the 1840s then, Western-educated Africans began to establish foundations for the colonial intelligentsia.[1]

However, these dramatic expeditions should not convey the sense that the history of the colonial intelligentsia stems neatly from these implantations in Nigerian soil. First, the Saro colonists arrived in societies undergoing and seeking to understand many momentous changes and quickly became enmeshed in these changes and discussions, especially as the returnees often had ties to their host societies. Further, as among the Efik of Calabar, European education predated the arrival of the Saro. Tied to the Atlantic economy from the sixteenth century, coastal notables hired foreign teachers or sought education overseas to better equip themselves for trade. By the early nineteenth century, one Calabar town had even established a school for English and accountancy. These early pupils of Western ways were not foreigners but often were closely tied to powerful families, whose interests they advanced jointly with their unlettered peers. The pioneer Saro settlements then were not planted in barren ground but in dense growth. Second, the educated immigrants themselves had connections through Sierra Leone to diverse parts of Africa and the Atlantic world. Freetown long remained an important nucleus of colonial West African society. Its Krio culture was formed in a context set by the indigenous Mende and Temne, among whom settled a community comprised of England's black poor, free Africans from colonial America via Nova Scotia, and Jamaican Maroons, complemented by liberated slaves from throughout West Africa. The Krio diaspora contained wealthy and poor, missionaries and farmers, literate Moslems and unschooled Christians. In Lagos further contributions came from returning freedmen from Brazil (known as Amaro) and the Caribbean, as well as American blacks concentrated in Liberia but also circulating along the coast.[2] Thus diversity, not least of political and religious traditions, long marked the Nigerian educated community. The ideas of the colonial intelligentsia have roots in discussions that reach beyond the narrow confines of colonial settlements, intertwining with various traditions of thought.

Rather than trace a single elegant stem, this study attempts to make some sense of profuse growth derived and nurtured from many sources. It does this by focusing on the colonial intelligentsia as a group within Nigerian society, but not as a group apart. They have strong links to the Saro immigrants but also to other communities involved in the precolonial Atlantic economy. Their local connections – unbroken, new, and renewed – divided and guided them through diverse histories. Yet they are a recognizable group because they share a cluster of attributes. They held the English language, the Christian church, British law, international commerce, and Western education as institutions relevant – but not always necessary – to their lives. By virtue of their Western education they shared a set of opportunities, roles, and dilemmas. In their printing presses, mission organizations, schools, and mercantile ventures, through intermarriage and family connections, they developed an identifiable tradition of engagement with the modern world. From the 1840s until British colonial conquerors swept through southern Nigeria in the 1880s, the intelligentsia established themselves as critical agents of a project to bring 'Western civilization' to 'Africa.' They were products of the emergent colonial system, but neither simple nor prefigured ones. Constructing a place for themselves necessarily from the cultures around them, they drew on ideas from all sides to pursue their material and intellectual interests. As a still small and insecure community, they found strength in the civilizing project proffered by contemporary European and Black Atlantic thinkers. But if their lives and ideas in the mid-nineteenth century stressed Africa's need for foreign inspiration, they never forgot their identity as 'Africans,' however little they may have inquired into the deeper contours of this still largely geographical category.

Minor clerks to merchant princes

The Western-educated community was dynamic, spreading geographically as it grew in size, thus gradually altering its significance and position within Nigerian society. But up to the 1880s it remained small, even in Lagos, and more closely connected to communities abroad than within Nigeria. Lagos in 1861 had a total population of about 25,000. This included perhaps 3,000, and no more than 5,000, 'native foreigners' – comprised mostly of Saro and Amaro in about equal numbers augmented by West Indians and Liberians – and a few educated indigenes. By 1891 some 5,200 Lagosians were deemed able to read and write and another 3,500 able to read, totaling perhaps 8,700 literates in a township of under 33,000. Although none of the census categories correspond exactly to the educated community, they suggest that it had grown by the 1880s to at most one-quarter of the urban Lagos population. Despite a doubling of Christians in the Lagos Township during the 1870s, traditionalists still outnumbered them six to one by 1881, and Moslems by four to three. If literacy in English was on the rise, so was literacy in Yoruba, while Portuguese remained popular among Amaro. The educated communities outside Lagos taken together did not equal it in numbers or significance. Abeokuta was another important center, with perhaps 600 Saro in 1842 and at most 6,000 Christians (not all educated) by the 1880s. There were less than 100 educated Africans in Old Calabar in 1862. Perhaps 400 Krio and Gold Coast commercial staff worked in both the Niger Delta and up-river in the 1870s.[3] Literacy is not an exact measure of the bounds of the colonial intelligentsia, but it is a skill central to the development of the community. Nigerians not literate in English were not necessarily excluded: the printed word could be spoken, and the spoken word inscribed. But literacy in English made direct participation possible and allowed membership in a group with special opportunities within the colonial order. Even those with only minimal education could both express their views in print and provide a readership for others.

Mission schools appeared quickly to start Nigerian roots for these communities. The first was founded at Badagry in 1843; others soon followed in Abeokuta, Lagos, and other southwestern towns. From the 1850s mission schools in the east spread from centers such as Calabar, Bonny, Qua Iboe, and Onitsha. Antecedent institutions in Sierra Leone, Ghana, and the West Indies provided their teaching staff for some time. Nigerian schools only slowly developed the ability to expand under their own power, even though many graduates became teachers. Missionaries founded schools as tools of evangelism; the colonial government needed them to train clerks. But growth depended above all on African interest. Sierra Leonean repatriates were keen, supplying most of the 3,000 primary students in Lagos by 1891 and sending others to Freetown. For most Nigerians the benefits of Western education remained less than obvious. The protection offered by the mission house first attracted ex-slaves and outcasts; missionaries among the Yoruba redeemed children who had been pawned. Some were drawn by the commercial value of literacy and accounting skills. School attendance dropped in Calabar when missionaries began to offer Scripture lessons in Efik instead of English, the language of commerce. Even so, family heads often sent slaves or dependents to acquire new skills, not their own children. Only as the colonial order became ensconced and the opportunities opened by Western education became obvious, did interest in schools expand rapidly. First in places such as Lagos and Calabar, but only after the 1880s in towns more protected from the colonial impact, the problem of education gradually shifted from finding recruits to finding space for them. Women were by no means treated equally; their curriculum tended toward domestic rather than literary training. But in relative proportions at least they fared better in these years than they would until the end of the colonial period, in part because the early missionaries and Saro held that educated women were integral to successful Christian families. An all girls' school opened in Onitsha as early as 1858. Early Lagos primary schools had three male students for every two females; as primary education spread to rural communities, the ratio rose to five to one.[4]

These schools offered little more than basic education in Christian and European ways. Secondary schools, following the curriculum and structure of British grammar schools, were much less common or widespread. The first secondary school appeared in Freetown in 1845; Lagos had one by 1859 and four by 1880, one of which was for girls. Secondary education abroad was expensive. The training offered West African elite girls by a London institute in the 1860s approximately equaled the annual salary of a lower-class government clerk or three months' salary for a first-class clerk.[5] Although this meant perhaps only one in twelve primary graduates in western Nigeria might find a place in secondary school, the road would narrow even more sharply for future cohorts, as primary education expanded far faster than secondary in the early colonial period.

Very few Africans had postsecondary education in mid-nineteenth-century Nigeria, especially women. Only those with wealthy families or generous mission sponsors could afford the travel abroad this required. For men, careers in the church were both more popular and more accessible than in law or medicine, not least because Fourah Bay College in Sierra Leone offered training. Founded in 1827, primarily to train African workers for the Church Missionary Society and affiliated with the University of Durham in 1876, it attracted many Saro. Perhaps 180 students from Yoruba families were admitted to Fourah Bay before 1900. It is not clear, however, how many graduated or pursued careers in Nigeria. The early clergy, doctors, and lawyers were from the Gold Coast or the African diaspora, slowly joined first by Sierra Leoneans and then Saro. The first medical doctors – Sierra Leoneans Africanus Horton and W.B. Davies – qualified in London with CMS and British government support in 1858. Of the seven who qualified in the quarter century following 1874, six were born in Sierra Leone and one in Lagos; six also had Yoruba family backgrounds. C. Sapara Williams, the first Yoruba and Nigerian lawyer, returned from the Gold Coast in 1886. Sir Kitoyi Ajasa, the first Lagos-born lawyer, returned only in 1894. Up to the 1880s, 'native foreigners' commanded the heights of the educational pyramid. Their links to the culture of the Black Atlantic also dominated colonial intellectual life.

The elite few who did sojourn in Britain in the mid-nineteenth century entered a society in which people of African descent were found in a variety of circumstances.[6] After slavery was abolished at the turn of the nineteenth century, many of those who had been domestic slaves continued as servants. The less fortunate formed the black poor; black musicians, especially in military bands, enjoyed a higher status. A few had risen from slavery to active roles in the abolitionist movement, in the manner of Olaudah Equiano and Ottobah Cugoano. Such men could associate with other abolitionist leaders among the middle classes. In the mid-nineteenth century, black American abolitionists joined these circles. Already Britain was a meeting place within the African diaspora. Racial prejudices existed; but for blacks with education and social connections, barriers were more permeable than they would become through the period of Britain's imperial dominance in Africa. Educated Africans were still objects of curiosity rather than contempt and were evaluated more by class than by color. Early university students clustered at London and Edinburgh, expanding later to Oxford and Cambridge. When men such as Horton came to study with government and CMS support, or when others came with personal or family funding, they therefore found a relatively congenial setting. The West African elite of the later nineteenth century could holiday in Britain, marry there, and carry some of their status with them. Queen Victoria was godmother to the first child of Saro merchant J.P.L. Davies and his wife Sarah. Self-proclaimed friends of Africa, such as Ferdinand Fitzgerald of the African Aid Association and the *African Times* or Thomas Hodgkin, a founder of the Aborigines Protection Society, were also part of Africans' social network, in addition to their commercial relationships. Some twenty-three West Africans visited Britain under CMS auspices between 1840 and 1883. A long-standing pattern was established early on. Britons interested in African affairs, for commercial, scholarly, or philanthropic reasons, linked up through such figures as Hodgkin and Fitzgerald with Africans on the coast and in Britain to pursue these interests. Interests often overlapped, as in the project to spread the gospel and promote trade. Through such exchanges the West African intelligentsia kept themselves abreast of current British thought pertinent to their situation. Nigeria's missionary and commercial contacts with America were much weaker than with Britain, but not absent. Few West Africans traveled to America until late in the century, but connections were established from the early decades through back-to-Africa movements in Liberia, and members of both communities intersected in England. The most direct evidence of connection was the tour of the American Martin Delany and the Jamaican Robert Campbell among the Yoruba in 1859 and 1860, undertaken with an eye to promoting African-American settlement. Campbell returned in 1862 to establish a newspaper in Lagos.

Uncertain Victorians

Life in Lagos in these decades was precarious. This was especially true for the educated immigrants attached to the nascent colonial order. The cession of Lagos in 1861 promised to strengthen the colonial presence, but the immediate effect was to provoke local suspicion of British power, with which the educated Africans were associated. Britain's commitment to the colony seemed hesitant, as British politicians discussed reducing their West African possessions, and the official seat of administration rested from 1866 to 1874 in Sierra Leone, then until 1886 in the Gold Coast. Trade conditions fluctuated frequently, often sharply. Citizens of property were plagued by both criminal and accidental fires; chronically underfunded public hygiene left noxious odors and threatened worse. The judicial system, according to Adewoye, long remained 'characterized by improvisation.' The Saro missionary James Johnson was unimpressed with the architecture and amenities when he arrived in Lagos from Freetown in 1874. Inland the threats were even more direct. Typically, the early returnees were treated with suspicion or disdain in their areas of origin, which they had often left as slaves. British antislavery policies in particular aroused the resentment of interior slaveholding notables and inspired a group of Lagos Saro to petition the government in 1864 for more tolerance of the way 'the natives look upon and hold their domestic slaves in the same light and manner as civilized nations [do] their real and personal property.' Anti-British feeling, they made clear, was threatening Saro interests:

> During the protectorate the British name was venerated, confidence placed to an unlimited extent, so much so that then the dress of an Englishman was a sufficient passport to any man to travel through these parts inland, as far as the banks of the Niger . . . but since the cession of Lagos the interior is closed against us, either for commerce or exploration. We are looked upon as spies

and deceivers, the British name has become odious, our lives are not even safe among the natives.[7]

At Brass in 1873 the killing of a totem animal led to assaults on church property and Christian converts, indicative of a persistent antipathy. Abeokuta, a town recently founded by the Egba in the midst of the Yoruba wars, was something of an exception. There were many Egba among the Saro, and many were welcomed back to Abeokuta as a means of strengthening the fledgling city against its rivals. But even here Egba disagreement with the British antislavery agenda and their sense that the Lagos government favored British over African traders inspired the violent expulsion of colonial agents in 1867. Some returnees chose to confine themselves to Lagos rather than face such hostility. But hostility was balanced with the recognition that the educated community could play an invaluable role mediating between hinterland states and British authorities, especially for Yoruba leaders facing the simultaneous problems of civil war and British penetration. Even isolationist Ijebu maintained contact with Ijebu Saro in Lagos, in spite of distaste at seeing compatriots adopt European ways.

These divisions were overlaid by a thick covering of Victorian culture, a feature which struck European observers most forcefully. In Calabar wealthy chiefs imported prefabricated houses from Liverpool and stuffed them with foreign furnishings. In frock coats and elaborate dresses, the Lagos elite organized and attended music recitals, soirees, levees, cricket matches, elaborate church weddings, the Queen's Birthday Ball, and jubilees. High street fashions from England shaped high style on the marina. Lagos even sported a musical merry-go-round in the early 1880s. Fraternal societies, such as the Masonic lodge founded in 1868, rounded out the picture. Their connections to Europe and even America were close in timing as well as spirit. J.A.O. Payne was the first African member of a civil servants' Prayer Union which had been founded in Britain in 1872. In 1887 he helped form a similar union in Lagos. The Independent Order of Good Templars, established in the United States in 1851, opened a Lagos chapter in 1868 with African members. At least some of the 100 or so Europeans in Lagos shared parts of their social life with the elite. Prominent families such as the Coleses, Moores, Randles, and Williamses dined at Government House and exchanged social calls among their intertwined families. A scattering of debating, literary, and scientific societies appeared bespeaking Victorian middle-class interest in science and improvement. An Old Calabar Literary Society was active in Duke Town in 1864 and 1865. Another early effort was the Lagos Academy proposed by prominent merchants in 1866 to foster the study of arts and science. Bishop Samuel Ajayi Crowther, the famous CMS missionary, was the patron; Payne was a member. The academy seems to have had at best a short life. But its vice president, Robert Campbell, who became 'one of the leading intellectuals of Lagos' in these decades, organized the Lagos Science Society in the 1860s, which at least hosted some lectures.[8] Campbell, with Nathaniel King, was again active in the Lagos Mutual Improvement Society established in 1879. It had 150 members by 1884, including a European president, and lasted until at least 1890. Churches and schoolrooms were popular venues for public meetings and lectures; Glover Memorial Hall, founded in 1887, quickly became a favorite site.

They also made efforts to secure contemporary books and journals. The evangelical and educational literature that arrived with the early missionaries was complemented by a wider selection of English books by the 1860s. The CMS bookstore and press established in 1869 soon proved reliably profitable, dealing in some secular texts along with its religious publications. It quickly faced competition from a book section in J.P. Haastrup's retail establishment. By the 1880s Lagosians could order books with relative ease, from America as well as from Britain. Libraries reveal less steady growth. At least three attempts were made to found lending libraries in the 1860s, by among others the academy and Governor Glover. The Young Men's Christian Association, which also sponsored lectures and debates, had some success with a lending library around 1874, but public libraries seem to have remained only proposals until at least the end of the century. Efforts to produce printed material were more successful. The first presses came with the Presbyterian mission to Calabar in 1846 and the CMS outpost in Abeokuta in 1854. Both were used to train printers while producing educational and religious material. The earliest newspaper, printed mostly in Yoruba, came from the CMS Abeokuta mission between 1859 and 1867. Robert Campbell used his press to train apprentices and produce the Anglo-African newspaper in Lagos from 1863 to 1865; the Lagos Times in 1880 initiated the continuous history of the Lagos newspaper press. The wealthy merchant Blaize opened a commercial printing press in 1875; by 1880 there were at least five printing establishments in Lagos alone.[9]

But these Victorian social habits are only part of the story. As Kopytoff observes, the Sierra Leoneans early on made clear that they did not 'look upon the new and the old cultural practices as mutually exclusive alternatives.'[10] The Catholic Brazilians and Muslim Yoruba among the social elite did not fit British Victorian norms; neither did Saro family trees. As Mann's research shows, economic change and kinship structures in Lagos inspired a variety of marriage practices, combining Christian and Yoruba patterns, which better suited contemporary reality than Yoruba or Victorian forms. The extended family remained central to social relations. The bride and groom of a high society wedding in 1886 graciously received both a silver teapot and locally woven cloth as gifts. While some merchants imported prefabricated houses, others devised styles of housing drawing variously upon British, local, and Brazilian models, adapted to the climate and materials of the coast. Mission converts in Abeokuta joined the Ogboni Society by 1861, a traditional Egba body of considerable secular authority. Challenged by European missionaries, the Ogboni members refused to accept that they were in any way repudiating their Christian faith. Returnees and converts in Abeokuta acquired titles and pawns in traditional ways. So too, Saro merchants could conspire with Abeokuta chiefs to attack European merchants threatening their trade or harassing British expeditions harboring their escaped slaves. There was no clean opposition here between Victorian and African ways.

Why this incomplete reproduction of Victorian society? The conventional explanation has been that the educated community was a transitional group moving from the 'African' world toward the 'modern.' They supposedly aspired to become 'Western' instead of 'traditional.' Thus Mahmud Tukur can argue that this group was becoming 'fundamentally and essentially Anglo-Saxon.' In the meantime they remained 'suspended . . . between two possible world views,' neither here nor there.[11] Ultimately, of course, they are held to have failed to bridge the chasm. But posing this kind of opposition obscures historical understanding. The educated community was situated in societies in flux, not resting in tradition, and never would move along Western lines. It did exist at the interface between the European colonial presence and African society. The culture that developed in this space did include elements from both worlds. As Baker sees them, the Saro stood:

> between the two worlds of European and African culture . . . collectively distinguished from other Lagosians by their unique cultural background. They

emulated English behaviour and mannerisms, rejected native authority, and adopted Christianity; but most Saros were also fully conscious of their Yoruba origins.[12]

The mistake is to see this as a culture suspended between two possible realities, with no possibilities of its own. The educated community was not moving from the African to the European but rather was seeking to define itself within an emergent Nigerian society. This was not an unstable transitional society waiting to find order by absorbing Western norms but an admittedly changeable society engaged in an ongoing – and unending – process of living through problems as it met them. As their culture developed it did not become more modern but rather more Nigerian, more profoundly a product of its own history. It used elements of both not to construct a bridge between them but to create a habitat distinct from both. There were many degrees of attraction to British culture within the educated community, but very few members sought full assimilation. Even if they did, few Europeans in Nigeria or abroad were willing wholly to accept them. Nor were many of the educated inclined simply to join their illiterate compatriots. Rather, they sought the unique advantages that came with the territory between. Western acculturation opened opportunities unavailable to the mass of the population and established an elite status. Connections to African societies gave them leverage with colonial authorities and advantages in trade. Remaining in this medial position, not getting beyond it, made the educated a special and increasingly enviable group.

It is more useful to think of invented identities here than of cultural transitions, of innovative fluidity rather than inevitable flow. The educated clearly were not intent on reproducing Victorian society but on using it. They were operating in a very competitive trading economy, where variable identities could be very useful. When politicking in Lagos or London, an elite Lagosian might be very English. When settling family disputes or politicking in the village, the same person might be very Yoruba. Yoruba in Brazil dressed in Yoruba fashions to stress their distinct identity but adopted a Brazilian style in Lagos to set themselves apart from the Saro.[13] The garden parties and the Victorian parlors so prominent in mid-nineteenth-century Lagos were important expressions of ambition and status. They projected attributes that set the educated community apart from other Africans and closer to European merchants and administrators. But they were not the essence of this group or foretokens of their future. These Victorian performances were one part of a much more diverse repertoire. If Victorian material played better in the middle of the nineteenth century than it would at the end, the simple explanation is that this identity allied them with the burgeoning power of Britain at a time when it promised much against their insecurities and uncertainties.

Civilizing schemes

What kinds of ideas occupied the intelligentsia situated in this society? By virtue of their Western education, the intelligentsia were introduced to contemporary European ideas about Africa. The circulation of ideas and people in the African diaspora introduced similar notions. Africa was more central to the latter than the former, but when it was discussed, questions of its present condition and future prospects were foremost. In general, judgments about its condition were not flattering. Africa was seen as benighted. Isolated, backward, and weak in itself, it had been further degraded by the Atlantic slave trade. Some thought this condition was more or less permanent; Africans were simply destined to be an inferior 'race.' Most, however, believed that great change was imminent. Various interested parties competed to promote their preferred future; this competition would not end with partition. Merchants tried to maximize their trade profits; administrators sought limited and inexpensive changes that would improve trade more generally and end slaving. Abolitionists and missionaries in particular had more potent plans to lighten Africa's burden, involving nothing less than remodeling tropical civilization. For them Africa might be suffering, but it had the potential to be redeemed. The core of this 'civilizing mission' was set forth most coherently by Thomas Fowell Buxton in *The African Slave Trade and Its Remedy*. Slavery had to be eradicated within Africa through the joint agency of Christian enlightenment and trade in the produce of free African labor. Under British protection, connected to foreign commerce, and reformed through missionary efforts, West Africa would develop a class of industrious and progressive farmers, traders, and teachers to be the vanguard of a new progressive civilization. Because Europeans could not thrive in the West African climate, educated West Indian blacks and slaves liberated at Freetown were recommended as the willing and available agents for this project. Christianity loomed large in this proposal. It was further developed in numerous missionary programs, most extensively by Henry Venn, lay secretary of the CMS from 1841 to 1872. Accepting the necessity of Christianity and African agency, Venn argued that Africans should assume control of their own church as soon as possible. This not only would facilitate the growth of a truly African church adapted to 'national peculiarities' but also would afford them valuable experience in managing their own affairs. In time this independence would extend to the secular realm, as mission schools spawned a skilled middle class. The Sierra Leone 'Native Pastorate' from 1861 and the consecration of Samuel Crowther as bishop for West Africa in 1864 were widely proclaimed applications of these ideals.[14]

This civilizing mission had a more secular version as well. Generally, British administrative policies in West Africa were the product of expedience rather than any long-term strategy. But as their West African commitments formed, the British resorted to imperial precedent and, from the 1840s, established crown colonies with executive and legislative councils to assist governors in their tasks. Lagos was thus constituted after its annexation in 1861. While official policy avoided predicting the distant future, for some such arrangements were seeds from which full-scale parliaments might someday grow. The third Earl Grey, colonial secretary from 1846 to 1852, clearly connected the 'rude Negro Parliament' he had promoted in the Gold Coast with this vision. A legislative assembly including local chiefs, he believed, had 'converted a number of barbarous tribes . . . into a nation, with a regularly organized authority.' Britain's duty, Grey argued, was:

> gradually to train the inhabitants of this part of Africa in the arts of civilization and government, until they shall grow into a nation capable of protecting themselves and of managing their own affairs, so that the interference and assistance of the British authorities may by degrees be less and less required.[15]

When a British Parliamentary Select Committee in 1865 endorsed a gradual withdrawal from West African commitments, it evoked the spirit of this dream, recommending that Africans be encouraged to acquire the skills required for running their own governments.

Similar ideas informed the attitudes of African Americans, evident among the settlers in Liberia or the expedition to Nigeria undertaken by Delany and Campbell in 1859. Africa's great potential needed the enlightened leadership of their black Christian brethren who had been exposed to civilization in America. At the very least Africa needed spiritual and industrial missionaries; a minority favored the return of black Americans *en masse* as agents uniquely suited by race, sentiment, and sympathy to 'introduce, in an effective manner, all the well-regulated pursuits of civilized life.'[16]

These ideas from the Atlantic world painted, at least in broad strokes, a West African future in which a native elite would create and control a new outpost of British civilization. They were focused and propagated from London by the African Aid Society, which was established in 1860 by prominent philanthropists inspired by Delany's expedition and backed by industrial interests hoping to promote West African cotton production. The *African Times*, the society's organ, acted as 'the public advocate in England' of the 'educated African.' It was clear that 'educated natives . . . are and will be indispensable as a vanguard of the great army of civilization that must be projected upon the ignorant barbarism of heathen Africa.'[17] Of all the proponents of this future, the West African educated community had the most obvious reasons to promote it; not surprisingly they quickly adopted the civilizing mission as their own. Its elements were not yet worked out in detail, let alone universally accepted. Elaborating and defending the civilizing mission were the central problems of the mid-nineteenth-century intelligentsia.

But merely adopting, defending, and applying the civilizing mission could not meet the needs of the intelligentsia, seeking as they were to understand their new role in an emergent social order. They also shaped it along more congenial lines. Venn of the CMS and others spoke of the need to adapt Christian ways to African life, but European missionaries were not well equipped – and often not inclined to disentangle the essentials of their faith from the trappings of their culture or to view African societies with empathy. African missionaries were both more equipped and more inclined. Crowther argued that African polygamy would have to be replaced by European monogamy but also held fast to the policy that the role of Christianity was only 'to abolish and supersede all false religions,' not 'to destroy national assimilations.' 'Heathen' aspects of African societies that were 'not immoral or indecent' should be 'improved upon and enriched from foreign stocks as civilization advances.' Crowther and his European and African colleagues devised written texts for six southern Nigerian languages by the 1880s and made careful studies of the history and culture of their prospective flocks, including Muslim communities, hoping to generate a Christian culture with some African forms.[18]

One of the most striking cases of adapting the civilizing mission was the Egba United Board of Management, which operated in Abeokuta between 1865 and 1874. It was the inspiration of G.W. Johnson, an Egba Saro. Suspicions about British expansion had soured early Egba eagerness to strengthen themselves through missionary connections. Johnson, leading a faction of the Saro community, sought to strengthen Abeokuta against British and other threats by having African leaders adapt European ideas of government without European aid. The Board of Management tried to unite the notoriously fractious political structure of Abeokuta under a single authority and for a time succeeded in implementing postal services and bureaucratic revenue collection. Plagued by British and internal opposition, its power faded, to be revived in the 1890s. Johnson, apparently undaunted, continued to propagate his ideas of independent African modernization in the West African press.[19]

The intelligentsia not only reshaped European ideas of the civilizing mission, injecting them with concern for African realities and attempting to situate local facts in European forms. They also moved beyond them, engaging ideas provided not by European and American discourse about Africa but rather by the African societies to which they were connected. The discourse of the colonial intelligentsia was not born afresh from the colonial situation and the mission school; it had roots beyond these institutions, as it would have through colonial times. The intelligentsia sometimes were introduced to these problems as they settled into local situations, for example, as missionaries or diplomats sent forth into the Yoruba wars. They also, as it were, grew up with them. Local recruits, even more than Krio returnees, brought their domestic or local intellectual problems with them through the schoolyard gate to address in the light of their new education. Often, ideas that engaged them most were those which intersected issues raised by the civilizing mission, but this is not to say that these issues were important only because foreigners made them so. The ideational links between the early colonial intelligentsia and their mid-nineteenth-century peers are faintly registered in the historical record and difficult to reconstruct. We can, however, recognize a few points of connection.

'Black Englishmen', Africa's advocates

Both the cultural and intellectual lives of the intelligentsia up to the 1880s are aptly encapsulated in the title 'black Englishmen,' a new breed drawing on diverse sources but aspiring to be neither wholly black nor wholly English. In certain contexts they saw themselves as outsiders, like the British, bringing illumination to Africa and Africa to illumination. One Lagos paper, for example, promised to save space especially:

> for the insertion of any reliable information of the Interior countries . . . which may throw some light into the degree of civilization and religion they had attained to, before the light of Christian civilization began to dawn upon them.[20]

The intelligentsia were the elite vanguard of a foreign civilization. This elitism was founded on their education in and emulation of European ways. At the same time, clear distinctions were maintained between Africans and Europeans, a difference which becoming 'civilized' would not erase. If African agency had initially been required by a climate inhospitable for Europeans, it was soon raised to the status of prescription. As one Krio clergyman wrote in 1844, 'If Africa could be raised from its present degraded state . . . Africans themselves must be the principal harbingers of peace.' Merchant Henry Robbin declined becoming a commercial agent for Lagos in 1857 because, as government dependents, 'intelligent Africans will continue to be servants and the spirit for promoting our country's and our own interest with independent authority will lie dormant and still.'[21] Further, many among the intelligentsia saw themselves as 'Africans,' as a vanguard of the race now spread around the Atlantic. This promised role, which must have seemed doubly enticing to the ex-slaves and outcasts among them, reflected their often direct ties to Sierra Leone and the diaspora, where the specific cultural divisions of Africa were swept aside by the grand notion of 'Africa' as a geographical and racial category, accepting the grand European division of the world by continent and somatic type.

This was an identity rich in ambiguity. As Michael Echeruo has remarked, the Anglo-African used 'us' to refer to both Africans and to the 'civilizing' British, even in a single editorial. It also pointed out that 'we in Africa . . . do not hold ourselves amenable to all the formalities and exactions of fashionable life in Europe' but rather recognize 'our veritable gentlemen' in either African or European dress.[22] But it was always anchored in a clear sense of the medial position and mediating role of the intelligentsia. As one Sierra Leonean told a missionary in 1865, 'We have always considered ourselves as Middlemen between you and the Egbas.' J.A.O. Payne, writing against the CMS policy on polygamy, stood firmly in this middle ground in 1887. 'We are here on behalf of the heathen, for it is for us to speak on their behalf.' It made sense to sustain both identities as part of their medial role. They did not intend to efface Africa but to refashion it. They were the agents of improvement, racially allied to but culturally distinct from the people to be elevated. Africa, it was understood, someday would be for the Africans. Martin Delany urged this in 1860; G.W. Johnson affirmed it in Abeokuta. Crowther, familiar with both the Egba United Board of Management and Delany, cautioned that 'to claim Africa for the Africans alone, is to claim for her the right of a continued ignorance.' But he was equally insistent that Africans had their special role in the redemption of their continent. Although African culture would be subordinate to European- and especially Christian-standards, the principle was adaptation, not displacement. European aid was necessary, but not European domination. The poles, then, were between a minority seeking African improvement along foreign lines under African guidance and the mainstream, seeking African improvement with variable amounts of European aid.[23]

This opposition of 'European' against 'African' was not altogether convenient for an educated community that was clearly neither, but these were the poles offered to it by the Atlantic community in which they were embedded. The intelligentsia was obliged to deal with these terms – in the mid-nineteenth century as through the colonial period – because they were colonial subjects, beholden to a British presence backed by commerce and cannonry. This limitation on Nigerian intellectual life must not be forgotten; it is not a tradition of thought developed under the range of choice that obtained, for example, within European discourse about Europe. Ideas about Africa were imposed. To ignore them was to be severed from the civilizing mission itself; to accept them was to receive premises that set the task of understanding Nigerian societies profoundly askew. The Africa imposed here was primitive and benighted, undeniably different from 'civilized' societies, housing false gods. Mid-century Victorian thought did not hold Africa to be mysteriously different – it was after all subject to redemption and liable to civilization – but neither did Victorian categories always fit African institutions. If pawns were not free, they were slaves; if marriages were not monogamous, they were not civilized. Africa was seen as subordinate, deserving to learn from Europe but not to teach it. The early intelligentsia attempted to adapt European discourse about Africa to their needs, to render from imposed categories something more suited to their medial position between imperial discourse and African realities. These impositions were more congenial now than they would soon become. The barrier between 'Africa' and 'Europe' was still held to be cultural and historical rather than racial, still surmountable by commerce and Christianity. 'African civilization' was not the oxymoron it would later become in racist imperialist discourse based not on mutual commercial development but on blunt imperial control. Co-operation between white and black missionaries – by no means untroubled – bespoke a certain common Christian ideal which rose above race and culture. Yet even later, these impositions were not as debilitating as one might expect. Imperial ideas about civilization, economic development, or morality could be rendered useful for other purposes.

That the intelligentsia did work with these ideas is an eloquent argument against those who would dismiss them as mere colonized copyists, unable to conceive or pursue their own interests. They were, to be sure, strongly inclined toward Victorian culture and ideas in the mid-nineteenth century, but not just because these ideas were entwined with the civilizing mission. They were attracted to Victorian ideas, as to Victorian culture, as a potent source of power within West Africa. They strove to have their input into the foreign institutions they helped build. They also exercised some choice, and effected some changes, in their search for a suitable world view, built with ill-suited ideas. They always remained 'African,' always ready to assert a special relation to the continent which diasporan Africans might share, but which Europeans could not. Nevertheless, the early Nigerian intelligentsia were more preoccupied with promoting the civilizing mission than questioning it, and it is not clear that the meaning of being 'African' was deeply probed. Their immediate need was to establish a new social order and a place for themselves, to support European expansion while resisting European deviation from the promise of the civilizing mission. Neither understanding exactly how the 'black' and the 'English' could be joined nor separating the kernel of Christian teachings from its European shell was a pressing question. The intelligentsia's connection to African sources of ideas would become more conscious, active, and direct in the cultural nationalist climate of the approaching decades. But this was not a wholly new orientation for them; Africa was not exactly a new discovery. From the start they had attended to African ideas in their race to civilize. The difference was that in the mid-nineteenth century, for the most part, they looked upon things African with a different attitude. Civilization would come from abroad. Africa was relevant because it marked what had to be improved, and it was not to be discarded wholesale. But it was to be judged according to external standards. As circumstances changed, the civilizing mission was given many different shapes and meanings. The rise of European racism imposed the need to define their 'African' identity more explicitly and to ask hard questions about the nature of 'black Englishmen' and Christianity in Africa. In the cultural nationalist phase, the interest and connection to things African would continue, but with a sense that Africa might set the standards of what was relevant. Between the wars conditions allowed for more balanced inquiry. In the late colonial rush toward the nation-state, external standards would again be invoked.

Notes

1   This chapter draws on a large body of published literature on the Western-educated community in West Africa.
2   K.K. Nair, *Politics and Society in South Eastern Nigeria, 1841–1906* (London, 1972) 66–9; D. Forde (ed.), *Efik Traders of Old Calabar* (London, 1956) viii; P.E.H. Hair, 'Africanism. The Freetown Contribution' *Journal of Modern African Studies*, 1967, 5.
3   The intriguing colonial term *Native Foreigner* referred to 'any person (not being a native of Nigeria) whose parents were members of a tribe or tribes indigenous to some part of Africa and the descendants of such a person, and shall include any person one of whose parents was a member of such tribe,' P.A. Talbot, *Peoples of Southern Nigeria*, 4 vols (London, 1926) 4: 19. Informed guesses about the early Lagos population vary.
4   On early colonial education, see Babs Fafunwa, *History of Education in Nigeria* (London, 1974) 81–91; A.E. Afigbo, 'The Background to the Southern Nigerian Education Code' *Journal of*

the Historical Society of Nigeria, 1968, 4; Nair, *Politics and Society*, 68; Kristin Mann, *Marrying Well: Marriage, Status and Social Change* (Cambridge, 1985) 18. On women's education, see LaRay Denzer, 'Women in Government Service in Colonial Nigeria' Working Papers in African Studies no. 136 (Boston University, 1989), 3–4; S.N. Nwabara, *Iboland* (Atlantic Highlands, NJ, 1978) 49.

5   Titlola Euba, 'Dress and Status in 19th Century Lagos', in Ade Adefuye *et al.* (eds) *Peoples of Lagos State* (Lagos, 1987), 152; Spencer Hunter Brown, 'A History of the People of Lagos,' PhD Diss. (Northwestern University, 1964) 133–8.

6   On blacks in Britain generally, including this period, available surveys are: Peter Fryer, *Staying Power* (London, 1984); Douglas Lorimer, *Colour, Class and the Victorians* (Leicester, 1978); Edward Scobie, *Black Britannia* (Chicago, 1972); James Walvin, *Black and White* (London, 1973); see also Ian Duffield, 'Skilled Workers or Marginalized Poor?' *Immigrants and Minorities*, 1993, 12. On early organizational links, see Immanuel Geiss, *The Pan-African Movement* (London, 1974) 166–9; Brown, 'People of Lagos,' 210–30. On Delany and Campbell, see R.J.M. Blackett, 'Return to the Motherland' *Phylon*, 1979, 40.

7   Omoniye Adewoye, *The Judicial System in Southern Nigeria, 1854–1954* (London, 1978), 48–52, 73–6; *Anglo-African*, 7 January 1865. On Lagos conditions, see E.A. Ayandele, *Holy Johnson: Pioneer of African Nationalism* (London, 1970) 85–7, 114–15; C.O. Nwanunobi, 'Incendiarism and other Fires in 19th Century Lagos' *Africa*, 1990, 60; Spencer Hunter Brown, 'Public Health in Lagos, 1850–1900' *International Journal of African Historical Studies*, 1992, 25. On Abeokuta, see Agenta Pallinder-Law, 'Government in Abeokuta, 1830–1914' PhD Diss. (Uppsala University, 1973) 21–2; Hakeem B. Harunah, 'Lagos-Abeokuta Relations' in Adefuye *et al. Peoples*; Saburi O. Biobaku, *Egba and Their Neighbors, 1842–1872* (Oxford, 1957). See also Nwabara, *Iboland*, 50; A.E. Ayandele, *The Educated Elite in the Nigerian Society* (Ibadan, 1974) 11–12; Ayandele, *The Ijebu of Yorubaland, 1850–1950* (Ibadan, 1992) 8.

8   Blackett, 'Return to the Motherland,' 384; *Anglo-African*, 14 January 1865. A.B. Ellis describes the merry-go-round in *Land of Fetish*, 1883, repr. (Westport, CT. 1970) 82–3. Their Victorian attributes have been colorfully detailed, for example, by Brown, 'People of Lagos,' 242–7, 254–70, or more recently by Michael Echeruo, *Victorian Lagos* (London, 1978) both sources for my account.

9   On bookshops and libraries, see H.B. Thomas, *History of Nigeria Bookshops*, typescript (Royal Commonwealth Society, 1969) 1–2; Brown, 'People of Lagos,' 232–53, 278–81; Lagos Institute, *Proceedings of Inaugural Meeting* (Lagos, 1901) 1. On presses, see J.F. Ade Ajayi, *Christian Missions in Nigeria, 1841–1891* (London, 1966) 158–9; Fred I.A. Omu, *Press and Politics in Nigeria, 1880–1937* (London, 1978) 106, 252.

10   Jean Herskovits Kopytoff, *A Preface to Modern Nigeria* (Madison, 1965) 127. On social habits, see Mann, *Marrying Well*, 110–27; Euba, 'Dress and Status,' 153–4; Brown, 'People of Lagos,' 153–65; Babatunde Agiri, 'Architecture as a Source for History: The Lagos example' in Adefuye *et al.*, *Peoples*, 341–50. On alliances with the interior, see E. Adeniyi Oroge, 'The Fugitive Slave Question in Anglo-Egba Relations' *Journal of the Historical Society of Nigeria*, 1975, 8.

11   Mohamed Tukur, 'A Critical Evaluation of Ayendele's *Educated Elite*', in *The Essential Mahmud: Selected Writings* (Zaria, 1990) 81; Elizabeth Isichei, *The Ibo People and the Europeans* (London, 1973) 179.

12   Pauline Baker, *Urbanization and Political Change: The Politics of Lagos, 1917–1967* (Los Angeles, 1974) 27.

13   Euba, 'Dress and Status,' 150–1.

14   Thomas Fowell Buxton, *The African Slave Trade*, 2nd edn. 1840 repr. (London, 1968); Henry S. Wilson (ed.), *Origins of West African Nationalism* (London, 1969) 121–52, reprints statements of Venn and similar missionary thinkers.

15   Henry George Grey, *The Colonial Policy of Lord John Russell's Administration*, 2 vols (London, 1853) 2: 287.

16   E.g. Martin Delany, *Official Report of the Niger Valley Exploring Party* 1861, repr. In H.M. Bell (ed.) *Search for a Place* (Ann Arbor, 1971) 110; Alexander Crummell, 'The Progress of Civilization along the West Coast of Africa' in *The Future of Africa*, 1861, repr. (New York, 1969).

17   *African Times*, 23 May 1863, 1 July 1880.

18   Samuel Crowther, 'Charge at Lokoja' (1869), quoted in Ajayi, *Missions*, 224; Crowther and John Christopher Taylor, *The Gospel on the Banks of the Niger 1859*, repr. (London, 1968) 227–39. See also Crowther, *A Grammar and Vocabulary of the Yoruba Language* (London, 1852) i–vii; Crowther, *Journal of an Expedition up the Niger and Tshadda Rivers*, 1855, repr. (London, 1970) 62–3; and the bibliography of early missionary writing in Ajayi, *Missions*, 285–9.

19   See Pallinder-Law, 'Abeokuta,' 51–2, 94, 179; 'Pallinder-Law, Aborted Modernization in West Africa?' *Journal of African History*, 1974, 15; Robert W. July, *The Origins of Modern African Thought* (New York, 1967) 196–207.

20   *Lagos Times*, 14 February 1891; prospectus of the *Miscellany*, in the *Eagle and Lagos Critic*, 28 April 1883, quoted in Echeruo, *Victorian Lagos,* 7.

21   George Nicol to J. Warburton, 12 April 1844, CMS CAll 0614, quoted in Wilson, *Origins*, 129; Henry Robbin to Henry Venn (1857), CMS CA 2/080, quoted in Kopytoff, *Preface*, 97.

22   *Anglo African*, 14 November 1863; Echeruo, *Victorian Lagos*, 99–100; see also Omu, 'The Anglo-African, 1863–65' *Nigeria Magazine*, 1966, 90.

23   John Craig, quoted in Echeruo, *Victorian Lagos*, 35; J.A.O. Payne, in Keyinde Okoro (ed.) *Views of Some Native Christians of West Africa on the Subject of Polygamy* (Lagos, 1887) 5, quoted in Kopytoff, *Preface*, 252; Crowther, 'Charge at Lokoja' (1869), quoted in Wilson, *Origins*, 150. Delany's vision is expressed in *Niger Valley*, 121. Kopytoff carefully delineates various positions in *Preface*, 272–8.

PART 5

Feminism, gender studies, histories of the body

Chapter 12

Ann Laura Stoler

CARNAL KNOWLEDGE AND IMPERIAL POWER: RACE AND THE INTIMATE IN COLONIAL RULE

Ann Laura Stoler has been among the most innovative and important historians of gender roles and relations in colonial situations, especially the 'intimate politics' of sexuality, and this is one of her greatest essays in that field. Here even more than with some of the other pieces reproduced here, it was sadly necessary for reasons of space to leave out much of the rich empirical detail of her analysis, and most of the references.

Stephen Howe

OVER THE PAST FIFTEEN YEARS, the anthropology of women has fundamentally altered an understanding of colonial expansion and its consequences for the colonized. In identifying how European conquest affected valuations of women's work and redefined their proper domains, feminist scholars have sought to explain how changes in household organization, the sexual division of labor, and the gender-specific control of resources within it have modified and shaped how colonial appropriations of land, labor, and resources were obtained. Much of this research has focused on indigenous gendered patterns of economic activity, political participation, and social knowledge and on the agency of those confronted with European rule – but less on the distinct agency of those women and men who carried it out.

More recent attention to the structures of colonial authority has placed new emphasis on the quotidian assertion of European dominance in the colonies, on imperial interventions in domestic life, and thus on the cultural prescriptions by which European women and men lived. From an earlier focus on how colonizers have viewed the indigenous Other, more work is beginning to sort out how Europeans in the colonies imagined themselves and constructed communities built on asymmetries of race, class, and gender-entities significantly at odds with the European models on which they were drawn.

Feminist attempts to engage the gender politics of Dutch, French, and British imperial cultures converge on some strikingly similar observations; namely, that European women in these colonies experienced the cleavages of racial dominance and internal social distinctions very differently than men precisely because of their ambiguous positions, as both subordinates in colonial hierarchies and as agents of empire in their own right. Concomitantly, the majority of European women who left for the colonies in the late nineteenth and early twentieth century confronted frequent constraint on their domestic, economic, and political options, more limiting than those in metropolitan Europe at the time and in sharp contrast to the opportunities open to colonial men.[1]

In varied form these studies raise a basic question: in what ways were gender inequalities essential to the structure of colonial racism and imperial authority? Was the strident misogyny of imperial thinkers and colonial agents a by-product of received metropolitan values ('they just brought it with them'), a reaction to contemporary feminist demands in Europe ('women need to be put back in their breeding place'), or a novel and pragmatic response to the conditions of conquest? Was the assertion of European supremacy in terms of patriotic manhood and racial virility an expression of imperial domination or a defining feature of it?

In this chapter I further pursue the premise that imperial authority and racial distinctions were fundamentally structured in gendered terms. I look at the administrative and medical discourse and management of European sexual activity, reproduction, and marriage as part of the apparatus of colonial control. Here I attend more to the dominant male discourse (less to women's perceptions of the constraints placed on them), arguing that it was how women's needs were defined, not by but for them, that most directly shaped specific policies. The very categories 'colonizer' and 'colonized' were secured through forms of sexual control that defined the domestic arrangements of Europeans and the cultural investments by which they identified themselves. Treating the sexual and conjugal tensions of colonial life as more than a political trope for the tensions of empire writ small but as a part of the latter in socially profound and strategic ways, this chapter examines how gender-specific sexual sanctions and prohibitions not only demarcated positions of power but also prescribed the personal and public boundaries of race.

Colonial authority was constructed on two powerful but false premises. The first was the notion that Europeans in the colonies made up an easily identifiable and discrete biological and social entity – a 'natural' community of common class interests, racial attributes, political affinities, and superior culture. The second was the related notion that the boundaries separating colonizer from colonized were thus self-evident and easily drawn. Neither premise reflected colonial realities. Settler colonies such as those in Rhodesia and Algeria excepted – where inter-European conflicts were violent and overt – tensions between bureaucrats and planters, settlers and transients, missionaries and metropolitan policy-makers, and *petits blancs* and monied entrepreneurs have always made European colonial communities more socially fractious and politically fragile than many of their members professed. Internal divisions grew out of competing economic and political agendas – conflicts over access to indigenous resources, frictions over appropriate methods for safeguarding European privilege and power, competing criteria for reproducing a colonial elite and for restricting its membership.

The shift away from viewing colonial elites as homogenous communities of common interest marks an important trajectory in the anthropology of empire, signaling a major rethinking of gender relations within it. The markers of European identity and the criteria for community membership no longer appear as fixed but emerge as a more obviously fluid, permeable, and historically disputed terrain. The colonial politics of exclusion was contingent on constructing categories. Colonial control was predicated on identifying who was 'white,' who was 'native,' and which children could become citizens rather than subjects, on which were legitimate progeny and which were not.

What mattered was not only one's physical properties but also who counted as 'European' and by what measure? Skin shade was too ambiguous. Bank accounts were mercurial. Religious belief and education were crucial markers but never clear enough. Social and legal standing derived from the cultural prism through which color was viewed, from the silences, acknowledgments, and denials of the social circumstances in which one's parents had sex. Sexual unions based on concubinage, prostitution, or church marriage derived from the hierarchies of rule. But, in turn, they were provisional relations, based on contested classifications, that could alter individual fates and the very structure of colonial society's ultimately, inclusion or exclusion required regulating the sexual, conjugal, and domestic life of both European colonials and their subjects.

Political messages and sexual metaphors

Colonial observers and participants in the imperial enterprise appear to have had unlimited interest in the sexual interface of the colonial encounter. No subject is discussed more than sex in colonial literature and no subject more frequently invoked to foster the racist stereotypes of European society. The tropics provided a site for European pornographic fantasies long before conquest was under way, with lurid descriptions of sexual license, promiscuity, gynecological aberrations, and general perversion marking the Otherness of the colonized for metropolitan consumption. Noting the rigid sexual protocols of nineteenth-century Europe, some colonial historians, such as Ronald Hyam, have suggested that imperial expansion itself was derived from the export of male sexual energy.[2] Gann and Duignan saw colonialism as 'a sublimation or alternative to sex [for European men].'[3] Both statements misconstrue the case, but one thing is clear: with the sustained presence of Europeans in the colonies, sexual prescriptions of varied sorts and targeting different actors became increasingly central to social policy and subject to new forms of scrutiny by colonial states.

The salience of sexual symbols as graphic representations of colonial dominance is relatively unambiguous and well established. Edward Said, for example, argued that the sexual submission and possession of Oriental women by European men 'fairly *stands for* the pattern of relative strength between East and West, and the discourse about the Orient that it enabled.'[4] Orientalism was described as a 'male perception of the world . . . a male power fantasy,' 'an exclusively male province,' in which the Orient was penetrated, silenced, and possessed.[5] Sexuality, then, serves as a loaded metaphor for domination, but Said's critique was not (nor did it claim to be) about those relations between women and men. Sexual images illustrate the iconography of rule, not its pragmatics. Sexual asymmetries and visions convey what is 'really' going on elsewhere, at another political epicenter. They are tropes to depict other centers of power.

If Asian women are centerfolds for the imperial voyeur, European women often appear in male colonial writings only as a reverse image fulfilling not sexual but other power fantasies of European men.[6] Whether portrayed as paragons of morality or as parasitic and passive actors on the imperial stage, they are rarely the object of European male desire. To assume that European men and women participated equally in the prejudices and pleasures that colonial privilege bestowed on them eschews the fact that European women took part in colonial relations in ways that imposed fundamentally different restrictions on them.

Sexual domination has been more often considered as a discursive symbol, instrumental in the conveyance of other meanings, but less often as the substance of imperial policy. Was sexual dominance, then, merely a graphic substantiation of who was on the bottom and who was on the top? Was the medium the message, or did sexual relations always 'mean' something else, stand in for other relations, evoke the sense of *other* (pecuniary, political, or some possibly more subliminal) desires? This analytic slippage between the sexual symbols of power and the politics of sex runs throughout the colonial record – as well as through contemporary commentaries on it. Some of this may reflect the polyvalent quality of sexuality – symbolically rich and socially salient at the same time. But sexual control was more than a convenient metaphor for colonial domination. It was a fundamental class and racial marker implicated in a wider set of relations of power.

As a critical interface of sexuality and the wider political order, the relationship between gender prescriptions and racial boundaries is a subject that remains unevenly unexplored. While recent work shows clearly that European women of different classes experienced the colonial venture very differently from one another and from men, we still know relatively little about the distinct investments they had in a racism they shared. Feminist scholars have made efforts to sort out the distinct colonial experience of European women, how they were incorporated into, resisted, and affected the politics of their men. Studies of the intervention of state, business, and religious institutions in the reproductive decisions of colonized populations are now joined by those that examine the work of European women in these programs, the influence of European welfare programs on colonial medicine, and the reproductive constraints on colonial women themselves.

This notion of sexuality as a core aspect of social identity has figured importantly in analyses of the psychological motivation of and injuries incurred by colonial rule. Here, sexual submission substantiates colonial racism, imposing fundamental limits on personal liberation. Among colonial and postcolonial male authors, questions of virility and definitions of manliness have been placed at political center stage. The demasculinization of colonized men and the hypermasculinity of European males are understood as key elements in the assertion of white supremacy. But these are studies concerned with the psychological salience of women and sex in the subordination of men by men. They only incidentally deal with sexism and racism as well as racism and sex.

An overlapping set of discourses has provided the psychological and economic underpinnings for colonial distinctions of difference. These discourses tie fears of sexual contamination, physical danger, climatic incompatibility, and moral breakdown to the security of a European national identity with a racist and class-specific core. Colonial scientific reports and the popular press are filled with assertions varying on a common theme: native women bear contagions, white women become sterile in the colonies, colonial men are susceptible to physical, moral, and mental degeneration when they remain in the tropics too long. What work do such statements perform? To what degree are they medically or politically grounded? We need to unpack what is metaphor, what is perceived as dangerous (is it disease, culture, climate, or sex?), and what is not.

Sex and other categories of colonial control

The regulation of sexual relations was central to the development of particular kinds of colonial settlements and to the allocation of economic activity within them. Who bedded and wedded whom in the colonies of France, England, Holland, and Iberia was never left to chance. Unions between Annamite women and French men, between Portuguese women and Dutch men, between Inca women and Spanish men produced offspring with claims to privilege, whose rights and status had to be determined and prescribed. From the early 1600s through the twentieth century the sexual sanctions and conjugal prohibitions of colonial agents were rigorously debated and carefully codified. It is in these debates over matrimony and morality that trading and plantation company officials, missionaries, investment bankers, military high commands, and agents of the colonial state confronted one another's visions of empire and the settlement patterns on which it would rest.

In 1622 the Dutch East Indies Company (VOC) arranged for the transport of six poor but marriageable young Dutch women to Java, providing them with clothing, a dowry on marriage, and a contract binding them to five years in the Indies. Aside from this and one other short-lived experiment, immigration of European women was explicitly restricted for the next two hundred years. VOC shareholders argued against female emigration on multiple counts. First, they maintained that the transportation costs for married women and daughters were too high. Second, they argued that Dutch women (with stronger ties than men to the Netherlands?) might hinder initiatives for permanent European settlement. By goading their burgher husbands to quick profits through nefarious trade, they would then press for repatriation to display their newfound wealth.[8] Third, the VOC feared that Dutch women might engage in private trade and encroach on the company's monopoly. Fourth, the objection was raised that European children would become sickly, force families to repatriate, and deplete the font of permanent settlers.[9]

The East Indies Company regulated against female migration by selecting bachelors as their European recruits and by promoting both extramarital relations and legal unions between low-ranking employees and imported slave women.[10] There were some Euro-Asian marriages among the colonial elite, but government regulations made concubinage a more attractive option by prohibiting European men from returning to the Netherlands with native wives and children. For the middling colonial staff, the East Indies Company firmly discouraged Euro-Asian marriages. Households based on Euro-Asian *unions*, by contrast, were seen to bear distinct advantages. Individual employees would bear the costs of dependents, mixed unions would produce healthier children, and Asian women would make fewer financial and affective demands. Finally, men would be more likely to remain if they established families with local roots.

Concubinage served colonial interests in other ways. It permitted permanent settlement and rapid growth by a cheaper means than the importation of European women. Salaries of European recruits to the colonial armies, bureaucracies, plantation companies, and trading enterprises were carefully calibrated and kept artificially low. Eliminating expenses for family support and transportation costs was only part of the story. As important, local women provided domestic services for which new European recruits would otherwise have had to pay. In the mid-nineteenth century such arrangements were *de rigueur* for young civil servants intent on setting up households on their own. Despite clerical opposition (the church never attained a secure and independent foothold in the Indies), by the nineteenth century concubinage was the most prevalent living arrangement for European men. Nearly half of the Indies' European male population in the 1880s were unmarried and living with Asian women. Government decrees designed to limit barrack concubinage in 1903 were never enforced. It was only in the early twentieth century that concubinage was more actively condemned.

The administrative arguments from the 1600s invoked to curb the immigration of European women, on the one hand, and to condone sexual access to indigenous women, on the other, bear a striking resemblance to the sexual politics of colonial expansion in other times and places. Colonized women living as the concubines of European men — referred to as *nyai* in Java and Sumatra, *congai* in Indochina, and *petite epouse* throughout the French empire — formed the dominant domestic arrangement in colonial cultures through the early twentieth century. Unlike prostitution, which could and often did increase the number of syphilitic and therefore non-productive European men, concubinage was considered to stabilize political order and colonial health. It kept men in their barracks and bungalows rather than in brothels or hospitals or, worse, in 'unnatural' liaisons with one another. Although prostitution served some of the colonies for some of the time, it often proved medically and socially problematic. It had little appeal for those administrations bent on promoting permanent settlement, and venereal disease was difficult to check, even with the elaborate system of lock hospitals and contagious-disease acts developed in parts of the British empire.

Across Asia and Africa, colonial decision makers counted on the social services that local women supplied as 'useful guides to the language and other mysteries of the local societies.'[11] Their medical and cultural know-how was credited with keeping many European men alive in their initial, precarious confrontation with tropical life. Handbooks for incoming plantation staff bound for Tonkin, Sumatra, and Malaya urged men to find a bed-servant as a prerequisite to quick acclimatization. In Malaysia, commercial companies encouraged their European staff to procure local 'companions' for psychological and physical well-being, as protection against the ill health that sexual abstention, isolation, and boredom were thought to bring. Even in the British empire, where the colonial office officially banned concubinage in 1910, it was tacitly condoned and practiced long after. In the Indies a similar sanction against concubinage among civil servants was only selectively enforced. It had little effect on domestic arrangements outside of Java and no real impact in Sumatra's new plantation belt where Javanese and Japanese *huishoudsters* (as Asian mistresses were sometimes called; lit. 'housekeeper') remained the rule rather than the exception.

Concubinage was the prevalent term for cohabitation outside marriage between European men and Asian women. But the term ambiguously covered a wide range of arrangements that included sexual access to a non-European woman as well as demands on her labor and legal rights to the children she bore. If glossed as companionship or cohabitation outside marriage, it suggests more social privileges than most women who were involved in such relations would have enjoyed. They could be dismissed without reason, notice, or severance pay. They might be exchanged among Europeans and 'passed on' when men left for leave or retirement in Europe. The Indies Civil Code of 1848 made their position poignantly clear: native women 'had no rights over children recognized by a white man.'[12] Some women combined sexual and domestic service with the abject status of slave or coolie and lived in separate quarters. On East Sumatra's plantations, where such arrangements were structured into company labor policies, Javanese women picked from the coolie ranks often retained their original labor contracts for the duration of their sexual and domestic service.

Most of these women remained servants, sharing only the beds of European staff. But some combined their service with varied degrees of independence and authority and used their positions to enhance their economic and political standing. In Indochina and the Indies, officials complained that local women provided employment to their own kin, making sure that the houses in which they served were peopled with gardeners, washerwomen, and night watchmen from their own families. Working for colonial men of higher station, these *huishoudsters* might run parts of the businesses of the men with whom they had arrangements, hire and fire the servants, and manage shopping budgets and other household affairs. Javanese women (like the European-born in a later period) were called on to keep men physically and psychologically fit for work, to keep them satisfied without distracting them or urging them out of line. Women who worked in such capacities in remote districts and plantation areas provided for the daily needs of the lower-level European staff without imposing the emotional and financial obligations that European family life would demand.

Concubinage reinforced the hierarchies on which colonial societies were based and made those distinctions more problematic at the same time. In North Sumatra, grossly uneven sex ratios often made for intense competition among male workers and their European supervisors for women who would perform these services. Javanese women were not the only ones requisitioned for such jobs. Elsewhere in the Indies, impoverished Indo-European women lived in situations that blurred the boundaries between companionship, concubinage, and paid-for sex. And it was that very blurring that disturbed the racial sensibilities of the Dutch-born elite. Metropolitan critics were openly disdainful of these liaisons on moral grounds – all the more so when these unions became sustained and emotionally significant relationships. Such affective ties defied the racial premise of concubinage as no more than an emotionally unfettered convenience.

The tension between concubinage as a confirmation of racial hierarchy and as a threatening compromise to that order was nowhere more visible than in reactions to the progeny that it produced. Mixed-bloods, poor Indos, and abandoned *mitis* children straddled the division of ruler and ruled as they threatened to blur that divide. Referred to by the common Dutch term *voorkinderen* (children from a previous marriage or union), in the colonies the term was racially marked to signal illegitimate children of a mixed union. Economically disadvantaged and socially invisible, they were sent 'back' to native *kampongs* or shuttled into the shoddy compounds of impoverished whites.

Concubinage was a domestic arrangement based on sexual service and gender inequalities that 'worked' efficiently by some criteria and badly by others. When European identity and supremacy were thought to be vulnerable, in jeopardy, or less than convincing, concubinage came under more direct attack. At the turn of the century and increasingly through the 1920s, colonial elites responded by clarifying the cultural criteria of privilege and the moral premises of their unity. Sex in the politically safe context of prostitution and where possible in the more desirable context of marriage between 'full-blooded' Europeans, replaced concubinage. As in other colonial regions, the ban on concubinage was not always expressed in explicit racist language. On the contrary, difference and distance were often coded to mark race in culturally clear but nuanced terms.

Restrictions on European women in the colonies

Most accounts of colonial conquest and settlement concur in suggesting that European women chose to avoid early pioneering ventures, but the choice was rarely their own. In the Indies, a government ordinance of 1872 made it impossible for any soldier below the rank of sergeant major to marry. Even above that rank, conditions were very restrictive. In the Indies army, marriage was a privilege of the officer corps, with barracks concubinage instituted and regulated for the rank and file. In the twentieth century, formal and informal prohibitions set by banks, estates, and government services operating in Africa, India, and Southeast Asia restricted marriage during the first three to five years of service, while some prohibited it altogether. In Malaya, the major British banks required their employees to sign contracts agreeing to request permission to marry, with the understanding that it would not be granted in less than eight years.

Many historians assume that these bans on employee marriage and on the immigration of European women lifted when specific colonies were politically stable, medically upgraded, and economically secure. But marriage restrictions lasted well into the twentieth century, long after rough living and a scarcity of amenities had become conditions of the past. In India, as late as 1929, British employees in the political service were still recruited at the age of twenty-six and then prohibited from marriage during their first three probationary years. In the army, marriage allowances were also denied until the same age, while in the commercial houses, restrictions were frequent but less overt. On the Ivory Coast, employment contracts in the 1920s denied marriage with European women before the third tour, which meant a minimum of five years' service, so that many men remained unmarried past the age of thirty.

European demographics in the colonies were shaped by these economic and political exigencies and thus were enormously skewed by sex. Among the laboring immigrant and native populations as well as among Europeans in the late nineteenth and early twentieth century, the number of men was, at the very least, double that of women and sometimes exceeded it by twenty-five times. Although in the Indies the overall ratio of European women to men rose from 47:100 to 88:100 between 1900 and 1930, representing an absolute increase from 4,000 to 26,000 Dutch women, in outlying islands the ratios were kept far more uneven. On Sumatra's plantation belt in 1920, there were still only 61 European women per 100 men. On Africa's Ivory Coast, European sex ratios through 1921 were still 1:25. In Tonkin, European men sharply outnumbered European women as late as 1931, when there were 14,085 European men (including military) to 3,083 European women. While these imbalances were usually attributed to the physical hazards of life in the tropics, political explanations are more compelling. In controlling the availability of European women and the sorts of sexual access allowed, colonial state and corporate authorities avoided salary increases as well as the proliferation of a lower-class European settler population. Such policies did not mute the internal class distinctions within the European communities. On the contrary, they shaped the social geography of the colonies by fixing the conditions under which European privileges could be attained and reproduced.

As in North Sumatra, the marriage prohibition was both a political and an economic issue, defining the social contours of colonial communities and the standards of living in them. But, as importantly, it revealed how strongly the conduct of private life and the sexual proclivities individuals expressed were tied to corporate profits and the security of the colonial state. Irregular domestic arrangements were thought to encourage subversion as strongly as acceptable unions could avert it. Family stability and sexual 'normalcy' were thus concretely linked to political agitation or quiescence.

Domestic arrangements varied as government officials and private businesses weighed the economic versus political costs of one arrangement over another, but such calculations were invariably meshed. Those in high office saw white prestige and profits as inextricably linked, and attitudes toward concubinage reflected that concern. Colonial morality and the place of concubinage in it was relative. Thus in Malaya through the 1920s, concubinage was tolerated precisely because 'poor whites' were not. Government and plantation administrators argued that white prestige would be imperiled if European men became impoverished in attempting to maintain middle-class lifestyles and European wives. In late-nineteenth-century Java, in contrast, concubinage itself was considered a major source of white pauperism, condemned at precisely the same time that a new colonial morality passively condoned illegal brothels.

What constituted morality vacillated, as did what defined white prestige – and what its defense should entail. No description of European colonial communities fails to note the obsession with white prestige as a basic feature of colonial thinking. Its protection looms as the primary cause of a long list of otherwise inexplicable postures, prejudices, fears, and violences. But what upheld that prestige was not a constant; concubinage was socially lauded at one time and seen as a political menace at another. White prestige was a gloss for different intensities of racist practice, gender-specific and culturally coded. Although many accounts contend that white women brought an end to concubinage, its decline came with a much wider shift in colonial relations along more racially segregated lines – in which the definitions of prestige shifted and in which Asian, creole, and European-born women were to play new roles.

Colonial communities were not generic; sharp demographic, social, and political differences existed among them. Colonies based on small administrative centers of Europeans (as on Africa's Gold Coast) differed from plantation colonies with sizable enclave European communities (as in Malaya and Sumatra) and still more from settler colonies (as in Algeria) with large, heterogeneous, and permanent European populations. But these 'types' were less fixed than some students of colonial history suggest, such as Winthrop Jordan, who argued that the 'bedrock demographics' of whites to blacks and the sexual composition of the latter 'powerfully influenced, perhaps even determined the kind of society which emerged in each colony.'[13] North Sumatra's European-oriented, overwhelmingly male colonial population, for example, contrasted with the more sexually balanced mestizo culture that emerged in the seventeenth and eighteenth centuries in colonial Java.

But these demographics were not the bedrock of social relations from which all else followed. Sex ratios themselves derived from the particular way in which administrative strategies of social engineering collided with and constrained people's personal choices and private lives. These demographic differences, and the social configurations to which they gave rise, still need to be explained, as do some of the common politically charged issues that a range of colonial societies shared. Some of the similar – and counter – intuitive ways in which the construction of racial categories and the management of sexuality were inscribed indicate new efforts to modernize colonial control.

European women and racial boundaries

Little is as striking in the sociological accounts of European colonial communities as the extraordinary changes that are said to accompany the entry of white women. These adjustments are described as shifts in one direction: toward European lifestyles accentuating the refinements of privilege and new etiquettes of racial difference. The presence of European women was said to put new demands on the white communities to tighten their ranks, clarify their boundaries, and mark out their social space. The material culture of European settlements in Saigon, outposts in New Guinea, and estate complexes in Sumatra were re-tailored to accommodate the physical and moral requirements of a middle-class and respectable feminine contingent. Housing structures in the Indies were partitioned, residential compounds in the Solomon Islands enclosed, servant relations in Hawaii formalized, dress codes in Java altered, food and social taboos in Rhodesia and the Ivory Coast codified. Taken together these changes encouraged new kinds of consumption and new social services that catered to these new demands.

The arrival of large numbers of European women coincided with new bourgeois trappings and notions of privacy in colonial communities. And these, in turn, were accompanied by new distinctions based on race. European women supposedly required more metropolitan amenities than did men and more spacious surroundings for them. Women were claimed to have more delicate sensibilities and therefore needed suitable quarters – discrete and enclosed. Their psychological and physical constitutions were considered more fragile, demanding more servants for the chores they should be spared. In short, white women needed to be maintained at elevated standards of living, in insulated social spaces cushioned with the cultural artifacts of 'being European.' Whether women or men set these new standards and why they might have both done so (and for different reasons) is left unclear. Who exhibited a 'need for' segregation? In Indochina, male doctors advised French women to build their homes with separate domestic and kitchen quarters. Segregationist standards were what women 'deserved' and, more important, what white male prestige required that they maintain.

Racist but moral women, innocent but immoral men

Recent feminist scholarship has challenged the universally negative stereotype of the colonial wife in one of two ways: either by showing the structural reasons why European women were racially intolerant, socially vicious, abusive to servants, and prone to illness and boredom, or by demonstrating that they really were not. Some scholars have attempted to confront what Margaret Strobel calls the 'myth of the destructive female' to show that these women were not detriments to colonial relations but crucial to bolstering a failing empire and to maintaining the daily rituals of racialized rule.[14]

Colonial discourses about white women were full of contradictions. At the same time that new female immigrants were chided for not respecting the racial distance of local convention, an equal number of colonial observers accused them of being more committed racists in their own right. Insecure and jealous of the sexual liaisons of European men with native women, bound to their provincial visions and cultural norms, European women, it was and is argued, constructed the major cleavages on which colonial stratification would rest. Writing about French women in Algeria, the French historian Pierre Nora once claimed that these 'parasites of the colonial relationship in which they do not participate directly, are generally more racist than men and contribute strongly to prohibiting contact between the two societies.'[15] Similarly, Octavio Mannoni noted 'the astonishing fact' that European women in Madagascar were 'far more racialist than the men.'[16] For the Indies, 'it was jealousy of the dusky sirens . . . but more likely some say . . . it was . . . plain feminine scandalization at free and easy sex relations' that caused a decline in miscegenation.[17]

What underwrites these assessments? Are we to believe that sexual intimacy with European men yielded social mobility and political rights for colonized women? Or less likely, that because British civil servants bedded Indian women, Indian men had more 'in common' with British men and enjoyed more parity? Colonized women could sometimes parlay their positions into personal profit and small rewards, but these were *individual* negotiations with no social, legal, or cumulative claims. Sex was not a leveling mechanism but a site in which social asymmetries were instantiated and expressed.

European women were positioned as the bearers of a redefined colonial morality. But to suggest that they fashioned this racism out of whole cloth is to miss the political chronology in which new intensities of racist practice arose. In the African and Asian contexts already mentioned, the arrival of large numbers of European wives, particularly the need for their protection, followed from new terms and tensions in the colonial contract. Their presence and safety was repeatedly invoked to clarify racial lines. It coincided with perceived threats to European prestige, increased racial conflict, covert challenges to colonial politics, outright expressions of nationalist resistance, and internal dissension among whites themselves.

If white women were the force behind the decline of concubinage, as is often claimed, they did so as participants in a broader racial realignment and political plan. This is not to suggest that they were passive in this process, as the dominant preoccupations in many of their novels attest. Many European women opposed concubinage but not because they were categorically jealous of and threatened by Asian women. More likely, it was because of the double standard concubinage condoned for European men. Some Dutch women championed the cause of the wronged *nyai*, while others urged improved protection for non-provisioned native women and children as they did for themselves. Still, few went so far as to advocate the legitimation of these mixed unions in legal marriage. Significantly, what European women had to say had little resonance and little effect until their objections coincided with a realignment in both racial and class politics in which they were strategic.

Race and the politics of sexual peril

If the gender-specific requirements for colonial living imposed specific restrictions on women, they were also racialized assessments of danger that assigned a heightened sexuality to colonized men. Although novels and memoirs position European women as categorically absent from the sexual fantasies of European men, these very men imagined their women to be desired and seductive figures to others. Within this frame, European women needed protection from the 'primitive' sexual urges aroused by the sight of them. In some colonies that sexual threat remained an unlabeled potential. In others, it was given a specific name. The 'Black Peril' referred throughout Africa and much of the British empire to the professed dangers of sexual assault on white women by black men.

In southern Rhodesia and Kenya in the 1920s and 1930s, preoccupations with the Black Peril prompted the creation of citizens' militias, ladies' riflery clubs, and commissions to investigate whether African female domestic servants would not be safer to employ than men. Some colonial states went further still: in New Guinea the White Women's Protection Ordinance of 1926 provided 'the death penalty for any person convicted for the crime of rape or attempted rape upon a European woman or girl'[18] and in the Solomon Islands authorities introduced public flogging in 1934 as punishment for 'criminal assaults on [white] females.'[19]

What do these cases have in common? First, the proliferation of discourse about sexual assault and the measures used to prevent it had virtually no correlation with actual incidences of rape of European women by men of calor. Just the contrary: there was often no *ex post facto* evidence, or any at the time, that rapes were committed or attempted. Sexual assaults may have occurred, but their incidence had little to do with the fluctuations in anxiety about them. Moreover, the rape laws were race-specific. Sexual abuse of black women was not classified as rape and therefore was not legally actionable, nor did rapes committed by white men lead to prosecution. If these accusations of sexual threat were not prompted by the fact of rape, what did they signal, and to what were they tied?

Allusions to political and sexual subversion of the colonial system went hand in hand. The term 'Black Peril' referred to sexual threats, but it also connoted the fear of insurgence, and of perceived non-acquiescence to colonial control more generally. Concern over protection of white women intensified during real and perceived crises of control-threats to the internal cohesion of the European communities or infringements on its borders. Thus colonial accounts of the rebellion in India in 1857 contain detailed descriptions of the sexual mutilation of British women by Indian men although no rapes were recorded. In Africa too, although the chronologies of the Black Peril differ – on the Rand in South Africa peaking a full twenty years earlier than elsewhere – we can still identify a patterned sequence of events. In New Guinea, the White Women's Protection Ordinance followed a large influx of acculturated Papuans into Port Moresby in the 1920s. Resistant to the constraints imposed on their dress, movement, and education, whites perceived them as arrogant, 'cheeky,' and without respect. In post-World War I Algeria, the political unease of *pieds noirs* (local French settlers) in the face of 'a whole new series of [Muslim] demands' manifested itself in a popular culture newly infused with strong images of sexually aggressive Algerian men.[20]

Second, rape charges against colonized men were often based on perceived transgressions of social space. 'Attempted rapes' turned out to be 'incidents' of a Papuan man 'discovered' in the vicinity of a white residence, a Fijian man who entered a European patient's room, or a male servant poised at the bedroom door of a European woman asleep or in half-dress.[21] With such a broad range of behaviors defined as dangerous, most colonized men were potentially threatening as sexual and political aggressors.

Third, accusations of sexual assault frequently followed on heightened tensions within European communities – and renewed efforts to find consensus within them. Rape accusations in South Africa, for example, coincided with a rash of strikes between 1890 and 1914 by both African and white miners. Similarly, in Rhodesia, after a strike of white railway workers in 1929, otherwise conflicting members of the European community came together in a common cause. The threat of native rebellion produced a 'solidarity [that] found sustenance in the threat of racial destruction.'[22] When labor actions by Indonesian workers and European staff were most intense, Sumatra's white community did the same. They expanded their vigilante groups, intelligence networks, and demands for police protection to ensure their women were safe and their workers 'in hand.'

White degeneracy, motherhood, and the eugenics of empire

European women were vital to the colonial enterprise and the solidification of racial boundaries in ways that repeatedly tied their supportive and subordinate posture to community cohesion and colonial security. That contribution was reinforced at the turn of the century by a metropolitan bourgeois discourse (and an eminently anthropological one) intensely concerned with notions of 'degeneracy.' Middle-class morality, manliness, and motherhood were seen as endangered by the related fears of 'degeneration' and miscegenation in scientifically construed racist beliefs. Degeneration was defined as 'departures from the normal human type . . . transmitted through inheritance and lead[ing] progressively to destruction.'[23] Degeneracy, brought on by environmental, physical, and moral factors, could be averted by positive eugenic selection or, negatively, by eliminating the 'unfit' or the environmental and more specifically cultural contagions that gave rise to them. Eugenic discourse has usually been associated with Social Darwinian notions of 'selection,' with the strong influence of Lamarckian thinking reserved for its French variant. However, the notion of 'cultural contamination' runs throughout the British, US, French, and Dutch eugenic traditions. Eugenic arguments used to explain the social malaise of industrialization, immigration, and urbanization derived from notions that acquired characteristics were inheritable and thus that poverty, vagrancy, and promiscuity were class-linked biological traits, tied to genetic material as directly as night blindness and blond hair. This Lamarckian feature of eugenic thinking in its colonial expression linked racial degeneracy to the sexual transmission of cultural contagions and to the political instability of imperial rule.

Appealing to a broad political and scientific constituency, Euro-American eugenic societies included advocates of infant welfare programs, liberal intellectuals, conservative businessmen, Fabians, and physicians with social concerns. By the 1920s, however, it contained an increasingly vocal number of those who called for and put into law if not practice the sterilization of what were considered the mentally, morally, or physically unfit members of the British, German, and North American underclass.

Eugenics reverberated in the colonies in predictable and unexpected forms. The moral, biological, and sexual referents of 'degeneracy' (distinct in the dictionary citation above) were fused in how the concept was actually deployed. The 'colonial branch' of eugenics focused on the vulnerabilities of white rule and measures to safeguard European superiority. Eugenics was designed to control the procreation of the 'unfit' lower orders and to target 'the poor, the colonized, or unpopular strangers.'[24] But eugenic thinking reached further. It permeated how metropolitan observers viewed the degenerate lifestyle of colonials and how colonial elites admonished the behavior of degenerates among themselves. Whereas European and US studies focused on the inherent propensity of the impoverished classes to criminality, in the Indies delinquency among 'European' children was linked to the proportion of 'native blood' that children of mixed unions had inherited from their native mothers. Eugenics provided not so much a new vocabulary as a new biological idiom in which to ground the medical and moral basis for anxieties over European hegemony and white prestige. It reopened debates over segregated residence and education, new standards of morality, sexual vigilance, and the rights of *certain* Europeans to rule.

Eugenic thinking manifested itself, not in the direct importation of metropolitan practices such as sterilization, but in a translation of the political *principles* and the social values that eugenics implied. In defining what was unacceptable, eugenics also identified what constituted a 'valuable life' and 'a gender-specific work and productivity, described in social, medical and psychiatric terms.'[25] Applied to European colonials, eugenic statements pronounced what kind of people should represent Dutch or French rule, how they should bring up their children, and with whom they should socialize. Those concerned with issues of racial survival and racial purity invoked the moral duty of European colonial women to fulfil an alternative set of imperial imperatives. They were to 'uplift' colonial subjects through educational and domestic management and attend to the family environment of their men. Sometimes they were simply encouraged to remain in the metropole and to stay at home. The point is that a common gender discourse was mapped onto different imperial situations that celebrated motherhood and domesticity.

If in Britain racial deterioration was conceived of as a result of the moral turpitude and the ignorance of working-class mothers, in the colonies the dangers were more pervasive, the possibilities of contamination worse. Proposals to secure European rule pushed in two directions. On the one hand, they pushed away from ambiguous racial genres and open domestic arrangements. On the other hand, they pressed for an upgrade and homogenization of European standards as well as a clearer delineation of them. The impulse was clear: away from miscegenation toward white endogamy; away from concubinage toward family formation and legal marriage; away from, as in the case of the Indies, mestizo customs and toward metropolitan norms. As stated in the bulletin of the Netherlands Indies Eugenics Society, 'eugenics is nothing other than belief in the possibility of preventing degenerative symptoms in the body of our beloved *moedervolken* [people, populace], or in cases where they may already be present, of counteracting them.'[26]

Like the modernization of colonialism itself, with its scientific management and educated technocrats with limited local knowledge, colonial communities of the early twentieth century were rethinking the ways in which their authority should be expressed. This rethinking took the form of asserting a distinct colonial morality, explicit in its reorientation to the racial and class markers of being European. It emphasized transnational racial commonalities despite national differences. Not least it distilled a notion of *Homo europceus* for whom superior health, wealth, and education were tied to racial endowments and a White Man's norm. Thus, Eugene Pujarniscle, a novelist and participant observer in France's colonial venture, wrote: '[O]ne might be surprised that my pen always returns to the words *blanc* [white] or "European" and never to "Francais" . . . in effect colonial solidarity and the obligations that it entails allies all the peoples of the white races.'[27]

Such sensibilities colored imperial policy in nearly all domains. Fears of physical contamination gave new credence to fears of political vulnerability. Whites had to guard their ranks, to increase their numbers, and to ensure that their members respected the biological and political boundaries on which their power was thought to rest. In Europe the socially and physically 'unfit,' the poor, the indigent, and the insane, were either to be sterilized or prevented from marriage. In the colonies it was these very groups among Europeans who were either excluded from entry or institutionalized while they were there and eventually sent home.

To sustain the notion that good health, virility, and the ability to rule were inherent features of being European, colonial rulers invested in a politics of exclusion that policed their members as well as the colonized. Such strategies and concerns were not new to the

1920s. In the 1750s the East Indies Company had already taken 'draconian measures' to control pauperism among 'Dutchmen of mixed blood.'[28] In the same period, the British East Indies Company enforced policies that discouraged lower-class European migration and settlement and argued that such populations would destroy Indian respect for 'the superiority of the European character.'[29] Patriotic calls to populate Java with poor Dutch farmers were also blocked for similar reasons in the mid-1800s and then again with new urgency in the following century as successive challenges to European rule were felt more profoundly.

Measures were taken both to avoid poor white migration and to produce a colonial profile that highlighted the manliness, well-being, and productivity of European men. In this equation, evidence of manliness, national identity, and racial superiority were meshed. Thus British colonial administrators were retired by the age of fifty-five, ensuring that 'no Oriental was ever allowed to see a Westerner as he ages and degenerated, just as no Westerner needed ever to see himself, mirrored in the eyes of the subject race, as anything but a vigorous, rational, ever-alert young Raj.'[30] In the twentieth century, these 'men of class' and 'men of character' embodied a modernized and renovated image of rule. They were to safeguard the colonies against the physical weakness, moral decay, and inevitable degeneration that long residence in the colonies encouraged and against the temptations that interracial domestic situations had allowed.

The strategies of rule and sexual morality

The political etymology of colonizer and colonized was gender- and class-specific. The exclusionary politics of colonialism demarcated not just external boundaries but also interior frontiers, specifying internal conformity and order among Europeans themselves. The categories of colonizer and colonized were secured through notions of racial difference constructed in gender terms. Redefinitions of acceptable sexual behavior and morality emerged during crises of colonial control precisely because they called into question the tenuous artifices of rule *within* European communities and what marked their borders.

Even from the limited cases reviewed here, several patterns emerge. First and most obviously, colonial sexual prohibitions were racially asymmetric and gender coded. Sexual relations might be forbidden between white women and men of color but not the other way around. On the contrary, interracial unions (as opposed to marriage) between European men and colonized women aided the long-term settlement of European men in the colonies while ensuring that colonial patrimony stayed in limited and selective hands. Second, interdictions against interracial unions were rarely a primary impulse in the strategies of rule. For India, Indochina, and South Africa, colonial contexts usually associated with sharp social sanctions against interracial unions, 'mixing' in the initial period of colonialization was tolerated and even condoned.

The focus here has been on late colonialism in Asia, but colonial elite intervention in the sexual life of their agents and subjects was not condoned to this place or period. In sixteenth-century Mexico, mixed marriages between Spanish men and Christianized Indian women were encouraged by the crown until mid-century, when colonists felt that 'the rising numbers of their own mestizo progeny threatened the prerogatives of a narrowing elite sector.'[31] In eighteenth- and early-nineteenth-century Cuba, mild opposition to interracial marriage gave way to a 'virtual prohibition' from 1864 to 1874 when 'merchants, slave dealers and the colonial powers opposed [it] in order to preserve slavery.'[32]

Changes in sexual access and domestic arrangements have invariably accompanied major efforts to reassert the internal coherence of European communities and to redefine the boundaries of privilege across the colonial divide. But sexual union in itself did not automatically produce a larger population legally classified as 'European.' On the contrary, even in early twentieth-century Brazil – where miscegenation had made for a refined system of gradations, 'most mixing [took] place outside of marriage.'[33] The important point is that miscegenation signaled neither the presence nor the absence of racial discrimination. Hierarchies of privilege and power were written into the *condoning* of interracial unions, as well as into their condemnation.

The chronologies vary from one context to another, but parallel shifts are evident in the strategies of rule and in sexual morality. Concubinage fell into moral disfavor at the same time that new emphasis was placed on the standardization of European administration. This occurred in some colonies by the early twentieth century and in others later on, but the correspondence between rationalized rule, bourgeois respectability, and the custodial power of European women to protect their men seems strongest during the interwar years. The success of Western technological achievements was being questioned. British, French, and Dutch policy makers had moved from an assimilationist to a more segrega-tionist, separatist stance. The reorganization of colonial investments along corporate and multinational lines brought with it a push for a restructured and more highly productive labor force. With it came more vocal nationalist and labor movements resisting those demands.

An increasing rationalization of colonial management produced radical shifts in notions of how empires should be run, how agents of empire should rule, and where, how, and with whom they should live. Thus French debates concerning the need to systematize colonial management and dissolve the provincial and personalized satraps of 'the old-time colon' invariably targeted and condemned the unseemly domestic arrangements in which they lived. British high officials in Africa imposed new 'character' requirements on their subordinates, designating specific class attributes and conjugal ties that such a selection implied. Critical to this restructuring was a new disdain for colonials too adapted to local custom, too removed from the local European community, and too encumbered with intimate native ties. As in Sumatra, this hands-off policy distanced Europeans in more than one sense. It forbade European staff both from personal confrontations with their Asian field hands and from the limited local knowledge they gained through sexual and domestic arrangements.

Medical expertise increasingly confirmed the salubrious benefits of European camaraderie and frequent home leaves. A *cordon sanitaire* surrounded European enclaves, was wrapped around mind and body, around each European man and his home. White prestige became redefined by the conventions that would safeguard the moral, cultural, and physical well-being of its agents, with which European women were charged. Colonial politics locked European men and women into routinized protection of their physical health and social space in ways that bound gender prescriptions to the racial cleavages between 'us' and 'them.'

It may be, however, that we should not be searching for congruent colonial chronologies attached to specific dates but rather for similar shifts in the rhythms of rule and sexual management, for similar internal patterns within specific colonial histories themselves. For example, following the Great Rebellion in India, political subversion was tied to sexual impropriety in new ways. Colonial politicians and moral reforms stipulated new codes of conduct that emphasized respectability, domesticity, and a more carefully segregated use of space. All of these measures focused on European women. Virtually all resonate with those developed in Africa and Southeast Asia but were instituted a half century earlier than in colonies elsewhere. Looking to a somewhat longer *durée* than the colonial crises of the early twentieth century, we might consider British responses to the 1857 rebellion not as an exception but as a template for colonial responses elsewhere. The modular quality of colonial perceptions and policies was built on new international standards of empire and specific metropolitan priorities. New standards in turn were responsive to local challenges of those who contested life and labor under European rule.

Sexual control figured in the substance, as well as the iconography, of colonialism's racial policies. But colonial politics was not just concerned with sex; nor did sexual relations reduce to colonial politics. Sex in the colonies had to do with sexual access and reproduction, class distinctions and racial demarcations, nationalism and European identity – in different measure and not all at the same time. Major shifts in the positioning of women were not, as we might expect, signaled by the penetration of capitalism *per se* but by subtler changes in class politics and imperial morality and in response to the failures of specific colonial projects. Ethnographies of empire should attend both to changing sensibilities and to sex, to racialized regimes that were realized on a macro- and micro-scale. They may begin to capture how European culture and class politics resonated in colonial settings, how class and gender discriminations were transposed into racial distinctions that reverberated in the metropole as they were fortified on colonial ground. Such investigations may show that sexual control was both an instrumental image for the body politic – a salient part standing for the whole – and itself fundamental to how racial policies were secured and how colonial projects were carried out.

Notes

1   Some women's sojourns in the colonies did allow them to pursue career possibilities and independent lifestyles barred to them in metropolitan Europe at the time. However, the experience of professional women in South Asia and Africa highlights how quickly they were shaped into 'cultural missionaries' or, in resisting that impulse, were marginalized in their work and social life.

2   Ronald Hyam, 'Concubinage and the Colonial Service: The Crewe Circular (1909),' *Journal of Imperial and Commonwealth History*, 1986, 1:4(3), 170–86.

3   Lewis H. Gann and Peter Duignan, *The Rulers of British Africa, 1870–1914* (London: Croom Helm, 1978) 240.

4   Edward W. Said, *Orientalism* (New York: Pantheon Books, 1978) 6; my emphasis.

5   ibid., 207.

6   In Dutch and French colonial novels of the nineteenth century, heightened sensuality is the recognized reserve of Asian and Indo-European mistresses and only of those European women born in the colonies and loosened by its moral environment. See P.A. Daum, *Ups and Downs of Life in the Indies*, trans. Elsje Qualms Sturtevant and Donald W. Sturtevant (Amherst: University of Massachusetts Press, 1987); Loutfi, *Litterature.*

7   Leonard Blusse, *Strange Company: Chinese Settlers, Mestizo Women and the Dutch in VOC Batavia* (Riverton, NJ: Foris Publications, 1986) 161.

8   Jean Taylor, *The Social World of Batavia: Europeans and Eurasians in Dutch Asia* (Madison, University of Wisconsin Press, 1983) 14.

9   Taylor, *Social World*, 14.

10   ibid., 16. European-born women also were excluded from much of the Portuguese empire from the sixteenth through the eighteenth centuries. C.R. Boxer, *The Portuguese Seaborne Empire, 1415–1825* (New York: Knopf, 1969) 129–30.

11   Louis Malleret, *L' exotisme indochinois dans la literature francaise depuis 1860* (Paris: Larose, 1934), 216; William B. Cohen, *Rulers of Empire: The French Colonial Service in Africa* (Stanford, CA: Hoover Institution Press, 1971) 122.

12   Taylor, *Social World*, 148.

13   Winthrop D. Jordan, *White over Black: American Attitudes Toward the Negro, 1550–1822* (Chapel Hill: University of North Carolina Press, 1968) 140. Carl N. Degler made a similar point when contrasting the shortage of European women in the Portuguese colonies to the family emigration policy of the British in North America. He argued that the former gave rise to widespread miscegenation and a vast population of *mulattos*, the 'key' to contrasting race relations in the United States and Brazil (*Neither Black nor White: Slavery and Race Relations in Brazil and the United States* (New York: Macmillan, [1971] 1986), 226–38.

14   Strobel, 'Gender and Race in the 19th and 20th Century British Empire' in Renate Bridenthal *et al.* (eds) *Becoming Visible: Women in European History*, 2nd edn (Boston: Houghton Mifflin, 1987) 378–79.

15   Pierre Nora, *Les francais d'Algerie* (Paris: R. Juillard, 1961) 174.

16   Octave Mannoni, *Prospero and Caliban* (New York: Praeger, 1956) 115.

17   Raymond Kennedy, *The Ageless Indies* (New York: John Day, 1947) 164.

18   Amirah Inglis, *The White Women's Protective Ordinance: Sexual Anxiety and Politics in Papua* (London: Sussex University Press, 1975) vi.

19   James Boutilier, 'European Women in the Solomon Islands,' in Denise O'Brien and Sharon Tiffany (eds), *Rethinking Women's Roles: Perspectives from the Pacific* (Berkeley: University of California Press, 1984) 197.

20   Emmanuel Sivan, *Interpretations of Islam, Past and Present* (Princeton: Darwin Press, 1983) 178.

21   Boutilier, 'European Women,' 197; Inglis, *White Women's Protective Ordinance,* 11.

22   Dane Kennedy, *Islands of White: Settler Society and Culture in Kenya and Southern Rhodesia,* (Durham, NC: Duke University Press, 1987) 138.

23   E.D. Morel, quoted in George L. Mosse, *Toward the Final Solution: A History of European Racism* (New York: Fertig, 1978) 83.

24   Eric Hobsbawm, *The Age of Empire, 1875–1914* (London: Weidenfeld and Nicolson, 1987) 253.

25   Gisela Bock, 'Racism and Sexism in Nazi Germany' in Renate Bridenthal *et al.* (eds) *When Biology Becomes Destiny: Women in Weimar and Nazi Germany* (New York: *Monthly Review*, 1984) 274.

26   Ernest Rodenwaldt, 'Eugenetisch Problemen in Nederlandisch-Indie' in *Ons Nageslacht*, 1928, 1–8, 1.

27   Eugene Pujarniscle, *Philoxene ou la literature coloniale* (Paris: Firmin-Dudot, 1931) 72; also see Robert Louis Delavignette, *Service africain* (Paris: Gallimard, 1946) 41.

28   *Encyclopaedie van Nederland-Indie*, 2nd edn. (The Hague: Martinus Nijhoff and E.J. Brill, [1919] 1921) 367.

29   Quoted in David Arnold, 'White Colonization and Labour in Nineteenth-Century India,' *Journal of Imperial and Commonwealth History*, 1983, 10(2), 139.

30   Said, *Orientalism*, 42.

31   June Nash, 'Aztec Women: The Transition from Status to Class in Empire and Colony,' in Etienne and Leacock, *Women and Colonization*, 140.

32   Verena Martinez-Alier, *Marriage, Class and Colour in 19th-Century Cuba* (Cambridge: Cambridge University Press, 1974) 39.

33   Degler, *Neither Black nor White*, 185.

Chapter 13

Kathleen Wilson

THINKING BACK: GENDER MISRECOGNITION AND POLYNESIAN SUBVERSIONS ABOARD THE COOK VOYAGES

Focusing on the eighteenth century as against Ann Laura Stoler's 19th and 20th centuries, Kathleen Wilson's work has also cast new light on ideas about sex, gender and the body in colonial encounters. James Cook's South Sea voyages have been debated from almost every conceivable angle – including some famously ill-tempered arguments among anthropologists – but here Wilson explores new territory including contending notions of masculinity and homosexuality.

Stephen Howe

BETWEEN 1768 AND 1780, CAPTAIN JAMES COOK and his crews embarked upon a set of voyages of discovery that would transform the face of the world. The achievements of the voyages, of course, have been celebrated and critiqued by an array of anthropologists, historical ethnographers, historians, art historians, literary critics, and scholars of subaltern and performance studies, illuminating both indigenous and British Enlightenment cultures and ecologies.[1] This chapter proposes to take a different tack, and address some of the confusions engendered by Cook's encounters with South Pacific peoples, focusing on the disruptions and silences produced by the arts and accounts of 'discovery.' The point of such an effort is not to try to 'unmask' the veracity of British empirical observation or 'speak' for eighteenth-century Polynesians by assigning them a western subjectivity irrelevant to their concerns. Rather, it is to recognize that the practices and epistemologies of Pacific peoples impressed themselves upon the explorers and the imperial archive in ways that altered both their substance and hence our ways of knowing them. For, despite the best intentions of men who believed themselves to be positioned at the cutting edge of History, Polynesian actors made their presence known in ways that could not and still cannot be assimilable within that history's narrative. I will focus in particular on the intriguing roles of gender misrecognition and the entanglements of desire evinced in some of the voyage journals and accounts, focusing on 'conjunctures' rather than 'cultures' *per se* [2] and taking seriously the mutual confusions that abounded as Cook and his men attempted to use gender and sexual practice as guides to Pacific social systems, and the Pacific islanders themselves tried in turn to map their cosmogonies on to European bodies. Far from exhibiting some unilateral process of 'othering' at work in the art of discovery, our exploration of gender misrecognition and Polynesian subversions highlights the intricate interplay of local modes of understanding on a global stage, and the dialogic nature of colonial encounter. The complex fields of identification at work in the crucible of first contact thus make visible the *unwriting* of History through the aporia of cultural translation.

Women in the history of man

Cook's mission of mapping and discovering the South Pacific took place in a period of growing political, intellectual, and cultural ferment in Britain, the global dimensions of which would become clear as the three voyages (1768–1771, 1772–1775, 1776–1780) unfolded. War, conquest, imperial supremacy, and expeditions to 'undiscovered' parts of the globe had created new responsibilities and anxieties for metropolitan and colonial peoples alike; these developments had also circulated new information about the diversity of humankind and the relative positions of Britons, Europeans, and indigenous peoples across the globe.[3] Ideas about natural and historical time were also changing, leading to the emergence of notions of 'deep time' that required the adjustment of humanity's cosmological, social, and biological location. As natural historians and philosophers came under greater pressure to found the study of human society upon a firm empirical base, travelers, colonizers, and explorers alike eagerly embraced the new national mission to describe and explain differences among the peoples of the world. The new history of humanity melded time and space to generalize and extend History to encompass the globe and reconceptualize relationships between parts of the world as temporal ones.[4] It also prompted competing theories about the ways in which different nations developed in relation to climate and 'race,' inventing ways to define 'race' through migration and language, and novel opportunities to debate the status of gender and sexual difference as social or natural categories.[5] In particular, the unruliness of 'talk,' the effeminizing impact of empire on the national character and its spirit of inquiry and compassion, and both female sexual agency and male effeminacy were canvassed in public forums, and became issues which the cult of sensibility and Enlightenment progressivism ('the natural history of man') strove to explain. The latter concomitantly reconfigured ideas about empire, the position of women and their roles as signs and agents of social progress.[6] In this context, the voyages to the South Pacific provided an occasion not only to prove British altruism and expertise in the arts of discovery, but also to verify men's and women's 'nature' and status through a widening comparative frame, constructed through first-hand, 'eye-witness' observation.[7]

Cook's celebrated explorations were thus stridently gendered as well as intensely nationalistic. They were also powerfully imbued with a historicist mission to turn their work and its subjects into 'History,' providing the 'facts' about new peoples that would help establish 'permanent truths in the history of Man.'[8] That the journals and logs of the senior and petty officers would be collected and used by the Admiralty for their 'official' accounts of the voyages gave credibility to crew members' rather inflated sense of their own roles in turning the voyages into History. Twinning the sensibility of enlightened masculinity and non-aristocratic morality with the benevolent and humanitarian goals of 'discovery,' the voyages sought to bring indigenous peoples 'within the pale of the offices of humanity . . . to relieve the wants of their imperfect state of society,' and so evince British modernity and achievement.[9] These achievements were recorded in the explorers' journals and relayed in voyage accounts to the British public in a naturalist reportage that combined features of travelogue and empirical description, even in its tales of the exotic and erotic.[10] The distinguished naturalists and artists on board (including Joseph Banks and Sydney Parkinson on the first voyage, Johann Reinhold Forster, his son, George, and William Hodges on the second, and John Webber on the third), as well as Cook and his crew, were well armed with Enlightenment social theory to gauge the 'stage' of material and civil progress of each new society encountered.

Central to this taxonomic effort was the assessment of the place of women. 'It is the practice of all uncivilized nations to deny their women the common privileges of humans beings,' George Forster noted. 'The ideas of finding happiness and comfort in the bosom of a companion only arise with a higher degree of culture.' Indeed, women, their physical and moral attributes and social status, were more enthusiastically studied than in any previous colonial encounter, and became vital, for example, to the Forsters' influential distinction between the two 'races' in the South Pacific.[11] Yet the apparently successful incorporation of Pacific women into the 'History of Man' masked the confusion and chaos that these encounters had engendered, a good deal of which stemmed from the apparently insatiable desire of the women in question for British officers and tars (which was more troublesome from the men's theoretical perspective, apparently, than the officers' and tars' desire for them).

Tahitian women, for example, had quickly become legendary for their beauty and their supposed proclivities for 'free love.' The overtly erotic dances and ceremonial disrobing performed by young Tahitian women, the polygamous sexual antics among the *arioi*, the elite group of performers and religious chiefs associated with the war god, Oro, and the more exogamous sexual trysts of their non-elite sisters with British tars sparked fantasies in English, as French, minds about the lack of guilt in the 'state of nature.' Yet in the everyday interactions of 'discovery,' the Tahitian women's character generated debate among the voyagers and wreaked havoc with the performance of appropriate masculinity by British and (in British eyes) Oceanic men alike. The gallant naturalist Joseph Banks, for example, revelled in the sexual alterity of Polynesian life to a degree that was taken to compromise his philosophical detachment. 'In the Island of Otaheitie,' he wrote in one account, echoing the rhapsodies of Bougainville, 'Love is the Chief Occupation, the favourite, nay almost the Sole Luxury of the inhabitants.'[12] His observations on the 'civilities' and 'politeness' of the women, who 'sometimes by force seat[ed] themselves and us upon the mats' to pursue carnal pleasures, his amorous connection to 'Oberea,' the putative 'queen' of Wallis's voyage, as well as his eagerness to act as 'participant anthropologist' in local erotic rites, were gleefully lampooned by pundits in London as examples of the libertinage and depravity of aristocratic and savage sensibilities alike.'[13] Banks' activities also raised hackles among some other officers aboard ship, not least for his exhibition of a marked disregard of masculine and bourgeois self-restraint as well as scientific curiosity.

In the event, Banks' judgments about Tahitians were not necessarily authoritative. Some observers defended Tahitian women's greater nonchalance towards matters of the flesh as a product of class (e.g. aristocratic luxury or lower-class depravity). The prosaic astronomer William Wales, of the second voyage, claimed that most married and unmarried women observed 'proprieties' and that the women who offered themselves to the sailors were common whores. 'A stranger who visits England might with equal justice draw the character of the Ladies there,' Wales asserted, 'from those which he might meet with on board the Ships in Plymouth Sound, at Spithead, or in the Thames; on the Point at Portsmouth, or in the Purlieus of Wapping.'[14] Quaker and artist Sydney Parkinson disagreed, arguing that neither married nor unmarried women had 'a very delicate sense of modesty: their husbands will allow you any liberty with their wives, except the last, which they do not approve' – yet he held the British to be as culpable for the (to him) disgraceful sexual traffic underway as the women. Characteristically Captain Cook was more measured in his assessments of the ladies, while also seeking to understand them within a global view of uniform human nature. He agreed that 'Chastity indeed is but little Valued,' but expressed horror at the *arioi* practice of infanticide, which allowed them to enjoy 'free liberty in love without being troubled or disturbed by its consequences.' On the second voyage, however, Cook defended Tahitian women against the charges of free love, and even argued that lower-class women had 'learned' morality since the last visit, 'on the whole I think the women in general were less free with their favours now than formerly' – although how they could have done so through contact with insatiable European crews remains obscure.[15]

Of course, the alleged 'libertinage' of the native, mixed-race, or enslaved woman was a well-entrenched trope of British colonization and exploration narratives, elaborated on by fur traders, settlers, planters, merchants, and missionaries in the New World.[16] Yet under the weight of the voyages' imperative to close observation and comparison, and in the face of local societies still intact enough to translate novelty in their own terms, the yardstick of Enlightenment gender roles could not cope with the complexities of Polynesian sexual and social practices. British tars were certainly delighted that the favors of Tahitian beauties could be won by bits of ribbon or mirror. But what appeared to them to be the 'libertinism' of Polynesian women was, in the women's eyes, a traffic in men that allowed them to exploit the arrival of boatloads of strangers for their own advantage.

For Polynesians had their own ethnography and histories of travel, ones that were intertwined with a cosmogony linking sexual intercourse with access to divine power and social advancement.[17] Women's offering themselves to British sailors may have been influenced by their beliefs that as foreigners they had close links to this sacred power and the offspring sired by them would give the women access to supernatural benefits in the form of ancestral *mana* (supernatural power). As Polynesian historians and anthropologists have argued, sex for Polynesians 'was everything: rank, power, wealth, land and the security of all these,' and sexual acts were conceived of as engaging men and women in a common opposition to the divine, allowing women in particular to 'attract and transform the divine generative forces.'[18] Hence the women involved seemed determined at all costs to seize the opportunity offered them by the arrival of shiploads of strangers. This was often executed against the will of their objects, the British tars. '[We] found all the Women of these Island but little influenced by interested motives in their intercourse with us, as they would almost use violence to force you into their Embrace regardless whether we gave them any thing or not,' Welsh surgeon's mate David Samwell complained at one point.[19]

As Polynesian women mapped their culture on to the European male body, they made that body the object in the process of their own spiritual and political aggrandizement. Alternately, when this illusion had waned, women would then offer themselves in return for 'curiosities,' displaying an avidity for ethnographic investigation themselves. Significantly, a large part of Cook's authority as commander rested upon his refusal to participate in this traffic as object or subject. His romantic disinterest and sexual self-control, however, elicited contempt from the women themselves. Hence at Tonga in June 1774 when Cook declined a beautiful young girl offered by her mother for his 'personal use,' he was roundly abused: 'I understood very little of what she said, but her actions were expressive enough and shew'd that her words were to this effect, Sneering in my face and saying, what sort of a man are you thus to refuse the embraces of so fine a young Woman.'[20]

The perception of a predatory sexual appetite of the women and the corresponding lack (so it was thought) of male authority over them troubled the voyagers exceedingly. They accordingly sought to exert their own masculine power and prowess through on-the-spot modification of 'universal laws' that presupposed a normative European morality. John Marra, gunner's mate on the *Resolution's* second voyage, theorized based on his experience that Society Islanders were 'an effeminate race, intoxicated with pleasure, and enfeebled by indulgence.'[21] Cook himself ventured a universal law on female chastity when, on the third voyage, contrary to expectations, the women of Van Diemen's Land (Tasmania) refused the tars' advances:

> I believe it has generally been found amongst uncivilized people that where the Women are easy of access, the Men are the first who offer them to strangers, and where this is not the case they are not easily come at, neither large presents nor privacy will induce them to violate the laws of chastity or custom. [22]

And J.R. Forster, who argued in his influential *Observations Made During a Voyage Round the World* (1778) that Polynesian women's good treatment by their men and quick sensibilities made them embodiments of their societies' progress towards civilization, still saw fit to upbraid the women in his journal for both their lack of chastity and their refusal to engage straightforwardly in sexual commerce:

> the [Tahitian] women coquet in the most impudent manner, and shew uncommon fondness for Foreigners, but are all Jilts and coax the Foreigners out of anything they can get: and will not comply to sleep with them, unless . . . the bribe very great and tempting.[23]

The journal accounts thus make visible the power of the women's gaze to destabilize that of the explorers by turning the seamen into the objects of Polynesian categories of difference.

Manly effeminacy

Male sexuality was another area where misrecognition confounded the voyagers' encounters with Pacific islanders. Let's listen to Wales talk about his attempts to put to rest among his own men the fear that the 'natives' were 'sodomites.' Recording the details of his exploration of the island of Tana (Vanuatu) in the New Hebrides – one of the islands of the western Pacific that was universally regarded by Cook and his crew to be lagging far behind the Tahitians in civilization and physical beauty – Wales reported that some of his men had been followed into the bushes by ni-Vanuatu males 'for a purpose I need not mention,' and then remarked:

> there are People who . . . are not capable of defending the Whims they Adopt otherwise than by *It is so – I know it* . . . and some of this Cast have asserted, and I make no doubt *written down* . . . that most of the People we have lately been among are Sodomites, or Cannibals, or both . . . [yet] no person had been attempted who had not either a softness in his features, or whose employment it was to Carry bundles of one kind or other which is the Office of their own Women.

Here Wales, like Cook a bluff and self-made Yorkshireman, tries to use his well-trained powers of observation to combat the prejudices of his crew and chalk up the miscues of the Tannese to gender confusion.[24] The visual and corporeal cues upon which European order depended were insufficient, it seems, in antipodean encounters, where British tars projected their own fears of sodomitical desire on to the ni-Vanuatu, and the ni-Vanuatu mapped their own culture on the European male body. From the ni-Vanuatu perspective, in a culture where women did most (though certainly not all) the carrying, and were in George Forster's view obliged 'to perform all sorts of laborious, and humiliating operations,' European men who did women's work looked like women or could be used as women. Equally possible is that the ni-Vanuatu could not conceive that shiploads of men could appear without women in tow to do their carrying for them. Significantly, Wales himself put the burden of proof of masculinity back on the British tars themselves, admitting that the 'softness' of features of some contributed to their misrecognition by the natives. Here he reflects a widely held view in Britain that 'the prevalency of this passion [for sodomy] has for its object effeminate delicate beings only.'[25]

Perhaps, as Gananath Obeyesekere has argued about Pacific cannibalism, the British sailors' suspicions about sodomy, arising after several months' incarceration in the cramped and homosocial holds of two sloops, revealed more about the practices aboard ship than they would like to think. Alternately, to follow this line of inquiry may be to treat these texts to what Lee Edelman has called, following Foucault, a 'hermeneutics of suspicion,' through which any sexual practice and all forms of homosociality become doubled, permeable, and suspect, and homosexuality is called into being through the forensic investigation of 'subtexts.'[26] Yet I would contend that a (non-homophobic) hermeneutics of suspicion may be precisely what is needed in order to illuminate what is at issue in these accounts: the dense sites of signification that nationalized bodies were made to bear, the failure (from the enlightened explorers' perspective) of native bodies to speak for themselves, and the murkiness created when cultures of identity circulate between nations at the point of contact. From this perspective, Wales's entry speaks to an array of issues surrounding sodomy and masculinity, both in English culture and in the arts of discovery, when for a variety of historical reasons the homophobic hermeneutics of suspicion that entangled the ship was projected on to indigenous societies.

For British seamen's prejudices seem to have been founded on the *terra firma* of metropolitan antipathy to 'effeminates' that was a marked feature of the social and political landscape in the 1770s. Within England, sodomy was increasingly identified with aristocratic debauchery and excess or, still worse, with the perception of depraved and degenerate character. Randolph Trumbach's recent argument that sodomy was becoming the touchstone of a gender revolution that legislated heterosexuality as the norm receives solid empirical support by the evidence of a rise in the expression of English hostility to sodomy in the last quarter of the eighteenth century, a hostility that exceeded perhaps anywhere else in Europe. In this period, bi- or homosexual men were banished to the continent by their families, and the numbers of pardons for the capital crime of sodomy steadily diminished. There was also an upsurge in formal charges of sodomy that began in the 1770s and reached a peak in the early 1800s, reflecting a backlash in England over non-procreative forms of sex in general.[27]

Obviously, the exploration of foreign territories and bodies invoked the concomitant fear of being explored. In such scenarios – and there are many such scenes of gender confusion in the journals of the voyages, working across many social terrains – gender, sexual practice, and 'national' difference seemed easily confused, underlining the degree to which the *familiarity* of bodies was the foundation for more complex and elaborate forms of classification and distinction. What is much less remarked upon is the circulation of subjectivity in such scenarios: as in these examples, who is the explorer and who the explored? Polynesians certainly had their own doubts about the virility of their visitors, finding the homosociality of the explorers' sloop suspect and derisive, in some cases even undertaking investigations to discover if they were 'whole men,' and raising questions about their inclinations and civility that the British themselves could never quite satisfactorily answer!

Wales's journal entry invites us further into this tangled circuitry of colonial identification, alterity, exchange, and transformation. He goes on to elaborate his theory about the gender confusion that gave rise to the unfortunate misapprehension that the ni-Vanuatu were sodomites, while also making clear that the purpose he 'need not mention' was universally recognized, and *could* be signed without difficulty in the gestural economy of encounter:

> The Man who carried Mr. Forster's Plant Bag had, I was told, been two or three times attemp[t]ed, and he happening to go into the Bushes on some occasion or other whilst we were set down drinking our Cocoa-nuts etc, I pointed it out to the Natives who sat round us, with a sort of sly look and significant action at the same time, on which two of them jump'd up and were following him with great glee; but some of our Parry bursting out into a laugh, those who were by . . . called out Erramange! Erramange! (its a Man! Its a Man!) on which the others returned, very much abashed on the Occasion.

The 'sly look and *significant action*' were both conveyed through gestural signs common in encounters in which neither party spoke the other's language; yet the acceptance of gestural language as a reliable indicator of sexual intention is, and was, clearly problematical. The Forsters would also hypothesize, entirely on the basis of such gestural signs, that the ni-Vanuatu were also eaters of human flesh. Wales, however, initially refused to believe that Maori were 'cannibals' despite mounting 'evidence' (the pantomime of cannibalism put on by the Maori) and the conviction to the contrary of all the rest of the company. He protested 'how far we are liable to be misled by Signs, report and prejudice.'[28] In the passage above, however, Wales indicates both that gestural sign (of sodomy? or heterosexual intercourse? it is unclear which sign was being made, or indeed if they were different) could convey the truth both to and of the ni-Vanuatu, and that the suspicious traffic flowed both ways. What should we make of this exchange?

European prejudices were both inverted and confirmed in this social performance. As previously noted, while sodomy and same-sex desire were by no means seen as unitary in the last quarter of the eighteenth century, both were, to varying degrees, coming to be attached to the same object of suspicion: the 'effeminate' man. In Britain, this (usually elite-identified) individual was the product of spending too much time around women or, as Millar theorized, of societies where women had too much civil or political power; in either case, he was beginning to be thought to be the most likely to harbor same-sex desires. There was an increasing, although not invariable, convergence, in other words, between gender and sexual practice, and a demand for men that the outward performance of gender be matched by inner desire. Hence the great surprise and alarm among the British public at the sodomy prosecution and subsequent exile of the manly Isaac Bickerstaffe, playwright and collaborator of Garrick.[29] In the encounter above, however, same-sex or sodomitical desire is feared as a function of primitive, rather than advanced and corrupted, sensibilities, which would require, according to late eighteenth-century stadial models of social development, that it had been there all along, a part of humanity in its 'original' as in its 'advanced' state (a view which anticipated missionaries' condemnation of sodomy as a 'heathenish' practice at all levels). That the ni-Vanuatu were in a 'primitive' state was not in doubt, although the Forsters theorized that their nation may have degenerated from the happiness of the Tahitians due to their less advantageous climate. And certainly gestural sign was associated by some with cultural primitiveness. The case had been made very eloquently by Rousseau, who argued that 'if the only needs we ever experience were physical, we should most likely never have been able to speak; we would fully express our meanings by the language of gestures alone.' On the other hand, on the basis of evidence culled from the voyages of Bougainville and Cook, as well as European communities of the deaf, some Enlightenment thinkers had elevated gestural sign to the level of a philosophical artifact, as a 'natural' and possibly even universal language.[30] From that perspective, sign language did seem to provide in first contact a theatrical, if provisional, 'mode of exchange, a physical and symbolic space inscribed with meaning,' as Paul Carter has argued of contact performances in general.[31] Yet what that meaning was to the different parties remains elusive. In other words, the indeterminacy of both sign and sodomy are glossed in Wales's account of the encounter: in the state of nature being enacted for the British in western Polynesia through a gestural economy, even the most stalwart empiricist was led to believe the 'unnatural crime' was not only recognized but could be made intelligible through a sort of *kin est he tic lingua franca*, the wink and the nod. Communication is achieved as meaning is deferred, and sodomy becomes the place were civilized and savage meet – a predilection of those with too much luxury and too much contact with women (as the British had long believed of Islamic nations)[32] as well as, apparently, those who neither spent time with nor appreciated women. Clearly, the enlightened explorers identified themselves with neither camp.

The traffic in men transformed the enlightened explorers into the objects of Polynesian knowledge, who thereby read their own culture on the European male body. But this exchange is of much broader historical significance. The 'crime that can never be mentioned' but was everywhere suspected points to the circuitry of identity, alterity, exchange, and transformation that was both charged and recuperated by the systems of observation and empirical recording. Who is the object and who the subject of these exchanges? Who is ethnographer and who the 'primitive'? The fragments through which the narrative of 'discovery' emerged highlight the epistemic violence visited through the multiple acts of cultural translation. There is no 'whole' in these accounts or perspectives, only fragments which suggest 'knowledge forms that are not tied to the will that produces the state,' and all of which 'challenge, not only the idea of wholeness, but the very idea of the fragment itself.'[33] The attempted imposition of British 'order,' by the explorers or their historians, can only temporarily divert attention from what Michael Taussig has called in another context the 'unstable interplay *of* truth and illusion.'[34]

Cook and his men aimed to discover and record empirical facts about an unknown world, and their cultural as well as topographical mappings changed the world in the process. The psychic impact of these processes on the colonizers and their forms of knowledge has received, perhaps, too little direct attention. Fantasy conditioned empirical observation, and vice versa. The empirical 'facts' of territorial and sexual conquest clearly summoned up the fantasy of being taken, as well as taking; and as desire, identification, and dis-identification worked to naturalize conquest and allay its anxieties, the unnatural nature of the act of conquest comes back to haunt in the figure of the sodomite – the absent presence (or present absence) on all the voyages. Perhaps these examples suggest that through the arts of discovery the emergence of the modern sexual regime was indeed being felt and fabricated across the world. But it is also clear that suspect practices could not necessarily produce and certainly could not prove the essentialized identities that such a regime required. The multiple images of Oceanic and British bodies reveal the fictive nature and irresolvable tensions within those categories of difference invented in the crucible of first contact. The same accounts that inaugurate the labor of colonial discourse in the South Pacific thus raise the central question: who was looking at whom? What was seen in the act of looking and who was the discoverer? Looking at natives looking back at them, could the scientific explorers of Cook's voyages be so sure they were not looking at themselves? From this perspective, gender misrecognition and Polynesian subversions marked the unwriting of nationality and gender into History, and the indeterminacies of sexual practices – in the time of the great Captain Cook, as well as in our own.

Notes

1 E.g. Christopher B. Balme, 'Sexual Spectacles: Theatricality and the Performance of Sex in Early Encounters in the Pacific,' *The Drama Review*, 2000, 44, 67–85; Greg Dening, *Mr. Bligh's Bad Language: Passion, Power and Theatre on the Bounty* (Cambridge University Press, 1992); Rod Edmond, *Representing the South Pacific: Colonial Discourse from Cook to Gauguin* (Cambridge University Press, 1997); John Gascoigne, *Joseph Banks and the English Enlightenment: Useful Knowledge and Polite Culture* (Cambridge University Press, 1994); Richard Grove, *Green Imperialism: Colonial Expansion, Tropical Island Eden and the Origin of Environmentalism, 1660–1860*

(Cambridge University Press, 1995); David Mackay, *In the Wake of Cook: Exploration, Science and Empire* (New York: St. Martin's Press, 1985); Gananath Obeyesekere, *The Apotheosis of Captain Cook: European Mythmaking in the Pacific* (Princeton University Press, 1992); Roy Porter, 'The Exotic as Erotic' in G.S. Rousseau and Roy Porter (eds) *Exoticism in the Enlightenment* (Manchester University Press, 1986) 117–44; Margaret Jolly and Martha Macintyre (eds), *Family and Gender in the South Pacific: Domestic Contradictions and the Colonial Impact* (Cambridge University Press, 1989); Leonore Manderson and Margaret Jolly (eds) *Sites of Desire: Economies of Pleasure: Sexualities in Asia and the Pacific* (University of Chicago Press, 1997); Bridget Orr, 'Southern Passions Mix with Northern Art: Miscegenation on the *Endeavour* Voyage,' *Eighteenth Century Life*, 1994, 18, 212–31; Marshall Sahlins, *Islands of History* (University of Chicago Press, 1985); Marshall Sahlins, *How 'Natives' Think: About Captain Cook, For Example* (University of Chicago Press, 1995); Nicholas Thomas, *Oceania: Visions, Artifacts, Histories* (Durham: Duke University Press, 1997); Kathleen Wilson, *The Island Race: Englishness, Empire and Gender in the Eighteenth Century* (London: Routledge, 2003).

2   This distinction is borrowed from James Clifford in his scintillating essay, 'Taking Identity Politics Seriously: "the Contradictory, Stony Ground . . ."' in Paul Gilroy, Lawrence Grossberg, and Angela McRobbie (eds) *Without Guarantees: In Honour of Stuart Hall* (London: Verso, 2000) 98. For conjunctural ethnography, see James Clifford, *The Predicament of Culture* (Cambridge, MA: Harvard University Press, 1998); and Kamala Visweswaran, *Fictions of Feminist Ethnography* (Minneapolis: University of Minnesota Press, 1994).

3   For details, see Wilson, *Island Race*, ch. 2.

4   Johannes Fabian, *Time and the Other: How Anthropology Makes its Objects* (New York: Columbia University Press, 1983).

5   Grove, *Green Imperialism*, 230–5; Wilson, *Island Race*, 8–9.

6   See Wilson, *Island Race*, 18–27; Kathleen Wilson, 'Empire, Gender and Modernity in the Eighteenth Century,' in Philippa Levine (ed.) *Gender and Empire* (Oxford University Press, 2004).

7   Jonathan Lamb, *Preserving the Self in the South Seas 1680–1840* (University of Chicago, 2001).

8   Samuel Stanhope Smith, *An Essay on the Causes of the Variety of Complexion and Figure in the Human Species* (Edinburgh, 1788) v–vi.

9   Andrew Kippis, *The Lift of Captain James Cook* (Basle, 1788) 371.

10   Wilson, *Island Race*, 55–6.

11   George Forster, *A Voyage Round the World During the Years 1772–1775* (2 vols, London, 1777) 11, 324; Harriet Guest, 'Looking at Women,' in Johann Reinhold Forster, *Observations Made on a Voyage Round the World*, Nicholas Thomas, Harriet Guest, and Michael Oettelbach (eds) (Honolulu: University of Hawaii Press, 1996), xli–liv.

12   Joseph Banks, 'Thoughts on the Manners of the Women of Otaheite,' MS 94, National Library of Australia.

13   Joseph Banks, *Endeavour Journal 1769–70*, J.C. Beaglehole (ed.) (2 vols, Sydney: Angus and Robertson, 1962), I, 254; Porter, 'The Exotic as Erotic,' 118; Off, 'Southern Passions,' 212–31.

14   *The Journals of Captain Cook*, J.C. Beaglehole (ed.) (3 vols, Cambridge University Press, 1957–1965) 11, 797.

15   Sydney Parkinson, *Journal of a Voyage to the South Seas in His Majesty's Ship the Endeavour* (London, 1773) 25; *Journals of Captain Cook*, I, 127–8; II, 236–7.

16   Wilson, 'Gender, Empire and Modernity'; Gunlog Fur, 'Some Women are Wiser than Some Men: Gender and Native American History,' in Nancy Shoemaker (ed.) *Clearing a Path: Theorizing the Past in Native American Studies* (London: Routledge, 1996) 75–101. See also Kathleen Wilson, 'The Female Rake: Gender, Libertinism and Enlightenment,' in Lisa O'Connell and Peter Cryle (eds) *Libertinism and Enlightenment* (Basingstoke: Palgrave, 2003).

17   The historical-ethnographic analysis in this chapter is much indebted to Douglas Oliver, *Ancient Tahitian Society* (3 vols, Honolulu: University of Hawaii Press, 1974) esp. vol. 11.

18   Sahlins, *Islands of History*, 26, 7–8; Caroline Ralston, 'Polyandry, Pollution, Prostitution: The Problems of Eurocentrism and Androcentrism in Polynesian Studies,' in Barbara Coine and E.A. Grosz (eds), *Crossing Boundaries: Feminisms and the Critique of Knowledge* (Sydney: Alien and Unwin, 1988) 71–80.

19   *Journals of Captain Cook*, III, 1085.

20   ibid., II, 444.

21   [John Marra] *Journal of the Resolution's Voyage in 1772, 1773, 1774 and 1775 on Discovery in the Southern Hemisphere* (London, 1775) 54.

22   *Journals of Captain Cook*, III, 56.

23   Johann Reinhold Forster, *The Resolution Journal*, Michael Hoare (ed.) (London, 1982) II, 356–7.

24   *Journals of Captain Cook*, II, 858–9, 790, 819.

25   *The Phoenix of Sodom or the Vere Street Coterie* (London, 1813) 2.

26   Gananath Obeyesekere, '"British Cannibals": Contemplation of an Event in the Death and Resurrection of James Cook, Explorer,' in Kwame Anthony Appiah and Henry Louis Gates, Jr. (eds) *Identities* (University of Chicago Press, 1995), 7–31; Lee Edelman, 'Homographesis,' *Yale Journal of Criticism*, 1993, 3, 192.

27   Randolph Trumbach, *Sex and the Gender Revolution, vol. 1 Heterosexuality and the Third Gender in Enlightenment London* (University of Chicago Press, 1998); Wilson, *Island Race*, 190–1 and refs there.

28   E.g. James Cook and James King, *A Voyage to the Pacific Ocean*, 2nd edn (3 vols, London, 1785) III, 26; *Journals of Captain Cook*, III, 815–20; W.D. Ellis, *An authentic narrative of a voyage performed by Captain Cook* (London, 1782) n, 153.

29   Philip Carter, *Men and the Emergence of Polite Society in Britain 1660–1800* (Basingstoke: Macmillan, 2001); Michele Cohen, *Fashioning Masculinity* (London: Routledge, 1998); Laurence Senelick, 'Mollies or Men of Mode? Sodomy and the Eighteenth-Century London Stage,' *Journal of the History of Sexuality*, I (1974–1976), 33–67.

30   For this, see Nicholas Mirzoeff, *Silent Poetry: Deafness, Sign and Visual Culture in Modern France* (Princeton University Press, 1995) 30–5; quotation from Rousseau's *Essays on the Origin of Language* (1749) is on 53.

31   Paul Carter, 'Making Contact: History and Performance,' in Carter, *Living in a New Country: History, Travelling and Language* (London: Faber, 1992) 163.

32   For which, see Nabil Matar, *Turks, Moors and Englishmen, Vol. I: The Age of Discovery* (New York: Columbia University Press, 1999).

33   Dipesh Chakrabarty, *Habitations of Modernity* (University of Chicago Press, 2002) 34–5.

34   Michael Taussig, *Shamanism, Colonialism and the Wild Man: A Story in Terror and Healing* (University of Chicago Press, 1987) 121.

PART 6

Ecological history

Chapter 14

Richard H. Grove

THE COLONIAL STATE AND THE ORIGINS OF WESTERN ENVIRONMENTALISM

> For evident contemporary reasons, ecological and environmental issues have drawn ever increasing attention from historians. Imperial and colonial studies are no exception, and are indeed in the forefront of this. Richard Grove has been one of the most important pioneers. Here, in passages from the last part of his major book *Green Imperialism*, he seeks to summarise some of his core arguments about the relationship between empire and ecology.
>
> Stephen Howe

I HAVE AIMED IN THIS CHAPTER to recount some of the main milestones in the intellectual development of the global environmental consciousness which emerged in the context of European colonial expansion between 1660 and 1860. This new kind of consciousness can now be observed to have arisen virtually simultaneously with the trade and territorial expansion of the Venetian, Dutch, English and French maritime powers. It was characterised by a connected and coherent intellectual evolution of ideas and concepts which had complex and yet identifiable roots in an Edenic and Orientalist search and in the encounters of a whole variety of innovative thinkers with the drastic ecological consequences of colonial rule and capitalist penetration.

The early phase of territorial expansion along the great trade routes to India and China undoubtedly provided the critical stimulus to the emergence of colonial environmental sensibilities. While the early oceanic island colonies provided the setting for well-documented episodes of rapid ecological deterioration, they also witnessed some of the first deliberate attempts to counteract the process artificially. The isolated settlement at the Cape Colony provided an analogous context for the formulation of conservationist attitudes.[1] The colonisation of the oceanic islands was especially significant in the evolution of remarkably sophisticated insights into the mechanisms and processes of ecological change brought about by the introduction of European settler agriculture in both freeholder and slave-plantation manifestations. Prior to 1700, episodes of deforestation and soil erosion in Europe, the Canary Islands, the Caribbean and South America had rarely elicited sophisticated insights into process, nor did they give rise to the kinds of programmes for environmental control which developed on St. Helena and Mauritius and in the Eastern Caribbean during the eighteenth century.

Environmental deterioration particularly threatened the island economies and the security of supplies for the ships of the new European companies trading to India. The responses of the different nations and their companies to the process were not uniform in character. Nevertheless, a shared heritage of intellectual and scientific developments, the product of late Renaissance literature and science, proved an influential stimulus to a new valuing of the tropical environment in literary, scientific and economic terms. The institutional development of the colonial botanical garden, particularly as it was developed by the Dutch at the Cape, the French on Mauritius and the British on St. Vincent, formed the basis for a new kind of learning, information collecting and networking in the tropical environment. This learning was global in its approach and in its aims. Above all, the colonial botanical garden provided the basis for the institutional emergence of environmentalist ideas.

Some of the first systematic attempts at forest and soil conservation in colonies began on St. Helena and created significant precedents for later East India Company land-use ideology. At first, however, the lack of any credible expertise or corpus of intellectual justification to explain the ecological decline set in train by settlement meant that the English East India Company only very slowly became cognisant of the nature of the physical problems which its 'improvement' programmes and trade requirements engendered. Eventually St. Helena became disproportionately significant in stimulating a wider intellectual awareness of the rate at which the European might degrade the tropical environment and bring about species extinctions.[2]

In the course of the emergence of colonial state conservation, the significance of initiatives taken by local actors on the basis of local and indigenous knowledge cannot be overestimated. By contrast, the writings of better-known western environmentalists writing outside the colonial context (G.P. Marsh is a noteworthy case in point) were of surprisingly little import in the formation of state policy. Instead the experience of perceiving and countering deforestation and land degradation at first hand, especially on tropical islands, proved to be far more influential. The centrality of the colonial periphery in stimulating environmental innovation was strongly reinforced both by the growing cultural significance of island environments and by the growing preoccupations of Orientalist and Humboldtian thinkers with the non-European 'other' of the tropics. The considerable importance of the tropical island as a cultural metaphor for the newly 'discovered' world as well as for the projection of discontents and Utopias helped to heighten awareness of the efficacy of man as an environmental agent. Here again St. Helena played a key role, not least in Godwin's *Man in the Moone*, in providing a model for later Utopian discourses, both scientific and otherwise, and in highlighting a new awareness of isolation, extinctions, race and gender, often coupled with increasingly global perceptions of natural processes. This literary interest in islands and isolation was crystallised ambiguously in Defoe's *Robinson Crusoe*, a work which not least provided a model for the French cult of the Utopian South Sea island which flowered in the wake of the writings of Rousseau, Commerson,

Bougainville and Bernardin de Saint-Pierre in the 1760s and 1770s. The seminal influence of the works of both Godwin and Defoe was indicative of a two-way process by which particular literary discourses powerfully shaped changing perceptions of nature and the globe, and in which literature was, in its turn, increasingly influenced by new understandings and 'discoveries' in an expanding European world system of economic dominion and ruling discourses.

Thus, in the same way that European expansion entailed the encompassing of vast new territories under a European economic yoke, it also opened up a vast new mental domain. Expansion of this domain followed and facilitated the growth of trade, but it also fostered an exchange of experiences and ideas about the environment that became progressively complex and global in scope as trade and colonial dominion became global in reach. The tropical island, however, remained critical to the focusing of these ideas. The way in which this focusing occurred was largely dependent on the nature of the relationship between the emerging body of natural philosophers or scientists and the colonial states that they served. This relationship was much closer in French colonies than in those of England or the Netherlands.[3] This close relationship is one of the reasons why it was the French management of Mauritius which saw the first comprehensive attempts by colonial scientists to analyse rigorously and then to attempt to control the environmental consequences of European economic rule – or, more specifically, to control the ecological impact of a capital-intensive, slave-utilising plantation economy.

The initiation of a major programme of conservation on Mauritius arose out of the coincidence of a specialised set of circumstances very specifically related to the objectives and structures of the French polity. This was due mainly to the success of physiocracy as a land-use ideology guiding the policies of the colonial state, coupled with the wish to play out a particular kind of insular and Utopian vision. Thus it is on Mauritius that one can observe the emergence of an environmental policy which, while not inspired by the state alone, increasingly relied on the state for its execution. The conservationism espoused by the physiocratic regime on Mauritius demonstrated for the first time the very significant effect of a new kind of valuing of the environment by an influential elite in checking the progress of ecological transition.

The mental image of Mauritius as both a tropical island paradise and as a hoped-for location for a physiocratic moral economy or Utopia came to occupy a surprisingly dominant role in the mainstream of intellectual discourse in France itself wherever the relationship between man and nature was the object of discussion. This philosophical nexus between Mauritius and Europe can be attributed almost entirely to the popularity of the fictional and non-fictional texts of Bernardin de Saint-Pierre. Indeed, it contributed greatly to the way in which a romantic environmentalism actually emerged as a vital precondition to the realisation of a social Utopia. However, this alone would not have been sufficient to ensure the involvement of the state in an environmentalist programme which required a set of rather more empirical justifications for obeying the 'laws of nature'. These were supplied by a physiocratic science.

Pierre Poivre, in particular, was able to perceive the vital importance of being able to utilise a society of established experts to make the new ecological risks credible and, indeed, dangerous in the eyes of the state. The strong institutional connections that developed in the French colonial system among the state, the tropical botanical garden and the Parisian botanical establishment facilitated the availability of such experts on Mauritius. Furthermore, the initiation of the physiocratic conservation programme on

Mauritius demonstrated the peculiar suitability of the colonial state in providing a context within which independent scientists and conservationists could work. Placed in an alien environment, they were still able to take advantage of a considerable pool of intellectual experience. This meant that as early as 1770 the conservation lobby on Mauritius could draw upon published literature dealing with the environmental thinking of Europeans in locations as far apart as Europe, North America, South America, India and China.

Working within the milieu of the innately insecure fabric of the colonial state, the new scientific interest group, directly employed by the state for the first time on Mauritius, was able to exercise political leverage unheard of in metropolitan Europe. Environmentalism on Mauritius took advantage of two coupled phenomona: the demonstrable vulnerability of a small island to the rigours of plantation agriculture and an emerging literature on the interconnections among climate, trees and society that was used increasingly to imply a connection between climatic 'virtue' and social or political virtue. The latter connection became especially important in the years immediately preceding the French Revolution. The sense of insular vulnerability was made more concrete by the emergence, before the end of the eighteenth century, of a knowledge of plant types and distributions which was global in scope. This new expertise was personified, particularly in Philibert Commerson. Apart from any Utopian and literary connection, it had its roots, as did much of the developing global awareness of the potential impact of the European on the environment and on other societies, in the scientific circumnavigations of the world by Bougainville and Cook.

While problems of forest degradation and soil erosion were easily understood on Mauritius, it was not long before the concept of species extinction also gathered a new momentum on the island. This was an important development, since it permitted the making of a direct theoretical link between perceptions of the vulnerability of the island and insights into the role of man as a destructive agent on a world scale. A third and most important component of ancien-regime conservationism concerned the re-emergence of desiccation theories. These theories, linking forest cover and deforestation to rainfall and rainfall change, had long existed, not least in the minds of Theophrastus and Christopher Columbus. On Mauritius, and also in the Eastern Caribbean, the revival of such desiccation theories formed the main justification for the participation of the state in environmental control. The close institutional connection which developed in the mid-eighteenth century between the Royal Society and the Academie des Sciences was directly instrumental in the revival of desiccationism. It meant, for example, that such physiocrats as Pierre Poivre were able to reinforce climatic ideas co-opted from eastern thought by reference to the plant-physiological researches of Stephen Hales and the English Newtonians.

At another level the success of physiocratic conservation demonstrated the growing efficacy of the Hippocratic outlook. Medical perceptions were an essential component of physiocratic thinking, in which climate, environment and the human condition were closely related. In a similar way, desiccation theories had themselves originated in a medical concern with the nature of the relationship between health and the wider physical environment. On Mauritius desiccation theories were first used as a persuasive scientific and social lever by pioneering professional scientists (and were also used by individual ministers in government to secure a particular course of action by the state). In this sense the colonial state, with its overbearing economic and strategic preoccupations, actually constituted a more persuadable kind of institution than did the state in Europe. Later it only required the very deliberate and authoritative application of global climatic and atmospheric theories by Joseph Priestley and Alexander von Humboldt to make the desiccation argument politically powerful for scientists working on regional or national scales. Where the scientists were a powerful group of medically trained individuals, as they were in the Indian medical service, it was only a matter of time before global theories of desiccation became politically effective on a sub-continental scale, namely in India.

Early colonial conservation policies were almost always perceived as being a legitimate concern of the state rather than of the individual. Moreover, they often resulted in governments' attempting to restrict the activities of private capital or its direct and indirect agents in the prior, and longer-term, interests of the state. In essence, however, the emergence of a conservation policy related to a perception by the colonial authorities of the unacceptable risks implied in retaining an unrestricted *status quo*. In this respect one is dealing with a paradoxical kind of development, both in discovering that environmentalist ideas and policies emerged earlier at the colonial periphery than at the metropolitan centre and in the realisation that the colonial state was so readily influenced by independent groups of scientists. Moreover, it is perfectly clear that the motivations of those specialists who proposed controls (and who were critical of the ecological degradation which they saw happening) were by no means always identical to those of the state. On the contrary, they were sometimes actively anti-colonial.

Initially the European colonial invaders of the tropics were frequently forced to deal with a highly unfamiliar set of circumstances in which risks in the physical environment (in terms of disease, soils, water supply and fuel provision) were paralleled only by the dangers apprehended as being posed by an often equally poorly understood indigenous population. The instability of power relations between coloniser and colonised was thus frequently paralleled by the terms of a new dispensation of power defined in terms of an unknown ecology. In other words, an unfamiliar environment and populace might both present untold risks in knowing and controlling. This, of course, was a main part of the highly precocious message of Shakespeare's *Tempest*.

Above all, the course of future events was made unpredictable. As Mary Douglas has demonstrated, the problem of knowing about the risks which face it is a critical one in the self-regulation and stability of a society.[4] As a result, a minimal knowledge of future risks is required. It was this requirement which led to the conspicuous prominence of the scientist in the colonial context. The way in which the state treats the interpretation of risk offered by the specialist thus becomes of particular importance, since the expert has access to a knowledge of risks in the new environment not available to the lay person, or even to the lay state, for that matter. In an unfamiliar environment, empirical knowledge is at a premium. The traditional conventions evolved in a relatively stable and known relationship between people and land in Europe were not sufficient or apt when transferred to the tropics. Tradition had thus to give way to empirical knowledge or to local indigenous knowledge co-opted for colonial use. Prospero in *The Tempest*, it might be recalled, needed to undergo the transition from magician to natural scientist.

One might argue that the sheer speed of ecological change implicit in the activities of capital in the context of colonial expansion made environmentalist ideas and conservation policies inevitable simply to protect European capital or settler investments. However, there are problems with this argument in its simplest form. Above all, rates of ecological change were not significant in eliciting intervention until they could be noticed, quantified and then worried about. In general, only the 'scientist' could effectively do the latter. This was why islands were important in the evolution of early environmental sensibilities and why the colonial state became so utterly dependent on the observations and then the predictions of scientists. Without observation or interpretation, any objective notion of rates of ecological change was politically irrelevant. Far more significant was the way in which the very nature of the colonial state and its privileged network of connections for the diffusion of information effectively promoted a sophisticated environmental critique, and, furthermore, one which was effective in encouraging the colonial state to enlarge its role far beyond that known to states in Europe. A growing interest in long-term environmental security ensured both continuity in policy and the evolution of an apparently contradictory role in land management for the colonial state. In this context, botanical gardens served a crucial purpose as symbolic texts, centres of calculation and repositories of information and expertise.

The social leverage acquired by the emerging scientific elite of the colonial state with respect to the environment demands some further exploration. Entirely contradictory motivations and ideologies could survive together, at least for a while, or even within the same state apparatus. For example, the extensive building of botanical gardens in the sixteenth and seventeenth centuries, first in Europe and then in the new colonies, arose out of plural motivations. On the one hand, there were medical and economic motivations; on the other, the botanical garden fulfilled a more complex sociological role in the recreation of an earthly paradise. The early colonisation of sub-tropical and tropical islands undoubtedly involved economic motives. But, as constructed in literature, islands also served a mental and projective purpose, as the writings of Dante, Columbus, More, Godwin, Shakespeare, Marvell and Defoe are sufficient to demonstrate. Increasingly, then, while the process of expansion continued to serve the purposes of capital and the European market, it also began to promote a longer-term project. This consisted, after about 1700, in the search for the normative location for social Utopias and the simultaneous formulation of an environmental critique. In other words, the attempt to reconcile the human ecological impact with the laws of nature manifested itself both in environmentalism and in searches for better and more 'natural' (or even revolutionary) social dispensations.

Governor Roberts, for example, advocated conservation and opposed the 'improvement' plans of the East India Company on St. Helena. Later Pierre Poivre wished to create a new moral economy of nature and society on Mauritius. Similarly, Bernardin de Saint-Pierre started to couple his pleas for ecological restraint with pleas for the release of slaves. In the West Indies, Alexander Anderson argued for forest protection while criticising the treatment of the Caribs. In India, Colonel Kyd advocated the production of famine-resistant crops and opposed continued territorial expansion in areas west of Bengal. In much the same fashion, Edward Balfour (quoting Bernardin de Saint-Pierre) advocated forest protection to fight the famines provoked by colonial revenue demands. While the reforms advocated in the conservation, public-health and medical fields by the surgeons of the EIC Medical Service were ostensibly motivated by a distinctly Benthamite utilitarianism, their policy prescriptions were also undoubtedly affected by the interventionist and radical ideas of Joseph Priestley and Joseph Hume.

Quite consistently, then, those who criticised colonial *laissez-faire* policies pertaining to deforestation, soil erosion and species extinctions tended also to be those who deprecated colonial exacerbation of famine and disease patterns and the treatment meted out to indigenous peoples. In this respect colonial scientists such as Bernardin de Saint-Pierre on Mauritius, Balfour in India, Dieffenbach in New Zealand and Strzelecki in Australia are all good exemplars of the close connections between nascent environmentalism and the social reformism of physiocracy and the Enlightenment.[5] The fact that the scientists employed by the British were frequently either Scottish or Central European, and thus inherently peripheral to the imperial social establishment, only served to strengthen this connection. Much later the same dualism was to recur at the metropole. For example, Octavia Hill, the founder of the National Trust and an early advocate of landscape protection, was also the leading figure in urban housing reform in Britain.[6] The emergence of a duality in social reform plus a mirroring environmental critique was just as distinctive at the colonial periphery. Undoubtedly, it reached its most sophisticated level on Mauritius, thanks to the combination of a physiocratic ethos and a pre-Revolutionary Rousseauist and Romantic critique of European society.

One has to recognise here that concern about the environment mirrored social concerns and positions. Thus, while the environment may be at risk, it is the social form which demands inspection.[7] Similarly, a specialised view of the environment may reflect a sectarian view of society.[8] A survey of the evolution of perceptions of the environment by colonial scientists indicates that for some groups the tropical environment had acquired a highly loaded symbolic value. The manifest threat posed by western economic transformation to this image mirrored the social threats and insecurities felt by those individuals who had promoted a high valuing of the environment in the first place and who had in some instances actively sought careers away from the European centre. The isolationist career of Burchell on St. Helena, for example, can be seen in this light.[9] In Europe the growth of a 'green language' as a form of social response to the alienating social and economic consequences of capitalism has been eloquently described by Raymond Williams.[10] At the colonial periphery this 'language' was even more conspicuous. Indeed, for a highly educated intelligentsia the colonial state offered great scope for the expression of unconventional environmental views in terms of active policy and lobbying power. Moreover, whether or not scientists shared sectarian social views, the sheer tyranny of physical and mental distance from the centre contributed to the growth of peripheral or even sectarian sympathies. Even colonial governments became peripheral in their attitudes.[11]

The intellectual history of environmental consciousness in the context of European colonial expansion appears to exhibit several important kinds of elements. At one level, environmentalist discourses related to physical well-being and bodily survival. This is the element developed principally as part of a medical critique of environmental change, leading to concerns about climate, disease, the hydrological state and, by extension, famine. At another level, a new valuing of the environment related more strongly to the mental domain of the (sometimes 'Orientalist') 'other' represented by the newly colonised or 'explored' world. This second set of notions was stimulated by literary evocations of Eden, Paradise, Utopia and New Cytheria and by Romantic images of the 'Sublime' and 'Wilderness'.[12] Such notions were strongly connected to ideas about a moral economy or even to more utilitarian ideals about the desirability of new state structures or roles. Both preoccupations, in the physical (medical) and the mental realms, were ultimately constructed as ways of dealing with anxieties about the survival, nature and integrity of the human individual and human society. The one might have been physically at risk; the other, at risk in a more complex existential, emotional or even political sense. Historically, a growing awareness of extinction processes, especially on islands, served to unite these concerns towards the end of the eighteenth century. Increasingly, too, the literature and environmentalist texts associated with islands stimulated thinking about the dynamics of species change and human origins. The writings of David Corneille, Alexander Anderson,

William Burchell, W.H. Webster, Joseph Hooker, Hugh Strickland and, not least, Charles Darwin are indicators of this long-evolving connection between insular discourses and the dynamics of species formation and extinction processes. As in the closely related evolution of environmentalism, the actual and psychological *isolation* of organisms and people on oceanic islands played a vital part in the formulation of new ideas. By 1859 the publication by Darwin of a theory of natural selection had completed this story of existential isolation and anxiety, so that even in Europe, where the dangers of extinction in a biological sense were less easy to demonstrate, the entire social order had become threatened by a theory which questioned the whole fabric of traditional beliefs and structures justifying and explaining man's place in the world and in time.[13]

Finally, one might ask how the apparently radical or extreme opinions of a peripheral minority, albeit an intellectual and vociferous one, could so sway the policy of the colonial state in regard to the environment. The answer is that, directly, they did not. Instead the ability of peripheral conservation lobbies to carry out their social prescriptions can be seen as a measure of their success in threatening the centralised colonial state with death, disease, famine and economic ruin. Increasingly, between about 1760 and 1850, the scientific lobby was able to make these threats credible in the tropics. This was particularly so after the El Niño-caused global drought of 1791–1792, an extreme event which gave a decisive advantage to environmental advocacy. In other words, the state could be made to act by persuading it of the dangers to its own survival. These dangers were easily represented on islands. At a continental scale, in India or in Southern Africa, for instance, the passage of such extreme events as famines, depletions caused by war, or disease episodes tended to facilitate the task of a 'sectarian' scientific lobby.[14] Fears of chronic social instability in the colonies, stirred up by contemporary political events in Europe, were another facilitating factor. But more important than these factors was the growing ability of the colonial conservation lobby to appeal to the credibility of evidence of a global threat to the environment from human activity. Initially this was made possible by the emergence of an internationally diffused scientific literature. Later, international and intercolonial contacts among scientists reinforced the growth of a sense of a global environmental crisis. The proceedings of supra-colonial scientific meetings, such as those of the British Association for the Advancement of Science in 1851 and the Royal Geographical Society in 1865 and 1866, reinforced the strength of the desiccation threats wielded by colonial scientists and gave them a new source of authority which no single colonial state could safely decide to ignore.

At some periods, departments or agents of the colonial state have themselves taken on a sectarian or peripheral role in countering the complacency of a metropolitan centre unable or undisposed to be sensitive to the environmental risks perceived in the peripheral colonial state. The governments of St. Helena, for example, entered this category in their relations with the EIC Court of Directors. Later the Madras Presidency government adopted scientific conservation propaganda to press its case with the government of India. The articulation of a threat of social breakdown on top of climatic or economic disaster was an effective political weapon in these cases.

Colonial environmental policies arose, therefore, between 1650 and 1850, as a product of highly structured tensions between colonial periphery and metropolitan centre and between the insecure colonial state and the climatic environmentalism of the new scientific conservation elites. In recognising the contradictions which arose in this way, one needs to reconsider the nature of the early colonial state and its relationship with science.

It may also seem prudent to question some of the simplistic assumptions that have been made about the degree to which science itself has genuinely been subordinated to the interests of capital and the colonial state. Clearly in so doing one needs to be aware of the variety of levels of discourse, disguise and argument with which scientific elites have historically encountered the problem of influencing governments about environmental risk. In a much broader sense, our older assumptions about the philosophical and geographical origins of current environmental concerns need to be entirely reconsidered. It is now clear that modern environmentalism, rather than being exclusively a product of European or North American predicaments and philosophies, emerged as a direct response to the destructive social and ecological conditions of colonial rule. Its colonial advocates, and their texts, were deeply influenced by a growing European consciousness of natural processes in the tropics and by a distinctive awareness of non-European epistemologies of nature.

Notes

1   See Grove, 'Early themes in African conservation' in D. Anderson and R.H. Grove (eds) *Conservation in Africa*, (Cambridge, 1987); and 'Scottish missionaries, evangelical discourses and the origins of conservation thinking in Southern Africa', *Journal of Southern African Studies*, 1989, 15.

2   Taking St. Helena and Ascension Island together, one can see that before 1870 the experience on those islands was taken up in turn in the theories of J.R. Forster (1774), Bernardin de Saint-Pierre (1769–1796), Alexander Beatson (1816), J.B. Boussingault (1837), L. Bouton (1837), J.D. Hooker (1842), E.G. Balfour (1849), Charles Darwin (1859), C.G.B. Daubeny (1863), Etienne de Clave (1863), G.P. Marsh (1864) and N.A. Dalzell (1869) (dates refer to publication in English).

3   Of these three maritime powers, the discontinuity between science and state was greatest in England in the second half of the seventeenth and the beginning of the eighteenth century. There is some irony in this, since it was in England that Francis Bacon had first extensively elaborated on the need for natural philosophy to serve the interests of and to be controlled by the state. The onset of the Commonwealth prevented this development from taking place and ensured that the Royal Society remained relatively independent and relatively weak. In France, however (under Colbert), the Baconian approach became incorporated in state policy; hence the nature and scope of the 1669 Forest Ordinance and its colonial inheritors, including the Mauritius forest legislation of 1769. I am indebted to Dr. Julian Martin for a discussion of this. One may argue that the East India Company itself acquired a more distinctly 'Baconian' role in science than the British Crown ever itself did before 1857.

4   Mary Douglas, *Implicit Meanings: Essays in Anthropology*, (London, 1979) 245–7.

5   Thus Bernardin de Saint-Pierre was a pioneering figure in the French anti-slavery movement; Edward Balfour was a leading advocate of the medical education of women in India; and Ernst Dielfenbach and P.E. Strzelecki were both vociferous propagandists for the rights of indigenous peoples under colonial rule. Strzelecki, an advocate of soil conservation in South Australia and defender of the rights of Aborigines, was also later a severe critic of British famine policy in Ireland. [. . .]All these individuals, with the possible exception of Balfour, can be described confidently as having been strongly anti-colonialist in sentiment, and Dielfenbach was also specifically anti-missionary; see *Travels in New Zealand*, 372.

6   W.H. Williams, *The Commons, Open Spaces and Footpaths Preservation Society 1865–1965: A short history of the society and its work* (London, 1965) 1–29; Octavia Hill, *Our Common Land: Open spaces and the future of the commons* (London, 1877). The connections between public health and housing reformers (such as Octavia Hill), urban liberal reformers, Quakerism and the commons-preservation movement have yet to be fully researched. Both George Shaw-Lefevre and John Stuart Mill were committee members of the Commons Preservation

Society; see Lord Eversley (George Shaw-Lefevre), *Forests, Commons and Footpaths* (London, 1910) 27, 98, 187, 319.

7   For a useful discussion of this, see Douglas, *Implicit Meanings*, 247.

8   M. Douglas and A. Wildavsky, *Risk and Culture* (London, 1982) 3–55.

9   See W.J. Burchell, *Travels in the Interior of Southern Africa* (London, 1822) 1–13.

10   Raymond Williams, *The Country and the City* (London, 1972) esp. 287–306.

11   The stand taken by the government of Madras after 1847 was a case in point, as was the critical position taken by Governor Roberts on St. Helena after 1708. However, probably the most important tensions set up between metropolitan centre and colonial government periphery arose when colonial officials were themselves enthusiasts for natural history. The stands taken by two successive colonial secretaries on Mauritius, Rawson W. Rawson (prior to 1853) and Edward Newton (after 1862), are good examples of this; see Grove, 'Early themes in African conservation', 26.

12   In fact, the history and etymology of 'Wilderness' is largely irrelevant to the story of early or colonial environmentalism in the Old World. For the American context, where it is more relevant, see R. Nash, *Wilderness and the American Mind* (New Haven, CT, 1967).

13   Darwin, *Origin of Species;* see also J. Turner, *Reckoning with the Beast* (London, 1980) 60–6; G. Himmelfarb, *Darwin and the Darwinian Revolution* (New York, 1959) 236–42, 280, 290–3. The response to publication of the *Origin* became particularly conducive to the efforts of those activists anxious to promote the preservation of species, especially threatened bird species. Alfred Newton, the professor of comparative anatomy at Cambridge (and the brother of Edward Newton, colonial secretary of Mauritius and a keen enthusiast of fossil ornithology and the protection of indigenous species), was the chief architect of the first bird-protection legislation in Britain; see J. Sheail, *Nature in Trust: The history of nature conservation in Britain* (London, 1976) 22–6. Alfred Newton (followed a little later by J.D. Hooker and T.H. Huxley) was the first natural scientist to recognise the validity of Darwin's work and had maintained a considerable correspondence with Darwin in the years preceding publication of the *Origin*; see Newton-Darwin correspondence and papers in the Balfour Library, Department of Zoology, Cambridge University. In this sense Newton can be compared to other early species preservationists who were affected by their extensive correspondence with Darwin, e.g. E. Dieffenbach (New Zealand), L. Bouton (Mauritius) and J. Forbes Royle (India). Apart from recognising the uniqueness of the St. Helena flora, Darwin was himself remarkably unconcerned, or seemingly so, to advocate the prevention of extinctions or the preservation of forests. He thus stands in stark contrast to his co-author and colleague Alfred Russell Wallace, a strong supporter of conservation ideas. Wallace wrote in 1863: 'If this is not done [conservation proceeded with] future ages will certainly look back upon us as a people so immersed in the pursuit of wealth as to be blind to higher considerations. They will charge us with having culpably allowed the destruction of some of these records of creation which we had it in our power to preserve and while professing to regard every living thing as the direct handiwork of the creator': A.R. Wallace, 'On the physical geography of the Malay archipelago', *Journal of the Royal Geographical Society*, 1863, 32, 127–37.

14   The famines of 1838/9 in India and 1862 in South Africa were instrumental in creating the climate for conservation legislation; see Grove, 'Early themes in African conservation', 28. Similarly, the great famine in India in 1877–9 brought about first the monolithic proceedings of the Famine Commission of 1880 and then a spate of related infrastructural reforms affecting environmental and famine management, such as (to name a few) the famine codes, the formation of an all-India Department of Agriculture and the Meteorological Department, and the strengthening of watershed and forest-protection legislation; see Government of India, *Famine Commission*, vol. 4. On Mauritius the serious outbreaks of malaria in the mid 1860s led almost immediately to the strengthening of forest protection; see R. Thompson, *Report on the Forests of Mauritius Port Louos, 1880*. C.J. Glacken argues, in a more general sense, that the great Lisbon earthquake of 1755 had a long-lasting influence in opening the eyes of European scientists to the vulnerability of man to natural hazards: *Traces on the Rhodian Shore* (Berkeley, 1967) 521–2.

Chapter 15

Nancy J. Jacobs

RETROSPECTIVES ON SOCIO-ENVIRONMENTAL HISTORY AND SOCIO-ENVIRONMENTAL JUSTICE

> Richard Grove's main attention is to the ideas and actions of colonizers.
> By contrast Nancy Jacobs here looks at the lives and thoughts of formerly
> colonized people, in the Kuruman region of South Africa.
>
> Stephen Howe

L IKE A PHOTOGRAPHIC PRINT IN the processing bath, an unrecognized
history in Kuruman comes into sight when human society and the biophysical
environment are mixed in the developing solution. It emerges that the quiet thornveld
and quiescent people there share a complex history. For more than 200 years, people
interacted in varying and changing ways with the landscape and each other. The point of
this chapter, however, has not been to vindicate Kuruman as a scene of dynamism. More
importantly, this history of the edge of the Kalahari yields new perspectives on the wider
field of southern African history. We have seen that the environment is a locus of struggle
between people. Moreover, the different ways people relate to biophysical conditions and
processes help shape structured inequalities in society. Images developed through the socio-
environmental approach to the history of Kuruman will be reflected in histories of other
places – in southern Africa and in other parts of the continent. These include Bantu speakers
consigned to a foraging class; agro-pastoralists who are receptive to, yet discriminating
of, innovations introduced from Europe; Africans being transformed into colonial subjects
through environmental processes; migrant workers who herd and garden; and an
environmentally interventionist state acting on the food production of the colonized.

As a retrospective on the larger meanings suggested by a socio-environmental study
of Kuruman, I will comment on several points it raises about the interpretation of South
African rural history. First, the collapse of the extensive subsistence system around 1900
and the gradual abandonment of supplementary production in the mid- to late-twentieth

century raises the question of whether the disappearance of old ways led to a declining quality of life. The second point involves assessing the inability to intensify. The perseverance of extensive techniques and the attrition of food production raises the question of to what extent extensive production was a shortcoming. The final point has the greatest scope: certain people in every period held power, sought to increase it, and exercised it in the realm of how they and others interacted with the environment. This raises the question of power in environmental history. In answering it, I will begin with explanations given by people in Kuruman and then close with my own.

Histories of decline and adaptation

> NJ: Do you think there is a future for people who are not plowing?
> IS: There is no future for *us*. If the mine shuts down what are you going to do? You can't depend on the mines, but plowing is from Adam and Eve to today.[1]

> What we are telling you here is what our mothers used to do. As we grew things changed and our lives got better.[2]

The first environmental histories of colonized peoples tended to emphasize the decline of their culture, population, autonomy, and ways of living in the environment. *The Roots of Dependency*, by Richard White, describing the collapse of indigenous systems of environmental management in the United States, was a powerful influence on my early thought. In fact, initially, I envisioned my study of Kuruman ending with the collapse of extensive subsistence production at the turn of the twentieth century. It became clear, however, that environmental history continued after that collapse and that people adjusted in interesting ways worthy of consideration. Additionally, the critique of the 'received wisdom' on degradation alerted me that where colonial observers saw environmental degradation and destruction, it was possible to see innovation, such as in the adaptation to bushes and use of donkeys. It was clear that even after the collapse of indigenous environmental management, people were engaged in specific and deliberate practices to mitigate their poverty and dependency on the cash economy, for example, in the Transvaal maize harvest, and tributary asbestos mining. This is not to say that colonized Africans exercised agency without constraints or that all their activities were environmentally friendly; the point is that they worked creatively and deliberately to mitigate their circumstances and to persevere. Their efforts, and the measure of success they found, are worthy of consideration. In Kuruman, these innovative relations with the environment showed that black rural areas were not stagnant in the wake of a process of under-development. Eventually, however, food production supplementing wage labor also diminished. Despite this broad trend, even today, some people who do not qualify as cattle barons still raise animals – a few cattle or more goats and some donkeys. Some people even cultivate, showing that people responded to the disincentives to food production in varied ways that belie inexorable decline.

Social stratification is another factor arguing against a declensionist interpretation. *Balala* lived in very hard circumstances and would not have mourned the passing of the old order as a loss. In fact, by irrigating and leaving to work in mines, they contributed to its end. Eventually, the prescriptions about the ways men and women related to the environment receded, and so today some widows control their families' herds. Emphatically, gender remains a critical social factor, but gendered distinctions in the sphere of relations with the environment have receded. In the twentieth century, racial categorization had a totalizing effect on people's experiences, but even within the category of blacks, some people benefited as class divisions reappeared. Different categories of people experienced the transition from one dispensation to the next differently, so describing a universal trajectory of decline flattens the variety of experience.

Clearly, Kuruman people experienced trauma and loss, as they did at the turn of the twentieth century. At times, they had very little room to maneuver and were victims more than agents, as when they suffered forced removals. Changes in their environment, such as increasing stock disease, the growing density of bushes, and the loss of water to the municipality, made it difficult to continue cultivation and cattle herding as they had. Hard times, however, do not dictate that history be about decline, degradation, or victimization. As might be expected, some older informants, such as Isaac Seamecho, quoted at the beginning of this section, stressed the deterioration from older days, but others, such as a woman in a group interview, also quoted above, considered that their lives were easier since they found new ways to support themselves. People held differing opinions on which ways to support themselves were the best. In one interview, my research assistants asked a group to make a matrix showing change over time in ways of working for a living, including food production. Interview participants showed stock keeping and cultivation declining in importance after the 1930s, with cultivation declining to the point of be coming negligible. Working in mines and as domestic servants peaked in the 1960s and declined thereafter. The jobs that became more prevalent in the 1980s and 1990s were sewing, harvesting grapes on Orange River farms, selling beer, making bricks, and trading hides. When asked to rank the jobs according to their advantages and disadvantages, individuals gave different answers. Some people preferred the independence of farming, selling beer, or sewing, because miners were vulnerable to retrenchment. Others preferred the regular salary of a steady job. One woman preferred grape harvesting, simply because that was what she knew best.[3] These different experiences, perceptions, and priorities warn against over-generalization in the evaluation of well-being.

People expressed these differences of opinion and experience when they postulated overall historical trends. Many people had a nuanced interpretation of enhanced or eroded well-being. Understandably, they communicated discouragement about the currently high levels of unemployment, and some people conveyed perceptions of general impoverishment over time.[4] Nurses who had worked at the Batlharos hospital before the 1960s, however, recalled severe malnutrition at that time, especially during drought, and stated that nutrition had improved with increasing education.[5] A group of women who lived in Ga-Mopedi contradicted this, asserting that their health and nutrition were better when they produced more themselves, but they understood that things had improved for people who lived near the hospital and schools or had jobs.[6] Some told us that the hardship of poor people was relatively greater now than it had been, but understood that class stratification had always existed and that not everyone was now poor.[7] Also I was told that the physical demands of food production were high. A woman whose parents had worked in others' fields recalled: 'It was no joke that they had difficulties. It was really tough during those days.'[8] They also had mixed memories of the diet of past days. People today still eat *veldkos*, but one man explained why he preferred the taste of foods from the shop: 'Wild foods have a disadvantage in the sense that if you eat them you will get sick and sometimes they taste bad. Unlike before, they didn't taste bad. Maybe that is because of civilization.'[9] Even though people regretted the loss of old ways, many conveyed that the changes entailed differing costs and benefits for different people.

The endurance of extensive production

Regarding the ways people related to their biophysical environment, I have stressed that production was extensive. To do this, I have relied upon European sources criticizing African production; however, by no means have I characterized extensive production as backward or the absence of intensification as a failure. At first, people did not intensify because they had no reason to do so and many good reasons not to. Later, they simply could not. Before 1800, the recent establishment of agro-pastoralism, the small population, and the low rainfall all worked to make food production reliant upon wide areas and low labor inputs. The Cape frontier introduced new types of land use, irrigation, and commercial hunting, and people adapted these to their existing ways of working the environment. The tragic irony of this history is that colonial land alienation created pressures to intensify only as impoverishment and political disinheritance made it impossible for people to do so. As supplementary food production decreased by the mid-twentieth century, low production became an excuse for the segregationist state to deny black people their land and water. Under Betterment, the state imposed more intensive habitation and pastoralism by investing capital to develop the necessary infrastructure. Empty expanses were populated with people and stock, even as the percentage of people who practiced food production declined. The decrease in the farming population would not be a problem any more than it was in affluent societies in the developed world, except that many non-farmers in Kuruman had an insecure claim on entitlements.

What is the future of human interactions with the environment on communal lands in the southern Kalahari? Would some form of intensive land-use provide more people with more of their sustenance? Many black people in the Kuruman River Valley hope that water from the Kuruman Eye will be restored to them and dream of intensive cultivation. Some gifted gardeners still do remarkable work. I recall a beautifully manicured plot in Seodin-Lareng and seeing many well-tended vegetable gardens on a walk along the river to Batlharos. In Ga-Mopedi, we saw a wheat field guarded by a woman and her children against birds, and in a nearby field donkeys and young male relatives plowed for an older woman. There was a veritable orchard next to the bone-dry river in Sedibeng, and even in Betterment villages, we saw a few healthy kitchen gardens watered by private boreholes.

If we agree with Ester Boserup, who argued that population growth is the major condition for agricultural growth, then we would expect intensification to occur if enough people need to produce more food.[10] However, Boserup identifies the logic of agricultural growth – labor aversion offset by the need for higher yields – more convincingly than she does its conditions. A more realistic assessment of agricultural growth acknowledges that in any given environment, certain human uses are possible and others are not. Few people would argue that semi-arid environments can sustain the same intensification as humid ones, and perhaps in spite of its eyes, the semi-arid thornveld will not see more intensive land use. The extremely low level of phosphates in the soil and the high price of fertilizer, not to mention the lack of water, suggest that cultivation will not be a cost-effective option in the near future. Rather than widespread capital- and labor-intensive production, the concern should be sustainable and affordable production. Sustainable production might involve sorghum, goats, and donkeys, even if they are not valuable enough to merit intensive commercial production.

Indigenous theories of environmental justice

> We are afraid to go to the trust farms because there will not be any work for our children and the graves of our grandfathers are here at Dakwen. The drought is being caused by white people.[11]

> I was once asked at work by a white man why it was that when the white men became rich, he gave his donkeys to blacks, but why when blacks were rich, they did not give the donkeys to people who are poor, but they decided to kill them?[12]

My final, farthest-reaching question addresses the role of power. Concentrations of power create structured inequalities between people in different racial, class, and gender categories, and this history has shown that the inequalities between these categories are fundamental to the ways people relate to the environment. Thus, power is a necessary consideration in environmental history, and in order to understand the historical dynamic between people and the biophysical environment, it is necessary to identify influence, authority, and material advantages in society. However, the consideration of power is more than a historical exercise; it is a moral process, involving reflection about how humans should live on this earth. Among environmental thinkers in the northern industrial world, moral reflection raises issues of the human impact on ecosystems and species and the disproportionate distribution of pollution among poor people and people of color.

Likewise, human-environmental relations provoked moral consideration in my interviews, and my informants explained past environmental relations with theories about the exercise of power and its repercussions – theories about environmental injustice and justice. This was particularly evident in two spheres. First, people frequently testified that drought has become more common in the thornveld and suggested that the improper exercise of power has caused drought. Thus, people's assertion of progressive desiccation, while reflecting a near-universal tendency to romanticize old times, also provides commentary on the rank abuses of power in their lifetimes. Second, people conveyed a well-defined populist vision of the propriety of donkey herding, maintaining that proper environmental relations must be democratically determined and must bring benefit to poor people.

In my interviews, people asserted with a nearly unanimous voice that progressive desiccation has occurred in Kuruman, although meteorological records indicate that this is not the case. A group who had lived at Konong even asserted that they had no droughts in their old home.[13] Even as they described the decline of *letsema* and the economic developments that discouraged plowing, they still maintained that a major reason more people did not cultivate or keep many animals today was the decline in rainfall. 'The reason we buy food from the shop is that there is no more rain and we don't have seed to plant. In the olden days our parents never bought food from the shop but only coffee and salt.'[14] Of course, there is a tendency of popular memory to idealize the past.[15] As with other sources, historians who use oral data must critique, but not dismiss, stories of a halcyon past, including the humid conditions. However, climatological records do not indicate that Kuruman experienced progressive desiccation in the period of historical record. Furthermore, in 1997, when I was told that rainfall was declining, the area had seen six years of increasing rainfall. Although the early 1980s had been terribly dry, the average annual rainfall for the decade 1987/8 to 1996/7 was 444 millimeters, above the yearly mean of 416 millimeters for the period beginning 1931/2. Under these conditions, what led people to say that rainfall had decreased?

One possibility is that the incidence and severity of drought have remained constant, but that people cannot adapt to it as they once did. Herding remains the most significant economic activity in this environment, but the vegetation has changed. When people compare the amount of grass to that present in earlier times, then the effects of drought seem all the more acute if the veld is bushier than it was. Stock populations are also much higher than they once were, and when it withers, there is more competition for the grass that remains. During drought people must purchase more fodder, the cost of which they feel acutely. Because human populations are large, access to the open veld has shrunk and people cannot gain much sustenance from foraging in hard times. Additionally, because of taste preferences and new demands upon household labor, maize replaced sorghum as the staple, although it is more sensitive to drought and more difficult to cultivate in this area. Therefore, people who cultivate maize today will be more frustrated by drought than sorghum farmers in the past. In one interview, a matrix on the history of rain showed many droughts in the past, yet people asserted progressive desiccation as a cause for the cessation of cultivation. I asked how this could be: if droughts in the past did not keep people from plowing, why did they do so today? I was told that drought was more serious today because other factors compounded it: 'In the olden days even if you had no rain, you had enough stock . . . Today it is difficult. Even if you have stock you worry people will steal it.'[16] Because of historical changes, droughts have a sharper impact on food production than they once did, even if they become no more frequent or severe. Another factor contributes to the discrepancy between memories of rain and records of the rain gauge; people believe that human disharmony, which they have witnessed in abundance, can cause drought.

Among Tswana people, *pula*, or rain, is a metaphor for blessings. This connects to a metaphorical aspect of testimony about increasing drought. I came even to believe that people used 'drought' as a code for hard times of social and environmental origin. But, drought is more than a symbol; it is believed to result from social hardship. In a neat reversal of environmental determinists who would attribute their level of development to the dry thornveld environment, my informants suggested that discordant social relations *created* the increasingly dry thornveld. Steven Feierman's elucidation of the ideas of *kuzifa shi* and *kubana shi* in Shambaai, Tanzania, provides a related example of social determinism. The concepts *kuzifa shi*, 'healing the land,' and *kubana shi*, 'harming the land,' describe social and political behavior with climatological and environmental repercussions. People in Shambaai believe the land is harmed when the king does not maintain proper relations with the people and when his power is inadequate to repel harmful forces, leading to drought and famine. The land is healed when proper relations between the king and his subjects are restored or when competition between the ruler and challengers is ended, restoring rainfall and plenty. Other scholars have observed similar beliefs among Tswana people that human, particularly chiefly, behavior will affect rainfall.[17]

Socio-environmental history and socio-environmental justice

> Men move boundary stones; the pasture flocks they have stolen. They drive
> away the orphan's donkey and take the widow's ox in pledge. They thrust the
> needy from the path and force all the poor of the land into hiding.
>
> Like the wild donkeys in the desert, the poor go about their labor of foraging
> food; the wasteland provides food for their children. They gather fodder in
> the fields and glean in the vineyards of the wicked.
>
> Job 24: 2–6 (NIV)

'Land alienation, loss of stock, foraging by the poor, labor in others' fields' – this passage
from Job encapsulates much of the environmental history of the thornveld. Like Kuruman
people, Job has a moral assessment of how people influence others' relations with the
environment. No stranger to suffering himself, Job speaks plainly: the perpetrators of
environmental injustice are simply 'the wicked.' Wickedness, however, does not offer
strong enough explanatory power to sustain the conclusion of an academic study. That is
not to say that social scientists are morally detached from their subjects. Both North
American environmental and South African social historians write of injustice by those
holding power, in destruction of the biophysical world and exploitation and repression
of people. Abundant examples in both fields qualify as good history after Cronon's
observation: 'At its best, historical storytelling keeps us morally engaged with the world
by showing us how to care about it and its origins in ways we had not done before.'[18]

As Cronon notes, historians explain change, but also evaluate it. The preceding
chapters describe environmental and social change. Much of the story has turned on the
exercise of power, and the evaluation has rested on questions of inequality and justice.
The evaluation of ecological change is particularly difficult. As a subject of others' power,
the environment has in some ways been resilient, but in other ways it has been transformed.
Following the lead of disequilibrium range ecology, I have been cautious about describing
change as ecological degradation. The thornveld became bushier, but tendencies toward
bushiness always existed, and herders were not entirely responsible for the change.
Whatever the cause, it will qualify as degradation if it is irreversible and involves a loss
of biodiversity. That question is for researchers in other disciplines to determine
experimentally. This history included other changes in the biophysical world. The eyes
continued to flow; however, people now capture streams as they emerge from the earth,
and a major anthropogenic change in the biota of the river valleys has resulted. Probably,
the wild animals once inhabiting the thornveld have lost the most in this history. Large
herbivores and carnivores are gone, and the loss of wetlands must have reduced birdlife.
Donkeys, although they are domesticated, also suffered as a species at the hands of people.
Today, there is a protected space for wildlife, but that is not to say that local people co-
exist with other species. The luxury private desert game reserve 'Tswalu' covers 1,000
square kilometers in the Kalahari northwest of Kuruman. At 4,000 rand per night per
person, it caters to a market few can afford, let alone black residents of communal reserves
who might like to view the local fauna.[19]

Despite the drastic changes suffered by plants and animals, in this chapter I have been
more occupied with changes in the ways different categories of humans interacted with
the environment. Class, gender, and racial categories are unequally sized receptacles of
power, all of which determine different people's relations with the biophysical world. Social

power has a reciprocal relationship with the environment. People both gain power from and use the biophysical world as an instrument of power over others. This study upholds C.S. Lewis's assertion that 'Man's power over Nature turns out to be a power exercised by some men over other men with Nature as its instrument.'[20] On the agro-pastoral frontier, chiefs confiscated stock, pelts, and wild plant food to maintain their advantage in the ecological cycle. The colonial state hindered Africans' food production by restricting their land in order to secure a labor force. The twentieth-century state, both the central government and Bophuthatswana, assailed black people's relations with the environment, in part, to maintain control as it implemented the plan of segregation. However, the environment was more than an instrument in this history; it provided a material base for the power to dominate others. At the same time it gave power to endure domination.

I do not mean that immediate relations with the environment are the ultimate source of power. For example, divisions by gender arise from cultural norms while expressed and realized in environmental relations. Although, white South Africans' power over blacks rested on their control over the bedrock, water, and topsoil, the inequalities of colonialism and segregation arose from many factors in the long history of interactions between Europe and Africa. In the modern world, people from different continents and countries interacted according to many contingencies, including religions, political systems, economies, and racial prejudices, as well as the environmental relations of the parties.[21] Environmental interpretations are necessary but not sufficient explanations for the acquisition of power in chiefdoms, colonies, or capitalist economies. That said, South African historiography has not sufficiently integrated the necessary environmental explanations.

Has environmental injustice been more severe in some dispensations than in others? Were there times when people in Kuruman lived with fewer environmental inequities? Imbalances of power always existed in the ways people related to the environment. On the agro-pastoral frontier, rich men had advantages over women and *balala*. Yet women retained control over one form of production, and while *balala* may have had the harshest physical existence of anyone in this history, they had more freedom when they avoided towns, and had a remote possibility of rising to the level of the powerful. On the Cape frontier, the introduction of irrigation and trading opened new routes to the accumulation of wealth and power. In the period before the imposition of colonial restrictions, male *balala* and food-producing male commoners had new opportunities to establish themselves, but women did not. A few men who took up irrigation independent of chiefs or hunted commercially paid wages to workers, but reciprocal and client labor remained the rule. In this period, capitalist inequalities did not replace those of the agro-pastoral society.

In the colonial period, the locus of power shifted from those defined by their gender and class to those defined by their origins, culture, and race, and Europeans gained power over Africans. The subjugation of Africans expressed itself in their inability to continue their production practices, and they became more dependent on the cash economy than on the environment. This dependence on the white-controlled economy entailed a collective subordination to another race. Yet European rule not only lowered but also leveled African society. When imperial annexation undermined indigenous ways of governing, of accumulating wealth and power, the result was some flattening of class and a blurring of gender. After the collapse of subsistence production, the thornveld on communal lands and the river valleys became less of a basis of power for one class or one gender. Rather, relations with the local environment came to mitigate the inequalities that people of a marginalized race experienced in national society.

The economic and political subordination of one race is not the same as segregation, the policy that exacerbated and hardened differences. Racial segregation concentrated power and made weaker people subject to new levels of abuse. Like earlier imbalances of class and gender, the aggregation of power in racial categories was expressed in the ways people related to the environment. Under segregation, those who had once functioned as men and women, fully entitled Tlhaping and Tlharo or *balala*, Christians, commercial hunters or woodcutters, colonial subjects, migrant laborers, asbestos producers, herders, and farmers became first of all black South Africans. Thus classified, their ability to act according to any other identity and to exercise power accruing to any other category was limited. Racial classification was totalizing and brought extreme restrictions to the ways blacks interacted with the nonhuman world. Many actually lost the right to stay in their homes and were deposited in harsher environments. However, forced removals are not the only environmental expression of racial imbalance. Through the policy of Betterment, segregation also restricted how black people could use the environments they were allowed to live in. The irony of this racially driven policy was that it redeveloped class as a receptacle for power, as the donkey massacre shows.

Thus, even in Apartheid South Africa, race was not the only salient division in the ways people related to the environment. The inequalities and injustices were undoubtedly most extreme in the segregationist period, when more wealth existed and the mechanisms of disenfranchisement were strongest. There were high physical and emotional costs for the black people of Kuruman, including the lives of children at Bendell. Nevertheless, toward the end of that period, food security improved. There had been famines throughout the early nineteenth and twentieth centuries, but the last one was in 1941. The transition from seasonal hunger to chronic malnutrition is a familiar one among the disadvantaged in southern Africa, but senior Batlharos nurses we interviewed in 1997 believed that malnutrition had also decreased since the 1960s.[22] This does not mean that every individual had secure entitlements, but that someone was sharing his or her wages or pension with family in Kuruman. Although unemployment caused hardship, people in the 1990s were getting by, perhaps better than many before them had. The AIDS pandemic will make this more difficult.

The political liberation of 1994 was a cause for joy and some improvements. In its wake, there have been projects to improve the infrastructure, and people who suffered forced removals have filed land claims. However, majority rule will not necessarily redeem the history of Kuruman from environmental inequalities. What it provides is an opportunity to mitigate the ill effects of the colonial heritage. Mamdani has observed that in much of independent Africa, the colonial institutions of Indirect Rule in the countryside have not been democratized and 'customary' tribal structures have not been opened to community participation.[23] Unless this occurs in South Africa, people on communal lands in Kuruman and elsewhere will remain vulnerable to unjust state intervention, however progressive the national constitution. The political will to develop democracy and invest in poor rural people remains to be demonstrated. Moreover, because South Africa is a poor country with under-developed traditions of participation, the necessary resources for these developments are scarce. Future sustainable development in Kuruman will involve the following specific improvements: restoring people to or compensating them for land they lost during segregation; encouraging small stock ownership among the many rather than cattle production among the few; cleaning up the deadly asbestos litter; distributing the water from the Kuruman Eye equitably; and helping people with affordable, small-scale cultivation – possibly of sorghum – on dry lands. Most fundamentally, however, it is necessary to recognize that environmental and social justice are linked and that power imbalances will determine the ways men and women, rich and poor, and blacks and whites live with each other and the natural world.

Notes

1   Interview B with Isaac Seamecho. 'NJ' is Nancy Jacobs.
2   Interview A at Batlharos.
3   Interview A at Maiphiniki.
4   Interviews C and D at Churchill.
5   Interview F at Batlharos. Interview with Vera Albutt.
6   Interview B at Batlharos.
7   Interview F at Batlharos.
8   Interview D at Ncweng.
9   Interview C at Ncweng.
10   Ester Boserup, *The Conditions of Agricultural Growth* (1965).
11   National Archives Repository [Pretoria] NTS 7933 165/337, minutes of meeting, December 10, 1948.
12   Interview C.
13   Interview B.
14   Interview C at Ncweng. See also Interview A at Ga-Sebolao, Interview B at Sedibeng, and Interview I at Ga-Mopedi; Interview with Gladys Motshabe and Interview with Joseph Kopman.
15   CPSAA Mackenzie Papers no. 1575, Mackenzie, October 20, 1887.
16   Interview A at Maiphiniki.
17   Steven Feierman, *Peasant Intellectuals* (1990). Regarding the Tswana, see Schapera, *Rainmaking Rites of Tswana Tribes* (Leiden: Afrika-Studiecentrurn, 1971) 17–42, 133–8; Paul Landau, *Realm of the Word* (1995) 25.
18   William Cronon, 'A Place for Stories,' *The Journal of American History*, 1992, 78, 1375.
19   www.explore-southafrica.co.za/explore/gameparks/tswalu/front.htm.
20   C.S. Lewis, *The Abolition of Man* (1946) 40.
21   For environmental explanations for colonialism and disparities of development, see Alfred Crosby, *Ecological Imperialism* (1986); Jared Diamond, *Guns, Germs and Steel* (New York: Norton, 1997).
22   Wylie, 'The Changing Face of Hunger,' *Past and Present*, 1989, 122. On malnutrition in South Africa in the 1980s, see Francis Wilson and Mamphela Ramphele, *Uprooting Poverty: The South African Challenge* (Cape Town: David Philip, 1989) 100–120.
23   Mamdani, *Citizen and Subject*, 1996, 24–5, 288–9.

PART 7

Racial imaginings

Chapter 16

Tony Ballantyne

KNOWLEDGE, EMPIRE, GLOBALIZATION

> Ballantyne has been another prime mover in developing the idea of 'imperial networks'. The particular ones under investigation are those by which ideas of 'race', and especially of 'Aryanism' traveled across the British-imperial world. Here, in the concluding part of his book *Orientalism and Race*, he sums up some of the wide implications of tracing those connections across time and space.
>
> Stephen Howe

THIS STUDY HAS DEMONSTRATED the centrality of aryanism in British imperial culture, not only in British India, but also in Southeast Asia, the Pacific and Britain itself. Within the British empire in the long nineteenth century Aryanism became a crucial heuristic device in colonial politics, popular journalism and imperial ethnology. Sir William Jones's ethnological essays, which insisted on a common cultural genealogy shared by Indians and Europeans, did not locate European origins in a 'harmless and distant' Orient as Said suggests: rather it fundamentally unsettled divisions between Europe and Asia, Britain and India, colonizer and colonized. The Aryan idea was both powerful and troubling. It seemed to unlock the broad sweep of universal history (and the place of the British empire within that grand narrative), but also caused much anxiety. What cultural bonds did Britons and Indians (or Polynesians) really share? If these ties of kinship were substantial, on what basis could imperial authority be constructed? The divergent visions of the Aryan theory examined in this study and the intensity of the debates that surrounded this notion reflected the moral and political weight of these questions.

Sir William Jones's discovery of linguistic affinities between Sanskrit, Latin and Greek was the basis for a fundamental reconceptualization of Indian history and culture. In 'unlocking' the mysteries of Sanskrit, in tracing the affinities between Greco-Roman mythology and Hindu tradition and in locating ancient Indian history within a Judeo-Christian chronological framework, Jones disciplined India, making it amenable to the emergent disciplines of history and ethnology. But Jones's legacy was ambivalent: his work did not simply inscribe colonial authority by proclaiming British ascendancy over Indian knowledge. Rather, Jones's research established a new comparative framework for the writing of universal history, a model that located Asia, and India specifically, at the very heart of the history of civilization, shattering the images of a wild and exotic India that haunted the European imagination from the Renaissance through to the mid-eighteenth century.

Within a colonial context, where racial boundaries were strictly policed and imperial authority carefully protected, Jones's discovery of Indo-European commonalities was particularly challenging. Administrators, historians, journalists and ethnographers attempted to impose order onto the Indian past and to reduce the complexity of South Asian culture into meaningful interpretations. Where late eighteenth-century Orientalists such as Jones celebrated the sophistication of the Vedic period and its contributions to 'Civilization' (while frequently decrying the 'decayed' nature of contemporary Indian society), from the 1820s these ancient glories and the authority of the Jonesian tradition itself were increasingly undercut as evangelical and utilitarian reformers pushed for the East India Company to assume a more aggressive position towards indigenous customs. Within this context, the cultural affinities between Indians and Britons were frequently downplayed or the Aryan theory was used to naturalize, justify and celebrate British colonialism of South Asia: Britain, younger and more energetic, was reinvigorating the increasingly decrepit culture of its ailing relative.

As British interpretations of India's increasingly privileged race, British scholars and administrators dwelt not only on racial differences between Indians and Europeans, but also placed greater emphasis on the clash between Aryan and Dravidian elements in Indian history. Within the fraught terrain of colonial life 'Aryan' and 'Dravidian' increasingly functioned as racial, rather than linguistic, signifiers. Although race never completely supplanted language as an analytical tool, as George Grierson's monumental *Linguistic Survey of India* illustrates, race did increasingly dominate popular, administrative and academic discourses on India. This centrality of race was enshrined in the *Imperial Gazetteer of India*: in the 1909 edition British understandings of India were so racialized that even the geology of India was divided into Dravidian and Aryan periods![1]

I have suggested that these debates over Aryan origins had an important impact in Britain itself in a period where the history and boundaries of 'Britishness' were openly debated. Although most Britons, like Europeans more generally, might have invested local traditions and regional identities with the greatest importance, elite groups were increasingly concerned with the national and racial past.[2] The very nature of the Aryan idea, which suggested that cultural bonds linked diverse European and non-European peoples, engaged the interest of a wide variety of scholars, politicians and religious thinkers in Europe. This idea was adopted and deployed unevenly: compared to their Scottish and German counterparts, English scholars were generally slow to show an interest in the idea or its methodological basis – comparative philology. While Scottish scholars quickly deployed the comparative method to refine their developmental models for the history of civilization, both Orientalism and philology were slow to make an impact south of the border. The Aryan idea finally gained some influence in England through the work of James Cowles Prichard, whose training in Scotland and a profound interest in German thought underpinned his engagement with Orientalism. In the face of the Anglo-Saxon revival and the rise of polygenist anthropology, Prichard used the Aryan concept to not only posit shared origins for 'Celtic' and 'Anglo-Saxon' Britons, but also to insist on an ancient cultural link between Britain and India. Prichard's vision of a shared Aryan history underpinning the empire jostled with older notions of the British as Teutons, Israelites or 'a Mongrel half-bred Race . . . In whose hot Veins now Mixtures quickly ran'.[3]

Although Victorian Britons could not arrive at a consensus regarding the ultimate origins of their ethnic stock, it is clear that the cultural entanglements of empire, where migration, military service and missionary projects brought Britons to the colonies and colonials to Britain, made questions of ethnic origins and the boundaries between peoples urgent. Thus history and ethnology were invested with particular cultural significance as they were central in the definition of both national and imperial identities. In suggesting that the encounter with India had important consequences for identities in the metropole, this study reaffirms recent works that suggest that metropolitan society was not insulated from the effects of empire, rather the imperial venture played a pivotal role in the constitution of material culture, cultural patterns and identities in Britain itself.[4]

We have also seen the divergent ways in which the Aryan idea was inserted into various forms of colonial nationalism, indigenous social reform and anti-colonial prophetic movements. For some Indian reformers, such as Dayananda Sarasvati, Orientalism's stress on the glories of the ancient Aryans was an important source for arguments that urged a return to the 'pure' Hinduism of the Vedas. But it was a short journey from Dayananda's celebration of Indo-Aryan purity to the more militant proclamations of Hindu superiority made by later Arya Samajis and nationalists such as Har Bilas Sarda.[5] Bengali Hindu reformers and intellectuals embraced Aryan theory particularly enthusiastically, using it to attack British stereotypes of the effeminate *babu*, reclaiming a 'virile history' which drew heavy inspiration from the work of the Orientalist James Tod.[6] While this study has added further depth to our knowledge of Bengali and Arya Samaji views of history and race, it has also shown that the Aryan theory was harnessed by a largely overlooked group of Indian Christians and administrators. For these groups who had vested material and social interest in British power, the Aryan idea allowed them to construct a vision of a harmonious and egalitarian colonial society characterized by Indian loyalty to the Crown and racial fraternity. Even these 'loyalists', therefore, offered a critique of British racial thought, proclaiming Indian equality as the bedrock of their distinctive social and religious agenda. Thus, the notion of an Aryan racial community was both profoundly contested and highly flexible, and any attempt to see it simply as a metropolitan ideology that could be transplanted to colonial contexts to justify British superiority is misleading.[7]

Maori leaders exhibited limited interest in the ongoing Pakeha debates over the location of Hawaiki and the ultimate source of Maori culture. For the Maori, theories that cast them as migrants from India, whether from the Aryan north, from the Dravidian south or from the strongholds of tribal culture, had little appeal. Instead, a succession of leaders, from Te Ua, the founder of Pai Marire, to Te Kooti, the great prophet-warrior, through to the later prophet-reformers Te Whiti and Rua Kenana, insisted that the Maori were 'Tiu' or 'Hurai' (Jews) or 'Iharaira' (the Israelites). Their arguments were both an appeal to the power of Old Testament narratives of deliverance and the result of the interweaving of Biblical knowledge and Maori political idioms. The most telling evidence of this imbrication was the assimilation of Noah and Shem into Maori *whakapapa* (genealogies), the basis for both individual and community identity. While we can see this identification with the Israelites as testament to the transformative power of colonialism and missionary activity, it was also a discourse of resistance and empowerment that countered the authority claims of Pakeha history and ethnology.

These various interpretations and counter-interpretations of the Aryan idea must be located within the specific cultural contexts from which they were fashioned. In particular, this study has insisted that we must place these ethnological and historical texts within the changing patterns of knowledge production. Through the studious maintenance of Indo-Islamic courtly tradition, the Company cast itself as a patron of learning and an upholder of cultural continuity, while simultaneously exerting growing pressure on regional kingdoms and local economies. The colonial state thus set about opening up new reservoirs of knowledge in addition to new sources of revenue as it keenly appreciated the value of military intelligence, commercial information and a 'mastery' of local customs. In a similar vein, the shift to Indocentric interpretations of Maori culture initiated by Richard Taylor was dependent upon economic, technological and social forces that underpinned the textualization of Maori culture. Once collected, edited, translated and printed, Maori traditions were effectively disembodied and, as such, they were amenable to comparative analysis, allowing Taylor to identify a shared Aryan heritage as an antidote to racial conflict.

Thus, it is clear that we must pay close attention to the diverse forces that shaped the production of historical and ethnological texts. We must not reduce colonial knowledge to being an instrument deployed at will to protect and maintain imperial authority. Neither the painless transplantation of metropolitan ideology nor the uncontested imposition of administrational exigency, colonial knowledge must be seen as the product of complex local engagements (whether in Bengal, Punjab, the Bay of Islands or even in Britain itself), struggles over meaning and power enacted within the unequal power relations of colonialism. As Eugene Irschick has insisted, the colonial social order was 'a negotiated, heteroglot construction shaped by both weak and strong, the colonized and colonizer, from the present to the past.'[8] Irschick's study of land tenure in the Madras hinterland traces the interplay between the demands of colonial administrators and the authority of indigenous knowledge traditions, stressing the 'dialogic' nature of British colonial knowledge. He warns that 'we can no longer presume' that British understandings of India were the 'product of an "imposition" by the hegemonic colonial power onto a mindless and subordinate society.'[9] Local aspirations and colonial agendas were in a constant dialogue, a dynamic process of exchange where claim and counter-claim led each interest group to modify its position almost constantly.

Such local engagements, however, occurred within a wider imperial world. The localized bodies of knowledge examined here must also be read as part of an Enlightenment and post-Enlightenment project that attempted to produce a detailed picture of the 'great map of mankind'.

Chronologically, this study began in the 1760s with the penetration of British commercial and scientific agents into parts of Asia and the Pacific that Europeans knew little about. The cluster of scholars at the forefront of this project (Cook, Banks, the Forsters, Jones) were central in constructing a global picture of both natural and human history. Detailed ethnographic observation in India and the Pacific, the translation of new languages, and the collection and analysis of indigenous traditions, allowed Europeans to study human variation and trace cultural affinities in greater detail. By 1800, European scholars had firmly established linguistic ties between north India and Europe and the fundamental affinity of the languages of the central and eastern Pacific, and had begun to explore the historical relationships between Eurasia and the Pacific.

Most importantly, we have seen that this global project was facilitated by a series of intellectual exchanges created by publication, correspondence and the foundation of new scholarly societies dedicated to the production of ethnographic and historical knowledge. Many of these individuals, institutions and networks were closely related to the agents of British expansion (the East India Company, the Royal Society, missionary organizations and colonial learned societies), and these imperial networks facilitated the rapid transmission of ideas and information. These networks thickened and multiplied in the nineteenth century, quickening the pace of the intellectual transactions within the empire. Extensive collections of ethnographic material had been gathered by European explorers, traders and missionaries in Asia and the Pacific by 1850, creating variegated bodies of knowledge which could be used to create increasingly sophisticated comparative studies of 'primitive cultures' and human history.

This knowledge underpinned the work of metropolitan synthesizers such as E.B. Tylor or Max Muller and, equally importantly, it also allowed ethnographers in the colonies to locate their studies within a broader comparative context. But, even as this process of accessing indigenous knowledge was in its infancy, important new models emerged in the 'peripheries'. While Sir William Jones's innovative comparative vision drew on his classical education and his extensive knowledge of Persian, it was fundamentally dependent on his engagement with Sanskritic and Indo-Islamic traditions. Innovative work was also carried out on the New Zealand frontier: Richard Taylor's identification of Maori as fellow Aryans in the midst of the racial hatred unleashed by the New Zealand Wars was not only an attempt to counteract the centrifugal forces that threatened the colony, but also reoriented the analysis of Maori culture toward India. Colonial officials, surveyors and anthropologists devoted greater effort to tracing affinities between Maori religion and Hinduism. By the 1890s and early 1900s, *tapu* had been identified as a transplanted form of caste, Elsdon Best had uncovered phallus worship among the Tuhoe, Alfred Newman had identified some 70 Hindu gods and 38 Hindu goddesses in Polynesia, and (from Assam) Samuel Peal had argued that Maori were descendants of the Nagas of the Gangetic basin and upper Burma.

These examples remind us that, by its very nature, colonial knowledge was itself profoundly hybridized at two levels. Firstly, British understandings of both South Asian and Maori society were dependent on indigenous expertise, as these forms of 'local' knowledge were not only believed to be more effective guides to policy-making, but were also more likely to be accepted by indigenous communities. Through their use of indigenous language, institutions and customs, colonial authorities hoped that their policies would be invested with authority and would gain greater cultural and political purchase. Secondly, the flows of personnel, policies and ideas that gave the empire its fundamental structure shaped the development of colonial cultures in ways that we are only beginning to understand. Because of their very nature as colonial societies, the development of India or New Zealand was never solely driven by internal forces; rather the reality of their integration into the webs of empire continued to mould their economic fortunes, social structures and cultural patterns.

Finally, it is important to conclude by underlining the central methodological emphases of this study. The importance of the cultural traffic and imperial networks uncovered in this work means that we must move beyond the nation-state as the organizing unit for the writing of the history of imperialism. In its place I have advocated a multi-sited imperial history that uses webs as its organizing analytical metaphor, an approach that views empires as integrative structures that knit, often forcibly, previously disparate and unconnected points together into a shared space.

The metaphor of the web also embodies the multiple positions that any given location might occupy within the structure of empire: one culture, city or institution could simultaneously be subordinate to the metropole, but in turn function as a important hub of its own set of important networks. This argument was stimulated by recent work on Ireland's place within the empire. It is increasingly clear that Ireland was both, in some senses at least, a colony but also an imperial centre in its own right. While the west of Ireland, for example, felt the full brunt of British power and was particularly impoverished during the famine years, it also became an important node within the imperial system. The East India Company army had recruited soldiers from the region since the late eighteenth century and with the foundation of the Queen's College in Galway in 1845 the British drew upon the small middle-class of the region. A steady flow of men from the west, both Catholic and Protestant, used their college education as preparation for imperial service, becoming colonial officials, administrators of prisons, asylums and hospitals, and, in the case of M.A. Macauliffe, a leading Orientalist.[10]

This study has made similar points with regard to New Zealand, which dominated Pacific studies and increasingly assumed the mantle of an imperial power in the Pacific islands, while remaining a British colony and a vital larder for Britain. Even more markedly, British India was the site of imperial innovation and intellectual endeavour, standing at the centre of numerous imperial circuits of exchange, including the expansive and dense personal, publishing, governmental and cultural networks that transmitted Aryanism from British India into Southeast Asia, the Pacific and beyond.[11]

Such networks were powerful agents of globalization. Throughout this study I have suggested that globalization offers a useful analytical lens for imperial history: an argument grounded in a belief that globalization itself has multiple histories, pasts that were embedded in the processes of empire building.[12] The imperial globalization generated by British commerce, conquest and colonization had two important effects. First, and most obviously, imperial networks brought previously unconnected regions together into a system, albeit a highly uneven one, of exchange and movement. Second, it transformed worldviews: globalization was (and is) as much a state of mind as a series of capital flows or migratory movements. The British empire transformed the ways in which people, both in Britain and in the colonies, thought about the world. From the 1760s, largely because of the drive of British interests into the Pacific and Asia, which was so pivotal in constructing a truly global picture of geography, Britons were not only able to comprehend the world as (more fully) global, but also increasingly saw their empire in global terms. This sense of global interconnectedness reached beyond the political and commercial elite. An author of a popular volume of 'improving literature' observed in 1786:

> [b]y the amazing progress of navigation and commerce, within the last two or three centuries, all parts of the world are now connected: the most distant people are become well acquainted, who for thousands of years, never heard of one another's existence.[13]

The discourses of Aryanism were an important product of these new 'connections'. Born out of the colonial encounter in South Asia, the Aryan idea became a crucial element of the culture of empire, whether in British India, Southeast Asia, the Pacific or in Britain itself, as it seemed to offer a powerful framework for explaining both the past and present of the empire. In charting the transmission of the theory and the ways in which it was quickly reworked and indigenized in various colonial contexts, this study has begun to construct a fuller picture of the long history of the idea, a global history that is fundamentally entwined with the British empire's reach into the Asia-Pacific region.

Notes

1   *The Imperial Gazetteer of India. The Indian Empire*: vol. I Descriptive, 26 vols (Oxford, 1907–1909) 64–102.
2   cf. Linda Colley, *Britons: Forging the Nation, 1707–1837* (London, 1992) 373.
3   Daniel Defoe, 'The True Born Englishman', from frontispiece, Benedict Anderson, *Imagined Communities. Reflections on the Origin and Spread of Nationalism*, rev. edn (London, 1991).
4   E.g. Antoinette Burton, *At the Heart of the Empire: Indians and the Colonial Encounter in Late-Victorian Britain* (Berkeley, CA, 1998); Michael Fisher (eds) *The Travels of Dean Mahomet* (Berkeley, CA, 1997); Rozina Visram, *Ayahs, Lascars and Princes* (London, 1986).
5   Har Bilas Sarda, *Hindu Superiority – An Attempt to Determine the Position of the Hindu Race in the Scale of Nations* (New Delhi, 1975 [1906]).
6   Indira Chowdhury Sengupta, *The Frail Hero and Virile History: Gender and the Politics of Culture in Colonial Bengal* (Delhi, 1998).
7   E.g. James Belich, 'Myth, race and identity in New Zealand', *New Zealand Journal of History*, 1997, 31, 9–22.
8   Eugene F. Irschick, *Dialogue and History: Constructing South India, 1795–1895* (Berkeley, CA, 1994) 10.
9   Ibid., 8.
10 Tadhg Foley, *From Queen's College to National University: Essays Towards an Academic History of NUI, Galway* (Galway, 1999).
11 But Indians themselves, we must note, had limited success in accessing these networks, in part because of the racialized reinterpretation of the Aryan idea (forwarded by Hunter, Risley and others) which denied the intellectual and political equality of South Asians.
12 A.G. Hopkins, 'Back to the future: from national history to imperial history', *Past and Present*, 1999, 164, 198–243.
13 Hester Chapone, *Letters on the Improvement of the Mind and Miscellanies in Prose and Verse*, 2 vols (Dublin, 1786) I, 145.

Chapter 17

Jonathon Glassman

SLOWER THAN A MASSACRE: THE MULTIPLE SOURCES OF RACIAL THOUGHT IN COLONIAL AFRICA

'Racial' ideas were far from being the sole preserve of colonisers and their intellectual supporters. Historically important, complex and too-often overlooked currents of racialised thought developed too—albeit often under a degree of European influence—among the colonised, sometimes with monstrous consequences. Here Jonathon Glassman (in an article from which again, alas, much of the close detail and the apparatus of references could not be included in this selection) both offers an overview, and investigates one major particular case, in colonial Zanzibar.

Stephen Howe

Educated Africans are continually agitating to be given more responsibility, but I submit to you . . . that you will be unable to take that part unless and until you have inculcated in your own people a pride of race. Without this, education is useless.

W. Norris, in *Mazungumzo ya Walimu*, 1930.[1]

Soap and education are not as sudden as a massacre, but they are more deadly in the long run.

Mark Twain, quoted in *Mazungumzo ya Walimu*, 1957.[2]

THE ABOVE INSIGHTS appeared in *Mazungumzo ya Walimu* (Teachers' Conversations), a magazine published by schoolteachers in colonial Zanzibar, an island sultanate just off the East African coast.[3] While unusual for having been written by

Westerners rather than Zanzibaris, the quotes represent *Mazungumzo*'s overall faith in the power of education to advance the goals of moral improvement. But Twain's aphorism also fits in a way that was unintended, and is chilling. It appeared in 1957, the opening year of the *Zama za Siasa* or 'Time of Politics,' when the sultanate became gripped by mounting racial tensions as nationalist parties vied in elections meant to prepare it for independence. Even though the schoolteachers believed their thirty-year project of uplift and nation-building had been as salutary as the teaching of modern hygiene, their rhetoric in fact contributed to the atmosphere of racial hatred that culminated during the early 1960s in pogroms against the so-called Arab elite, including those accompanying the racial revolution that overthrew the sultanate in January 1964, a few weeks after independence.[4] Outsiders viewed the massacres as emblematic of the 'primordial attachments' that blocked the way of those who wished to build nations in the former colonies.[5] But, in many ways, the obstacle had been created by the nation-builders themselves.

The schoolteachers and their rhetoric typify the elite intelligentsia who dominated mainstream nationalism throughout Africa in the middle decades of the twentieth century. In suggesting that Zanzibar's postwar racial hatred was rooted in the political discourse they authored, I am going against several currents in the literature on exterminationist ethnic violence in the colonial and postcolonial world. Much of that literature assumes that ethnic conflict arose more or less automatically from social structures that had been bolstered or even created outright by colonial rule. Its emphasis, then, is not on indigenous political thinkers but on European policymakers who defined and divided their subjects by race and ethnicity.[6] Historians who do take cognizance of indigenous racial thinkers usually portray them as marginal figures, the tools of colonial mentors. The result is that the intellectuals who incited dehumanizing violence are treated as aberrations, 'sub-nationalist' demagogues isolated from the anti-colonial mainstream of nationalist thought.[7]

Authors who give any consideration to the role of local thinkers in the rise of Zanzibari racial politics (they are remarkably few, for reasons to be explored below) generally bypass the intelligentsia altogether and focus instead on the poorly-educated ideologues of the African Association and its successor, the Afro-Shirazi Party (ASP), whose virulent racial populism informed most of the pogroms. These subaltern intellectuals came late to the political scene, as did the migrant workers and urban poor who constituted the core of their constituents, and their rhetoric is usually assumed to have been derived from external sources, especially the abolitionist history taught in colonial schools. The intelligentsia, in contrast, were the pioneers of nationalism, first in the Arab Association and later in the islands' first viable political party, the Zanzibar National Party (ZNP). For decades, they had advocated an inclusive form of national identity that bridged racial and class divides by enjoining common loyalty to the sultan and to the long-standing traditions of Islamic civilization that he supposedly represented. This unifying message steadily gained support throughout the 1940s and 1950s (according to the standard account), only to run aground on the racial fears whipped up by the ASP during the Time of Politics of 1957–1963.[8]

Although it is undeniable that ASP demagoguery lay behind much of the violence of the Time of Politics, the racial thinking from which it emerged, and which made so many Zanzibaris susceptible to its seductions, was fairly pervasive and as such is unlikely to be traced to a single cause. On the contrary, as Ann Laura Stoler has observed, a 'scholarly quest for origins'—a quest for the moment of 'original sin' when 'the die of race was cast'—can only obscure a full understanding of the etiology of racial thought.[9] Such quests assume what Loïc Wacquant describes as 'the logic of the trial,' with investigators seeking to name 'victims and culprits' rather than understand complex historical processes.[10]

A pointed illustration of the dangers involved can be found in the literature on Rwanda, a case that parallels Zanzibar's in many ways.[11] In a recent synthesis, Mahmood Mamdani focuses on the processes by which notions of difference became racialized during the colonial era. This concept of racialization can be indispensable, for it prompts us to ask how diverse forms of ethnic and national thought can become invested with racial meanings.[12] Yet, like many authors, Mamdani traces the racialization process back to a single source, the actions of the colonial state.[13] The result is a view of colonial intellectual history in which Europeans are the only actors, inventing and imposing identities as prompted by administrative needs.

The literature on colonial Africa is rife with such interpretations. To understand why this is so, one must confront a cluster of misapprehensions about the nature of race and associated forms of ethnic and national thought, some specific to the study of Africa, others more general. Only then can one craft a strategy that does not underestimate the role played by African thinkers in the construction of race.

The first of these misapprehensions is a lingering tendency toward what Robert Miles calls the 'conceptual inflation' of race into an element of social structure; this is especially pronounced in studies of the colonial world. Most sociologists now reject that tendency, preferring instead to understand race as a mode of thought—in constant interplay with social structures and political processes, to be sure, but best approached as a topic of intellectual history. This understanding stresses that the history of race has involved the 'production and reproduction of meanings,' specifically, meanings concerning particular ways of categorizing humanity.

However, most studies of the history of racial thought limit themselves by regarding their subject only as a specific corpus of ideas: a 'doctrine' that categorizes and ranks humanity in terms of biology. Racial thought is thus usually approached as a school of Western science ('raciology,' as it once was called), which realized its classic distillations in nineteenth-century Europe. To be sure, some authors have recognized the limits of such a view, since, even at the height of raciology's academic respectability, few *pogromschiki* or lynch-mob members would have been conversant with the writings of Joseph-Arthur de Gobineau or Houston Stewart Chamberlain. More pointedly, over the past twenty years, a substantial literature has taken cognizance of postscientific forms that have flourished in the wake of raciology's postwar academic demise. These 'new racisms' demonstrate that racial thought need not be manifested in a scientific idiom or entail a comprehensive ranking of racial categories. There now exists a 'racism without races,' writes Etienne Balibar, 'a racism whose dominant theme is not biological heredity but the insurmountability of cultural differences.'[14]

Yet even the literature on the 'new racism' portrays it as a holdover from classic raciology or, more precisely, as a deteriorated version of that ideology, which once existed in a pristine, originary state. Such literature is mistaken both in its depiction of the supposed newness of culturalist racial thought and in its depiction of the older forms, which in fact were neither invariably hierarchical nor invariably built around a core of biological theory. Past social practices that are universally accepted as classic examples of 'racism,' including colonial racisms, were informed by a wide variety of ideologies, many of which had little to do with racial science. Far more influential than raciology, for example, was the anthropological concept of clearly bounded 'cultural monads,' a concept directly connected with contemporary culturalist thought. As Balibar recognizes, the idea of 'racism without races' is far from revolutionary.[15]

In succumbing to the search for origins, scholars overlook a central theme of the historical literature on racial science itself, which charts the latter's own varied and multiple sources, including many that were neither 'racial' (in the conventional sense) nor scientific. Perhaps most significant of these sources was the concept of 'barbarism' and its foil, 'civilization,' from which modern race-thinkers inherited the project of comparing all humanity according to a single, universal standard. It should be axiomatic that the history of a phenomenon cannot be found solely by looking for its earliest manifestations as it is defined *a priori*; to paraphrase Friedrich Nietzsche, in defining a phenomenon we deny it a history. Many scholars nevertheless insist on an absolute divide between racial thought and the concepts that contributed to it, and search doggedly for the precise moment that race emerged from (for example) the discourse of barbarism. As Stoler archly observes, they come up with widely divergent dates.[16]

One of the implications for the study of the colonial world should be clear. If 'race' is assumed to arise solely from scientific doctrines, then its presence in the non-Western world must be traced solely to the West. And that, in fact, has become a standard narrative. Building on a set of functionalist assumptions often associated with Immanuel Wallerstein, authors describe how Western expansion called racial thought into being as a way of structuring the worldwide division of labor between the subservient 'periphery' and the ruling 'core.' In tying race so mechanistically to the structures of global capitalism, such analyses remove it from the realm of intellectual history. The result is the kind of conceptual inflation Miles warns against; indeed, several authors explicitly insist that race can be defined only in terms of the 'inequalities . . . inherent in a social structure' of Western conquest. Again, such explanations are undermined by a historical literature on the multiple sources of Western racial thought, sources that included, for example, seminal debates about *European* difference. Still, despite disagreements concerning the precise relationship between imperial expansion and the rise of racial thought, there is wide consensus that race was invented in the West and carried to the rest of the world in the toolbox of colonial rulers.

What happens if we abandon the fixation on scientific doctrines and instead recognize racial thought as a shifting field of discourse, a general set of assumptions that humankind is divided among constituent categories, each of which is distinguished by inherited traits and characteristics? ('Racism,' a belief that racial qualities can be ranked according to moral status and other criteria, will then be seen as but a possible form of 'racial thought.') Raciology and other Western racisms then appear as historically specific manifestations of a much broader trend in Western thought—and in human thought generally. Relatively few of the intellectual currents that contributed to raciology were peculiar to the West: drawing boundaries between peoples or ethnicities and even ranking them according to universalizing registers of inferiority and superiority have been far from unusual in world-historical terms. Concepts convergent with the ideal of civilization, ostensibly inclusive yet contributing to hierarchical beliefs and practices that look uncomfortably like 'racism,' have occurred in many non-Western intellectual traditions, Zanzibar's among them. Indeed, Igor Kopytoff has argued that discourses of civilization and barbarism—including tropes marking barbarians as physically different—have been so common in sub-Saharan oral traditions that one might almost speak of them as part of a continent-wide political culture.[17]

Still, the approaches we have been discussing all assume that race can be fundamentally distinguished from other ways of categorizing difference, such as ethnicity or xenophobia, by the central conceit that cultural identities, and hence cultural boundaries, are fixed in the body, or the 'blood.' The ubiquity of this distinction is surprising, since it is of recent vintage: it came into its own only after World War II, as social scientists strove to isolate raciology, recently discredited by the Nazis, from more general concepts of ethnic and national difference. ('Ethnicity,' in fact, was something of a neologism.) Yet the distinction is misleading, for it obscures the fact that all these modes of thought build on the same two core elements. First is the assumption that humanity consists of a discontinuous series of authentic cultural wholes, each internally homogeneous, the creation and property of a distinct 'people.' Second is the metaphor of descent, that is, the general idea that the peoples who are the guardians of these discrete cultures are somehow linked by consanguinity. Such 'blood ties' are imagined with greater or lesser degrees of vagueness. Language we call 'race' places more explicit emphasis on the metaphor of descent—or, indeed, on the conviction that the 'blood relationship' is more than mere metaphor— than does language we call 'ethnicity.' The distinction between 'race' and 'ethnicity', then, is one of degree not kind; and rather than regard them as qualitatively distinct, it is more useful to recognize them as modes of thought that fall toward opposing ends of a single continuum, the 'aura of descent' hovering around them all.

I do not mean to deny the usefulness in historical analysis of distinguishing *descriptively* between doctrines or political ideologies based on explicitly racial concepts and those based on other kinds of ethnic criteria. (So, for example, contrary to the claims of neo-conservative critics, one must acknowledge the historical specificity of white supremacy and the unique forms of oppression it has produced.) But it should be recognized that at any particular historical juncture all such doctrines are part of a common discourse of difference that categorizes humanity via metaphors of descent. The 'family resemblance'[18] among them must be grasped if we are to understand how virtually any form of ethnic thought carries implications that are capable of being elaborated in terms of qualities fixed in the 'blood.' Such elaboration—the process of racialization—is rarely the work of a unified cadre, inspired by a single coherent doctrine. Rather, it emerges from the debates of a diverse range of intellectuals, drawing on multiple and overlapping sources, united only by the general assumptions of racial/ethnic discourse.

Nationalism is one variant of ethnic thought that has proven especially susceptible to racialization. By the mid-twentieth century, the politics of the nation-state had become a global 'categorical order,' a set of concepts taken for granted by leading political thinkers throughout the colonial world. Of course, this did not automatically lead to unity. Nations have never been defined by any single set of criteria, and conflicts have always been rife among nationalist ideologues over who, precisely, belongs to the national community. It has become a truism that nations are defined as much by exclusion as inclusion, that is, in terms of who does *not* belong. When such exclusionary rhetoric is considered alongside the genealogical metaphors that underlie all ethnic discourse, one can understand how virtually any form of national thought—including, as we shall see, thought based on an ostensibly inclusive, universalizing language of civilization—might be interpreted in ways that denigrate certain categories of people by dint of their descent. There is no firm line between national thought and racial thought, and a racial paradigm of exclusion and dehumanization is implicit in virtually all nationalist projects, even the most liberal.

The misconceptions I have been highlighting are especially common in the literature on Africa, much of which continues to approach ethnicity, race, and nation as analytically distinct. There is a tendency to regard only the last of these as the product of ideologies consciously crafted by African thinkers. Ethnicity and race, on the other hand, are often inflated into 'sociological facts,' nowadays usually explained instrumentally. Some scholars, as we have seen, dismiss ethnic thought as little more than a European invention, accepted by Africans in order to secure access to resources controlled by missionaries and the colonial state. Others, more persuasively, recognize the role played by African intellectuals, who cast ethnic appeals in ways calculated to resonate with concerns that had been shaped by labor migration, clientelism, and other processes associated with the construction of the colonial political economy. Yet even these authors assume that ethnic rhetoric can be traced to European origins; hence, as Leroy Vail argues in an often-cited overview, African intellectuals should be seen as 'brokers.' More fundamentally, these authors stress that the power of ethnic appeals can be explained only in terms of material need. In downplaying all other factors, which Vail dismisses as 'non-rational' and therefore irrelevant, they minimize the impact of the content of ethnic thought, even while focusing on the intellectuals themselves.[19]

The continuing assumption of a strict analytic divide between nationalism and other forms of ethnic thought is part of a more general failure to break fully with the nationalist paradigm that has shaped African historical studies for the past forty years. And this has prevented historians of Africa from addressing the kind of questions that have marked other literatures on ethnic politics. Those other literatures have examined how intellectuals crafted locally compelling languages of belonging and exclusion whose affective power rarely had much to do with utilitarian logics. In contrast, the Africa literature has largely treated political thinkers 'empirically,' describing their roles in creating and leading parties and associations, but reducing the content of their thought to the formulae of a nationalist calculus: 'nationalism' as inherently inclusive and liberatory, 'ethnicity' as the divisive legacy of colonialism. The result is a history written from the perspective of the nationalists who took control of the state from the departing colonial powers.

Many of these shortcomings have been remedied in the past decade or so with the emergence of a new literature that seriously engages with the thought of African intellectuals who debated the public good in ethnically specific discourses that were once dismissed as 'tribalism' or 'sub-nationalism.' Rather than force ethnic thought onto a Procrustean bed of utilitarian 'rationality,' these studies reconstruct alternative rationalities that did not necessarily rest on logics of straightforward material advantage. By tracing the deep histories of these discourses, they demonstrate the limits of colonial-era 'invention.' They also demonstrate that ethnic thought had a multiplicity of sources, not just the material demands created by the colonial state as interpreted by instrumentally minded political entrepreneurs, let alone the ideological constructs imposed by colonial rulers. Thus they avoid what Nancy Hunt calls the cliché of the colonial encounter, the nationalist paradigm that interprets modern African history in Manichean terms.[20]

But studies of the racialization of African ethnic thought, and of the exterminatory violence it has at times engendered, have proven stubbornly resistant to this kind of analysis. Most studies of African ethnicity deal with vertical or regional divisions that were once commonly described as 'tribes': ethnic categories that are imagined to exist side by side, each an 'incipient whole society.' Genocide and other forms of exterminatory violence, on the other hand, tend to be accompanied by rhetoric in which ethnic categories are imagined as hierarchical strata, linked to one another in relationships that structure the entire society; the violence itself is prompted either by the subordinate group's attempt to throw off those it sees as its oppressors or the dominant group's attempt to pre-empt such a revolt. Such situations of 'ranked' ethnic stratification parallel the Western experience of race; in fact, there is a sociological literature that distinguishes 'race' from 'ethnicity' precisely by the presence of such ranking. A recognition of those parallels is what has prompted several authors, including Mamdani, to write of 'race' when describing clashes such as those in Rwanda or Zanzibar. But, combined with the persistent assumption of an originary distinction between 'race' and 'ethnicity,' as well as the assumption that race is a Western invention, the parallels have also prompted many of the same authors to assume that the primary force behind racialization was colonial indoctrination.

As a result, relatively little attention has been paid to African initiatives in the racialization of 'ranked' ethnic thought. One suspects that many authors are immobilized by a set of political scruples borne of the assumption that all racial thought originates in white supremacy; in short, they don't want to appear to be blaming the victim. That assumption and those scruples seem confirmed by the undoubted influence that Western teachings had on African racial thinkers, as well as by the fact that the antagonists in some of these conflicts, including the 'Arabs' and 'Africans' who fought for political advantage in Zanzibar, defined themselves in terms that converged with major categories of Western racial thought.

These characteristics are amply displayed in the Zanzibar literature, much of which portrays race as a peculiarly Western disease, introduced to the islands by the effects of colonial rule and even the deliberate machinations of European officials and educators.[21] Authors vary in their identification of the malady's local vectors. Many focus on immigrants from the African mainland, reputedly the ASP's most militant loyalists. Mainlanders presumably were more susceptible to European influences, including mission education, than were people rooted in the islands' Islamic communities, who in contrast continued to nurture more flexible local concepts of belonging. Other authors blame the ruling 'Arabs,' who championed British policies that propped them up as a racial elite.[22] Both variants reflect the political scruples already mentioned, borne of postcolonial politics. In their cruder forms, they constitute nationalist orthodoxies—one supportive of the revolutionary government, the other of the opposition—in which politicians who before independence took the lead in fomenting racial politics absolve themselves of all responsibility by simply blaming the colonial state and its stooges. Whether crude or scholarly, such interpretations depict African intellectuals as having either too little autonomy or too much: either dupes whose thinking was easily molded by British mentors or steadfast anti-imperialists who clung to an authentic subaltern consciousness. Neither circle spoke to the other, and the anti-imperialists avoided all contamination from colonial thought.

Below, I will illustrate how these assumptions might be subverted by reconstructing the precise conversations and debates from which racial thought emerged, a task that requires abandoning images of authentic indigenous discourses and imported infections, and the 'logic of the trial' that goes with them. Such a reconstruction reveals that indigenous intellectuals spoke to one another more than they addressed the colonial state or responded to its demands, and that their impact on the emergence of racial thought was arguably greater, and certainly more direct, than that of colonial educators. (As Anthony Appiah has observed, the colonizers were never as fully in control of intellectual life as the nationalist elite subsequently made them appear.[23]) I have suggested elsewhere that the

ASP's racial rhetoric emerged within a discursive framework of nationalism whose terms had been set not by colonial officers but by members of Zanzibar's elite intelligentsia.[24] Although the idea of the nation-state may ultimately be traced to the West, its pervasiveness in Zanzibar largely resulted from the influence of local intellectuals, who by the 1950s had persuaded thinkers across the spectrum that politics was about the rights of national groups. Zanzibaris disagreed only over how those groups should be defined.

Yet the intelligentsia's role in the racialization of political thought went still further: their own definition of the nation, despite its inclusiveness, directly contributed to the emergence of the Asp's more explicitly racial nationalism. The process was catalyzed by class factors. In its earliest manifestations, ZNP nationalism was liberal and inclusive, growing from a deep intellectual tradition that defined local communities of belonging in terms of an expansive 'civilization' marked by the attributes of an Arabcentric urban high culture. But because the cultural criteria used to mark this civilization were largely class based (that is, beyond the reach of the poor), stressing them as marks of national identity risked dividing the very nation that the nationalists aspired to unify. Balibar has observed that this is why proponents of 'civilizing' nationalisms often turn their constituents' attention to the threat of 'false nationals' ('Jews,' 'wogs,' 'immigrants') who threaten the nation from within.[25] In Zanzibar, as elsewhere, the concept of civilization became an effective tool of nationalist mobilization when it was used to define barbarians to be purged.

Long before the Time of Politics, Zanzibar's elite intellectuals had devoted much energy to reflecting on the history of the Islamic civilization of the Swahili coast, of which they considered Zanzibar the exemplar. This civilization, they argued, distinguished the coast and islands from the rest of East Africa. In the 1950s, the implications of their historical narratives were noticed by the less cultured activists of the African Association/ASP, who accused the intelligentsia of seeking to exclude anyone who did not fully identify with urban high culture, particularly agricultural workers and the urban poor, many of whom traced their roots to the African mainland. To the intelligentsia's invocation of an Arab-driven history of civilization, African Association propagandists responded with historical narratives of Arab conquest and enslavement, and with an alternative definition of national identity based on race rather than civilization. By the late 1950s, ASP charges of racial blood guilt were routinely met by ZNP charges of innate barbarism. The resulting rancor spiraled into every corner of society, contributing directly to racial violence. Thus any attempt to trace the history of popular racial nationalism must begin, paradoxically, with the intelligentsia's rhetoric of history and civilization.

Of course, it would be misguided to neglect the impact of Western thought, including general Western concepts of ethnicity and nation. But such concepts were usually introduced indirectly and only after much reworking. The key actors were local intellectuals, for whom Western thought was but one of many influences, of many provenances; only they were capable of innovating versions of national thought that were locally compelling in ways that pallid imitations of Western discourse could not be. The potential complexities are well illustrated by Zanzibar's political intelligentsia, a vibrant and self-conscious intellectual community that was hardly susceptible to colonial control. The most prestigious intellectual circles were drawn from town-based elite families who considered themselves ethnically Arab. Their main idiom of discourse was Islamic, although, as we shall see, a new cadre of secular intelligentsia began to emerge early in the twentieth century, often from the same families that dominated the ranks of the *ulamaa* (religious scholars). The most learned knew Arabic, with which they read not only religious texts but also Cairo newspapers that championed Islamic modernism and Arab nationalism. Families were especially proud if they could send their children to study in Cairo. Intellectual accomplishment was an important component of family pride and, given the kind of learning that was most valued, it is not surprising that such accomplishment was closely connected to a family's ability to claim elite status as Arabs.

Zanzibar's intelligentsia, then, were keenly cosmopolitan—more so, in many ways, than their European rulers and sometime teachers—and, though not isolated from colonial discourse, they had ample intellectual resources to be able to engage with the ideas of nationalism without merely parroting Western ideas. In fact, influence flowed in more than one direction: Zanzibari intellectuals had a marked impact on the thinking of British educators and administrators. Colonial historians acknowledged the influence of their local informants far more readily than is consistent with the image of a discrete and overpowering colonial discourse. The lower echelons of the provincial administration were staffed almost entirely by members of local elite families, who were especially prominent as *mudirs*, the rough equivalent of district officers in other British colonies. These men were routinely commissioned to write reports on local customs and history, which were then circulated throughout the colonial bureaucracy.

In sum, it is just as misleading to speak of two discrete spheres of discourse—one colonial, the other indigenous—as it is to speak of the colonial state's domination of its subjects' consciousness. It is equally misleading to assume that popular discourse existed in isolation from that of the elite intelligentsia. The subalterns who would later support the ASP were not as lacking in political awareness in the interwar years as the standard sources assume; they were listening to and arguing about many of the same issues that propelled the urban intelligentsia. Like any change in political culture, new ways of thinking of ethnic difference emerged from circuits of discourse in which diverse intellectuals spoke to one another—elite and popular, European and African—and in which their ideas were interpreted and debated by the population at large. Thus the history of the popular racial nationalism of the 1950s must be traced to the elite intellectual discourse of a generation before.

It is ironic that Islam, with its well-deserved reputation for condemning all ethnic distinctions, should have provided some of the language with which the intelligentsia constructed their chauvinist rhetoric; it is also a powerful index of the breadth of sources on which racial thought can draw. Yet the irony is not unheard of: like all universalizing creeds (including Enlightenment ideals of civilization and progress), Islamic ideologies have often been used to express difference. In Zanzibar, locally inherited concepts of Arab hegemony were compounded by the teachings of Cairo-based modernists who made an exception for Arab ethnic solidarity, arguing that it alone was sanctioned and even encouraged by Islam as necessary for the well-being of the faith. In the societies where they originated, such teachings gave religious support to calls for national unity. But in a place such as Zanzibar, they were divisive. They told islanders that, in order to be moral beings according to the religious ideals they themselves held dear, they had to accept the leadership of an ethnically distinct Arab elite.

Because the intelligentsia's interwar teachings on Arab superiority also stressed the lesson of coastal exceptionalism, their impact on indigenous islanders was ambivalent. But the message conveyed to African mainlanders was straightforward. Mainlanders were described unreflectively as *washenzi* and hence automatically excluded from any community built on the values of *ustaarabu*. The Arab Association was particularly plain spoken. Its weekly paper *Al-Falaq*, with which the *Mazungumzo* circle had close connections, frequently stressed the inherent differences between islanders and mainlanders: whereas islanders had become 'sufficiently Arabianized' to have lost most of the qualities of African barbarism, mainlanders are but 'primitive natives . . . whose culture and history are in process of formation only now.'[26] These themes became pronounced during the association's first attempt at mass political mobilization in the late 1930s, when, locked in a bitter conflict with the Indian merchants who purchased most of the clove crop, its activists sought to enlist islanders' support for boycotts of all Indian businesses. They did so with a deeply chauvinist rhetoric that made purge categories of both Indians and mainland Africans. Even though Indians were the activists' primary targets at the time, the dehumanizing rhetoric about mainlanders was to have a more potent afterlife in the racial divisions that racked the islands during the Time of Politics.

Hovering around all the paternalist rhetoric about how islanders had been civilized by Arab tutelage was the specter of slavery, a specter that would haunt some of the worst violence of the later years. In accordance with local sensibilities, slavery was rarely mentioned openly before the 1950s. Yet, in their historical essays, the intelligentsia sometimes referred delicately to the 'help' slaves had given Arab settlers in building up the wealth of Zanzibar's 'Great Arabic Empire,'[27] or indulged in the kind of apologies for 'Arab slavery' that would later become standard fare in ZNP journalism. (In a prominent 1937 polemic, the young man who would later found the ZNP argued that 'such was the happy state of slaves, that they loathed freedom.'[28]) In 1938, *Al-Falaq* went even further, obliquely suggesting that slavery was the very institution that had done the most to civilize African 'natives,' imposing the control necessary to channel their anarchic energy into productive labor.[29]

These ideas reflect with particular clarity how multiple intellectual strands became densely intertwined in Zanzibari discourses of difference. Bringing barbarians into the light of religion and civilization had once been the key justification of enslavement in Islamic doctrine. *Al-Falaq*'s rhetoric shows that doctrine lingering in postemancipation Zanzibar, complemented by European concepts of labor-discipline. It also shows the influence of pan-Arabist journalism, in which the contrast between a supposedly benign 'Arab slavery' and the cruelties of its Western counterpart was a key point in the defense of national honor. Such apologies grew out of two separate historical misunderstandings. First is the assumption that, despite its long and varied history, an institution such as slavery could be characterized and labeled in fixed terms: even though slavery in the Arab Middle East (and Islamic Africa) was indeed often 'benign' relative to New World forms, the East African experience shows that such relaxed relations of bondage could become transformed over time. So the label 'Arab slavery' in fact corresponded to no single set of practices. Yet such labeling was central to nationalist understandings of history, in which institutions were said to reflect discrete national spirits. In this case, the history of Zanzibar slavery was said to demonstrate the humane paternalism of Arab civilization.

Second, whatever slavery looked like in Zanzibar at any given moment, there was nothing particularly 'Arab' about it: contrary to conventional assumptions, many masters were Africans. This misunderstanding stemmed not from imported nationalist philosophies but from local usages, in which the claim of Arab status connoted descent from the planter elite and the absence of slave ancestry. Memories of slavery, in other words, were central to local understandings of Arab identity, and that placed the intelligentsia in the uncomfortable position of having to apologize for it. Given the bitterness with which ASP nationalists would later accuse them of the inherited sin of slavery, it is ironic that the intelligentsia chose to use slavery's history as a narrative tool in their construction of an Arabcentric national identity. But the choice was virtually forced on them by past practices in the construction of ethnic difference.

The acute racialization of political discourse was an aspect of the nationalist mobilization that only began in earnest during and after World War II. The intelligentsia were the pioneers of that mobilization, and their language of civilization, nation, and modernity had a more direct impact on it than did more esoteric notions of raciology. Yet this impact was profoundly contradictory. Most ambivalent were the responses elicited from the village non-elites who were widely regarded as indigenous to the islands. Arab Association activists invited indigenous islanders to participate in the nation-building project, telling them that they were destined to join ranks with Arabs because of their shared history of *ustaarabu* and Islam. But the invitation was unmistakably condescending for, although the intelligentsia encouraged islanders to consider themselves superior to mainland barbarians, they also implied that Arabs alone were in full command of the civilizing arts. That condescension can be read obliquely in the tone of the few Swahili items that *Al-Falaq* began to carry in 1946. (Before then, the paper had published only in English and Arabic.) It can be read more directly in the paper's assumption that Arab leadership was the norm in all affairs, civil and political, and that, unless Arabs are in charge, 'any institution established . . . by Natives' was doomed to fail.[30]

Given such rhetoric, it is easy to understand why the hegemony of Arabcentric notions of *ustaarabu* did not translate into simple consent for Arab leadership but, on the contrary, sometimes encouraged racial resentments against Arabs. This was dramatically revealed by a wartime surge of Shirazi ethnic nationalism in southern and eastern Zanzibar Island, a development that, as the outcome of several converging intellectual trends, provides an excellent illustration of the diverse sources of racial thought.

Before the war, villagers in these agriculturally marginal areas had commonly called themselves 'Hadimu,' an ethnonym that reflected historical memories of vassalage to the Omani sultans. It was derived from an Arabic word for 'servant' or 'slave.' During the nineteenth century, Hadimu cultivators were pushed out of the fertile central and western portions of the island by Arab settlers who established large estates of clove and coconut trees. By World War II, their villages had become reserves of seasonal plantation labor, in good years extruding the majority of their male population to assist in the clove harvest. Not surprisingly, the intelligentsia's historical narratives skirted the processes by which the expansion of the Arab-dominated plantation sector had relegated the Hadimu to the island's rockiest fringes. The most common ploy was simply to deny that tensions had ever existed and to explain the Hadimu's present-day poverty in terms of their innate fecklessness, typical of 'natives.'

The discourse of Shirazi ethnic revival, then, arose from an amalgam of sources, some strictly local, such as the dreams of community revival, others borrowed from the subaltern intellectuals of the SA, whose rhetoric in turn was derived from their opponents among the intelligentsia. Yet, despite this diversity of origins, and despite the anti-Arab resentments expressed by SA supporters in the Hadimu fringe, Shirazi identity was founded on the same distinction between civilization and barbarism that had been elaborated by the secular intelligentsia. And that meant that the category most commonly excluded from the SA's vision of the nation were not Arabs but mainlanders. This was most apparent in Pemba, the birthplace and stronghold of the Shirazi Association (SA). Because ownership of clove estates was more evenly distributed there than in Zanzibar Island, Pemba was not plagued by the economic tensions that plagued the Hadimu fringe. Hence in Pemba, enmity toward Arabs never overtook the hostility to mainlanders that had prompted creation of the Shirazi Association in the first place.

By the end of the war, the intelligentsia had set many of the basic terms of political discourse, including discourse used to express resentment of elite Arabs themselves. Even the subaltern intellectuals of the African Association, who claimed to speak for mainlanders, accepted the intelligentsia's teachings that the nation must be built on the values of civilization and modernity, that those values had been introduced to Africa from abroad, and that upcountry Africans had received them late, from Europeans rather than Arabs. Historical narratives written by African Association journalists differed from the intelligentsia's mainly in their abolitionist perspective—their emphasis that the British had brought Africans not only enlightenment but also redemption from Arab oppression. But even this was not simply a matter of parroting British teachings. Colonial historiography, in fact, more closely resembled the intelligentsia's whitewashing of 'Islamic slavery' and glorification of the civilizing effects of Arab rule. In contrast, the racial nationalists of the African Association told the story of Arab rule almost purely as one of conquest and enslavement, which tied mainlanders together in a history of shared victimhood.[31]

African Association propagandists thus seized on elite historical narratives and made their racial undertones explicit, complementing them with notions borrowed in part from the rhetoric of pan-Africanism. In a sad irony, though, instead of following the pan-Africanists' quest for the African roots of 'civilization,' they accepted a reactionary Eurocentric vision. This move enabled them to craft more straightforward appeals to anti-Arab sentiments than the SA's ambivalent rhetoric of *ustaarabu*. With its emphasis on skin color and 'blood purity,' their propaganda advocated a hardening of the flexible boundaries between ethnic categories, arguing that God himself had decreed that the races and nations be kept separate. An interpretation inflected by the nationalist paradigm might emphasize that this move revealed the influence of Western racial philosophies. That was no doubt true for pan-Africanism itself. But few of the African Association propagandists were well read, and most derived their pan-Africanism second- or third-hand. And whatever the ultimate derivation of pan-Africanist ideas, local intellectuals were the ones who did the job of elaborating them in a local idiom and applying them to the circumstances of local politics.

The African Association's rhetoric of racial solidarity appealed most directly to mainlanders but, with the introduction of electoral politics, its activists also used it in efforts to win support from indigenous islanders. The contest between the two rival visions of the nation—one based on *ustaarabu*, the other on race—was most hotly fought in the Hadimu fringe, owing to the intense ambivalence there about Shirazi identity. In 1957, Ameri Tajo and other Makunduchi activists led a portion of the Shirazi Association to unite with the African Association, thus forming the ASP. Tajo embraced his new partners' stress on racial unity, and together they excoriated Arabs as oppressive aliens. The partnership proved brittle, however, and two years later Tajo and his associates left the ASP to form the anti-mainlander Zanzibar and Pemba People's Party (ZPPP), which allied itself to the ZNP. In marked contrast to his former party, Tajo's new one vilified mainlanders as barbarians, and at rallies he shared the stage with members of the intelligentsia who used history lessons to persuade listeners that by origin and essence

Shirazi were the same as Arabs.[32] In the 1961 and 1963 elections, the ZPPP and ASP battled fiercely and violently for Makunduchi's votes.

As the pace of political mobilization accelerated after 1957, members of the intelligentsia, who in their youth had written high-minded essays on civilization and uplift took to blaming mainlanders for a wide array of ills. Such rhetoric appeared even in *Mwongozi*, postwar Zanzibar's most sophisticated political weekly. Published by two former Hollingsworth students and closely affiliated with the ZNP, *Mwongozi* had been a voice of Islamic modernism, ecumenical tolerance, and anti-racialism. Yet its essays on history and culture were imbued with all the assumptions of coastal exceptionalism, increasingly expressed as contempt for mainlander savagery. So, for example, adapting to its purposes a deeply rooted popular discourse about criminality and difference, *Mwongozi* blamed crime on immigration policies that admitted too many mainlanders (and ASP supporters), 'foreigners who have been allowed to pour into our islands as if this were a rubbish-heap for every type of filth,' and castigated its political rivals for wanting to 'leave the door open to . . . thieves, cannibals, and naked people.' By the eve of independence, the paper was regularly vilifying mainlanders as enemies of Islam and warning that under a ZNP government their 'beastialities' (*sic*) would not be tolerated.[33]

Thus both sides engaged in the spiral of reciprocal dehumanization that culminated in bloodshed. Of the two, only the subaltern intellectuals of the ASP espoused a politics that was 'racial' in the conventional sense, focusing on the divinely ordained solidarities of common origin manifested by bodily markers; ZNP propagandists, in contrast, remained more preoccupied with the intellectual traditions that had shaped their youthful essays for *Mazungumzo*, stressing the lessons of Islamic universalism and the distinctions between civilization and barbarism. But in terms of their dehumanizing impact, it is difficult to discern between these two rhetorics. And, no matter who was most to blame for the rising intensity of racial politics, it is clear that the discourses of civilization and race informed and fed off one another.

In focusing on the elite intelligentsia who came of age between the wars, I have told only a small part of the story, slighting the ASP demagoguery that contributed most directly to the bloodshed of the early 1960s and omitting entirely the processes, far from inevitable, by which racial thought was transformed into popular conceptions capable of motivating transgressive violence. But because the intelligentsia exerted such an overwhelming influence on Zanzibari political culture, this focus is an essential starting point. It is pertinent in other ways as well. Of all Zanzibaris, the intelligentsia experienced the most direct and sustained influence of colonial education. Reconstructing the development of their thought thus offers a pointed demonstration of the limits of colonial indoctrination. It also demonstrates how even the most liberal and mainstream of nationalist rhetorics might become racialized, not by the sinister workings of colonial mentors (throughout the postwar years, in fact, British officials strove to damp down ethnic conflicts, not fan them), but by political actors responding to political opportunities. Neither the convergence of African and European idioms of ranked difference nor the interplay between them, as in the rich intellectual cross-fertilization that took place between Teachers Training School graduates and their British mentors, is sufficient to justify the assumption that African concepts of racial politics originated solely in the European imagination.

This emphasis on the limits of European indoctrination should not be taken to imply that Zanzibar's racial clashes were manifestations of some ancient, inbred enmity. That, in effect, is the false choice proposed in much of the instrumentalist literature on African ethnicity: since it is plainly ahistorical to view tribalism as primordial, one must therefore see it as a consequence of colonialism. Yet, even though the links between colonial rule and contemporary ethnic politics are unmistakable, they alone are not sufficient for explaining the often profound resonance of ethnic demagoguery, especially its ability to evoke ethnic violence. For that, one needs a historical perspective that is both deeper and broader than a simple focus on the colonial state. The racialization of Zanzibari ethnic thought was indeed a modern process, accomplished by modern thinkers, Zanzibari as well as British. But the modes of thought subjected to the process were neither invented from whole cloth nor imported anew; many had been inherited from precolonial intellectual traditions. At the same time (and contrary to primordialist assumptions), those traditions had always been given to innovation, adaptation, and change. So, for example, although distinctions between Shirazi and other islanders were rooted in precolonial thought, their meanings had changed dramatically in the nineteenth century, with the rise of the plantation sector and Omani rule, and again in the twentieth, with the imposition of the colonial state and the rise of nationalist politics. At the same time, memories of historical events placed limits on innovators' ability to invent new political traditions: this appears with particular clarity in the dilemma faced by elite intellectuals who found themselves having to apologize for 'Arab slavery.'

As in other parts of the colonial world, racial thought in Zanzibar was derived from a multiplicity of sources, foreign and domestic, and the innovators who rethought and combined them came from many walks of life. Such diversity implies that we cannot universalize any one path toward racial thought. Yet many studies of the non-Western world still reflect a tendency to universalize the experience of the West and, in particular, the United States. Hence the continued assumption that ethnicity and race had separate origins, the latter arising from imported European doctrines. Although it is undeniable that the divide between 'race' and 'ethnicity' is fundamental to contemporary American political discourse, that discourse is the product of a long and complex history, which we cannot assume to have been replicated anywhere in identical terms. Abandoning such self-centered assumptions is a necessary first step toward a precise understanding of how racial thought developed elsewhere in the world. And that in turn may help us relinquish the last vestiges of the racial thought in which we ourselves have been schooled: the assumption that racial boundaries have any basis in phenomena that exist apart from the subjective perceptions shaped by our several histories.

Notes

1   A.W. Norris, 'Pride of Race,' *Normal Magazine*, April 1930, 4(4), 30–3. The magazine was later renamed *Mazungumzo ya Walimu*, hereafter *Maz.*

2   *Maz.*, n.s. May 1957, 1(3), 14.

3   Zanzibar consists of two main islands, Zanzibar (or Unguja) and Pemba. From 1890 to December 1963, it was a British protectorate, its official head of state chosen from the Omani Arab dynasty that had established the sultanate early in the nineteenth century. Shortly after independence, the sultan was overthrown by forces loyal to the Afro-Shirazi Party. In April 1964, Zanzibar and the mainland nation of Tanganyika united to form the United Republic of Tanzania.

4   To describe the revolution in this way is to take a stand on an issue that has aroused much contention. The extent of racial violence in 1964 is undeniable, yet several authors have argued that 'so-called ethnic divisions' merely masked the fundamental fact that the coup

was 'not an ethnic, but a social revolution.' This distinction between 'ethnic' and 'social' phenomena is, of course, false. I fully endorse these authors' contention that racial identities are mere 'images people have of themselves and others.' But the events of 1957–1964 are eloquent testimony to the impact such images can have on people's thoughts and actions, and it is imperative that the historian try to account for how they were constructed. Quotes are from L. Rey, 'The Revolution in Zanzibar,' in Lionel Cliffe and John Saul (eds), *Socialism in Tanzania* (Dar es Salaam, 1972) 1: 30; and (for 'images') Abdul Sheriff, 'A Materialist Approach to Zanzibar's History,' in A. Sheriff and Ed Ferguson (eds) *Zanzibar Under Colonial Rule* (London, 1991) 7.

5   For a forceful statement, see Michael Lofchie, 'Zanzibar,' in James Coleman and Carl Rosberg (eds) *Political Parties and National Integration in Tropical Africa* (Berkeley, CA, 1964) 506. The quoted phrase is from Clifford Geertz, 'The Integrative Revolution: Primordial Sentiments and Civil Politics in the New States,' in Geertz (ed.) *Old Societies and New States* (New York, 1963). Prominent examples of Western perceptions of the Zanzibar violence include V. S. Naipaul's 1979 novel, *A Bend in the River*, and Gualtiero Jacopetti's 1966 film, *Africa Addio*.

6   I will consider the African literature below. The classic argument for South Asia is Gyanendra Pandey, *The Construction of Communalism in Colonial North India* (Delhi, 1990); for broad critiques, see Sudhir Kakar, *The Colors of Violence: Cultural Identities, Religion, and Conflict* (Chicago, 1996) 12–24; C.A. Bayly, *Origins of Nationality in South Asia: Patriotism and Ethical Government in the Making of Modern India* (Delhi, 1998); Rosalind O'Hanlon, 'Historical Approaches to Communalism: Perspectives from Western India,' in Peter Robb (ed.) *Society and Ideology: Essays in South Asian History* (Delhi, 1993) 247–66.

7   See the suggestive comments in Michael Chege, 'Africa's Murderous Professors,' *The National Interest* 46 (Winter 1996); also Gyanendra Pandey, 'In Defense of the Fragment: Writing about Hindu-Muslim Riots in India Today,' *Representations*, 1992, 37, 27–55.

8   Allowing for the oversimplification necessary in summing up a complex and nuanced work, this stands as a fair representation of the argument in Michael Lofchie, *Zanzibar: Background to Revolution* (Princeton, NJ, 1965). Anthony Clayton criticizes Lofchie for underestimating the divisiveness of ZNP rhetoric; his own account of the Time of Politics serves as a useful corrective: *The Zanzibar Revolution and its Aftermath* (London, 1981) 37–49. Lofchie's study remains the standard account of the islands' political history, although subsequent authors have emphasized more the colonial derivation of Zanzibari racial thought: for example, Alamin Mazrui and Ibrahim Noor Shariff, *The Swahili: Idiom and Identity of an African People* (Trenton, NJ, 1994); Laura Fair, *Pastimes and Politics: Culture, Community and Identity in Post-Abolition Urban Zanzibar* (Athens, OH, 2001). For a fuller discussion of the ASP's racial rhetoric, see Jonathon Glassman, 'Sorting Out the Tribes: The Creation of Racial Identities in Colonial Zanzibar's Newspaper Wars,' *Journal of African History*, 2000, 41, 395–428.

9   Ann Laura Stoler, 'Racial Histories and Their Regimes of Truth,' *Political Power and Social Theory*, 1997, 11, 183–206, quotes from 185.

10   Loïc Wacquant, 'For an Analytic of Racial Domination,' *Political Power and Social Theory*, 1997, 11, 221–34, quote from 222.

11   René Lemarchand, 'Revolutionary Phenomena in Stratified Societies: Rwanda and Zanzibar,' *Civilisations* 1968, 5(10); Catharine Newbury, 'Colonialism, Ethnicity and Rural Political Protest: Rwanda and Zanzibar in Comparative Perspective,' *Comparative Politics*, 1983, 15, 253–80.

12   The concept is often associated with the sociologist Michael Banton, *The Idea of Race* (London, 1977); Jean-Pierre Chrétien makes use of it in his studies of Rwandan intellectual history, some of which are cited below.

13   Villia Jefremovas observes that most authors neglect the role of elite indigenous intellectuals: 'Treacherous Waters: The Politics of History and the Politics of Genocide in Rwanda and Burundi,' *Africa*, 2000, 70(20), 298–308.

14 Etienne Balibar, 'Is There a "Neo-Racism'?" in Balibar and Immanuel Wallerstein, *Race, Nation, Class: Ambiguous Identities*, Chris Turner, trans. (London, 1991) 21. This literature first arose in response to the arguments of Banton and other British sociologists that the anti-immigrant rhetoric of Tory politicians in the postcolonial UK could not properly be deemed 'racism.'

15 Balibar, 'Is There a "Neo-Racism"?' 23.

16 Stoler, 'Racial Histories.' An example is Ivan Hannaford, *Race: The History of an Idea in the West* (Baltimore, 1996). The first half of Hannaford's book is an erudite exercise in correcting for the opposite error, that is, the assumption through backward induction that an act of apparent racism from the pre-modern past was the product of raciological doctrines.

17 Igor Kopytoff, 'The Internal African Frontier: The Making of African Political Culture,' in Kopytoff, *African Frontier*, esp. 49–50, 56–7. Kopytoff notes that discourses of civilization and barbarism shaped the competing claims of peoples who met at the continent's many internal frontiers.

18 Donald L. Horowitz, *Ethnic Groups in Conflict* (Berkeley, CA, 1985) uses this phrase to describe similarities between idioms of kinship and ethnicity.

19 Leroy Vail, 'Introduction: Ethnicity in Southern African History,' in Vail, *Creation of Tribalism*, 1–19.

20 Despite Young's plea of fifteen years ago, this cliché has been abandoned less quickly in studies of ethnic and nationalist politics than in studies of social history.

21 Nancy Rose Hunt, *A Colonial Lexicon of Birth Ritual, Medicalization, and Mobility in the Congo* (Durham, NC, 1999); Frederick Cooper and Ann Laura Stoler, 'Between Metropole and Colony: Rethinking a Research Agenda,' in Cooper and Stoler (eds) *Tensions of Empire: Colonial Cultures in a Bourgeois World* (Berkeley, CA, 1997) 1–56.
   Hence the leading authority on Zanzibari history, in language similar to that used by many authors, explains ethnic divisions by invoking British 'preferences' informed by policies of 'divide and rule': Abdul Sheriff, 'Race and Class in the Politics of Zanzibar,' *Afrika Spectrum*, 2001, 36(3), 307–8.

22 For a pronounced version of the first interpretation, see Alamin Mazrui and Ibrahim Noor Shariff, *The Swahili: Idiom and Identity of an African People* (Trenton, NJ, 1994); for the second, B.D. Bowles, 'The Struggle for Independence,' in Sheriff and Ferguson, *Zanzibar under Colonial Rule*, esp. 86, 92; B.F. Mrina and W.T. Mattoke, *Mapambano ya Ukombozi Zanzibar* (Dar es Salaam, 1980).

23 Appiah, *In My Father's House*, 7.

24 Glassman, 'Sorting Out the Tribes.'

25 Balibar, 'Racism and Nationalism,' 60.

26 'Our New Educational Chief,' *Al-Falaq*, May 20, 1939; 'Native Trusteeship (1),' *Al-Falaq*, July 29, 1939; 'Memorandum by the Arab Association,' February 5, 1934, CO 618/60/15, PRO; 'Report on Zanzibar Education (II),' *Al-Falaq*, October 1, 1938.

27 *Al-Falaq*, June 15, 1940; M.A. el-Haj, 'Hadimu Land Tenure,' May 1940, AK 33/294, ZNA.

28 Ali Muhsin, 'Slavery as It Used to Be Practiced in Zanzibar,' *Makerere College Magazine*, August 1937, 1(4), 111. Muhsin's essay was celebrated in *Al-Falaq*; for a full discussion, see Glassman, 'Sorting Out the Tribes.' Six decades later, Muhsin continued to issue similar apologies: *Conflicts and Harmony*, 177–86.

29 'The So-Called Native Lethargy,' *Al-Falaq*, September 3, 1938. The article was published as part of an ongoing campaign to persuade the authorities to create the legal apparatus by which estate owners might more effectively control agricultural labor.

30 'Itihad-el-Watani,' *Al-Falaq*, February 11, 1939.

31 The discussion of African Association rhetoric in this and the next two paragraphs is based mostly on Glassman, 'Sorting Out the Tribes.' For the British defense of 'Islamic slavery' generally, see Paul E. Lovejoy, *Transformations in Slavery: A History of Slavery in Africa* (Cambridge, 1983) 261–8; and Morton, *Children of Ham*; the views of several Zanzibari officials can be found in Sir Arthur Henry Hardinge, *A Diplomatist in the East* (London, 1928).

32   Anti-mainlander sentiments can be found in the ZPPP news sheet *Sauti ya Wananchi*, among other sources; see AK 20/1, ZNA; also Saud A. Busaidy (DC Urban), March 6, 1963, AK 31/15, ZNA. In a particularly telling moment, Tajo shared the stage with Zam Ali Abbas, long a figure on *Mazungumzo*'s editorial board; their speeches are summarized in 'Umma Hay!' *Mwongozi*, April 21, 1961.

33   Quotes from 'Barua,' by 'Mzanzibari,' *Mwongozi*, May 3, 1957; 'Yepi Yaliyowaleta Pamoja Wananchi na Wazalendo,' *Mwongozi*, March 3, 1961; 'Declaration from Lamu,' *Mwongozi*, September 13, 1963. Similar rhetoric can be found in an official ZNP statement from October 1957, CO 822/1377, PRO.

Chapter 18

Jonathan Hyslop

THE IMPERIAL WORKING CLASS MAKES ITSELF 'WHITE': WHITE LABOURISM IN BRITAIN, AUSTRALIA, AND SOUTH AFRICA BEFORE THE FIRST WORLD WAR

Here too the intricate interconnections between metropole and colony, and among different colonies of settlement, are under scrutiny. 'Whiteness studies' have had something of a vogue, mainly in North American history. Hyslop argues that a distinctive, powerful idea of 'whiteness' took form in Britain and its colonies – indeed especially in its colonies – and not least among working class and trades union activists.

Stephen Howe

Introduction

ON 1 MARCH 1914, THE BIGGEST British Labour demonstration of the early twentieth century flooded into London's Hyde Park in a seven-mile-long column. Estimates of the size of the crowd ran as high as half a million. The Socialist papers were 'euphoric.' R.B. Suthers wrote in *The Clarion* (6 March 1914):

Never in my long experience of Hyde Park, have I seen such countless multitudes pouring into its confines and gathering around the speakers and the platforms. Never have I seen so impressive a crowd, never have I seen so unanimous and earnest a mass meeting.

The publication of the engineering workers' union described the gathering as 'the greatest and most impressive of its kind that has ever taken place in the heart of the Empire' (ASEMJR February 1914).[1]

One would imagine that such an event would have been the focus of considerable attention by the legions of British labour historians. But to my knowledge only one – Logie Barrow (1989) – has given a careful analysis of the significance of that day's events. It is easy to suggest a reason for this strange absence of comment. For the demonstration was in a cause embarrassing in the extreme to later twentieth-century historians of labour sympathies. The march manifested the solidarity of British trade unionists and Socialists with the cause of white workers in South Africa.

Following a white workers' general strike in the Johannesburg area in June 1913, and a second, attempted one, in January 1914, nine leaders (seven of them British born) had been deported to Britain by the government of General Louis Botha and his right-hand man, General Jan Smuts. The deportees' unions were ones which demanded the exclusion of Black and Asian workers from skilled jobs. Support for these unions and their leaders was the occasion of the Hyde Park demonstration.

In this chapter I want to account for the extraordinary British labour response to events in South Africa by advancing the following argument. First, the white working classes in the pre-First World War British Empire were not composed of 'nationally' discrete entities, but were bound together into an imperial working class, by flows of population which traversed the world. Second, the labour movements based on this imperial working class produced and disseminated a common ideology of White Labourism. In this ideology, the element of the critique of exploitation and the element of racism were inextricably intermingled. This was an era of radical labour militancy, of profound ideological hostility to capitalism, of widespread influence of syndicalist doctrines in the unions. But these trends fused with the notion that employers were attempting to sap the organised power of white workers internationally by subjecting them to the competition of cheap Asian labour. This internationally constructed synthesis of militant labour and racist visions was a major cultural source of the rise of working class racism in turn-of-the-century Britain, of the beginning of South African industrial segregation, and of the politics of the 'White Australia' policy. These phenomena were not separate, but rather, part of a single story.

The approach which lies behind these arguments derives in part from the illuminating recent discussion of the historiography of colonial societies by Stoler and Cooper (1997). The tendency for historians of labour within Britain and its former Empire to look at their subject in a 'national' framework can be profoundly misleading and anachronistic, for lateral connections within the Empire were extremely important in the formation of labour movements. As Stoler and Cooper (1997: 22) argue 'The "nation-state" has become too centred in conceptions of European history since the late eighteenth century, and "empire" not centred enough.' Thus I take the British Empire, not its successor states, as the relevant geo-social framework for this chapter.

The direction which a national labour movement took cannot be understood purely in terms of the conditions prevailing inside a single country, but must also be viewed in its connection with the international flows of political culture. South African scholars, for example, have been very good at describing the structural factors encouraging the creation of state-sponsored labour segregation, but less good at accounting for the mind-set of the white working class (Legassick 1974; Davies et al. 1976; Davies 1979; Yudelman 1983). This, I would suggest, is because they tend to leave out the vital international sources of white workers' political culture. The political concerns of white labour were carried around the empire by persons, by newspapers, and by organisational links. As Stoler and Cooper

(1997: 28) put it, 'The circuit of personnel around empires grounded the idea of empire in global experiences.' It is necessary and possible to show the specific pathways along which the ideas of the imperial working class circulated.

The tendency of the various national labour literatures to present racism as simply an unfortunate ideological infection of a previously robust proletarian identity is misguided. Not only in South Africa and Australia, but also in Britain itself, the development of labour identity was inextricably tangled with notions of race. In Stoler and Cooper's (1997: 16–17) words: 'Cultural domination, racial exclusivity and violence were written into modernizing, nationalist and Socialist projects.'

My chapter's approach also derives partly from the American historical work of the 1990s on the relationship between the construction of 'whiteness' and the politics of class (Saxton 1990; Roediger 1994; Allen 1994; Ignatiev 1995). This literature emphasises that conceptions of 'whiteness' are socially constructed, and therefore have histories which can be investigated. Ignatiev (1995: 180) suggests that American labour historians had previously tended to avoid the question of the role of white labour in promoting racial divisions amongst the workforce. The newer work redresses the balance by examining the ideological construction of race in various historical contexts of American working class formation and organization. This chapter shares this concern with the history of how combinations of racism and labour identity have been built. However, I see the historical development of labour racism in the British Empire as possessing dynamics distinct from those of D.S. labour. The imperial framework was central in shaping the self-conceptions of British and colonial workers before 1914. In that period, notions of Britishness were crucial to the labour racism of Britain, Australia, and South Africa.

Three vectors of White Labourism

In the remainder of this chapter I want to substantiate the claims I have made about the existence of an imperial working class and its White Labourist ideology. I will show how various social threads crossed the world, helping to weave the pattern which was to be visible in the racial solidarity of 1914. In doing so I will trace three particular strands, amongst the many which existed. First, I will show how the Australian labour movement played a fundamental role in the generation of a White Labourist political model, and how this was disseminated through the empire, especially to South Africa. Second, I will explore how the industrial world of the Cornish miners was crucial in connecting the racial labour politics of Britain, Australia, and South Africa. Lastly, I will look at the similar unifying role played by a British union which operated internationally, the Amalgamated Society of Engineers (ASE). Each of these were important 'vectors' through which White Labourism spread. The word 'vector' is used to emphasise that there were specific, identifiable lines of direction along which White Labourism travelled across the world. I do not suggest that the three vectors I identify were by any means the only ones; there are certainly many others yet to be charted. This chapter ends with an exploration of the British labour movement response to the 1914 deportations, which seeks to show how integral to that movement the conceptions of White Labourism had become by then.

In order to link this argument with my claims about the significance of the 1914 events, I must first provide the reader with a little more detail on the background of the Hyde Park demonstration. The nine deportees included some of the most important figures of a period of white worker militancy which had gradually built up on the gold mining Witwatersrand region, around Johannesburg, in the period since the Boer War. This militancy was fuelled by many factors, including the hideous death rate from industrial lung disease and attempts by owners to increase the pace of work (Katz 1976, 1990). But the underlying theme of the work of the union movement was the demand for the protection of white workers' monopoly of skilled jobs against the competition of Asian and African labour. Initially, after the Boer war, white labour's focus was on the exclusion of Chinese labour from the mines (Richardson 1982). But once this issue had been won with the coming to power of the 1906 Liberal government in Britain, on a platform of opposition to Chinese labour, the white workers' focus changed. Now their fear was that they would be replaced by African workers. This fear was all the more real, because with the introduction of revolutionary new drill technology, a considerable deskilling of mining work was taking place, which meant that new workers could be trained fairly quickly. In 1907, the resulting attempts by mine owners to change production practices precipitated an unsuccessful white mine workers' strike on the Rand (Dawe 1998: 217–34). In the subsequent period, the basic issue at stake remained, with mine owners seeking ways to raise profits through labour market and work process reorganisation, and the white miners resisting this. Between 1909 and 1912, the South African Labour Party, led by F.H.P. Creswell, emerged as a unified political voice for White Labourism. In June 1913, a general strike of white labour broke out in Johannesburg. Smuts, the key figure in Louis Botha's government, called out the British garrison. On 4th June, clashes between strikers and the police erupted, leading to rioting by white workers and the unemployed in Johannesburg. On 5th June, British troops fired indiscriminately into the crowds, causing more than twenty fatalities and scores of injuries. Smuts and Botha then entered Johannesburg to negotiate with the strike leaders at the Carlton Hotel. Once the meeting had started, strike supporters surged around the British troops guarding the hotel. At this point, according to some versions of the event, a union leader, J.T. Bain, and one of his companions, threatened to shoot Smuts and Botha if the soldiers fired on the crowds again. In order to extricate themselves from the situation, Smuts and Botha signed a nonvictimisation agreement which they regarded as a complete capitulation to the strikers. Smuts, furious at what had happened, laid plans to deal with the union movement. In January 1914, the government deliberately precipitated a railway strike, leading to a general strike. Smuts used this as an excuse to proclaim martial law, calling out the newly constituted Union Defence Force. A large number of labour leaders were arrested, and nine of them, including Bain, were rushed to Durban and placed on the *SS. Umgeni*, bound for England. Smuts freely admitted that he had little legal basis for his actions and attempted to cover his tracks with a bill indemnifying the government (*Clarion*, 20th February 1914; Cope n.d.: 88–161; Hepple n.d.: 153–7; Walker and Weinbren 1961: 22–58; Katz 1976; Hirson and Williams 1995: 101–26).

The Australian vector

The formation of the international Labour movement in the late nineteenth century, fuelled by the human rivers of migration flowing around and out of Europe, occurred at the same moment as an enormous outflow of migrants from the Fukien and Kwantung provinces of China and from India. It was this conjuncture which created a context in which defining themselves and their labour market interests as 'white' could seem an advantageous option to organised workers. Faced with potentially highly competitive labour markets, one possibility for workers of European origin was to seek economic protection from the state by appealing to the idea that they were racial partners in empire. This formed the ideological basis for advocating differential sets of rules governing access to labour markets for white workers as against Asians and Africans. Although the clashes between white and Asian labour on the west coast of North America in this era are well known, in neither the US nor Canada did exclusion of Asian workers become the central issue in national politics. In Australia it did. The 'White Australia' policy was the result.

The political processes taking Australia in that direction began shortly after Chinese workers entered the Australian goldfields in the 1850s. Within a few years, violent clashes were taking place between white and Chinese diggers. Exclusionary measures against Chinese were first introduced in Victoria in the 1850s, following racial violence in the Bendigo area in 1854. This culminated in the imposition of penal taxation against the Chinese in Victoria in 1857. From here a pattern developed in which one Australian colony after another pushed Chinese labour out through taxation; legislation aimed at doing this was introduced in New South Wales in the early 1860s and in Queensland in 1877 (Johanson 1962: 5–6).

From the start, White Labourism's weird combination of racism and egalitarianism was present. In December 1861, the Miner's Protective League issued its manifesto at Lambing Flat, New South Wales, in the build-up to a particularly notorious anti-Chinese pogrom. The document called for the white diggers to 'drive the moon-faced barbarians away,' while at the same time urging 'men of all nations' to join the League and calling 'upon every man whose spirit yearns for equality, fraternity and glorious liberty'(Ebbels and Churchward 1960: 74–6). Emerging labour organisations took this path. The employment of Chinese labour was a central grievance in the Sydney seaman's strike of 1878 (Ebbels and Churchward 1960:103–5). In 1890, the Sheep Shearers' Union, which in the next year would launch possibly the most symbolically significant strike in Australian history, forbade the recruitment of new Chinese members (Ebbels and Churchward 1960: 114–6). Unions played a major role in bringing about the passage of Exclusion Acts in the various Australian colonies in 1888, aimed at shutting out Chinese immigration (Rolls 1993: 471–503). In the 1890s, economic recession gave a considerable impetus to the development of labour parliamentary politics in Australia (White 1981: 86). Persisting white fears of immigrant competition, especially from Japanese, Indian, and 'Kanaka' (Pacific Islander) workers, made yet tighter immigration restrictions a crucial plank of Australian Laborism.

At the elections which led to the formation of the Australian Commonwealth in 1901, although there was a broad consensus on the notion of White Australia, Labor suspected the other parties of being prepared to renege on this 'principle.' Labor made the passage of a 'White Australia' policy a condition for supporting the 'middle way' government of Edmund Barton (Clark 1993: 411). In the debate on the bill at the first Commonwealth parliament, Labor's leader, J.C. Watson, posed the question of immigration at the elevated level of 'whether we would desire our sisters or brothers to be married into any of these races to which we object' (Ebbels and Churchward 1960: 234–5). Interestingly, Labor MPs were actually more likely to be British born and more likely to be recent immigrants than the MPs of other parties (White 1981: 87). So the sense of where racial lines were to be drawn seems not to have been stronger amongst the Australian-born than amongst immigrants. Thus Bonnett's implied view that racial lines were initially clearer in the colonial than in the British mind seems dubious (Bonnett 1998).

What Australian labour created at the turn of the century was a militantly egalitarian polity, protected by an interventionist state. Local industry would be protected by tariffs, worker's rights by the arbitration system, the vulnerable and aged through pensions, and children through maternity benefits. And white workers' jobs would be protected by 'White Australian' exclusion of all 'other' races from the labour market. The boundaries of the social-democratic project would be racially defined (White 1981: 144–5; MacIntyre 1997).

It was this political 'ideal' that many Australian workers brought to the Witwatersrand. The depression in Australian mining during the 1890s coincided with the rapid development of the South African gold fields, resulting in a flow of Australians to the Transvaal. After that, many of the 16,000-strong Australian military contingent in the Boer War stayed on in South Africa after their service was completed. By 1904, there were over 5,000 Australians in the Johannesburg area, most of whom were miners or artisans (Kennedy 1984: 2–6).

Australians played a major role in white trade unionism around Johannesburg, in the years from 1902 to 1914. Katz was the first to draw scholarly attention to the importance of these Australian unionists (Katz 1976: 16, 449). This was not just a question of their physical presence, but also of the prestige which the Australian political model enjoyed more widely amongst the ranks of the imperial working class (Katz 1976: 2).

There is abundant evidence of this crucial Australian role and of the extent to which it was linked to attempts to import the racial-utopian vision of 'White Australia.' When James Ramsay MacDonald, then a London County Councillor, visited Johannesburg in 1902, he found 'an Australian trooper' had been the author of a 'platform' which had been circulated from the engineers' union to labour groupings for their support. This document included a number of strongly anti-capitalist provisions, but also had an Australian White Labourist tinge. It contained proposals for a franchise which excluded blacks, for legislation to prevent the introduction of 'Asiatic' labour on the mines, and for the arbitration system in labour relations (MacDonald 1902: 112–3).

Peter Whiteside, the Ballarat-born President of the Witwatersrand Trades and Labour Council, took a lead in opposing the importation of Chinese labour and in subsequently campaigning for the deportation of the Chinese miners. An Australian, J. Forrester Brown, was a leading figure in the white mine workers' union. Robert Burns Waterston, born in Bendigo, was one of the nine unionists deported by Smuts. At the time he was secretary of the South African Labour Party. The prominent Johannesburg unionist, John Joseph Ware, had been a member of the Operative Masons' Society in Australia, and had represented that union at the founding conference of the Australian Labor Party. He ended his career as a Senator representing the South African Labour Party. Paramatta born James Briggs' South African career took him through leadership of the bricklayers union, the presidency of Pretoria Trades Council, and also to a Senate seat. Tom Kneebone, a militant organiser of the Associated Society of Engineers in South Africa, was also born in Australia. Frederick Swan, the leader of the South African banking employees, was born in London but had grown up in Queensland and had his first job at Brisbane Post Office (Gitsham and Trembath 1926: 159–79). O.H. Evans, another president of the Witwatersrand Trades and Labour Council, was another British-born unionist who had worked in Australia (Katz 1976: 485).

The direct impact of the domestic politics of 'White Australia' was also felt in South Africa. In 1904, the Australian Prime Minister, Alfred Deakin, found himself reliant on the goodwill of Labour MPs for the survival of his government in office. At this juncture he was approached by the Labour government of New Zealand to make a joint protest to the imperial government over the importation of Chinese labour into the Transvaal. Deakin was personally very unenthusiastic about this proposal, but felt obliged to join in, because of fear of a possible Labor Party revolt if he failed to do so (Jebb 1905: 130).

The Australian model was one which aroused not only the admiration of South African labour activists, but also the fears of mining magnates, who saw it as system in which working class interests had attained an excessively powerful position. Percy Tarbutt, a director of Consolidated Goldfields, wrote from London to F.H.P. Creswell in 1903, explaining his opposition to the latter's proposal for the use of whites in unskilled work on the mines on the grounds that business feared:

> the same trouble will arise as is now prevalent in the Australian colonies. viz. that the combination of the labour classes will become so strong as to be able, more or less, to dictate not only the question of wages, but also the political questions by the power of their votes when a representative government is established.
>
> (Hepple n.d.: 145).

Thus mining magnates were suspicious of any measure that would increase white worker numbers or security. It has been seriously suggested by at least one academic commentator that fear of white labour unrest was a key motive in employers' support for developing a Chinese work force (Adam Smith 1965: 158). Although this claim should be treated with scepticism, there seems to be no doubt that business interests viewed the example of the Australian polity with some alarm.

The success of the Australian activists in influencing the South African labour movement arises from the way that their model squared with the aspirations and prejudices of trade union supporters, whilst also helping to resolve the dilemmas of egalitarian-minded activists. As the fascinating recent work of Lucien van der Walt (1999) has shown, some of the small, white left-wing groups in South Africa in this era were in close touch with syndicalist movements in Europe and North America, and they did think seriously about the position of black workers, and they did begin to establish common organisations with black activists. However, where white Socialists took leadership positions in the white labour movement, they found themselves pushed toward a white labourist project. Some left-wing union leaders were able to reconcile themselves to this fate by way of the circuitous reasoning that although African workers should have political rights in principle, in a situation in which Africans were living in an unfree condition, and could thus be forced to perform cheap labour, the wage and welfare gains of white workers needed to be protected against 'unfair' competition. It was at this point that the Australian model offered itself as a solution to white leftists' difficulties. The white mine workers' leader Tom Matthews explained how he had decided that the Australian strategy was imperative, despite his more broadly democratic sympathies:

> I hold that the Kaffir should be allowed to get free, but in the interim, as he is here only as a semi-slave, I have a right to fight him and oust him just as the Australians ousted the Chinamen and the Kanakas.
>
> (Simons and Simons 1969: 95).

What Avner Offer wrote of Canada and Australia seems true of South Africa in an even more sinister way: 'It is wrong to regard exclusion as a 'dark side' of colonial societies. Rather racism arose directly out of their virtues of democracy, civic equality and solidarity' (Offer 1988: 235).

The Cornish vector

A central component of the imperial working class was provided by the mining communities originating in Cornwall. In the late nineteenth and early twentieth century, the extraordinary international mobility of the Cornish, the demand for their specific mining skills, and their social cohesion abroad gave them a social impact which was out of all proportion to their relatively small numbers in England itself. In this section I will seek to demonstrate, firstly, the remarkable reach and strong collective identity of the Cornish diaspora; secondly, how it became unionised and mobilised abroad; and, thirdly, how its White Labourism connected back into British politics. Cornish White Labourism had peculiar features. The Cornish working class was not very responsive to the rise of Labour parliamentary activity in Britain. In the period under discussion, they voted largely for the Radical Liberals. It was partly as a consequence of this that the Radical Liberals were to take such a strong anti-Chinese labour position. At a time when the shift of British working class allegiance from Radical Liberalism to Labour still had a very long way to run, this situation helped to ensure that Labour could not take any sort of non-racial position on imperial labour questions without threatening its own ability to continue winning new support.

From the middle of the nineteenth century, the exhaustion of some of the Cornish ore deposits, combined with the opening elsewhere in the world of cheaper and more plentiful sources of copper and tin, and the lure of the gold rushes, produced a vast Cornish mining diaspora. From the 1830s, there was a massive population movement to North America and, from the late 1840s, to Australia. In South Africa, a trickle of Cornish miners to the mines of Namaqualand and Kimberley turned into a flood with the opening of the Witwatersrand in 1886 (Burke 1984: 59). In these migrations, the Cornish emigrants did not necessarily just move to one area of settlement, but often shifted around the world, from one site to another, as new mineral fields opened and declined. As Philip Payton (1996: 244) has observed, this generated the construction of an international industrial culture rooted in a network of Cornish communities around the world.

This was an example, perhaps *the* example, of what James Belich (1996) has called 'Crew Culture,' the characteristic workers' social formation of the nineteenth-century gold-rushes. Crews shared 'the same manners, customs, slang, prejudices, dress, leisure habits, virtues, and vices – the same subculture . . . Crews were prefabricated communities into which new members could easily slot' (Belich 1996: 428). It was a culture which valued 'strength, toughness and manual skills' (Belich 1996: 431).

Cornish identity can usefully be understood in this framework because it was a culture which defined itself industrially; mining skills were at its core. It was not an ethnic-nationalist identity despite the fact that the Cornish language had only recently faded away, and despite the very strong regional sense in Cornwall (Payton 1992: 112–14). Cornish nationalism only began to be developed in the late nineteenth century, by Anglican clerics and intellectuals, whose ideas had little appeal for their Methodist, proletarian countrymen (Payton 1996: 260–8). Crew culture, on the other hand, was well adapted to miners' competing needs in the Cornish diaspora, for both mobility and solidarity. Migrants could fit into a crew culture grouping wherever they arrived, and crew culture also provided the informal networks which could be used to exclude unwanted competitors in the labour market.

On the Rand, Cornishmen participated in what initially was a classic migrant labour system. In the South African case, Cornish miners were much less likely to bring their families with them than they had been in America and Australia (Burke 1984: 67). Many worked for several long periods on the Rand, punctuated by return visits to Cornwall. Early Johannesburg was perhaps the ultimate example of the crew culture world of 'binge centres, red-light districts and shabby boarding houses' of which Belich (1996: 436) writes. In 1905, there were about 7,000 Cornish miners on the Rand, out of perhaps 16,000 white mine workers. The emigrants, mostly men, single or separated from their families, sent back about a million pounds Sterling in remittances to Cornwall each year (Dawe 1998: 211). Many of them returned to Cornwall only to die of phthisis as the crystalline quartzite dust of the Rand tore up their lungs (Katz 1990).

This migrancy created a bizarrely close connection between Cornwall and the Rand. The historian A.L. Rowse wrote in his memoir of his working class boyhood in Cornwall before the First World War that:

> At home people knew what was going on in South Africa often rather better than what was happening 'up the country': the journey across the seas to another continent was more familiar to them than going very far 'up the country,' say as far as London.
>
> (Rowse 1942: 35)

In the depressed condition of the turn of the century Cornish economy, a kind of dependence upon the Rand developed. When the 'African Mail' bearing the postal orders arrived at Redruth-Camborne, people would flock into town from the surrounding villages to collect their money, and business in local shops would boom (Barton 1974: 162, Payton 1996: 245).

The white working class on the South African goldfields, the Cornish working class and the miners of Australia were not just connected. To a very great extent, one is actually talking, in these three cases, of the same globally mobile individuals, linked in a transcontinental network. At home, the Cornish miners displayed remarkably little interest in trade unionism. This is linked to two factors. One was the Cornish mining industry's tradition of 'tributing,' a practice in which a miner would bid against his fellow workers in an auction, to work a pitch of rock at a particular rate. Thus tendencies toward solidarism were undermined by a sense of private enterprise. A second feature was that it was only late in the nineteenth century that technological change even began to threaten the craft skills of the 'hard rock' miners. Rock drill technology only started to be used after 1875. In contrast, in British coal mines the deskilling process began decades earlier (Burke 1984: 66–72).

Abroad, whether in Australia, America or elsewhere, changes in working conditions rapidly broke down the Cornish reluctance to organize collectively. In Australia, the initial wave of Cornish mining migrants was particularly concentrated at the Burra Burra copper mine in South Australia, which flourished from 1845 to 1860. Already in 1848, a major strike took place. A second Cornish copper mining concentration formed in the 1860s in the Moonta-Kadina Wallaroo area of South Australia; so heavy was the Cornish dominance there that it became known as 'Little Cornwall.' Significant strikes broke out in that area in 1863 and 1874. So Cornish miners participated in the emerging labour movement of Australia from the beginning. Those who came to South Africa with a background of Australian mining had experience of a labour movement which was propagating its 'White Labourist' position. And significant numbers of the Cornish did move through Australia to South Africa. The South Australian mines entered a steep decline in the 1880s, which meant that the labour market there was closing up just as the Rand gold rush started in 1886 (Payton 1978; 1984: 89–94).

The Cornish, whether they came via other countries, or direct to South Africa, played a remarkable role in the initial emergence of White Labourist union organisation in that country. When the Miners Association was started on the Rand in 1902, its founding leader was the Cornishman, Tom Matthews, whose mining career in the United States had included being elected as the only Socialist member of the Montana legislature (Dawe 1998: 197). A unionist whose personal history is emblematic of the influence of the global Cornish diaspora on South Africa (although not himself a miner) was Benjamin Caddy. Caddy's father had emigrated from Cornwall to Australia with his parents in 1854. Caddy was born in Ballarat and trained as a boiler-maker. Coming to South Africa with the Australian contingent in the Boer War, Caddy stayed on and became a leader in the unionisation of the boilermakers. He participated in all the major actions of the era of white worker militancy, including the 1913 and 1914 strikes, the 1919 worker occupation of the Johannesburg municipality and the 1922 strike (Verwey 1995: 34–5).

The strength of the crew culture of the Cornish on the Rand gave them an ability to implement racially and ethnically exclusionary labour practices. In the first two decades of Rand mining they were able, through their informal social networks, to exercise a remarkable degree of control over recruitment of skilled labour, shutting out not only black and Asian workers, but also Afrikaners and other whites who had not been initiated into the world of crew culture. This power was usually exercised through Cornish foremen, in whose hands management often placed the control of recruitment of skilled personnel. This had some remarkable results; in one Rand mine, Ferreira Deep, the entire white workforce was made up of workers from a single Cornish pit, Dolcoath (Payton 1996: 242). Other mines also had a reputation for exclusively hiring Cornishmen as skilled workers (Dawe 1986: 75–6). Even after the failure of the 1907 strike loosened this control, enabling management to bring in substantial numbers of Afrikaner workers, the Cornish influence remained strong.

From the turn of the century, White Labourism became the dominant electoral issue in the mining areas of Cornwall, largely because of the area's close links to South Africa. Although the supporters of Joseph Chamberlain had made some political headway in the area in the 1890s (Payton 1992: 153–4). Chamberlain's backing for the use of Chinese labour in South Africa ensured that miners would not be available to support his Unionist deviation from Liberalism (Chamberlain's inability to question the educational policies of his Conservative allies, which were unfavourably regarded by religious non-conformity, was an added disadvantage in Methodist Cornwall). In the 1900 election, the Radical Liberal W.S. Caine won the mining division of Cornwall on the basis of a campaign against the still hypothetical possibility of the importation of Chinese labour to the Transvaal. This was a particularly burning question in that year, because of the presence in the constituency of many miners who had fled the Rand at the outbreak of the Boer War, and were anxious as to the future of their jobs. Following Caine's death in 1903, another anti-Chinese candidate, Wilfred Lawson, defeated the experienced Unionist, Arthur Strauss (Dawe 1998: 193–215).

In 1906, Transvaal Chinese Labour became an important national issue in the British elections. The issue played a big part in tipping Cornwall as a whole firmly into the Liberal camp and certainly also helped the Liberal cause in other parts of the country (Payton 1992: 154). Unionist arguments that Chinese labour, by boosting the production of the mines, would create jobs for Cornishmen, were rejected by the voters of the mining division, who returned yet another radical Liberal, A.E. Dunn (Dawe 1998: 193–215).

The rising Labour movement was very ready to assure the Cornish miners of their reliability on the Chinese labour issue. From the beginning of the Transvaal Chinese labour scheme, the Trades Union Congress campaigned against it. In March 1904, a labour-led demonstration of 80,000 people against the Chinese labour scheme took place in Hyde Park (Yap and Leong Man 1996: 106–7). Will Crooks, the Labour MP and famous union organiser, campaigned in Cornwall against Chinese labour during the initial crisis on the issue of 1904. In 1906, Labour stood in Cornwall for the first time (Dawe 1998: 193–215).

The politics of this era demonstrate one of the difficulties in Bonnett's arguments. If any faction of the upper classes had a coherent project of creating a sense of national community in Britain, it was surely Chamberlain and his followers. Yet they were not as firm on drawing the boundaries of 'whiteness' against Chinese labour as were working class supporters of the Radical Liberals and the Labour Party. Thus, to a significant extent, the pressure for a stronger boundary to 'whiteness' came from below, and was not imposed by upper class advocates of 'national community,' as Bonnett's view implies. The anti-Unionist election campaign of 1906, in which 'Chinese Slavery' was an important slogan, exemplified the way in which Radical Liberal and Labour thought in Britain and the empire managed to combine racism with an appearance of altruism. This critique of 'slavery' directed venom against the Randlords' exploitation of the Chinese, apparently demanding the liberation of those who would in fact be deprived of work. The effect was to protect white skilled workers against 'cheap' labour competition while wrapping this cause in a cloak of morality.

The Engineers' vector

A major way in which the Imperial working class was socially unified was through the practice of several important British unions of maintaining branch structures abroad. A significant example of this was the Amalgamated Society of Engineers (ASE), described in 1898 by John Burns as '57,000 skilled artisans combined in the strongest trade union in the world' (Kapp 1979: 313). The ASE had branches throughout North America and Australasia, and a scattering of branches more widely in the empire. While the union could devolve some functions to regional councils, all branches continued to report and send fees to the London head office, and the London-based executive committee ensured that the benefits, voting procedures, contribution payments, and entrance requirements conformed strictly to British practice. In return, all overseas branches could draw on the union's centralised funds (Jefferys 1945: 172). This created a structure which facilitated the mobility of engineering workers around the empire, and in which UK-trained members often took the leadership of overseas branches. The success of this form of organisation in the pre-First World War period strengthens my case for the existence of an imperial working class.[2] In Australia and New Zealand, the ASE expanded from twenty-four branches with 2,600 members in 1890, to eighty-two branches with 11,000 members in 1913 (Jefferys, 1945:128). Similarly, in South Africa the ASE, after maintaining only a handful of struggling branches in South Africa in the 1890s, proliferated branches in the Transvaal in the immediate post-Boer War period. By 1913 it had twenty-six South African branches with 2,800 members (Jefferys 1945: 128). That there was an organizational dynamic specific to the Empire is suggested by the fact that the union did not make similar progress in the United States. Before 1890, British artisans had established a number of ASE branches in the US, especially in the New England industrial centres. But after that date, the union ceased to make any American headway (Jefferys 1945: 128).

In all the countries where the ASE was active, the high levels of training and literacy of their members made the organization particularly well-placed to produce leadership figures in the wider union movement. Some of the major leaders of white labour in South Africa, including J.T. Bain and W.H. Andrews (later an important member of the Communist Party), came out of the ASE. But despite the relative lack of personal racism on the part of these two leaders, the logic of white unionism tended to trap such men in racist positions. Thus, in its submission to the Transvaal Mining Regulations commission, the ASE presented it as self-evident that, 'the growing practice of placing kaffirs and other coloured persons in charge of winches, engines and other machinery' was a safety hazard and that this would reduce 'the sphere of employment for European labour without which the colony cannot progress' (Simons and Simons 1969: 90). In a submission to the 1908 Transvaal mine commission, supervised by Andrews, the ASE explained its support for the exclusion of blacks from skilled jobs, and the introduction of whites into skilled jobs on the basis that the African 'has no interest in the country except to earn his living here' (Simons and Simons 1969: 89).

British unionism was directly involved in the creation of South African industrial segregation. For anyone inclined to seek the roots of labour racism in Afrikaner racial ideologies, it is worth noting that, at the first conference of the South African Labour Party in 1909, there was not a single Afrikaans speaking delegate present (Hepple n.d.: 153).

White Labourism in Britain, 1914

In this last section, I will use an exploration of the solidarity movement which greeted the deportees from South Africa in 1914 to show the depth and intensity of the support for White Labourism in the British working class movement at that time. I will start by demonstrating the extraordinary unanimity of labour in taking this position of solidarity, and then go on to examine the discourse of the statements put forward in support of the deportees.

The deportations created a remarkable wave of unity amongst the ever factious British left. The deportees' ship was greeted at Gravesend by a senior Labour delegation, led by Arthur Henderson who came alongside the *Umgeni* in a small boat to persuade the group to come ashore (rather than remaining on board in protest) (*Cornubian*, 16th February 1914). The deportees were entertained to dinner at the House of Commons by the Labour MPs (*Forward*, 7th March 1914). They were feted at a dinner given by the staff of *The Clarion* (*Clarion*, 13th March 1914). Three of the deportees were welcomed at a public meeting of 3,000 in Glasgow, addressed by the renowned union leader Bob Smillie, and the legendary revolutionary activist, John MacLean (*Forward*, 4th April 1914). The campaign was taken to Cornwall, where some of the deportees spoke at Penzance (Dawe 1998: 204). At a London public meeting held at the Opera House before the great demonstration, the labour movement wheeled out its big guns to share the platform with the deportees: Henderson, Keir Hardie, Ramsay MacDonald and Trades Union Congress President, J.A. Seddon (MacDonald suffered from Suffragette heckling) (*Clarion*, 6th March 1914).

The ASE was well to the forefront of the agitation. A delegation of the deportees led by Bain was welcomed by the union's executive for discussions at ASE headquarters. Numerous British branches sent in resolutions to the head office, supporting the recall of the Governor-General of South Africa, Lord Gladstone. Three thousand ASE members from the London branches alone participated in the Hyde Park march (*ASEMJR* February and March 1914). The trade union demonstration was followed by a broadly-based union conference of protest in London, on the subsequent weekend (*ASEMJR* May 1914).

The discourse of the reception is revealing as to how far the assumptions of White Labourism were part of the fabric of the British labour movement by 1914. First, it is clear that, for most activists, the working class which they sought to defend was the diasporic 'British' working class. At its worst, the Socialist response to the deportations merged with the discourse of biological racism, to the extent that the cause of the working class and that of whiteness were conflated. This is exemplified by a contribution in one of the left papers, the Glasgow *Forward*, by J. O'Connor Kessack. Kessack was then involved in the leadership of a campaign, under the auspices of the transport workers' federation, to exclude 'Lascars' – Asian and African seamen – from employment on British ships. Kessack wrote that:

> The coloured man's life is low, his food simple and inexpensive, and his clothing so scanty as to be financially negligible. He costs the Capitalist a mere fraction compared with the white man. He is squeezing the white man out. That is the real Yellow Peril. The standard of life is in danger and the white man must either fight the evil influence or go under and carry white civilization with him. (*Forward*, 11th April 1914).

For Kessack, the labour conflicts on the Rand were: 'the preliminary skirmishes of the great battle which will determine whether African and Asiatic shall displace White' (*Forward*, 11th April 1914).

Second, the labour movement was often presented as defending British liberties, which should apply to white imperial citizens, against erosion by authoritarian government. The labour movement was seen to have an interest in the constitutional integrity of the Empire. Labour could thus be presented as the true defenders of the Imperial enterprise against self-interested capitalists who were betraying it. Victor Fisher, the Secretary of a British committee set up to contest the legal basis of the deportations, wrote that it was the Botha government 'who have acted unconstitutionally, they who have pursued a revolutionary policy. We are the constitutional party. We vindicate the privileges of an ancient Imperial state' (*Clarion*, 13th February 1914).

Third, the threat to the working class was seen as coming from all the social forces that could be represented as non-British; not only the primary threat of Asian and African labour, but also white 'others.' In the left press's coverage of the deportation incident, anti-semitism was a common feature of the characterisation of the Rand mine-owners.

Thus, in a cartoon in the Glasgow *Forward*, a stereotypic, fat Jewish capitalist is shown kissing an armed Boer, while a clean-cut manacled worker looks on the background (*Forward*, 21 February 1914).

Finally, the extent to which white workers had been subject to repression in South Africa was seen as a breaching of the thresholds of violence which could acceptably be used against white British citizens. It was taken as presaging a threat to the British labour movement in a way in which repression of African or Asian colonial subjects was not. Thus the ASE's official publication wrote that 'Russianised methods of government in a British colony cannot be tolerated by the trade union movement' (*ASEMJR* February 1914). The ASE journal also contended that Botha, with the connivance of the Governor-General, 'has ridden rough-shod over the hard won charter of British freedom' (*ASEMJR* March 1914). This charter clearly did not extend to the Black workers in South Africa, whom the ASE had played a prominent part in excluding from skilled employment.

Conclusion

This chapter has shown that the imperial working class was a social reality of the pre-First World War world. Space has only permitted me to indicate a few of the multiple threads that held it together, but the strength of its global connections should be apparent. Although the ideologies of its social world were many and complex, it should be clear that one of the dominating and unifying ones was White Labourism. Throughout the empire there were movements of labour fighting for their members to be recognised as 'white.' Whiteness was not so much imposed from above as demanded from below. The imperial working class did not 'become white': it made *itself* 'white.' The imperial working class of the pre-First World War era was unable to separate its hostility to its own exploitation from its aspiration to incorporation in the dominant racial structure. The consequence was an egalitarian racism which sought to construct racially bounded 'democracy.' However incomprehensible this ambiguous universalism may be to the early twenty-first-century observer, to those who participated in it, it made perfect sense.

The most notorious moment in South African labour history came in the 1922 white miner's strike, when the strikers (literally) marched under the banner 'Workers of the World, Fight and Unite for a White South Africa' (see the photographs in Glanville, 1922). This slogan is often treated as evidence of the illogicality of Rand white labour's thinking, and of the specifically South African character of their movement. This chapter has indicated that it proves neither point. The notion of 'Workers of the World' that the slogan expressed was that which had prevailed in the British Empire labour movement before the First World War. The cause of international labour was seen as identical with the cause of the globalised white British labour diaspora. And the 'White South Africa' which the banner advocated was the analogue of the 'White Australia' which had been the 'achievement' of the Australian labour movement.

Notes

1   The abbreviation *ASEMJR* is given for *Amalgamated Society of Engineers Monthly Journal and Report*. These periodicals are available at the Modern Records Centre, University of Warwick, series MSS 259/4.

2   The story of the international development of the ASE can be followed in its fascinating branch reports, on which I have drawn here. These reports are housed in the Modern Records Centre, University of Warwick, series MSS 259/2/1.

References

Adam Smith, J. 1965. *John Buchan*. London: Rupert Hart-Davis.

Allen, T.W. 1994. *The Invention of the White Race: Volume 1: Racial Oppression and Social Control*. New York: Verso.

Barrow, L. 1989. 'White Solidarity in 1914.' In R. Samuel (ed.) *Patriotism: The Making and Unmaking of British National Identity: Vol. 1: History and Politics*. London: Routledge.

Barton, R. (ed.) 1974. *Life in Cornwall at the End of the Nineteenth Century: Being Extracts from the West Briton Newspaper in the Years from 1876 to 1899*. Truro: D. Bradford Barton.

Belich, J. 1996. *Making Peoples: A History of New Zealanders from Polynesian Settlement to the End of the Nineteenth Century*. Auckland: Penguin.

Benn, C. 1992. *Keir Hardie*. London: Hutchinson.

Bonnett, A. 1998. 'How the British Working Class Became White: The Symbolic Re-formation of Racialised Capitalism.' *The Journal of Historical Sociology*, 11(3), 16–340.

Burke, G. 1984. 'The Cornish Diaspora of the Nineteenth Century.' In S. Marks and P. Richardson (eds) *International Migration: Historical Perspectives*. London: Maurice Temple Smith.

Clark, M. 1993. *History of Australia*. London: Chatto & Windus.

Cope, R.K. n.d. *Comrade Bill: The Life and Times of WH. Andrews, Workers' Leader*. Cape Town: Stewart.

Davies, R, D. Kaplan, M. Morris and D. O'Meara. 1976. 'Class Struggle in South Africa.' *Review of African Political Economy*, 7: 4–30.

Davies, R.H. 1979. *Capital, State and White Labour in South Africa 1900–1960: An Historical Materialist Analysis of Class Formation and Class Relations*. Brighton: The Harvester Press.

Dawe, R.D. 1986. 'The Role and Influence of the Cornish in South Africa.' MA dissertation. Middlesex Polytechnic.

Dawe, R.D. 1998. *Cornish Pioneers in South Africa: 'Gold and Diamonds, Copper and Blood*. St. Austell: Cornish Hillside Publications.

Ebbels, R.N. and L.G. Churchward (eds). 1960. *The Australian Labour Movement 1850–1907*. Sydney: Australian Book Society.

Gitsham, E. and J.F. Trembath. 1926. *A First Account of Labour Organisation in South Africa*. Durban: E.P. & Commercial.

Glanville, E. 1922. *Through the Red Revolt on The Rand*. Johannesburg: The Star.

Hepple, A. n.d. 'The South African Labour Movement: A Memoir.' Unpublished manuscript. Institute of Commonwealth Studies Library, University of London.

Hirson, B. and G. Williams. 1995. *The Delegate for Africa: David Ivon Jones 1883–1924*. London: Core.

Ignatiev, N. 1995. *How the Irish Became White*. New York: Routledge.

Jebb, R. 1905. *Studies in Colonial Nationalism*. London: Edward Arnold.

Jeffreys, J.B. 1945. *The Story of the Engineers, 1800–1945*. London: Lawrence & Wishart.

Johanson, D. 1962. 'History of the White Australia Policy.' In K. Rivett (ed.) *Immigration: Control or Colour Bar*. Melbourne: Melbourne University Press.

Kapp, Y. 1979. *Eleanor Marx: Volume I: The Crowded Years*. London: Virago.

Katz, E. 1976. *A Trade Union Aristocracy: A History of White Workers in the Transvaal and the General Strike of 1913*. Johannesburg: African Studies Institute.

Katz, E. 1990. *The White Death: Silicosis (Miner's Phthisis) on the Witwatersrand Gold Mines 1886–1910*. PhD thesis. University of the Witwatersrand.

Kennedy, B. 1984. *A Tale of Two Mining Cities: Johannesburg and Broken Hill 1885–1925*. Melbourne: Melbourne University Press.

Legassick, M. 1974. 'South Africa: Capital Accumulation and Violence.' *Economy and Society* 3: 253–91.

MacDonald, J.R. 1902. *What I Saw in South Africa*. London: The Echo.

MacIntyre, S. 1997. *The Succeeding Age 1901–1942: The Oxford History of Australia, Vol. 4*. Melbourne: Oxford University Press.

Offer, A. 1988. 'Pacific Rim Societies: Asian Labour and White Nationalism.' In J. Eddy and D. Schreuder (eds) *The Rise of Colonial Nationalism*. Sydney: Allen & Unwin.

Payton, P. 1978. *Pictorial History of Australia's Little Cornwall*. Adelaide: Rigby.

Payton, P. 1984. *The Cornish Miner in Australia: Cousin Jack Down Under*. Treolsta: Dyllansow Truran.

Payton, P. 1992. *The Making of Modern Cornwall: Historical Experience and the Persistence of Difference*. Redruth: Dyllansow Truran.

Payton, P. 1996 *Cornwall*. Fowley: Alexander Associates.

Richardson, P. 1982. *Chinese Labour in the Transvaal*. London: Macmillan.

Roediger, D. 1994. *Towards the Abolition of Whiteness: Essays on Race, Politics, and Working Class History*. London: Verso.

Rolls, E. 1993. *Sojourners: Flowers and the Wide Sea: The Epic Story of China's Centuries-old Relationship with Australia*. St. Lucia: University of Queensland Press.

Rowse, A.L. 1942. *A Cornish Boyhood*. London: Cape.

Saxton, A. 1990. *The Rise and Fall of the White Republic: Class Politics and Mass Culture in Nineteenth Century America*. London: Verso.

Simons, H.J. and R.E. Simons. 1969. *Class and Colour in South Africa 1850–1950*. Harmondsworth: Penguin.

Stoler, A.L. and F. Cooper. 1997. 'Between Metropole and Colony: Rethinking a Research Agenda.' In F. Cooper and A.L. Stoler (eds) *Tensions of Empire: Colonial Cultures in a Bourgeois World*. Berkeley: University of California Press.

Van de Walt, Lucien. 'The industrial union of the embryo of the Socialist Commonwealth: The International Socialist League and revolutionary syndicalism in South Africa, 1915–1920,' *Comparative Studies of South Asia, Africa and the Middle East*, 1999, XIX(1), 5–28.

Verwey, E.J. (ed.) 1995. *New Dictionary of South African Biography, Volume 1*. Pretoria: HSRC.

Walker, L.L. and B. Weinbren. 1961. *2000 Casualties: A History of the South African Labour Movement*. Johannesburg: South African Trade Union Council.

White, R. 1981. *Inventing Australia: Images and Identity 1688–1980*. St. Leonard's: Allen & Unwin.

Yap, M. and D. Leong Man. 1996. *Colour, Confusion and Concessions: The History of the Chinese in South Africa*. Hong Kong: Hong Kong University Press.

Yudelman, D. 1983. *The Emergence of Modern South Africa: State, Capital and the Incorporation of Organised Labour on the South African Gold Fields, 1902–1939*. Cape Town: David Philip.

PART 8

The impact of colonialism's cultures on metropoles

Chapter 19

John M. MacKenzie

THE PERSISTENCE OF EMPIRE
IN METROPOLITAN CULTURE

Still another major theme in 'new imperial histories' has been investigation of how empire impacted upon the colony-owning powers, their politics, cultures and social lives. Such work has been most prolific and longest-established in relation to Britain and its empire, though scholars working on many other countries in and beyond Europe are now undertaking similar studies. For Britain, John MacKenzie was the undisputed initiator in writing on this topic.

Stephen Howe

THE SCHOLARLY LITERATURE ON THE end of the British Empire is brimming with all kinds of evocative metaphors. To take just a small sample of this penchant for coining the all-encompassing phrase, we have leading titles such as *Imperial Sunset* (Max Beloff, 1969), *Eclipse of Empire* (D.A. Low, 1991), *Imperialism at Bay* (W.R. Louis, 1977), *Escape from Empire* (R.J. Moore, 1979), *Unscrambling an Empire* (W.P. Kirkman, 1966), *The Contraction of England* (D.A. Low, 1983), *The Retreat from Empire* (John Darwin, 1988) and *Britannia Overruled* (David Reynolds, 1991) – all of which, to some extent, convey the respective authors' particular view of imperial decline. More recently, decolonisation has been described as the 'Implosion of Empire', in order to convey a sense of the political upheavals on the colonial periphery reverberating inwards on metropolitan society.[1] Implosion is a dramatic word. It means 'bursting inwards'. It conjures up parts of the anatomy, such as the appendix; or what happens to a vacuum flask when its skin is damaged. It is something which happens rapidly, dramatically, and indeed painfully. Perhaps there were some signs of implosion in the Dutch Empire in Indonesia or the French Empire in Indo-China and later Algeria, but the British Empire was so astonishingly vast that its decolonisation took place in stages from the inter-war years right down to the 1990s. If we leave aside the American seizure of independence in the 1770s and the handing back of the Ionian islands to Greece in 1864, decolonisation (at least in formal constitutional terms) began for the so-called white Dominions with the Statute of Westminster in 1931, and for other territories with the ending of the mandate in Iraq in 1932, and the treaty which permitted Egypt's entry into the League of Nations in 1936. Although imperial territories remain, the process can be seen as climaxing with the handover of Hong Kong to China in 1997.

If a sixty-year implosion sounds something like a contradiction in terms, perhaps we can think instead of a sequence of implosions, possibly ultimately detonating each other. Certainly, the years 1947–1948 looked rather like an implosion with rapid decolonisations in India, Pakistan, Burma and Sri Lanka, the departure of Ireland from the Commonwealth, and the scuttle, implosion and explosion all at once in Palestine leading to the dramatic formation of the state of Israel. Then there was almost a decade's pause. Many have seen the Suez crisis as involving a sort of implosion of confidence, a moment of truth when the British realised that they could no longer discipline the 'awkward squad' at the periphery in the way that they had in the nineteenth century. Egypt is indeed a fascinating case, for the story starts with a colonel and it ends with a colonel. In 1882, the British had little difficulty in dealing with Colonel Urubi Pasha: they, alone, defeated him at Tel el Kebir; propped up their puppet the Khedive Tewfik; established their veiled Protectorate under one of the great pro-consuls of the age (Sir Evelyn Baring, often known as 'Over-Baring'); and sent the Colonel into exile. In 1956, a mere seventy-four years later, they could do nothing with Colonel Nasser, who had overthrown King Farouk and nationalised the Canal Company with impunity. Even in league with France and Israel, it was now painfully apparent that the British could only flex imperial muscles with American support. Without them, Anthony Eden's fixation with Munich and the notion that 'dictators' should be dealt with firmly was as nought. Within months of Suez, though seemingly unrelated, the British were starting to decolonise in West Africa (Ghana) and Southeast Asia (Malaya and Singapore). They were also agonising about their capacity to maintain any presence east of Suez. So perhaps we can identify implosion number two in 1956/1957.[2]

The third implosion came in the massive wave of acts of decolonisation which took place throughout Africa in the years 1961 to 1965, quickening particularly in 1963 to 1965. The colonies of West and East Africa were cut adrift and the Central African Federation was broken up. By then the decolonising problems came not from blacks and browns, but from whites. Some 250,000 white settlers clung to a tenuous independence in Rhodesia/Zimbabwe for another fifteen years, until the Lancaster House agreements of 1980. South Africa seemed like an altogether different proposition. Paul Kennedy saw the Soviet Empire as being much longer-lasting and more intractable than the other declining great powers.[3] Yet both that Soviet Empire and the apartheid-ruled South Africa proceeded to implode in 1989/90.

The Falklands War of 1982 seemed very like a nineteenth-century imperial campaign, though the issues here were unquestionably more complex. The Thatcher Government had presented all the wrong signals; the aggressor was a dictator; and the inhabitants of the islands were quite clear that they wished to remain attached to a distant imperial mother. Here was certainly a distant explosion rather than an implosion. The handover of Hong Kong was decidedly not an implosion either and some would see it as the opposite of an act of decolonisation. Here was a carefully planned transmission of authority from one imperial power to another, which had been on the cards ever since the British had secured the ninety-nine-year lease to Kowloon and the New Territories in 1898, land without which their more permanent settlement on Victoria Island was entirely untenable. Though complicated by a democratically posturing and bullish final governor, this piece of the end of empire theatre is best symbolised by that astonishing display of synchronised hand-waving put on by sailors in the Chinese navy. It was intended as an act of friendship and encouragement, but it came over as a threatening instance of formidable collective action.

There was a similar paradox on the British side. The delivery of Hong Kong to the Chinese was presented as a piece of imperial theatre, taking its place with jubilees and coronations. The ceremonies, the troops, the hauling down of the flag, the images of Prince Charles and Governor Chris Patten on the beautiful royal yacht *Britannia*, significantly towards the end of a career which had started when the British still had imperial pretensions in the early 1950s, seemed to lead if anything to a swelling of national pride. Largely irrelevant to the lives of most people in Britain, this was the end of empire as a rather agreeable 'docu-soap', a television spectacle that had positive rather than negative resonances. Even in an act of departure and decline, the British could put on a 'good show'.

So a few islands are left, in the Caribbean, the Atlantic and the Pacific together with the ever-anomalous Gibraltar. There are still imperial stamp issues, and the British find themselves complicit with off-shore tax havens, playgrounds for the rich, and maritime 'flags of convenience'. The mighty empire on which the sun never set is now a good deal smaller than that of Denmark in Greenland, although problems like the issue of the distribution of land in Zimbabwe still come back to haunt the British. So, given that we have a complicated mix of implosions, explosions, and small sputterings ranging from largish fireworks to happenings not much greater than Roman candles or hand-held sparklers, what cultural significance can be read into this sequence of events that runs over several decades?

Two points are worth making straight away. The first is that the notion that the British were indifferent to their Empire and accepted decolonisation with total equanimity constitutes an interesting piece of right-wing propaganda. It has been much put about by such figures as the late Lord Beloff, who argued into his eighties that an empire acquired in a fit of absence of mind could equally be lost by an indifferent oversight. Because the British had never developed a theory of empire, because they were fundamentally not an imperial people, they could view the loss of their imperial baubles with equanimity.[4] Not for them the reactions of the over-emotional French or Portuguese, who contemplated decolonisation with a series of domestic implosions, with revolutions, *coups d'etat*, assassinations and new constitutions. Not for the British that Gallic spectacle of overwrought French motorists driving round and round Paris beating out on their horns 'Alger-ie francaise'. The English language does not have the beat; the British have not got the rhythm; and their cars probably do not have the horns.

Clearly, this notion of the utterly indifferent British is something of a self-justificatory and consolatory travesty. If it were true, then decolonisation would have had almost no cultural effects upon the British and the fundamental point of this book would be undermined. It also implies that decolonisation was foreseen in its entirety and that the British were able to prepare themselves psychologically and culturally for it. In fact it is hard to sustain such a proposition. In considering the long sequence of implosions and explosions that I have identified, we must be careful not to let the benefit of hindsight influence our assessment of the manner in which the British and others viewed the future of empire in the post-Second World War years. That the South Asian ring could not be held had been perfectly obvious to most intelligent observers since the 1930s. Even if Churchill huffed and puffed about the revolting spectacle of the half-naked fakir meeting the representative of the King-Emperor (that is, the encounters between M.K. Gandhi and viceroys of the inter-war years), or later declaimed that with the loss of India the British would immediately collapse to the status of a third-rate power, it was perfectly obvious to all perceptive observers that the Attlee Government had no alternative. The imperial fabric in India was thoroughly rotted through. To change the metaphor, a creeping decolonisation had been taking place for years, not only through constitutional change but also through personnel substitution. By the 1940s, it was Indians who were largely running the British Empire in India. As far back as the 1840s General Napier had said that the British ruled India by an astonishing act of bluff. With the end of the Second World War and the removal of the repressive military clamps, that bluff had become yet more transparent. Even if Mountbatten had his own reasons, it is not surprising that he speeded up the process of departure. The intriguing affair between Jawaharlal Nehru and Edwina Mountbatten somehow symbolised this dramatic reversal of fortunes. No wonder Mountbatten was eager to be off.

But when that Asian implosion was over and the British were desperately trying to warm themselves up after the horrendous winter of 1947/48, to what extent did they really think that the end of their Empire was on the cards, let alone that it was collapsing like a pack of cards? As they struggled to get coal and electricity supplies back, there were fresh horrors to come in Palestine and elsewhere.[5] But was this really the end?

There is a great deal of evidence to suggest that the British carefully subdivided their Empire and that this sectionalisation implied deep chronological differences. The Indian Empire was an old empire inherited in 1858 from a commercial company. Since the 1830s, the so-called Anglicist school, led by Lord Macaulay, had trumpeted that Indian independence, under the leadership of Indians who were English in tastes, in morals and in intellect, would be the greatest day in English history. Nehru, educated at Harrow and Cambridge, who heralded independence with a radio speech in the clipped and elegant expression of the Edwardian upper classes, seemed to symbolise the working out of that policy. Its western-educated elite had its origins in the early nineteenth century. British-style universities had been founded in the 1850s and graduates had been turned out by the countless thousand. However much an 'illusion of permanence' had developed for some in the later nineteenth century, the restoration of some form of independence remained within the logic of the British imperial system in India.[6]

But the rest of the Empire was not like that. It comprised either the white Dominions, vast territories inhabited by the kith and kin of the imperial race, or dependent territories – and notice the implication of that word dependent – where economic re-orientation to western forms, infra-structural development and elite formation seemed so much less advanced than in India. Although it has been argued that the presence of Arthur Creech Jones as Colonial Secretary in the Attlee Government and of a number of radical and far-sighted officials in the Colonial Office, such as Sir Andrew Cohen, implied that full decolonisation was now recognised as a necessary policy option, I do not think that it seemed that way to the ordinary Briton on the streets.[7]

Many found that the end of the Second World War, as with the First, did not so much produce a land fit for heroes, as a period of depression and anxiety. Wartime rationing continued until the early 1950s. Although the postwar boom was to provide something of an illusion of full employment, British industry suffered from major under-investment and restructuring difficulties. Postwar Britain, as I know from my native Glasgow, looked not unlike that of the 1890s. There were extensive slums, grimy tenements coated in coal dust and smoke. Since coal remained the prime energy source, fogs and smogs were common. Many of the working class still struggled to make ends meet and retain respectability. The trams, those gondolas of the working classes, still trundled through the streets, many of them actually dating from before the First World War. When the sirens sounded, waves of workers still flooded out of the shipyards, docks, factories, iron foundries and steel works. In Glasgow, small ferries still plied back and forth across the river every hundred metres or so transporting (without charge) the workers from tenement homes to places of employment. The night sky was still ablaze with the flames of the foundries and noisy with the sirens, hooters and whistles of works, trains and ships. This was essentially a nineteenth-century world, not a brave new postwar dispensation. It is not surprising that in those conditions, the thoughts of the British should once again turn to empire as a solution to their social and economic problems.

As the great imperial shipping lines received their surviving ships back from troop transportation or built new tonnage, they still thought in terms of conveying emigrant hordes.[8] The mighty Cunard, Union-Castle and P&O lines again advertised their cabins for emigrants, often on assisted passages. P&O continued to operate in this trade right through the 1950s, although by now southern Europeans, often Italians or Greeks, were joining the British in heading for Australia. The *Daily Express* continued to try to persuade its readership to emigrate to South Africa throughout the 1950s. In Zimbabwean history, following the Cecil Rhodes example of 1890, we often joke about the 1947 pioneer column. My own father, fresh out of the wartime army and disillusioned with opportunities in Britain, joined that column and, as a result, part of my childhood was spent in Northern Rhodesia, now Zambia. When we arrived on the Union-Castle liner at Cape Town, we boarded a train for the four-day journey through Cape Province, Bechuanaland (Botswana) and Southern Rhodesia (Zimbabwe) to Northern Rhodesia. The British seemed in command of the region, at least outside Afrikaner nationalist South Africa. Everywhere, including Afrikaner-ruled South Africa, English was spoken and the currency was the pound. In the same period, other Scottish relatives were leaving for Canada and the United States.[9]

Thus in the 1940s and 1950s, Britons were still convinced that the British Empire in the Dominions and in Africa would endure. The popular press certainly gave them this impression. So indeed did the policy-makers in Government. During my childhood in the town of Ndola, Northern Rhodesia was part of the Federation of Rhodesia and Nyasaland, the ill-fated Central African Federation which was dreamed up by the Labour Government and brought into being by the Conservatives in 1953. This federation was based on three premises: first, that the territories concerned could not achieve independence under black rule for a considerable period; second, that they constituted complementary economies which would work better if brought together under white rule; and third, that there was an opportunity to create a new white Dominion to stand against the one that appeared to have been lost to the Afrikaners in South Africa. No one predicted that that Federation would encounter revolt and emergency as early as 1959 and that it would be broken up by 1964. It was camouflaged with propaganda about racial partnership, but the first federal Prime Minister, Sir Godfrey Huggins, later Lord Malvern, blew that particular cover by referring to it as the partnership of the rider and the horse.[10] I have a clear recollection of seeing a family displaying themselves as the Central African Federation in a fancy-dress parade on a Union Castle liner: the father personified the white patriarchal Southern

Rhodesia; he towed a trolley on which reclined his wife, clothed and painted in yellow to symbolise the copper riches of Northern Rhodesia, while his son, blacked up, walked alongside to represent the labour migrants of the poorer Nyasaland (Malawi). The gendering of the three territories was intriguing, for many saw the Federation as an opportunity for the Southern Rhodesian whites to exploit the riches of the North. Little did that family know how well they had represented it or how soon they would be split asunder.

Even in East Africa, where a policy of African paramountcy had been in place since the 1920s, there was little indication that black nationalist victory would soon be the rule rather than the exception. At the end of the Second World War, white authority seemed to be enhanced and Europeans in the Kenyan so-called white Highlands had been given full local self-government on a sort of county council basis. When Jomo Kenyatta returned to Kenya, he was advised by the Governor to involve himself in local government rather than nationalist politics. Throughout East and Central Africa, Africans continued to be denied the franchise since, as one authority has put it, the policy of 'multi-racialism' was 'too ingenious for electoral tests';[11] Nationalists themselves, even Julius Nyerere in the former League mandate and UN trusteeship territory of Tanganyika, were to be taken by surprise by the speed of decolonisation from the late 1950s.

Pacific mandates arising from the defeat of Germany in the First World War were held by Australia and New Zealand, and their rule in those territories was if anything even more imperial and unthinking of the future than that of Britain itself.[12] For many observers of the world in the period, decolonisation in South and Southeast Asia could seem like an exception rather than the norm. Certainly, the great majority of the British and the Dominions press gave little indication that the imperial game was up until at least 1959.

In Britain, the Conservative and Unionist Party continued to use imperial symbolism right through that decade. So too did such right-wing Dominion politicians as Sir Robert Menzies in Australia. Even the Americans were sending out confusing signals. If, after the Second World War, US policy-makers had been convinced that European imperialism presented an invitation to communist advance in Asia, in the Cold War conditions of the 1950s they were more inclined to think that some areas of surviving empire could act as a bulwark. Moreover, it is significant that when, in 1959, the Mau Mau campaign and the Hola Camp massacre, together with the emergency in Central Africa, convinced the radical Tory Iain Macleod that the British had to decolonise in Africa, the Prime Minister Harold Macmillan advised caution. It was not until after Macmillan had won a majority of over 100 seats in the British general election of 8 October 1959 that he put Macleod into the Colonial Office and unleashed 'the wind of change' with such a storm force that he enraged and alienated his own right wing. By that time, the British Government had significantly made the decision that Britain required a fully professional army. All those born after 1940 would no longer have to do national service. As campaigns raged in Kenya, Cyprus, Malaya, Borneo and later Aden, it was abundantly apparent that the British could no longer sustain a succession of colonial revolts.

It seems to me that it is this third implosion of empire, as I have characterised it, between 1959 and 1964, which is actually more important in cultural terms than the first one of the 1940s. It is true that in the 1940s there was good evidence that the British were exceptionally ignorant about their Empire. When the Colonial Office conducted polls in 1947 and 1948, they discovered that very few people could name a single colony. One man apparently suggested Lincolnshire. Given the intense rivalry between the adjacent counties, I think he must have been a Yorkshireman. Interestingly, 3 per cent of those polled thought that the United States was still in the Empire. And no one could define the difference between a dominion and a colony.[13]

Yet in that same decade the BBC was still projecting a confident image of imperial development. The Christmas Day flagship programmes on radio continued to tour the Empire, depicting a healthy and mutually beneficial economic imperialism, until as late as the 1950s. For example, the groundnut scheme in Tanganyika, shortly to be the graveyard of so many colonial developmental schemes, was heralded on these programmes as the great economic hope of the future. In 1947, it was described as 'offering solid ground for hope, hundreds of miles of jungle cleared by science and the bulldozer with a real promise of a better life for African and European'. In 1948, British groundnutters (unfortunate word) were celebrated as 'English families under canvas or in huts' to a background of African drumming and chanting. In 1951 the programme *The Gifts of Christmas* featured 'Zulu voices raised in thanksgiving', no doubt rejoicing at the development of the apartheid policies of the Afrikaner nationalists. There was also a section on the Gold Coast, including the commentary: 'once the white man's coming here meant terror and slavery; now he comes bringing gifts – gifts of learning – spelling the way to a fuller life'. And that very Gold Coast was only six years off full independence. Something of the importance of these programmes is conveyed by the fact that they were narrated by figures such as Laurence Olivier, Robert Donat and John Gielgud, while composers of the eminence of William Alwyn, Benjamin Britten and Walter Goehr wrote the background music.[14]

Yet in other aspects of ceremony and exhibition, the Empire and Commonwealth appeared to continue to be supremely important. In 1951, the Imperial Institute in South Kensington mounted an exhibition entitled 'Focus on Colonial Progress' as part of the Festival of Britain, although it received many fewer visitors than the main show. 'Queen and Commonwealth' exhibitions were held in association with the coronation in 1953.

There was a good reason for the need for these exhibitions to continue in their propagandist role. This was the renewed emergence of a strategy of colonial development and welfare after the war. This belated policy of government investment in imperial development had its origins in 1929, but it was only from 1945 that it became truly significant in both British and French efforts to regenerate their empires. As with the Tanganyika groundnut scheme, the policy was promoted with considerable optimism. Empire could at last be justified on the grounds of enlightened official notions of welfare, investment and development. The implication was that the Empire was now genuinely about trusteeship, partnership and state-sponsored investment. The ideals of the inter-war years had at last captured the high ground, some would think in pursuit of a self-interested containment. This same sense runs through Lord Hailey's monumental *African Survey*, first published in 1938 and revised in 1956 for publication in 1957.[15] Medicine, science, economics and education could now all be harnessed for the benefit of Africa and Africans. A renewed sense of the redemptive power of science had begun to emerge before the Second World War and it was thought that the postwar imperial world would be the setting for the enlightened activities of the 'expert'. Experts would transform agriculture, forestry, the environment and the world of work.[16]

It has often been remarked that this same sense of optimism surrounded the coronation of Queen Elizabeth II in 1953. Symbolically, it was accompanied by that distinctive imperial event, the conquest of Everest.[17] That military metaphor reflects the extent to which the British and other imperial powers had seen the planting of the flag on the greatest mountain tops of the world as a vital ambition of the imperial spirit. Many times attempted in the twentieth century, it was now achieved by the perfect combination of the New Zealander Edmund Hillary and the Nepalese Tenzing Norgay. After all, Nepal had a special relationship with the British Empire through the recruitment of Gurkhas to the ranks of its army, where they remain to this day.

In publishing, imperial traditions also seemed to be alive and well. The works of G.A. Henty, Sir Henry Rider Haggard and R.M. Ballantyne, among many others, remained in print and still constituted some of the prime elements of the prize and present market for children.[18] A new tradition of youthful reading had yet to establish itself. Oral evidence suggests that many missionaries, settlers, politicians and soldiers continued to be influenced by such childhood reading experiences.[19] It was only from the early 1960s that a wholly new style of modern comics, concentrating on more futuristic themes such as space travel, was to establish itself. Imperial hagiographical biographies continued to be read right through the 1950s. This is certainly true, for example, of the missionary-explorer David Livingstone. In Scotland, his national memorial at Blantyre remained a place of popular resort for schools and Sunday schools throughout that decade.[20] Only later did its visitor numbers begin to fall off. Indeed, it was not until 1973 that Livingstone received his first fully debunking biography; a very inadequate one by Tim Jeal.[21]

Moreover, it is possible to find an imperial tradition surviving in historical scholarship into the 1950s. Yet once more, it is to the 1960s that we look for the origins of a new history; pursuing more radical theorisation or searching for the hidden histories of indigenous peoples. Only then did resistance and revolt in Asia and Africa come to be interpreted in new and sympathetic ways. Even the supposedly radical Robinson and Gallagher continued to refer to colonial revolts as late as 1961 as romantic and backward-looking movements of peoples 'who would not be comforted'. By the end of the 1960s, such revolts were being formulated in very different ways.[22]

In all of these ways it does seem to me that an illusion of imperial power, underpinned by popular cultural reflections, continued to be projected throughout the 1950s. Of course it was an illusion, in all sorts of ways. It was an illusion in military terms, as Suez and colonial revolts amply demonstrated. It was an illusion in economic terms, for the concept of a fully complementary empire, which really only flourished briefly after the 1932 Ottawa agreements, dissipated with great speed after the war. British indebtedness, including its major debts to its own Empire, ensured a continuing weakness when much of the rest of Europe was regenerating on Marshall Aid. The formerly mighty sterling area was now under considerable pressure. The pound was exceptionally weak in the face of the ever-strengthening dollar; as was again demonstrated in the Suez crisis. Imperial markets were no longer protected by culture and sentiment. Import substitution was rampant everywhere and the Treaty of Rome and new economic alliances in Europe soon indicated further writing on the wall for Britain.

But popular culture can have precisely this role of projecting illusion when a different form of reality has taken over. There comes a moment, however, when the illusion is exposed and its forms crumble. That moment came, not in the 1940s or the 1950s, but only in the early 1960s. It was only then that it became cruelly apparent that the British could no longer trade off (in both literal and metaphorical terms) a richly powerful imperial past. Thus it seems to me that both popular and intellectual culture only became fully aware of the underlying realities of power; of the extent to which empire was over in economic, political, military and conceptual terms, once the third implosion of the British Empire had occurred.

It was only after that third implosion that the stresses within the British state became truly apparent. It was only in the 1960s that domestic racial tensions became fully significant, taking up a central place in British political debate through the agency of Enoch Powell and the National Front. Those tensions produced legislation that restricted immigration, but also legislation that brought the weight of the law to bear against racial discrimination. The 'troubles' broke out in Northern Ireland in the last years of that decade, heralding a searing thirty-year struggle. Restless nationalisms in Scotland and Wales became more active, although I think that the relationship between Celtic nationalism and empire is often more complex and subtle than is sometimes suggested.[23] The British also realised that their preoccupation with empire had caused them to miss the European economic bus. The 1960s saw them desperately trying to run after it and jump on. Even the Thatcherite free market, monetarist experiment was in many ways a reaction to the loss of empire. However much she invoked the Tory icons of Disraeli and Churchill, she was of course, in economic terms, a Gladstonian.[24] Not for her the state controls and investment policies of empire. The fact is, for example, that most railway systems in the Empire were state-run in the nineteenth century. Nationalisation was a classic imperial policy. In Thatcher, imperial rhetoric and economic practice were totally at odds. Moreover, from at least the 1890s, empire had been largely bi-partisan. Conservatives, Liberals and Labour had all been sucked into its seductive patriotisms. Empire was the forerunner of the so-called Butskellite (that is, left Tory and right Labour) consensus which Thatcher railed against. Whereas the possession of empire had tended towards a degree of class conciliation, Thatcher was prepared to raise the standard of economic and social civil war in intoning her cry of 'the enemy within'. It may also be the case that empire had preserved some of the rigidities of the British class system.[25]

To conclude, we can see imperial popular cultural forms as much as economic policies sailing serenely on through the first implosion of the late 1940s, one that was expected and was not regarded as heralding the rest. The second implosion of the mid- to late 1950s began to check a dominant popular culture which had been in place since at least the 1890s. Only by the third implosion, of the 1960s, was British culture being channelled into wholly new grooves. Even then, as the excitements of the Falklands War of 1982 demonstrated, imperial pride was not wholly shattered. The 'heat and lust' school of internationally successful films and British television serials set in India continued to offer nostalgic images of an empire lost.

However, it is perhaps significant that a television series about Cecil Rhodes in 1996 was a good deal less successful, partly because the plotting was so complex that few viewers comprehended what was actually going on.[26] By then, as street 'vox pop' interviews revealed, no one in Britain seemed to have heard of Rhodes, the mighty Colossus of the late nineteenth century. The name had become inseparably associated with a television chef called Rhodes, with the distinctly unimperial first name of Gary. This culinary connection seems eminently appropriate. If the Empire never knew a Sir Gary as Governor or even as rampantly expansionist entrepreneur Britain's imperial past had now come to be symbolised in that phenomenon known as 'the Empire strikes back'. From the late 1940s, with the arrival of that significantly named vessel from the West Indies, the *Empire Windrush*, the processes of migration had been dramatically reversed. Blacks and Asians from the West Indies, West and East Africa, South Asia, Hong Kong, and elsewhere colonised British cities, creating a new and lively multiculturalism. That ultimate joke of Europe, British cuisine, suddenly became cosmopolitan and exciting, even if adapted for

British tastes. Ex-imperial peoples at last showed signs of bringing global civilisation to bear upon the ever-insular British.

Notes

1   This was the title of a conference at the University of Southern Denmark in February 1999, when this paper was originally given as an introductory lecture. Although this is a revised version, some of the informalities of that occasion have been retained, both as a matter of record and in the hope that some of the author's experiences constitute a form of historical source. *Implosion of Empire* is also the title of a forthcoming book by Lars Ole Sauerberg, to be published by Palgrave.

2   There is now a considerable literature on decolonisation, although this work is almost exclusively political and diplomatic in content. Little or nothing has been written about the cultural changes wrought by the end of the Empire and the transition to Commonwealth. See particularly John Darwin, *Britain and Decolonisation: The Retreat from Empire in the Post-War World* (London, Macmillan, 1988) and *The End of the British Empire: The Historical Debate* (Oxford, Blackwell, 1991); J.D. Hargreaves, *Decolonization in Africa* (London, Longman, 1988). For the Suez crisis, see W.R. Louis and Roger Owen (eds) *Suez 1956: The Crisis and its Consequences* (Oxford, Clarendon Press, 1989). Several chapters on aspects of decolonisation and the end of empire can be found in W. Roger Louis and Judith M. Brown (eds) *The Oxford History of the British Empire, Vol. IV: The Twentieth Century* (Oxford, Oxford University Press, 1999).

3   Paul M. Kennedy, *The Rise and Fall of the Great Powers* (London, Unwin Hyman, 1988).

4   Max Beloff, *Imperial Sunset, Vol. 1: Britain's Liberal Empire, 1897–1921* (London, Methuen, 1969) p. 19 and many newspaper articles. Lord Beloff was very critical of the Oxford History of the British Empire project, which he saw as representing a modern and, to him, unsympathetic historiography. For a discussion of the significance of empire to British domestic history, see P.J. Marshall, 'Imperial Britain' (the Creighton Lecture, 1994) published in the *Journal of Imperial and Commonwealth History,* 1995, 23(3), 379–94.

5   For the Palestine crisis, see W.R. Louis, *The British Empire in the Middle East*, 1945, 51 (Oxford, Clarendon Press, 1984) and W.R. Louis and Robert W. Stookey (eds) *The End of the Palestine Mandate* (London, I.B. Tauris, 1986). For the 1947 winter fuel crisis, see Alex J. Robertson, *The Bleak Midwinter* (Manchester, Manchester University Press, 1987).

6   Francis G. Hutchins, *The Illusion of Permanence: British Imperialism in India* (Princeton, Princeton University Press, 1967). See also Thomas R. Metcalf, *Ideologies of the Raj* (Cambridge, Cambridge University Press, 1995).

7   Robert D. Pearce, *The Turning Point in Africa: British Colonial Policy, 1938–48* (London, Frank Cass, 1982).

8   For postwar migrant patterns, including inward migration to the UK, see Stephen Constantine, 'Migrants and Settlers', in Louis and Brown (eds) *Oxford History of the British Empire,* 163–87.

9   The background to these movements can be surveyed in Stephen Constantine (ed.), *Emigrants and Empire* (Manchester, Manchester University Press, 1991); see also Marjory Harper, *Emigration from Scotland Between the Wars* (Manchester, Manchester University Press, 1998).

10   For contemporary polemics relating to the Federation, see Sir Roy Welensky, *Welensky's 4000 Days: The Life and Death of the Federation of Rhodesia and Nyasaland* (London, Collins, 1964) and Patrick Keatley, *The Politics of Partnership* (Harmondsworth, Penguin, 1963).

11   John Lonsdale, 'East Africa', in Louis and Brown (eds) *Oxford History of the British Empire,* 541.

12   I.C. Campbell, *A History of the Pacific Islands* (Christchurch, Canterbury University Press, 1989), esp. chs 15 and 16; A.M. Healy, 'Colonial Law as Metropolitan Defence: The

Curious Case of Australia in New Guinea', in Hermann J. Hiery and John M. MacKenzie (eds) *European Impact and Pacific Influence: British and German Colonial Policy in the Pacific Islands and the Indigenous Response* (London, I.B. Tauris, 1997) 214–30.

13 David Goldsworthy, *Colonial Issues in British Politics*, 1945–61 (Oxford, Clarendon Press, 1971) 399.

14 John M. MacKenzie, 'In Touch with the Infinite: The BBC and the Empire, 1923–53', in John M. MacKenzie (ed.) *Imperialism and Popular Culture* (Manchester, Manchester University Press, 1986) 182–3.

15 Lord Hailey, *An African Survey* (London, Oxford University Press, 1938 and 1957).

16 Something of the flavour of the expert's optimism can be derived from E.B. Worthington, *Science in Africa: A Review of Scientific Research Relating to Tropical and Southern Africa* (London, Oxford University Press, 1938). Worthington's book was compiled as part of Hailey's great survey project.

17 See also Gordon T. Stewart, 'Tenzing's Two Wrist Watches: The Everest Expedition and Late Imperial Culture in Britain 1921–1953', *Past and Present* (November 1995), 149, 170–97. For a general discussion of the significance of mountaineering in British imperialism, see Peter H. Hansen, 'Vertical Boundaries, National Identities: British Mountaineering on the Frontiers of Europe and the Empire, 1868–1914', *Journal of Imperial and Commonwealth History*, 1996, 24(1), 48–71.

18 Jeffrey Richards (ed.) *Imperialism and Juvenile Literature* (Manchester, Manchester University Press, 1989).

19 See the compilations of Charles Allen, *Plain Tales from the Raj* (London, Andre Deutsch, 1975) and *Tales from the Dark Continent* (London, Deutsch for the BBC, 1979) and of Jeremy Weston for the University of Edinburgh (2000, private communication) .

20 John M. MacKenzie, 'David Livingstone: The Construction of the Myth', in Graham Walker and Tom Gallagher (eds) *Sermons and Battle Hymns: Protestant Popular Culture in Modern Scotland* (Edinburgh, Edinburgh University Press, 1990) 24–42.

21 Tim Jeal, *Livingstone* (London, Heinemann, 1973).

22 T.O. Ranger, *Revolt in Southern Rhodesia, 1896–97* (London, Heinemann, 1967).

23 Tom Nairn, *The Break-Up of Britain: Crisis and Neo-Nationalism* (London, Verso, 1981); John M. MacKenzie, 'On Scotland and the Empire', *International History Review*, 1993, 15(4), 714–39.

24 For discussions of Margaret Thatcher and 'Victorian values', see Eric M. Sigsworth (ed.) *In Search of Victorian Values: Aspects of Nineteenth-Century Thought and Society* (Manchester, Manchester University Press, 1988) and Eric J. Evans, *Thatcher and Thatcherism* (London, Routledge, 1997).

25 David Cannadine, 'Empire and Social Hierarchy in Modern Britain', the Esmee Fairbairn lecture at the University of Lancaster, 4 November 1999, privately printed.

26 Antony Thomas, *Rhodes: The Race for Africa* (London, BBC, 1996) was the book of the series, which was also issued on video.

Chapter 20

Wendy Webster

'THERE'LL ALWAYS BE AN ENGLAND': REPRESENTATIONS OF COLONIAL WARS AND IMMIGRATION, 1948–1968

If attention to gender and its imagery has been one major stream feeding into 'new imperial histories' and interest in the metropolitan effects of empire another, a third has been the coming together of literary, film and other cultural studies with historical research. Wendy Webster combines all these emphases, in looking at how British cinema depicted the end and aftermaths of empire, and how sexual imaginings and fears were at the heart of this.

Stephen Howe

'IN MALAYA,' THE *DAILY MAIL* NOTED IN 1953, 'three and a half years of danger have given the planters time to convert their previously pleasant homes into miniature fortresses, with sandbag parapets, wire entanglements, and searchlights.'[1] The image of the home as fortress and a juxtaposition of the domestic with menace and terror were central to British media representations of colonial wars in Malaya and Kenya in the 1950s. The repertoire of imagery deployed in the *Daily Mail* for the 'miniature fortress' in Malaya was extended to Kenya, where the newspaper noted wire over domestic windows, guns beside wine glasses, the charming hostess in her black silk dress with 'an automatic pistol hanging at her hip.' Such images of English domesticity threatened by an alien other were also central to immigration discourse in the 1950s and 1960s. In the context of the decline of British colonial rule after 1945, representations of the empire and its legacy—resistance to colonial rule in empire and 'immigrants' in the metropolis—increasingly converged on a common theme: the violation of domestic sanctuaries.

Colonial wars of the late 1940s and 1950s have received little attention in literatures on national identity in early postwar Britain, but the articulation of racial difference through immigration discourse, and its significance in redefining the postimperial British national community have been widely recognized.[2] As Chris Waters has suggested in his work on discourses of race and nation between 1947 and 1963, these years saw questions of race become central to questions of national belonging. Waters explores the race relations literature of this period to review the ways in which the idea of a 'little England' was used against a black migrant 'other.'[3] The myth of 'little England,' as he notes, can be traced back to the Edwardian period, when it was often used as an anti-imperial image. It was in the context of anxieties about national weakness, provoked by the Anglo-Boer war (1899–1902), that G.K. Chesterton, in a symposium of papers by the Patriots' Club, advocated a return to 'our ancient interest in England' as opposed to 'our quite modern and quite frivolous interest in everywhere else,' in tracing the 'error in our recent South African politics.'[4] As Alison Light's work has shown, the imagery of 'little England' was developed in the interwar period, when national identity was increasingly domesticated, emphasizing hearth, home, and herbaceous border.[5] After 1945, Waters argues, this version of nation was reworked against the migrant other—'an other perceived as a "stranger" to those customs and conventions taken to be at the heart of Britishness itself.'[6]

Bill Schwarz's work also explores what he calls a 're-racialization' of England in the late 1950s and early 1960s, but his focus is on the impact of decolonization on the metropolis and, in reviewing the history of white settler communities in empire, he is concerned to trace a range of connections between empire and 'home.'[7] One connection is what he describes as 'a battle between two irreconcilable Englands,' exemplified most starkly by Ian Smith's unilateral declaration of independence in Rhodesia in 1965. But another is the convergence of the language of white settler communities in empire and white opponents of black immigration in the metropolis, as both identified themselves as beleaguered, vulnerable, and embattled:

> With immigration, the colonial frontier came 'home.' When this happened, the language of the colonies was reworked and came with it . . . two inter-related sentiments slowly cohered, unevenly and partially. First, whites were coming to imagine themselves as historic victims; and second—commensurably—blacks were believed to be acquiring a status of supremacy.[8]

While literatures on national identity have focused on questions of race, literatures on gender and sexuality have noted the pervasive anxieties about white masculinity in this period. Such anxieties manifested themselves in various forms. A preoccupation with the new 'home-centered' working-class man expressed concern that he was becoming apolitical, with declining participation in public life of all kinds, whether in trade unions or public houses. The intense homophobia of the 1950s saw a rash of criminal prosecutions of gay men, some of them extensively publicized. A key anxiety about black migrants in Britain concerned 'miscegenation'—a notion that was highly gendered, focusing on fears that black men were stealing 'our women.'[9] Work on cultural representations of gender in film and drama has analyzed the ways in which such anxieties were addressed through a misogynistic discourse that showed white women emasculating men.[10] However, the connections between such anxieties and national identity have rarely been explored.[11]

The notion that loss of imperial power had any impact on the metropolis has generally gone unrecognized, with the conventional historiography of decolonization presenting—in Bill Schwarz's memorable phrase—'a stunning lack of curiosity' in this area.[12] If Gayatri

Spivak's comment that 'empire messes with identity' has generally been taken to apply to colonized rather than colonizing nations, there has been a particular absence of attention to the way empire messed with British/English identities in a period of decolonization.[13] In this article, I share Schwarz's concern to make connections between empire and 'home.' But I also attempt to make connections between aspects of the literatures on national identity, which emphasize the racialization of Britain in the 1950s, and the literatures on gender and sexuality, which emphasize the anxieties surrounding white masculinity. The convergence of discourses of colonial wars and immigration on the image of a threatened domestic sanctuary suggests that it is important to explore questions of gender and their intersections with questions of race, as an area that is central to a consideration of the impact of loss of imperial power on narratives of Britishness and Englishness.

Representations of colonial wars and immigration in the mainstream British media are a rich source for exploring such questions and demonstrate the extent to which racial difference was articulated in Britain in the 1950s not only in immigration discourse, but also through images of empire. Benedict Anderson's work has argued that the development of printed media was an important factor in the process by which individuals were able to imagine a shared experience of identification with the nation as an 'imagined community.'[14] But the development of visual media, as well as a popular press, in the nineteenth and twentieth centuries dramatically increased the audiences who could be involved in such identification. James Ryan's work has shown the importance of photography to the production of imperial spectacle in Britain and its empire in the nineteenth and early twentieth centuries, in a traffic of images between home and away.[15] The development of motion pictures in the twentieth century meant that visual images became increasingly significant in the projection of national imagery and reached a wider audience. As Bill Schwarz comments, 'Increasingly through the middle decades of the twentieth century, the imagination of the nation has been inscribed first and foremost in its cinema.'[16]

In this article, I examine imagery in the mainstream British media to explore the complexity and ambivalence of the theme of a domestic sanctuary, threatened with violation, and its interplay of ideas of racial and gender differences. I argue that while both representations of colonial wars and immigration showed black men invading white territory, this was a territory that was characteristically defined in terms of home and family. Domestic order thus became an increasingly important marker of Englishness, and one which was strongly gendered, showing black as a male category, while white women were foregrounded as symbols of a nation under siege. The absence of black women from these images enforced the association between Englishness and domestic order, constructing both home and family as white. But the foregrounding of white women was ambivalent. They were shown defending their homes alongside men in empire, while in the metropolis they were assigned roles as guardians of internal frontiers against 'miscegenation' and 'blacks next door.' At the same time, they were seen as points of entry for national weakness, as they were blamed for loss of imperial power, while fears of 'miscegenation' focused on relationships between black men and white women.

These images domesticated the frontier, providing a focus on a 'little England'— 'an idea that was associated with fears of national decline and that developed between the wars, when colonial rule was contested, particularly through the War of Independence and the rise of Indian nationalism. Before 1939, however, although sometimes used as an anti-imperialist image, 'little England' also co-existed with notions of imperial identity. It could be invoked to characterize white settler communities creating English homes and gardens in Kenya or Rhodesia, or as a place from which adventure heroes journeyed to exciting masculine exploits on far-off frontiers.[17] What is striking about the 1950s is the increasing identification of the frontier as the herbaceous border or the privet hedge. In representations of colonial wars, genres that, before 1945, had usually been sharply differentiated—the domestic and the adventure narrative—began to merge.

This domestication of the frontier and the image of a threatened domestic sanctuary, with its suggestions of national vulnerability, point to the many tensions involved in redefining England as postcolonial. Chief among these tensions were anxieties about white masculinity as the frontiers where, in pre-1939 imperial narratives, British men had found and demonstrated their manhood disappeared. The classic frontier hero of imperial imagery became an increasingly embattled figure, as colonial war imagery showed white men pinned down in domestic settings, defending their homes alongside women. Such images disrupted the distinction between 'home' and 'empire,' as Britishness in far-off territories was increasingly constructed in terms of 'home,' and domestic order and harmony became key signs of 'civilization'—'away' as well as at 'home'— 'constructed against the savagery of the colonized and the immigrant. Moves to counter anxieties about white British masculinity included not only a misogynistic discourse, blaming women, but also a prolific genre of Second World War nostalgia that transposed the soldier hero from an imperial setting to a Second World War setting.

'There'll always be an England while there's a country lane' announced the popular song, much-quoted in discussions of dominant images of rurality in ideas of Englishness. References to empire in the song's refrain—'the empire too, we can depend on you'— are generally ignored. How were narratives of nation reworked when they could no longer depend on 'the empire too'—in a period when colonial rule was widely contested, the process of decolonization gathered pace, and Britain made the transition from colonial power to postcolonial nation? What was the impact on narratives of Britishness and Englishness of a diminution of British territories and a contraction of its frontiers? In addressing these questions, this article considers various ways in which the relationship between England and empire in the song were reconfigured after 1945. Since empire and its legacy were increasingly portrayed as a threat to Englishness, the song's refrain and its idea of imperial connections became problematic. While 'There'll Always Be an England' was strongly asserted in the early postwar period, 'the empire too' began to be forgotten, disavowed, or denied.

Colonial wars and the Second World War

In films made during the war 'There'll Always Be an England' is sung by female British internees in Occupied France in *Two Thousand Women* (1944) and whistled by male British prisoners of war as they march into prison camp in *The Captive Heart* (1946).[18] Representations of Britain during the war insistently referred to traditional rural images of Englishness.[19] But this notion of a gentle, peaceful land was also disrupted by images of the home front as a place of danger in the blackout and the blitz, and as a place where women were mobile, abandoning domesticity to serve in aircraft factories, the services, and the land army, as shown in films such as *Millions Like Us* (1943), *The Gentle Sex* (1943), and *A Canterbury Tale* (1944).[20]

'There'll Always Be an England' is a song that aptly encapsulates the England evoked in *The Captive Heart*—one that captivates Captain Hasek (Michael Redgrave), a Czechoslovakian man who has become a prisoner of war by masquerading as a British soldier to escape return to a concentration camp. Hasek falls in love with the idea of Celia Mitchell (Rachel Kempson), the wife of the man whose identity he has assumed, through the photographs and letters that he receives from her at the camp. He also falls in love with the idea of England that she conjures in these letters. She is shown writing to him—speaking the words of her letter against scenes of English village life—church, country station, and cricket match. The film cuts to a scene of another cricket match, played by British prisoners of war in the camp. As the cricketers return, enthusiastically discussing the game, they are reduced to silence as Hasek reads her letter to them: 'The apple trees are in full blossom, already making the orchard look like a sheet of fleecy snow. And ten-acre meadow is all white too, because this year that's where the ewes are pastured with their lambs. Soon the garden will be filled with the scent and colour of the may and beyond the river you can see the first vivid green of the larches in the bluebell wood.'

This association of the home front with women in domestic settings, often located in rural scenes, marks a shift in ideas of home in films that were made as the war was coming to an end. Both *The Captive Heart* and *Diary for Timothy* (1946) mark a transitional moment between war and postwar, portraying home as a place of safety where women have spent the war passively waiting for their men to return.[21] *Diary for Timothy* foregrounds gentle, domestic images as its central character—a baby boy—is shown the story of what has been happening in Britain in the first six months of his life and is entrusted with the task of making a different world when the war is over. He is shown home as a place of danger for other people as they shelter from doodlebugs under their kitchen table, and a team goes out to rescue those buried in the rubble that had been their home. But home is a place of safety and security for him, as he lies warm and comfortable in his mother's arms. In *The Captive Heart*, home is represented in opposition to the hardships of the prisoner-of-war camp—a haven that the prisoners, including Hasek, long to see. Although both films are careful to emphasize an inclusive British identity incorporating Welsh and Scottish characters, and urban as well as rural locations, both associate the idea of home as peaceful haven against war, not only with a dominant image of English rurality, but also with women and domesticity.

Women, moreover, are portrayed as passive figures. The messages for the baby boy in *Diary for Timothy* are all from men in a film where the script by E.M. Forster is spoken by Michael Redgrave. Timothy's mother says virtually nothing, is portrayed mainly in a domestic setting, and is waiting for her husband's return. Although this return is not shown in the film it is promised through the voice of Timothy's father in a letter promising that 'we will all be together again.' In *The Captive Heart*, the return is shown through the early release of some of the prisoners, and resolves the anxiety and pain of the men in the prison camp, as one receives news of his wife's love affair, another of his wife's death in childbirth, and a third feels obliged to break off his engagement because he has lost his sight. As the audience knows, however, women have been guarding the home during the war—for apart from one shot of a mobile woman in uniform saying farewell to her family as she boards a train, they are shown in domestic settings. Women have been faithful to men, or unfaithful only through unfortunate misunderstandings, and are waiting for them to come home—a notion that is extended to incorporate Hasek as he journeys to England on release from prisoner-of-war camp to find Celia Mitchell, and the film ends with the promise of their happiness. As the men return, order is restored, and all is well.[22]

The place of home in films, portrayed during the war as a potentially dangerous front line where women were active, and shifting by 1945 to an image of a place of safety where women patiently waited for their men, changed once again in the rash of Second World War texts that were produced in the 1950s. As Marcia Landy observes, these films were 'prone to presenting the women as faithless creatures, as negligible, or as insubstantial, focusing on the male group.'[23] This tendency is evident in the way servicewomen—with one or two exceptions, such as *Odette* (1950) and *Carve Her Name With Pride* (1958)—generally featured only as a backdrop to scenes of male heroism.[24] As John Ramsden comments:

> Whole hours of these films go by without a woman even uttering a word, and, if they are there at all, it is in roles without responsibility, pushing flags around RAF maps in *Angels One Five*, . . . or doing the same job a decade later at the Admiralty while Kenneth More plots to *Sink the Bismarck*.[25]

It is evident also in the way in which the home front faded from view, and war was generally sealed off from domestic imagery. Prisoner-of-war films in the 1950s, as Marcia Landy comments, offered 'no space for fantasies of home,' in striking contrast to *The Captive Heart*.[26] Women, whether in the armed forces, in factories, or in a domestic setting, generally faded from view, and the emphasis was on homosocial worlds of active service or the prisoner-of-war camp.

Representations of colonial wars in the 1950s have attracted little attention by comparison with these Second World War texts.[27] Yet colonial wars—Malaya (1948–1958), Kenya (1952–1956), Cyprus (1954–1959)—were widely reported in newspapers during the 1950s and represented in a range of films, including *The Planter's Wife* (1952) set in Malaya, and *Simba* (1955), set in Kenya, both made by Rank.[28] In paying tribute to the courage of the planter in Malaya and the farmer in Kenya, both these films conformed broadly with the aim of government propaganda. The images in *Simba* of Mau Mau ransacking and burning white farms, and butchering farmers, fitted government concerns that this aspect of the war should receive substantial coverage, to counter any impression of 'Africans being manhandled and oppressed by white imperialists.'[29] The casting of Claudette Colbert, an American star, as the heroine of *The Planter's Wife* fitted government concerns to bring British efforts against Communism in Malaya to American attention, and the Rank publicity release expressed the hope that the film would 'help make the American people as a whole more aware of the part Britain is playing against Communism in the Far East.'[30] At the same time, such casting was also intended to secure commercial success for the films, in both Britain and America, reflecting Rank's designs on the American market, as well as its concern to challenge Hollywood's dominance of British box-office receipts. The choice of Jack Hawkins to play the male lead in *The Planter's Wife* was probably an important factor in its box-office success in Britain. In the year after its release he was voted the most popular male star in Britain, while Dirk Bogarde, who played the male lead in *Simba*, had displaced Hawkins as most popular male star in Britain by 1955.[31]

Colonial war films took an opposite trajectory from Second World War films of the 1950s. The latter transposed the adventure hero from an imperial to a war setting, and took up many of the themes of pre-war imperial films—a homosocial world where men were removed from the domestic scene, and demonstrated courage, endurance, and humor in faraway places. Postwar imperial films, however, unless they were set in the past, portrayed heroes whose capacity for action was increasingly eroded, and moved toward a concern with home fronts and with women. When in the Korda imperial classic, *The Drum* (1938), produced just before the war, the question is posed, 'do you think you can conquer the English?,' and the reply is, 'I tell you the empire is just waiting to be carved to pieces,' a British audience can be confident that someone who utters these words is an evil, devious villain—probably a fanatic too—who will get his come-uppance during the course of the film.[32] It is a measure of how quickly British colonial rule declined that there can be no such confidence in the 1950s. Although the army arrives in the nick of time to save the day in *The Planter's Wife* and *Simba*—as it does in *The Drum*—neither film shows much confidence that the British can continue to maintain control for very long. Both portray a time on the cusp between British resolve to stay on and maintain colonial rule and the end of empire.

Where texts of imperialism had generally shown the hero sealed off from domestic settings, exploring and conquering vast territory, the hero of post 1945 colonial war films was a distinctly embattled and beleaguered figure. *The Planter's Wife* is framed by sequences of violence against planters' homes. Beginning with shots of 'bandits' crawling on their bellies from the night-time jungle, killing a planter as he emerges in pajamas from his bungalow, and then setting fire to it, the film ends with a long sequence of another planter's bungalow under siege on the following night by 'bandits,' who cut the barbed wire, occupy the sand-bagged parapets, and shoot the searchlights. The main theme of *Simba* is similarly the threat to white homes, families, and settlement in Kenya from the Mau Mau. Early sequences of the film show British homes under threat. Allan Howard (Dirk Bogarde), on a visit to his brother from England, is met at the airport by Mary Crawford (Virginia McKenna), but the moment of arrival at his brother's farm is disrupted by the sight of police outside. The movement into a white home becomes a revelation of the Mau Mau, who have ransacked the house and killed Allan's brother. The film ends with a scene of conflagration as this farm, now run by Allan, is destroyed by a black mob.

As the title of *The Planter's Wife* suggests, British women occupied an important place in representations of colonial wars. Liz Frazer (Claudette Colbert), the wife of the title, is shown like her husband Jim (Jack Hawkins) living under constant threat of death and ambush, surrounded by menace, and in particular danger within the home. While Jim wants to pack her off to safety in England, she determines to stay with him. This image of the plucky white British woman, staying on despite the danger, was common to media representations of colonial wars in this period. The *Daily Mail* celebrated another planter's wife in Malaya in 1948:

> Mary . . . will not leave her husband because his labourers are watching for the first signs of weakness in the master's bungalow. Her departure would be so construed and could panic the coolies who are openly anti-Communist and fearful of the Communist-led guerillas.[33]

Where England as home was represented in *The Captive Heart* as a place to which the prisoners of war longed to return, the notion of return was more ambivalent in images of colonial wars, for return represented retreat—in the language of the popular press 'scuttling.' In *The Planter's Wife* Jim agrees to let Liz stay on, but she also successfully persuades him to 'take some leave.' In *Simba* the notion of return is also coded as 'taking leave' as Mary's father is shown telling his wife about his plans to do so over their midday meal, just before he is murdered in a Mau Mau attack. England in both films stands for a safe haven away from the violence of colonial wars—but neither portrays a return, celebrating instead the courage of those who stay on.

An emphasis on women as heroines was also characteristic of newspaper reports of war in Kenya. The story of Mrs. Dorothy Raynes-Simson and Mrs. Kitty Heselburger attracted particular attention. Killing three Mau Mau who attacked them in their sitting room, and wounding a fourth, they were widely celebrated as 'the two bravest women in Africa.'[34] The *Daily Express* compared them both to heroines of Westerns and to male heroes of the Second World War:

> If you are a woman of Kenya out on the lonely farms in the black zones you wear slacks all day, you have a holster on your hip, and you look like the heroine of a Western film . . . Britain! Do you remember the way you reached out in love and praise to the men of Arnhem, embattled and faithful? Today give your hearts to the women of Kenya. They are surrounded by menace but they do not budge.[35]

However, taboo in a Second World War context, the armed British woman, shooting to kill, was a recurrent image of female courage in colonial wars, and women killing non-white men became a sign of strength rather than pathology. In *The Planter's Wife* Liz Frazer shoots a 'bandit' in the compound of her bungalow against the background of domestic animals and a washing-line, drawing a gun from the folds of her dress. Later, when her home is attacked at night she is behind a machine gun. Mary, the heroine of *Simba*, is shown behind a machine gun as a white farm is attacked by the Mau Mau.

This image of the woman fighting to defend her home against attackers was not only associated with strength and courage but also with vulnerability. After she has killed the 'bandit' in the compound, Liz Frazer swoons and is taken up in the arms of Jim, who carries her into the bungalow. Newspaper reports stressed themes of female vulnerability as well as female heroism. When Dr. Dorothy Meiklejohn and her husband were attacked by Mau Mau, the *Daily Express* reported:

> Dr. Dorothy pulled herself from the floor by clutching the furniture and crawled upstairs. There she tore pillow cases and tried to staunch her many wounds. There is no telephone in the house. So alone, unarmed, and only half-conscious she drove along the empty track for help.[36]

In the reporting of Dorothy Raynes-Simson and Kitty Heselburger's killings of three Mau Mau there was emphasis on their friends as well as themselves 'all living alone and all middle-aged or old.'[37]

The domestic world on which such images focused was also ambivalent—one that marked the civilization of the British against those who resisted their rule, but which also threatened to feminize British masculinity. The heroes in colonial war films are still men of action taking on all comers, but the shadow of the decline of British colonial rule hangs heavily over this image. John Newsinger, analyzing military memoirs of British soldiers who served in Malaya in the 1950s, comments that they tell 'a story of colonial warfare waged by young white men in an exotic locale against an alien foe: the very stuff of the imperial imagination.'[38] In media images, however, civilians were usually the focus of interest, especially when there were attacks on women, and when the home front was foregrounded there was an elaboration of domestic detail that suggested male vulnerability as well as female. Pajamas frequently figured as a sign of unpreparedness for attack—in the opening of *The Planter's Wife*, and in newspaper reports from Kenya where men were killed 'eating their New Year's Day dinner in pyjamas and dressing gown' and 'in pyjamas, taking his nightly last look round with his 32-year-old wife.'[39] In *Simba*, the Mau Mau kill a British farmer in his kitchen as he goes to investigate noises that interrupt his mid-day meal. The hero of *The Planter's Wife* is first shown in his bedroom, awakened from sleep by a telephone call—the police checking on his safety—introducing both the notion that his home is under threat and the domestic setting in which he is pinned down during the main action of the film, defending it against attack. As a man of action, he is nevertheless closely associated with this domestic world as he turns the bungalow into a military fortification, and it is this bungalow that is the scene of battle. It is perhaps in an attempt to align him more closely with the traditional adventure hero of imperial films—whose struggles and conquests were in vast territory—that he is shown at daybreak, crawling under the barbed wire that surrounds his home in an attempt to save his rubber trees from attack. However, even in this sequence, he is still in sight of the bungalow.

In *Guns at Batasi* (1964), a film set somewhere unspecified in postcolonial Africa, the British soldier is removed even further from the traditional hero.[40] The film explores the impact of loss of empire on British masculinity, showing soldiers who are immobilized by the process of decolonization, pinned down in barracks. When they do take action it is to move only a few yards, still within sight of the mess. The film continuously asserts the racial superiority of the British and at the same time shows that such superiority no longer provides any guarantee of authority or power. *Guns at Batasi* is an elegy for the soldier hero, particularly the imperial soldier, and is infused by imperial nostalgia.

Guns at Batasi invokes British racial superiority particularly through a contrast between African mayhem and British order. In early sequences of the film, all the action is African as Africans stage a coup, demonstrating on the streets and setting fire to cars. This action extends to the barracks, where the British colonel (Jack Hawkins) hands over command to the African Captain Abraham (Earl Cameron), in line with a policy of non-involvement. Led by Lieutenant Boniface (Errol John), supporters of the coup take Abraham prisoner and raid an ammunition store to arm themselves. Shot from a white British perspective, Africans are shown as a threatening mob in the opening sequence of the film, as British soldiers driving an army truck encounter African demonstrators, and in a later sequence that shows African demonstrators attacking a car from the point of view of whites inside it. Following both these sequences there are cuts to the barracks and the mess as places where the British maintain order. Such order is symbolized by Sergeant Major Lauderdale (Richard Attenborough) who rules the mess with a rod of iron. In the first mess sequence a soldier takes down a portrait of the queen, betting that Lauderdale will notice its absence within two minutes of arrival, and he wins the bet. In the second mess sequence this order is connected with pre-1945 British colonial rule as the men swap stories about 'best stations,' recalling 'church parade in Singapore before the war,' and India—'Jewel of the East they used to call it—what a pity they had to give it away.'

As in colonial war films, the emphasis on the domestic world inhabited by the British provides an ambivalent image, for the mess is not only a place of British order but also the place where, throughout the first half of the film, British soldiers are confined, under orders from their colonel to stay there until what he calls 'this little spot of bother' blows over. Against scenes of African action, they are shown indoors, drinking, chatting, and playing billiards. Their passivity is emphasized by the comments of one soldier: 'Bloody marvellous! Two hot chocolates chuck bricks at each other and the whole British army is immobilized.' As the men dine in the mess on the queen's birthday and a loyal toast is proposed, African mayhem disrupts the orderly scene as Abraham, who has been wounded while escaping, bursts in, collapsing on the billiard table. This is the watershed of the film. Thereafter the British move away from confinement, immobilization, and impotence. Defending his men, his mess, and Captain Abraham, against what he sees as Boniface's 'mutiny,' Lauderdale takes action that culminates in his movement out of the mess to blow up guns trained on it by Lieutenant Boniface. The image of a British soldier resisting a mutineer is linked to images of other British soldier heroes by Lauderdale who, in a confrontation with Boniface, recalls reading about their exploits on the northwest frontier, with 'beads of sweat pouring down my face from a battle two hundred years old.'

If Lauderdale symbolizes the values of old imperial Britain, it is Miss Barker-Wise (Flora Robson), a member of Parliament who comes to Africa on a visit, who symbolizes the new era of loss of imperial power. The contrast between them is thus represented through sexual difference—a contrast in which the idea of a postimperial Britain is feminized and presented as decidedly unattractive, for Miss Barker-Wise is a bossy middle-aged woman with a cigarette permanently hanging from the corner of her mouth. Lauderdale—no youth himself—calls her an 'old bag,' and this is a verdict that the film endorses. Miss Barker-Wise occupies a female role that was common in texts that explored British postwar malaise, for while women were incorporated into the story of nation in Malaya or Kenya to stand for both heroism and vulnerability, they were also blamed for national weakness and decline in a range of texts that showed them either attempting to emasculate men or championing liberal causes.[41] Miss Barker-Wise does both. She attempts to order Lauderdale around and champions Africans in general and Lieutenant Boniface in particular—describing him to Lauderdale as 'a civilised and cultured man.' The film shows Boniface as cruel and untrustworthy, and Miss Barker-Wise eventually discovers her own error of judgement. In the closing sequence of the film she admits her error to Lauderdale.

Lauderdale may win a small victory over a woman, but the values he represents are shown as otherwise defeated in a postimperial world. It is not Lauderdale but Boniface who has the last word, for the coup is successful and Boniface demands that Lauderdale leave the country. The British colonel's own impotence is shown as he orders Lauderdale to return to England by the next available plane, at the same time admitting that in Lauderdale's place he too would have resisted. The action of the soldier hero in the aftermath of loss of empire is thus shown as more likely to earn punishment than medals. In a brief moment of frustration and anger, Lauderdale disrupts British order, hurling a glass at the main symbol of authority in the mess—the portrait of the queen. He then quickly reverts to his own meticulous standards, sweeping up the shattered glass, straightening the portrait, and marching briskly—even jauntily—away from the mess. Despite its closing image of an undaunted Lauderdale, *Guns at Batasi* is imbued with sadness for a lost world and shows the British army profoundly affected by decolonization—its capacity for action eroded to the point of immobility, its authority diminished, and its soldier heroes unhonored.

Guns at Batasi was dedicated to 'the Warrant Officers and Non Commissioned Officers of the British Army, past and present, who have at all times upheld the high traditions of the service.' *The Planter's Wife* was 'dedicated to the rubber planters of Malaya, where only the jungle is neutral, and where the planters are daily defending the rubber trees with their lives.' Such dedications announced the films' celebration of the courage and service of the ordinary British civilian or soldier, embattled in empire or former empire, and suggested that their record went otherwise unacknowledged. Quoting an advertisement for *The Planter's Wife*—'There are few medals for the people of Malaya, the police, the military, the planter and the planter's wife'—*The Times* commented that the film 'sets about distributing them.'[42] Colonial wars, however, like the texts that portrayed them, were generally forgotten once over. In contrast, the celebration of the heroism of the British forces in the Second World War became a major industry. On Nicholas Pronay's count, eighty-five films made between 1946 and 1960 were devoted to this theme. It was an industry that also produced numerous best-selling novels, autobiographies, biographies, memoirs, and stories in children's literature and comics.[43] Most of these texts produced representations that were sealed off from the present, securing an image of British heroism. When they were juxtaposed against the present, as in *The Ship That Died of Shame* (1955), they were pervaded by anxieties about British masculinity.[44] This film, opening with scenes of male camaraderie and heroism in the war, shows men who are aimless and adrift once it is over, and who attempt to recapture something of the spirit of the war by putting their former ship into service once again. As they use the ship for increasingly illicit purposes—contraband, forged currency, gun-running, and finally harboring a child-murderer—the ship registers its shame at what the men have become. As its engines die and it finally disintegrates, the ship offers an image of England calling men back to duty and honor in a postwar world characterized by a malaise which is specifically identified as masculine.

Colonial wars and decolonization are an important context for understanding the immediate nostalgia for the Second World War, and the speed with which the war assumed a major place in ideas of national identity, once it was over. The soldier or adventure hero was increasingly difficult to produce in an imperial setting. Only a few 1950s' texts continued to celebrate his exploits in empire, and these were generally set in the nineteenth or early twentieth centuries. The much wider range of Second World War texts, which were often highly popular, could provide an image of British male heroism set in the recent past. Against the beleaguered hero of colonial war films, the loss of British male authority and power in *Guns at Batasi*, and the postwar masculine malaise of *The Ship That Died of Shame*, they offered a reassuring representation of British masculinity where heroic struggles could be transposed from an imperial to a Second World War setting and resolved in the knowledge of the outcome of the war: a famous victory.

Domestic order

'Not a day passes but English families are ruthlessly turned out to make room for foreign invaders,' William Gordon, MP for Stepney, stated in 1902 in the House of Commons, advocating the control of Jewish immigration to Britain. 'Out they go to make room for Rumanians, Russians and Poles . . . It is only a matter of time before the population becomes entirely foreign.'[45] As Gordon's speech suggests, the idea of an English home and family, threatened by an alien other, was not confined to images of colonial wars and was current in immigration discourse before 1945. It was in the 1950s, however, that representations of empire and its legacy—resistance to British colonial rule in empire and 'immigrants' in the metropolis—increasingly converged on a common theme: the threat to an Englishness symbolized by the idea of 'home.'

Representations of Englishness that made reference to the small-scale and familiar—the privacy of domestic and familial life—invoked a particular exclusive and intimate identity. They were developed between the wars when, as Alison Light's work has shown, in contrast to the expansive rhetoric of empire, the English were also imagined as inward-looking—decent, but quiet and private. This version of Englishness not only celebrated the female sphere of domesticity, but also the quiet, pipe-smoking Englishman, tending his garden.[46] It was extended during the Second World War when, as Light comments, Britain could be seen as 'a sporting little country batting away against the Great Dictators.'[47] J.B. Priestley, in his *Postscripts*, broadcast on radio in 1940, exemplified the pipe-smoking Englishman, as he offered his audience a version of a fireside chat—the intimacy and homeliness of the occasion reinforced by his slow delivery in a Yorkshire accent. He also celebrated homely virtues—as, for example, in his broadcast on Dunkirk, which told the story of the 'little holiday steamers' and their associations in a pre-war world with ordinary, innocent pleasures when 'the gents' were full of 'high spirits and bottled beer,' while 'the ladies ate pork pies.' These were the steamers that, to rescue British soldiers, had 'made an excursion to hell and came back glorious.'[48]

After 1945, in the context of the reversal of the colonial encounter through migration to Britain from colonies and former colonies, this version of national identity was increasingly mobilized to construct both 'family' and 'home' as white. In the 1950s, oppositions between the 'immigrant' and Englishness were gendered as well as raced—the immigrant generally represented as a black man and Englishness frequently embodied in the figure of a white woman. The black man was often seen as transient and adrift, rarely represented as having family or a settled home, and characterized in terms of an incapacity for domestic and familial life. The white woman embodied Englishness as domestic and familial life, and the notions of the rootedness and stability—belonging, attachment, and settlement—that this life suggested.

Representations of the alien other as male were common before 1939, particularly in the image of a male horde descending to attack the British—a commonplace of imperial narratives.[49] But the characteristic absence of women from such images took on new significance as the frontier moved from the battlefield to the domestic interior—the planter's bungalow in empire or the privet hedge in metropolis. Home and family became much more important as markers of difference between colonizers and colonized, English and 'immigrant.' In immigration discourse, the foregrounding of domesticity worked to suggest 'immigrants' as people who did not belong in Britain, and the absence of women from these representations before the early 1960s reinforced a disassociation from ideas of family or domesticity. In contrast, in representations of colonial wars, domesticity and family were images of white civilization that worked to suggest whites as settlers who belonged in Malaya and Kenya through a network of attachments to their families and to the land that they owned and cultivated. The colonized—never shown in domestic settings apart from in their role as the tamed and domesticated 'house boys' of the British in Kenya—were associated with bestial imagery: as denizens of the jungle in *The Planter's Wife*, as primitive savages in *Simba*, as wild animals in the *Daily Express* report of the attack on Raynes-Simson and Heselburger through quotation of their comment that 'they came silently like panthers with incredible swiftness.'[50]

In both empire and metropolis, alien others were not only disassociated from domestic life, but also shown violating English domestic boundaries. The domestication of the frontier is particularly apparent in the elaboration of domestic detail to signify Englishness. In newspaper reports of Raynes-Simson and Heselberger killing three Mau Mau in Kenya, photographs and text reconstructed the moment of attack: the women in their lounge, one cracking a Christmas nut against a background of Christmas cards arranged on the mantelpiece, both close to the radio listening to the nine o'clock BBC news.[51] In immigration discourse there was a similar proliferation of domestic imagery as homes and streets in the metropolis were described in detail, with a particular attention to boundary objects—clean lace curtains, clean windows, tidy dustbins, washed front door steps, neat house fronts.[52] These scenes of domestic order became images of Englishness under threat. The *Daily Express* commented on the Kenyan interior:

> The house is warm with the comfort of good books and nice things—if you don't brood on the bullet hole under the old Dutch clock. This could be Carshalton instead of *No Woman's Land*.[53]

The *Daily Mail* noted the:

> warm Kenya sun beating down on a lovely English-looking garden . . . It might have been Worcestershire or Herefordshire in deep summer. The Mau Mau terror has been poised to strike at their homestead—any British homestead— for months. They were not afraid.[54]

In Sheila Patterson's account of West Indians in Brixton, neat house fronts stood for what she called 'our ways—a conformity to certain standards of order, cleanliness, quietness, privacy and propriety,' and she noted that 'no immigrant group has in the mass so signally failed to conform to these expectations and patterns as have the West Indians.'[55] Elspeth Huxley, in a series of articles on 'immigrants' first published in *Punch* in 1963, chose the 'quiet street' and 'privet hedge' as emblems of Englishness threatened by 'immigrants.' West Indians in particular, she noted, disrupted English quiet and order by playing loud music and keeping late hours at weekends. They also violated boundaries, leaving yards and front steps filthy and windows unwashed, and lying in bed with their feet sticking out of the window.[56]

In Kenya a particular symbol of threat to homesteads was the disloyal servant, either himself a member of the Mau Mau or someone who would let the Mau Mau into his employer's home.[57] Richard Dyer has noted the rigid binarism around which *Simba* is organized, where white stands for modernity, reason, order, and stability, and black for backwardness, irrationality, chaos, and violence.[58] But it is also worth noting that stability and order are represented mainly through images of home, so that treachery is associated with the domestic, not the political or military, and is thus a particularly intimate betrayal. The distinction between different black masculinities represented in the film—the tamed and domesticated 'houseboys' and the atavistic and murderous Mau Mau—is blurred by white anxieties about whether 'houseboys' will betray them. These are anxieties that are shown as justified. There remains a distinction between loyal and disloyal servants since the film shows an attack on a white farm where some let the Mau Mau in, while others are themselves murdered. Mary's mother, whose husband is killed in this attack, has defended her servants against charges of possible disloyalty by arguing that they are each 'one of the family,' reinforcing the idea of an intimate betrayal. The master or mistress and servant relationship stood for the wider authority and control of white over black, as well as the idea that black men could be tamed. This scene of white domestic order invaded by black violence, through treachery from within, could be read as a particularly telling instance of the violation of a domestic sanctuary signifying loss of imperial power.

The notion of Englishness threatened from within also appeared in immigration discourse, where it was developed through a focus on internal frontiers—homes, neighborhoods, streets—where English families and homes were under siege from 'blacks next door.' In the late 1940s and 1950s, a focus on 'miscegenation' in discourses on immigration foregrounded relationships between black men and white women. Like the image of the English family under threat, fears of 'miscegenation' had also surfaced in various contexts in the first half of the century, but in the 1950s they intensified and were always highly gendered.[59] Characteristic questions were those posed by *Picture Post* in 1954, 'Would you let your daughter marry a negro?'; by Colin MacInnes in 1956, 'What of these tales of coloured men corrupting our young girls?'; and by the *Daily Express* in 1956, 'Would you let your daughter marry a black man?'[60] If black migration to Britain brought a fear of the collapse of the boundaries between colonizers and colonized, black and white, it was particularly through the breaching of this internal frontier that such a collapse was imagined.

Flame in the Streets (1961), a film representing a wide range of conflicts between white English and black 'immigrants' in the metropolis, exemplifies many of these anxieties.[61] The action of the film, contained within Guy Fawkes Day, is set against the background noise of fireworks, as bangers are thrown and rockets go up, reinforcing a pervasive sense of tension. In the workplace, white men abuse black. In the streets, white teddy boys attack black men, disrupting the community bonfire party. But the central conflict of the film is in a white working-class home inhabited by the Palmer family—Kathy (Sylvia Sims), her mother, Nell (Brenda de Banzie), her father, Jacko (John Mills) and her grandfather (Wilfred Bramble)—and is provoked by Kathy's announcement that she plans to marry Peter Lincoln (Johnny Seka), her black teacher colleague. Nell is the guardian of internal frontiers, and it is her reaction to Kathy's plans that prompts much of the action of the film.

Nell is herself strongly associated with domesticity. Throughout the film she is characterized by her aspirations for a better home in a better district—one with a bathroom. Apart from one shot at the garden gate that shows her anxiously looking out for Kathy, she ventures from the home only once—to find Jacko, who is in a trade union meeting, and tell him of Kathy's plans. The film is infused with liberal attitudes, and the representation of Nell draws on notions of the neurotic and materialistic housewife, while her outbursts against Kathy are presented as hysterically racist. But her warnings to Kathy are nevertheless reinforced by the film's images. She has told Kathy that 'you're no better that the whores in the high street,' and as Kathy leaves home to wander the streets in search of Peter's house she passes a white whore on the arm of a black man. She has told Kathy that 'they live like animals—six, eight, ten to a room,' and when Kathy enters the house it is to find multi-occupied rooms, peeling wallpaper, stained walls, washing hanging from the ceiling. As Kathy tries to find Peter's room, she becomes a voyeur, catching glimpses of black life within the rooms she enters, and encounters a scene that even Nell had perhaps not imagined—a black man in bed with a black woman who invites Kathy to join them. Finally on the landing she encounters Judy, a white woman married to a black man and pregnant by him. What Judy tells her reinforces Nell's message. Gesturing at the domestic disorder she says with heavy irony, 'It's a great life—look around.'

Domestic order not only became a central image of Englishness, but also frequently the only resolution narratives offered to the conflicts they portrayed. *The Times*, reviewing *Simba*, wondered whether there was something distasteful in making a record of the violence and blood shed in Kenya and 'tacking on to that record a conventional film love story.' As this comment suggests, in representations of colonial wars domestic and adventure narratives began to merge. The imperial adventure, although occasionally incorporating themes of heterosexual romance, had formerly been resolved mainly by the restoration of British military and political order. Now reconciliations on the home front became the main resolution. In *The Planter's Wife* the impact of colonial war in Malaya is explored primarily through the damage it has done to the relationship between Liz and Jim Frazer. The sign of this damage—Liz's decision not to return to Malaya if she goes back to England to take their son to boarding school—is part of her recognition of the breakdown of their marriage as a result of the war. As she acts to save her marriage and stay by Jim's side, the movement of the film is toward a reconciliation between husband and wife. The final image—where they stand together happily united on a station platform, waving farewell to their son who is being taken back to England by friends, and not by Liz—seals the notion of reunion. But the wider conflict in Malaya remains unresolved, and it is the restoration of their marriage that provides the only resolution in the film. As *The Times* commented, 'The film is sensible enough not to pretend that, because husband and wife kiss and make up, all is well in Malaya.[62]

Flame in the Streets also offers reconciliation between white husband and wife as its only resolution. The film undercuts its association of Nell with hysteria through the detailed attention given to her point of view in her conflict with Jacko. As she tells him that he had no time for her, treated her like part of the fixtures, turned the front room into an office, even made love to her as though he were taking a quick drink, Jacko is reduced to tears. His efforts to make amends and reunite the family are demonstrated when he accepts Nell's instructions to go and find Kathy and bring her home. As he fulfils his mission and Kathy comes home bringing Peter with her, racial violence erupts, and white teddy boys push a black man into a lighted bonfire and badly injure him. The fate of this man, the conflict on the streets, as well as the central problem that the film poses— whether Kathy can bring Peter home and incorporate him into white family life through marriage—all remain unresolved. As Peter crosses the boundary of the Palmer home for the first time, and Jacko brings Nell downstairs to meet him, the film ends on an uneasy image: Jacko and Nell are on one side of the family hearth and Kathy and Peter on the other, in a shot that is angled to show them separated by the whole width of the room. Whatever the future, however, Jacko and Nell have been reunited. In offering reconciliation between Nell and Jacko as its only resolution, the film heightens its use of family and home as emblems of white life, and of Englishness.

It is significant that the home and family used as emblems of Englishness in *Flame in the Streets* are white, urban, and working class. Nineteenth- and early twentieth-century texts on the white urban poor in the metropolis had produced a pattern of associations between class and race, deploying a repertoire of racial imagery that linked 'darkest

England' and 'darkest Africa,' and portrayed 'colonies of heathens and savages in the heart of our capital.'[63] The urban crowd was associated with fears of unrest and disorder in the metropolis.[64] In postwar immigration discourse, however, 'immigrants' took the place formerly assigned to the urban poor, and it was the urban working classes who were used to represent order and belonging. In both Patterson's and Huxley's accounts of Brixton, the contrast between the neat English house fronts and the domestic barbarism of 'immigrants' is embedded in an opposition between 'immigrants' and 'residents.'[65] The representation of the Palmers' home in *Flame in the Streets* is characteristic of immigration discourse. Its neat house front and privet hedge contrasted to the chaos and noise of 'immigrant' housing stand for the propriety and order that are so closely guarded by Nell. The symbols of Englishness in such texts were not the pastoral but the urban or suburban—the 'quiet street.'

Henry Mayhew had commented on the London poor in 1851 that as 'vagabonds and outcasts' they lacked 'hearth and rootedness . . . sacred symbols to all civilised races.' His notion of the urban poor as rootless was developed by other nineteenth-century writers who portrayed them as 'wandering hordes' and 'nomadic tribes.'[66] But in the 1950s, it was the urban working classes who were used to represent the values of the 'hearth' against 'immigrants.' In *Flame in the Streets* such rootedness is suggested in the detailed portrayal of the Palmer family, across the generations, and in the character of Jacko who still lives in the house where he was born and takes on the mantle of his father, a founder of the trade union, in his work as a shop steward. In contrast, none of the black characters in the film is endowed with family connections. The representation of 'immigrants' as transient, rootless, and adrift was common in the 1950s—as sailors on the point of moving on to another port in *Pool of London* (1950) and *A Taste of Honey* (1961), as 'drifters' in Colin MacInnes's novel, *City of Spades* (1957) where they inhabit a world of prostitution, illicit drinking, gambling, drugs, and violence.[67] In 1950s texts 'dark strangers,' 'wandering hordes,' and 'alien races' in the metropolis are no longer the white urban poor but 'immigrants.' England itself, constructed against 'immigrants,' takes on increasing significance as a place standing for order.

Imperial identities

In 1966, *The Sunday Times* reported Ian Smith's claim that:

> if Sir Winston Churchill were alive today, I believe he would probably emigrate to Rhodesia—because I believe that all those admirable qualities and characteristics of the British that we believed in, loved and preached to our children, no longer exist in Britain.[68]

In neatly reversing the notion of Britain as the heartland of empire, Smith positioned himself as a true defender of the nation against the metropolis. He did this paradoxically through rebellion against British rule in Rhodesia. The identity that he was defending was imperial, exemplified by Winston Churchill who had died in the year that Smith declared unilateral independence in Rhodesia and whose funeral Smith had attended. In claiming Rhodesia as the heartland of empire—a place to which Churchill would now emigrate—Smith constructed white Rhodesians, embodying exemplary British qualities, against a metropolis that had given up on imperial rule. Smith's disavowal of Britain as the center of empire was given particularly dramatic form through the Unilateral Declaration of Independence, but it was a view shared by other white settler communities in Africa, many of which identified themselves as bearers of true Britishness, and true defenders of the nation, against a metropolis that they accused of betraying the cause of empire.[69]

In 1968, Enoch Powell also wrestled with the question of Britain's imperial identity in addressing the question, 'why, in retrospect, our history of the last 20 years seems to have been one long series of retreats and humiliations, from Suez to Aden, from Cyprus to Rhodesia.'[70] Unlike Smith, however, Powell chose to disavow not Britain as the heartland of imperial identity, but imperial identity itself. This was the culmination of a long journey Powell had made from an intense attachment to such identity—one where the shock of the news of imminent Indian independence had proved so severe that 'I remember spending the whole of one night walking the streets of London trying to come to terms with it.'[71] The empire, he had claimed in the same year, 'is the structure on which we are dependent for our very existence.' In his 1951 electoral address to constituents he had insisted that 'I BELIEVE IN THE BRITISH EMPIRE. Without the Empire, Britain would be like a head without a body.'[72] Yet by 1968, Powell had moved to a position where, in a startling formulation, 'retreats' and 'humiliations' were out of the question since Britain—with the possible exception of rule in India—had never been an imperial power.

Both Smith's disavowal of England as the center of the empire and Powell's dismissal of that empire as a 'myth' came at a moment when the process of decolonization was virtually complete. Taken together they suggest some interesting ways in which imperial identities affected narratives of nation. In breaking with Britain, Smith represents himself as a defender of imperial identity. Powell in some ways suggests the appropriateness of such a move, since, in the interests of denying 'humiliations' and 'defeats,' he manages to produce a version of Britain that is shorn of an imperial identity, not through the process of decolonization, but through dismissal of its imperial past as 'myth.'[73] But although these two stories appear completely contradictory they have a major theme in common. Both construct the idea of England against empire. England, in Smith's version of this opposition becomes a place that betrays the values of empire since, like Miss Barker-Wise in *Guns at Batasi*, it can no longer be relied on to uphold white rule over blacks and contemplates a move, however gradual, to black majority rule in an independent Rhodesia. In Powell's version, England becomes a place to which 'our generation . . . comes home again from years of distant wandering.' This is the domestic sanctuary that Powell had once thought dependent on empire for the very structure of its existence, but which he now finds to be characterized by 'the continuity of her existence . . . unbroken when the looser connections which had linked her with distant continents and strange races fell away.' The empire, if it ever existed—and Powell has considerable problems in altogether denying this—has been a distraction, but fortunately 'the nationhood of the mother country remained unaltered through it all.'[74] Powell has forgotten the refrain of the song, 'the empire too, we can depend on you,' but not its main theme: 'There'll Always Be an England.'

Powell's speech on the illusion of empire received little media coverage. His 'Rivers of Blood' speech on immigration in 1968, however, received very extensive coverage, and has become the most well-known text in British immigration discourse. Powell may have confidently announced in 1964 that England had 'remained unaltered' by an imperial past that he simultaneously denied, but in 1968 he represented 'immigrants'—by which he meant black and Asian immigrants—as a major threat to Englishness. A main symbol of this threat in his speech was the familiar idea of the violation of domestic sanctuaries. Domestic order, guarded by an English woman, is disrupted by 'immigrants' who turn her 'quiet street' into a 'a place of noise and confusion.' They threaten the boundaries of her home—pushing excreta through her letter box, breaking her windows. Reversing the story of imperial identity—expansive, active, masculine—Powell tells a story about nation that foregrounds a white woman and that evokes powerlessness and vulnerability at home in a quiet English street. The violation of a domestic sanctuary becomes a symbol of a nation under siege.[75]

Powell's 'Rivers of Blood' speech and its reverberations bring into sharp focus the main ways in which imperial identities affected narratives of nation once colonial wars were forgotten and decolonization was more or less complete. But there were other narratives that developed the construction of Englishness against empire; narratives that, in representing decolonization as a moment of ruin for former colonies, celebrated rather than denied an imperial past. Chief among these was an opposition between British order and disorder in former British colonies—a theme strongly developed in colonial nostalgia. In *Guns at Batasi*, African mayhem is represented as inevitable when not contained by British rule. A British soldier comments at the outset, 'They got rid of our government, now they want to get rid of their own,' and the film, in tracing the story of a successful coup, shows an African country being taken over by a violent mob. Evocations of British order against disorder in former colonies could work to suggest empire as a historical burden for the British that had mercifully been lifted or as a blessing bestowed on people who were naturally disposed to the violence that erupted once the British departed. In either case they represented decolonization as a disaster for former colonies.

I have argued here that the image of a domestic sanctuary, threatened with violation, signifies loss of imperial power. Despite his dismissal of the empire as a 'myth,' Powell's 'Rivers of Blood' speech demonstrates the continuing importance of empire in imaginings of Englishness and, as this chapter has demonstrated, draws on imagery that had gained wide currency in the British mainstream media in the post-1945 period. In its emphasis on domestic boundary markers—letter boxes, windows—the reworkings of England's frontiers are particularly apparent. This emphasis suggests how far the decline of British imperial power, and the collapse of Britain's imperial frontiers, prompted fears of a wider collapse, of boundaries between colonizers and colonized, black and white. Powell's 'quiet street,' like the English home of colonial war imagery and Nell's neat house front and privet hedge in *Flame in the Streets*, is a place where a white woman guards boundaries. The emphasis on women suggests how far frontiers were re-imagined in terms of domestic space and national vulnerability. The domestication of the frontier in this imagery deprives frontiers of associations with expansiveness and enterprise, and virile and active masculinity.

The image of a threatened domestic sanctuary, however, not only suggests the fear of collapse of boundaries, signifying loss of imperial power, but also works to deny the notion of collapse. Its emphasis on domestic order affirms Englishness as stable and rooted—an image rein forced by disruptions of that order by 'terrorists' in empire and 'immigrants' at home. As the English home and family are constructed as symbols of that order, against black as a male category, dissociated from family or domesticity, a national identity is invoked that is intimate, private, exclusive, white—Englishness not Britishness. This version of Englishness shows an England that is threatened by empire and its legacy.

But at the same time it provides reassurance that boundaries cannot be breached, since England itself is imagined as a domestic sanctuary, against empire and former empire. There is no longer 'the empire too,' but there will 'always be an England.'

Notes

1   *Daily Mail*, 26 January 1953.
2   See esp. Paul Gilroy, *'There Ain't No Black in the Union Jack': The Cultural Politics of Race and Nation* (London, 1987); Bill Schwarz, 'The Only White Man in There: The Re-racialisation of England, 1956–1968,' *Race and Class*, 1996, 38, 65–78; Chris Waters, 'Dark Strangers in Our Midst: Discourses of Race and Nation in Britain, 1947–1963,' *Journal of British Studies*, 1997, 36, 207–38; Kathleen Paul, *Whitewashing Britain: Race and Citizenship in the Postwar Era* (Ithaca, NY, 1997); Wendy Webster, *Imagining Home: Gender, 'Race' and National Identity, 1945–64* (London, 1998).
3   Waters '"Dark Strangers" in Our Midst,' 208.
4   Quoted in Martin Wiener, *English Culture and the Decline of the Industrial Spirit, 1850–1980* (Cambridge, 1981) 60.
5   Alison Light, *Forever England: Femininity, Literature and Conservatism between the Wars* (London, 1991).
6   Waters '"Dark Strangers" in Our Midst,' 208.
7   Bill Schwarz, 'The Only White Man in There, Black Metropolis, White England,' in *Modern Times: Reflections on a Century of English Modernity*, Mica Nava and Alan O'Shea (eds) (London, 1996) 182–207, and 'Reveries of Race: The Closing of the Imperial Moment,' in *Moments of Modernity: Reconstructing Britain, 1945–1964*, Becky Conekin, Frank Mort, and Chris Waters (eds) (London, 1999) 189–207.
8   Schwarz 'The Only White Man in There,' 73.
9   Lynn Segal, 'Look Back in Anger: Men in the Fifties,' in *Male Order: Unwrapping Masculinity*, Rowena Chapman and Jonathan Rutherford (eds) (London, 1988) 68–96; Alan Sinfield, *Literature, Politics and Culture in Postwar Britain* (Oxford, 1989); Sheila Jeffreys, *Anticlimax: A Feminist Perspective on the Sexual Revolution* (London, 1990); Chris Waters, 'Disorders of the Mind, Disorders of the Body Social: Peter Wildeblood and the Making of the Modern Homosexual,' in *Moments of Modernity*, Conekin, Mort, and Waters (eds), 134–51.
10   John Hill, 'Working-Class Realism and Sexual Reaction: Some Theses on the British New Wave,' in *British Cinema History*, (eds) James Curran and Vincent Porter (London, 1983) 303–11, and *Sex, Class and Realism: British Cinema, 1956–1963* (London, 1986); Micheline Wandor, *Look Back in Gender: Sexuality and the Family in Postwar British Drama* (London, 1987); Terry Lovell, 'Landscapes and Stones in 1960s British Realism,' *Screen*, 1990, 31, 357–76.
11   But see Richard Dyer, *White* (London, 1997) esp. 184–206; Webster, *Imagining Home*.
12   Schwarz 'The Only White Man in There,' 65.
13   Gayatri Spivak, *Outside in the Teaching Machine* (New York, 1993) 226.
14   Benedict Anderson, *Imagined Communities: Reflections on the Origin and Spread of Nationalism* (London, 1983).
15   James Ryan, *Picturing Empire: Photography and the Visualisation of the British Empire* (London, 1997).
16   Bill Schwarz, 'Politics and Rhetoric in the Age of Mass Culture,' *History Workshop Journal*, 1998, 46, 139.
17   For a discussion of this imagery, see Graham Dawson, *Soldier Heroes: British Adventure, Empire and the Imagining of Masculinities* (London, 1994) esp. 58–76.
18   *Two Thousand Women* (Frank Launder, 1944); *The Captive Heart* (Basil Dearden, 1946).
19   Jeffrey Richards, *Films and British National Identity: From Dickens to Dad's Army* (Manchester, 1997) 97–104. Richards records that *This England* (1941) was retitled *Our Heritage* for its Scottish release, 97.

20   *Millions Like Us* (Frank Launder and Sidney Gilliat, 1943); *The Gentle Sex* (Leslie Howard and Maurice Elvey, 1943); *A Canterbury Tale* (Michael Powell and Emeric Pressburger, 1944). For a discussion of the image of the mobile woman in wartime British cinema, see Antonia Lant, *Blackout: Reinventing Women for Wartime British Cinema* (Princeton, NJ. 1991) esp. ch. 2.

21   *Diary for Timothy* (Humphrey Jennings, 1945).

22   In *Frieda* (Basil Dearden, 1947), return is represented as more problematic. In this film, a peaceful rural English home and community is disrupted by the return of fighter pilot Bob Dawson (David Farrer) accompanied by the German nurse Frieda (Mai Zetterling) who has helped him to escape. But the film resolves the problem posed by Frieda's presence as she is shown increasingly accepted and incorporated into the community, reinforcing the idea of English tolerance.

23   Landy, *British Genres: Cinema and Society, 1930–1960* (Princeton, NJ, 1991) 178.

24   *Odette* (Herbert Wilcox, 1950); *Carve Her Name with Pride* (Lewis Gilbert, 1958).

25   John Ramsden, 'Refocusing the People's War: British War Films of the 1950s,' *Journal of Contemporary History*, 1998, 33, 57.

26   Landy, *British Genres*, 176.

27   Andy Medhurst, '1950s War Films,' in *National Fictions*, Geoff Hurd (ed.) (London, 1984) 35–9; Nicholas Pronay, 'The British Post-bellum Cinema: A Survey of the Films Relating to World War II Made in Britain between 1945 and 1960,' *Historical Journal of Film, Radio and Television*, 1988, 8, 39–54; Neil Rattigan, 'The Last Gasp of the Middle Class: British War Films of the 1950s,' in *Reviewing British Cinema, 1900–1992*, Wheeler Dixon (ed.) (New York, 1994) 143–52; Ramsden, 'Refocusing The People's War.' Ramsden notes a dearth of studies of British postwar films about the war of 1939 to 1945, by comparison with films made during the war.

28   *The Planter's Wife* (Ken Annakin, 1952); *Simba* (Brian Desmond Hurst, 1955). There is discussion of *Simba* in Richard Dyer, 'White,' *Screen*, 1988, 29, 44–64; Webster, *Imagining Home*, 52–5.

29   See Susan Carruthers, *Winning Hearts and Minds: British Governments, the Media and Colonial Counter-Insurgency, 1944–1960* (London, 1995) 167–8.

30   ibid. p. 112.

31   See Andrew Spicer, 'Male Stars, Masculinity and British Cinema, 1945–1960,' in *The British Cinema Book*, Robert Murphy (ed.) (London, 1997) 144–53. Dirk Bogarde also starred in *The High Bright Sun* (Ralph Thomas, 1965), a colonial war film, set in Cyprus. *The Planter's Wife* was one of Rank's biggest box-office successes in 1952. See Vincent Porter, 'Methodism versus the Market Place: The Rank Organisation and British Cinema,' in *The British Cinema Book*, Murphy (ed.) 126.

32   *The Drum* (Zoltan Korda, 1938). There are discussions of pre-1939 imperial films in Jeffrey Richards, 'Boy's Own Empire: Feature Films and Imperialism in the 1930s,' in *Imperialism and Popular Culture*, John MacKenzie (ed.)(Manchester, 1986) 140–64; Landy, *British Genres*, 101–10; Lola Young, *Fear of the Dark, Race, Gender and Sexuality in the Cinema* (London, 1996) 55–83; Richards, *Films and British National Identity*, 31–81

33   *Daily Mail*,16 August 1948.

34   *Daily Mail*, January 1953.

35   *Daily Express*, 7 January 1953.

36   *Daily Express*, 24 November 1952.

37   *Daily Express*, 7 January 1953.

38   John Newsinger, 'The Military Memoir in British Imperial Culture: The Case of Malaya,' *Race and Class*, 1994, 35, 48.

39   *Daily Express*, 3 January 1953; *Daily Express*, 26 January 1952.

40   *Guns at Batasi*, John Guillermin, 1964.

41   See Webster, *Imagining Home*, ch. 4.

42   *The Times*, 19 September 1952.

43   Pronay 'The British Post-bellum Cinema,' 39.

44   *The Ship That Died of Shame* (Basil Dearden, 1955).

45   Quoted in Steve Cohen, 'Anti-semitism, Immigration Controls and the Welfare State,' *Critical Social Policy*, 1985, 13, 74.

46   Light, *Forever England*, esp.1–19.

47   ibid. p. 8.

48   J.B. Priestley, *Postscripts* (London, 1940) 1–4.

49   This image had particular currency in Hollywood 'British' empire films, such as *Gunga Din* (George Stevens, 1939), which focused on the northwest frontier and the soldier hero. It was also a common image in British imperial films such as *The Drum*.

50   *Daily Express*, 5 January 1953.

51   E.g. *Daily Express*, 5 January 1953; *Daily Mail*, 5 January 1953; *Illustrated London News*, 17 January 1953.

52   E.g. Sheila Patterson, *Dark Strangers: A Sociological Study of the Absorption of a Recent West Indian Migrant Group in Brixton, South London* (London, 1963) 198–9.

53   *Daily Express*, 7 January 1953.

54   *Daily Mail*, 5 January 1953. Some newspapers reported that Raynes-Simson was South African, but this did not disrupt the connections made between images of a peaceful home and garden and Englishness.

55   Patterson, *Dark Strangers*, 198–9.

56   Elsbeth Huxley, *Back Street New Worlds: A Look at Immigrants in Britain* (London, 1964) 46–7.

57   For a discussion of the way this image was deployed in representations of the Indian Rebellion of 1857, see Dawson, *Soldier Heroes*, 91.

58   Dyer 'White,' 49.

59   A newspaper headline in 1906— 'tainting the race'—referred to the employment of Chinese seamen and resulting settlement of Chinese communities in London and other ports, and spoke of the results of interracial mixing between Chinese men and English women as 'swarms of half-bred children to be seen in the district.' See John Gabriel, *Whitewash: Racialized Politics and the Media* (London, 1998) 58. The chief constable of Cardiff's proposal of a legal ban on 'miscegenation' in 1929 referred to the employment of African and Indian seamen, and resulting settlement in ports such as Cardiff and Liverpool. See Paul Rich, *Race and Empire in British Politics* (Cambridge, 1990) 130. Although interracial sex was never made illegal, fears of 'tainting the race' were extended during the Second World War as black British and American soldiers served in Britain. See Marika Sherwood, *Many Struggles: West Indian Workers and Service Personnel in Britain* (London, 1985); Ben Bousquet and Cohn Douglas, *West Indian Women at War: British Racism in World War II* (London, 1991); Sonya Rose, 'Sex, Citizenship, and the Nation in World War II Britain,' *American Historical Review*, 1998, 103, 1147–76.

60   Trevor Philpott, 'Would You Let Your Daughter Many a Negro?' *Picture Post*, 30 October 1954; Colin Machines, 'A Short Guide for Jumbles to the Life of Their Coloured Brethren in England,' in his *England: Half English* (London, 1961) 25 (originally published in 1956); *Daily Express*, 18 July 1956.

61   *Flame in the Streets* (Roy Baker, 1961). This film is discussed in Young, *Fear of the Dark*, ch. 4; Webster, *Imagining Home*, ch. 3.

62   *The Times*, 19 September 1952.

63   For discussion of this imagery see Ann Stoler, *Race and the Education of Desire: Foucault's History of Sexuality and the Colonial Order of Things* (Durham, NC, 1995) ch. 4.

64   See Anne McClintock, *Imperial Leather: Race, Gender and Sexuality in the Colonial Contest* (London, 1995) 118–22.

65   Patterson, *Dark Strangers*, 98; Huxley, *Back Street*, 47. While Patterson calls 'our ways' those of 'residents,' Huxley calls them those of 'Brixtonians.'

66   Quoted in Stoler, *Race and the Education of Desire*, 128. For a discussion of this imagery, see Ian Baucom, *Out of Place: Englishness, Empire and the Locations of Identity* (Princeton, NJ, 1999) 55–62.

67 *Pool of London* (Basil Dearden, 1950); *A Taste of Honey* (Tony Richardson, 1961).

68 *The Sunday Times*, 6 November 1966.

69 Schwarz, 'The Only White Man In There.'

70 Enoch Powell, 'Myth and Reality,' in *Freedom and Reality*, John Wood (ed.) (London, 1969) 243.

71 Quoted in Simon Heffer, *Like the Roman: The Life of Enoch Powell* (London, 1998) 115.

72 Quoted in Humphrey Berkeley, *The Odyssey of Enoch: A Political Memoir* (London, 1977) 52; Heifer, *Like the Roman*, 169.

73 Enoch Powell, 'Myth and Reality,' 245–50.

74 ibid. p. 255.

75 Enoch Powell, 'Immigration,' in Wood (ed.) *Freedom and Reality*, 213–19.

Chapter 21

Andrew S. Thompson

THE LANGUAGE OF IMPERIALISM
AND THE MEANINGS OF EMPIRE

Another historian who has made a huge contribution to thinking about how empire helped shape 'domestic' British politics and culture is Andrew Thompson. Here he inspects how Fabians and Conservatives thought about empire, and sought to bring their ideas to a wider public, around the turn of the 19th–20th centuries. We have had to exclude much of Thompson's equally fascinating discussion of Liberal attitudes in the same article.

Stephen Howe

The forthcoming General Election will turn, we are told, mainly on the popularity of Imperialism. If this be so, it is important that voters should make up their minds what Imperialism means.[1]

George Bernard Shaw

THUS WROTE GEORGE BERNARD SHAW on behalf of the Fabian Society in October 1900. Shaw recognized what many historians have subsequently failed to see: the meaning of imperialism inside British politics was not fixed.[2] Rather, the terms 'empire' and 'imperialism' were like empty boxes that were continuously being filled up and emptied of their meanings.[3] Of course, the same was true of other political concepts: the idea of patriotism, for instance, was constantly being reinvented by politicians.[4] But the idea of empire was all the more vulnerable to this sort of treatment because it was sensitive to changing circumstances at home and abroad and because it had to take account of a colonial as well as a British audience. Furthermore, the fact that opinion in Britain was widely felt to be ignorant or indifferent to the empire meant that politicians had to be particularly careful in deciding what sort of imperial language to use.

This chapter will consider what contemporaries meant when they spoke of empire, how its meaning varied between different political groups in Britain, and whether it is possible to point to a prevailing vision of empire during the period between the launch of the Jameson Raid in December 1895 and the outbreak of the Great War in 1914. It will discuss these issues with reference to the activities of the imperial lobbies and pressure groups that proliferated during the late Victorian and Edwardian period.[5] Many of these organizations were intent on constructing a national political agenda around the empire, and hence it was often in an extraparliamentary context that issues of imperial politics were most openly and vigorously debated. In their determination to reach a wider public, imperial lobbies and pressure groups made use of a variety of media, including the platform and periodical press, mass pamphleting and leafleting, lantern lectures and cinematographs, musical evenings, garden parties, and plays.[6]

The significance of these organizations is further underlined by their close relationships with the political parties. The emergence of a number of pressure groups on the right of British politics in the late nineteenth and early twentieth centuries was linked to imperial debates within the Conservative party. For example, a group such as the Imperial South Africa Association (ISAA), which was quasi-governmental, saw its role as the mobilization of public opinion in Britain behind the South African policy of Joseph Chamberlain and Alfred Milner. In contrast, a group such as the Navy League was more critical of the Conservative leadership, which was thought to have failed to respond to the threats to Britain's position as a world power. The League was formed in 1894 and projected itself as a nonparty organization, but the configuration of its parliamentary and executive committees was unmistakably skewed toward the Conservative party. It aimed to promote the command of the sea as the primary object of national policy and to preserve the maritime supremacy of the empire. The ISAA spoke for a Conservative elite, while the propaganda of the Navy League was broadly representative of Conservatism in its more popular form.

There were also a number of groups on the left of British politics that addressed themselves to the question of Britain's responsibilities as an imperial power. Many of these organizations were either active in, or associated with, the National Liberal Federation (NLF), a body formed in 1877 to generate demands for radical policies and to incorporate single-group agitations into a nationwide political structure.[7] In view of the centrality of the NLF to extra-parliamentary Liberal politics,[8] it is important to pay some attention to the proceedings of its annual meetings, particularly during the Boer War, before examining the attitudes of two of the pressure groups connected to it. The organizations to be considered are the Increased Armaments Protest Committee (IAPC), formed in 1896 to protest against increasing expenditure on the navy, and the British Committee of the Indian National Congress (BCINC), formed in 1889 to advance the cause of Indian reform in Parliament. The NLF, IAPC, and BCINC expressed the views of Radical Liberals toward the empire.[9]

Another group on the left of British politics that was forced to define its position toward the empire during this period was the Fabian Society. The political alignment of the Fabian Society was more ambiguous than that of the organizations mentioned above. Notwithstanding their decision to affiliate with the Labour Representation Committee, middle-class Fabians could not agree on whether the best hope of political influence lay in 'permeating' the Liberal party or supporting independent Labour politics.[10] This dilemma was raised most painfully during the Boer War when a number of Fabians who belonged to the Independent Labour party, some of whom were also active in the pro-Boer movement, resigned over the society's refusal to make a public pronouncement against British intervention in the Transvaal. Meanwhile the rest of the society turned to Lord Rosebery and the Liberal Imperialists as the 'most likely potential executors of their domestic programme.[11] The views of imperially minded Fabians are considered below, and finally the views of three Fabians who were more critical of British imperial policy—John Clifford, Sydney Olivier, and Ramsay MacDonald—are referred to in the examination of Radical Liberalism. This first section also discusses the ideas of the economist and publicist J.A. Hobson and the writer and politician J.M. Robertson, both of whom were major contributors to Radical Liberal thinking about the empire, especially through their journalism.[12] Although Hobson and Robertson did not actively participate in the IAPC or BCINC—Robertson sometimes spoke at meetings of the latter—they were members of a small progressive community in London, centered around the Rainbow Circle and thus moved in the same political circles as many of the Radical Liberals who did participate in them.[13]

Before exploring the contribution of these extraparliamentary organizations to imperial discourse in the period from 1895 to 1914, some preliminary remarks are necessary. First of all, it is important to remember that when people thought about empire they were trying to make sense of a diverse collection of colonies, acquired for a wide range of reasons, and governed in significantly different ways. The empire was not a single entity, and the very term was in some sense delusive. Moreover, when contemporaries wrote or spoke about empire, they were not usually contemplating it in a detached fashion. More likely, they were involved in concrete political battles, the outcome of which turned on such rhetorical struggles. Hence language was very much a part of the political process, and the meaning of words such as 'empire' and 'imperialism' was continually being contested both between and within the Liberal and Conservative parties.

Second, as far as the meaning of empire is concerned, the Boer War was clearly an event of considerable importance. Events in South Africa touched the British population in a way it is now difficult to appreciate, so much so that some have made comparisons between this conflict and that of America in Vietnam: both wars had significant domestic consequences.[14] Perhaps the most lasting effect of the Boer War was to stifle the so-called new imperialism of the 1890s. After the turn of the century nobody seems seriously to have advocated that the empire grow any bigger. Indeed, it seemed pointless to contemplate further conquest and expansion when the British army had been barely adequate to the task of bringing a small community of Dutch farmers to heel. In the light of the military weaknesses exposed during the war, therefore, the problem facing imperialists was understood to be one of consolidation. Somehow the empire had to be reorganized so that it could continue to compete with states such as Germany and America that had huge resource bases and growing populations. Many believed that the way forward lay in drawing the self-governing Dominions closer to Britain in order to augment its strength. And the imperial sentiment displayed by Canadian and Australian troops in South Africa afforded a striking example of such cooperation, suggesting that the time might be ripe for some form of imperial federation.

The tendency to regard Anglo-Dominion relations as the key to imperial problems was not without its consequences for other areas of the empire, particularly India. In the aftermath of the Boer War, imperialists of the Curzon school, as well as many critics of the Raj, pleaded for a proper appreciation of India's place in the imperial system and warned of the dangers of a misplaced emphasis on the Dominions.[15] George Curzon complained that India's participation in the war effort had been ignored and that discussions about the empire were increasingly being conducted without reference to its largest and most powerful unit. Radical Liberals, meanwhile, spoke out against the racial ideal of empire manifest during the war, believing that it threatened to unite in opposition all of those colonies which fell outside its scope.[16] Events in South Africa were therefore relevant to other areas of the empire, for in raising the profile of the Dominions, they also marginalized India and Britain's other tropical colonies in imperial debate.

Finally, the Boer War affected public sentiment toward the empire. The blanket of public enthusiasm that had enveloped Britain's imperial enterprise during the 1890s was torn away during the latter stages of the conflict, with the result that it was no longer possible to assume that the empire commanded widespread support. It is now necessary to examine more closely the impact of the different stages of the war on the idea of empire and the changing meanings of imperialism between 1895 and 1914.

The Conservative vision of empire, intended to justify the decision of the government to go to war with the Transvaal in December 1899, was expressed by the ISAA, which declared its intention to uphold British supremacy in South Africa and to promote the interests of British subjects in the region.[17] It was in close touch with organizations in South Africa that defended the interests of the British community there, and its aim was to keep a united South Africa inside the British empire and out of the hands of rival powers, particularly Germany. The organization had close links with the government, and its defense of British policy mirrored that of Chamberlain and Milner, who attempted to concentrate the public gaze on the political grievances of the Uitlanders, thereby giving effect to 'the sentiment of kinship . . . which I believe is deep in the heart of every Briton.'[18]

The Uitlanders were a community of predominantly British immigrants who moved into the Transvaal in the years following the gold discoveries of the 1880s but who did not enjoy the franchise.[19] That Chamberlain presented the situation in South Africa in this way is perhaps not surprising. As early as 1886, his opposition to Irish home rule was developing along such lines. Insisting that Ireland was not a homogeneous community, and that it consisted of two separate races and religions, Chamberlain protested that Gladstone's proposals failed to protect the interests of Irish Protestants.[20] Similarly, Chamberlain and Milner correctly judged the issue of the Uitlander franchise to be the safest way to put the question of British supremacy in South Africa onto the political agenda since it avoided polluting the debate on the war with discussions of 'Randlordism' and the matter of the mining industry.

Likewise, it was the self-proclaimed object of the ISAA to promote the interests of British subjects in South Africa. George Wyndham, the first chairman of the association, wrote to Milner in the months preceding the outbreak of war discussing its work in these terms, arguing that it was a matter of getting MPs and public alike to see South Africa as a question of British supremacy.[21] Wyndham described the Uitlander petition of March 1899 as 'a very proper mode of expression for a very natural and proper feeling,' but stressed how it had to be repeated again and again if the Uitlanders were to be believed.[22] The ISAA organized a series of meetings as a response to the petition, urging the government to take up the Uitlanders' case. By May, Wyndham was confident enough to inform Milner that nothing short of the franchise would satisfy the people back home.[23] Geoffrey Drage, Wyndham's successor as chairman, also focused his attention on the Uitlander question. In a speech in Derby following the outbreak of war, Drage told his audience that its immediate cause had been the grievances of the Uitlanders and the determination of the British government to obtain redress for them.[24]

The policies advocated by the ISAA were designed to support and strengthen the British population in the Transvaal and the Orange Free State, particularly its land settlement schemes. The ISAA believed that it was the inherent right of the British to send settlers to its colonies, especially those acquired at considerable cost, and it attempted to settle immigrants in the countryside as well as the towns.[25] Milner often stressed that what concerned him most was the land question and the predominance of the Dutch in agricultural terms.[26] The ISAA responded by forming a Land Settlement Committee, which organized a scheme of rural emigration to the Orange River Colony (O.R.C.)[27] and also worked closely with a number of voluntary emigration societies.[28]

The purpose of the ISAA was to persuade the electorate to identify with the interests of British subjects in South Africa. The association's propaganda repeatedly emphasized that the Uitlanders were 'fellow countrymen' and 'our own people' and that it was 'British supremacy' and the plight of 'British citizens' that were at stake. The vision of empire this entailed was one of settler colonies—British communities transplanted abroad. It rests uneasily with Hugh Cunningham's claim that Conservatives failed to devise a language of patriotism that was both English and imperial, and thus 'Englishness' dominated.[29] This is a misunderstanding. The Conservative vision of empire, as expounded by the ISAA, was essentially a British one.[30] That is not to say that a sense of Britishness supplanted all other political loyalties or that Britain emerged in this period as a blending of the different national cultures which composed the English-speaking empire. Both Celtic and colonial identities were asserted within an imperial framework.[31] Nevertheless, when set in a wider imperial context, it was the similarities rather than the differences between the different parts of the English-speaking empire that were more striking. As Linda Colley has argued, we should not underestimate the effect of the outside world, as Britons experienced and imagined it, on national identity: 'we usually decide who we are by reference to who and what we are not.[32]

Even the monarchy, which Cunningham cites as evidence that late nineteenth-century patriotism was primarily English, was arguably a symbol of both nation and empire in this period. At the 1897 Diamond Jubilee, for example, it was the onward march of empire that epitomized the progress experienced under Victoria's reign. Contemporaries emphasized how the occasion was celebrated all over the world by 'Britishers' and pointed to the representation of imperial troops from every part of the empire at the ceremony in London.[33] No doubt there were different languages of patriotism, just as there were different languages of empire. But the language of imperialism articulated by Chamberlain, Milner, and the ISAA was the 'lingua franca' of public debate during and after the Boer War, and as Cunningham acknowledges, by the 1890s it was difficult to separate patriotism and imperialism.

For a while, the Conservative vision of empire, expressed by the ISAA, enjoyed some success. In the general election of October 1900, the Unionists won a 134 seat majority. It is hard to believe that this is not partly to be explained by the propaganda of the right after the Jameson Raid and the careful timing of polling day to coincide with the wave of imperial patriotism that appears to have swept the country in the summer of that year. However, the imperial propaganda of the ISAA, and the right more generally, proved too limited and failed to answer a number of questions raised by the poor performance of the British army on the South African veldt. As A.P. Thornton observes, 'It cost the country £250 million to subdue a Boer male population which did not outnumber that of Brighton, and to deal with them conclusively we were forced to employ 400,000 troops.'[34] Precisely the same point was made by the manifesto *Fabianism and the Empire*, prepared during the summer months of 1900 and written in the belief that after the relief of Kimberley, Ladysmith, and Mafeking, the public mood was changing. The status of the Fabian Society was largely derived from the quality of such publications, which played an important role in publicizing the organization and familiarizing an educated public with the arguments for Fabian collectivism.[35] Although imperialism had been debated among Fabians during the Diamond Jubilee in 1897, it was not until 1899 that the Society decided to publish a manifesto on the subject. The manifesto observed that 'the brief days of window-breaking and hat-blocking, exhilarating to our selves, but unspeakably ridiculous to the European spectator, have passed; and we are now asking ourselves . . . Are we a nation of Fools?'[36] As earlier euphoria subsided, attention turned to why the army of an imperial power had suffered a series of disastrous defeats at the hands of the Boer peasant farmer during the 'black week' of December 1899. Was this symptomatic of a wider decay and decline? If so, what could be done to reverse it? New concerns had emerged among the British public which the vision of empire developed by Conservatives during the war did not address. It was in this atmosphere that the Fabian Society saw an opportunity to break a near Conservative monopoly over imperial propaganda.

Shaw's bid for the language of imperialism required a delicate balancing act. On the one hand, he argued that 'the word was entitled to have a most favourable construction and it was idle to force a base interpretation and lavish virtuous indignation on it.'[37] Behind this argument lay the belief that the Boer War had catapulted imperialism to the top of the political agenda and that it was impossible for the Fabian Society to conduct an election campaign without reference to it. On the other hand, Shaw claimed for the society and 'the stream of tendency it represents' the invention of imperialism 'in its best sense.' Shaw thought that the best chance for 'khaki' at the election was not its own popularity but the absence of any alternative: it was incumbent on Fabians to provide the electorate with such an alternative.

This was first presented by Shaw in a lecture to Fabians in February 1900, reported by the *Daily Chronicle* in an article entitled 'Sane Imperialism. As defined by Mr. G. Bernard Shaw.'[38] Shaw claimed that the principal danger to empire did not come from an external attack but from mismanagement within, as exemplified during the war when Britain had failed to bring the mines into public ownership and deferred to the wishes of speculators and financiers. The manifesto claimed that Britain was becoming parasitic on her colonies and living unproductively on foreign labor and predicted that if this state of affairs persisted the British empire would follow in the footsteps of Rome. From this diagnosis sprang the following prescription: vital reforms at home and the insistence that civilization as well as trade must follow the flag abroad.

In attempting to redefine the idea of empire, Shaw was forced to fight a war on two fronts. He wanted to wrest the language of imperialism from the hands of Conservatives and to cement an alliance with the Liberal Imperialists on a platform of social imperialism— a policy that promised to combine a patriotic approach to imperial affairs, entrusted to an expert imperial ruling elite, with a limited measure of welfare collectivism.[39] It was hoped that, with the encouragement and assistance of Richard Haldane, the Fabian Society might elaborate the domestic side of this program for the Liberal Imperialist group. But to achieve this the Liberal League would have to out-maneuver the Liberal Forwards, an organization formed in 1896 to act as a mouthpiece for the Radical section of the Liberal party on foreign and imperial questions.[40] Shaw sought to discredit what Fabians saw as the old, decaying vision of Liberalism propounded by Gladstonians, maintaining that these Liberals 'still cling to the fixed-frontier ideals of an individualist republicanism, non-interference, and nationalism, long since demonstrated to be inapplicable to our present situation.'[41] However, it is clear that Shaw's predatory view of international affairs was also influenced by Social Darwinist thinking and in particular the ideas of Benjamin Kidd. In a lecture to the Fabian Society in May 1904, Kidd argued that the 'Old World' conditions were ending and that nations must now organize themselves on a larger scale. 'Efficient' nations, Kidd submitted, were entirely justified in overriding the territorial claims of a backward people. Shaw accepted the broad thrust of Kidd' s 'external social Darwinism' and likewise pictured the world as being divided into explicitly hostile communities, only the most competitive of which would survive.[42] In the words of the manifesto, 'the world is to the big and powerful by necessity and the little ones must come within their borders or be crushed out of existence.'[43] At the same time, Fabians were ambivalent toward the specifically eugenicist implications of Social Darwinism drawn out by Karl Pearson and Francis Galton. This was because most members of the society understood environment rather than heredity to be of greatest significance in determining individual characteristics. For instance, despite his concern about the declining birth rate among the 'abler' classes, Sidney Webb's rhetoric of social efficiency was intended to advance the concept of a 'National Minimum' '—a countrywide standard of living below which the government should allow no citizen to fall—and not to point the way to a program of eugenicist legislation which would discourage the reproduction of the 'unfit' and thereby prevent racial deterioration.[44]

There is evidence that Shaw's notion of 'sane imperialism' found much sympathy in the Fabian Society. In March 1900 a self-confessed Little Englander, H.W. Paul, lectured to the society and was apparently received like a 'Daniel among lions.' Paul spoke against the Imperialist section of the Liberal party and in support of Richard Cobden, John Bright, and William Gladstone. Fabians were not impressed with the 'antique' version of Liberalism they were offered from this 'early Victorian,' 'young in years but wonderfully ancient in ideas.'[45] Yet the Fabian vision of empire offered by Shaw was held to ridicule by other elements of the Labour movement. The weekly New Age, which was best known for its literary and artistic commentary but also took an interest in Labour policy on foreign and imperial affairs, took delight in observing how the smooth waters of Fabianism had recently been troubled by modest storms. It argued that the Fabian was a 'Socialist who was not really a Socialist . . . but presumably something else, possibly an Imperialist, a Jingo.'[46] Shaw's word games had clearly cut no ice with the paper, but what impact, if any, did the idea of 'sane imperialism' have elsewhere?

In the short term the notion of 'sane imperialism' did not catch on. Why was this? No doubt it owed much to the fact that the manifesto was seen for what it partly was: a piece of naked political opportunism. The manifesto was obviously aimed at the general election and attempted to promote Fabian policies under the pretence that they were relevant to the empire. The rest of the Labour movement strongly criticized the Fabian leadership for trying to tie its domestic program to imperialist concerns. Leo Amery, a cofounder of the Oxford branch of the Fabian Society, explained the problem in his autobiography when he described the Webbs as:

an indefatigable pair . . . more concerned with getting their ideas of the welfare state put into practice by anyone who might be prepared to help, even on the most modest scale, than with the early triumph of an avowedly Socialist Party.[47]

As far as the Fabians' middle-class audience was concerned, the manifesto was in all probability premature. In the autumn of 1900 Milner warned Chamberlain that the public mood was in the process of turning: 'If the present discouraging phase of the war had been realised at home—I cannot help but feel it would have had a mischievous effect on public opinion.'[48] Milner's fears were well-founded. During the summer months of 1901, as news of the military camps filtered back to England—particularly through the reports and later the addresses of Emily Hobhouse—the public became impatient with a war that showed little prospect of ending. It was not until 1902, however, that this shift in popular opinion was anything like complete. This difficulty was acknowledged by the manifesto itself, which in practice was not all that critical of the present state of imperial policy and which failed to offer a radically different alternative. In fact, there was a conscious decision not to follow such a course because it was recognized that the public was unlikely to be sympathetic. In October 1899 the Fabian Publishing Committee recommended the society publish a tract sketching the outlines of a 'true' imperialism. This tract was to be a wide-ranging inquiry into the compatibility of imperial expansion and Liberal principles, and the influence of capitalism on empire.[49] A week later, however, the Fabian executive decided to withdraw the report of the Publishing Committee.[50] It was also unlikely that Fabian ideas would enjoy popular appeal. Fabian propaganda was aimed at an educated, middle-class public. It sought to persuade by reason rather than polemics. This restricted its circulation, and the manifesto probably sold no more than two thousand copies.[51]

By whom might the idea of 'sane imperialism' have been embraced? Clearly, the notion of the inevitability of imperial expansion was repugnant to a majority of Radicals. At the other end of the political spectrum, many Conservatives and Liberal Unionists were dismissive of Fabian measures of social reform. Moreover, tariff reform was a stumbling block to cooperation with many such politicians, and Fabian criticisms of the government during the war were unlikely to ingratiate the society with the right. This left the Liberal Imperialists. In February 1902, Beatrice Webb commented that 'we are at present very thick with the Limps,' while Sidney Webb had recently become a member of the Literature Committee of the Liberal League.[52] Unfortunately, this alliance was short-lived, and the prospect of Rosebery and company recasting the Liberal party as an imperial one was never more than remote.

The reluctance of the Liberal Imperialists to take up the domestic side of the social-imperialist program in which the Fabians had instructed it was revealed during debates on the Education Bill in 1902. The bill put denominational schools on the rates and thereby brought the voluntary sector under a degree of state control. Sidney Webb had stressed the need for such legislation in his tract *Twentieth Century Politics: A Policy of National Efficiency*.[53] The tract argued that Britain was not sufficiently organized to retain her status as a great power. Without a strong, healthy, and well-trained population, its author warned, the nation would not be equal to the demands of the empire. Various domestic reforms were then outlined, including improvements in public education. Thus the 1902 bill became something of an acid test for the viability of the Liberal Imperialist program. But Liberal Imperialists greatly under-estimated the opposition of grassroots Nonconformity to the bill. The Baptist leader, John Clifford, organized a campaign of nonpayment of rates, and Robert Perks, founder of the Nonconformist parliamentary committee and treasurer of the Liberal League, pressured Rosebery to withdraw his support. Rosebery capitulated. Evidently, it was sectional rather than national interests that had captured the Liberal party again, and it appeared unlikely that the Liberal Imperialists had the inclination or influence to push through the type of legislation advocated by Fabians.

The first line of defense for Conservatives was a traditional and predictable one, though nonetheless effective for that. It involved a renewed assault on the alleged unpatriotic tendencies of Radical Liberalism. The labels 'Little Englander,' 'pro-Boer,' and 'anti-imperialist' were some of the terms of abuse which Conservatives used to denigrate Radical attitudes to foreign and imperial policy. These charges remained an integral part of the Conservative bid for the language of imperialism precisely because they exposed the dilemma facing many Radicals from the 1890s: it was difficult for them to speak simultaneously the language of imperialism and the language of peace. For example, the apparent success of arbitration in resolving conflicts between Britain and America in Venezuela, first in 1895 and later in 1902, was contrasted with the Moroccan crises of 1905/6 and 1911, which confirmed to many Radicals that the deteriorating international situation was in no small part the result of colonial rivalries in Africa.

It is true that there were counter-currents. The apparent success of the grant of self-government to the Transvaal and O.R.C. was believed by Liberals to vindicate the party's commitment to an empire where power was devolved and government decentralized. After 1906, precedent suggested that liberalism might be reconciled with empire. However, a close study of Liberal speeches and writings on empire makes it clear that even if South Africa was a source of pride and Ireland one of hope, the party as a whole did not exploit these opportunities to project itself as an imperial one. Granted, the Liberal Imperialists attempted to project the party in this way, but the 'Limps' were something of a spent force by 1906 and never had a large following in the constituencies anyway. This being the case, there was little chance of them converting the rest of the party. It was the language of peace rather than imperialism that came instinctively to the lips of the parliamentary and constituency Liberal party during the Edwardian period:

> since the beginning of the twentieth century . . . a policy of peace and of moderation in armaments has become an outstanding mark of British Liberalism as against Conservatism.[54]

The second line of defense for Conservatives was to try to popularize the language of imperialism first fashioned by imperial federationists in the 1870s and 1880s and rehabilitated by those who defended Milner and Chamberlain's decision to go to war in 1899. This explains the strong continuity of approach in the imperial propaganda of the ISAA and the Navy League. The Navy League aimed to put pressure on government to maintain the two-power standard and to prevent the withdrawal of the fleet from the Mediterranean and Pacific waters. It was a populist pressure group with an extensive network of local branches, the largest of which were located in towns and cities with a strong naval heritage such as Bristol and Liverpool.[55] Like the ISAA, the Navy League developed a vision of empire to which the settler colonies were central and which largely ignored acquisitions made in tropical Africa. By focusing attention on the white Dominions, the Navy League hoped to revive the liberal and democratic ideal of empire, an ideal which appeared to have been lost sight of in military campaigns of the 1890s. For the

Dominions had successfully advanced to self-government under Britain's tutelage and were a place where, in the words of one Navy Leaguer, men were 'born free,' to be contrasted with the German empire where 'everything was by rule.'[56] Following a tour around the Dominions, the Navy League's colonial envoy, Harold Wyatt, spoke of how 'the whole British people throughout the world constitute a great democracy.'[57]

The question of empire played a central role in the Navy League's propaganda, and the league assumed that invoking empire was a good way to extend support among the working classes. At the same time, Navy Leaguers did not take the popularity of empire for granted and often complained that working men tended not to look beyond their own immediate, material interests. Although it was possible to appeal to such interests by relating naval supremacy to the question of food supply and popular living standards, thereby stressing the commercial as well as strategic benefits of naval supremacy, the Navy League saw that it was inevitable that social reforms would eventually come into conflict with the defense budget, and it was right. In the spring of 1908, Asquith announced the government's intention to introduce old age pensions as the first major measure of social reform, and a crisis erupted in the Liberal cabinet in the winter of 1908/9 over the naval estimates for the following year.

Unlike other imperialist organizations, the Navy League did not try to establish a link between empire and social reform. It separated the problems of domestic and imperial reconstruction and appealed more directly to the imperial sentiment of the working classes in an attempt to broaden their political perspectives. As Robert Yerburgh remarked:

> Within a short span the ignorance of our own democracy might destroy our empire, which it has taken a thousand years to build up. Their horizon is limited, their views are short. We have to teach them to take longer views.[58]

HTC Knox put the problem more pithily when he described it as the 'parish pump' mentality. Thus the League tried to change the perspective of the working man.[59] Like the ISAA, it believed that by the skilful use of political propaganda it was possible to influence not only the way electors thought about particular issues but their collective political belongings too. As Sir John Colomb exhorted those attending the annual dinner in 1905, 'every citizen must no longer think merely in terms of his own hearth or shore but must survey the empire to behold his home.'[60] It was the same Anglo-Saxon imperialism, which the ISAA had begun to reshape during the Boer War, which the Navy League saw as the key to changing the outlook of working-class voters.

Was the fashioning of an imperial identity really as deliberate and purposeful as this suggests? Certainly there are no minutes from the Navy League's literature and propaganda committees that discuss its strategy in such terms. Then again, such committees were largely concerned with more mundane matters, and it was unusual for them to take a long-term view. The company that the Navy League kept lends some weight to the argument. Its close connections with Lord Meath's Empire Day Movement and strong interest in imperial education in the schools indicate that it was aware of the advantage of laying the foundations of such an identity at an early age. But such evidence is no more than suggestive and is insufficient to support such an interpretation. It is not the testimony of Navy League propagandists that propels one to such a conclusion but the type of political language with which Navy Leaguers shaped imperial appeals. Recent work on nationalism has stressed how such identities are constructs.'[61] There is nothing inevitable about the emergence of these collective belongings; they are painstakingly and slowly established by language over a period of time.'[62] Language has been central to this process of getting people to envisage themselves as belonging to larger communities, and in the case of empire, language was particularly important since the vast majority of the population had never visited the colonies and had to experience them imaginatively. At the same time, the language of imperialism was rooted in a specific historical setting and was inseparable from the cut and thrust of political life.[63] In other words, language was not a completely autonomous domain; it was intrinsic to the question of what imperial propagandists were trying to do, and we must turn to politics to find out why they were trying to do it.

In his *Imagined Communities*, Benedict Anderson argued that 'if nation-states are widely conceded to be "new" and "historical," the nations to which they give political expression always loom out of an immemorial past, and, still more important, glide into a limitless future.'[64] As with nations, so with empires. The language of imperialism developed by the Navy League was highly charged with a sense of history and drew heavily on the notions of legacy and heritage that had been so central to the discourse of an earlier generation of Victorian imperialists. Empire was discussed in three tenses: past, present, and future. Speeches and articles sought to cultivate an awareness of Britain's imperial past, and the growth of the empire was associated with the great personalities of British history. Wyatt talked of how the foundations of empire had been laid under Elizabeth and Sir Francis Drake and how they had stood throughout the Napoleonic wars by the work of those such as Nelson.[65] Knox reminded an audience that they belonged 'to a large Empire, one hundred times the size of the island in which we live, won for us by other people to whom we should be grateful,' while referring to the Crimean War, the Indian Mutiny, and General Gordon as being instrumental in 'winning the Empire.'[66] Navy League propaganda also reminded audiences of their responsibilities to past and future generations: 'being only life renters we must hand it [the empire] on to our successors.'[67] The charter of the league stressed the importance of maintaining 'intact in territory, and untarnished in honour, the splendid inheritance received from our forefathers.'[68]

Racial awareness was another important component of this identity. The British were frequently referred to as an 'imperial race,' and racial ties with the Dominions were seen as a cornerstone of empire. The Navy League expressed the opinion that the affection of the 'British race' for its 'motherland' was an asset of 'incalculable value' in the continuity of imperial unity and goodwill,[69] and Knox praised the willingness of those 'Britons overseas' to rally behind the mother country in South Africa.[70] The League insisted that it was 'criminal folly' to palter over the spending of a few millions on the naval estimates when the stake was the 'great heritage received from our fathers, the Empire we have won and peopled, the land we love, and the welfare of the very race to which we belong.'[71]

This language also had an imperial purpose. As we have seen, after the Boer War the reorganization of the English-speaking empire had become a pressing concern. Even a pressure group such as the ISAA, whose attention was focused on a particular region of empire, had a Canadian Committee and took pride in the sound work it had done to build up unity of thought in the Dominions and United Kingdom.[72] The Navy League spoke a familial language of imperialism with this objective in mind. The concept of community was of central importance to this language, and its close association with imperial discourse can be traced back to at least the 1870s. The concept of community was in turn underpinned by the rhetoric of domesticity and gender, a rhetoric which came to enjoy a wider currency during the Edwardian period as the Tory appeal to notions of male identity was downplayed in favor of a less male-centered, and more domestically orientated, Conservatism, associated with organizations such as the Primrose League. Using the metaphor of the family, Navy Leaguers described the Dominions as 'sister nations' or 'daughter dominions' of the 'mother country,' which, with the help of their 'parent,' had grown up from 'childhood' through 'adolescence' to the 'maturity' of self-government. A branch secretary of the league recommended instructing the young in the 'practical and serious meaning of the word empire,' making them aware that 'the ships are going across the sea to their brothers and sisters whose fathers and mothers are out in other parts of the empire growing the material for their clothes, the corn for their bread.'[73] Such language suggested an imperial partnership whereby the Dominions would accept the lead of Britain in matters of defense and foreign policy, and Britain in return would be sensitive to the wishes of the Dominions and consult their opinion.

Of course, the Navy League was plugging into a fairly well established rhetoric, and I am not trying to suggest that it had anything particularly original to contribute to the form of this discourse. It borrowed unashamedly the idioms and metaphors of its Victorian predecessors, sustaining and popularizing a familial language of imperialism rather than shaping it in any distinctive way. Nevertheless, the Navy League was associated with an increasing politicization of imperial discourse from the late 1890s, and the vision of empire it espoused served to widen the rift between the white colonies and the dependencies, much to the chagrin of Indian reformers.[74]

What, if anything, is it possible to claim for the imperial propaganda of the ISAA and the Navy League? It is true that there were a number of extraparliamentary organizations operating on the fringes of the Conservative party between 1900 and 1914 and that these organizations may have preached different messages. Moreover, of course, propaganda mediated is not necessarily propaganda received. The question of how such identities were reinterpreted or rejected by their audience is a difficult one. The propaganda of the ISAA and the Navy League gives an indirect approach to this problem, allowing us to establish some of the assumptions these groups made about their audience: the more influential they were, the more likely that some of these assumptions were correct. Beyond this there is the problem of those competing and overlapping identities of Edwardian Britain: region, nation, gender, class, populist, and others perhaps, too, which vied with empire to catch the popular imagination. The question of how far the popularization of an imperial identity worked to suppress other social belongings is extremely difficult to answer, although it should be remembered that it was possible to inhabit more than one of these identities and that the articulation of such belongings depended on place and time.

Yet even if the Conservative vision of empire enjoyed only partial recognition, it had become central to the political debate of the period. It was a vision that, as we have seen, helped to sustain the image of Conservatives as the party of empire from the heady days of imperial enthusiasm in the 1890s, through the vagaries of the Boer War, to a very different climate in the years that followed. It revolved around the Dominions and struggled to accommodate India and Britain's dependencies in Africa and Asia. It stressed racial and linguistic ties but in a way which largely avoided the xenophobia often associated with such belongings. It was confident about past achievements but anxious for the future.[75] Finally, as far as the economy is concerned, it was a holistic vision of empire, which was neither biased toward the service sector nor expressive of the civic virtues and codes of honor which P.J. Cain and A.G. Hopkins have associated with 'gentlemanly capitalism.'[76] However, there was nothing preordained or automatic about the Conservatives' possession of this language. At the beginning of this article we saw how the meaning of empire was sensitive to what was happening overseas. Many Liberals, particularly those on the Radical wing of the party, seized on events in South Africa to expose the weaknesses of the definition of empire propounded by the right. As a result, the hold of Conservatives on the language of imperialism was far more precarious than often assumed in the years immediately following the Boer War. For a brief spell in the 1890s the right had enjoyed its monopoly; it was fortunate for Conservatives that they were far less complacent than historians about the decade that followed.

Notes

1   *Fabianism and the Empire: A Manifesto by the Fabian Society* (London, 1900) 1.
2   The fluidity of the language of imperialism was also appreciated by J.A. Hobson, *Imperialism: A Study* (London, 1902) 1.
3   For an overview of the subject, see R. Koebner and H.D. Schmidt, *Imperialism: The Story and Significance of a Political Word, 1840–1960* (Cambridge, 1964) xiii–xvi. The authors claim to identify twelve changes in the meaning of the term between the 1840s and the 1960s.
4   D. Eastwood, 'Robert Southey and the Meanings of Patriotism,' *Journal of British Studies, 1992*, 31, 265–87; H. Cunningham, 'The Language of Patriotism, 1750–1914,' *History Workshop Journal*, 1981, 12, 8–33.
5   For the proliferation of nationalist and social-imperialist extraparliamentary organizations, see F. Coetzee, *For Party or Country? Nationalism and the Dilemmas of Popular Conservatism in Edwardian England* (Oxford, 1990); B. Semmel, *Imperialism and Social Reform: English Social-Imperialist Thought, 1895–1914* (London, 1960); R.J. Scally, *The Origins of the Lloyd George Coalition: The Politics of Social-Imperialism, 1900–1918* (Princeton, NJ, 1975).
6   The way in which these organizations disseminated their propaganda is discussed at greater length in my doctoral thesis, A.S. Thompson, 'Thinking Imperially? Imperial Pressure Groups and the Idea of Empire in Late-Victorian and Edwardian Britain' (DPhil thesis, Oxford University, 1994), chs 2 and 3.
7   On the relationship between Radical pressure groups and the NLF, see D.A. Hamer, *The Politics of Electoral Pressure: A Study in the History of Victorian Reform Agitations* (Sussex, 1977) ch. 4; P. Auspos, 'Radicalism, Pressure Groups, and Party Politics: From the National Education League to the National Liberal Federation,' *Journal of British Studies*, 1980, 20, 184–204.
8   For the view that the NLF was the organization of the Liberal party's rank and file, see G.L. Bernstein, *Liberalism and Liberal Politics in Edwardian England*, London, 1986, 10, 23–24.
9   For the growing importance of the Radical movement within the parliamentary Liberal party, see T.W. Heyck, *The Dimensions of British Radicalism: The Case of Ireland, 1874–95* (Urbana, Ill., 1974) 6–11, 154–5. Between 1874 and 1885 about one-third of Liberals in the House of Commons could be identified as Radicals by the causes they supported. Between 1886 and 1895 the number had increased to more than 70 per cent.
10   For a fuller discussion of the political alignment of the Fabians, see A.M. McBriar, *Fabian Socialism and English Politics, 1884–1918* (Cambridge, 1962), chs 9, 10, 11.
11   Semmel, 66.
12   Hobson went to South Africa in 1899 as a special correspondent for the *Manchester Guardian*, and Robertson was sent to South Africa by the *Morning Post* in 1900 to report on the operation of martial law.
13   For the political milieu of the Rainbow Circle, see the introduction to M. Freeden (ed.) *Minutes of the Rainbow Circle, 1894–1924* (London, 1989).
14   The comparison with Vietnam is made by Robert Blake in *The Conservative Party from Peel to Thatcher* (London, 1979) 166. For the importance of the Boer War in terms of its impact

on British society, see R. Price, *An Imperial War and the British Working Class: Working Class Responses to the Boer War, 1899–1902* (Bristol, 1972), who suggests that the Boer War was unique in scale and significance—a 'little war' that involved the whole nation. Similar claims are made by B. Porter in 'The Edwardians and Their Empire,' in *Edwardian England*, D. Read (ed.) (London, 1982) 128–9, who regards the Boer War as a profoundly disturbing experience for most Britons who lived through it. A.P. Thornton considers the implications of the Boer War for the imperial idea in *Britain in the Imperial Idea and its Enemies: A Study in British Power* (London, 1959) 109, arguing that after the war imperialism 'suffered a contraction, a loss of moral content, from which it never completely recovered.' In their study, *Imperialism*, 221, 248–9, Koebner and Schmidt (no. 3 above) identify the reversion of the word 'imperialism' to the status of a partizan abuse at the beginning of the twentieth century with the Boer War.

15   Curzon's political activities after returning to England from India in 1905 are discussed most extensively by D. Gilmour in *Curzon* (London, 1994) chs 22–5.

16   This was a recurring theme of India (the newspaper of the BCINC) during and after the Boer War. The purpose of the paper was to provide a continuous commentary on Indian affairs in the British press. Its paid circulation was quite small, but advanced proofs were sent to editors and nearly one thousand free copies were distributed to politicians and political associations.

17   Few records of the ISAA survive and most of those that do are printed. Its four successive chairmen were George Wyndham, Geoffrey Drage, Alfred Lyttelton, and Gilbert Parker. The ISAA organized public meetings in working men's clubs, distributed large amounts of political literature, and formed three branches in Manchester, Newcastle, and Scotland. Its general council and colonial parliamentary committee were overwhelmingly Conservative in complexion. See Thompson (no. 6 above) chs 2 and 3.

18   Chamberlain's speech at the Royal Colonial Institute, March 31, 1897, quoted in W.D. Handcock (ed.) *English Historical Documents, 1874–1914* (London, 1977) 390.

19   A.N. Porter, *The Origins of the South African War: Joseph Chamberlain and the Diplomacy of Imperialism* (Manchester, 1980) 58.

20   J. Chamberlain, *Home Rule and the Irish Question* (London, 1887); J. Loughlin, 'Joseph Chamberlain, English Nationalism and the Ulster Question,' *History*, 1992, 77, 202–19. Admittedly, there was no franchise grievance in Ulster, but there was the fear that under a Dublin parliament Ulster Protestants would be politically dispossessed. It was not until later, however, that the rest of the Unionist party committed themselves to defending the Union on such grounds.

21   There is an interesting parallel between the work of Milner as high commissioner in South Africa (January 1897–March 1905) and Wyndham as chief secretary for Ireland (November 1900–March 1905): both men saw themselves protecting minority British populations who looked to the British government for support.

22   George Wyndham to Alfred Milner, April 28, 1899, *Milner Papers*, dep. 209, fols. 123–6, Bodleian Library, Oxford University.

23   Wyndham to Milner, May 18, 1899, *Milner Papers*, dep. 209, fols. 99–100, Bodleian.

24   'Real Causes of the War, and Some Reasons for the Final Settlement,' speech by Mr. Drage MP at the Drill Hall, Derby, December 7, 1899, ISAA pamphlet, copy contained in the Geoffrey Drage Papers, Christ Church Library, Oxford University.

25   Resolution of Sir Gilbert Parker on land settlement in the *Annual Report of the ISAA* (Cambridge, 1905/6); resolution of Sir John Gilmour on land settlement in the *Report of the AGM of ISAA* (London, 1903). The author consulted the reports in the library of the Royal Commonwealth Society in London. Since then, the archive of the Royal Commonwealth Society has been moved to Cambridge University Library.

26   Milner to George Parkin, July 13, 1901, *Milner Papers*, dep. 180, fol. 64, Bodleian.

27   Annual Report of ISAA (1903/4); ISAA pamphlet no. 9, *South Africa: Orange River Colony Land Settlement Scheme for Country Settlements*, nd., Drage Papers, Christ Church Library, Oxford University.

28   Such as the South African Colonisation Society and British Women's Emigration League. See the *Annual Report of ISAA* (1904/5).

29   H. Cunningham, 'The Conservative Party and Patriotism,' in *Englishness: Politics and Political Culture, 1880–1920*, R. Colls and P. Dodd (eds) (London, 1986).

30   Ross McKibbin comments that 'it is hard to escape the conclusion that a sense of being British was widely and positively felt in the working classes.' See R. McKibbin, 'Why Was There No Marxism in Great Britain?' *English Historical Review*, 1984, 391, 316.

31   See here K. Robbins, *Nineteenth Century Britain: Integration and Diversity* (Oxford, 1988); J.M. Mackenzie, 'Essay and Reflection: On Scotland and the Empire,' *International History Review*, 1993, 15(7), 14–39; L. Colley, *Britons: Forging the Nation, 1707–1837* (London, 1992).

32   L. Colley, 'Britishness and Otherness,' *Journal of British Studies*, 1992, 31, 311; Colley, *Britons*, 1–9.

33   See the effusion of Jubilee literature, including W.T. Stead, *Her Majesty the Queen. Studies of the Sovereign and the Reign. A Memorial Volume of the Great Jubilee* (London, 1897); 'London Illustrated News,' *Her Majesty's Glorious Jubilee* (London, 1897); *The Diamond Jubilee of Victoria* (London, 1897); *All About the Diamond Jubilee* (London, 1897).

34   Thornton (no. 14 above), 106.

35   The Fabian Society was not a large organization, and its peak membership in this period was two thousand and seven hundred in 1913. The Fabian strategy was not therefore to mobilize mass support. Rather the Society exerted influence through its publications, through the work of its members in local government, and through the relationships the Webbs cultivated with officials, journalists, and politicians at their 'political salon' in Grovesnor Road. See McBriar (n. 10 above) chs 8–9.

36   *Fabianism and the Empire* (no. 1 above) 98.

37   Minutes of members' meetings, February 23, 1900, *Fabian Society Papers* C39, Nuffield College Library, Oxford University; *Fabian News* (February 1900), *Fabian Society Papers*, Nuffield College.

38   Extract from *Daily Chronicle*, in the minutes of the Fabian Society members' meeting, February 23, 1900, *Fabian Society Papers* C39, Nuffield College.

39   Semmel (no. 5 above) ch. 3; Scally, *The Origins of the Lloyd George Coalition*, esp. pp. 26–7.

40   The Liberal League was formed by Liberal Imperialists in February 1902. Its predecessor was the Imperial Liberal Council, which was formed in April 1900. The Transvaal Committee was an offshoot of the Liberal Forwards and monitored the activities of the Colonial Office in an attempt to rouse public opinion against going to war with the Transvaal.

41   *Fabianism and the Empire*, 7.

42   Semmel, esp. pp. 29–31. For a fuller discussion of the legacy of Darwinism for theories of war and human aggression, see P. Crook, *Darwinism, War and History: The Debate over the Biology of War from the 'Origin of Species' to the First World War* (Cambridge, 1994).

43   *Fabianism and the Empire*, 50.

44   McBriar (no. 10 above), ch. 4. Given the importance Fabians attached to the environment, they were inclined to support the Lamarckian view that habit produced modifications of structure in organisms and that these modifications were inherited by progeny. Crook, 73.

45   Minutes of the Fabian Society members' meeting, March 10, 1899, *Fabian Society Papers* C39, Nuffield College. Paul was a leader writer for the *Daily News*.

46   'Strange Case of the Fabian Society,' *New Age*, December 16, 1899, in minutes of the Fabian Society members' meeting, December 12, 1899, *Fabian Society Papers* C39, Nuffield College.

47   L.S. Amery, *My Political Life: England before the Storm, 1896–1914* (London, 1953) 1: 223.

48   Quoted in H.H. Hewison, *Hedge of Wild Almonds: South Africa and the Quaker Conscience, 1890–1910* (Portsmouth, 1989) 122.

49   Minutes of the Fabian Society executive committee, October 20, 1899, *Fabian Society Papers* C7, Nuffield College.

50   Minutes of the Fabian Society executive committee, October 27, 1899, *Fabian Society Papers* C7, Nuffield College.

51   The Society approached the publishers on a number of occasions between 1901 and 1903 and offered to buy back the remaining stock at a reduced price. See Minutes of the Fabian Society executive committee, May 10, 1901, October 28, 1902, and June 12, 1903, *Fabian Society Papers* C8, Nuffield College.

52   H.C.G. Matthew, *The Liberal Imperialists: The Ideas and Politics of a Post Gladstonian Elite* (London, 1973) 89.

53   Tract no. 108, November 1901, *Fabian Society Papers*, Nuffield College.

54   Robertson, *The Meaning of Empire*, 126.

55   The official membership of the Navy League was recorded at 12,000 members in 1901, 20,000 members in 1908, and 127,000 members in 1914. Coetzee (no. 5 above) *Navy*, September 1914, 25, 138.

56   Marshall Pike, 'Are Our Wage-Earners Imperialists?' *Navy*, April 1914, 139.

57   *Navy League Journal*, November 1904) 284.

58   *Navy League Journal*, June 1906, 139.

59   *Navy League Journal*, February 1907.

60   *Navy League Journal*, November 1905, 279.

61   B. Anderson, *Imagined Communities: Reflections on the Origins and Spread of Nationalism* (London, 1983) 13–16; E.J. Hobsbawm, *Nations and Nationalism since 1870: Programme, Myth and Reality* (Cambridge, 1990) 9–13.

62   E.g. see G. Stedman Jones on the Chartist movement and working-class consciousness, 'Rethinking Chartism,' in *The Languages of Class: Studies in English Working-Class History, 1832–1982* (Cambridge, 1983).

63   Eastwood (no. 4 above) 265–6.

64   Anderson, 19.

65   'Envoy to the Colonies,' *Navy League Journal*, February 1904.

66   *Navy League Journal*, May 1904, 142.

67   *Navy*, January 1912, 22.

68   'The Objects of the Navy League,' not dated, copy contained in the *Patrick Hannon Papers*, House of Lords Record Office, London.

69   *Navy*, January 1914, 1.

70   Lecture given in Oxford, Branch Reports, *Navy*, April 1912, 110.

71   *Navy*, September 1912, 241.

72   Annual Report of the ISAA (1899–1900); 'Speech by Gilbert Parker to the AGM of the ISAA,' July 1905 in the *Annual Report of the ISAA* (1905).

73   *Navy League Annual* (1908–9).

74   See here the response of Lord Curzon discussed in S.R. Mehrotra, *India and the Commonwealth, 1885–1929* (London, 1965) 243–4. Curzon's complaint about the marginalization of India in Edwardian imperial discourse can also be explored in G.N. Curzon, *The Place of India in the Empire: Address Delivered before the Philosophical Institute of Edinburgh, October 19th, 1909* (London, 1909).

75   While I have sketched the main lines along which this vision was developed, there is little doubt that different social groups managed to inflect imperialism with further meanings. Empire may have been used by the lower middle class to counter status anxieties, see R. Price, 'Society, Status and Jingoism: The Social Roots of Lower Middle-Class Patriotism, 1870–1900,' in *The Lower Middle Class in Britain 1870–1914*, G. Crossick (ed.) (London, 1977). For ardent imperialists anxious about the consequences of a terminal decline in Christian belief, such as Cecil Rhodes, imperialism could become a sort of surrogate faith. The call for universal military training from the 'Diehards'—those politically active peers from the landed classes—was made with a view to lowering class barriers and dampening social antagonisms as well as protecting the empire, see G. Phillips, *The Diehards: Aristocratic Society and Politics in Edwardian England* (London, 1979). Finally, one might consider the extent to which the imperial business community was particularly susceptible to moralizing empire through the idea of a civilizing mission, thereby downplaying the other purposes

their capital served (such as Patrick Hannon and Alan Burgoyne of the Navy League and Lord Lovat of the ISAA). This accretion of meanings helps to explain why empire was picked up with varying degrees of enthusiasm by different groups. Conservative propaganda usually resisted these accretions: the fear was that they would confuse the main vision of empire.

76   P.J. Cain and A.G. Hopkins, *British Imperialism: Innovation and Expansion: 1688–1914* (London, 1993) ch. 1.

PART 9

Colonialism's afterlives

Chapter 22

Paul Gilroy

HAS IT COME TO THIS?

There are few, if any, more important and stimulating thinkers about Britishness, notably in its affiliation to ideas about 'race' – or indeed about the concept of race in general – than Paul Gilroy. Here, in an extract from his remarkable book *After Empire*, he turns his attention more fully than before to the specifically imperial and postcolonial dimensions of these questions.

Stephen Howe

TALES OF HEROISM BY THE BRAVE PILOTS of Spitfires and Hurricanes were important to my postwar childhood. Their anti-Nazi action established one dimension of my moral universe. Yet, when the World War II airplanes thundered overhead during the pageantry that attended the Queen Mother's burial in 2002, it was impossible not to wonder why that particular mythic moment of national becoming and community has been able to endure and retain such a special grip on Britain's culture and self-understanding. Why are those martial images – the Battle of Britain, the Blitz, and the war against Hitler – still circulating and, more importantly, still defining the nation's finest hour? How is it that their potency can be undiminished by the passage of time, and why do they alone provide the touchstone for the desirable forms of togetherness that are used continually to evaluate the chaotic, multicultural present and find it lacking?

Any worthwhile explanation for Britain's postmodern nationalism has to be complex enough to answer those questions. It must also be able to acknowledge that exceptionally powerful feelings of comfort and compensation are produced by the prospect of even a partial restoration of the country's long-vanished homogeneity. Repairing that aching loss is usually signified by the recovery or preservation of endangered whiteness – and the exhilarating triumph over chaos and strangeness which that victory entails. If this partial explanation is to become valid, it will have to account for how Britain's nationalism has interfaced with its racism and its xenophobia, but there is another interpretative challenge here. We need to know how the warm glow that results from the nation's wholesome militarism has combined pleasurably with the unchallenging moral architecture of a Manichaean world in which a number of dualistic pairings – black and white, savage and civilized, nature and culture, bad and good – can all be tidily superimposed upon one another. We will have to consider the pleasures that result from the experience of being happy, glorious, and victorious in a setting where the nation's characteristic ethnic blend of luck, pluck, and resilience can be identified and affirmed. Revisiting the feeling of victory in war supplies the best evidence that Britain's endangered civilization is in progressive motion toward its historic completion.

These distinctive combinations of sentiment and affect result in the anti-Nazi war being invoked even now. This is done so that Brits can know who we are as well as who we were and then become certain that we are still good while our uncivilized enemies are irredeemably evil. However, it is not obvious how and why the country's downbeat martial values still make sense to generations for whom the war itself is more myth and fantasy than memory. Political citations of World War II in pursuit of other more recent ends – the reconquest of the Falklands or the overthrow of Saddam Hussein – have stretched official anti-Fascist history so thin that it cannot possibly accomplish all the important cultural work it is increasingly relied upon to do. An uncertain generation for whom all knowledge of the conflict arrives on very long loops, usually via Hollywood, is still required to use expensively manufactured surrogate memory of World War II as the favored means to find and even to restore an ebbing sense of what it is to be English. Under these conditions, it has become instructive to ask why that war above all can connect people to the fading core of a culture and a history that is confronting a loss of certainty about its own distinctive content and its noble world mission. After all, the United Kingdom has been in plenty of other wars since the great triumph of 1945. Its troops have been dispatched to fight in the Netherlands East Indies, Palestine, Malaya, Korea, Kenya, Suez, Cyprus, Oman and Muscat, Brunei and Borneo, Saudi Arabia and Aden, Dofar, Ireland, the Falklands, the Persian Gulf, and then the Balkans. None of those conflicts – even the chronic warfare in Northern Ireland and the functional immediacy of Mrs. Thatcher's Falklands victory – can command a comparable ideological and mythological space. Scale, duration, and the remoteness of some of these battlefields from the homeland are insufficient explanations of why these conflicts have largely disappeared from view. The historical and conceptual problems they raise become more complex once we appreciate that the totemic power of the great anti-Nazi war seems to have increased even as its veterans have died out. On the other hand, the mysterious evacuation of Britain's postcolonial conflicts from national consciousness has become a significant cultural and historical event in its own right. Those forgotten wars have left significant marks on the body politic, but the memory of them appears to have been collapsed into the overarching figuration of Britain at war against the Nazis, under attack, yet stalwart and ultimately triumphant. That image, produced with apparent spontaneity from below and sometimes engineered politically from above by crown and government, has underpinned the country's unstable post-1945 settlement. It is addressed to what has become a perennial crisis of national identity, which lately reached a notable point of transition and decision in popular resistance to joining the US invasion of Iraq and the debate over the terms upon which that special but dubious alliance with George Bush's superpower should now proceed.

Cultures of melancholia and the pathology of greatness

I think that there is something neurotic about Britain's continued citation of the anti-Nazi war. Making it a privileged point of entry into national identity and self-understanding reveals a desire to find a way back to the point where the national culture – operating on a more manageable scale of community and social life – was, irrespective of the suffering involved in the conflict, both comprehensible and habitable. That memory of the country at war against foes who are simply, tidily, and uncomplicatedly evil has recently acquired the status of an ethnic myth. It explains not only how the nation remade itself through war and victory but can also be understood as a rejection or deferral of its present problems. That process is driven by the need to get back to the place or moment before the country lost its moral and cultural bearings. Neither the appeal of homogeneity nor the antipathy toward immigrants and strangers who represent the involution of national culture can be separated from that underlying hunger for reorientation. Turning back in this direction is also a turning away from the perceived dangers of pluralism and from the irreversible fact of multiculture.

The immediate roots of this situation reside in the way that Britain snatched a wider cultural and psychological defeat from the jaws of its victory over Hitlerism in 1945. I want to show that since then the life of the nation has been dominated by an inability even to face, nevermind actually mourn, the profound change in circumstances and moods that followed the end of the Empire and consequent loss of imperial prestige. That inability has been intertwined with the apprehension of successive political and economic crises, with the gradual breakup of the United Kingdom, with the arrival of substantial numbers of postcolonial citizen-migrants, and with the shock and anxiety that followed from a loss of any sense that the national collective was bound by a coherent and distinctive culture. Once the history of the Empire became a source of discomfort, shame, and perplexity, its complexities and ambiguities were readily set aside. Rather than work through those feelings, that unsettling history was diminished, denied, and then, if possible, actively forgotten. The resulting silence feeds an additional catastrophe: the error of imagining that postcolonial people are only unwanted alien intruders without any substantive historical, political, or cultural connections to the collective life of their fellow subjects.

These extraordinary failures have obstructed the arterial system of Britain's political body in many ways. They deserve the proper name 'postimperial melancholia' in order simultaneously to underline this syndrome's links with the past and its pathological character. This is a complex ailment with multiple symptoms that build upon and divert earlier patterns of imperial melancholy from which they make a decisive break. An older, more dignified sadness that was born in the nineteenth century should be sharply distinguished from the guilt-ridden loathing and depression that have come to characterize Britain's xenophobic responses to the strangers who have intruded upon it more recently.

Matthew Arnold helped to create the special 'ethnic' space between Hebraism and Hellenism from which the country's Victorian racial destiny could be divined. By staging his famous poetic reflections on Britain's modern predicament at the frontier of Dover Beach, where today's asylum seekers still fear to tread, he made it clear that proximity to the alien presence of the French had helped to concentrate his mind with regard to the country's historic responsibilities as well as its relationship to the classical world that had supplied the template for its global imperium. The historic mission to civilize and uplift the world was England's unavoidable destiny, but he sensed that it would bring neither comfort nor happiness. That imperial mission re-created the national community in a modern form but then drew it immediately into a terrible web of war and suffering, polluting its beautiful dreams, confusing and destabilizing it. For Arnold, the unchanging cliffs of England were glimmering and vast when compared to an ephemeral gleam of light visible on the nearby French coast. The distinctive island ecology of land and sea were operating on a geological tempo to which he gives the reader access. With the right dosage of Hellenic inspiration, the landscape/seascape could not only produce a deep geo-piety but also speak uniquely to the country's modern predicament and, of course, to the difficult position of the poet who bore a resigned witness to it. His apprehensions were aligned with those of the larger social body, but, as he heard and felt the shingle start to move beneath his feet, he opted to turn away from those public concerns and seek consolation in the private and intimate places where romantic love and fidelity could offset the worst effects of warfare, turbulence, and vanished certitude. The accompanying inward turn was a defensive gesture, and it was morally justifiable only when it promoted a self-conscious struggle with the historic sources of the tendency to become sad and pensive in the face of the Empire's demanding geopolitical responsibilities.

We can say that Arnold's articulate melancholy was shaped by the culture of that Empire in its emergent phase. It combined with and was complemented by the older melancholy of the poor, the expropriated, the empressed and the abjected which is still remembered in the folk music of England. An altogether different pattern became visible once the imperial system shifted into undeniable decline. Victorian melancholy started to yield to melancholia as soon as the natives and savages began to appear and make demands for recognition in the Empire's metropolitan core. The change was complete when the limits of the political project involved in subordinating colonial peoples were communicated to their apprehensive racial betters by baffling ingratitude and a stubborn appetite for independence. At home, a novel conception of where the boundaries of British culture would fall was contoured by a new arrangement in which immigration, war, and national identity began to challenge class hierarchy as the most significant themes from which the national identity would be assembled. Until very recently, even the horrible shock of the World War I, which engulfed thousands and thousands of colonial soldiers, was recovered and preserved in an exclusionary form as a wholly private or domestic matter from which non-whites were shut out by the force of the class conflicts that bound authentic Britons to each other in the man-made storm of military absurdity that made their divided lives expendable.

The end of external hostilities demanded a new map of the nation's internal fractures and divisions. The conflict between Celts and Anglo-Saxons was no longer adequate to the task of managing the inflow of aliens and their disruptive presence in the cities. Paul Foot drew attention long ago to the xenophobic populism swirling around the passage of the 1919 Aliens Act. He cites a powerful speech made in the House of Commons by Josiah Wedgwood, who set standards that today's Labour members of parliament have clearly been unable to maintain:

> Generally speaking, aliens are always hated by the people of this country. Usually speaking, there has been a mob which has been opposed to them, but that mob has always had leaders in high places. The Flemings were persecuted and hunted, and the Lombards were hunted down by the London mob. Then it was the turn of the French Protestants. I think that the same feelings holds

good on this subject today. You always have a mob of uneducated people who will hunt down foreigners, and you always have people who will make use of the passions of this mob in order to get their own ends politically.[1]

The lingering effects of this traditional xenophobia are registered not only in the antipathy toward alien settlers of all kinds but also in the country's intense political and emotional responses to its residual colonial responsibilities in Zimbabwe, Kenya, Diego Garcia, and elsewhere. Britain's ambivalence about its empire is especially evident in its reactions to the fragments of brutal colonial history that emerge occasionally to unsettle the remembrance of the imperial project by undermining its moral legitimacy and damaging the national self-esteem. The terrifying folk knowledge of what is actually involved in being on the receiving end of imperial power has also been preserved and finds expression elsewhere – above all, in the country's intermittent fears of itself becoming a colonial dependency of the United States. This apprehension was expressed most vividly by Peter Kilfoyle, MP, during the summer of 2003, when the disastrous character of the invasion of Iraq was becoming apparent. He pointed out that 'the defence secretary Geoff Hoon, has acknowledged that we are to be to the US armed forces what the sepoys were to the British Indian Army.'[2]

Each of the historical examples I have mentioned in passing can supply a detailed case study in support of my larger arguments. For example, the revelations about the brutal conduct of the war against 'Mau Mau' insurgents in Kenya that emerged on the fiftieth anniversary of the declaration of the eight-year 'emergency' in that country warrant close attention in their own right, but they are also typical of the drip of embarrassing and uncomfortable information about imperial and colonial governance that has begun to leak into the public debate and challenge the country's instinctive sense that its imperial ambitions were always good and its political methods for realizing them, morally and legally defensible. This particular example involved allegations of brutality, torture, and killing, which may compare favorably to the dismal record of other European powers elsewhere in Africa but nonetheless raised a host of issues about the abuse of human rights and the characteristic manner in which colonial wars were conducted. The shock involved in trying to accept that British colonial administrators and soldiers, as well as the officials who controlled them from Whitehall, could have been routinely involved in such horrible practices did not exhaust the nation's feelings of discomfort and shame at the conduct of its empire. Indeed, sticking with the Kenyan case, those responses have been extended and amplified by various postcolonial conflicts. They have recently been compounded by another layer of trauma that is directly relevant to the theme of this chapter. Though their disturbing claims have been clouded by accusations of fraud, Kenyan women from several generations have launched a legal action against the British Ministry of Defence, which alleges that they were subjected to sexual assault by UK troops stationed in the area to conduct 'training exercises.' Though the women involved were, unlike the insurgents of the earlier period, Masai rather than Kikuyu, these allegations suggest governmental continuities between colonial and postcolonial administrations that are united by a view of the natives as infra-human creatures to be preyed upon for sexual gratification. The women's controversial claims also included the additional charge that the British Army had, over a thirty-year period, refused to investigate repeated allegations of rape.

My argument is not principally concerned with the details involved in these or various other similar legal actions, or indeed with the methodological and moral shifts that follow from approaching Britain's imperial history through its victims' decisions to seek financial compensation for their injuries by legal means. I am interested instead in the way that British political culture has had to adapt in order to make sense of the catalogue of horror that extends into the present from Morant Bay and Lucknow via Londonderry and Dol Dol. I want us to consider the political and psychological reactions which attend the discovery that imperial administration was, against all the ethnic mythology that projects empire as essentially a form of sport, necessarily a violent, dirty, and immoral business. We need to know how that deeply disturbing realization has been managed and, in particular, to consider what consequences follow from the need to maintain the moral pre-eminence and progressive momentum that define colonial power as the redemptive extension of civilization into barbarity and chaos?

It is not only that the greatness of the British nation is evidently still at stake in the contested history of its difficult relationships with its colonial subjects. Repressed and buried knowledge of the cruelty and injustice that recur in diverse accounts of imperial administration can only be denied at a considerable moral and psychological cost. That knowledge creates a discomfiting complicity. Both are active in shaping the hostile responses to strangers and settlers and in constructing the intractable political problems that flow from understanding immigration as being akin to war and invasion. The hidden, shameful store of imperial horrors has been an unacknowledged presence in British political and cultural life during the second half of the twentieth century. It is not too dramatic to say that the quality of the country's multicultural future depends on what is now done with it. The history of empire directs attention to the practical mechanisms of racial hierarchy and the ideology of white supremacy, but that is not its only value to contemporary debates. Once those encounters have begun and a revised account of the nature of imperial statecraft has been folded into critical reflections on national life, the possibility of healing and reconciliation come into view. Sadly, the pressure of the past upon the present means that these difficulties are usually resolved in other, less fruitful directions. The invitation to revise and reassess often triggers a chain of defensive argumentation that seeks first to minimize the extent of the Empire, then to deny or justify its brutal character, and finally, to present the British themselves as the ultimate tragic victims of their extraordinary imperial successes. This outlook reaches its apogee in the work of Linda Colley, where it is combined with a great reluctance to see contemporary British racism as a product of imperial and colonial power. While I am with her when she stresses that 'the British need to know much more about their impact in the past upon different regions of the world,'[3] we part company where the emphasis falls on the fact that Brits were passive 'captives' of their imperial project and on the suggestion that their extensive global power was so multifaceted and locally complex that any generalizations about its uniformity, its racism, its ethics, and its military disposition must be postponed until it has been somehow fully understood. The desire to judge the Empire harshly gets drowned in a swamp of squeamish equivocation:

> Africans transported as slaves across the Atlantic experienced an atrocity that was not peculiar to the British empire, but was certainly fostered by it. In other contexts, however, the impact of empire was more uneven, sometimes very shallow and far more slow. Environments, economies, customs, power relations, and lives were sometimes devastated; but by no means always, because these intruders were frequently limited in number, and dependent often on a measure of indigenous tolerance.[4]

These telling words illuminate a larger cultural problem. They encapsulate what has become a widespread desire to allocate a large measure of blame for the Empire to its victims and then seek to usurp their honored place of suffering, winning many immediate political and psychological benefits in the process. Much of this embarrassing sentiment is today held captive by an unhealthy and destructive postimperial hungering for renewed greatness. Colley is again right in seeing that during the twentieth century, this desire feeds Britain's vicarious investments in US pre-eminence. She is not, however, inclined to connect the desire for recovered greatness with the magical appeal of restored racial and ethnic homogeneity. The appeal of being great again was central to Mrs. Thatcher's premiership, particularly after her South Atlantic triumph, but it did not vanish with her. It has endured and mutated and emerged again as one significant element that propelled a largely reluctant country to war against Iraq in 2003. There was much more to this outcome than the New Labour info-warriors' desire to mimic the populist tempo of Thatcher's long and damaging political experiment. On the occasion of the anti-Saddam war, the geopolitical logic of Tony Blair's postideological oligarchy was running in a different direction from the spontaneous gestures of a not-yet-plural nation that desperately seemed to want to become something different, something less great but more noble, more consistent, and more autonomous.

Into The Streets

Mike Skinner of 'The Streets' has explicitly voiced the alternative desire not to recover or repeat the conceits of empire but to shift into a different state of being in the world and 'turn the page' of Britain's national history. In the year-long build-up to the outbreak of war, his poetic attempts to make the country more habitable by giving value to its ability to operate on a less-than-imperial scale were a notable counterpart to the totalizing ambitions of megapolitical government. Built upon the continuing aftershock of 'Rock Against Racism,' which was a formative experience for the post-1968 generation, Skinner's songs share with Eliza Carthy's album 'Anglicana' and Maggie Holland's Music Hall folk song 'A Place Called England,' a precious ability to transport English ethnicity into the present.[5] All of these interventions show that what Orwell would have regarded as an authentically geo-pious Anglo patriotism can, in fact, be adapted to the demands of multicultural society. The singer Billy Bragg is another one of these awkward voices to have carried the debate over the cultural forms of the emergent, postimperial nation into the world of art-criticism. His rather worthy effort, 'Take Down the Union Jack' redeems itself with his request for assent to the idea that 'Gilbert and George are taking the piss.' Certainly, the argument about postcolonial melancholia can place the nihilism of these and other, younger British artists in a very different setting. Unnoticed either by government or overground media culture, the emergent Britain for which Skinner's The Streets supplied a witty and ambivalent mouthpiece mobilized traditional ideas of self-reliance and caution, insularity and fairness in order to make a range of bold, and in my view healthier claims about the condition of the country and the state of racial politics. These wittily delivered vernacular pronouncements were aimed toward the establishment of more modest and more explicitly democratic specifications of a revised national identity that is easier to appreciate and enjoy when it has removed itself from the world stage. This little England owes something to its nativist predecessors. It certainly shares their commitment to the relocalization of the world, but it has expanded their horizons and overcome their xenophobia. Racial difference is not feared. Exposure to it is not ethnic jeopardy but rather an unremarkable principle of metropolitan life. Race is essentially insignificant, at least when compared either to the hazards involved in urban survival or to the desperate pleasures of the postcolonial city: 'sex and drugs and on the dole.'

In The Streets' playful ontology, race is not an identity that can fix or contain individuals; it is a practice that can be understood through a comparison with the strategic choice of drug that a variety of person opts for in a particular situation: 'whether you're white or black; smoke weed, chase brown, toot rock.' More importantly, in this view of the nation the balance between its internal and external relations has been decisively adjusted. The imperial profile has become less appealing and, though the memory of war remains important, it is adapted to other purposes. The Streets' song 'Turn the Page' suggests that the hope of a new national identity rests upon its re-interpretation. The song recasts the formative, traumatic memory of World War II as a rave. It is also compelling for the way that it refigures an English pastoral consciousness in an *urban* setting, breaking down the opposition between country and city and framing postcolonial Englishness with a recognizable trace of Orwell signaled by some casual ornithology:

> The sky turns white it all becomes clear
> they felt lifted from their fears
> they shed tears in the light after six dark years
> young bold soldiers the fire burns cracks and smoulders, the war is over,
>   the bells ring
> memories fading, soldiers slaying
> looks like geezers raving
> the hazy fog over The Bullring the lazy ways the birds sing . . .[6]

Skinner's fundamental concern with national collectivity is signaled by the song's shift from London to Birmingham. Along the way, the country has been actively reimagined as an ordered polity in a moral world of similar states capable of acting beyond self-interest in the spirit of cosmopolitan or, more accurately, planetary obligations that are opposed to the manifest injustices of globalization as Americanization: 'round 'ere' he whines in a Brummie-Cockney hybrid accent, that emphatically asserts the priority of these local codes, 'we say birds, not bitches.'

The unexpected tide of popular opposition in 2003 to the British government's support for U.S. military power created opportunities to develop this revised conception of England and its adjusted role in the world. At that moment, it not only became possible to query the authoritarian versions of emancipatory modernization that had been served up in bad faith by New Labour but to imagine what it would be like to depart from the political and cultural templates of the nationalist mindset that Anthony Barnett identified long ago as 'Churchillism.' Churchill's name provided an especially appropriate term for this knot of imperial ideas and feelings because he had identified the uniqueness of Britain with its position at the junction of three distinct geopolitical formations: the north Atlantic world; the empire in its transition toward being a commonwealth; and Europe. This special location defined Britain's obligations and specified what had to be done in order to be and remain a great power. The rewards to the country would be substantial, especially if the disabling, socialistic habits of what we might now call 'old Labour' could be disposed of. First, the

Empire/Commonwealth and then the acquisition of nuclear weapons were critical in maintaining the stature of the country and in justifying its presence at the world's 'top table.' Postwar political administrations awarded different priorities to the various elements involved in managing this tripartite scheme, but its basic elements and their imagined relationship to the greatness that distinguishes Britain's character and genius have remained constant. Tony Blair's puzzling enthusiasm for gunboat diplomacy needs to be seen in this context. His resort to those old tactics registers the end of the political order in which the Soviet Union's global influence balanced American power and interests, but it is much better understood as the latest episode in a much longer and sorrier tale of the desperate things that British governments have done in order to mediate the worst effects of their inexorable decline. We should seize the chance to break with the Churchillist view of our nation and its interests before other campaigns, against Iran and Syria or even more simply against asylum seekers, who are the latest enemy within, drag us back in the same depressing direction once again. What follows is concerned with the cultural context and manifestations of this pathological formation and, of course, with the vibrant, ordinary multiculture that now opposes it.

Melancholia

The concept of melancholia essayed here and adapted to Britain's postcolonial conditions does not come into my arguments directly from its Freudian sources in discussions of narcissism, group psychology, and bereavement. It has arrived via the creative *use* made of those difficult insights in the pioneering social psychology of the German psychoanalysts Alexander and Margarete Mitscherlich. Their interpretation of social, psychological, and political behavior in postwar West Germany endeavored to understand the German people's melancholic reactions to the death of Hitler and to fathom the postwar demand that they face and work through the larger evil of which their love for him had been part. Faced with a sudden and radical loss of its moral legitimacy, the German nation warded off a collective process of mourning for what they had loved and lost by means of a depressed reaction that inhibited any capacity for responsible reconstructive practice.

The nation's accumulated guilt had been projected narrowly onto its fallen leader and his immediate accomplices. Bolstered by denial of the destructiveness and wickedness of Germany's war aims, that guilt intervened to block and defer the country's comprehension of its history. The ability to recall whole segments of the national past faded away, leaving destructive blank spaces in individual autobiographies and creating patterns of intergenerational complicity and conflict that contributed to a culture of alienation from and indifference not only to the past but 'to anything that entails responsibility.'[7]

The Mitscherlichs made a long, contentious, and complex argument, and I must inevitably oversimplify it here. They warn that melancholic reactions are prompted by 'the loss of a fantasy of omnipotence' and suggest that the racial and national fantasies that imperial and colonial power required were, like those of the Aryan master race, predominantly narcissistic. From this perspective, before the British people can adjust to the horrors of their own modern history and start to build a new national identity from the debris of their broken narcissism, they will have to learn to appreciate the brutalities of colonial rule enacted in their name and to their benefit, to understand the damage it did to their political culture at home and abroad, and to consider the extent of their country's complex investments in the ethnic absolutism that has sustained it. The multilayered trauma – economic and cultural as well as political and psychological – involved in accepting the loss of the Empire would therefore be compounded by a number of additional shocks. Among them are the painful obligations to work through the grim details of imperial and colonial history and to transform paralyzing guilt into a more productive shame that would be conducive to the building of a multicultural nationality that is no longer phobic about the prospect of exposure to either strangers or otherness.

This new phase of psychological and ethical maturity has emerged very slowly and unevenly among the political class. In marked contrast, the reflexive position outlined by The Streets and other similar voices has been unexpectedly close to the center of Britain's vernacular dissidence, lending energy to an ordinary, demotic multiculturalism that is not the outcome of governmental drift and institutional indifference but of concrete oppositional work: political, aesthetic, cultural, scholarly. This pressure from below has enriched and expanded the country's public sphere. I would like to bring about a new appreciation of this unheralded multiculture, which is distinguished by some notable demands for hospitality, conviviality, tolerance, justice, and mutual care.

Healthier patterns, in which Britain renounces its pursuit of greatness and reaps immediate benefits in civil society, are addressed to the very same historical moment and awareness that have solicited and even institutionalized the melancholic reaction I have been criticizing. The multiculturalism they articulate can usefully be identified with a mature response to diversity, plurality, and differentiation. It is oriented by routine, everyday exposure to difference. Postimperial melancholia, on the other hand, is associated with the neo-traditional pathology of what, in the British setting, Patrick Wright, who is its most acute observer, has identified as the morbidity of heritage.

I should emphasize that I do not see the larger mechanism at work here as something that is uniquely relevant to Britain. The modern histories of numerous other European countries, particularly Belgium, France, Spain, Italy, and the Netherlands, might also be used to construct equivalent arguments amidst the wreckage of their colonial extensions and the injustices of their inconsistent responses to immigration. These analyses would be based upon their obvious difficulties in acknowledging the pains and the gains that were involved in imperial adventures and upon the problems that have arisen from their inability to disentangle the disruptive results supposedly produced by an immigrant presence from the residual but potent effects of lingering but usually unspoken colonial relationships and imperial fantasies.

The historical experience of British world dominance and the accompanying habituation to imperial pre-eminence have no single iconic human cipher. Winston Churchill comes closer than Raleigh, Rhodes, Hawkins, or Nelson to being their imaginary embodiment, but perhaps because of the Empire's extraordinary reach and duration, even his superhuman figure cannot stand in for it. The imperial domination with which his name has become synonymous generated an unprecedented condition of security and privilege. Today, those qualities have faded, but the imperial power that produced them is unmourned even when its potent residues intervene to make the restoration of British greatness imperative. The fragility of national life and the real value of empire would only be disclosed in the country's darkest and finest hours, from which Britain would be rescued by the sacrifice of its colonial soldiery.

Freud might have diagnosed this arrangement as an effect of the cultural urges that are capable of tipping whole civilizations or epochs into a neurotic state. In order to illuminate this 'pathology of cultural communities' and to make sense of the way it has shaped the political fate of contemporary Britain, I want to propose that it is the infrahuman political body of the immigrant rather than the body of the sovereign that comes to represent all the discomforting ambiguities of the Empire's painful and shameful but apparently nonetheless exhilarating history. The immigrant is now here because Britain, Europe, was once out there; that basic fact of global history is not usually deniable. And yet its grudging recognition provides a stimulus for forms of hostility rooted in the associated realization that today's unwanted settlers carry all the ambivalence of empire with them. They project it into the unhappy consciousness of their fearful and anxious hosts and neighbors. Indeed, the incomers may be unwanted and feared precisely because they are the unwitting bearers of the imperial and colonial past.

In this precarious national state, individual and group identifications converge not on the body of the leader or other iconic national object Britannia recast in the guise of gym-trim Diana, the equally immortal Queen Mum, David Beckham's various haircuts, or even the beaming, sweaty figure of Prime Minister Blair himself – but in opposition to the intrusive presence of the incoming strangers who, trapped inside our perverse local logic of race, nation, and ethnic absolutism not only *represent* the vanished empire but also refer consciousness to the unacknowledged pain of its loss and the unsettling shame of its bloody management.

An important displacement mechanism becomes evident here. The arrival of these incomers, even when they were protected by their tenure of formal citizenship was, as I have already said, understood to be an act of invasive warfare. That structure of feeling governs the continuing antipathy toward all would-be settlers. Later groups of immigrants may not, of course, be connected with the history of empire and colony in any way whatsoever. However, they experience the misfortune of being caught up in a pattern of hostility and conflict that belongs emphatically to its lingering aftermath. Once they recognize the salience of racial categories to their perilous predicament, it should not be surprising if these people try to follow the well-trodden path pioneered by the most vulnerable and marginal members of the host community. They too will seek salvation by trying to embrace and inflate the ebbing privileges of whiteness. That racialized identification is presumably the best way to prove they are not really immigrants at all but somehow already belong to the home-space in ways that the black and brown people against whom they have to compete in the labor market will never be recognized as doing.

As is well known, Enoch Powell's notorious speeches on immigration played with these powerful feelings of aggression, guilt, and fear and articulated them as a violent racist politics. We should think back to his memorable imagery not of the 'rivers of blood,' which in 1968 he predicted would be the catastrophic outcome of all Britain's mistaken attempts to mix the races, but of the even more terrifying prospect of a wholesale reversal of the proper ordering of colonial power. A plain-speaking, Brummie informant provided the point of departure for Powell's whole argument with a racist warning that 'in this country in fifteen or twenty years time the black man will have the whip hand over the white man.'[8] That awful prospect was intended to be scary. It has subsequently provided the justification for many a pre-emptive strike like the one that took Stephen Lawrence's life in 1993.

In practice, the colonial strangers' disturbingly intimate association with their mother country was always qualified by the exclusionary workings of informal institutions such as the 'Colour Bar.' Nevertheless, the citizen-settlers appeared confident that their reasonable requests for hospitality would eventually be heard and understood. They had no idea that those demands were impossible to fulfil within the fantastic structures of the melancholic island race. The requests for fairness only increased the problems because the inevitable refusals precipitated a further cycle of violence and guilt. This was itself intensified by feelings of resentment, rejection, and fear at the prospect of open interaction with an otherness, which could only be imagined as loss and jeopardy.

Britain's inability to mourn its loss of empire and accommodate the Empire's consequences developed slowly. Its unfolding revealed an extensively fragmented national collective that has not so far been able to meet the elemental challenge represented by the social, cultural, and political transition with which the presence of postcolonial and other sanctuary-seeking people has been unwittingly bound up. Instead, racist violence provides an easy means to 'purify' and rehomogenize the nation. As one might anticipate, postimperial and postcolonial melancholia characteristically intercut this violence and the shame-faced tides of self-scrutiny and self-loathing that follow among decent folk, with outbursts of manic euphoria.

Racist and nationalist responses that were pioneered by populist opposition to commonwealth immigration during the 1950s and 1960s remain the backbone of this resistance to convivial culture. The same kind of symptomatic contradiction can even be noted in the conclusions to Sir William MacPherson's celebrated report of inquiry into the murder of Stephen Lawrence, the official document that marked the latest event in the fitful emergence of the country's racial conscience. MacPherson's epoch-making report anchored the most recent phase of reforms and helped to bring anti-racist goals closer to the governmental process. His well-publicized adjustments to the concept of institutional racism have become legendary, but they are also marked by postcolonial melancholia. Though the good judge acknowledged that prejudice was indeed present in Britain's system of criminal justice, he then emphasized the idea that this dysfunctional racism was 'unwitting.' He was saying, in effect, that racism's perpetrators should not be seen as wholly responsible for the outcome of their actions. To be sure, he identified institutional racism with collective organizational failures of British legal and governmental agencies, but he then provided a definition of what counted as racist that was so narrowly and tightly drawn that it excluded almost everybody and left the sources of these persistent but mysterious failures inaccessible to all but the most sophisticated management consultants. Similar oscillations can be detected in other pronouncements and policies. Indeed, those characteristic oscillations are audible wherever race and absolute ethnicity have been made intelligible as matters of law and government.

These patterns have been swirling around in debates over black criminality for decades. Many of the continuing responses to MacPherson's report reveal similar aspects or suggest melancholia's signature combination of manic elation with misery, self-loathing, and ambivalence. Hostility to the proposition that racist violence and institutional indifference are normal and recurrent features of British social and political life gets intermingled with absolute and sincere surprise at the nastiness of racism and the extent of the anger and resentment that it can cause. Antipathy toward asylum seekers and refugees cannot be concealed, but the idea that it has anything to do with racism or ultra-nationalism remains shocking and induces yet more guilt. This confusion and disorientation result from a situation in which melancholic Britain can concede that it does not like blacks and wants to get rid of them but then becomes uncomfortable because it does not like the things it learns about itself when it gives vent to feelings of hostility and hatred.

The other end of this chain of meaning has for the last few years lain in anxiety over the fate of Britain's abandoned colonial kith and kin in the Falklands, in Africa, and particularly in Robert Mugabe's Zimbabwe. This too is a long story. The repetition of tragic southern African themes – the interminable saga of Julie Ward's murder, the massive coverage for sexual and other violent assaults on holidaymakers and tourists[9] – are a notable feature of this moment not only because they convey the catastrophic consequences of intermixture and the severe problems that arise once colonial order has been withdrawn or sacrificed but because, like Linda Colley's recent work and Enoch Powell's 'rivers of blood' speech, they are deployed to contest and then seize the position of victim. Taking possession of that coveted role can also be linked to a sustained academic attempt to rehabilitate the imperial idea and enhance colonial history so that it can play a proper role in the redefinition of national sovereignty, a move required by the military humanism of the gunboat diplomats who, in the words of Tony Blair's adviser, the diplomat Robert Cooper, promote the application of 'double standards.' There is now one law for the 'postmodern' West, another for the chaotic world of failed, incompetent, and pre-modern states. For Cooper, these operations now involve a self-conscious reversion to 'the rougher methods of an earlier era-force, pre-emptive attack, deception, whatever is necessary to deal with those who still live in the nineteenth-century world of every state for itself.'[10]

The very ease with which the ideologues of this strategy reach for the concept of empire as a benign and dynamic guarantor of progress betrays how much ground they still have to cover if they are ever to work through its history and, once melancholia has been succeeded by mourning, start to produce a new image of the nation that can accommodate its colonial dimensions. Again, this is not just a British problem. In France, the publication of General Paul Aussaresses' popular memoir of the war in Algeria, with its unrepentant defense of torture as practical political technique, has created a recognizable pattern of equivocation, denial, and mock horror.[11] It bears repetition that retelling these colonial stories projects the imperial nation as the primary victim rather than the principal beneficiary of its vanished colonial dominance. This variety of discourse is also common to the populist politicians who now profess an inability even to recognize our country since the arrival of postcolonial aliens has decisively altered its moral and cultural topography. I should emphasize that these problems precede and underpin the poetics of *racial*, *national*, and ethnic difference that makes them comprehensible. I must also insist that the country's persistent failure to be hospitable is about far more than just managing the internal effects of mass immigration. It cannot be said too often that this is not, at source, a matter of 'race,' even though, for many people, it is understood and lived as such. It is the workings of racism that produce the order of racial truths and not the other way around.

The consolidation of postcolonial melancholia suggests an even more disturbing possibility, namely that many people in Britain have actually come to need 'race' and perhaps to welcome its certainties as one sure way to keep their bearings in a world they experience as increasingly confusing. For them, there can be no working through this problem because the melancholic pattern has become the mechanism that sustains the unstable edifice of increasingly brittle and empty national identity. The nation's intermittent racial tragedies become part of an eventful history. They punctuate the boredom of chronic national decline with a functional anguish. The loss of empire – and the additional loss of certainty about the limits of national and racial identity that result from it – have begun, ironically, to sustain people, providing them with both pleasure and distraction. The historical approach tentatively pioneered here tries to seek out a less regular narrative rhythm than strict, even oscillation between identification with the victims of racism, a guilty dislike of them and the changes they have made to the country, and tormented self-disgust at the prospect of being implicated either in the problems they import or in their colonial and postcolonial sufferings.

Notes

1   Cited in Paul Foot, *Immigration and Race in British Politics* (Harmondsworth: Penguin, 1965) 106.
2   Peter Kilfoyle, 'With Friends Like These,' the *Guardian*, August 18, 2003.
3   Linda Colley, *Captives* (New York: Pantheon, 2002) 18.
4   Colley, *Captives*, 377.
5   England is not flag or Empire, it is not money and it is not blood.
    It's limestone gorge and granite fell, it's Wealden clay and Severn mud,
    Blackbird singing from the may tree, lark ascending through the scales.
    Robin watching from your spade and English earth beneath your nails.
    From 'A Place Called England,' written by Maggie Holland (© Moose Music, 1999).
6   These words come from the song 'Turn the Page.'
7   Alexander and Margarete Mitscherlich, *The Inability to Mourn: Principles of Collective Behavior*, trans. Beverly R. Paczek (1967; reprint, New York: Grove Press, 1975) xx.
8   Quoted in Enoch Powell, *Freedom and Reality* (Surrey: Elliot Right Way Books, 1969) 282.
9   E.g. the lurid coverage of the horrible assault on Norman and Cathy Green from Dorset, Terry Kirby, 'Gang Stabs British Tourist on Remote South African Beach,' the *Independent*, November 27, 2002. At one point, it was rumored that the Foreign Office had advised UK visitors to South Africa to take out 'rape insurance.'
10 Robert Cooper, *The Postmodern State and the World Order* (London: Demos, 2000) 39.
11 This text, which has attracted a lot of interest in the 'post-9/11' climate, is published in English as *The Battle of the Casbah: Terrorism and Counter-Terrorism in Algeria, 1955–1957* (New York: Enigma Books, 2002).

Chapter 23

Bill Schwarz

CLAUDIA JONES AND THE *WEST INDIAN GAZETTE*: REFLECTIONS ON THE EMERGENCE OF POSTCOLONIAL BRITAIN

> If Paul Gilroy has a 'friendly rival' for title of the most stimulating modern thinker about migration, racial identities and Britishness, it would be Bill Schwarz. This essay uncovers a whole world of half-forgotten ideas and activities — seemingly a small world, but one with huge implications for national, imperial and postcolonial histories.
>
> Stephen Howe

THE IDEA OF POSTCOLONIAL BRITAIN, on the face of it obvious enough, proves more elusive than we might expect. 'Postcolonial' arrived in the academy — as a specific object of intellectual inquiry — coupled with that familiar, but ever-awkward, adjunct 'theory'. As readers will know, postcolonial theory was often theory-with-a-vengeance, locked into the kind of abstraction which is inimical to historical thought. Translating these concerns into a properly historiographical mode, as the notion postcolonial Britain requires, has proved the source of much dispute.

The best of the early historiography on decolonization, deriving from quite different intellectual procedures, always sought to weigh up the respective balance between external (colonial and international) and internal (metropolitan) factors.[1] When the domestic has been considered, it is largely the question of economic and political institutions which figure most prominently.[2] But if we choose to accept the legitimacy of the term 'postcolonial Britain', this presses us into addressing the domestic dimensions of decolonization in their cultural or symbolic manifestations, for the idea of the postcolonial, in this context, carries with it an implied question: is Britain yet — or fully — postcolonial? Palpably, to all intents and purposes, the colonial Empire no longer exists. But there is no reason why we should suppose that mentalities, formed in an earlier colonial history, punctually terminate at the pre-ordained moment when the Empire itself disappears. It is this question which the notion of postcolonial Britain raises most sharply.

Research in this field of inquiry is in its earliest stages, and many difficulties present themselves. How can we possibly connect the events of far-away colonial lands, barely known at all by domestic Britons, to the everyday lives of those in the metropolis? What would such a historical reconstruction look like?

Yet it may be that it is in the domain of mental life ('culture'), particularly, that we can establish connections between the end of the Empire and transformations in the domestic scene. It is true that many difficulties arise, above all in methodology. For the native inhabitants of Britain, decolonization was, in contrast to France or Portugal, largely an invisible or heavily mediated phenomenon – seen principally through that strange medium of the newsreel. Even those Britons most dedicated to the cause of decolonization conventionally perceived it to be an issue concerning the colonized, in which the citizens of the metropole were only indirectly implicated.[3] Perhaps, in this instance, the job of the historian is to make visible or conscious assumptions which hitherto have been invisible or unconscious. This requires, in turn, deploying a mode of historical inquiry alert to the full complexities of mental life, in which displacement and the jamming together of different historical times represent the normal workings of the imagination. In short, the search for postcolonial Britain may take us to some unexpected places.

As I have argued elsewhere, the aboriginal philosopher of postcolonial Britain was Enoch Powell, and – paradoxically – an early moment in postcolonial Britain was manifest in a xenophobic movement of the radical right, turning on the resurrection of the remembered, colonial figure of the white man.[4] Clearly, this is not an argument in which strict, separable historical causes can be adumbrated. Decolonization is only one of the many inchoate histories of postcolonial Britain. But the difficulties of thinking through the domestic consequences of decolonization – invisibility, displacement, the simultaneous existence of competing historical times – should not tempt us to give up. In this respect, the postcolonial theorists were right: to explain these things we need a history of a rather different kind.

As my concern with Powell may indicate, I think questions of ethnic or racial identifications ('Where do I belong?'; or, in its transposed form, 'Where are you from?') have a privileged role in these colonial and postcolonial imaginings of subjective life. My own understanding is that during decolonization and in its aftermath, a consciousness of being white intensified for a significant number of indigenous Britons – those who took to identifying themselves, for example, in letters to the local press or to prominent politicians, such as Powell, explicitly as a 'white man'.[5] No one would doubt that the most proximate cause of the intensification of these sentiments was black immigration. While I would argue that these modes of self-identification drew heavily from colonial cultures – particularly from the political sensibilities of the white tribunes of the old settler societies – others would choose to reserve judgement. But insofar as these issues have now moved into the historiography, discussion about the relations between decolonization and the metropolis has principally (and for good reason) turned on the role of white Britons.[6] My purpose here is to turn this around and to explore this question from the vantage point of black Britons, resident in Britain: specifically those who had recently emigrated from the Caribbean.

This emigrant culture was important in many respects.[7] West Indians coming to Britain in the 1940s and 1950s were juridically British, regarded themselves as British, and regularly expressed enthusiasm for diverse aspects of the civilization of the British. The institutional cultures of their home nations – in schooling, sport, language, literature, religion – were unusually close to those of native Britons. Yet, at the same time, they came from societies well advanced in the prerequisites of breaking with colonialism. The majority would have had memories, as adults or children, of the cataclysmic labour riots which tore through the Caribbean in the late 1930s.[8] As a consequence of oral tradition, some memories went back much further – to the bloodletting of Governor Eyre, for example, in 1865.[9] Moreover, having arrived physically in the mother country, by virtue of the fact that they were not white, they experienced their Britishness, in all its deep, affective forms, as something precarious: both as resource and as liability. Located in British civilization, they found themselves simultaneously dislocated from its privileges.

In the postwar world, affiliation to the imperatives of Britishness diminished across all the old domains of what once represented Greater Britain – in the dominions, in the colonies and, as we can witness from the rather later apprehensions of the break-up of Britain, in Britain itself. Smuts, Churchill, Menzies: these were the Titans of this disappearing global civilization, who spent their later lives fighting many a rearguard action. In part, the disintegration of this transnational British world represents the symbolic dimensions of decolonization, the undoing of that civilization whose origins have been charted by Linda Colley.[10] The West Indians who crossed the seas and travelled to the mother country found themselves, against all expectations, living on the unofficial front line of this larger struggle for decolonization. Expatriate involvement in the political campaign to transfer power was one part of this, though perhaps a subordinate one. More significantly, West Indians in Britain were positioned such that – simply in going about their daily lives, navigating their way through the lore of the metropolis – they discovered themselves having to interrogate the lived culture of the colonizers, in order to comprehend their own discrepant experiences. If the British were unable to confront, in this sense, who they were and what they did, the marginal Britons from the Caribbean would have to do their work for them, in order that both could be free.[11] The West Indian emigrant – or immigrant, as he or she became the moment they disembarked – became an important, if often reluctant, agent in imagining a future for Britain after colonialism.

There are two aspects to this. The first can properly be called conceptual, in which intellectuals organic to the emigrant West Indian communities provided the formal means to think through these issues. The second, more informal and more difficult to locate, but just as significant, was manifest in the lived relations the West Indians brought with them, and which came – unevenly – to result in the incipient creolization of aspects of the metropolitan culture. The line between the two cannot easily be drawn.

Where, during the key years of decolonization, could one find located within Britain an intellectual culture which explicitly drew upon Frantz Fanon, W.E.B. DuBois, Kwame Nkrumah, Jomo Kenyatta, Martin Luther King, Paul Robeson, Nelson Mandela, and James Baldwin, and upon the traditions exemplified by *Presence africaine*?

Some of these influences registered in the various publications of the emergent New Left. As agents of sedition, many or all of these figures would have been the object of state surveillance, accruing weighty files – though even the most curious employee of the secret state would have to concede that the purpose of such surveillance could hardly be construed as intellectual. A more complete, if not entirely exclusive, answer is in the pages of the *West Indian Gazette*. It is worth exploring this more closely.

The *Gazette* was launched in the spring of 1958, taking as its full title the *West Indian Gazette and Afro-Asian Caribbean News*. It came out monthly; it fluctuated in size, though it was generally anything between eight and sixteen pages; it cost sixpence (in the currency of the time); and its offices were based in Brixton.

Its inspiration was Claudia Jones.[12] Jones had been born in Port of Spain in 1915, and as a child emigrated with her family to Harlem. There she was drawn into the Young Communist League, and Harlem radicalism entered her soul. She was repeatedly arraigned, harassed by the authorities, and suffered a spell in prison. In 1955 it was finally ruled that she be deported but, as the colonial government in Trinidad wanted nothing to do with her, she was shipped to Britain, where she arrived – appropriately, in a fog of Stygian density – in December. In contrast to her send-off from New York, the British Communist Party barely noticed her arrival; King Street, it seems, was unnerved by this Harlem tyro. Nonetheless, she threw herself into tireless political activity, determining to animate the specifically West Indian culture of the emigrant on the home territory of Britain itself. The *Gazette*, in her own mind, worked as the principal means by which this would be achieved. Like many such ventures, it was the product of imagination, colossal human energy (hers, mainly), and minimal material back-up.

The *West Indian Gazette* was founded a matter of months before white riots broke out in Notting Hill and in Nottingham, in late August and September 1958.[13] It is difficult to retrieve the full impact of the collective violence unleashed on the local immigrant communities. In popular memory these events are conventionally recorded through the fiction of Colin MacInnes and the cinema of Julien Temple.[14] In their different ways, these catch important truths. But neither quite conveys the pitch and extent of visceral racial hatred.[15] In the aftermath many hundreds of West Indians chose to return home.[16] Those who remained did so on the understanding that initial hopes of integrating into the mainstream of British society had become severely curtailed. In an unanticipated ruse of history, this new situation in which the West Indian immigrants found themselves proved the making of the *Gazette*. If the prospect of integration were to be postponed to some distant future, and if its desirability had become compromised as a consequence of the experience of racial terror, those who chose to stay did so in the realization that, in the future, the only cultural resources they could call upon were those they made their own, summoned from a long collective memory of fear and violence. The *West Indian Gazette* attempted to invent a public voice which could articulate these hopes and fears.[17]

Much of the originality of the *Gazette* was to be found in its attempt to connect the local with the global: to link, say, the specific neighbourhood concerns of its readers in Notting Hill to the wider global world of anticolonialism and the Civil Rights movement. Much is revealed by the juxtaposition of stories which, according to the journalistic conventions of the time, should have had nothing in common. The combination of these reports supplied a view of the world unlike any other. In November 1959, for example, photographs showing Guinea's Sekou Toure arriving at London airport sit side by side with a report that the Afro-Asian WI Nurses' Association had just been launched in Balham. Or again, in April 1961, the lead story on the front page comprised an account of a Ladbroke Grove pub which was imposing a colour bar. This competed with publication of Patrice Lumumba's last letter; reports about protests against Kenyatta's continuing imprisonment; news that a nineteen-year-old Jamaican nurse in London, Cherry Larman, had replaced Marlene Walker as carnival queen; and the announcement that Mr David Pitt was to contest Stoke Newington in the forthcoming London County Council elections.

There was one advertisement, addressed to those who had 'the West Indian or African appetite', publicizing ENCO imported foodstuffs; and two notices: one for the Africa Day Concert at the Festival Hall, with Paul Robeson and Humphrey Lyttleton, and one announcing a seventy-two-hour vigil at Lancaster House to campaign against apartheid, under the banner 'Verwoerd Must Go!'

All newspapers, according to Benedict Anderson in his analysis of the workings of imagined communities, produce a sense of 'simultaneity'. The sum total of published stories, by connecting events which otherwise would remain disconnected, works to create the possibility for imagining a larger collectivity as a community, as in some manner – knowable.[18] From this point of view, placing Lumumba's last letter, or stories about Kenyatta, alongside a report of David Pitt's hopes for Stoke Newington gives each an equivalence, integrating the local with the global; or even (in this instance) effacing all difference between them. Each becomes an episode in a larger story.

Despite the frequent invocation of the roll-call of the great anti-colonial figures of the age, the *Gazette's* conception of the global also carried the feel of the local. Almost exclusively, the global embraced the political world of the black Atlantic. Cape Town, Accra, Birmingham, Alabama: these were proximate locales in the mental maps generated in the pages of the *Gazette*. Personalities were important. In the manner of the Communist press of the time, the *Gazette* declared (in December 1959) that its 'Heroine of the Year' was 'brave mother of 11, Mrs Elizabeth Mafeking', the President of the South African Agricultural and Cannery Workers. Paul Robeson – close friend to Claudia Jones from Harlem days and staunch supporter of the *Gazette* – was a continual presence. Cultural events in Harlem received detailed reporting, as did the shows (and political activities) of Harry Belafonte and, with rather more circumspection, Sammy Davis Jr. News from the Caribbean featured prominently – especially from Jamaica, and most especially from Kingston. Local matters of interest to the inhabitants of Kingston (the burning of Henderson's, a city store, for example) came, for the majority of the paper's readers, as a story from afar; but for those who had once lived in Kingston, even though they might now be inhabiting a British city, this remained a story of neighbourhood. The experience of diaspora, which the *Gazette* strained to voice, turned the polarities of local and global inside-out.

By extension, the local which the *West Indian Gazette* brought into being was, resolutely, a black local. Readers might feel that their new neighbourhoods in urban Britain were, by jostling in the pages of the paper with other known locations of the black Atlantic world, accorded a measure of recognition, or validation. But the local was never subsumed by this larger world. The *Gazette* carried the flavour of its dispossessed Brixton and South London environment. (One of the most regular advertisements carried by the paper promoted the services of Prof. T.A. Wheeler of 175 Stockwell Road, 'London's greatest authority on all diseases of the hair and skin'.) Attempts to reach out to cover black life in Birmingham and the Midlands were frequent, but the tone of the paper stubbornly reproduced its South London and Notting Hill axis. For all the echoes of the global world, its local was as local as any provincial newspaper. Except, critically, for the issue of race, an interview with a schoolboy footballer – in form – could have come from any local newspaper, as could the photographs of the weddings. For a while Claudia Jones ran the story of two orphaned London twins, who were dubbed 'The St. Lucia Babes', and sought to raise cash from what was in the process of becoming 'the black community'. Recognition that this was a community in the making also required that public voice be given to the indignities of daily life – to the accumulating forces which conspired to prevent expatriate West Indians from becoming a community. Thus, for example, in September 1960 the fate of Norman Taylor was reported. He had just moved into Reservoir Road, Brockley – the first Caribbean to do so – and within days of his arrival his van was set alight.

Through the evolution of the *Gazette* it is possible to witness the slow emergence of this black locality, and to plot its urban topographies. It came to life at seemingly random points in the city, fashioned out of what was to hand. By the end of 1960, for example, it was announced that the *Gazette* was obtainable from the following locations: Desmond's Reliable Furniture, Denmark Hill; Deins's Food Store, Shepherd's Bush; Theo's Record Shop, Brixton Road; Carmen's Beauty Shop, Hollywood Road, SW10; Lewis Stores, Lower Clapton Road; Paddington Travel Bureau; Martyn's Barber Shop, Coldharbour Lane; Monica's Beauty Salon, Lowfield Road, N3; Rainbow Travel, Edgware Road. In London, these nondescript outlets served as the improvized institutions of a nascent, ramshackle black civil society.

They also represented another, significant phase in a process which had been occurring as long as colonialism: the gradual, uneven creolization of the metropolis, in which the cultural forms of the periphery moved to, and subsequently transformed, the centre. The movement of vernacular musics from the West Indies to Britain – most especially of Trinidadian calypso and of ska, the specifically Jamaican rendition of rhythm and blues – proved to be of historic significance, creating within Britain a new syncretic culture. Theo's Record Shop, or shops like it, worked to create new urban soundscapes for both West Indians and indigenous Britons.[19] For much of the 1950s and even in the early 1960s, this was largely a subterranean process, though there were occasions when more public manifestations could be spotted. Alongside the bowler-hatted trad jazz bands on the CND marches, for example, the *Gazette* reported the presence of West Indian calypsonians. Famously, Cy Grant fronted the topical calypsos on BBC's television programme, *Tonight* (first broadcast in 1957) – though the integrity of the form may be open to doubt in this case, given the fact that they were scripted by an Englishman of deeply English sensibilities, Bernard Levin.[20] From the late 1940s, South London had been the venue for many formal inter-racial dances – some of which were hosted by the Brixton MP, Marcus Lipton, who, while relatively tolerant on the issue of black immigration, held a fanatical distaste for the infiltration of 'African' musical forms into Britain.[21] The *Gazette* promoted inter-racial dances on this model, and at the end of 1960 an 'Inter-racial Talent Contest', with early rounds taking place in Lambeth, Stoke Newington, and Kensington town halls, and the 'Grand Final' at St. Pancras Town Hall. It also supported the British-Caribbean Annual Christmas Ball which, in 1960, featured Cleo Laine and the Dudley Moore Sextet, with Mr. and Mrs. Iain Macleod invited as guests of honour.

But these activities were peripheral compared with the energies poured into the launching of carnival. Claudia Jones was one of the principal figures, maybe even the principal figure, in re-inventing traditional Trinidadian carnival for the West Indian diaspora in Britain. The *West Indian Gazette* functioned as the effective public organizer of carnival. In Claudia Jones's imagination these two institutions – the *Gazette* and carnival – worked to the same purpose: they were to become the means by which a West Indian community conscious of its history was to be born on British soil. The idea of creating carnival in Britain – if not yet a 'British' carnival, an unimaginable concept then – came about as a direct response to the white riots of August and September 1958. Out of a situation of fear and hatred, carnival was to be revived as collective testament to the elemental human worth of the colonized and formerly enslaved, a tribute rooted deeply in traditions of popular music and dance, adornment, masquerade, and burlesque. London's first carnival was held in the chilly, municipal environment of St. Pancras Town Hall in February 1959 – billed to coincide with carnival in the Caribbean, not with more appropriate climactic conditions in the UK. The BBC was persuaded to televise it, though (most likely due to the fact that it must have been filmed live) no footage seems to have survived. Here, too, the complex reverberations of the local and the global can be felt. For the new residents of London, St. Pancras Town Hall was eminently, immediately local – as far removed from the streets of Port of Spain as could be imagined. But in Claudia Jones's mind, at least, West Indians in London were a constituent part of the emergent, larger West Indian nation. Carnival may have been inspired by the particular conditions of London, following the Notting Hill riots, but it was also conceived as an organic part of the movement for colonial independence, and of the ambitions to transform the West Indian Federation into an active, living, cultural reality. She wrote in the 1959 souvenir programme:

> A pride in being West Indian is undoubtedly at the root of this unity: a pride that has its origin in the drama of nascent nationhood, and that pride encompasses not only the creativeness, uniqueness and originality of West Indian mime, song and dance – but is the genesis of the nation itself.[22]

The carnival organizers determined that the event should be West Indian; but they did not mean it to be exclusive. The fact that it was to be relayed by television to the homes of white Britons was perceived to be an important breakthrough in establishing the public credentials of West Indians in Britain. In January 1960, in reporting the news that the BBC had agreed to televise the second carnival, the *Gazette* noted that this would 'infuse the Carnival spirit of Friendship, Gaiety and Joy into every British home'. The tone of optimism was characteristic. But Jones herself was always keen that native Britons should be involved. In 1961 the carnival queen judges included two MPs, Marcus Lipton and Nigel Fisher; the following year, the playwright John Osborne and the theatre-director Joan Littlewood were recruited.

In retrospect, it is difficult to decide who presents the more incongruous judge of a Caribbean carnival queen contest – John Osborne, whose views on the new world that he himself had been significant in proclaiming, a while earlier, were becoming increasingly sour; or Joan Littlewood, whose spirited, anarchic feminism would not appear to have made her a likely arbiter on feminine convention.[23] There is no hint of anticipation in the pages of the *Gazette*, or elsewhere for that matter, of the outrage which would compel a later generation of white women, in 1970, to hurl flour-bombs at Bob Hope while he compered the Miss World competition. The carnival queen contest, in 1959 and in the early 1960s, was imagined by all to be an essential part of carnival, and an exercise in affirming the qualities of black femininity, demonstrating that black could indeed be beautiful. As a cadre in the Communist Party of the USA, Claudia Jones had written fierce words about what she described as the super-exploitation of black women.[24] It was precisely due to her recognition of this experience of women's denigration in economic and social life that Jones, and others, could look on carnival queen contests as an affirmative act.[25]

It is difficult to overestimate the significance of the carnival queen contests. Carnival itself was a major event. No doubt, the *West Indian Gazette* accorded it more influence in the lives of the Caribbean diaspora than it merited – as we may suppose from the wishful belief that a televised carnival would bring the virtue of friendship into British homes. In absolute terms, the numbers who attended were not huge. In 1961 there were an estimated 1,800 people – out of an overall West Indian population in London of some 60,000.[26] And yet, as an occasion which combined maximal good times with a measure of political purpose, it was unrivalled. By the 1962 carnival – edging forward in the calendar to March – the organizers were able to fly Mighty Sparrow over from Trinidad. This marked an impressive coup. Sparrow was a popular intellectual of great renown, who conveyed in the vernacular the hopes of independence from colonial rule. C.L.R. James declared of him that: 'He is living proof that there is a West Indian nation'.[27] More traditionally accredited intellectuals had their role to play as well. In 1960, while Claudia Jones was charged with awarding the tombola prizes and Sylvia Wynter narrated the events, as MC, the carnival queen contest was judged by George Lamming, Jan Carew, Sam Selvon, and Pearl Connor. This line-up represented a sensational ensemble of West Indian intellectuals, whose collective thought still resonates in the Caribbean today. That the reason for their congregating was carnival, and more particularly the carnival queen contest, is instructive. Throughout the year the *Gazette* provided extensive coverage of the carnival queen, publishing photographs of the contestants in the lead-up; announcing the winner; and then following the activities of the carnival queen through the summer months. In 1960 the prize awarded to Marlene Walker comprised a return-trip home to the Caribbean. Reports of her departure from London, in June, and her arrival back in August, were carried with accompanying photographs. The *Gazette* turned Marlene Walker into big news, projecting her as their own West Indian star. She played out her symbolic role as figurehead, or queen, of the emergent community. This followed the conventions of many such carnivals, separated widely in time and space, but we might speculate that something more was happening on this occasion. Perhaps the crowning of the carnival queen allowed the home nations of the West Indies to be remembered, through the figure of the female icon, by those destined to remain. Or in a sharper rendition, given the choice of prize, we might surmise that she could act out for her symbolic subjects what they could only dream: going home.

Marlene Walker had *style*. Carnival was an occasion not only for music but also for fashion, as the competition for the best-dressed bands confirms. It is clear from the advertisements placed in the *Gazette* that male fashion constituted an important dimension of the lives of the new emigrants. Arnold's, for example, of Blackstock Road, catered for the impecunious man of fashion, offering 'West Indian Style Suits' on 'Pay As You Wear' terms. Female fashion, and the feminine world, were addressed in (irregularly appearing) women's pages. 'Beauty Tropical', by Carmen, was one such feature. The issue of December 1960 proffered advice on deportment and charm (and correct lip-shades) to 'The Smart West Indian Woman' around London, reminding readers that 'Your appearance gets a close scrutiny'. Style was a contradictory phenomenon. It cannot be read, retrospectively, simply as a conscious vehicle for subverting the codes of respectable Britain, though at times – in its male, zoot incarnation – it was just that. For, equally, it could serve as a means to proclaim the conviction that the immigrant was as smart or as respectable as any native Briton.[28] But even with respectability to the fore, the conscious inhabitation of convention does not preclude the disturbance of its boundaries as, from a different sector of the national culture, the mods were about to reveal. Style implies being one step ahead in the game; minimally, it carries with it a subtext of excess. The photographic evidence of West Indians in Britain in the 1950s and early 1960s suggests the degree to which style, in this sense, was lived.[29]

Alongside fashion tips, the women's pages in the *Gazette* offered information on Caribbean cooking. One of the most consistent refrains of the diasporic fiction of the 1950s turns on the absence of home dishes, and the lengths the new emigrants would go to get hold of familiar produce, including not only foodstuffs, but favoured brands of rum. The dearth of these clearly proved painful. As late as 1960, a bottle of pepper-sauce was priced at two-and-six (a hefty sum). In the same year, an advertisement made a point of emphasizing the fact that fresh West Indian food was available from an outlet in the Victoria Dock Road – some distance from the usual Caribbean neighbourhoods. We may assume, as a consequence, that fresh items were hard to come by elsewhere. The situation seems to have changed fairly rapidly thereafter, with new shops opening and more regular supplies of Caribbean fare arriving in the new black neighbourhoods of British cities. The attention given in the pages of the *Gazette* to the introduction of Mount Gay Rum and Red Stripe beer is notable. The first advertisement for Mount Gay Rum appeared in June 1960, followed (in August) by a full report welcoming its arrival; subsequent advertisements listed all the shops in Britain which stocked it, allowing again the new local topographies to be charted – in London and the Midlands particularly. A year later the *Gazette* indicated that Red Stripe had come, pondering the fact that although it was promoted as a West Indian beer, it would only have been known, up until then, to Jamaicans – implying, perhaps, the degree to which a collective West Indian identity could take root, with peculiar force, in the diaspora. The fate of Red Stripe in Britain continued to be of concern to the *Gazette* for some months after its introduction.

These issues raise questions about the place of early West Indian entrepreneurship in Britain, about which too little is known. More particularly, though, they remind us that the market in West Indian commodities was not only an economic phenomenon. Through these commercial initiatives the lived cultures of the Caribbean came to be embedded in urban Britain. Creolization, though, supposes something more than this, suggesting a significant measure of transformation of the civilization of the metropolis itself.

On this the *Gazette* was characteristically up-beat, confident that the values of its own West Indian societies were percolating through to the British. In December 1959 it reported a poll, originating from the *Sunday Times*, which revealed that the celebrity whom British teenagers most wanted to meet was Norman Manley. (The discredited runners-up included Churchill, Montgomery, the Duke of Edinburgh, Kruschev, Albert Schweitzer, the Queen, Fidel Castro, Laurence Olivier, Louis Armstrong, and Elvis.) This is a surprising, even quirky, finding. It is of some consequence, as it followed Manley's well-publicized journey to London – Notting Hill included – in the aftermath of the white riots, in order to speak for the West Indians resident in Britain, who otherwise experienced emigration as little different from a re-imposition of colonial disenfranchisement. But without further corroborative evidence, not too much can be made of it.

In itself, the extension of Caribbean cultures into the metropole did not necessarily work to creolize the metropolitan civilization, nor was creolization the only means by which a new domestic postcolonial order arrived. When I first became interested in these themes, and asked students to consider the cultural consequences of the end of the Empire in Britain, they invariably came to write about the proliferation of different cuisines, anticipating Robin Cook's enthusiasm for the fact the most popular national dish has come to be Chicken Tikka Massala. In itself, this does not really get us anywhere. Even if we could point to an increase in the consumption of yams among native Britons in Notting Hill or Brixton in the early 1960s, or to an increasing preference for Mount Gay Rum rather than Johnnie Walker, we would be hard pressed to draw any significant conclusions. We need only call to mind William Hague. A few years back, as leader of the Conservative opposition, he was photo-called with his wife-to-be in matching, sparklingly laundered safari gear – sipping over-the-top cocktails at carnival in Notting Hill. This multicultural pastime did nothing to halt his expatiating on the dangers of an England which (he warned) was on the point of becoming a foreign land. In themselves, yams or, in a later age, ditzy cocktails are not the issue.

Vernacular musical forms, and the varied presentations of the self which accompany them, may suggest a more complex phenomenon. Here there is a strong case for arguing that cultures which originated on the colonial periphery did move to the centre and restructure metropolitan life, while the anti-colonial credentials of calypso and ska are evident. Carnival, in its journey from municipal St. Pancras in February 1959 to the current free-for-all extravaganza, represents a profound transformation of Britain itself. Even if one doubts the commitments of William Hague, the fact that he felt impelled to make the visit is significant. But even here, methodological questions remain. The most convincing, sophisticated account of the impact of Caribbean and black musics on Britain in this period – Dick Hebdige's *Subculture* – concedes that the creolization he unearths took the form of a 'phantom history'.[30] By this he means that the forms of indigenous British musics and style which emerged in the 1960s were in a perpetual, if often unspoken, dialogue with their black counterparts, appropriating, adapting, and refusing as the moment demanded. Hebdige makes it clear that this is a form of historical explanation which, while empirically located, depends on interpretative readings of particular symbolic forms. In the manner of Carlo Ginzburg's morphological histories, it cannot finally decide an argument, in the sense of staking a strict demarcation between truth and falsity. In other words, it cannot conform to the positivist injunction: 'Make it true and real!' But an approach 'such as this can open new lines of thought, and illuminate unseen patterns and connections in the past'.[31] Cultural histories of this sort may help in working through the problem of postcolonial Britain.

One methodological problem remains which I will not attempt to answer here. I assume that the domestic culture of the metropolis in the postwar period can be understood to be (in some way) colonial. Sceptics may see in this assumption an unwarranted stretching of the concept of colonial. I would say only that to a degree (how, when, how much: all remains open) the conception of civilization which Britain embodied was cast not only in the metropole but in the colonies and overseas empire. In the twentieth century, Smuts, Menzies and many more were not just adjuncts to an already-given idea of Britain, but were active creators in making this a conception of civilization which lived.[32] Particularly, it was in Britain 'overseas' that the work was done which ensured that the deepest values of the British came to be encoded as the special preserve of the white race. The movement of these philosophies – these conceptions of civilization – from overseas to metropolitan Britain was a complex one, which in turn presents another layer of methodological difficulty. But it did happen.

It is in this context that we can understand creolization. The non-white world represented by the *West Indian Gazette* had been formed in the codes of British civilization, and knew its inner forms with a lifelong intimacy. As even its most conservative intellectuals acknowledged, commitment to the idea of Britain in the Caribbean could simultaneously be experienced as profoundly meaningful and as a kind of ventriloquism, never quite working as it should. Some of the early fiction of V.S. Naipaul describes this very well.

This discrepant experience redoubled when emigration to the metropolis occurred, opening up both old wounds and new possibilities. West Indian Britishness in Britain was a historically specific amalgam of competing pressures, and was peculiarly volatile. It marked a lived form of Britishness which was in the process of imploding. In this lay its creativity, and its dangers too. In themselves, the opening of Desmond's Reliable Furniture store on Denmark Hill, the arrival of Mount Gay Rum, or even the adventures of Marlene Walker may not signal much of historical consequence. But in the larger context, and in combination, I think they do. They capture the lived expressions of this emigrant world. But they were also touched by a vigorous anti-colonial intellectual culture. Which brings us back to Fanon, DuBois, Nkrumah . . .

At the same time that the *West Indian Gazette* devoted its coverage to carnival queen contests, or to the import of home liquors, it was a medium of uncompromising anti-colonialism. This was an anti-colonialism which inherited the tradition of Pan-Africanism that had, in London in the 1930s, been closely identified with the activities of West Indians, among whom George Padmore and C.L.R. James were the most influential. In turn, in the *Gazette* this tradition had become allied to the body of thought then emerging from the USA in the early phases of the Civil Rights movement. This reflected a political universe whose boundaries were determined by the black Atlantic. A notable exception came about as a result of Claudia Jones's growing enthusiasm for China, which may have been the cause of further difficulties between her and the British Communists. Kenyatta, co-conspirator with Padmore and James in the 1930s, was a prominent figure, and was interviewed by the paper when he was in London in December 1961. The fate of Nkrumah's Ghana was closely observed, the paper filing reports from Amy Ashwood Garvey – Marcus Garvey's first wife and a named editor of the *Gazette* – while, in October 1962, Nkrumah contributed his own account. Fiery stories about the collapse of the Central African Federation were carried, as they were about the deepening repression within South Africa. Sekou Toure was translated from *Presence africaine*, writing on the emancipation of women (December 1959), and DuBois extolled the socialist advances achieved by China (September 1959). The deaths of Fanon and DuBois brought, in July 1962 and June 1963, respectively, admiring appreciations. When the crucible of US Civil Rights shifted to Birmingham, Alabama in the spring of 1963, the *Gazette* provided regular coverage. There was much more in similar vein. Optimism of the will worked in conjunction with a comprehensive vision of anti-colonial imperatives.

The Caribbean, as one would have expected, represented the most active concerns of the *Gazette*. The Cuban Revolution was regarded as a decisive moment in Caribbean history, eliciting copy from one established distinguished historian, E. Hobsbawm (in December 1960, recounting his first trip to a Caribbean island), and from one future distinguished historian, Walter Rodney (in May 1962). In the aftermath of the Bay of Pigs the paper was quick to promote the 'Hands Off Cuba!' campaign. The *Gazette* celebrated every advance of anti-colonialism and 'progress' in the British West Indies (Trinidad's first native-born governor; the first woman barrister in Antigua, which made front-page news), and saw each sporting success as a sign of readiness for independence. It advocated with passion West Indian Federation, publishing frantic pleas (September 1961) designed to dissuade Jamaica from seceding and, effectively, from destroying future prospects for a pan-Caribbean unity.[33]

More particularly, the *West Indian Gazette* served as the house-paper for a generation of Caribbean intellectuals who had made the journey to London. Here, too, a sense of locality was expressed. The successes of local (London-Caribbean) writers and activists were relayed with evident pride – much like the sporting achievements of their compatriots back home. In June 1960 the paper announced that David Pitt had been elected to the London Labour Party Executive and that Andrew Salkey had given up teaching in order to devote more time to his writing. In November it reported that Salkey had won a Guggenheim scholarship. That same month, under the heading 'To Local Artists', readers were informed that V.S. Naipaul had received a residential scholarship in the West Indies, launched to persuade native artists to return home: Naipaul was quoted as offering the unlikely sentiment that 'It is a fine example of a Government recognizing local talent'. The following May it was the turn of George Lamming, invited to Canada to attend an international conference of the arts. These were local figures, 'local talent' in Naipaul's words, articulating the essentials of a knowable community. In the pages of the *Gazette* the novels of this small expatriate intelligentsia were reviewed, the poems and paintings reproduced. Claudia Jones herself, Amy Ashwood Garvey, Eric Williams, John La Rose, George Lamming, Jan Carew, Aubrey Williams, Ronald Moody, Sam Selvon, Walter Rodney, Richard Hart, Arthur Lewis: all were represented.

They spoke in a plurality of idioms; some were drawn to a firebrand politics, others to quieter contemplation of the aesthetic. They all shared, though, a belief in the necessity of independence from colonial rule, as an elemental moral requirement, and a faith – in varying degrees – in the future of the West Indian people.

Contention was rife. Certain themes, though, recur. Many of these thinkers, for example, felt impelled – as part of their anti-colonial sympathies – to explore anew the historical past. This registers, in the fiction and in the critical writings, across the entire West Indian intellectual formation of the period. The *West Indian Gazette* saw itself as a popular educator in the field, presenting short accounts of key events of the past (the issue of November 1959, for example, told of the Morant Bay Rebellion). There was evident soul-searching about the best means to constitute a specifically Caribbean history, free from colonial perspectives.[34] Interesting, though, is the manner in which these formal intellectual arguments blended into more popular sensibilities, in which Africa and a specifically black past assumed a new imaginative fascination in the present. The insights West Indian visitors brought back from newly independent Ghana were influential in providing an immediacy to these longer, collective memories – a sense of which can be gauged from the vernacular musics of the time. But there are hints elsewhere as well. In the *Gazette* there appeared correspondence proposing the introduction of Yoruba as an official language of the Caribbean (in January 1960). The paper picked up on a research report (September 1960) produced by academics at the University College of the West Indies, which had investigated the emergence of the Rastafarian movement in Jamaica, concluding that alarm about the Rastafarians had been manufactured by the police and that there was no need for them to be perceived as seditious. Norman Manley was prevailed upon to meet with an official delegation. In September 1961, Claudia Jones discussed the revival of Garveyism in Jamaica. There were also more poignant indications of the extent of this rediscovered remembrance of Africa. In October 1959, Roy Prince, a barber of Blenheim Crescent, Notting Hill, and four of his friends decided that they would explore the idea of 'returning' to Africa by making a preliminary trip to Guinea. They got as far as southern Morocco only to realize the difficulties which further travel across the desert would entail. They remained in Casablanca for three weeks, and then came back to Notting Hill.[35]

Garveyism, Rastafarianism, Africa: these powerful, imagined categories, brought into the present, worked to articulate the experience of being black. Or more precisely, they made it possible to *be* black. 'I became black in London, not Kingston', as Stuart Hall has put it.[36] This represents a critical moment, for it anticipates the symbolic shift in Caribbean cultures from an ascription defined principally in terms of being West Indian to one which was moved to claim itself as black. These categories made speakable what, in the recent history of the British West Indies, had been rendered unspeakable, or what had only been thinkable in terms of the uneasy projections of an individual pathology: the fact of blackness itself. This is a transformation which has many dimensions. But its specifically British conditions – the conditions of a diasporic locality – can, I think, be gleaned from the pages of the *Gazette*.

The white riots of 1958 and the murder of Kelso Cochrane early in 1959 did much to define the purpose of the *West Indian Gazette*. But even in the midst of racial violence, the prospect of independence and, in Britain, the success of carnival made possible a belief in a future. Claudia Jones died at the end of 1964. The paper continued for a while after her death, but then wound up. The tone of the *Gazette* is rather different at the end of her editorship than in its earlier years. The defeat of the West Indian Federation proved a bitter blow. But the situation in Britain also provoked darker forebodings. It is clear from the later coverage that the paper began to address a Caribbean population which was becoming more settled and, so far as we can judge, more prosperous. Advertisements proffered the full range of consumer durables which, from the late 1950s, had begun to be marketed on a mass basis. From 1961 there appeared advice on how to buy property and (slightly later) information on the mortgage company which David Pitt had organized to serve Caribbean residents in London. Articles on schooling appeared for the first time. But this determination to settle and build a family life in Britain, combined perhaps with increased purchasing power, triggered new tensions, for new domains of discrimination opened up. The *Gazette* began to report on racism in the education system (June 1963). Increasing attention was given to police harassment, and to the need for black families to know their legal rights. From November 1961 a series of stories covered the arrest and subsequent assault of six West Indians – four women and two men – in Brixton. In February the following year the *Gazette* printed Claudia Jones's own story 'I Spend A Night in Notting Hill Police Station' – in which she related how a black companion, driving through London, was stopped by the police and arrested. With typical gutsiness, Jones insisted the police arrest her as well – hence the night of incarceration. Both had spent the evening celebrating the opening of Red Stripe House.

The *Gazette* denounced (in August 1960) Sir Oswald Mosley's rally in Brixton, at which he called for all 'Jamaicans' to be sent home. Earlier in the year the paper's offices had received threatening calls from a neo-Nazi group; in May 1961 the offices were ransacked, and faeces smeared throughout. The same month that the Mosley rally had been reported, the *Gazette* started monitoring the speeches of the Conservative MP Cyril Osborne, who had determined to lift the issue of black immigration into a matter of major public concern. The fact that Osborne was knighted in the Queen's Birthday Honours of 1961 was perceived by the *Gazette* as a serious, dangerous affront. But the honour for Osborne coincided with increasing indications that the government was about to introduce legislation designed to clamp down on non-white immigration to the UK. Legislation of this sort had been mooted since the mid-1950s, but on each occasion had been shelved for fear that provision determined purely by race would prove so fiercely controversial that there could be no likelihood of success.[37] The draft of the Commonwealth Immigration Bill, however, was made public in the autumn of 1961. Its proposals demonstrated that what previously had been deemed impossible had now become merely a technical or pragmatic matter, or that the government felt able to ride out any consequent moral censure. Claudia Jones condemned the bill as 'monstrous' (November 1961), convinced that the only possible rationale for its introduction was racist. The *Gazette* campaigned against it, drawing into its pages white opponents – of whom Fenner Brockway was the most prominent. The failure of this campaign, and the passing of the legislation, coming in the immediate aftermath of the destruction of the Federation, marked a cruel time. Future prospects looked grim.

These developments were experienced by some as a reassertion of colonial mentalities within Britain – as the organization of a system devoted to the segregation of 'second class citizens' (December 1961) – just at the moment when independence was in the process of being granted in the Caribbean. The riots of 1958 had principally brought racial violence onto the streets and into particular neighbourhoods. In some respects, the passing of the Commonwealth Immigration Bill represented an assault of more comprehensive proportions, in which the home civilization of the British, from top to bottom, proved culpable. For the emigrant, or now more properly settler, population these transformations signalled an acute dislocation in the relations of Britishness, in the heartland of Britain itself. The effects were far-reaching. In intellectual terms they encouraged, I think, an inward-turn: a shift in analytical focus that was increasingly drawn to examine the internal modes of power within the civilization of the metropole; and a shift too to the inner life of Britishness, to the subjective realities of former colonized and former colonizers alike.

In the same issue that Claudia Jones recounted her arrest, George Lamming reflected on these themes. He told of a visit to a working-class neighbour in Chiswick, and contrasted this experience to dinner at high-table at a Cambridge college. Dinner at the high-table brought home to him the intractable complexity of the unspoken rituals of upper-class England. His hosts at Cambridge represented, he believed, a culture which was entirely located, entirely centred, conscious only of the fact that those whose lives fell outside its boundaries were somehow aberrant, lacking in refinement, reason, and civilization. Lamming's friend in Chiswick inhabited that different universe. He told Lamming that when he listened to the wireless he only tuned in to the Light Programme, 'knowing' that the other programmes devoted to Shakespeare, as he had got it into his mind, were not for him. Lamming wrote:

> I realised that almost two-thirds of the population of this country were in a colonial relation to the culture and traditions which were called England. And it was at this point that my own process of decolonisation began.

This is a moving moment. It charts an instant of recognition in which a conception of civilization ('the traditions which were called England') falls away, allowing a new future to be imagined. Lamming poses this in a manner which domestic critics of cultural hierarchies at that time did not: in terms of colonialism. Decolonization signals here not only a formal critique of the public curriculum of the civilization of the British, but a more difficult inquiry into lived and subjective forms: into 'my own process' of decolonization. This short passage also conveys, literally, the sense that this work of internal decolonization has been initiated by the former colonized – shipped into the metropolis, and bringing into the heartlands a sense of future possibility. It marks a fleeting instance of Britain becoming postcolonial.

These ideas were first presented at a session of the Postcolonial Britain conference, organized by the Institute of Contemporary British History in July 2002. With thanks to Simon Gikandi, Stephen Howe, and Wendy Webster, and especially to Catherine Hall.

Notes

1   The most analytically convincing engagement remains John Darwin, *Britain and Decolonization. The Retreat from Empire in the Postwar World* (London, 1988); see too his 'Decolonization and the End of Empire', in Robin Winks (ed.) *The Oxford History of the British Empire. Vol. V, Historiography* (Oxford, 1999). Largely complementary in approach is R.F. Holland, *European Decolonization, 1918–1981: An Introductory Survey* (London, 1985).

2   On economic institutions, pre-eminent in synoptic power is P.J. Cain and A.G. Hopkins, *British Imperialism: Crisis and Deconstruction, 1914–1990* (London, 1993). On the political arena, see John Darwin, 'Fear of Falling: British Politics and Imperial Decline since 1900', *Transactions of the Royal Historical Society*, 1986, 36, 27–43; David Goldsworthy, *Colonial Issues in British Politics, 1945–1961* (Oxford, 1971); Miles Kahler, *Decolonization in Britain and France: The Domestic Consequences of International Relations* (Princeton, 1984); Stephen Howe, *Anticolonialism in British Politics. The Left and the End of Empire* (Oxford, 1993); and Philip Murphy, *Party Politics and Decolonization: The Conservative Party and British Colonial Policy in Tropical Africa, 1951–1964* (Oxford, 1995). An important attempt to read race in these terms was Paul B. Rich, *Race and Empire in British Politics* (Cambridge, 1986).

3   When the Movement for Colonial Freedom was launched in April 1954, in the draft of the inaugural policy statement Jennie Lee noted that 'Our immediate objective must be to create a psychological revolution throughout the colonies'. This projection of the issue outwards was symptomatic. Quoted in Howe, *Anticolonialism in British Politics*, 234.

4   Bill Schwarz, 'Actually Existing Postcolonialism', *Radical Philosophy*, 2000, 104, 16–24.

5   Bill Schwarz, 'The only white man in there. The re-racialization of Britain, 1956–68', *Race and Class*, 1996, 38, 65–78.

6   Representative is the fine collection edited by Stuart Ward, *British Culture and the End of Empire* (Manchester, 2001) and the equally important findings of Wendy Webster, especially 'There'll Always Be an England: Representations of Colonial Wars and Immigration, 1948–1968', *Journal of British Studies*, 2001, 40.

7   I discuss this more fully in 'Crossing the Seas', in Bill Schwarz (ed.), *West Indian Intellectuals in Britain* (Manchester, 2003); and its more theoretical implications in 'Unspeakable Histories. Diasporic Lives in Old England', in Peter Osborne and Stella Sandford (eds) *Philosophies of Race and Ethnicity* (London, 2002).

8   In this respect, George Lamming's novel, *In The Castle of My Skin,* written in England and first published in 1953, is representative.

9   See Donald Hinds, *Journey to an Illusion. The West Indian in Britain* (London, 1966) 24.

10 *Britons. Forging the Nation, 1707–1837* (London, 1992).

11 This I take to be the position adumbrated by that renowned West Indian, C.L.R. James, in his *80th Birthday Lectures* (London, 1981), esp. 48.

12 For information on Jones, see Marika Sherwood, with Donald Hinds and Colin Prescod, *Claudia Jones. A Life in Exile* (London, 1999) and Buzz Johnson, *'I Think of My Mother.' Notes on the Life and Times of Claudia Jones* (London, 1985). The *Gazette* is notoriously difficult to get hold of. It seems that no complete run of the paper exists. I have relied on poor microfilm reproductions of what remains. These can be consulted at the Library of the Institute of Race Relations in London.

13 The long-awaited release of the Metropolitan Police documents relating to the riots do not prove as revealing as one might have hoped: they principally contain the reports of the arresting officers, which conform to very familiar generic conventions. What they do show, though, is evidence of the popular white sentiment that the police were 'all for' the blacks. Public Records Office, MEPO 1/9838.

14 I am thinking especially of MacInnes's justly regarded novel, *Absolute Beginners* (London, 1959) and the movie of the same name made by Temple in 1987.

15 For an indication, see 'The Habit of Violence: Notting Hill Documents', *Universities and Left Review*, 1958, 5, 4–5, which reproduces the views of local white schoolchildren.

16 In 1959, 6,000 West Indians returned to the Caribbean from the UK; in 1960, this figure was 7,500, and in 1961 it was 8,300. This steady rise continued the pattern of the late 1950s. There is no way of establishing a direct correlation between the events of 1958 and the migrants' reasons for departing. See Ceri Peach, *West Indian Migration to Britain. A Social Geography* (London, 1968) 50.

17 These effects of Notting Hill are discussed in Edward Pilkington, *Beyond the Mother Country: West Indians and the Notting Hill White Riots* (London, 1988) and are recalled first-hand in Mike Phillips and Trevor Phillips, *Windrush: The Irresistible Rise of Multiracial Britain* (London, 1998). One of the most insightful black responses from the time can be found in George Lamming, *The Pleasures of Exile* (London, 1960).

18 Benedict Anderson's stimulating comments occur in a section entitled 'Apprehensions of Time' in his *Imagined Communities* (London, 1983) 22–6.

19 See especially the marvellous arguments marshalled by Dick Hebdige in *Subculture. The Meaning of Style* (London, 1979). An inspirational example of the resultant syncretic forms can be heard on the CD collection, *London is the Place for Me. Trinidadian Calypso in London, 1950–1956* (London, 2002), discussed by Stuart Hall, 'Calypso Kings', *Guardian*, 28 June 2002.

20 Asa Briggs, *The History of Broadcasting in the United Kingdom. Vol. V. Competition* (Oxford, 1995) 163, depicts Grant's presence as a pleasingly early instance of a warm-hearted multi-culturalism.

21 See *Melody Maker*, 30 June 1956.

22 Quoted in Sherwood, *Claudia Jones*, 157.

23 The respective political stances of Osborne and Littlewood can be followed in their contributions to the theatre of the time, and also in John Osborne, *Almost a Gentleman. Autobiography. Vol. II* (London, 1991) and Joan Littlewood, *Joan's Book. Joan Littlewood's Peculiar History as She Tells It* (London, 1995). The June 1960 issue of the *Gazette* reported Littlewood's plans to establish a Negro theatre in London.

24 *An End to the Neglect of Negro Women* (New York, 1949).

25 The only whisper of criticism came from one John Harris, a correspondent to the *Gazette* who, in April 1963, wrote in to claim that the judges were swayed by the preponderance of Jamaicans attending carnival, unjustly favouring the Jamaican contestants.

26 This figure is provided by Sheila Patterson, *Dark Strangers* (London, 1963) 420.

27 James, 'The Might Sparrow' in *The Future in the Present* (London, 1977) 191.

28 The influence of West Indians on male fashion was noted from as early as 1948. See Steve Chibnall, 'Whistle and Zoot: The Changing Meaning of a Suit of Clothes', *History Workshop Journal*, 1985, 20, 71.

29 See especially Stuart Hall, 'Reconstruction Work', *Ten: 8*, 1984, 16. Instructive too was the exhibition at the Photographers' Gallery, London, in October–November 2002, which presented the work of the high-street Brixton photographer, Harry Jacobs, spanning the period from the 1950s to the 1990s.

30 Hebdige, *Subculture*, 45. See too the same author's *Cut 'n' Mix. Culture, Identity and Caribbean Music* (London, 1987).

31 For a comparable study which explores decolonization in France from this angle of vision, see Kristin Ross, *Fast Cars and Clean Bodies. Decolonization and the Reordering of French Culture* (Cambridge, MA, 1995).

32 I follow here Simon Gikandi in his paper to the ICBH Postcolonial Britain conference. My own initial argument on Smuts appeared in 'Reveries of Race. The Closing of the Imperial Moment', in Becky Conklin, Frank Mort and Chris Waters (eds), *Moments of Modernity?* (London, 1990).

33 The 'external' determinations analysed by David Killingray in his 'The West Indian Federation and Decolonization in the British Caribbean', *Journal of Caribbean History*, 2000, 34, needs to be integrated into this 'internal' reading.

34 For the broader context, see Howard Johnson, 'Decolonisation and the History Curriculum in the Anglophone Caribbean', *Journal of Imperial and Commonwealth History*, 30.

35 In the November 1960 issue, a plea from a Ghanaian diplomat, Frances Cann, was reproduced in the *Gazette* imploring Rastafarians to stay at home.

36 'Postscript' *Soundings*, 1998, 10, 190.

37 This can be followed in Kathleen Paul, *Whitewashing Britain. Race and Citizenship in the Postwar Era* (Ithaca, 1997).

PART 10

Africa and the Caribbean

Chapter 24

Joan Dayan

HAITI, HISTORY, AND THE GODS

Haiti's revolution, from 1791 onward, had a world-historical significance which is perhaps only now beginning properly to be appreciated and explored. Its echoes have sounded across more than two centuries, and not only in the Caribbean or in France (though its significance for the latter is explored further by Laurent Dubois in his contribution to this volume and much other work), but globally. Joan Dayan looks at aspects of this, including the parts played by gendered and racialised imaginings, and by the voudun religion.

Stephen Howe

The child of savage Africa,
Sold to fall under the colonist's whip,
Founded independence on the soil of slavery,
And the Hill, in its voice, echoed the language of Racine and Fenelon!
M. Chauvet, Chant lyrique, 1825[1]

'**R**ID US OF THESE GILDED AFRICANS,** and we shall have nothing more to wish,' Napoleon wrote to his brother-in-law General Leclerc in 1802. Though successful in Guadeloupe and Martinique, Napoleon's soldiers, commanded first by Leclerc and then by Rochambeau, failed to re-establish slavery in Saint-Domingue. The only locale in history of a successful slave revolution, Saint-Domingue became the first black republic in 1804. Dessalines tore the white from the French tricolor – 'Mouche, chire blanc lá qui lan drapeau-lá' (Tear out the white from the flag, Monsieur)[2] – as he would remove the name 'Saint-Domingue' from the former colony. He called the new nation 'Haiti,' from the original Amer-Indian word (*Ayti*) for the island, which meant 'mountainous lands.'

Called 'Black France' by one nineteenth-century observer (Jules Michelet) or this 'France with frizzy hair' by another (Maxine Raybaud) or merely a 'tropical dog-kennel and pestiferous jungle' by Thomas Carlyle, Haiti forced imagination high and low: expression moved uneasily between the extremes of idealization and debasement. In the background of this textualized and cursedly mimetic Haiti, however, remained certain legends, blurred but persistent oral traditions that resisted such coercive dichotomies as genteel and brute, master and slave, precious language and common voice. Though Haiti's 'Africanness,' like its 'Frenchness,' would be used by writers for differing purposes, the business of *being Haitian* was more complex, and the slippages and uneasy alliances between contradictions more pronounced than most writerly representations of Haiti ever allowed.

Romancing the dark world

A series of articles on Haiti appeared in the *Petite Presse* in Paris from September 8 to December 31, 1881. Written by a black Martiniquais M. Cochinat, the columns reported on everything from vodou to the military, calling attention to the Haitians' love of artifice, their propensity to exaggerate and mime, and their apparent indifference to the bloody revolutions that followed independence in 1804. Cochinat also turned to vodou and to tales of cannibalism and magic in order to prove to his French audience that Haiti remained unregenerate.[3]

Louis-Joseph Janvier published his alternately strident and elegiac response to Cochinat in Paris in 1883.[4] Janvier, born in Port-au-Prince, was the first in his family to be educated. In 1877, when he was twenty-two, he received a scholarship from the Haitian government to study in France. There he remained, for twenty-eight years, until 1905. His collection of meditations, called *La Republique d'Hai'ti et ses visiteurs, 1840–1882*, contained long passages from the abolitionist Victor Schoelcher, Oliver Wendell Holmes, and M. Victor Meignan, and a preface packed with quotations from Michelet, Chateaubriand, Hugo, Renan, Danton, Lamartine, and Christophe. Janvier claimed that Haitians were on the road to civilization, arguing that the bloodiest political crimes in his country simply proved that 'Haiti always imitates Europe.'

> Be indulgent, oh sons of western Europe!
>
> Recall – I am citing at random, unconcerned about chronology – recall the Sicilien Vespers, the *holy* Inquisition . . . the Albegensian massacre, the war of the Two Roses, the massacre of Strelitz, the sacking of ghettos, the religious wars in England, which is to say the papists hanged by the anti-papists, and the anti-papists burned by the papists, Saint Barthelemy, the days of September 1792, the 10th of August, the red Terror, the 13th Vendémiaire, the 18th Brumaire, the white Terror, the June days of 1848, December 2, 1851; the month of May 1871 . . . be indulgent.

When Janvier wrote his defense of Haiti, about 90 per cent of the population were peasants. Romanticized for their pastoral innocence and endurance, those whom foreigners had condemned as remnants of 'dark Africa' were transformed by Janvier into French-speaking, God-fearing laborers. The ground upon which he constructed his fable of the Haitian nation – proud, vital, earthy, and black – they served as an appropriate symbol of the new Haiti: a gothic Eden resurrected on the ashes of colonial Saint-Domingue. Whether they inhabited the plains or the hills, the peasants Janvier idealized were fiercely independent, attached to their lands, and devoted to their gods. Yet Janvier's sense of 'the Haitian' depended on his refutation of vodou, which he denounced as 'primitive.' He assured his readers that all Haitians were now Catholic or Protestant, that all traces of barbarism had disappeared, and that most Haitians spoke French. After all, Janvier concluded, 'French prose, Haitian coffee, and the philosophical doctrines of the French Revolution are the best stimulants of the Haitian brain.'[5]

Black skin, white heart

The turning of Saint-Domingue into Haiti, colony into republic, demanded a new history that would be written by people who saw themselves as renewing the work of the French, who had once abolished slavery and declared slaves not only men but citizens. Yet the reactionary conceptual flotsam of the old regime, and the appropriate tags of 'civilization,' 'order,' and 'dignity,' would clash with a 'fanaticism' that had no proper language and no right to history. Could the history of the Haitian revolution be told in the language of France? As Haitian historians attempted to gain access to 'civilization,' someone else's language (and at least part of the history that went with it) was necessary to their entitlement.

If the justification of slavery depended on converting a biological fact into a metaphysical truth – black = savage/white = civilized – the descendant of slaves must not only pay tribute to those who enslaved, but make himself white, while remaining black. The complex working out of personal identity through a duplicity or doubling of color proves crucial to the making of a nation, and shapes the way the first two major Haitian historians, Thomas Madiou and Beaubrun Ardouin, introduced themselves. Though a mulatto who lived in Paris for ten years, Ardouin focused on his African ancestry. He announced himself in his 'Introduction' as 'Descendant of this African race that has been so long persecuted,' and at the end of his eleven-volume history (published in 1853–1860), he exclaimed: 'Glory to all these children of Africa . . . Honor to their memory!' Madiou, also mulatto, lived in France from the age of ten until he was twenty-one. Unlike Ardouin, who defended the class of *affranchis*, whether mulatto or black (ignoring their interest, after the decree of May 15, 1791, in preserving slavery), Madiou refused to account for Haitian history according to the 'official' mulatto view. He would later be claimed by Haitian ideologues as the *noiriste* historian of Haiti. His fiery assessment of Dessalines as a Haitian Robespierre, 'this angel of death,' based on interviews in the 1840s with former revolutionaries, departed from the critical disdain of the more moderate and elite *eclairees*. If Dessalines was savage, Madiou countered that he remained the 'Principle incarnate of Independence; he was barbaric against colonial barbarism.'

For both Madiou and Ardouin, the labor of writing history demanded that the historian be seen as human while remaining Haitian. They turned to France and the white world, but claimed blackness and repaired the image of Africa, by making Haiti, purified of superstition, sorcerers, and charms, the instrument of reclamation. Their ability to reclaim and represent their 'native land' to a foreign audience depended ultimately on their variously authentic and partly spurious claims of color but, most important, on the wielding of proper language. Both Madiou and Ardouin concluded their introductions by apologizing not for color but for style. In Ardouin's case, especially, the apology helped him prove his nationality, affirmed by nothing less than his resolutely faltering or broken French. He articulated, perhaps for the first time, what Edouard Glissant much later would name *antillanite*, and what Cesaire, speaking about his choice of writing poetry in French not Creole, would qualify as French with the *marque negre*: 'If this work finds some readers in Paris, they will see many infelicities of style, still more faults in the rules of grammar: it will offer them no literary merit. But they should not forget that, in general, Haitians stammer the words of the French language, in order to emphasize in some way their origin in the Antilles.'[6] Ardouin no doubt remembered his predecessor's conclusion to his introduction. In *Histoire d'Haiti* Madiou had addressed his readers:

> I beseech the reader to show himself indulgent concerning the style of my work; all I did was attempt to be correct, since at 1,800 leagues from the hearth of our language, in a country where nearly the entire population speaks Creole, it is quite impossible that French would not suffer the influence of those idioms I have meanwhile tried to avoid.[7]

Between civilization and barbarism

In Port-au-Prince on April 16, 1848, the very black and illiterate President Faustin Soulouque began the massacre of mulattoes he suspected as conspirators. In Paris a 'Prince President,' Louis Napoleon, who had just come out on the other side of the barricades and blood of the June 1848 revolution, exclaimed, 'Haiti, Haiti, pays de barbares!' The nephew of Napoleon, Marx's 'caricature of the old Napoleon' did not have it easy. When he declared himself emperor a year after the *coup d'etat* of December 2, 1851, he found himself not only described as Marx's caricature and Hugo's 'Napoleon le petit,' but compared to the Haitian Soulouque. The trivializing of revolution (in Haiti the 1843 and 1844 rebellions in the south) and the spectacle of reaction brought Haiti and France together in a knot of contamination.

Soulouque declared himself Emperor Faustin I on August 25, 1849. Spenser St. John thought this act typical of a racially particular obsession: 'All black chiefs have a hankering after the forms as well as the substance of despotic power.'[8] Imitating the genuine Bonaparte, Soulouque crowned himself, then crowned the empress, and created a nobility of four princes, fifty-nine dukes, two marquises, ninety counts, two hundred barons, and thirty chevaliers. About three years later, in France Louis Napoleon became emperor and brought the Second Republic to an end.

In *The Eighteenth Brumaire of Louis Bonaparte* (1851), Marx compared what he called 'the best' of Louis Napoleon's 'bunch of blokes' to 'a noisy, disreputable, rapacious boheme that crawls into galerooned coats with the same grotesque dignity as the high dignitaries of Soulouque.'[9] Referring to the hollow Bonaparte, Hugo wrote a poem about 'A monkey [who] dressed himself in a tiger's skin' ('Fable or History,' *Les Chatiments*, 1853). Though most obviously referring to the dubious royalty and bombast of Louis Napoleon, the horrific slaughters of Hugo's poem could not fail to remind readers of

Soulouque's outrages. Hugo's parting shot in 'Fable or History' could be taken as a product of racialist ideology: 'You are only a monkey!'

Gustave d'Alaux (pen name for Maxine Raybaud, the French consul during part of Soulouque's reign), wrote *L'Empereur Soulouque et son empire*, parts of which appeared as a series of articles in the metropolitan *Revue des deux-mondes* (1850–1851) and finally as a book in 1856. He introduced his readers to a place where you could find 'civilization and the Congo,' and 'newspapers and sorcerers.'[10] Even American abolitionist Wendell Phillips, rendering homage to Toussaint and the Haitian revolution in Boston and New York in 1861, reminded his listeners how much events in Haiti mattered to the new Napoleon in France: the present Napoleon . . . when the epigrammatists of Paris christened his wasteful and tasteless expense at Versailles, Soulouquerie, from the name of Soulouque, the Black Emperor, he deigned to issue a specific order forbidding the use of the word.[11]

A later Haitian historian, Dantes Bellegarde in *La Nation hatienne* (1938), lamented that the reputation of Soulouque suffered from the illegitimate actions of Louis Napoleon. Soulouque's character was defamed when the French made him the vessel for their disdain of their emperor. His words are crucial to understanding how different history might be if we jostle our ideas of cause and effect.

The crowning of the Emperor, celebrated with unmatched magnificence, resulted in cruel jokes about Soulouque in the liberal French press and thus avenged the *coup d'etat* of December 2, 1851 by the Prince-President Louis Napoleon. And when, by the plebiscite of November 20, 1852, he had himself proclaimed Emperor, they accused him of having aped [*singe*] Faustin I, and the more one blackened Soulouque, the more odious appeared the imitation of his grotesque act by the old member of the Italian Carbonari. The hatred of Napoleon the little, as the poet of the *Chatiments* referred to him, contributed much to giving the chief of the Haitian State his unfortunate reputation as a ridiculous and blood-thirsty sovereign.[12]

Re-reading events in France through the quizzing glass of Raiti is to clarify the reciprocal dependencies, the uncanny resemblances that no ideology of mastery can remove. Who is 'aping' whom? The question must have haunted Beaubrun Ardouin when he found himself in Paris, having escaped from the murderous Soulouque, happy to find himself in the 'Republic' he praised in a letter to Lamartine, only to see *liberty* turn again into *monarchy*: the country he had turned to as example for his 'young Haiti' flipping over, again, into empire.

No easy liberty

Ardouin appreciated the business of politics. Friend and partisan of the tough mulatto Major General Jean-Pierre Boyer (an *ancien affranchi*), who governed Haiti from 1820 to 1843, Ardouin as senator had negotiated the financial settlement with France in 1825: 150 million francs indemnity to be paid to the dispossessed French planters of Saint-Domingue in order to obtain French recognition of the independence of its former colony, which was given in a royal ordinance from King Charles X.

Madiou, never one to mince words, imagined what the heroes of the revolution would do if they left their tombs only to see the French flag flying in the cities of the new republic, while Haitians curried favor and became indebted to the descendants of colonial torturers. But it was Boyer's 1826 Code Rural that reduced most Haitians, especially those who did not occupy positions of rank in the military or civil branches of the state, to slave status. A small fraction of Haiti's population could live off the majority, collecting fees – with the help of their lackeys, the rural *chefs de section* – for produce, for the sale, travel, and butchering of animals, and even for the cutting of trees. In *Les Constitutions d'Haiti* (1886), addressed primarily to a Haitian audience, Janvier described Boyer's code as 'slavery without the whip.' Jonathan Brown, an American physician from New Hampshire who spent a year in Haiti, recalled his impressions of Boyer's regime in *The History and Present Condition of St. Domingo* (1837): 'The existing government of Hayti is a sort of republican monarchy sustained by the bayonet.'[13]

In 1843 and 1844 there were two revolutions that Ardouin would later describe as the 'tragedy' of his generation: the popular army of Praslin, led by Charles Riviere-Herard, and the next year, the Piquet rebellion, led by the black southerner and police lieutenant Louis Jean-Acaau 'to defend the interests of the poor of all classes.' The crises of 1843–1844 compelled Ardouin to write his history. The 'Proclamation de Praslin,' though ostensibly speaking for the people, and condemning Boyer's officials including Ardouin as traitors, was really a document contrived by Riviere-Herard and other mulattoes, disgruntled Boyarists who wanted some of the power. Acaau's *l'armée souffrante*, along with the resistance of members of the black elite such as Lysius Salomon, resulted in Riviere-Herard's overthrow. Salomon's petition to the provisional government of Riviere-Herard (June 22, 1843) is a marvel of recall and revision: 'Citizens! Dessalines and Petion cry out to you from the bottom of their graves; . . . Save Haiti, our communal mother; don't let her perish . . . save her . . . The abolitionists rejoice and applaud you.'[14]

Who is the true Haitian? Ardouin's answer to the question gives definition the utility of not defining. Though he claimed himself as 'Descendant of Africa' and condemned the injustices of the colonial government against 'the men of the black race which is my own,' he asserted that the road to being Haitian must progress away from the dark continent toward his present audience, those who represented enlightened France. He remained uncomfortable with 'oral and popular traditions,' and most of all, with 'superstitious practices derived from Africa,' summed up as 'the barbarism . . . that brutalizes souls.' Ardouin emphasized the attributes that made Haiti worthy of the France he esteemed (and identified Haitians who thought like him as most qualified to command): same religion, language, ideals, principles, customs, and he concluded, 'a taste preserved for French products.' For France 'has deposited the germ of its advanced civilization.' Now, with Napoleon III, under 'the reign of a monarch enlightened and just,' Haiti could profit from the 'lights *[les lumières]* of its former metropole.'

'Sucking from the breasts of France,' as Ardouin had once put it in a letter to Lamartine (who, as minister for foreign affairs in the provisional government of 1848, would definitively abolish slavery in the French colonies), Haiti would turn, emptied of its gods and its magic, to both 'the revolution of 1789 . . . this torch of French Genius' and to the Napoleonic eagle. On January 15, 1859, General Fabre Nicholas Geffrard overthrew Soulouque. Ardouin returned briefly to Haiti and then departed again for Paris as minister plenipotentiary.[15]

Dessalines, dessalines demanbre

On October 17, 1806, Jean-Jacques Dessalines, 'chef supreme des indigenes,' the first president and emperor of Haiti, was murdered in an ambush at Pont-Rouge by soldiers from the south on the road from Marchand (now Dessalines) to Port-au-Prince. The assassination order came from a clique of mulattoes and blacks from the west and south, including his friend General Pétion. Christophe knew of the plan. A young officer shot Dessalines. General Yayou stabbed him three times. Vaval filled him with bullets from two pistols. Then he was stripped naked; his fingers were cut off so that the jeweled rings could be removed. Stories vary about the details of the mutilation. Even Ardouin, not given to melodrama, hesitated before recounting what happened to the corpse after Dessalines was assassinated by the men with whom he had fought: 'one must pause at this appalling outrage.'[16]

By the time the body reached Port-au-Prince, after the two-mile journey, it could not be recognized. The head was shattered, the feet, hands and ears cut off. In some accounts, Dessalines was stoned and hacked to pieces by the crowd, and his remains variously described as 'scraps,' 'shapeless remains,' 'remnants,' or 'relics' – were thrown to the crowd. According to Madiou, American merchants hustled to buy his fingers with gold. 'They attached an importance to the relics of the founder of our Independence that Haitians, transported by such horrible fury, did not then feel.'[17] That foreign merchants bargained for Dessalines' fleshly remnants tells us something about the role of Dessalines as martyr of liberty. Yet this is only part of the story, for popular vengeance turned Dessalines into matter for resurrection. Dessalines, the most unregenerate of Haitian leaders, was made into a *lwa* (god, image, or spirit) by the Haitian people. The 'liberator' with his red silk scarf was the only 'Black Jacobin' to become a god. Neither the radical rationality of Toussaint nor the sovereign pomp of Christophe led to apotheosis. Yet Dessalines, so resistant to enlightened heroics, gradually acquired unequaled power in the Haitian imagination.

Dessalines was born on the Cormiers plantation in a parish now known as the Commune of Grande-Rivière du Nord sometime in 1758. In 1794 Dessalines became Toussaint's guide through Grande Riviere du Nord. At the time of the revolution, Toussaint was a literate coachman, and later steward of all the livestock on the Breda plantation. Christophe (born in Grenada) was a waiter, then a manager, and finally an owner of La Couronne, an inn at Cap Francois. Dessalines, first owned by a brutal white named Duclos, was then sold to a black master. Whenever Dessalines wanted to justify his hatred of the French, it is said that he liked to display his scar-covered back.[18] We should think for a moment about the problems in speaking about the figure of the hero who was once a slave, a man who would refer to himself as 'Duclos' (his name in servitude), recalling for his listeners, even as emperor, his identity as an item of property.

Rejecting things French, unconcerned about social graces, turning away from the customs, language, and principles Ardouin would see as that part of the Haitian inheritance that made his country worthy of recognition by 'civilized' Europe, Dessalines made a vexed entry into history. Perhaps more than either Toussaint (who had the habit of asking the women who visited him, in a tender but nasal twang, 'Have you taken communion this morning?') or Christophe, Dessalines recognized the temptations of civilization, which for him meant a new, more subtle servitude. He understood how easily rebels or republicans could themselves become masters. Speaking of the *anciens libres*, those freed before Sonthonax's General Emancipation decree of August 1793, which abolished slavery in Saint-Domingue, Dessalines declared, 'Beware, negroes and mulattoes! We have fought against the whites. The goods that we have won in spilling our blood belong to everyone. I intend that they be shared fairly.'[19] Madiou emphasized Dessalines' preference for steering clear of the established cities, 'so that European corruption could not reach him,' choosing to establish himself at Marchand, situated in the plain of the Artibonite at the foot of the Cahos hills.[20]

Spenser St. John recognized 'the only quality' of Dessalines as 'a kind of brute courage . . . he was nothing but an African savage.'[21] It is said that when Leclerc, who had earlier praised Dessalines as 'butcher of the blacks' in a letter to Napoleon in September 1802, learned of his defection from the French a month later, he cried out, 'How could I have been so deceived by a *barbare!*' The two most important twentieth-century poets of Martinique, Aime Cesaire and Edouard Glissant, do not write about Dessalines. Perhaps they had difficulty (in spite of their rhetoric or their desire) acknowledging the chief who called his people to arms with the command, 'Koupe tet, boule kay' (Cut off their heads, burn their houses). Glissant wrote the play *Monsieur Toussaint* (1961). Cesaire turned to Toussaint in his *Révolution francaise et le problème colonial* (1981), as well as writing *La Tragédie du Roi Christophe* (1963).

Haitians especially have had a difficult time writing about the general whose uncompromising ferocity had become legendary. More embarrassing still were stories of the surfeit and abandon of his reign. Surrounded by cunning ministers, Dessalines recognized too late the need to curb their excesses. Madiou and others recount Dessalines' passion for dancing and women, especially Couloute, his favorite mistress. The emperor's ardor inspired a celebrated and much popularized *carabinier* (a wilder, more energetic and undulating kind of *meringue*): 'The Emperor comes to see Couloute dance.'[22] At one particularly luxurious ball, when a dancing Dessalines leapt into the air and landed on his knee before Couloute, Christophe is reported to have remarked (loud enough for Dessalines to hear him): 'See His Majesty! Aren't you ashamed to have such a *sauteur* [meaning both 'jumper' and 'temporizer' or 'chameleon'] as our leader!'

Hyperbolized by Madiou as a 'thunderbolt of arbitrariness,' Dessalines fought at different times against the French and the African-born former slaves *neg bosal*, *neg ginen*, or *neg kongo* who never collaborated with the French. These *maroons*, such as Ti-Noel, Sans Souci, Macaya, Cacapoule, and other unnamed insurgents of the hills who formed armed bands of nearly a thousand men, refused to surrender to Leclerc as did Christophe and Dessalines after the loss of the battle of Crete-a-Pierrot and the removal of Toussaint in 1802.[23] According to historian Henock Trouillot, writing about Dessalines in the Haitian newspaper, *Le Nouvelliste*, 'His name alone, in spite of the contradictions of his attitude, became a symbol among blacks.'[24] In December 1802 his authority was so great that the mulatto general Petion knew he had no choice but to fight under the black who had, only two years before, under Toussaint's orders, bathed the south of Haiti in the blood of mulattos.

A number of oral traditions haunt the written remains of Dessalines, who would become general in chief of the Army of Independence. In a story reported by both Trouillot and Mentor Laurent, African bands called *takos*, including a rebel named Jean Zombi and 'other types full of fire,' surrounded Dessalines in Plaisance, refusing to listen to him and saying, 'We do not deal with whites.' According to Trouillot, Dessalines replied:

> Look at my face. Am I white? Don't you recognize the soldier of Crete-a-Pierrot? Was I white at the Petite-Riviere of the Artibonite when the expedition arrived? Ask these hills covered with French bones. They will nominate Dessalines as the hero of these trophies.[25]

Historians even disagree about the languages Dessalines could speak. Some say he spoke in 'Congo,' a general attribution for the specific African 'nations' or 'tribes' in Saint-Domingue (Arada, Nago, Congo, Fon, Ibo, Bambara) that came to designate 'African' or the 'secret' or 'magic' language of initiates in vodou. In *Les Limites du Créole dans notre enseignement*, Trouillot cites, from Antoine Metral's *Histoire de l'expédition francais au St. Domingue* words that suggest that even though he did not speak their language, Dessalines could gesturally, figurally become African: 'His savage eloquence was more in certain expressive signs than in words.' Trouillot concluded: 'By fantastic gestures Dessalines managed more than once to make himself understood by Africans, so it seemed, when he did not speak the dialect.'[26] We are dealing, therefore, with a Creole who could take on the role of an African as easily as he could serve the French.

Dessalines controlled his own passage between apparent extremes and thrived on the composite histories of his locale. According to Madiou, Dessalines called the populations subject to his authority 'Incas or children of the sun,' memorializing the 1780 Inca uprising in Peru. According to Haitian Marxist historian Etienne Charlier, when Dessalines called the new black republic 'Haiti,' retrieving its original Amerindian name, he 'transcend [ed] his race and present[ed] himself as the avenger of the Indians.'[27] Dessalines, also believed to have been a vodou adept (and in some stories, sorcerer), was known to have massacred cult leaders and their devotees. Yet Gustave d'Alaux in *L'Empereur Soulouque et son empire* explained that while Toussaint and Christophe, obsessed with the trappings of culture, pitilessly suppressed vodou practitioners, 'Dessalines, in spite of his either sincere or pretended infatuation with African savagery, was himself mixed up with the *papas* (conjure-men).' D'Alaux reported that once, before going into battle, Dessalines covered himself with magic talismans in order to become invulnerable. But wounded in the first discharge of fire, Dessalines beat up the 'sorcerer' and took back the money he had paid for the consultation.[28]

Two of the concerns that account for the admiration and disdain summoned by Dessalines' name are race and land. In the constitution of 1805, he declared that no white, whatever his nation, could set foot on the territory of Haiti as master or owner of property (Art. 12). Who could be Haitian? For Dessalines, certain whites could be naturalized as Haitians: for example, white women who had conceived or would bear Haitian children and those Germans and Poles who deserted Leclerc's army during 1802–1803 to fight with the *indigenes* (Art. 13). Further, Haitians, whatever their color, would be known as *blacks*, referred to 'only by the generic word *black*' (Art. 14).[29] Since the most problematic division in the new Haiti was that between *anciens libres* (mostly *gens de couleur*, mulattoes, and their offspring) and *nouveaux libres* (the newly free, who were mostly black), Dessalines attempted by linguistic means and by law to defuse the color issue.

But it was Dessalines' attempt to redefine the ownership of land that cost him his life. In 1804 he rescinded all transfers of property made after October 1802, thus removing mulatto claims to valuable plantations. In 1805 he decided that all land titles would have to be verified. Tradition has it that Dessalines would check for the authenticity of land titles by smelling them to discover those that had been smoked to make them *look old*: 'ca pas bon, ca senti fumee' (it's no good, it smells smoked). According to many this was a direct attack on the *anciens affranchis*, those who had taken, or had been given land formerly owned by their white planter fathers.

In his constitution Dessalines had given equal rights to both legitimate children and those recognized by their fathers but born out of wedlock, thus accepting the prevalence of *placage* or consensual union, not wishing to coerce his people, those he called 'natives of Haiti,' to follow the marital rituals of the whites. According to Madiou, Dessalines said it would be unjust to establish unequal rights in inheritance between men who had come out of servitude and degradation: 'the *indigenes* had all been . . . legitimized by the revolution.' However, for Dessalines there could be no kinship with a white colonist. No mulatto could claim that he was entitled to his father's land. Ardouin, a descendant of the disenfranchised *anciens affranchis*, argued that land reform was 'an attack on the sacred right of property.' But for Janvier, and other later Haitian historians, Dessalines 'wanted to make the genuine independence of the peasant possible by making him an owner of land.'[30]

When we ask what made possible the second coming of Dessalines as hero and god, we must attend to his vision of the *true* Haitian. He gave property to those slaves who had, only recently, been considered property. The division of land, his attempt to destroy 'false' property titles, and the violence with which he tried to carry out what has been called 'an impossible reform of the mentality of the ruling classes, and perhaps his own mentality,'[31] would make him the favorite of left-leaning, twentieth-century novelists such as Réne Depestre and Jacques-Stephen Alexis. As the sociologist and anthropologist Antenor Firmin put it in *De l'Égalité des races humaines*, his 1885 response to Gobineau's *De l'Inégalité des races humaines*:

> For us, sons of those who suffered the humiliations and martyrdom of slavery, we could see there [in Dessalines' actions] the first manifestation of the sentiment of racial equality, a sentiment which Dessalines still personifies in Haiti.[32]

Between Dessalines' death in 1806 and Lysius Salomon's (the finance minister during *la politique de doublure*) speech in memory of the 'emperor-martyr' in 1845, the transition from oblivion to glory had taken place. Speaking at the parish church in Cayes, October 17, 1845, Salomon proclaimed: 'Avenger of the black race, liberator of Haiti, founder of national independence, Emperor Dessalines! Today is your glory, the sun today burns for you as radiantly as it did in 1804.' Before Salomon's scandalous speech, which blamed 'the aristocracy of color' for Dessalines' death (and earned Salomon, who was later called 'the eater of mulattoes,' their lasting fury), previous governments had ignored or condemned 'The Liberator.'

One exception was the cunning political move by the mulatto Charles Riviere-Herard in January 1844, during the forty-first anniversary of the founding of the state of Haiti. As Madiou put it: 'He made a speech where, for the first time since the death of Dessalines in October 1806, these words came out of the mouth of a President of the Republic: 'It is to the glorious Dessalines, it is to his immortal comrades that the Country owes the new era into which she enters.' Madiou reminded his readers that Riviere-Herard was part of the class that despised Dessalines, the large landowners of Cayes, who had most to lose when Dessalines began his call for property reform. He:

> belonged to a class of citizens who saw in Dessalines nothing but a barbaric despot that they had sacrificed; but since they planned a *coup d'etat*, they had to draw on the sympathies of the people by glorifying the founder of independence.[33]

Yet, Madiou concluded, the people were not dupes of these 'empty words,' for they had heard that Dessalines' remains – unworthy of a mausoleum – still lay in a deserted grave, marked only by a brick tomb with the inscription in Creole: 'Ce-git Dessalines/Mort a 48 ans' (Here lies Dessalines/Dead at 48 years old).[34]

Some fifty years after Riviere-Herard used the figure of Dessalines for his political designs, President Florvil Hyppolite built in France a modest monument in memory of Dessalines. Later, for the centenary celebration of the Haitian nation, which actually marked the beginning of the state cult of Dessalines, Justin Lherison composed the national anthem, the 'Dessalinienne.' Sung for the first time on January 1, 1904, the song begins:

> For our Country
> For our Ancestors
> Let us march together
> No traitors in our ranks
> Let us be the only masters of the land.

But the monumentality that turned October 17 from a day that heralded liberation from a dictator to a day of mourning for his death was devised by literate Haitians in the cities. Repressive governments, such as that of Louis Borno under the US occupation (1915–1934), found the erection of a mausoleum for the Liberator easier than affording their subjects liberation from internal oppression and foreign control.

Called by the literate elite 'The Great One,' 'The Savior,' 'The Lover of Justice,' and 'The Liberator,' the Dessalines remembered by vodou initiates is far less comforting or instrumental. They know how unheroic the hero turned god could be. The image of Dessalines in the cult of the people remains equivocal and corruptible: a trace of what is absorbed by the mind and animated in the gut. How inevitable are the alternations back and forth from hero to detritus, from power to vulnerability, from awe to ridicule: a convertibility that vodou would keep working, viable, and necessary.

Not simply master or tyrant, but slave or supplicant, Dessalines and the religious rituals associated with him keep the ambiguities of power intact. Unlike the spectacles of sanctification endorsed by the urban literati and the politicians, the history reconstructed by the gods and their devotees is not always one of revolt and triumph. 'Do you have the heart to march in blood all the way to Cayes?' Dessalines asked the soldiers of his third brigade before his assassination in October 1806. Gods held in the mind and embodied in ceremony re-enact what historians often forget: the compulsion to serve, the potency and virtue of atrocity. The very suppressions, inarticulatenesses, and ruptures in ritual might say something about the ambivalences of *the* revolution: it was not so liberating as mythologizers or ideologues make it, and the dispossessed who continue to suffer and remember know this.

Dismemberment, naming, and divinity

Vodou enters written history as a weird set-piece: the ceremony of Bois-Cai'man. The story is retold by nearly every historian, especially those outsiders who enjoyed linking the first successful slave revolt to a gothic scene of blood, drinking and abandon. Though David Geggus has written in *Slavery, War and Revolution: The British Occupation of Saint*

Domingue, 1793–1798, that 'the earliest mention of the famous Bois Caiman ceremony seems to be in Dalmas' *Histoire* of 1814,' what matters is how necessary this story or myth remains to Haitians who continue to construct their identity by turning not only to the revolution of 1791, but by seeking its origins in a service quite possibly imagined by those who disdain it.[35]

On the stormy, lightning-filled night of August 14, 1791, in the middle of the Caiman woods, Boukman, an *oungan* (priest), and a *manbo* (priestess) conducted the ceremony that began the fight for independence. Madiou, though given to much melodramatic detail, did not include the ceremony in his history. But vodou, once displaced, reared its head a few pages following his descriptions of the uprising in the north. Madiou described Biassou, who with Jean-Francois led the revolt, surrounded by 'sorcerers' and 'magicians.' His tent was filled with multicolored cats, snakes, bones of the dead, and other objects of what Madiou calls 'African superstitions.'[36] Ardouin described the ceremony of Bois-Caiman, but told his readers that he was 'transcribing here an extract from the unedited works of Celigny Ardouin' that included information he received from an old soldier who resided in Saint Domingue, in service of the king of Spain.[37]

Both Madiou and Ardouin recounted how blacks – 'phantasies,' as Madiou put it, by sorcerers – threw themselves at cannons, believing the balls dust. When blown to pieces, they knew they would be reborn in Africa. The naturalist Descourtilz (his life was saved during the massacre of whites by Dessalines' wife, Claire Heureuse, who hid him under her bed) remembered how:

> the Congo Negroes and other Guineans were so superstitiously affected by the utterances of Dessalines that they even let him persuade them that to die fighting the French was only a blessing since it meant that they were immediately conveyed to Guinea, where, once again, they saw Papa Toussaint who was waiting for them to complete the army with which he proposed to reconquer Saint Domingue.[38]

To reconstruct a history of the spirits in Haiti is no easy matter. How does thought about a glorified, if ambiguous past become palpable? How do we get from now to then, to a history beyond the reach of written history? Until the American occupation – and one could argue, the publication of Jean Price-Mars' *Ainsi parla l'oncle* (1928) – the Haitian elite looked upon vodou as an embarrassment.[39] Even Duverneau Trouillot, who published his 'esquisse ethnographique' (ethnographic sketch), *Le Vaudoun: apercu historique et évolutions* in 1885, while listing (for the first time, as far as I know, the individual spirits), felt that vodou in Haiti demonstrated the inevitable degradation of ancestral practices, reduced to 'a tissue of rather ridiculous superstitions.' Trouillot prophesized that Christian civilization would soon absorb these atavistic 'remnants' or 'debris.'[40]

Born in Haiti, Dessalines is called a *lwa Kreyol* (Creole god). As 'Ogou Desalin,' he walks with the African Ogou, the gods of war and politics that remain in Haiti in their multiple aspects. Trouillot warned that after the revolution, African beliefs and rituals would continue to degenerate. But the old traditions and gods remained powerful, embracing the new events and leaders such as Dessalines. With independence, the underground opposition to the now defeated white oppressor did not disappear, for the spirits, and the people's need for them, was not contingent on being suppressed. On the contrary, vodou came, to some extent, out into the open to thrive. But haltingly so, as though the people were keeping some of the old secrets hidden, ready to serve in other repressive situations that did not fail to occur.

The history told by vodou defies our notions of identity and contradiction. A person or thing can be two or more things simultaneously. A word can be double, two-sided, and duplicitous. In spite of this instability, or what some argue to be the capriciousness of spirits and terminologies, something incontrovertible remains. In parts of contemporary Haiti the *demanbre* is fundamental to vodou. The piece of family land where the spirits reside, the *demanbre*, marks the spiritual heritage of the group.[41] Also defined as 'the basic unit of peasant religion,' 'the common family yard,' and 'the center of the veneration of the dead,' this sacred, ancestral land cannot be divided, sold, or given away.[42] Haiti was conceived as earth blooded with the purifying spirit of liberation. Dessalines, who thought of himself as father of all Haitians, the family henceforth to be known as 'blacks,' died for his attempt to give land to the disinherited. Serving Dessalines re-inspirits what many believe to have been his legacy: the indivisible land of Haiti, consecrated by the revolution. Having lost his personal identity, he becomes the place. The dismembered hero is resurrected as sacred locale.

To serve Dessalines is sometimes less a sign of good fortune than the record of a cruel and demanding intimacy. The song about Dessalines' *demanbre* joins the hero to a powerful 'she-devil' or 'sorceress,' known as *kita-demanbre*. The feared Marinette-Bwa-Cheche (Marinette-dry-bones, dry-wood, or brittle arms), said to 'mange moun' (eat people), is also called Marinette-Limen-dife (light-the-fire). Served with kerosene, pimento, and fire, she is the lwa who put the fire to the cannons used by Dessalines against the French. The other Petwo gods that bear the names of revolt, the traces of torture and revenge, such as Brise Pimba, Baron Ravage, General Brise, and Jean Zombi, recall the strange promiscuity between masters and slaves; white, black, and mulatto; old world and new. These rituals of memory could be seen as deposits of history. Shreds of bodies come back, remembered in ritual and seeking vengeance – whether blacks fed to the dogs by Rochambeau or whites massacred by Dessalines.

The lwa most often invoked by today's vodou practitioners do not go back to Africa; rather, they were born during the revolution. A historical streak in these spirits, entirely this side of metaphysics, reconstitutes the shadowy and powerful magical gods of Africa as everyday responses to the white master's arbitrary power. Driven underground, they survived and constituted a counterworld to white suppression. It is hardly surprising that when black deeds and national heroic action contested this mastery, something new would be added to the older traditions.

The dispossession accomplished by slavery became the model for possession in vodou, for making a man not into a thing but into a spirit. In 1804, during Dessalines' massacre of the French, Jean Zombi, a mulatto of Port-au-Prince, earned a reputation for brutality. Known to be one of the fiercest slaughterers, Madiou described his 'vile face,' 'red hair,' and 'wild eyes.' He would leave his house, wild with fury, stop a white, then strip him naked. In Madiou's words, he 'led him then to the steps of the government palace and thrust a dagger in his chest. This gesture horrified all the spectators, including Dessalines.'[43] Jean Zombi was also mentioned by Henock Trouillot as one of the *takos* who had earlier threatened Dessalines in Plaisance. Variously reconstituted and adaptable to varying events, Zombi crystallizes the crossing not only of spirit and man in vodou practices, but the intertwining of black and mulatto, African and Creole in the struggle for independence.

The ambiguities of traditions redefined by changing hopes, fears, and rememberings is exemplified by the brief mention of Jean Zombi in the 1950s by Milo Rigaud in *La Tradition voudoo et le voudoo haitien.* 'Jean Zombi is one of the most curious prototypes of vodoun tradition. He was one of those, who on Dessalines' order, massacred the most whites during the liberation of Haiti from the French yoke. Jean Zombi is actually one of the most influential mysteries of the vodoun pantheon: as lwa, he belongs to the Petwo rite.'[44] According to anthropologist Melville Herskovits, in Dahomean legend the zombi were beings without souls, 'whose death was not real but resulted from the machinations of sorcerers who made them appear as dead, and then, when buried, removed them from their grave and sold them into servitude in some faraway land.'[45]

In contemporary Haiti, however, the zombi calls up the most macabre figure in folk belief. No fate is more feared. The zombi, understood either as an evil spirit or the zombi in 'flesh and bones,' is the most powerful emblem of apathy, anonymity, and loss. This incarnation of negation or vacancy – what Jamaican novelist Erna Brodber has defined as 'flesh that takes directions from someone' – is as much a part of history as the man Jean Zombi. Zombification in its contemporary manifestations grew out of a twentieth-century history of forced labor, victimization, and denigration that became particularly acute during the American occupation of Haiti. As Haitians were forced to build roads, and thousands of peasants were brutalized and massacred, tales of zombies proliferated in the United States. The film *White Zombie* (1932) and books such as William Seabrook's *The Magic Island* (1929) or John Huston Craige's *Black Bagdad* (1933) helped justify the 'civilizing' presence of the marines in barbaric Haiti. This re-imagined zombi has now been absorbed into the texture of previous oral traditions, structurally reproducing the idea of slavery in a new context. As lwa, then, Jean Zombi embodies dead whites and blacks, staging again for those who serve him the sacrificial scene: the ritual of consecration that makes him god.

Let us return to Dessalines' constitution of 1805, and to the logic of the remnant turned god. 'The law does not permit one dominant religion' (Art. 50). 'The freedom of cults is tolerated' (Art. 51). Not again in the many constitutions of Haiti, until 1987, would freedom of religion be allowed. Both Toussaint and Christophe had recognized only Catholicism ('la religion Catholique, apostolique et romaine') as the religion of the state. Dessalines remained close to the practices of the Haitian majority. But according to Milo Rigaud, who does not give sources for his unique details of Dessalines possessed and punished, Dessalines suffered the vengeance of the spirits for ignoring their warnings not to go to Pont-Rouge.[46] Nor did the gods forget the general's attack on their servitors when he followed Toussaint's orders in 1802. But what Ardouin called the 'misfortunes' of popular vengeance on Dessalines could be a record of something less verifiable and more disturbing.

General Yayou, when he saw the body of Dessalines, proclaimed: 'Who would have said that this little wretch, only twenty minutes ago, made all of Haiti tremble!' When an initiate is possessed by the 'emperor,' the audience witnesses a double play of loss and gain. The 'horse' (in the idiom of possession the god mounts his horse) remains him/herself even when ridden, but stripped bare, as was Dessalines, of habitual characteristics, the lineaments of the everyday. The essential residue, the name remains. What emerges after the first moments of disequilibrium and convulsive movements is the ferocity commonly 'associated with Dessalines. It is as if the self is not so much annihilated as rendered piecemeal. Out of these remnants comes the god or mystery who overtakes what remains.

What does the conjunction of hero and madwoman tell us about Haitian history? The trope of long-suffering or mad *negresse* and powerful *noir* became a routine coupling in contemporary Haitian texts. The parallels between literary and historical writing raise questions about the myth of the Haitian nation and the kinds of symbols required to make a 'national' literature. Haitian history has been written by men, whether colonizers who distort or negate the past, or the colonized who reclaim what has been lost or denied. What is the name of the manbo who assisted the priest Boukman in the legendary ceremony of Bois Ca'iman? 'As history tells it she made the conspirators drink the blood of the animal she had slaughtered, while persuading them that therein lie the proof of their future invincibility in battle.'[47] Arlette Gautier has argued in *Les Soeurs de solitude* that, as opposed to the men of the revolution, women left no records. 'They have remained nameless except for Sanite Belair, Marie-Jeanne Lamartinière for Saint-Domingue and the mulatta Solitude in Guadeloupe.'[48]

Both Madiou and Ardouin mention women during the revolution. Not only the fierce Sanite Belaire who refused to be blindfolded during her execution and Marie-Jeanne who led the indigenes in the extraordinary battle of Crête-à-Pierrot, but also Claire Heureuse, the wife of Dessalines, who saved many of the French he had ordered massacred. Yet we need to consider how these women are mentioned, how their appearances work within the historical narrative. Their stories are something of an interlude in the business of *making history*. Bracketed off from the descriptions of significant loss or triumph, the *blanches* raped and butchered or the *noires ardent* and fearless became symbols for *la bonte*, *la ferocite*, or *la faiblesse*.

What happens to the unnamed black women during the repeated revolutions in Haiti when mythologized by men, metaphorized out of life into legend? The legend of *Sor Rose* or Sister Rose is a story of origins that depends for its force on rape. The Haitian nation began in the flanks of a black woman. I know of only two written references to this ancestress, both from the 1940s, complementary to the noiriste revolution of 1946: Timoleon Brutus' *l'Homme d'airain* (1946), his biography of Dessalines, and Dominique Hippolyte's play about Dessalines and the last years of the revolution (1802–1803), *Le Torrent* (1940). In *La Tradition voudoo* (1953), Milo Rigaud noted that the mulatto Andre Rigaud, ultimately Toussaint's enemy, issued from the coupling of a Frenchman and 'a pure negresse of the Arada or Rada race [in Dahomey]: Rose. On his habitation *Laborde*, he 'served' the rada mysteries [spirits] from whom his mother had recovered the cult.'[49]

Where did the lived experiences of women figure in the demands for black enlightenment? How did they respond to the call for black and mulatto equality? The legend of Rose, like the land Haiti, begins with a woman 'brutally fertilized,' as Brutus puts it, 'by a slave in heat or a drunken White, a criminal escaped from Cayenne [the French colonial prison]; or a degenerate from feudal nobility in quest of riches on the continent.' Summoning this myth of violation, Brutus argues that it is senseless to put mulatto over black or vice versa, since 'the origin of everyone is common.' No superiority can be extricated from the color and class chaos that began Haitian society. Yet in this locale of blacks, whites, mulattoes, criminals, slaves, and aristocrats, the 'black woman' is singular. In an amalgam of neutralized distinctions, she stands out as victim and martyr. In the legend of Sor Rose, *to give oneself to a man*, voluntarily or not, is *to give Haiti a history*.

But what kind of history? And who gets to claim it? In *La Femme* Michelet, who had praised Madiou's *Histoire*, greeted Haiti: 'Receive my best wishes, young State! And let us protect you, in expiation of the past!' Yet, while extolling the spirit of this 'great race, so cruelly slandered,' he turned to Haiti's 'charming women, so good and so intelligent.'[50] A few pages earlier, he had tried to show that those races believed to be inferior, simply 'need love.' Tenderness toward women, as colonial historians had argued in their justifications of slavery, was the attribute of civilized men alone. But Michelet extended the possibility of enlightenment to black women who want white men: 'The river thirsts for the clouds, the desert thirsts for the river, the black woman for the white man. She is in every way, the most amorous and the most generous.' Her beneficent desire entitles her, in Michelet's mind, to a particular kind of monumentalizing. Not only is she identified as icon of loving surrender, but she becomes land: generalized as an Africa named, tamed, and dedicated to serving Europe. 'Africa,' Michelet concluded, 'is a woman.'[51]

Michelet's words recall descriptions of the *femme de couleur* in colonial Saint Domingue – most pronounced in Moreau de St. Mery and Pierre de Vassiere, but found in 'natural histories' throughout the Caribbean. Not only sensual, but beings who lived for love, they embodied the forced intimacies and luxuriant concubinage of the colonial past. In Haiti, Michelet's Black Venus becomes Sor Rose, beautiful but violated. Yet, it remained for a Haitian, Janvier in his *La République d'Haiti et ses visiteurs*, to be explicit about the marvels of a history understood as courtship with one aim: possession.

The history of Haiti is such: difficult, arduous, thorny, but charming, filled with interpenetrating, simultaneous deeds, subtle, delicate, and entangled.
She is a virgin who must be violated, after long courtship; but how exquisite when you possess her! . . . She is astonishing and admirable.[52]

The recuperation of emblems for heroism or love in written histories of Haiti often appear as if caricatures or simulations of French 'civilization.' In this recycling of images, as in the case of Louis Napoleon and Soulouque, we are caught in a mimetic bind. The heterogeneity of vodou syncretism, however, offers an alternative to such blockage. Vodou does not oppose what we might construct as 'Western' or 'Christian,' but absorbs apparently hostile materials, taking in as much as it resists.

On May 18, 1803, at the Congress of Arcahaie, General-in-Chief Dessalines ripped the white out of the French tricolor that covered the table. Trampling it under his feet, he commanded that the red and blue – symbolizing the union of black and mulatto – be sewn together as the new flag and that '*Liberté ou la Mort*' (Liberty or Death) replace the old inscription, '*R.F.*' (*Republique Francaise*). In Leogane in the 1970s I heard people recount how Dessalines, possessed by Ogou, cut out the white strip of the French flag. Yet Brutus in *L'Homme d'airain* presents a more compelling version. He tells a story 'of undying memory,' heard and passed on by Justin Lherison in his history class at the Lycee Petion in Port-au-Prince in the 1930s. No spirit of African origins possessed Dessalines, but 'the Saint Virgin, protectress of the Blacks.' Then, Dessalines cursed in 'Congo language' (the sacred language for direct communication with the spirits), and 'then in French against the Whites who dared believe that the Independents wanted to remain French.' Brutus concludes, 'He was in a mystic trance, possessed by the spirit when he said: "*Monsieur, tear out the white from that flag.*"'

But who is this spirit? What is the Virgin Mary doing speaking in Congo and in French? Dessalines possessed speaks the language of the spirit who has entered his head. This Black Virgin speaks both French and the general term for African languages, or more specifically, the tongue of initiates. The inherently unreformable quality of this myth goes beyond sanctioned histories, and most important, de-idealizes a 'pure' type such as the Virgin. We can begin to understand what happens to the idea of virginity or violation when hooked into the system of local spirituality. If priests violated local women while teaching chastity, if they produced impurity, *the mixed blood*, while calling for purity, how was this violation absorbed into the birth of new gods?

One of the rebel Acaau's lieutenants named Frére Joseph was also a vodou practitioner who had great influence in Port-au-Prince during Soulouque's reign. According to Father P.A. Cabon, in *Notes sur l'histoire religieuse d'Haiti de la Révolution au Concordat (1789–1860)*, Joseph walked, candle in hand, amid Acaau's bands, edifying them with *novenas* to the Virgin, but believed by them because of his involvement with the vodou gods.[53] Madiou, writing about the struggle in 1845 between the two 'superstitious' or 'pagan' sects called *guyons* and *saints*, revealed how confused spirituality in Haiti had become after independence: bags with fetishes, human bones, and snakes were mixed up with Catholic rituals.[54] Duverneau Trouillot had argued that, after independence, vodou ceremonies had become so 'Frenchified' that the old cult would disappear under the weight of Christian civilization. The 'advantages of liberty' could not help but contribute to the disintegration of these increasingly disordered and noncodified beliefs and gods.[55]

But what Trouillot praised as the benefits of liberation were never available to the Haitian majority. For them, the gods, saints, and devils of French dogma had to be remade on Haitian soil. Endowed with new qualities, they lost their missionary or conquest functions. Remnants of texts and theologies, once re-interpreted by local tradition, articulated a new history. The Virgin who possessed the militant Dessalines or Frere Joseph would also haunt Haitians as the *djables* – the feared ghostly woman condemned to walk the earth for the sin of dying a virgin. In the Creole songs of Defilee, virgin and whore, purity and defilement became mutually adaptable.

To serve the spirits is to disrupt and complicate the sexual symbolism of the church and state. In answer to Janvier's correlation between the virgin, long desired and finally violated, and Haiti's history, intractable but ultimately apprehended, the most feared spirits, such as the most beloved Virgin, were formed out of the odd facts that made up the discourse of mastery permeated by the thought of subordination. A *vodou history* might be composed from these materials: oral accounts of Dessalines possessed and his emergence as Iwa, god, or spirit, as well as equally ambivalent accounts of figures such as Erzili, Jean Zombi, Defilee, Virgin or Djables. Sinkholes of excess, these crystallizations of unwritten history force us to acknowledge inventions of mind and memory that destroy the illusions of mastery, circumventing and confounding *any* master narrative.

Notes

1   A preliminary version of this essay was presented at the Davis Center for Historical Studies, February 15, 1991. My thanks to Natalie Davis, William Jordan, Fransçois Hoffmann, Gananath Obeyeskere, Richard Rathbone, and Drexel Woodson for their comments and criticisms.

2   M. Chauvet, *Chant lyrique* (Paris: Chez Delaforest, Libraire, 1825) 9. All French and Creole texts are my translations except where otherwise indicated.

3   Quoted in Timoleon Brutus, *L'Homme d'airain* (Port-au-Prince: Imp. NA Theodore, 1946) 1, 264.

4   In his *Description topographique, physique, civile, politique et historique de patrie francaise de l'isle Saint-Domingue*, Moreau de Saint-Méry depicts in detail, for the first time, the rites and religious practices of the slaves in colonial Saint-Domingue. He explains that 'Vaudoux means an all-powerful and supernatural being upon whom depends all of the events that come to

pass on earth.' In Moreau's texts 'vaudoux' also denotes a dance and/or practitioners of the 'cult.' I use the term 'vodou' to describe the belief system of the Haitian majority, though devotees, when asked about their traditional practices, simply say: 'I serve the gods.' See my 'Vodoun, or the Voice of the Gods,' *Raritan*, Winter 1991, 32–57.

5   Janvier published his first responses to Cochinat in the Port-au-Prince journal *L'Oeil*. Other articles appeared in Haiti in the journal *Perseverant*. The 636-page *La Republique d'Hai'ti et ses visiteurs, 1840–1882* (Pads: Marpon et Flammarion, 1883) was reprinted in Haiti in 1979 with the added title, *Un Peuple noir devant les peuples blancs (étude de politique et de sociologie comparées)*. Janvier, *La Republique d'Hai'ti*, pp. 319, 420.

6   Ardouin, *Études sur l'histoire d'Hai'ti, suivies de la vie du General J. –M, Borgella* (Port-au-Prince: Chez l'editeur, 1958) 1, 4.

7   Madiou, *Histoire d'Hai'ti* [1847–1848] (Port-au-Prince: Editions Henri Deschamps, 1989) xiii. The first three volumes of Madiou, published in Port-au-Prince with l'Imprimerie Joseph Courtois (1847–1848), began with the arrival of Columbus and ended with the struggles between Christophe and Petion in a divided Haiti. In 1904, on the one hundredth anniversary of independence, Madiou's descendants published a fourth volume dealing with the events of 1843–1846. In 1988 Maison Henri Deschamps undertook the publication of Madiou's complete works.

8   Spenser St. John, *Hayti or the Black Republic* [1884] (London: Frank Cass, 1971) 95–6.

9   Marx, *The 18th Brumaire of Louis Bonaparte* (New York: International Publishers, 1972) 134.

10   Gustave d'Alaux, *L'Empereur Soulouque et son empire* (Paris: Michel Levy Freres, Librairies-Editeurs, 1856) 1.

11   Wendell Phillips, *Speeches, Lectures, and Letters* (Boston: Lee and Shepard, 1892) 482.

12   Bellegarde, *La Nation hai'tienne* (Paris: J. DeGirord, editeur, 1938) 119.

13   Brown, *The History and Present Condition of St. Domingo* [1837] (London: Frank Cass, 1971) 259.

14   Salomon's speech is reprinted in the appendix of Leslie Manigat's *L'Avénement a la présidence d'Hai'ti du General Salomon: essai d'application d'un point de théorie d'histoi're* (Port-au-Prince: Imprimerie de l'Etat, 1957) 73–8.

15   For a superb analysis of Ardouin's work, see Henock Trouillot, *Beaubrun Ardouin: homme politique et l'historien* (Port-au-Prince: Instituto Pan Americano de Geografia e Historia, 1950).

16   Ardouin, *Études*, 6, 74.

17   Madiou, *Histoire*, 3, 405.

18   The gruesome details of Dessalines' life in servitude are described in Timoleon Brutus' *L'Homme d'airain*, 2 vols. (Port-au-Prince: Imprimerie de l'etat, 1947).

19   Ardouin, *Études*, 6, 45–6.

20   Madiou, *Histoire*, 3, 156.

21   Spenser St. John, *Hayti*, 79.

22   See Jean Fouchard, *La Meringue: danse nationale d'Hai'ti* (Ottawa: Editions Lemeac, 1974). 68–72, for his account of Couloute, Dessalines, and the *carabinier*.

23   In *Apercu sur la formation historique de la nation hai'tienne* (Port-au Prince: Les Presses Libres, 1954) Etienne Charlier, secretary-general of the Haitian Communist party in 1954, condemns historians who concentrate on the actions of 'a few great men' and ignore those he calls 'the only great midwives' (p. 284). Carolyn E. Fick, in *The Making of Haiti: The Saint Domingue Revolution from Below* (Knoxville: University of Tennessee Press, 1990), demonstrates how *marronage*, fugitive slave resistance by those individuals history has obscured, was crucial to the course of the revolution in Saint-Domingue. The most critical essay on 'silences' in the making of 'the world of 1804' is Michel-Rolph Trouillot, 'The Three Faces of Sans Souci: Glory and Silences in the Haitian Revolution,' unpublished ms., 1992.

24   Henock Trouillot, *Le Nouvelliste*, August 13, 1971, 5.

25   ibid.

26   Trouillot, *Les Limites du Créole dans notre enseignement* (Port-au-Prince: Imprimerie des Antilles, 1980) 67.

27   Charlier, *Apercu sur la formation historique de la nation hai'tienne*, 307.

28   D'Alaux, *Empereur Soulouque*, 239–40.

29   Janvier, *Les Constitutions d'Hai'ti (1801–1885)* (Paris: Marpon et Flammarion, 1886) 31–2.

30   Janvier, *Les Constitutions d'Hai'ti*, 1, 43.

31   Catts Pressoir, Ernst Trouillot, and Henock Trouillot, *Historiographie d'Hai'ti*, Publicacion numero 168 (Mexico: Instituto Panamericano de Geografia e Historia, 1953) 190.

32   Antenor Firmin, *De l'Égalité des races humaines (anthropologie positive)* (Paris: F. Pichon, 1885) 544.

33   Madiou, *Histoire*, 8, 77.

34   See *L'Homme d'airain: étude monographique sur Jean-Jacques Dessalines fondateur de la nation hai'tienne* (Port-au-Prince: Imprimerie de l'Etat, 1946) 2, 246–65, for details about the succession of monuments to Dessalines.

35   David P. Geggus, *Slavery, War, and Revolution: The British Occupation of Saint Domingue, 1793–1798* (Oxford: Clarendon, 1982) 40. See also François Hoffmann's 'Histoire, my the et ideologie: La ceremonie du Bois-Caiman,' *Etudes Creoles: culture, langue, societe*, 1990, 13 (I), 9–34, for his analysis of what he believes are the French sources of the legend, and of the stylized Haitian renditions of the story, which were then re-absorbed into oral tradition as national myth. Most recently, Geggus has responded to Hoffmann and deconstructed the 'exaggerated' mythologizing of 'the insurrection of August' in 'La ceremonie du Bois-Caiman,' *Chemins critiques*, May 1992, 2(3), 59–78.

36   Madiou, *Histoire*, 1, 96.

37   Ardouin, *Etudes*, 1, 50–1.

38   Michel Etienne Descourtilz, *Voyages d'un naturaliste* (Paris: Dufart Pere, 1809) cited in Alfred Metraux, *Voodoo in Haiti* (1959; repr. New York: Schocken Books, 1972) 48–50.

39   Price-Mars, *Ainsi parla l'oncle* (Compigne: Imprimerie de Compiegne, 1928).

40   Duverneau Trouillot, *Le Vaudoun: apercu historique et évolutions* (Port-au-Prince: Imprimerie R. Etheaart, 1885) 26, 30–1, 37.

41   Serge Larose, 'The Meaning of Africa in Haitian Vodu,' in *Symbols and Sentiments: Cross-Cultural Studies in Symbolism*, I.M. Lewis (ed.) (London: Academic, 1977) 97.

42   See Serge Larose, 'The Haitian Lakou, Land, Family, and Ritual,' in *Family and Kinship in Middle America and the Caribbean*, Arnaud F. Marks and Rene A. Rainer (eds) (Curapo, Netherlands Antilles: Institute of Higher Studies, 1978) 482–511 and Jean Maxius Bernard, 'Démanbré et croyances populaires,' *Bulletin du Bureau National d'Ethnologie*, 1984, 2, 35–42.

43   Madiou, *Histoire*, 3, 168–9.

44   Rigaud, *La Tradition voudoo et le voudoo hai'tien* (Paris: Editions Niclaus, 1953) 67.

45   Melville J. Herskovits, *Dahomey, An Ancient West African Kingdom* (New York, 1938) 243.

46   Moreau de Saint-Mery, *Description*, 1, 70.

47   J.B. Romain, *Quelques moeurs et coutumes des paysans hai'tiens* (Port-au-Prince: Imprimerie de l'Etat, 1959) 59.

48   Gautier, *Les Soeurs de solitude: la condition feminine dans l'esclavage aux Antilles du XVII au XIX siecle* (Paris: Editions Caribeenes, 1985) 221.

49   Rigaud, *La Tradition voudoo*, 66.

50   Michelet, *La Femme* [1859] (Paris: Flammarion, 1981) 184.

51   ibid., 180–1.

52   Janvier, *La Republique d'Haiti*, 1, 248.

53   Cabon, *Notes sur l'histoire religieuse d'Haiti de la Revolution au Concordat (1789–1860)* (Port-au-Prince: Petit Seminaire College Saint-Martial, 1933) 391. For other accounts of Frére Joseph as 'vodou prophet,' see Gustave d'Alaux, *L'Empereur Soulouque*, 71–2; Dante's Bellegarde, *Histoire du Peuple Haitien (1492–1952)* (Port-au-Prince: Collection du Tricinquantenaire de l'Independance d'Haiti, 1953) 150.

54   Madiou, *Histoire*, 8, 318–19.

55   Trouillot, *Le Vaudoun*, 31–2.

Chapter 25

Deborah A. Thomas

MODERN BLACKNESS: WHAT WE ARE AND WHAT WE HOPE TO BE

Taking off from a little-known, pioneering text of 'Black Consciousness' written in the 1880s, Deborah Thomas undertakes a multi-faceted journey through Jamaicans' ideas about themselves and the world, past and present, local and diasporic. This is a striking example of the innovative work published in the journal *Small Axe* under the inspiration of its editor, David Scott, whose own writings include some of the most powerful of all modern meditations on the meanings of decolonisation, postcoloniality – and what comes after those.

Stephen Howe

THIS IS A PROGRESSIVE TALE, or rather a tale of progress redefined in Jamaica. Like most tales, it has its various twists and turns, but I am going to focus here on the beginning and end of a long century – 1888 to 1998. These two dates bookend a shift in the public power of the ideologies, practices, and aesthetics of lower-class black Jamaicans. Contemporary public invocations of blackness and black progress in Jamaica have become increasingly unmoored from the notions of communal morality and (multiple) territoriality expressed by the first published black nationalists during the late nineteenth century. Central to this shift have been the intensification of transnational migration and the proliferation of media technologies, which have facilitated the amplification of a diasporic consciousness, and the increased political, economic, and social influence of the United States, which has allowed many black Jamaicans to evade the colonial class and race structures institutionalized by the British. These are, of course, not the only factors to consider, but I focus on them here in order to draw attention to another key shift that had taken place by the late 1990s: the diminishing influence of the sector of the professional middle classes that gained state power at independence and served as cultural and political brokers in the lives of poorer Jamaicans. This has occurred alongside significant changes in the ideological thrust of the political party that currently governs, as well as the Jamaican state's more general ability to control and structure public discourse. Consequently, as black Jamaicans have negotiated recent transformations in global capitalist development in order to chart new possibilities for their lives, their visions of progress and the media through which they express these visions have gained a new public prominence and even, to an extent, legitimacy.[1]

I will briefly outline two versions of a black nationalist theme. The first is drawn from a text published at the turn of the last century, a text whose contributors formed part of the emergent post-emancipation stratum of black middle-class Jamaicans. The teachers' and ministers' visions highlighted in the volume emphasize a locally rooted development model in which formerly enslaved black people, free from the physical and psychological bonds of the plantation, would continue to be transformed into a respectable peasantry and, eventually, a politically moderate citizenry, through diligent and 'enlightened' middle-class leadership. The second black nationalist theme is grounded in my own ethnographic research in a community in East Rural St. Andrew at the turn of this century. Here, what is emphasized is a more racialized, individualist, autonomous, and consumerist vision of progress whereby a great many lower-class black Jamaican men and women are increasingly bypassing local middle-class leadership to get what they need. Moreover, they are defining citizenship transnationally. My purpose here is not to compare these two visions of black nationalist progress because, being espoused by different sectors of the population, they are not directly analogous. Rather, I am attempting to clarify where these two visions stand in relation to the Creole multiracial nationalism that became hegemonic in Jamaica by the time of independence in 1962, and what this implies regarding the power of the postcolonial state in relation to the political economy of globalization.

Early black nationalism: *Jamaica's Jubilee*

The 1888 publication of *Jamaica's Jubilee; or, What We Are and What We Hope to Be* was the first published work by black Jamaicans that codified a critique of racism.[2] The book was geared toward demonstrating to a British audience the progress of former slaves in Jamaica during the fifty years since emancipation and toward assuring them that blacks held no feelings of revenge. The five authors, all of whom had substantial connections to the nonconformist missionary churches, attempted to convince their readership that fifty years of freedom and missionary effort had benefited the people of Jamaica who, with continued assistance, would progress even further:

> We launch [this book] forth upon a considerable public, in the earnest hope that it will, in this Jubilee year of our country's Emancipation, awaken in the bosoms of our friends in Britain and Jamaica a still livelier interest in us, and evoke still more persistent and hopeful efforts on our behalf; while we trust that the wholesome advice, the faithful admonitions, and the encouraging facts contained in it, will produce their legitimate effect on ourselves, the struggling children of Afric [sic] in the West.[3]

The book is divided into five essays, each of which tackles an aspect of Jamaica's past, present, and future, illuminating the meanings of freedom and progress for the authors at the turn of the century.

In their attempt to refute the widespread belief that black Jamaicans were incapable of possessing 'those mental and moral qualities so indispensably necessary to his rise in the scale of true civilisation,'[4] the authors outlined several advances since emancipation. The increase in elementary schools after the abolition of slavery was cited as evidence of the former slaves' ability and desire to learn. The authors also placed great emphasis upon the increased number of mutual improvement societies, reading clubs, and Christian associations; the proliferation of musical and social gatherings during Christmas time; and the increase of legal marriages. They felt that this type of progress was due to fifty years of 'social liberty and equality, of religious privileges, of educational advantages, and of intercourse in various ways with civilised and Christian men.'[5] The 'Jubilee Five' also cautioned the readership against censuring Jamaicans for not having advanced further in the fifty years since emancipation, arguing that 'no other people could, under similar circumstances, have reached a greater height on the ladder of social advancement within the same period of time.'[6]

> That a nation is not born in a day is a truth that holds good here. Those who are expecting to find our people higher up the moral, social, and intellectual ladder, have certainly forgotten how many centuries it took other nations and peoples enjoying superior advantages to be what they are today: notably, the British nation, now the foremost, on the whole, in science, art, commerce, literature, and religion.[7]

Notably, the authors attributed the post-emancipation developments in Jamaican society to the nonconformist missionaries, whom they viewed as having instilled in the slaves a desire for freedom and progress during slavery, and as having worked to counteract deleterious social phenomena such as laziness and apathy, which they felt had resulted from the slavery system. The British colonial government, on the other hand, was indicted for having abandoned the former slaves after emancipation and for having failed to initiate any policy that would have countered the destabilizing influences of slavery. The authors' view was that Britain left 'Africa and her children' derailed on the path to civilization:

> Has [the Jamaican Negro] been happily positioned since his introduction into this island? Have his advantages been of the best and most favourable kind? Has sufficient encouragement been held out to him? The only answer to these questions that can have any show of fairness and justice, must be in the negative.[8]

The authors' acceptance of an evolutionary paradigm with respect to progress – or, in the terminology of the day, civilization – is clear, but here they used Social Darwinism to critique post-emancipation British colonial policy. Further, their assertion that despite their African ancestry, black Jamaicans' positions as British subjects gave them the right to claim both a history and 'the interest, sympathy, and protection of those who were instrumental in effecting the expatriation of [their] ancestors'[9] indicated that they expected some degree of reparations based on their legal equality as British subjects.

The writers' vision for future progress can be divided into two categories, with the first addressing the need to strengthen Jamaica's infrastructure. In this respect, they called for more effective management of the colony, greater access to training in scientific agriculture, a greater reliance on locally grown goods rather than imports, and the construction of more and better parochial roads. The second category of the authors' vision for the future concerned the need to strengthen Jamaicans' values. Progress, as they saw it, rested on the pillars of industry (thoughtful and focused labor), economy (thrift and frugality), and godliness (Christian living). They located these values in the persona of the independent peasant, based on their view that working on the sugar estates exerted a demoralizing influence that ultimately would hinder the development of respectable practices and values. Respectability, here, was defined as owning a small plot of land in the mountains, being able to support a family through small-scale agricultural production, having a quiet disposition, and living simply.[10] In their elaboration of these values, the authors consistently evoked the principle that individual effort is related to national development, arguing that the cultivation of respectability would give black Jamaicans entrance into 'the brotherhood of nations.'[11]

> Our defamers shall be constrained to acknowledge us as, with themselves, the common denizens of a common world, the children of a common Father, the subjects of a common king, the servants of a common Maker; possessing the same rights, entitled to the same privileges, claiming the same regard and affection, and having the same destiny.[12]

Finally, the authors made a plea for greater unity among Jamaicans. They argued that 'internal jealousy' in the guise of racism and class prejudice 'prevents steady advancement as a civilised people'[13] and that unless blacks in Jamaica united, the development of a national spirit would be inhibited. Here, it is notable that though their argument is general, they are also speaking on behalf of their race, as it were: 'we form the bulk by far of Jamaica's people' and therefore, 'Jamaica is emphatically ours.'[14] The potential for the articulation of such a vision of ownership had terrified both the local elite and colonial administrators since the establishment of Jamaica as a plantation colony. The volume concludes on an optimistic note, proclaiming hope for Jamaica's future as a united and prosperous nation:

> We seem born to live! Other savage nations have perished under oppression and vanished before the advance of civilisation; but, in the most inhospitable climates of the globe, the children of Africa have lived and increased through centuries of different climates of the globe, and there treated as anything but men and women; and yet they have lived, and instead of being crushed beneath the tread of advancing civilisation, they have joined the ranks of progress, and are to-day marching after the nations already in the van . . . 'Ethiopia shall soon stretch her hands unto God.'[15]

Rebutting racism

There are several reasons why the publication of the *Jamaica's Jubilee* volume is so critical to an understanding of the development of Creole multiracial nationalism in mid-twentieth-century Jamaica. The first is that despite the authors' reproduction of Social Darwinist premises regarding progress through imperial guidance, the book offers a counterpoint to the revival of the racist prejudices of the old planter histories. James Anthony Froude's *The English in the West Indies*,[16] published in the same year as *Jamaica's Jubilee*, became the most popular reading material for English visitors during the long boat passage to the West Indies. As a tract against both imperial absenteeism and self-government for the Caribbean colonies, Froude's text was ultimately a plea for a change in British imperial policy for the West Indies toward the model of the British Raj in India. He viewed West Indian blacks as innately inferior – 'of another stock'[17] – and as incapable of ruling themselves, let alone whites. While Froude's work is generally seen as an aberration within the growing liberalism of the late nineteenth century, at the same time his association of imperialism with all that was new, modern, and civilized, and his conviction that the emancipation of black West Indians began with their removal from Africa as slaves,[18] reflects the growing ideology within Britain that Britain had an imperial responsibility, defined as both right and duty, to lead 'weak nations' toward true freedom.[19]

Froude's polemic did not go unanswered.[20] Nevertheless, even Froude's detractors tended to accept the conventional view that emancipation was an act of English benevolence.[21] This reveals the extent to which Social Darwinism, as an ideology of racial progress, pervaded the analyses of even the most progressive or purportedly sympathetic observers. Indeed, even the Jubilee Five, in their refutation of scientific racism, also framed their remarks within a vision of progress consistent with Social Darwinist ideas.[22] While this should underscore for us the difficulty of transcending context, it also points us toward consequences. By capitulating to the sectarian churches' view that the combination of religiously inspired behavioral and institutional change in conjunction with small (though significant) post-emancipation reforms would lead to improved conditions for the mass of the population, the Jubilee Five relegated both systemic overhaul and explicitly racial mobilization to back burners. In this way, the vindicationist arguments put forth by the authors of *Jamaica's Jubilee* ultimately foreshadowed those formulated by mid-twentieth-century nationalist elites.

Subjects and nationalists

The expansion of Crown lands during the 1880s and 1890s meant that the peasantry was increasingly unable to buy land and was therefore also increasingly exploited as proletariats.[23] Additionally, changes toward a more interventionist imperial policy by the late nineteenth century reflected the growing conviction within Britain that the state should play a greater role in the lives of its citizens. By the time the five *Jamaica's Jubilee* authors penned their essays, the concept of empire as a mobilizing ideology designed to bridge racial and class-based divisions both in the colonies and in England was reaching its peak.[24] This brings us to the third critical contribution of *Jamaica's Jubilee* to understanding the ideological and practical foundations of Creole nationalism in Jamaica: the simultaneous proclamation of loyalty to Jamaica and to Great Britain within the context of an emergent diasporic sensibility. The insistence that black people in Jamaica could claim a history based on their position as British subjects,[25] the vision of Queen Victoria as the Great Ruler of the Universe and of emancipation as a great act of elevation,[26] and the assertion that Britain – as 'the most enlightened Christian nation on the face of the earth' – has a duty to assist the former slaves[27] all reflect the identification of the British Crown (with whom many former slaves associated the Baptists), with benevolent and fair rule. The British government was viewed as protecting the interests of the former slaves from both direct persecution by local whites and from the planters' intermittent dalliances with the idea of annexation to the United States.[28] The former slaves' understanding of the relationship between the planters and the colonial government as antagonistic was long standing and would be long lasting.[29]

It is important to note, however, that identification of the British Crown as protector among the former slaves and their descendants did not necessarily translate into loyalty to British imperialism or colonialism as an economic and political system, either on the part of the mass population or the emergent black intelligentsia.[30] That the *Jamaica's Jubilee* authors ultimately regarded Jamaica as a nation, albeit an embryonic one, is incontrovertible. It is also apparent that their simultaneous loyalty to Britain and to Jamaica co-existed with their recognition that the position of blacks in Jamaica was part of a worldwide conception of blacks, Africa, and African civilization as having 'as yet achieved nothing.'[31] Indeed, this belief would lead many contemporary educated blacks to proselytize for the Christian church in Africa in an attempt to prove that blacks were capable of civilization, and that Africa, though currently wild and backward, could rise to prominence again with the transference of Western civilization. The *Jamaica's Jubilee* authors' identification with Africa was with its potential future rather than its present.[32] Of course, this is an attitude that would change after the emergence of Garveyism, which in its recognition of the significance of racism as a factor retarding black social, economic, and political progress presented a more radical challenge to hegemonic ideas regarding progress, consolidated around the tenets of Christianity. What emerges as most significant here, however, is that the authors' self-assessments as British, as Jamaican, and as 'children of Africa' were not presented as either/or propositions. Rather, they were able to express intense loyalty to all three aspects of their identity.[33]

What emerged was an increasingly diasporic consciousness and experience that provided the potential for an organized political movement from multiple loyalties and locations. Indeed, while the five authors of *Jamaica's Jubilee* put forth their arguments primarily in economic and socio-religious terms, other late-nineteenth- and early-twentieth-century black nationalists agitated for increased participation in electoral politics as well as for the establishment of alternative opportunities for political organization and involvement for black Jamaicans.[34] Moreover, the debates in which these nationalists were integral participants were some of the first regarding the relevance of race to political identity and participation and to socio-cultural and economic development.

While these early leaders struggled for post-emancipation economic and political development for the masses of Jamaicans, they nevertheless distanced themselves from these same masses both socially and culturally. This was, in part, a result of their own position within Jamaica's late-nineteenth-century black middle class, a relatively unstable grouping of teachers, religious ministers, small-scale farmers, artisans, and constables.[35] This grouping would ultimately produce the professional strata of black Jamaicans whose 'respectability' and status were based on their education and their adherence to an idealized Victorian middle-class gender and family ideology rather than on the ownership of either land or other means of capitalist production. As black intellectuals, the Jubilee Five insisted that they articulated important mass concerns on the basis of their shared blackness, but they distanced themselves from lower-class blacks and African-derived cultural expressions as a result of their own education and goals toward personal progress. The various ideological developments toward the end of the nineteenth century – the ascendance of Social Darwinism as a new justification for stratified race relations, the privileging of the formation of an independent peasantry, and the simultaneous assertion of allegiance to Great Britain and Jamaica within the context of an emerging diasporic consciousness – reinforced these class and cultural cleavages. Early nationalists, therefore, were in the precarious position of proving to local and international publics both their equality and their difference.

This was a trend that would continue among some sections of the nationalist movement. Indeed, the dual pillars upon which mid-twentieth-century Creole multiracial nationalism rested echoed late-nineteenth-century emphases on the moral economy of the peasant specifically, the formation of relatively self-sufficient nuclear families organized internally according to a Victorian gendered division of labor, and the consolidation of moderate middle-class leadership.

As Britain's empire was disintegrating, and as development policies pursued by successive Jamaican governments began to privilege the type of industrialization by invitation programs implemented in Puerto Rico, those liberal nationalists advocating Creole multiracialism found themselves in the contradictory position of reproducing the colonial value system that had been strengthened during the period of Crown Colony rule in order to legitimize their leadership and provide for their population. To do so they deflected active relationships to contemporary struggles in Africa, actively contained the development of other contemporary attempts to mobilize along class or racial lines, and emphasized social and economic reform instead of advocating either a socio-economic or political radicalism. This reformist tendency was consolidated during the period between the West Indies-wide labour rebellions in the late 1930s and the achievement of formal independence in 1962, despite the activism of sections of the Marxist movement (expelled from the People's National Party in 1952) and despite the emergence of alternative racialized perspectives and programs such as Bedwardism, Garveyism, Ethiopianism, and Rastafari. Indeed, these perspectives became marginalized within a public sphere dominated by the projection of territorially based multiracial harmony, and in this way Creole multiracial nationalism became knotted to middle-class respectability and cultural hybridity.

At the same time, where late-nineteenth-century nationalists were able to manipulate the racist ideology of imperialism as a civilizing mission to shame British imperial authorities into greater accountability toward their colonial subjects, mid-twentieth-century mobilizers also did so in order to argue for self-government. By proving their progress, both early black nationalists and later Creole nationalists were able to demand equality either as human beings within the 'brotherhood of Christians' or as citizens within the 'brotherhood of nations.' This is what has changed in the contemporary period. The context of globalization has facilitated the ascendance of a vision of progress that is unapologetically racialized and unrepentantly autonomous. The 'modern blackness' of the late twentieth and early twenty-first centuries is urban, migratory, based in youth-oriented popular culture and influenced by African American popular style, individualistic, radically consumerist, and ghetto feminist. Elsewhere, I probe the gendered dimensions of modern blackness that I am identifying as 'ghetto feminism.' Here, my primary concern will be to unpack the slickness of its other aspects.

Reconstituting an autonomous aesthetics and politics

First, the modern blackness of late-twentieth-century Jamaicans diverges from both 'folk' and 'revolutionary' blacknesses. In order to achieve their political goals, nineteenth-century black nationalists and mid-twentieth-century Creole nationalists spoke as 'insiders' to 'outsiders' in a manner that would be understood by those formulating policy that would affect their futures. However, as Kwame Dawes has pointed out in his recent book on the 'reggae aesthetic' in Jamaican literature, the 1970s in Jamaica was a watershed decade in terms of how black Jamaicans articulated and mobilized around their concerns.[36]

Dawes argues that reggae music, while garnering significant international appeal, was primarily a musical genre that spoke first to Jamaicans, in Jamaican language, and only secondarily to the rest of the world. Unlike earlier nationalists, these artists' portrayals of working-class lifestyles and philosophies were neither explanatory nor vindicationist. In this way, reggae musicians defined the terms of engagement with both the music and the messages encrypted within it.

Dancehall music, the soundtrack for modern blackness, has not diverged from this trend. Indeed, it takes it one step further to reassert, as Norman Stolzoff has argued, 'a distinctive black lower-class space, identity, and politics.'[37] This is an identity and political space less easily appropriated by other sectors of the society in the way that some middle-class Jamaicans who were politicized during the 1970s adopted reggae music to embrace their blackness and to champion the cause of Jamaica's 'sufferers.' 'Africa,' here, is largely absent, and dancehall music and culture have re-established a degree of autonomy for their lower-class black afficionados:

> The dancehall itself became a symbol of the division between . . . a music that was increasingly oriented to an international market (roots reggae) and one that spoke to the local sensibilities of a younger generation of dancehall fans. For example, the dancehall-style DJs relied on Patois to a much greater extent than did roots reggae singers. Also, the local space of the ghetto, in general, and the dancehall, in particular, became the subject of lyrical celebration rather than a return to the African motherland.[38]

This relative autonomy has been generated not only within the realm of aesthetics but also, to some extent, within politics. As political scientist Brian Meeks has argued, dancehall has provided 'an impenetrable retreat in which the poor spoke to the poor without the interpolation of the traditional Left, or any outside source with their preconfigured, structural, and linear view of progress.'[39] Because dancehall is not merely a response to hegemonic power but marks the changing aesthetic and political space that both contests and (re)produces broader relations of power, the space of dancehall – and of modern blackness more broadly – is not monolithic. As with any socio-cultural and political trend, there is a great deal of internal ideological debate.

If modern blackness is unlike both 'folk' and 'revolutionary' blacknesses, it is perhaps most similar to the Rude Boy phenomenon of the late 1960s and early 1970s. Prior to the ascendance of reggae's rejection of Babylon's vision of progress, Rudies – influenced by American westerns (and potentially also by the blaxploitation film genre) – had captured the imagination of lower-class black Jamaicans, especially those who were recent urban migrants. Emerging within a growing yet increasingly polarized economic climate and a progressively more violent political atmosphere, Rudies also challenged middle-class politics of respectability but in a drastically different political-economic context and, therefore, with different results. By this I mean that the Jamaican state of the 1960s was considerably more able than it is currently to suppress manifestations of black lower-class political, economic, and cultural mobilization that were considered threatening to the stability of multiracialism and the consolidation of a local capitalist class.

America the beautiful, or the belly of the beast?

The modern blackness of the late twentieth and early twenty-first centuries is also urban, migratory, based in youth-oriented popular culture, and influenced by African American popular style. Migration has long been central to the ways lower-class Jamaicans have constituted their economic lives and family networks and has shaped Jamaicans' consciousness of race, nationality, gender, and class. The United States has figured prominently in Jamaicans' aspirations, particularly during the second half of the twentieth century. Where the *Jamaica's Jubilee* authors envisioned a future in which 'America' would always be hungry enough to demand all that Jamaica produced, by the late 1990s it had become clear that what America had the ability to consume was Jamaican labor, male and female. Here, my focus is on the ways the intensified migration of the late twentieth century has shaped local meanings of 'America.' In the rural hillside community where I conducted my research, villagers' view of America as a 'land of opportunity' co-existed with the view of the United States as an 'evil empire.' The latter was, in large measure, due to its position in the global political economy and the impact this has had on economies such as Jamaica's. In fact, when villagers identified the 'global economy,' they typically spoke of 'America' (and very occasionally, Japan). America's appeal has clearly been ambivalent. For many of the poorer villagers, the 'American dream' has not been without its nightmarish qualities due to, in part, their familiarity with American-style racism and their awareness that intensified global capitalism has widened the gap between rich and poor, not only between the United States and the rest of the developing world but also within the United States itself. Moreover, 'Americanization' has often been seen as the latest in a long line of oppressions, and Americans have been viewed as degenerate cultural influences.[40] Indeed, villagers often attributed the perceived increases in consumerism, individualism, materialism, and a desire for instant gratification to American influence.[41] America was perceived as the place to 'make a living,' but Jamaica was where you would 'make life.'

The politics of modern blackness and hegemonic re-ordering in Jamaica

In re-reading the meanings of rationality, autonomy, reflection, subjectivity, and power from the slaves' point of view, Paul Gilroy has argued that black intellectual and expressive cultural production elaborates a 'counterculture of modernity.'[42] Gilroy has considered black music, in particular, to constitute an 'alternative public sphere.'[43] This is because among black Atlantic populations, the production and consumption of music and other expressive cultural forms has blurred modern Euro-American boundaries between ethics and aesthetics, life and art, and performer and crowd. Here, public expressions of blackness are correlated with the values of egalitarianism, community, and reciprocity. Insofar as these values represent challenges to dominant norms associated with the effects of slavery and capitalist development – hierarchy, individualism, and greed – they have been held up as evidence of resistance (with a capital 'R'). However, the popular music associated with dancehall culture represents and reproduces aspects of contemporary dominant systems of belief – such as 'making it' in the marketplace – that also embody particular political visions. This raises thorny questions for academics, policymakers, and activists concerned with the transformative potential of popular cultural production and representation. If modern blackness is supposed to be countercultural, where is its counter-hegemonic politics? If it marks a new kind of representation holding a new public power, does it embody a new mode of articulating protest? Does it carry a particular vision for the future?

These have long been questions that have animated research among subordinated populations. Indeed, several scholars have attempted to identify key aspects of popular political consciousness that have provided a foundation for counter-hegemonic material and ideological strategies among working-class Jamaicans over time.[44] In one of the more recent considerations, sociologist Obika Gray has located politics both inside and outside of formal party structures.[45] As a result he emphasizes an increased 'cultural confidence' among the urban poor after 1980, a confidence that has occasioned an 'expansion of their social autonomy, and a meteoric rise in their social power.'[46] Gray argues that methodologically, the politics of the poor is generated through informality, improvisation, attrition, and survivalism, and that it is largely a politics of identity designed to 'recover, defend, and preserve their sense of cultural respect and authority'[47] within the broader context of competition for wealth, power, and influence. Gray goes on to identify several channels through which poorer Jamaicans have defined and defended their politics. Among these are evasion and disengagement; 'social outlawry' and the rejection of dominant class morality; and the 'trespassing' and 'colonizing of social spaces,' including those spaces associated with party politics, the informal economy, and the domain of 'culture' – as he defines it, sports, music entertainment, dance forms, language, and religious expression.[48] Here, he is pointing to many of the same trends I am identifying as characteristic of modern blackness in the late 1990s. What I believe is critical to add to his formulation is the extent to which the intensified migration since 1980 has also shaped a transnational politics among poor and working-class Jamaicans.

By the end of the twentieth century in Jamaica, there had been a profound restructuring of the link between territory and nationalism that went beyond re-inscribing migrant populations into the nation and instead had come to ground the nation in individuals and their networks. Scholars have long asserted that transnational migration has led to both intensified racial and pan-Caribbean consciousness as well as to the development of multiple political, economic, and social ties.[49] While these processes have been ongoing, something new has also developed in the contemporary period. These ties are now as often embodied within individual networks of family and friends as they are in collective groups or organizations, particularly among a younger generation.[50] That is, today Jamaica is wherever Jamaicans are. This is a conceptualization of nationality that goes beyond identity politics to raise issues of citizenship and its associated rights and responsibilities, both within particular national territories and beyond them.[51] This emergent politics is neither univocal nor univalent but has the potential to alter Jamaicans' political and social possibilities in the twenty-first century as significantly as the explicit conceptualization of the African diaspora as a common community did in the late nineteenth and early twentieth. This is because it is a politics that is rooted in the changing ways people define community, in how they are restructuring their lives in order to survive, and in how they are reorganizing racialized, classed and gendered identities within the public sphere.

Within this context, modern blackness emerges as 'two-sided.' On the one hand, it provides visions for upward mobility within today's globalized economy that are alternative to those professed by professional middle-class Jamaicans. On the other, these visions do not necessarily open the door to long-term transformations in social, political, and economic hierarchies. For example, while the entrepreneurial zeal with which community members seek to take advantage of migratory possibilities has facilitated their relative success within a global labor market, it has also drained the community of young people with skills, has presented serious challenges to the development of leadership locally, has further disadvantaged those community members who are not able to migrate, and has perpetuated an outward outlook whereby local ambitions require foreign realization. At the same time, within a context where in spite of increased access to education, the ability of poorer Jamaicans to find sufficiently remunerative work locally that is related to their specific skills has declined, entering the migratory circuit becomes a welcomed opportunity. The 'two-sidedness' of modern blackness is also expressed within its popular representations, such as dancehall music and its associated culture. By this I mean that song lyrics and roots play scripts, often both celebrate the culture of dancehall and recuperate aspects of the culture of respectability.

In this way, modern blackness is both a part of and itself embodies the cultural duality that frames the range of ideological and political possibilities for contemporary Jamaicans. As such, it is less a stable and coherent ideological framework for action than a way of seeing, organizing, and imagining that exists alongside other ways of seeing, organizing, and imagining. It might be the counterpoint to the point, the reputation to the respectability, but it is as often the road not taken. Still, modern blackness embodies a public power previously unattained, one that encompasses a framework for facing the everyday 'double-sidedness' of Jamaica's position within the global economy. I mean to say that under conditions of a capitalist globalization that has intensified older hierarchies of race, class, gender, and nationality as well as created new ones, and within a context wherein the degree to which subordinated people have been able to exercise their own agency has been severely circumscribed by power structures over which they have very little control, the public ascendance of modern blackness signals a momentous change. This is true whether aspects of cultural production associated with modern blackness are evaluated as challenges or capitulations to dominant ideologies and practices. Popular cultural production in contemporary Jamaica, then, must be positioned neither as a kind of false consciousness nor as inherently or hopefully resistant or revolutionary, nor as contradictory. Instead we must take seriously the cultural dimensions of intensified globalization in Jamaica in order to more clearly apprehend the political implications of a shift not only in the balance of power between the respectable state and popular culture but also in the composition of these dimensions at specific moments in time.

Notes

1   For additional analyses of this shift, see Brian Meeks, 'The Political Moment in Jamaica: The Dimensions of Hegemonic Dissolution,' *Radical Caribbean* (Kingston: University of the West Indies Press, 1994) and *Narratives of Resistance* (Kingston: University of the West Indies Press, 2000); Don Robotham, 'Transnationalism in the Caribbean: Formal and Informal,' *American Ethnologist*, 1998, 25(2), 307–21; and David Scott, *Refashioning Futures* (Princeton: Princeton University Press, 1999) and 'The Permanence of Pluralism,' *Without Guarantees: In Honour of Stuart Hall*, Paul Gilroy, Lawrence Grossberg, and Angela McRobbie (eds) (London: Verso, 2000) 282–301.

2   'Colored' people – meaning mixed 'brown' folk – were not invited to contribute to this volume because of the view that black Jamaicans would more forcefully reflect the impact of emancipation and missionary activity on the population of former slaves. In the preface the authors insisted that they should not be seen as exceptions within the race. Rather, they wanted the British public to know that there were many others like them who also would have been able to write the book. Biographical information for contributors can be found

in C.A. Wilson, *Men of Vision: A Series of Biographical Sketches of Men Who Have Made Their Mark Upon Time* (Kingston: The Gleaner Co., 1929).

3   *Jamaica's Jubilee; or, What We Are and What We Hope to Be, By Five of Themselves* (London: S.W. Partridge, 1888).

4   ibid., 12.

5   ibid., 75.

6   ibid., 83, italics in original.

7   ibid., 16–17.

8   ibid., 13, italics in original.

9   ibid., 12.

10   Elsewhere, I discuss more fully the dynamic articulations of gender, colour, and class that under-girded this definition of respectability, and the ways the concept and practice of respectability have been implicated within diverse sectors of the nationalist project. *Modern Blackness: Nationalism, Globalism, and the Politics of Culture in Jamaica* (Durham, NC: Duke University Press, 2004). See also Diane Austin-Broos, *Jamaica Genesis* (Chicago: University of Chicago Press, 1997); Honor Ford-Smith, 'Ring Ding in a Tight Corner,' *Feminist Genealogies, Colonial Legacies, Democratic Futures*, Chandra T. Mohanty and M. Jacqui Alexander (eds) (New York: Routledge, 1997) 213–58; and Rhoda Reddock, *Women, Labour and Politics in Trinidad and Tobago* (London: Zed Books, 1994).

11   *Jamaica's Jubilee*, 48.

12   ibid., 21.

13   ibid., 30.

14   ibid., 111.

15   ibid., 115, 128.

16   James Anthony Froude, *The English in the West Indies, or The Bow of Ulysses* (London: Longmans, Green & Co. 1888).

17   ibid., 50

18   ibid., 236.

19   ibid., 207. See also W.P. Livingstone, *Black Jamaica* (London: Sampson Low, Marston, 1899) for a local representation of this view.

20   See John Jacob Thomas, *Froudacity* (London: New Beacon Books, 1969 [1889]) and T.E.S. Scholes, *The British Empire and Alliances, or Britain's Duty to Her Colonies and Subject Races* (London: Elliot Stock, 1899).

21   Thomas, *Froudacity*. See also Elizabeth Pullen-Berry, *Jamaica As It Is, 1903* (London: T. Fisher Unwin, 1903) 26.

22   Of course, these were not the only black intellectuals to find themselves and their arguments limited by the context in which they worked. See Lee Baker, *From Savage to Negro: Anthropology and the Construction of Race, 1896–1954* (Berkeley: University of California Press, 1998) 62; and Mia Bay, *The White Image in the Black Mind: African-American Ideas about White People, 1830–1925* (New York: Oxford University Press, 2000) for US examples.

23   By the mid-1890s, eighty-one individuals had become owners of 97 per cent of the area of rural land offered by the government for sale. Veront Satchell, *From Plots to Plantations: Land Transactions in Jamaica, 1866–1900* (Mona, Jamaica: Institute of Social and Economic Research, 1990) 21.

24   Patrick Bryan, *The Jamaican People, 1880–1902* (London: Macmillan Education, 1991).

25   *Jamaica's Jubilee*, 12.

26   ibid., 90.

27   ibid., 14.

28   This movement was re-asserted at various times throughout the second half of the nineteenth century, and particularly between 1880 and 1884 and between 1898 and 1902.

29   See Bryan Edwards, *The History, Civil and Commercial, of the British West Indies* (New York: AMS Press, 1966 [1792]) 553, for an early documentation of this sentiment.

30   See also Michael Craton, *Testing the Chains* (Ithaca: Cornell University Press, 1982) 16.

31   *Jamaica's Jubilee*, 111.

32   This would lead some diasporic blacks to discuss potential black colonization of Africa. The first attempt to resettle Africa from the Americas in 1899 combined a desire to provide land for entrepreneurial West Indians and other blacks with educational and missionary functions for Africans themselves. These early pan-Africanists, not surprisingly, used much of the language of the British imperialists. Bryan, *The Jamaican People*, 258.

33   This is an argument that Paul Gilroy also makes in his discussion of Martin Delany's ideas about pan-Africanism and black nationalism during the same time period in the United States. *The Black Atlantic; Modernity and Double Consciousness* (Cambridge: Harvard University Press, 1993).

34   For an example of political mobilization, see Joy Lumsden, 'Robert Love and Jamaican Politics' (PhD diss., University of the West Indies, 1987).

35   Bryan, *The Jamaican People*.

36   Kwame Dawes, *Natural Mysticism: Towards a New Reggae Aesthetic* (Leeds: Peepal Tree Press, 1999).

37   Norman Stolzoff, *Wake the Town and Tell the People: Dancehall Culture in Jamaica* (Durham: Duke University Press, 2000) 103.

38   ibid., 103.

39   Meeks, *Narratives of Resistance*, 12.

40   There is a long history to this perception of Americans as uncivilized. E.g. Frank Taylor, *To Hell with Paradise* (Pittsburgh: University of Pittsburgh Press, 1993).

41   Mary Waters makes similar arguments for West Indian migrants in the United States. *Black Identities: West Indian Dreams and Immigrant Realities* (Cambridge: Harvard University Press, 1999).

42   Paul Gilroy, *The Black Atlantic* (Cambridge: Harvard University Press, 1993) 1.

43   Paul Gilroy, *There Ain't No Black in the Union Jack* (Chicago: University of Chicago Press, 1991 [1987]) 215. See also Dick Hebdige, *Cut 'n' Mix* (New York: Routledge, 1990).

44   E.g. Jean Besson, 'Religion as Resistance in Jamaica Peasant Life,' *Rastafari and Other Afro-Caribbean Worldviews*, ed. Barry Chevannes (New Brunswick, NJ: Rutgers University Press, 1998) 43–76.

45   Obika Gray, 'Discovering the Social Power of the Poor,' *Social and Economic Studies*, 1994, 43(3), 69–89. This is a critical distinction also raised by Brian Meeks, who notes an increase in confrontational political action outside the structures of party politics that coincides with a decrease in participation within the formal politics of the state. As an example he notes that while popular participation in general elections declined from a high of 86.1 per cent in 1976 to 66.7 per cent in 1993 and 65.2 per cent in 1977. Meanwhile, the common tactic of mounting illegal roadblocks to draw attention to social and economic problems within communities has grown dramatically from twenty-three incidents per year in 1986 to two hundred and seven in 1997. *Narratives of Resistance*, 13.

46   Gray, 'Discovering the Social Power,' 177.

47   ibid., 182.

48   ibid., 197.

49   Regarding the development of racial and pan-Caribbean consciousness, see Austin-Broos, *Jamaica Genesis*; Winston James, *Inside Babylon* (New York: Verso, 1993); and *Holding Aloft the Banner of Ethiopia* (New York: Verso, 1998); and Constance Sutton and Sue Makiesky-Barrow, 'Migration and West Indian Racial and Ethnic Consciousness,' *Caribbean Life in New York City* (Staten Island: Center for Migration Studies, 1987). For examples of the kinds of multiple political, economic, and social links forged by transnational migrants, see Linda Basch, *et al.*, *Nations Unbound* (Langhorne, PA: Gordon and Breach, 1994).

50   See Nina Glick Schiller and Georges Fouron, *Georges Woke Up Laughing: Long Distance Nationalism and the Search for Home* (Durham: Duke Univers, Black Identity Press, 2001) for a similar discussion among West Indians in the United States.

51   See Saskia Sassen, *Globalization and Its Discontents* (New York: The New Press, 1998), esp. ch. 5.

Chapter 26

E.S. Atieno Odhiambo

RE-INTRODUCING THE ' PEOPLE WITHOUT HISTORY': AFRICAN HISTORIOGRAPHIES

Postcolonial studies and 'new imperial histories' have, thus far, often given more attention to South Asia, the Middle East and indeed to former imperial metropoles than they have to Africa. Thus it is important to be reminded how fertile and various is the historical work from and about Africa – including, as Atieno Odhiambo stresses in this overview – the work of 'amateur' local historians and of painters and other artists as well as that of academic historians. Here are yet more 'new imperial histories' not always borne enough in mind when such labels are used.

Stephen Howe

Introduction

IT HAS BECOME FASHIONABLE to think of continents, communities, identities, belonging, tradition, heritage and home as imagined, invented or created entities. The idea of Africa has been tantalizing to the West since Homer imagined the flight of the Greek gods from mount Olympus to Africa, there to feast with the blemishless Ethiopians. In the fifteenth century, a Papal Bull imagined Africa as a *terra nullius* and proceeded to divide it between Christian Spain and Portugal. The English poet Jonathan Swift imagined a 'yon Afrique' where geographers were wont to fill the blank spaces with elephants for want of towns. The partition of Africa at the Berlin West Africa Conference in 1884–1885 carved out Africa to European powers ostensibly because the continent had an ignoble history of slave trade and slavery which could only be stamped out through European colonization. Thus the former citizens and subjects of African kingdoms and of stateless communities were dubbed as the peoples without history. Instead it was asserted that there was only the history of Europeans in Africa. European authorship from Hegel down to H.R. Trevor-Roper asserted that Africa constituted a blank darkness, and 'darkness was no suitable subject for history' [Trevor-Roper 1966: 9]. The colonial period was a time of distortion through power: 'power was used to force Africans into distorting identities; power relations distorted colonial social science, rendering it incapable of doing more than reflecting colonial constructions '(Ranger 1995: 273). One of these distortions was that of Africans as peoples without history.

The other Africa, the actually existing Africa of the Africans, did not participate in this discourse. History being a record of man's past, and philosophy of history being second-order reflections on the thoughts of historians about the historical process, engaged the oral historian Mamadou Kouyate of the empire of Mali as much as it did the Moslem scholar of the same empire at the same time, Ibn Khaldun. This tradition of the production and engagement with the memory of their own histories continued through the ages into the twentieth century, the age of Africa's peasant intellectuals (Feierman 1990). By tradition, what is meant here:

> the socially consolidated versions of the past, and particularly accounts of origins of institutions, which served to define communities and underwrite authority in them. Memory refers to those traces of past experience present in the consciousness of every human being, which provided the essential but problematic basis for the sense of personal identity, as well as the constraining or enabling basis for future action. Tradition was social and hierarchical, memory was individual and open-access.
>
> Peel 1998: 77

Overview

Precolonial historiographies of Africa consisted of oral histories as well as written accounts. The oral histories included myths, legends, epic, poetry, parable as well as narrative. They varied from dynastic accounts and kinglists that were a record of the royal courts and the state elites to the clan histories of the stateless societies. Because of their selective valorization and silences they constituted historiographies in themselves. These oral renditions were the resources that the first Christian African elites drew on to write their histories in the nineteenth and early twentieth century: Apolo Kagwa in Buganda, John Nyakatura and Kabalega Winyi in Bunyoro, Samuel Johnson among the Yoruba, Akiga Sai among the Tiv and J. Egbarehva in Benin. Similarly among the stateless peoples the clan histories were to become the resources for writing the wider histories. The written sources of African history belong to three different historiographical traditions. First was the enormous corpus of Muslim sources from the eighth to the fifteenth centuries CE. Written by Islamic missionaries, travellers and scholars to Sudanic and the eastern coast of Africa these included the works of Al Masudi, Al Bakri, Al Idrisi, Ibn Batuta, Ibn Khaldun and Al Wazzan (Leo Africanus). These sources consisted of direct and reported observations of local societies. The sources were biased in favour of Muslim rulers and said little positive about the non-believers. After the sixteenth century African Islamic scholarship emerged that incorporated the local oral traditions in its renditions. This scholarship took centre-stage with the emergence of the Tarikh al Sudan by Al Sadi of Timbuktu in 1665, Tarikh al Fattash (1664), and Tarikh Mai Idris by Imam Ahmad Ibn

Fartuwa. As well, Swahili Islamic scholarship emerged from the eighteenth century, embodied in city-state histories such as the *Pate Chronicle* or in the nineteenth-century resistance poetry from Mombasa, Muyaka. The same happened in the Hausa states, giving rise to the *Kano Chronicle* as a generic format. These documents focused on state power rather than the wider social processes. In the nineteenth century, vigorous Islamic scholarship flourished in the *Sokoto Caliphate* as well, represented by the extensive writings of the founding Caliph Shehu, Usuman Dan Fodio and those of his successors.

The second corpus of written sources consisted of European traders and travellers' accounts dating from the fifteenth century. They imparted the image of the exotic as well as a primitive Africa often at war with itself, particularly in the nineteenth century. The third strand of scholarship came from the Africans in the Diaspora in the Americas, beginning with Olaudah Equiano in 1791 on to Edward Wilmot Blyden in the nineteenth century, and W.E.B. Dubois and Leo Hansberry in the twentieth century. This trend marked the opposite of the European endeavour: it sought to glorify the African past. Within Africa, Cheikh Anta Diop endeavoured to prove that the foundations of ancient Egyptian civilization was Black and African. This tendency has been seized upon by the school of Afrocentricity in the USA, led by Molefi K. Asante.

Colonial historiography produced its own knowledge of Africa, based on the premise of European superiority and the civilizing nature of its mission. Colonial historiography presented the Europeans as the main actors in any significant transformation of the African continent since its 'discovery', exploration and conquest. Elspeth Huxley's *Lord Delamere and the Making of Modern Kenya* (1935) was typical of this genre. The Africans were seen by the administrators, missionaries, historians and anthropologists alike as being static and primitive, the passive recipients of European progress. Africa's self-evident artistic achievements, its historic monuments, its political kingdoms that resembled any other western-type bureaucracy, and its complex religious institutions were attributed to foreigners, the Hamitic conquerors from the northeast. The 'Hamitic hypothesis' (Sanders 1969) was ubiquitous and was used to explain east coastal urbanization as well as the Yoruba myths of origin.

The external factor in the twentieth century was European colonialism, seen as a civilizing mission among inferior peoples. History served as an ideological legitimation of Europe in Africa. In the eyes of at least one African historian, this was 'bastard historiography' (Afigbo 1993: 46). The nationalist movement was in part a challenge to this notion of Africans as a people without history. With the attainment of independence in the 1960s emerged a postcolonial historiography centred within the continent but with significant external liberal support as well. Liberal historiography in the 1960s sought to help Africans recover and reclaim their own histories in consonance with the attainment of political independence; to distinguish the history of Europeans in Africa from the history of African peoples, and to write history from 'the African point of view'. Conceptually the liberals worked within an interdisciplinary framework alongside archaeologists, political scientists, and economic historians. Methodologically, they developed the field of oral history, and appropriated and extended the range of questions to be asked concerning social change by social anthropologists. The favourite theme of the period was African resistance and its opposite, African oppression.

The dyad of resistance and oppression (Cooper 1994) inspired magisterial research on Samori Toure by Yves Person, on the Maji Maji war in Tanganyika led by John Iliffe and Gilbert Gwassa, on the Chimurenga war in Southern Rhodesia (Zimbabwe) by T.O.

Ranger, and on the Herero/Nama revolt in Namibia by Helmut Bley. 'The people in African resistance' became a mantra for the period. An early demur suggested that within African communities there obtained a paradox of collaboration and resistance; that within the textures of African societies the resisters of today would be the collaborators of tomorrow, thus creating 'the paradox of collaboration' (Steinhart 1972; Atieno-Odhiambo 1974). Still the dyad held sway in African historiography in the 1980s.

In the 1960s, Dar-es-Salaam University became most associated with this enthusiasm for the recovery of African initiative. The Dar-es-Salaam school of history was created under T.O. Ranger. It sought to explicate the explanatory value of African history as a discipline; to give Tanzania its national history; and to engage in debates relating to the building of Ujamaa socialism in Tanzania. The short-lived (1965–1974) nationalist thrust of this historiography began to be challenged in the early 1970s for its failure to engage with the imperial and global contexts in which actions and agencies were undertaken; and with its tendency to narrow down complex strategies of multi-sized engagements with forces inside and outside the community into a single framework to emphasize African activity, African adaptation, African choice and African initiative.

This radical response to the paradigm was prompted by the emergence of Marxist historians, anthropologists and political scientists in the 1970s. It fore-grounded class analysts at the global and local levels (Rodney 1974). Economic history became the first locus of the liberal/radical debates. One school called for substantive analysis focused on culture as the operative force in African economic history, and applied western market analysis to African economic activity. The liberal approach privileged individual action; while the radical approach saw political power and economic constraints as the principal operative feature of the historical process (Newbury 1998: 304). The radicals traced the history of African poverty in the context of global capitalism.

The recovery of initiative

The setting up of western-type universities in Africa on the eve of independence marked a significant milestone in what African scholars came to regard as the recovery of African initiative. The new departments of history established the teaching of African rather than European history at the core of the curriculum, with a full commitment to the Africanization of learning through an African faculty, trained in Europe and the United States by individuals with backgrounds in imperial or mission history. In turn they assumed the leadership in African universities created at Ibadan (Nigeria), Legon (Ghana), Nairobi (Kenya), Dar-es-Salaam (Tanzania). Their biggest challenge was methodological: history as understood in the west was based on written documents. The greatest break came with the acceptance and refinement of the methodology of oral traditions as a means for recapturing the African voices from the past. Jan Vansina's *De la Tradition Orale* (1959) translated into English as *Oral Tradition* (1965) wielded enormous influence.

The traditions were treated as narratives, and later scholarship has defined them as comparable to primary written documents, and also as representations of secondary interpretations with kernels of original texts. The establishments of relative chronologies was another major innovation as calendric dating of events based on lists of rulers in African states, solar and lunar eclipses were correlated with written sources. Ancillary disciplines, particularly archaeology and historical linguistics, extended the timescale of the deep past as the C14 technique provided archaeologists with dates going back four millenia (Thornton 1997). As well, glotto-chronology and more complex comparative methodologies enabled historical linguists to provide dates going back two millennia in places such as eastern Africa. Thus the origins of ancient civilizations, the spread of iron working, Bantu migrations and settlements, key issues in the historical discourses of the period, found resonance in the allied disciplines (Ehret 1998). The acceptance of oral traditions facilitated tremendous expansion in graduate programmes at African Universities as the first generation of African scholars undertook the supervision of the many students who sought to give histories to the many ethnic groups that hitherto had no history. In addition, the requirement that undergraduate history majors complete a research dissertation enabled thousands of students to undertake oral and archival research, leading to an engagement with local histories as students spent two to three months interviewing oral experts in the field. This input brought academic history in contact with the wider society and helped to build links with the academy and the public over a period of twenty years before funds for the universities dried up in African universities. The existence of well over six thousand of these dissertations are a marker of the recovery of the initiative sought by the pioneers and to the institutionalisation of history within Africa. As well, the effort resulted in some quality essay publications (McIntosh 1969; Mutahaba 1969; Webster 1974; Atieno-Odhiambo 1975).

Thematic variations

From the beginning of the 1970s, African history branched into various specializations. Studies of the Atlantic slave trade, first inspired by P.D. Curtin's work (1969), flowered into debates about the numbers; the nature of domestic slavery in Africa before and after the Atlantic phase; the impact of the Atlantic slave trade on African economies, demographies and development; comparative slavery in the East African coast and in the new world; and the slow death of slavery in twentieth-century Africa. The historical study of African religions, Christian missionary, independent African Christians, and African traditional religions, attracted T.O. Ranger, Isaria Kimambo and B.A. Ogot. A.G. Hopkin's *Economic History of West Africa* (1973) applied the substantivist analysis to African economic behaviour. David Henige's journal, *History in Africa* emerged as the premier journal of method, critiquing the uncritical usage of both European and African traditions. *Ecology, Control and Economic Development in East Africa*, by Helge Kjeshus (1976), was the founding text on environmental history in East African historiography. Intent on restoring the people as agents of African initiatives, the author sketched how pre-colonial societies controlled their environment and were victors in the ecological struggle to the end of the nineteenth century when rinderpest and smallpox devastated both human and livestock populations. This breakdown was exacerbated by the violent conquest by the Germans, forced recruitment into the First World War and the British policies of forced settlements, labour recruitment, wildlife conservation and economic exploitation. The resulting population declines gave 'nature' the advantage, and tsetse fly infestation, sleeping sickness and decline in agricultural production set in.

In the ensuing two decades, this historiography has become more complex as both archival and oral histories have been used to illuminate the complex relations between environment, people, history, culture, and political and economic structures. In *Custodians of the Land* (Maddox and Gilbin 1996) colonized Africans are portrayed as pushing on in spite of colonial adversity, learning not only to survive, but to thrive under new sets of challenges. The work enriches the analysis of the relationship between population changes and political economy. In the opinion of a reviewer, it marks a state of the art research into the relations between ecology and history: suggesting that the present ecological condition is a product of a complex and contested interaction between the environment, local initiative and imperial drive over the past century. African demographic, medical and labour histories emerged, the latter driven by the Marxist structural interests in class struggles and the emergence of working-class consciousness (Cooper 1995). Peasant studies emerged with Colin Bundy's *Rise and Fall of the South African Peasantry* (1979) and commanded sustained elaboration in central and Eastern Africa. This field has become flourishing as Agricultural History (Vail and White 1980, Mandala 1990).

The global agenda on women inspired the first histories of women in Africa relating to women's role in economic development, and African women and the law. These were enriched by the multi-disciplinarity facilitated by feminist, gender and literary studies, resulting in a historiography that is distinct from the more orthodox specializations in its familiarity with conversations from other continents. The first wave of studies of women in the 1970s focused primarily on the economically productive activities and social agency of African women. This work turned on women in development, especially agrarian change, land tenure, urbanization, and women's role in formal and informal economies. The second wave focused on the colonial period, and studied questions relating to colonial domesticity, customary law, motherhood, reproduction, sexuality, and the body. Luise White's study of prostitution, *The Comforts of Home* (1990), is representative. The most recent cultural wave has covered gender and masculinity, social and institutional identities, and generational, homosocial struggles (Hunt 1996). The lexicon of cultural history has covered gender meanings, modernity, coloniality, postcoloniality, consumption and public culture. Thus there has been a paradigm shift from women's history to gender history, foregrounding gender as a set of social and symbolic relations (Cohen and Odhiambo 1992; Robertson 1997).

To summarize, from the vantage point of the end of the century, African historiography has moved from the institutional to the economic, then the social, and now cultural history. The rubric of social history captures much of the more recent historiography. Its strength has been its multidisciplinarity and its multivocality. The insights of history, political economy, historical anthropology, literary studies and other forms of social science have been combined to illuminate the following parameters of understanding: landscapes of memory and imagination; the constructions of identity; the colonization of consciousness; colonial texts and transcripts as social practices; the consumption of leisure; the production and risks of knowledge; the occult and imaginary; and the rituals of power. The anatomy of 'experience, identity and self expression which link the glories of past independence, the miseries of domination and poverty, and the hopes of a fully autonomous future' (Austen 1993: 213) are very much at the core of this endeavour, at 'Reinventing Africa', to borrow Andre Brink's apt title.

Nationalist history: Eastern Africa

The faithful phantom of Africanism can be represented in the two sides of a coin: with the state on one side and the nation on the other. Whether one tries to ignore it, work within it, or adore it, history, whether written or publicly recited, does not escape the state.

Jewsiewicki 1986: 14

The meta-narrative of the nationalist historiography begins with Thomas Hodgkin's *Nationalism in Tropical Africa* (1956), a populist text which sought to equate nationalism with any protest phenomenon generally. With the attainment of political independence, a nationalist historiography emerged. It sought to study the origins and course of African nationalism through the lenses of modernization theory, and emphasized the emergence of the African elites and the launching of western-style political parties. A strand of the genre sought to lay bare the connexions between the primary resisters to colonial conquest, the modernizing elites of the interwar years, and the later territorial nationalists of the 1950s that saw the goal of nationalism as being the attainment of political independence. This facilitated the writing of the history of the new states as the history of the 'African voice', and of this voice as the voice of these elites (Ranger 1970). These elites were conscious of the aspirations of the masses and were able to attract a broad following and to articulate popular concerns, speaking on behalf of 'those who had not spoken'. Radical rural movements were thus linked through the local notables such as the Samkange family in Southern Rhodesia to the wider canvas of nationalist discourses (Ranger 1996). Thus, in the case of Tanganyika, the political elites such as Julius Nyerere found common cause with local organizations challenging everything from unjust marketing regulations to restrictive crop controls, and from cattle dipping to further European land alienation. In the context of an imperial Britain that was ambivalent about its need to keep Tanganyika and anxious to stem the spread of Mau Mau-like activities there, Julius Nyerere and his allies in TANU galvanized the grassroots demand for independence (Illiffe 1979). The most recent historiography has criticized this narrative for its male-centeredness by arguing for the centrality of women in Tanzania's nationalist movement, emphasizing their role in rural and urban political party politics. Thus a more inclusive version that integrates the political, cultural and symbolic work of women into the past and present of nationalism has emerged.

The local antithesis of this British conquest narrative was anti-colonialism variously understood as African nationalism (Rosberg and Nottingham 1966), a peasants' revolt (Maloba 1993), African resistance against colonialism (Ogot and Ochieng' 1995), or as the historiography of the Mau Mau rebellion as a specifically central Kenyan phenomenon (Berman and Lonsdale 1992). The historiography of the revolt has increasingly moved from the nationalist narrative to the local levels, with significant focus on the squatters (Kanogo 1987), the Rift Valley (Furedi 1989), Muranga district (Throup 1987) and southern Kiambu district (Kershaw 1997). The participation of Kikuyu women in Mau Mau both as mobilizers and as combatants in south Kiambu have been made explicit (Presley 1992). The very power of the 'thick descriptions' of the local has thus created space for the development of intellectual history of central Kenya as a vital component of Kenya's historiography. The power of Mau Mau as a historical event with deep cultural and symbolic meanings for the Kikuyu themselves has been captured by John Lonsdale's work on the moral economy of Mau Mau, a work that gives it ethnic and historical specificity; and totally overthrows the possibility of re-inventing a Kenyan nationalist narrative (Berman and Lonsdale 1992). The Mau Mau narrative has other power manifested through the many public debates in the public arenas: it has been a trope for critiques of the postcolonial

state from below (Atieno-Odhiambo 1992). These concerns with the internal problema-
tiques do not consider nationalism to be a pre-requisite ideology for the construction of
a future nation-state (Atieno-Odhiambo 1999).

Beyond Kenya, fascination with Mau Mau has led to concerns with peasant
consciousness in the later liberation struggle in Zimbabwe, to debates on the meaning of
peasant consciousness, and to an engagement with the wider question of war and society
in Zimbabwe (Ranger 1985; Kriger 1992; Ranger and Bhebe 1996). A narrative of the
Zimbabwean society as a narrative of struggle has emerged; but so also has an undercurrent
critique that points to an unholy alliance of the ruling elites and the guerrillas at the
expense of the rest of society in the postcolonial dispensation (Ranger 1999).

The disappointments with the results of political independence from the mid-1960s
led to radical pessimism captured by the title of Oginga Odinga's book *Not yet Uhuru*
(1967), and to critiques of the nation-building projects that were inspired by Marxism,
underdevelopment theories and by the writings of Frantz Fanon and Kwame Nkrumah.
Walter Rodney's *How Europe Underdeveloped Africa* (1974) was a salient statement of the
underdevelopment thesis. This literature was significant for the radicalism that it injected
into academic and popular discourses; its impact on actual researches on the ground was
more limited. One unintended consequence of it was to raise the question of the possibility
of African history at all, given the fact that Africa's autonomous development had been
subverted for five hundred years according to the thesis. An orthodox variant of this
radical pessimism was marked by the shift in focus from the African elites to the study
of peasants and workers as the real wagers of the anti-colonialist struggles. Historians
read the works of anthropologists and political scientists as well as conducting oral histories:
the result was a major thrust in peasant studies (Bundy 1979; Klein 1980; Vail and White
1980; Mandala 1990), as well as in studies of rural struggles of squatters and sharecroppers
(Kanogo 1987; Onselen 1996).

Ordinary lives

> This is a biography of a man who, if one went by the official record alone,
> never was. It is the story of a family who have no documentary existence, of
> farming folk who lived out their lives in a part of South Africa few people
> loved, in a century that the country will always want to forget. The State
> Archives, supposedly the mainspring of the Union's memory, has but one line
> referring to Kas Maine. The Register of the Periodic Criminal Court at
> Makwassie records that on September 8, 1931, a thirty-four-year-old 'labourer'
> from Kareepoort named 'Kas Tau' appeared before the magistrate for
> contravening Section Two, Paragraph One of Act 23 of 1907. A heavy bound
> volume reveals that 'Tau', resident of Police District No. 41, was fined five
> shillings for being unable to produce a dog licence. Other than that, we know
> nothing of the man.
>
> Onselen 1996: 1

So begins Charles van Onselen's epic biography of Kas Maine, a South African sharecropper
on the northwestern Transvaal. In so doing, Onselen follows a tradition founded in the
same region eight decades earlier by Sol Plaatje whose writings captured the historical

conjuncture of African dispossession of their land in 1913 (Plaatje 1916). Kas Maine belongs to rural Africa, to ' the peoples without history', whose agency is all but invisible in the colonial archives much valorized by western scholarship. Historians of Kenya faced the challenge of this absence right from the early 1960s as they sought to re-write the Mau Mau into the narrative of the emergent nation. This effort continues to be controversial. A more accommmodating approach came with the almost simultaneous appropriation of Peasant Studies from anthropologists by historians of Southern Rhodesia, Kenya and South Africa (Arrighi 1967; Atieno-Odhiambo 1972; Bundy 1979). Subsequently historians of rural South Africa sought to recapture their worlds via oral interviews in the last two decades (Marks and Rathbone 1982; Marks and Trapido 1987). This has yielded details regarding the part played by Africans in the unfolding historical events, the dialectics of their own history and culturally reflexive accounts of their own experiences. Kas Maine's biography is the epitome of this restoration. Onselen succeeds in restoring Kas Maine to the mainstream of colonial history by excavating the landscapes of memory retained by the thousands of contacts, transactions, exchanges, fights and hatreds that the inhabitants of this region retained about their own personhood and agency in the making of their long century from the 1870s down to 1985 when his protagonist died. In the process he constructs a historical figure who was never far from comprehending his own sense of worth, and of the 'worth of ordinariness', emphasizing moral equity even in the ravines of race and class, calling on the common humanity of all (Cohen and Odhiambo 1989: 119–120).

Scholars of folklore studies have significantly explored this terrain as well, by emphasizing performance in context in their interpretation and understanding of oral texts. This approach has proven useful both for the gendered household and family histories in Southern Africa; as well as for the male politics of status and rank associated with the oral poetry of chieftaincy. Cumulatively we have had the re-introduction of the South African Black Africans through the foregrounding of their own perceptions of the unfolding events. The contrasting perspectives of the South African problem by the nationalist Nelson Mandela and the sharecropper Kas Maine are mutually reinforcing in this regard (Mandela 1994).

Indigenous historiographies

Beyond the historian's guild, the twentieth century has witnessed the production of popular historical literature in Africa, produced locally, often in non-western languages by individuals and collectivities believing in their past, giving themselves their own histories which tell of those pasts, and which have meaning, authority and significance for the local populations. The recognition of this popular work compels a movement from narrow understandings about the nature of history, historical evidence, and what should constitute other peoples' histories (Cohen 1994). One is led to multiple sites of historical telling: the song, praise poetry, the allegory in the folktale, the silences in the memory of the past, for example. There has been a continuous production of the oral histories of Africa, captured in the rendition that 'we live our lives as a tale that is told' (Hofmeyr 1994). At the same time, the advent of literacy has led to the proliferation of the realm of the written world.

Vernacular authors have sought to give their peoples a history. The first generation of Africa's modern men in the twentieth century appropriated the knowledge of the organic intellectuals of the previous century by bridging the gap between orality and literacy through publication. The foundations for this genre were laid early in the century by Apolo Kagwa in eastern Africa and Samuel Johnson in west Africa (Kiwanuka 1970; Ajayi 1998). They collected the oral traditions of their clans and kingdoms and in so doing created a master narrative for the Baganda and the Yoruba. In terms of method they occupied a fairly modern terrain. They interviewed knowledgeable informants, custodians of shrines, court historians and keepers of clan lores. Fifty years later the academy—Jan Vansina in the 1950s and B.A. Ogot in the 1960s—travelled along the same path, interviewing individual encyclopaedic informants, holding formal sessions with court historians and clan elders, as well as reading the missionary and colonial archives to arrive at a history of the Kuba or the Luo that accommodated every major lineage, or left enough room for the malleable accommodation of more recent incorporations into the putative genealogy of all Kuba or all Luo (Cohen and Odhiambo 1987). Johnson's work has spawned a century of Yoruba historiography (Falola 1991). Kagwa's work has influenced western scholarship in the fields of history, anthropology and religion in the region for a century, and spawned a specific Ganda historiography that continues to thrive (Reid 1997).

Critiques of these canons have emerged with revisionist interpretations. In the Great Lakes areas, historiography has moved from the original diffusionist conquest model—the Hamitic myth—into a concern with ecological change, and the contextualization of struggles over authority and wealth (Schoenbrun 1999; Willis 1999). A significant by-product of this accommodationist stance has been the production of regional as contrasted with state histories in both western and eastern Africa, as exemplified by case studies of the Mande and Luo worlds. The wider Mande canvas covers a period of seven centuries, from the rise of the Mali empire under Sundiata Keita in the fourteenth century down to the destruction of the state of Samory Toure by the French in late nineteenth century. During this period the cultural landscape remained recognizable as a Mande world, the locus moving southward away from the Sahel to the Atlantic coast as a result of the slave trade (Barry 1998).

Likewise, the Luo chronology has its epicentre in the cradleland of the central Sudan sometime around 1000 CE. Successive milestones in Luo historiography, from J.P. Crazzolara in the 1950s, Ogot in the 1960s, Cohen and Odhiambo in the 1980s and Ron Atkinson in the 1990s, all assume the constancy of the Luo world. Both Mande and Luo histories traverse several ethnicities, states and polities over the centuries without being confined to any single one of them. Acholi ethnicity evolved during the eighteenth century (Atkinson 1994). There were Mande and Luo nations and cultural spheres well before the incursion of the colonial state in the twentieth century. Their sense of multiple belongings to the various postcolonial states in the regions suggests an alternative paradigm for writing regional rather than state histories, an alternative that is closer to peoples' experiences with history in the long durée than the western historical practice and which throws up challenges for the student of Comparative History (Lorenz 1999).

The production of locality

In the recent past, the productions of local histories has flourished in the Niger delta as villages, neighbourhoods and administrative districts have laid a claim to the authority on their pasts. Local community histories comprise an autonomous corpus outside the academy. They consist of published books describing the history and culture of towns, villages, clans or geographical areas. Authored by amateurs they build on issues of identity, and locate individual citizens within the local developmental discourses and environment. This literature belongs to the genre of 'production of locality' from within the community outside the reach of the State. The production and intended consumption of this material remains local. The choice of the English language suggests that community histories are very much a product of modernity (Harmeit-Sievers 1997).

The authors consider that they are writing history, inscribing the essence of the existing society through history, culture and symbols of modernity. The format of these many books is often a narrative of the origins of the village, the arrival of the western missionaries, schools and hospitals, the emergence of the local notables and the latest developmental trends. It is the story of progress as lived and witnessed and lived. It is also a site of contestation. Guild historians, commissioned by the local communities to write them a history, are as often contested over their authority over the mastery of local history and on the veracity of the produced texts (Alagoa 1997).

Scopic representations

One version of vernacular history that constitutes a challenge to academic historiography has been genre paintings that emerged in the Belgian Congo from the 1920s. Its first stage marked African inventions of scopic regimes of modernity, the invention of the West in the African imagination via painting. The intellectual and artistic reading of the colonizing West on paper and on canvas began with Albert Lubaki and Tshyela Ntendu in the 1920s and 1930s:

> These painters tried to understand what colonial modernity meant, seeking to put the colonialists, their objects and their people on a meaningful framework— using the plastered walls of houses as well as paper to figure in paint their understanding of the Western perception of themselves and their universe.
>
> Jewsiewicki 1991: 139

The paintings depicted the goods and postures of modernity: the Missionary, man on a bicycle, family portraits, the colonial army, the telephone, typewriter, train, car and steamer. A later generation of the 1940s and 1950s represented by Mwenze Kibwanga and Pilipili were literate teachers of art in schools. The genre of urban painting was 'invented' by and for the literate petty bourgeoisie of the cities in the 1960s. They were characterized by the recollections of the violence of colonial conquest and domination, as well as by memories of the political violence after independence. A new generation rose in the 1970s that was dominated by worries of social justice, political arbitrariness, and new gender and generational conflicts. Its leading artists included Cheri Samba, Moke, Sim Simaro and Vuza Ntuko. Their creations are both chronicles of social and political life as well as materializations of the imagination and social memory. Cheri Samba is primarily a moralist and teacher. Bogumil Jewsiewicki reminds us that these are members of the urban petty bourgeoisie with bourgeois aspirations. One must therefore be careful when referring to these artists as 'popular' painters, for their hopes and tastes are bourgeois (Jewsiewicki 1991: 146). Each painting refers to a story and emits a narrative.

Tshibumba Kanda Matulu's conceptualization of his work is that by painting he is doing history. 'I don't write but I bring ideas, I show how a certain event happened. In a way I am producing a monument' (Fabian 1996: 14). The social significance of his painting emerges from his contention that he is a historian of his country and an educator of his people. Shibumba's *History of Zaire* is a narrative of over one hundred paintings that the painter regards as a book, part of Zaire's colonial and postcolonial historiography:

> As an interpreter of the history of his country Tshibumba competes with journalistic reporting and academic historiography over chronology and dating, and over contexts and interpretations of certain events. He regards his works as fixions with a message: to make his audience think.
>
> Fabian 1996

For the historian the challenge lies in integrating these representations of history into our scopic canvas.

References

Afigbo, A.E. 1993. 'Colonial Historiography'. In T. Falola (ed.) *African Historiography*, Harlow: Longman.

Ajayi, J.F.A. 1998. 'Samuel Johnson and Yoruba Historiography'. In Paul Jenkins (ed.) *The Recovery of the West African Past*. Basel: Basler Afrika Bibliographien, 57–68.

Alagoa, J. 1997. 'Village history in the Niger Delta'. Bellagio: Mimeo.

Arrighi, G. 1967. *The Political Economy of Rhodesia*. The Hague: Mouton.

Atieno-Odhiambo, E.S. 1999. *Ethnicity and Democracy in Kenya*. Lincoln, NE: University of Nebraska, Lincoln.

—— 1992. 'The Production of History in Kenya: The Mau Mau debates', *Canadian Journal of African Studies*, 25(2): 300–7.

—— 1975. 'Seek Ye First the Economic Kingdom: the early history of the Luo thrift and trading corporation (LUTATCO), 1945–1956'. In B.A. Ogot (ed.) *Hadith V: Economic and Social History of East Africa*. Nairobi: East African Publishing House, 218–56.

—— 1974. The *Paradox of Collaboration*. Nairobi: East African Publishing House.

—— 1972. 'The Rise and Fall of the Kenya Peasantry, 1888–1922', *East Africa Journal*, 5(2): 5–11.

Atkinson, Ronald R. 1994. *The Roots of Ethnicity: The Acholi of Uganda Before 1800*, Philadelphia: The University of Pennsylvania Press.

Austen, R. 1993. 'Africanist historiography and its critics: can there be an autonomous African history?' In T. Falola (ed.) *African Historiography*. Harlow: Longman, 203–18.

Barry, Boubacar. 1998. *Senegambia and the Atlantic Slave Trade*, Cambridge: Cambridge University Press.

Berman, B. and J. Lonsdale. 1992. *Unhappy Valley*. Athens: Ohio University Press.

Bundy, C. 1979. *The Rise and Fall of the South African Peasantry*. Berkeley: University of California Press.

Cohen, D.W. and E.S. Atieno-Odhiambo. 1992. *Burying S M: The Politics of Knowledge and the Sociology of Power in Africa*. Portmouth, NH: Heinemann.

—— 1989. *Siaya: The Historical Anthropology of an African Landscape*. London: James Currey.

—— 1987. 'Ogot, Ayany and Malo: Historians in Search of a Luo Nation', *Cahiers d' Etudes Africaines*, 107–108, XXVII(3–4): 269–86.

Cohen, David William. 1994. *The Combing of History*. Chicago: Chicago University Press.

Cooper, F. 1995. 'Work, Class and Empire: an African Historian's Retrospective on E.P. Thompson', *Social History*, 20(2): 235–41.

—— 1994. 'Conflict and Connection: Rethinking Colonial African History', *American Historical Review*, 99: 1516–25.

Curtin, P. 1969. *The Atlantic Slave Trade; A Census*. Madison: University of Wisconsin Press.

Ehret, C. 1998. *An African Classical Age: Eastern and Southern Africa from c. 1000 BC to 400 AD*. Charlottesville: University of Virginia Press.

Fabian, Johannes. 1996. *Remembering the Present*. Berkeley: The University of California Press.

—— (ed.) 1991. *Yoruba Historiography*. Madison: African Studies Center, University of Wisconsin.

Feierman, Steven. 1990. *Peasant Intellectuals*. Madison: University of Wisconsin Press.

Furedi, F. 1989. *The Mau Mau War in Perspective*. London: James Currey.

Harmeit-Sievers, Axel. 1997. 'Igbo Community Histories: Locality and History in Eastern Nigeria', Basel Africa Bibliographien, Working Paper No. 6.

Hodgkin, T. 1956. *Natialism in Colonial Africa*. London: Muller.

Hofmeyr, Elizabeth. 1994. *'We Live Our Lives as a Tale that is Told'*, New York: Little Brown.

Hopkins, A.G. 1973. *An Economic History of West Africa*. London: Longman.

Hunt, Nancy Rose. 1996. Introduction. *Gender and History*, 8(3): 323–37.

Huxley, Elspeth. 1935. *Race and Politics in Kenya*. London: Faber & Faber.

Iliffe, J. 1979. *A Modern History of Tanganika*. Cambridge: Cambridge University Press.

Jewsiewicki, B. 1986. 'One Historiography or Several? A Requiem for Africanism'. In Jewsiewicki, B. and Paul Lovejoy, *African Historiographies*. Beverly Hills: Sage, 9–17.

Jewsiewicki, Bogumil. 1991. 'Painting in Zaire: From the Invention of the West to the Representation of Social Self'. In Susan Vogel (ed.) *Africa Explores*. New York: The Center for African Art, 130–75.

Kanogo, Tabitha. 1987. *Squatters and the Roots of Mau Mau*. London: James Currey.

Kershaw, Greet. 1997. *Mau Mau From Below*. Athens: Ohio University Press.

Kiwanuka, M.S.M. 1970. *History of Buganda*. Harlow: Longman.

Kjeshus, H. 1976. *Ecology, Control and Economic Development in East Africa*. London, Heinemann.

Klein, M. (ed.) 1980. *Peasants in Africa*. Beverley Hills: Sage.

Kriger, Norma. 1992. *Zimbabwe's Guerrilla War: Peasant Voices*. New York: Cambridge University Press.

Lorenz, Chris. 1999. 'Comparative Historiography: Problems and Perspectives', *History and Theory*, 38(1): 25–39.

Maddox, G. and Gilbin, J.L. (eds) 1996. *Custodians of the Land*. Oxford: James Currey.

Maloba, W. 1993. *Mau Mau and Kenya*. Bloomington: Indiana University Press.

Mandala, E. 1990. *Work & Control in a Peasant Economy*. Madison: University of Wisconsin Press.

Mandela, N. 1994. *Long Walk to Freedom*. London: Little Brown.

Marks, Shula and S. Trapido. 1987. *The Politics of Race, Class & Nationalism in 20th Century South Africa*. London: Longman.

Marks, S. and Rathbone, R. 1982. *Industrialization & Social Change in South Africa*. New York: Longman.

McIntosh, B. 1969. *Ngano*. Nairobi: East African Publishing House.

Mutahaba, G. 1969. *Portrait of a Nationalist: the life of Ali Migeyo*. Nairobi: East African Publishing House.

Newbury, David. 1998. 'Historiography'. In J. Middleton (ed.) *Encyclopedia of Sub-Saharan Africa*, Vol. 2. New York: Martin Scribner's Sons, 299–304.

Ochieng, W.R. and B.A. Ogot. 1995. *Decolonization & Independence in Kenya*. London: James Currey.

Odinga, O. 1967. *Not Yet Uhuru*. London: Heinemann.

Onselen, Charles van. 1996. *The Seed is Mine: the life of Kas Maine, a South African sharecropper 1894–1985*. New York: Hill & Wang.

Peel, J.D.Y. 1998. 'Two Pastors and their "Histories". Samuel Johnson and C.C. Reindorf'. In Paul Jenkins (ed.) *The Recovery of the West African Past*. Basel: Basler Afrika Bibliographien, 69–81.

Plaatje, S. 1987 (1916). *Native Life in South Africa*. Harlow: Longman.

Presley, Cora A. 1992. *Kikuyu Women, the Mau Mau Revolt and Social Change*. Boulder: Westview.

Ranger, T.O. 1999. *Voices from the Rocks*. Oxford: James Currey.

—— 1996. 'Postscript: Colonial and Postcolonial Identities'. In T.O. Ranger and R. Werbner (eds) *Postcolonial Identities in Africa*. London: Zed books, 271–81.

—— 1995. *Are We Not Also Men?: the Samkange Family and African Politics in Rhodesia 1920–1964*. Portsmouth, NH: Heinemann.

—— 1985. *Peasant Consciousness and Guerrilla War*. London: James Currey.

—— 1970. *The African Voice in Southern Rhodesia*. London: Heinemann.

Ranger, T.O. and N. Bhebe. 1996. *Society in Zimbabwe's Liberation War*. Oxford: James Currey.

Reid, R. 1997. 'The Reign of Kabaka Nakibinge: Myth or Watershed?' *History in Africa*, 24: 287–97.

Robertson, Clare. 1997. *Trouble Showed the Way*. Bloomington: Indiana University Press.

Rodney, Walter. 1974. *How Europe Underdeveloped Africa*. Dar es salaam: Tanzania Publishing House.

Rosberg, C.G. and J. Nottingham. 1966. *The Myth of Mau Mau*. New York: Praeger.

Sanders, Edith R. 1969. The Hamitic Hypothesis: Its Origin and Function in Time Perspective, *Journal of African History*, 10, 4.

Schoenbrun, D. 1999. *A Green Place, A Good Place*. Kampala: Fountain Publishers.

Steinhart, E.I. 1972. *Conflict and Collaboration*. Princeton: Princeton University Press.

Thornton, J. 1997. 'Historiography in Africa'. In J.O. Vogel (ed.) *Encyclopedia of Precolonial Africa*, London: Sage, 54–8.

Trevor-Roper, H.R. 1966. *The Rise of Christian Europe*. London: Thames & Hudson.

Throup, D. 1987. *Economic & Social Origins of Mau Mau*. London: James Currey.

Vail, Leroy and L. White. 1980. *Capitalism & Colonialism in Mozambique*. Minneapolis: University of Minnesota Press.

Vansina, J. 1965. *Oral Tradition*. London: Routledge.

Webster, J.B. 1974. *The Iteso During the Asonya*. Nairobi: East African Publishing House.

White, L. 1990. *The Comforts of Home*. Chicago: University of Chicago Press.

Willis, J. 1999. 'Kinyonyi and Kateizi: The contested origins of pastoralism in south-western Uganda'. In J-P. Chretien et J-L. Triaud *Histoire d'Afrique: Les ejeux de memoire*. Paris: Karthala, 119–36.

PART 11

Other empires, other histories

Chapter 27

Selim Deringil

'THEY LIVE IN A STATE OF NOMADISM AND SAVAGERY': THE LATE OTTOMAN EMPIRE AND THE POSTCOLONIAL DEBATE

Too often, still, 'imperial history' even where 'new' has been taken to mean the histories of European seaborne empires; with the other imperial systems which have existed in modern history – not least the Ottoman – passed over too hastily or even quite literally forgotten. That is beginning to change, and comparative work such as that of Selim Deringil is among the welcome forces of change. Combining close 'local knowledge' (which, regretfully, cannot fully be represented here) with broad conceptual sophistication, he offers intriguing new insights on empire in general.

Stephen Howe

I was treated with respect by these savages, and subjected to the direst insults by this English race for which I had the greatest respect. Yet I am a reasonable man and I tried not to pass judgment on the whole of the English race on the basis of the misbehavior of a few officials.

Esref Kuscubasi, Turkish POW in Egypt, 1917

THE OTTOMAN EMPIRE was the last great Muslim world empire to survive into the age of modernity. The Ottoman state, together with its contemporaries, Habsburg Austria and Romanov Russia, was engaged in a struggle for survival in a world where it no longer made the rules. As the nineteenth century approached its last quarter, these rules were increasingly determined by the successful and aggressive world powers, Britain, France, and, after 1870, Germany.

As external pressure on the Ottoman Empire mounted from the second half of the century, the Ottoman center found itself obliged to squeeze manpower resources it had hitherto not tapped. Particularly nomadic populations, armed and already possessing the military skills required, now became a primary target for mobilization. This study is an attempt to come to grips with the 'civilizing mission' mentality of the late Ottomans and their 'project of modernity' as reflected in their provincial administration. It is the view of this writer that sometime in the nineteenth century the Ottoman elite adopted the mindset of their enemies, the arch-imperialists, and came to conceive of its periphery as a colonial setting.[1] It is my contention that the Ottoman elite conflated the ideas of modernity and colonialism, and applied the latter as a means of survival against an increasingly hostile world:

> Within its remaining territories, the Ottoman state began imitating the western colonial empires. The state consolidated the homogeneity of the core region, i.e.—the Anatolian peninsula and the eastern regions of Thrace . . . even as it pushed the periphery—principally the Arab provinces—into a colonial status.[2]

The novelty of the colonial idea meant that it had actually to be spelled out in books and pamphlets produced at the time.

In a book entitled, 'The New Africa' (Yeni Afrika), obviously written on an official commission, Mehmed Izzed, 'one of the official interpreters for the Imperial Palace,' felt that he had to clarify the mechanics of colonialism:

> The practice of 'colonialism' is one in which a civilized state sends settlers out to lands where people still live in a state of nomadism and savagery, developing these areas, and causing them to become a market for its goods.[3]

Where Mehmed Izzed refers to peoples and tribes living to the south of Ottoman Libya, his attitude can pretty much be summed up as the White Man's Burden wearing a fez: '[these people] who are savages and heretics can only be saved by an invitation into the True Faith.'[4]

Yet in their drive to achieve modernity, the Ottomans were not to build on a tabula rasa. In characteristically pragmatic fashion, the 'Romans of the Muslim world,' in the unforgettable words of Albert Hourani, were to dip into a whole grab bag of concepts, methods and tools of statecraft, prejudices, and practices that had been filtered down the ages.[5] It is this type of colonialism that I propose to call 'borrowed colonialism.'[6]

The empire that fell between the cracks

Some of the themes in this article were taken up in my book, *The Well Protected Domains. Ideology and the Legitimation of Power in the Ottoman Empire.*[7] However, that work was necessarily more descriptive than theoretical. I had postponed dealing with many of the questions coming to my mind at the time. Therefore none of the present discussion of issues such as the relationship of Ottoman studies and the postcolonial debate appeared in that volume, nor does much of the archival material, particularly that relating to Ottoman Libya and Yemen. Similarly, the memoir literature and biographical studies incorporated here are not found there.

In this chapter I will argue that as the nineteenth century neared its end, the Ottomans adopted a colonial stance toward the peoples of the periphery of their empire. Colonialism came to be seen as a modern way of being. For the Ottomans, colonialism was a survival tactic, and in this sense the Ottoman Empire can hardly be compared to the aggressive industrial empires of the West. In a sense theirs was much closer to the 'borrowed imperialism' of the Russian Empire, another 'also ran' compared to the British and the French.[8] It was a survival tactic because the Ottomans were fully aware that if they were not to become a colony themselves they had to at least qualify for such 'also ran' status.[9] It is this in-between status that I will refer to as the 'borrowed colonialism' of the Ottoman nineteenth century.[10] Although it covered a huge geography until its last days, and its study presents fruitful challenges to any student of colonialism and postcolonialism, the nineteenth-century Ottoman empire has been largely ignored by the literature covering these issues. Even in the work of as major a figure as Edward Said, the Ottoman Empire is dismissed as a sort of epiphenomenal (and dare one say it, quintessentially 'Oriental') creature. He comments on Eric Auerbach's presence in Istanbul as a 'critically important alienation from [Western cultural tradition]' and 'Oriental, non-Occidental exile,' and by doing so Said falls into much the same trap as the writers he critiques in his epic *Orientalism*. Eric Auerbach writes in *Mimesis* that his lack of access to the libraries of Europe in fact enabled his writing of the work. For Said, that Auerbach is in exile in Istanbul is doubly poignant—not only is he in exile from his sources, he is exile in the city that was the capital of the 'monster': 'For centuries Turkey and Islam hung over Europe like a gigantic composite monster, seeming to threaten Europe with destruction.'[11] That Auerbach was sitting in the city that was the seat of much of what stood for Western Civilization seems to have passed unnoticed by the authors of both *Mimesis* and *Orientalism*. Can it be that Homi Bhabha's famous, 'almost the same but not quite' dictum applies here in a way that he never imagined?[12] Dare one speculate that the reason the Ottoman phenomenon is ignored by both the Subalterns and their opponents is because it is precisely 'almost the same but not quite'? And to go even further, may we venture that the 'not quite' bit is the fact that it was a Muslim power?

The aim of this essay resonates with aspects of the postcolonial debate. The Subaltern Studies group as well as authors such as Benedict Anderson and Timothy Mitchell inevitably see nationalism as something that follows European colonialism. It is my view that in the case of Ottoman 'borrowed colonialism' we have something that develops side-by-side with it.[13] I would completely agree with Gyan Prakash in his assessment of the task of the Subaltern Studies group:

> These directions of postcolonial criticism make it an ambivalent practice, perched between traditional historiography and its failures, within the folds of dominant discourses and seeking to rearticulate their pregnant silence.[4]

In a similar way the study of the Ottoman empire also finds itself 'perched' between Western historiography on the one hand and the study of 'Muslims/Middle Easterners who matter' (i.e. Arabs, Jews, Iranians, Indians,) on the other. In other words, what Prakash notes for subalterns, that they fall between the 'fault lines' of the 'cracks of colonial archeology of knowledge' is largely true for the Ottoman.[15] Here I fully agree with Dipesh Chakrabarty when he states that European historians may (or rather used to in my view) get away with ignoring the historiography of Third World writers:

Third World historians feel a need to refer to works in European history; historians of Europe do not feel any the need to reciprocate.' This he elegantly terms, 'inequality of ignorance.'[16]

But I would have to say that the Subaltern group in its turn, locked in as it is on the ills of colonialism, completely ignores that there existed a major non-Western sovereign state whose destinies were in many ways intertwined with the destinies of India.[17] Even in a work by an Indian scholar which purports to be a study of 'the making of Europe' the focus is Christianity. This is perhaps not surprising, but what is surprising, is that it is Western Christianity, as if the Great Schism somehow wiped eastern Christianity off the map of 'Europe.'[18] Although I agree with Chakrabarty that we are still a long way from 'provincializing Europe,' and with Prakash that 'there is no alternative but to inhabit the discipline,' I feel that some significant steps have been taken in the direction of putting Ottoman studies on the world historiographical map.[19] One such example is Ussama Makdisi's work which engages the very subaltern debate itself, and situates the Ottoman Tanzimat reform process and reactions to it in the subaltern discourse.[20] My aim in this essay is to rise to the challenge of A. Hopkins:

> What is needed is a fundamental reappraisal of world history to bring out the extent to which, in recent centuries, it has been shaped by the interaction of several types of empire at various stages of development and decay. Such an approach would capture both the differences between empires and their dynamism, and would leave few parts of the globe untouched.[21]

At this point a few observations are in order to contextualize the Ottoman colonial project, and to establish some preliminary markers that set it off from Western colonialism. First, the Ottomans rulers and ruled discussed in this essay were of the same religion, and the ultimate legitimation for Ottoman rule rested on the position of the Ottoman Sultan as the Caliph of all of the world's Muslims. My query therefore is: at what point is common religion not enough of a differentiating factor in a comparative study of how Christian or Muslim powers relate to their respective subject peoples? At what points do the Ottoman version of colonialism and the Western version converge and diverge? In a sense, the Ottoman case is unique, since the Ottoman empire was the only sovereign Muslim state to survive into the height of the era of colonialism in the late nineteenth century, and to be recognized (albeit grudgingly) as a member of the club of Great Powers. One half of this borrowed colonialism was based on tried and true practices of Islamic Ottoman empire building; the Caliphate, the Sharia, Hanefi Islamic jurisprudence, guilds, and Turkish/Islamic law (kanun/yasa). The other half, or 'new' half, was a creature of the nineteenth-century positivist, Enlightenment-inspired centralizing reforms.[22] Particularly after the official declaration of the Tanzimat Edict of 1839, the state made it its business to permeate levels in society it had not reached before.

Yet, a word of caution is in order here: these two halves were not hermeneutic compartments sealed off by the bulkheads of 'reform.' What makes Ottoman borrowed colonialism interesting is this interpenetrated nature itself, the interpenetration, that is, of the pre-modern and the modern. Ussama Makdisi points out that the classic Subaltern misperception—the tendency to assume that all phenomena such as religious sectarianism are 'forms of colonialist knowledge' or are a throwback to some form of atavistic behavior—

leads to a failure to understand that sectarianism was indeed an aspect of modernity.[23] His assessment is that sectarianism has to be evaluated at two different levels:

> It is an intermingling of both precolonial (before the age of Ottoman reform) and postcolonial (during the age of reform) understandings, metaphors, and realities that has to be dissected at two overlapping and mutually reinforcing levels, of the elite and non-elite.[24]

My contention in this study is that what is true for religious sectarianism at a local level is also true for the elite's perception of itself and its peripheral populations, the same 'intermingling' is very much in evidence. Nor do I mean to imply that the Ottoman state and society previous to 1839 were static monolithic entities. Some valuable recent research is showing us that much of what was synthesized into the Ottoman modernity project was the result of historical processes and trends which were taking place already in the eighteenth century.[25] The hybrid unique nature of Ottoman colonialism may very well be a useful mirror to hold up to Western colonialism as a way of deepening our understanding of what is at the bottom of it all: power and the enforcement of rule over people who don't want you there in the first place. First, it will be useful to examine what the nineteenth-century Ottoman inherited from the past.

Nomadism as anathema for modernity

The attitude of the late Ottoman statesman to nomadic populations in the periphery of the Empire was informed by a combination of traditional and modern factors. A classical Ibn-Khaldounian view that all civilization advances as a confrontation of nomadism with settled life was combined with a distinct 'mission civilizatrice' that the Ottomans took right out of the Troisieme Republique.[26] The two modes of life were irreconcilable:

> The clash between nomads and urban dwellers generated the Ottoman cultivated man's stereotype that civilization was a contest between urbanization and nomadism, and that all things nomadic were only deserving of contempt.[27]

This contempt could range from out and out enmity to a relatively mild paternalism. The latter could even shade into an admiration for the 'noble savage.' Yet the basic belief was always the same, as was stated in the capsule phrase when it came to nomadic populations: 'they live in a state of nomadism and savagery' ('hal-i vahset ve bedeviyette yasarlar').[28] The term is inevitably the same with some mild variations such as 'they live in a state of ignorance and nomadism' ('hal-i cehalet ve bedeviyette yasarlar'). What had to be done, inevitably, was to 'gradually include them in the circle of civilization' ('pey der pey daire-i medeniyete idhal'), or they had to have 'civilization and progress brought to them' ('ürbanýn temeddün ve terakkileri'). But these people were never actually bad, they were always, 'simple folk who cannot tell good from evil' ('nik ve bed'i tefrik edemiyen sade dilan ahali'). The nomadic leaders or notables had to be treated carefully and all care was to be taken to avoid 'provoking their wild nature and hatred' ('tavahhus ve nefretlerini mucib olmak').[29] The Ottoman's constant use of the 'civilizing motif' was similar to the White Man's Burden as applied by the British Raj in India, where all opposition to British rule was dubbed, as by nature, 'fanatic' as in a 'fanatic Moulvi' who 'provoked the fanaticism of the natives.'[30] If at all possible, the leaders of the nomads or the provincial notables were to be won over by 'giving them a little something' ('bir mikdar sey') and 'flattering their leaders' ('elebas ýlarýný tatyib').[31] This too resembles the British practice of 'cajoling local leaders.'[32] Indeed the British themselves, when they came to apply their colonial rule to Egypt, felt that the Egyptian view of his new masters was that 'the English are Turks with the faculty of justice added.' The new masters were clear about who they were displacing, '[We] have only to reckon with the Osmanli of different degrees who have found a home in this country . . . These are the dominant races.'[33] There is little doubt that many an Ottoman provincial official would have envied the British their easy arrogance and sheer power to work their will.

The 'two faces' that Ussama Makdisi has noted in his study of the Ottoman Lebanon at mid-century are germane here:

> The violence of the Ottoman state in the Lebanese periphery may also be understood to have 'two faces' in the sense that it invoked the language of an ideal Islamic order that clearly discriminated against non-Muslims, while it tacitly acknowledged the impossibility of realizing such an ideal order in a religiously diverse region of Mount Lebanon.[34]

My point that builds on Makdisi here, is that the 'two faces'—official intolerance of diversity, and the reality of the need to tolerate such diversity—can be extended to those Muslims who 'live in a state of nomadism and savagery.' This is at the core of 'borrowed colonialism.' The face that had hitherto largely left the 'savage' to his own devices now, in a situation of dire need, turns into the face that will 'civilize' him and make him useful.

Memoirs and 'life worlds' as clues on borrowed colonialism

In the memoirs and biographies of people who lived through what turned out to be the death throes of an empire, we catch glimpses of the mentality outlined above. Habermas' concept of 'life world' is useful here in attempting to capture this mentality:

> [T]he lifeworld appears as a reservoir of taken-for-granteds, of unshaken convictions that participants in communication draw upon in cooperative processes of interpretation . . . We can think of the lifeworld as represented by a culturally transmitted and linguistically organized stock of interpretative patterns.[35]

In this context Naciye Neyyal Haným, the author of the memoir cited below, and the life stories of Yusuf Dia' and Ruhi Al Khalidi are instances of 'lifeworlds,' as a shared world in which 'interpretative patterns' and 'mutual understanding' would regulate the intellectual horizons within which these actors found themselves.'[36]

A remarkable example of the genre is the massive memoir of a woman (unusual in itself), the painter Naciye Neyyal Haným, whose life spanned the last days of the empire and the first days of the republic.[37] Her husband, Tevfik Bey, was the Ottoman mutasarrrýf (governor) of Jerusalem from 1897 to 1901. Naciye Haným accompanied him on his posting. A fellow passenger on their journey was the Minister of Customs, who disembarked when the ship first docked at Beirut:

> I saw a crowd of Arabs who had come to meet him. They were noisily kissing his hands, and in a great clamor they put him in a boat and rowed off shouting 'Allah! Allah!'[38] When it was their turn to disembark at their port of arrival, Jaffa, 'some twenty or twenty-five Arabs arrived in big boats to take us ashore and seized the oars shouting, 'Allah! Allah.'[39]

It is almost as though that by their 'nature' the Arabs must utter 'Allah! Allah!' After their arrival in Jerusalem, at some point Naciye Haným catches an eye infection from two Arab women vendors who have been let into the house. She points out that eye infections due to flies are 'very common among the Arabs.' When she welcomed her husband home in the evening:

> In those days, because of this confounded eye infection, I used to liken myself to those Arab women who go out to the gate together with their gummy eyed (çipil gözlü) child to meet their husbands. Accordingly I welcomed Tevfik Bey with the Arabic greeting, 'ahlan wa sahlan.' He smiled and replied, 'there we are, now you have become just like them' ('tam onlara benzemissin').[40]

Yet, the 'noble savage' is right around the corner in the shape of Sheikh Rashid Arikat, who is presented as, '[Formerly] a rebel against the state who then declared his obedience and was made responsible for keeping the peace in Riha.' The sheikh teaches Naciye Haným to ride, saves her life from a runaway horse, and she ends up by saying, 'He used to love me as a father.'

In describing her life as the young wife of a dashing Ottoman official Naciye Haným waxes poetic:

> I used to accompany Tevfik Bey everywhere he went, but in those days, even if one was man and wife, it would not do to be seen next to one another. Accordingly I followed at a distance of fifty, sixty or even one hundred metres. I was usually accompanied by gendarmes, just as he would be surrounded by soldiers and other official people. This life of ours, was something like the life of a prince and princess ruling a faraway kingdom . . .[41]

When Tevfik Bey went to Bir-i Sebi in the Negev desert, where he had been given instructions to form a *kaza*, Naciye Haným went with him. Here, in contrast to the words above, she emphasized how they won the hearts of Arabs by their modesty:

> The fact that, although we were the mutasarrýf, we mingled with them as a young husband and wife, without fanfare and ceremony and shared their life style, caused them to warm to us. I sensed that they liked us because, although they are savage, and live so far from civilization, they appreciate goodwill and know how to be thankful.[42]

Apparently, the *kaza* was a success. After the construction of the government building, Naciye Haným recorded that:

> [P]eople flocked to the government building to register themselves and to settle around it. They requested that a mosque be built alongside it as an imperial gift and that all the buildings should bear the name of the August Personage.[43]

The memoirs of Naciye Haným bear eloquent testimony to the 'half-and-half nature' of Ottoman colonialism. On the one hand, Naciye Haným feels that it was a mistake to let the Arab vendor women into the house because she 'caught an Arab disease' which caused her husband to tease her that 'she had become just like them.' On the other hand, Sheikh Arikat emerges from her memoirs as the heroic father figure. Yet, the scene in which she describes the official procession could have been a scene from 'Passage to India.' Her assessment of the Arabs who 'appreciate kindness and goodwill' is reminiscent of British lady travelers who praised the hospitality of 'savage peoples' into whose hands they entrusted their lives. Yet, the subtext of a shared religion is there in the need to be seen walking a respectful distance behind her husband.

It is at this point that I would like to engage Homi Bhabha's formulation of the colonial relationship as 'mimicry' and question its applicability to borrowed colonialism. In Babha's memorable wording: '[C]olonial mimicry is the desire for a reformed, recognizable Other, as a subject of difference that is almost the same but not quite.'[44] The concept of 'mimicry' or 'mimic man' as a threat to colonialism, '[T]he menace of mimicry' which ultimately becomes a threat because it threatens to do away with the difference,' would simply not apply in cases such as the Khalidis.[45] To continue to read Bhabha here: 'The ambivalence of mimicry—almost but not quite—suggests that the fetishized colonial culture is potentially and strategically an insurgent counter-appeal.' For the Khalidis or their other Arab Ottoman cohorts, mimicry of the Ottoman elite would not have been an issue, they were the Ottoman elite. The Khalidis would not have to 'mime' nor would they have to 'fetishize.' They, along with their Turkish, Albanian, Armenian, and Jewish fellow Young Turks or Young Ottomans, were already within the Ottoman system; Istanbul was not Gandhi's London or Ho Chin Minh's Paris—it was their city. Mimicry implies self-consciousness and inferiority, we will of course never know the psychological make up of these men, but it would appear that they were in no way consciously seeking to 'copy the Turk.' So where do we draw the line? Who was the center? In 1841 the Ottoman governor of the province of Trablus Garp became an affiliate of the Sanusiyyah dervish order, a situation which would have been considered an unthinkable case of 'going bush' in a white colonial context.[46]

So what remains of the other colonial half of borrowed colonialism? Where has the other 'half' gone? The answer lies in the limits of the pilgrimage. Only one Arab served as Grand Vizier in the nineteenth century, and he was of Circassian slave origin.[47] Prosopographies of Ottoman Grand Viziers in the Tanzimat and Hamidian periods show that '34 of the last 39 Grand Viziers of the Ottoman State were Turkish, meaning that they were Anatolian or Rumelian Muslims whose mother tongue was Turkish.' So that is where we find the 'gentlemen of the Home Counties.'[48] In the case of the Palestinian distinguished gentlemen, or even in the case of the leaders of the dervish order of the Sanusiyyah, the fact was that they were well within the Pale. They were part of the Civilizing Project as Civilizers. Those who were excluded of course were the tribal, nomadic element, until the state became desperate for manpower in the later half of the nineteenth century.

Conclusion

The question that arises is, what was the difference between the Ottoman attitude of, say, the eighteenth or even early nineteenth century toward their peoples and their attitude in the nineteenth century. In a word, what was 'Ottoman Colonialism'? I think the only succinct answer would be the new attitude of increased distance from the population. Here I speak of a moral distance whereby the fact that the population in question is Muslim is not of the first degree of importance. On the one hand, a moral appeal is made for Muslim solidarity against the Christian invader, yet on the other the peripheral people are seen as a resource in the material and positivist sense. The moral distance is paralleled by a will of unprecedented intensity to enforce the policies of the center.

It seems to me that the important difference between the pre-Tanzimat Ottoman state and the modern Ottoman state may well lie in the disappearance of the 'polite fictions.' In the pre-Tanzimat period, the official in any given locality, the Vali or the kaymakam, may very well not have needed to enforce the center's will. Both he and the local power holder (sheikh, agha notable, etc.) would go through the motions of a polite fiction. The Ottoman official would not unduly interfere with the inner workings of the local power holder's dominion. Polite forms would be observed, gifts exchanged, bribes given and taken, and, in return, the local power holder would acknowledge the suzerainty of the sultan. However, when the empire was being squeezed to an unprecedented extent, indeed was fighting for its life, there was no longer any space for the polite fictions. In the words of a Western contemporary observer:

> In the spasmodic attempts made by individual Sultans to reorganize the Empire, the nomads presented themselves as a difficulty that must be eliminated before organization could be achieved. It was part of the policy of Abd ul Hamid [sic] carrying out more effectively the tendencies which were inevitably produced by the centralizing tendencies began by Mahmud II about 1815, to bring about the uniformity of the Muslim population.[49]

Lamartine's 'Oriental Despotism' that Makdisi rightly exposes as a chimera, and the 'always reconfigured anomaly that was everyday Ottoman politics' that he points to as the reality on the ground, the 'perfectly routine and reciprocal, if hierarchical, intercourse between urban Ottoman governors on the one hand, and rural Druze chieftains and Maronite emirs on the other,' in other words my polite fiction, is replaced by a much more immediate presence that draws on European colonial experience.[50]

But in the final instance, borrowed colonialism was fated to remain an art of the possible. The center's weakness meant that it was dependent on the goodwill and co-operation of the Sanusi sheikh, the local notable, and the Bedouin. It was here that Islam came into play. Even the Parisian intellectual Osman Hamdi, deeply concerned about increasing British encroachment, declared that Ottoman ships should patrol the Persian Gulf and show the flag, 'To show that Turkey still lives, to show the Turkish and Muslim flag to all peoples.'[51] As was seen above, the census-takers in Tripoli were ordered 'not to frighten' the people, and the first preference in such situations was always the application of 'lenient and moderate measures' ('vesait-i leyyine ve mutedile').[52] These were cheaper and less destabilizing than the military option, which might not be available in any case. Standard practice usually followed a set pattern. First, an 'advisory commission' ('heyet-i nasiha or heyet-i tefhimiye') would be sent, usually including local notables or respected religious leaders. In the case of the Saharan Bedouin, it was hoped this role would be fulfilled by the Senusi sheikhs. In the case of the Hicaz and Yemen, Osman Nuri Pas'a made it clear that nothing could be accomplished without the co-operation of the tribal chiefs. The commission would, 'cajole the local leaders' with decorations and declarations that the Sultan was their 'affectionate father' ('peder-i müsfik'). Sometimes they would be invited to come to Istanbul as the Sultan's 'guests,' where they could on occasion be 'guests for life' under house-arrest.[53] Out-and-out bribes and presentation copies of the Qur'an usually, 'written in large (meaning easy to read) characters' were also used. If all else failed, then and only then was a 'punitive expedition' ('kuvve-i tedibiye') or a 'reformatory force' ('firkai ýslýahiye') sent to inflict what was hoped would be exemplary punishment. But a pardon was always on offer if the people mended their ways.[54] The Ottoman officials on station were in fact quite conscious of their 'new colonialism.' On one particular occasion in 1869, the Vali of Damascus, Mehmed Rasid Pasa, actually invited the French and British Consuls to accompany him on a pacification campaign against the Bedouin in the central Jordan valley.[55] When the Bedouin in the Karak region of the Jordan rose in rebellion against the Ottomans in 1911, they targeted specifically those elements that they saw as representing Ottoman rule: the census offices, the school, barracks, even the mosque built under Ottoman auspices.[56]

Another aspect of the relationship between the Ottoman center and the subject peoples that differed considerably from the British or French experience was the far greater negotiating power that the subject population had. What Beshara Doumani has pointed out in the case of Ottoman Nablus up to the mid-century holds largely true for the Ottoman center's relationship with other spheres: 'In their discourse, both forces seized on the long history of flexible and permeable boundaries between center and periphery as well as on the exigencies of rapidly changing political economic realities in order to expand their respective space for maneuvering and, in the process, to re-invent their mutual relationship.'[57] Yet, as his study shows, by 1860 the rules of the game had been radically altered as the Ottoman government ended the centuries-long autonomy of Jabal Nablus and, 'finally achieved a monopoly of the means of coercion and was able to impose direct political control.'[58] The Hamidian regime very closely resembled what Christopher Bayly has described as 'Curzonism,' with its emphasis on 'unity' and 'efficiency.' Abdul Hamid's Ottoman Empire, like Curzon's United Kingdom and India, used as its instruments 'public health, public works, and the taxonomizing imperatives of police anthropology.'[59]

As the century wound to its close, and particularly after the Young Turks seized absolute power after the rigged election of 1912, the Committee of Union and Progress alternated the policies of strong centrist rule with continued appeals to Islamic solidarity:

> The fact that they were of the same religion as the Arabs was not significant to the Young Turks. They saw themselves as bringing civilization to the tribal society of the Arabs and protecting it against Western Imperialism.[60]

As the debate between the 'Arabists' and the 'Turkists' in the Committee of Union and Progress heated up, some of the Arabists accused the CUP of:

> having been intent on concentrating the power of the state in Turkish hands and treating the non-Turkish elements in the Ottoman Empire just like colonial France treated the Algerians.[61]

After the Italian navy bombarded Arab provinces with impunity during the Italian-Ottoman War of 1912, and news reached Syria that Libya had fallen to the Italians, some Arab Ottomans began to think that the Ottoman state could no longer protect them against 'real' colonialism. Rafiq al-Azm, a prominent Syrian and president of the Ottoman Administrative Decentralization Party, wrote:

> Syria is Ottoman as long as the Ottoman state is capable of defending it. If, God Forbid, the Ottoman State collapses, . . . then Syria is an Arab country indivisible from Arab territory. Syria is Ottoman first, Arab second, and rejects any foreign interference. The Syrian nation holds fast to its Ottomanism and . . . does not wish for the policy of colonization to put an end to its national life.[62]

Therefore, in a paradoxical way, the Italian defeat was used as propaganda material by the Young Turks and served to push their appeal for unity and solidarity in the face of the colonialist threat.[63]

Situating the nineteenth-century Ottoman Empire in the postcolonial debate ultimately ends up showing us more clearly what we knew all along: the Ottoman state was never a colony. In order to avoid becoming a colony, and to stake a legitimate claim to existence in an increasingly hostile world, the Ottomans decided that they had to become like the enemy, to borrow his tools, so to speak. This brings me full circle to my query at the beginning, to paraphrase: at what point does the common religion cease to be a sufficiently differentiating condition in the relationship of the Ottomans to the 'native' population? I submit that it is at the point that the stance of moral superiority leads to a position of moral distance, this perceived sense of 'them' and 'us.' The paradox lies in the fact that this distance is establishing itself in the minds of the center at the very time that their dependence on their fellow Muslim subjects is increasing. Also, in the absence of real coercive power at the disposal of the center, the bargaining position of the tribal warrior is much stronger than the bargaining position of say, a jute worker in India, or a rubber gatherer in the Congo. When the Ottoman official approaches the Touareg, he still assumes as a given that the man is a 'savage' (noble or not), but he must make an argument, which is: 'the Christians are closing in on you.' Thus it could be said that as an empire, and a great power, and the only Muslim great power at that, the Ottomans rejected the subaltern role that the West seemed intent on making them adopt, but they could only do this by inviting (to put it euphemistically) 'their own' subalterns into history.

Seen from the position of the subaltern, on the other hand, the Ottomans and the British as imperial powers may well have looked rather similar. Karl Blind, in 1896, was to severely criticize Gladstone's comment that the 'Turks were the one great anti-human species of humanity' with the remark:

> How if he had been reminded by a member of the anti-human race that there are some Irish Home Rulers and Secessionists who in United Ireland, speak of England, on account of her rule of the Sister Isle and her many polyglot dominions as the 'Anglo-Saxon Grand Turk.'[64]

No doubt Abdulhamid would have considered this a compliment although the Irish could hardly have meant it as such.

Notes

1   My definition of colonialism here closely follows the Leninist position as in 'Imperialism the Highest Stage of Capitalism.' In my view, this is still one of the best and most succinct definitions of imperialism. After showing how the partition of the word accelerated in the 1880s, Lenin concludes, 'It is beyond doubt therefore, that capitalism's transition to the stage of monopoly capitalism, to finance capital, is connected with the intensification of the struggle for the partitioning of the world.' V. Lenin, *Selected Works* (Moscow: Progress Publishers 1977) 224.

2   See Edhem Eldem, 'Istanbul from Imperial to Peripheralized Capital,' in *The Ottoman City between the East and West*, Edhem Eldem, Daniel Goffman, and Bruce Masters (eds) (Cambridge, 1999) 200.

3   Mehmed Izzed, Interpreter for the Imperial Palace ('Saray-i Hümayun tercümanlarindan') *Yeni Afrika* (Der Saadet 1308/1890, 2).

4   ibid., 50.

5   Albert Hourani, 'How Should We Write the History of the Middle East,' *International Journal of Middle Eastern Studies*, 1991, 23, 125–36.

6   I am adapting this term from Dietrich Geyer's 'borrowed imperialism,' which he uses for late imperial Russia. See Dietrich Geyer, *Russian Imperialism. The Interaction of Domestic and Foreign Policy 1860–1914* (Leamington Spa, Hamburg, New York, 1987) 124.

7   Selim Deringil, *The Well Protected Domains. Ideology and the Legitimation of Power in the Ottoman Empire 1876–1909* (London and Oxford, 1998).

8   Dietrich Geyer, *Russian Imperialism*, esp. 125–49.

9   It is significant that Lenin also saw the Ottoman plight: 'I think it is useful, in order to present a complete picture of the division of the world, to add brief data on non-colonial and semi-colonial countries, in which category I place Persia, China and Turkey: the first of these countries is already almost completely a colony, the second and the third are becoming such.' V. Lenin, 'Imperialism, the Highest Stage of Capitalism,' 225.

10 The Russian Finance Minister, Sergei Ulevich Witte, was to specifically define Russia's position in the following words: 'Russia's economic relations with western Europe are still very similar to the relationship between colonies and their mother countries . . . To a certain extent Russia is still one of these hospitable colonies for all the industrially developed states . . . However there is one essential difference in comparison with the situation in the colonies: Russia is a powerful politically independent state. Russia itself wants to be a mother country ('metropoliya') . . .' See Dietrich Geyer, *Russian Imperialism*, 145–6.

11 Moustafa Bayoumi and Andrew Rubin, *The Edward Said Reader* (New York, 2000) 224–5. The quotations are from Edward Said's essay *Secular Criticism*. I would like to thank Charles Sabatos for drawing my attention to this paradox. Sabatos is about to publish an article on this topic in the journal *New Perspectives on Turkey*.

12 Homi K. Bhabha, 'Of Mimicry and Man. The Ambivalence of Colonial Discourse,' in *The Location of Culture* (New York, 1994) 85–92.

13 Benedict Anderson, *Imagined Communities* (London, 1991); Timothy Mitchell, *Colonizing Egypt* (Cambridge, 1991). I owe thanks to an anonymous CSSH reader for inviting me to emphasize this point.

14 Gyan Prakash, 'Subaltern Studies as Postcolonial Criticism,' *The American Historical Review*, 1994, 99, 1475–90.

15 Ibid, 1486. Even in studies that set out to be self-consciously 'comparative,' the Ottoman empire gets short shrift. See, for example, Michael Adas, 'Imperialism and Colonialism in a Comparative Perspective,' *The International History Review*, 1998, 20, 253–388. Although the author mentions the 'Ottomans' twice in the article, no sources are cited.

16 Dipesh Chakrabarty, 'Postcoloniality and the Artifice of History: Who Speaks for "Indian" Pasts?' *Representations*, 1992, 37, 1–26.

17   Witness the fact that there is no mention of the politics of pan-Islamism in *Subaltern Studies* vols. 1–10 (1982–1999). In all fairness, it must be admitted that Turkish historiography has also largely ignored India. After the legendary financial aid to the Kemalist movement during the 1919–1922 War of Liberation, which Indian Muslims sent to Turkish nationalists as a gesture of solidarity, and the interest of the Indian Muslims in the Caliphate (which in fact led to its demise), India (and even more surprisingly Pakistan) seem to drop off the map. On Indian Muslims and the nationalist cause see Bernard Lewis, *The Emergence of Modern Turkey* (Oxford, 1965) 241–3, 263.

18   Satish Saberwal, 'On the Making of Europe: Reflections from Delhi,' *History Workshop Journal*, 1992, 145–51.

19   Chakrabarty, op. cit., 20; Prakash, op. cit., 1489.

20   Ussama Makdisi, 'Corrupting the Sublime Sultanate: The Revolt of Tanyus Shahin in Nineteenth-Century Ottoman Lebanon,' *Comparative Studies in Society and History*, 2000, 42, 180–208.

21   A. Hopkins, 'Back to the Future: From National History to Imperial History,' *Past and Present*, 1999, 198–243.

22   Although I take note of the comment of an anonymous reviewer of the manuscript who correctly points out that 'a project of modernity is not necessarily a civilizing mission,' in the case of the late Ottoman provincial administration in the Arab provinces, the two were virtually synonymous.

23   Ussama Makdisi, *The Culture of Sectarianism. Community, History and Violence in Nineteenth-Century Ottoman Lebanon* (Berkeley, Los Angeles, and London, 2000) 7. Makdisi is referring here to Gyanendra Pandey's *The Construction of Communalism in Colonial North India* (Delhi, 1992).

24   ibid.

25   See, for example, Ariel Salzmann, 'An Ancien Regime Revisited: Privatization and Political Economy in the Eighteenth-Century Ottoman Empire,' *Politics and Society*, 1993, 21, 393–423. Salzmann's major contribution was to show that many of the trends that had been depicted as negative 'decentralizing' tendencies, such as the growth of locally powerful tax farmers, were in fact dynamic trends making for capital formation and the integration of a state elite into a new structure which was emerging. In this context see also Muge Göçek, *Rise of the Bourgeoisie, Demise of Empire: Ottoman Westernization and Social Changes* (New York, 1996). Also on the topic of Islamic origins of many of the modernizing trends see Butrus Abu Manneh, 'The Islamic Origins of the Gülhane Rescript,' *Die Welt Des Islams*, 1994, 34, 173–203.

26   Ibn Khaldun's cyclical conception of state power, whereby settled states matured, grew senile, and were destined to be overwhelmed by more virile nomadic peoples, informed much of the basic formation of Ottoman statesmen. Yet, there is also a side to Ibn Khaldun which admires the nomad. I have used the Turkish translation of the Mukaddimah; see Ibn Haldun, *Mukaddime* (Istanbul, 1979) 103, 331, 364.

27   Serif Mardin, 'Centre-Periphery Relations. A Key to Turkish Politics?' *Daedalus*, 1973, 102, 170–1. This attitude is very similar also to that of Russian travelers in the 'Orient' in the nineteenth century. For these men, keen to prove that Russians were much more 'European' than Turks or Arabs, '"[W]ild" meant the antithesis of European culture; where Europe penetrated "wildness" retreated.' See, Peter R. Weisensel, 'Russian Self-Identification and Travelers' Descriptions of the Ottoman Empire in the First Half of the Nineteenth Century,' *Central Asian Survey*, 1991, 10, 65–85. Weisensel calls this, 'The deep-seated Russian bias of agriculturalists against pastoralists.'

28   I have kept a database drawn on hundreds of documents dealing with nomadic populations. See my *The Well Protected Domains. Ideology and the Legitimation of Power in the Ottoman Empire 1876–1909* (London and Oxford, 1998), 'The Symbolism of Language in the Hamidian Era,' 39–42.

29   ibid. *The Redhouse Turkish—English Lexicon* (Beirut 1895) defines 'tevahhus' as: 'being or becoming timid like a wild beast.'

30   Ranajit Guha, 'The Prose of Counter Insurgency,' in *Selected Subaltern Studies* (Oxford, 1988) 46, 48, 49.

31   ibid. It was considered impolite to actually pronounce the word 'money.'

32   Peter Hardy, *The Muslims of British India* (Cambridge, 1972) 20.

33   Francis W. Rowsell, 'The English in Egypt', Cairo, 14 May 1883. *The Nineteenth Century*. 1883, 34, 1068.

34   Ussama Makdisi, 'Corrupting the Sublime Sultanate: The Revolt of Tanyus Shahin in Nineteenth-Century Ottoman Lebanon,' *Comparative Studies in Society and History*, 2000, 42, 180–210.

35   Jürgen Habermas, 'The Theory of Communicative Action,' Vol. 2: *Lifeworld and System* (Boston, 1989) 124.

36   ibid., 123.

37   Ressam Naciye Neyyal in *Mutlakiyet, Mesrutiyet ve Cumhuriyet Hatýralarý* (The memoirs of painter Naciye Neyyal regarding the Hamidian Young Turk and Republican Periods), prepared for publication by Fatma Rezan Hürmen (Istanbul, 2000). This memoir is based on diaries that Naciye Haným kept throughout her life. The book is some 600 pages in length and is virtually a day-by-day account of these years. The writer went on to become a prominent painter in the early republic. The volume was prepared for publication by her granddaughter.

38   ibid., 83.

39   ibid., 77–9.

40   ibid., 50.

41   ibid., 49.

42   ibid., 61.

43   ibid., 88–9. Present-day Beersheva in Israel.

44   Homi Bhabha, 'Of Mimicry and Man. The Ambivalence of Colonial Discourse,' in *The Location of Culture* (London and New York, 1994), 85–92. Emphasis in original.

45   ibid., 88–9.

46   Lisa Anderson, *The State and Social Transformation in Tunisia and Libya*, 73.

47   He was Tunuslu Hayreddin Pasa (Hayreddin Pasa the Tunisian) who served briefly as Grand Vizier under Abdulhamid II. On him, see *Ibnulemin Mahmud Kemal Inal, Osmanli Devrinde Son Sadrazamlar* (The last Grand Viziers of the Ottoman Empire) (Istanbul, 1984).

48   Sevan Nisanyan, 'Son Sadrazamlar. Kimdiler, Nereden Gelip Nereye Gittiler?' (The last Grand Veziers. Who were they? Where did they come from? Where did they go?) *Toplumsal Tarih*, 1997, 7, 36–46. See also Ibnulemin Mahmud Kemal Inal, *Son Sadrazamlar*. For the 'Home Counties' imagery, see Hopkins, 'Back to the Future,' 204–5: 'But the British Empire . . . was still run from London and managed by English gentlemen whose natural habitat was found in the Home Counties.' The natural habitat of the Ottoman Grand Viziers would have been their yalýs on the shores of the Bosphorous.

49   William Mitchell Ramsay, 'The intermixture of races in Asia Minor. Some of its causes and effects,' *Proceedings of the British Academy*, 1916, 7, 31.

50   Makdisi, 'Corrupting the Sublime Sultanate,' 190.

51   Eldem, 'Quelques lettres d'Osman Hamdi Bey,' 127. It is interesting that Osman Hamdi should have equated Muslim and Turkish in this way. Eldem's view is that he was not a particularly pious person.

52   For a detailed discussion of this, see my *The Well Protected Domains*, 68–92.

53   The Wahabi leader Ibn Su'ud was captured and sent to Istanbul in 1818, 'where many learned orthodox ulema tried to reason with him in his prison and to win him back to Islamic orthodoxy.' See, Howard Reed, 'The Destruction of the Janissaries by Mahmud II,' (PhD dissertation, Princeton University 1951), 34.

54   The punitive expeditions could sometimes be commanded by the highest ranking officials in the land. Ahmet Cevdet Pasa himself commanded such a force sent to quell rebellion

among the Kurds in Cilicia in 1864. See Cristoph Neuman, *Araç Tarih. Amaç Tanzimat* (Istanbul, 2000) 34. Similarly, no lesser a personage than Fuad Pasa, the Grand Vizier, was sent to restore order in Damascus after the 1860 riots. See, Leila Fawaz, *An Occasion for War* (London, 1994).

55 Eugene Rogan, *Frontiers of the State*, 51. The Pasa's aim was presumably to show off his efficiency. In this he was successful since the Bedouin submitted, and the French Consul duly reported back to his superiors.

56 ibid., 197–201.

57 Beshara Doumani, *Rediscovering Palestine. Merchants and Peasants in Jabal Nablus 1700–1900* (Berkeley, Los Angeles, and London, 1995), 217.

58 ibid., 234.

59 Christopher Bayly, 'Returning the British to South Asian History,' *South Asia*, 1994, 22, 1–25.

60 Sükrü Hanioglu, 'The Young Turks and the Arabs before the Revolution of 1908,' in *The Origins of Arab Nationalism*, Rashid Khalidi, Lisa Anderson, Reeva Simon and M. Muslih (eds) (New York, 1984) 31.

61 Mahmoud Haddad, 'The Rise of Arab Nationalism Reconsidered,' *International Journal of Middle Eastern Studies*, 1994, 26, 201–22.

62 ibid. Haddad is quoting an editorial by Rafiq Al Azm published in the *Al Muayyad* newspaper on 24 December 1912.

63 Hasan Kayali, *Arabs and Young Turks: Ottomanism, Arabism, and Islamism in the Ottoman Empire 1908–1918* (Berkeley, Los Angeles, and London, 1997) 129–43. Kayali's work shows that the relationship between the Young Turks and the Arab reform movement was much more nuanced than has hitherto to been believed.

64 Karl Blind, 'Young Turkey,' *Fortnightly Review* 66 (London, 1896) 840.

Chapter 28

Laurent Dubois

LA RÉPUBLIQUE MÉTISSÉE: CITIZENSHIP, COLONIALISM, AND THE BORDERS OF FRENCH HISTORY

> Many historians of Britain and its empire, as we've seen, are not only exploring but calling into question the boundaries between the 'imperial' and the 'domestic'. Such issues are now little less debated, and little if any less controversial in contemporary political terms, for France – and Laurent Dubois is among the most inventive of the writers involved. In rough parallel to Paul Gilroy's or Bill Schwarz's thinking about the relationship among imperial legacies, postcolonial migrations and national identities in Britain, Dubois offers stimulating ideas on how France too has been and is being shaped by its 'outside'.
>
> Stephen Howe

IN THE OPENING SCENE of Wim Wenders' 1994 film *Lisbonne Story*, Winter, the main character, travels from Germany to Portugal across a Europe 'without borders'. As he passes out of Germany the camera pans to the empty customs post as Winter begs 'Stop me! You can't imagine how much I'm smuggling!' He drives across the highways of Europe through night and day, sun and rain, to a soundtrack of radio chatter in different languages, of music from around the world – French rap, American pop – mixed with the eternal news of political scandal. Winter's car overheats just as he enters Portugal; but the border post is abandoned, so there is no one to help him. The phone doesn't even work. He is saved by a tour bus of Americans, who give him Coca-Cola to pour into his engine. In Lisbon, at the edge of an open Europe, he encounters the edge of representation; his filmmaker friend has abandoned all hope of producing unspoiled images, and spends his days making films that are to be preserved from the polluting and transforming gaze of the viewer. Winter ultimately coaxes his friend back from the edge, convincing him that it is still possible, at the end of the twentieth century, to make 'moving pictures'.

This evocation of 'Europe without borders' reverberates with the central political issues facing France and the rest of Europe today. The process of creating a European community – underfoot since the late 1980s, and intensified since 1992 – raises fundamental issues about the nature of the nations that will be part of this community. If the identity of European nations such as France was in many ways consolidated not only from the centre out but also from the periphery in, what happens when the border posts are abandoned, trade restrictions are lifted, and the border zones that were instrumental to the formation of nationality themselves vanish? Clearly the borders are far from gone, and national identity as an exclusionary concept is seemingly on the rise rather than the other way around. The opening of the territorial borders suggests not the elimination of borders and exclusions but their reconfiguration. Geographical border zones are less and less sites of the intensive policing of the territory that they once were; but the movement of people is nonetheless continually policed based on the 'probable cause' of the appearance of foreignness. As the more solid territorial border posts and checkpoints are abandoned, a thousand shifting borders are set up within the national territory of France.

One of the most heavily policed areas in Paris today is the RER train, which connects Paris' banlieue to the centre of the city. After a series of bombings, most notably an autumn 1997 attack on a RER train at the Port Royal Station, the French government instituted 'Operation Vigipirate', mobilizing troops to police the city, particularly the RER. The soldiers conduct extensive identity checks against those who 'look' foreign, concentrated in sites of transit which those who live in the banlieue must pass through each day on their way to work. The policing of the RER is a structural reassertion of the economic exclusion of those who live in the banlieue. Unlike in US cities, the poorer areas of Paris are largely concentrated on the peripheries of the city. In these communities, often an hour's train ride away from the centre of town, projects called HLMs (for Habitations à Loyers Modérés) were built starting in the late 1940s to provide housing for those left homeless after the Second World War. By the 1970s, these housing projects were increasingly populated by working-class immigrants. In recent years, the malaise of the banlieue has become a central subject of debate in French public life, as the youth of these neighbourhoods, many of whom are children of immigrants, have become an 'issue' through which problems of economic exclusion, cultural difference and national identity are discussed. The economic and social exclusion of these communities confronts French society with the limits of ideals of integration that have been traditionally the cement of Republican social policy. For many wealthier Parisians, the poorer banlieue is basically another world: the writer and editor François Maspero wrote a travel narrative, *Roissy Express*, about a two-week trip into the northern Paris suburbs, and their history, and presented it as an anthropological journey into a foreign land (Maspero 1994).

The young director Mathieu Kassovitz turned an ethnographic eye towards the texture of life in the banlieue in his 1995 film *La Haine*, the best known of a series of films about the suburbs that have been released in France in recent years. The film skilfully captures the social distance between the banlieue and the centre of Paris by telling the story of a day in the lives of a 'tricolour' group of underclass youths from the banlieue – an Arab North African named Said, a black West African named Hubert, and a white Jew named Vinz. As the film opens, Bob Marley's bass-heavy anthem 'Burnin' and Lootin'' mixes with footage of recent French riots, many of which have pitted police against youth in the banlieue. The film reverses the journey from Paris represented by Maspero's work, and places the viewer in the shoes of the youth of the banlieue as they make their way through a neighbourhood and a society policed against them. Its characters speak in the patois emerging from these communities – a French with its own accent, expanded with Arabic vocabulary and hip-hop terminology – and many French audiences had difficulty understanding the language, not to mention the sense of rage expressed in the film. The film sought to capture the culture of the banlieue, one in which US film and music – particularly rap – informs the banlieue's encounter with police brutality and economic exclusion. In one particularly skilful scene in the film, a young DJ sets up his speakers in the windows on top of one of the project's towers, mixing Edith Piaf's 'Je ne Regrette Rien' with a rap of 'Nique la Police', a French take-off of N.W.A.'s song 'Fuck the Police'.

The communities that live in the banlieue come from a variety of backgrounds – they are first- and second-generation immigrants from West Africa, the Maghreb, the Caribbean, they are whites of French ancestry returned from Algeria, they are Italian or Portuguese, they are Français de souche (the 'real' French). Their presence in France is the result of a long process of inter-European migration as well as the more recent waves of movement from former French colonies during the latter half of the twentieth century (Noiriel 1988). These populations do not live in communities according to their ethnicity: the group of friends in *La Haine* is aggressively multi-ethnic. Despite the multi-ethnic character of the banlieue communities, the process of their exclusion operates in ways that echo the racialization of policing and economic exclusion in the US. Yet the French engagement with issues of poverty, class and cultural identity differs in important ways from that of US society. This was made startlingly clear during the year before *La Haine* came out, when state officials passed a ban on the wearing of veils in public schools. Many in France, including those on the Left, supported the decision as a defence of the secularist tradition of Republicanism, in which education has been seen as a central institution in the production of the social equality central to citizenship. The decision, however, was also the expression of another, less acknowledged part of the Republican tradition – the colonial history through which universalism has been merged with the particularistic exclusion of 'others'. Though the administrative heritage of this colonial history is rarely recognized, understanding the conflicts over immigration and citizenship in France at the end of the twentieth century necessitates a journey into this often overlooked aspect of the genealogy of France's Republican political culture.

In this article, I draw on my research on the interwoven histories of France and the Caribbean to explore two moments of conflict over the meaning of national citizenship in the French Republic – the conflicts over the slavery that shook the French colonies at the end of the eighteenth century, and the contemporary struggles of undocumented immigrants in France calling themselves the sans-papiers. I do this not to correlate the two situations – clearly the experiences of eighteenth-century slaves and contemporary immigrants are vastly different – but rather to highlight continuities both in the forms of exclusion that have operated in French political culture and in the ways groups have struggled against these forms of exclusion. I also hope to suggest, through the specific stories I tell, some of the ways in which a better understanding of French colonial history is a vital foundation for an engagement with contemporary debates about race, immigration and national identity in France.

In *Vers un Multiculturalisme Français* (1996) the French anthropologist Jean-Loup Amselle argues that any project of imagining a 'multicultural' France must start with an understanding of the history of colonialism as one of the foundations for French national identity. The cover of his book is a scene from a public artistic event that sought to commemorate and create a vision of a united but culturally plural France – the 1989 Opéra Marseillaise that was the climax of the commemorations of the bicentennial of the French Revolution. This Opera was the work of the advertising impresario, Jean-Paul Goude, who in response to his mission of celebrating the heritage of the Revolution and of the universalist ideals of the 'rights of man', chose what he considered to be the modern-day, communication era equivalent to these ideals, the 'afro-occidental rhythm':

> I went to Bombay, to Brazil, to Moscow, to Hong-Kong. I realized that the youth had adopted the afro-occidental rhythm. English hip-hop, Chinese piliwu, American breakdance: all of it is the same thing. The 14th of July will be the consecration of this universal rhythm.
>
> Leruth 1995: 222

The celebration of this rhythm was, for Goude, the most appropriate tribute to the radical possibilities of the Revolution: 'To have groups of French traditional musicians play a symphony written by a composer of African origin who synthesizes Western and African rhythms, now that's revolutionary.' 'For me', he noted elsewhere, 'the true Revolution is the birth of a world sound' (Kaplan 1995: 286–9).

Given the political debates surrounding the problem of immigration and the question of cultural identity in France, the parade was a controversial hymn to 'métissage', figured both in the international mix of the dancers in the parade and in its percussive musical foundation arranged by the African musicians. One of the 'tableaux' (as the sections of the parade were named) was called the 'Tribes of France'. It was meant to evoke the Festival of the Federation of 14 July 1790, during which representatives from the entire nation gathered in the first national celebration of the new Republic. The 1989 version grouped together traditional musicians from throughout France in a percussive mix arranged by the Franco-Beninois composer Wally Badarou. The 'tableau' that followed was entitled 'the Arabs of Paris', and was composed of fifteen 'Maghrebian' waltzers in huge black gowns, each straddled by a small child representing the different peoples of the world. The African-American singer Jessie Norman, wrapped in the colours of the French flag, sang the Marseillaise; and the act that closed out the parade was the Texas A & M University marching band, which moonwalked backwards down the Champs-Elysée.

African culture was particularly showcased in ways that accentuated the complex past of colonialism and the French relationship to the image of 'Africanness', whose exoticization was both critiqued and re-inscribed in Goude's parade. In one tableau a giant staircase was topped by the Senegalese musician Doudou N'Diaye Rose, who was dressed in a white tuxedo and led an orchestra of percussionists. The float – presented in the official programme as 'an homage to Senegalese independence' – was surrounded by nearly three hundred torch-bearing men in 'colonial explorer uniforms', and topped by six Senegalese women in long blue, white and red gowns – the clearest and most striking representation of the French tricolour in the parade. The other African float, meant to represent all African countries (except South Africa), included a human pyramid of percussionists, including topless female drummers, accompanied by three hundred and sixty men (recruited among African workers in Paris) dressed as tirailleurs sénégalais – the colonial troops who fought both in the European World Wars and in the repression of colonial rebellions (Leruth 1995: 7–15; Kaplan 1995: 305–7).

Goude's parade provides a window into the complexities of French Republican mythology. It was presented by some as a cosmopolitan and internationalist gesture – as proof of France's continuing tolerance and openness. After all, how many countries would celebrate their national holiday through a parade composed largely of foreigners? Yet what kind of relationship did the parade actually posit between France – and the French Revolution – and its African excolonies? What did it mean to have a homage to Senegalese independence carried by men figured as colonial explorers? What exactly did the Senegalese women in blue, white and red stand for? Goude's artistic fascination with 'Africanness' was part of his broader artistic trajectory, which in many ways echoed the primitivism of the surrealists in the ways it celebrated the liberating possibilities of African aesthetics through a disturbingly exoticizing and sexist gaze. Goude – who was capable of claiming that his conception of blackness was 'free of all social connotations because I am European' – presented his parade as an anti-racist celebration of 'world culture' (Kaplan 1995: 288). Michael Leruth has written that it was a successful hymn to the possibilities of a plurivocal, postmodern 'pagan Republicanism' that is developing in French hip-hop and in the activism of the youth of the banlieue, for whom 'multiculturalism and tribalism are not always in contradiction with the French Republic' (Leruth 1995: 354–5). It also, however, placed the 'multiculturalism' of France's own history on display in a way that did not confront the broader structural contradictions of a system that has long celebrated its universalism and tolerance while maintaining structures of racial and economic exclusion.

In constituting his battalions of tirailleurs sénégalais, the organizers of the parade encountered the contradictions of their own mythology. Recruiting in Senegal itself was too expensive, and so the organizers turned to the workers' dormitories of Paris to find men who could perform in the parade. But the potential performers were worried. Sylla Samba, a representative for a group of Malians from one of these dormitories, asked for an official letter that would allow them to absent themselves from their work without losing their jobs. Others worried that the recruitment was in fact a ploy to get them out of the dormitories and on to one of the Mali-bound charter planes which the French government had been sending during the previous years (Kaplan 1995: 194). Africans were needed for the heart of France's bicentennial, and yet their very hesitation spoke profoundly of their exclusion from the universal rights which their presence was supposed to evoke. Any representation of Africa that takes place within France is fundamentally hemmed in by the broader structures of power that echo certain voices and silence others. Goude's parade in many ways courageously gestured towards a broader movement afoot within a variety of communities in France to redefine the meaning of citizenship and of rights. Yet it is not only in the birth of a 'world sound' that Africa and the Caribbean should be understood as present in France today, but in the very structures of the Republic itself.

The importance of métissage in the political history of the French Republic is highlighted by an examination of the French Revolution, which is commonly understood as the foundational moment not only of the modern French state but more broadly of modern-day practices of citizenship. In his now canonical work, Rogers Brubaker has argued that '[m]odern national citizenship was an invention of the French Revolution, which brought together a series of developments – including 'the establishment of civil equality', 'the institutionalization of political rights', and the creation of a 'link between citizenship and nationhood' – 'together for the first time' (Brubaker 1992: 35). These 'developments' in the culture of citizenship were of course the product of a complex series of struggles within metropolitan France. Yet they were also, as has less often been noted, crucially affected by developments outside of Europe, notably in the Caribbean colonies, which were seen by both England and France as of vital importance to the future. In particular, the ultimate content granted to the abstract ideas of 'universal rights' depended on the actions of the slaves turned citizens of the French Caribbean, who during the 1790s transformed the order of colonial society.

In 1789, at the beginning of the French Revolution, the Caribbean islands of Guadeloupe, Martinique and St. Domingue represented the world's most valuable colonial possessions. There, an order based on the enslavement of 90 per cent of the population produced sugar and other commodities for metropolitan consumption, powering the economic transformations of eighteenth-century France and the emergence of a new merchant bourgeoisie. Between 1789 and 1794, the social order of the most prosperous colonial possessions of the Americas was completely reversed. The rapidity and scope of the changes witnessed in the French Antilles during this period bewildered, frightened and fascinated observers. As Michel Rolph Trouillot has argued, the Haitian Revolution was at that time, and in many ways has remained since, an 'unthinkable history'. 'The events that shook up Saint Domingue from 1791 to 1804 constituted a sequence for which not even the extreme political left in France or in England had a conceptual frame of reference. They were 'unthinkable' facts in the framework of Western thought' (Trouillot 1995: 82). In the face of the 1791 insurrection, contemporaries constantly sought the roots of revolution outside the slave insurgents themselves, in the propaganda of abolitionists, the conspiracies of royalists, or the imperial designs of Spain or England. Even those who advocated slave emancipation were unprepared for the radical implications of the slave revolt of 1791, and tended to argue that political rights could only gradually be granted to ex-slaves. Indeed, by the time the massive revolt occurred in St. Domingue, little progress had been made, even on the issue of whether to grant gens de couleur – free people of African descent – political rights. Despite the activism of the famous Société des Amis des Noirs, no action had been taken at all in the direction of eliminating slavery.

Ultimately, emancipation was decreed locally in St. Domingue in 1793, and this decision was ratifed by the National Convention in Paris in 1794, so that slavery was abolished through the French empire in the first national experiment in slave emancipation. If this occurred, however, it was both because of the military and economic pressure placed on the French colonies by slave insurrection, and on the basis of political alliance put forward by slave insurgents themselves. In the early 1790s, slave insurgents were often inspired by rumours that metropolitan officials had abolished slavery and that local officials were blocking the application of the new law. Such prophetic rumours put forward the idea that an alliance between slave insurgents and metropolitan officials could offset the power of white planters. By 1792 and 1793, many white planters increasingly turned away from the Republic, and even made overtures to the English, promising to hand over the colonies to them. Besieged Republican officials found allies in the gens de couleur and eventually in slave insurgents themselves. In 1793, when hundreds of slaves rose up in Trois-Rivières, Guadeloupe, and killed twenty-three whites, they presented their actions to the officials of the island as an attack against the royalist conspiracies of their masters. 'We have come to save you', they told the whites, 'we want to fight for the republic, the law, the nation order'. Instead of punishing them, many whites called for the formation of a slave army to defend the island from English attack. The intervention of insurgents like these into the conflict over the meaning of Republican citizenship ultimately became official policy first in St. Domingue and then throughout the Antilles. The French Republic abolished slavery and mobilized armies of ex-slaves, and the call for slave liberation, as potent weapons in its global conflict with Britain.

In my work (Dubois 1998a,b) I have explored these events in order to argue that slave insurgents claiming Republican citizenship and racial equality during the early 1790s ultimately expanded – and 'universalized' – the idea of rights. The developments in the Antilles, I suggest, actually outran the political imagination of the metropole, transforming the possibilities embodied in the idea of citizenship. Though the intervention of European thinkers who had critiqued colonialism and slavery during the eighteenth century was of course an important part of this transformation, it was the slaves of the Caribbean who set in motion and defined the fundamental changes of the period. Out of alliances between slave insurgents and Republican officials in the Antilles, a new colonial order emerged, one in which the principles of universalism were put into effect through regimes that applied the same constitution in the metropole and the colony. The actions of slave insurgents, therefore, brought about the institutionalization of the idea that the rights of citizens were universally applicable to all people within the nation, regardless of race. This new colonial order, which marked a powerful blow to the system of slavery, was a crucial step in the broader march towards slave emancipation throughout the Americas and Europe. It was also the foundation for later attempts at colonial reform – most fully put into practice in 1946 – which were based on the idea of assimilating the colonies more fully into a metropolitan system of law.

This imperial expansion of France during the late nineteenth and early twentieth century depended on the myth that France was the mother, and repository, of the universalist language of rights and the practices of citizenship that flowed from it. This myth rested on the convenient elision of the complex history through which events in the colonial Caribbean had actually shaped the political ideas and practices presented as the pure, exportable product of France. Scholarship in colonial studies has in recent decades shown the profound importance of colonial history in shaping the economic and cultural development of the 'West', but it has been less remarked on how profoundly important was the colonial experience – more specifically the actions of people in the colonies – in the development of the political ideas commonly understood as the product of that 'West'. By returning to the history of the Caribbean during the 1790s, and so transcending the borders of French history as it has traditionally been written, we can undermine what Fernando Coronil calls the 'Occidentalism' of 'the West's self-fashioning as the self-made embodiment of modernity' (Coronil 1997: 13–14).

The conflicts over the meaning of citizenship in the French colonies during the late eighteenth century were of course only the first volley in a longer history of colonialism which forged the contemporary structures and meanings of Republican political culture. In the 1870s, the emergence of the Third Republic in France was interlinked with the creation of the overseas institutions surrounding colonial citizenship. In the 1920s and 1930s, the emergence of what Gary Wilder (1999) has called 'colonial humanism' through the work of colonial administrators and activists from Africa and the Caribbean reshaped the meaning of Republican citizenship, culminating after the Second World War in the 1946 Departmentalization Law which installed a formal equality of rights between metropole and colony. And through the struggles over decolonization, ideologies of universal rights were used against the self-contradictory colonial regimes which had claimed to espouse and protect them.

From the eighteenth century on, the profound challenges posed to the structures of French colonialism by insurgents forced administrators to respond in complex ways. During the 1790s, and again during the important French imperial expansion under the Third Republic, principles of universal inclusion became layered with practices of racial exclusion. Indeed, as has been noted again and again, universalism itself provided a powerful justification for colonial violence and oppression. In a recent article, Alice Conklin (1998) has explored how Republican principles animated the decisions of colonial administrators in West Africa at the turn of the twentieth century, and has argued that it is important for historians to take seriously the impact of universalist discourse on the process of colonialism. A better understanding of this history, she suggests, can help us meet 'the idea of universal human rights' as we disentangle the 'blind spots' of colonialists who saw themselves as Republicans. By studying the complex ways in which Republican thought was articulated within colonial regimes throughout French colonial history in Africa, Asia and the Caribbean, we can better understand the contradictions which continue to haunt contemporary struggles surrounding immigration and citizenship in France.

How does the abstract universality of the discourse of citizenship become layered with practices of exclusion? Etienne Balibar (1991) and Uday Mehta (1990) have both interestingly explored how various foundational texts of political theory carry within them contradictions which allow for particularistic exclusions within universalist systems. Yet to fully understand the development of practices of exclusion we need to turn to the complex colonial history out of which these practices emerged. For in fact these contradictions were in many ways also the product of the process of contestation through which the colonized confronted and transformed the language of rights and forced colonial powers to reformulate their own discourses as they sought to maintain their colonial regimes. Here again, the history of the French Caribbean provides a window into the development of practices of exclusion within a project of liberation.

The idea that certain people were simply not ready for citizenship is one that was at the heart of the contradictory regimes of emancipation established in the French Caribbean in both 1794 and 1848. In 1794, however, there were few earlier examples for administrators of emancipation to draw on, and so the development of their thinking provides a unique window into how universalist principles became layered with exclusionist policies. After slavery was abolished in 1794, the new juridical order raised serious philosophical and political problems for the administrators who had to oversee the transformation: how were slaves, who had consistently been denied all legal and social rights, to become citizens ready to use and defend these rights? And how was the colonial plantation economy, deemed central to the economy of France, to be maintained despite this transformation? The question of how to create a society in which the degrading yet necessary state of the labourer co-existed with the successful functioning of a democracy was a central problem in Revolutionary political theory. It was an issue which animated the conflicts over 'active' and 'passive' citizenship during the Revolution and the continued struggles over suffrage in the next centuries.

French Republican colonial regimes, from the time of the Revolution through the twentieth century, operated on the principle that the colonized – whether ex-slaves in the Caribbean, or 'natives' in Africa and Indochina – had the potential to be assimilated as citizens of the Republic only potentially. This assimilation depended on a process of transformation that could only take place gradually through education and a transformation from tradition to modernity (Conklin 1997; Wilder 1999). So citizenship, while possible for some among the elite, was for the most part deferred, a goal which justified the violence of colonialism through its promise. This complex of inclusion and exclusion, and of the deferral of the application of universal ideas, is the very 'Republican racism' which continues to haunt the contemporary discussions around immigration in France. The colonial history out of which French Republican political culture emerged highlights the continuing contradiction within the terms of citizenship, which carries both a promise of the expansion of rights and the constant possibility of a limitation on those rights. This history therefore posits a fundamental question: to what extent can the discourse of citizenship which has emerged out of colonial history serve to craft a better future for a France in the midst of economic and cultural reconfigurations at the end of the twentieth century?

In the past two years, the sans-papiers movement has actively crafted a response to this question. The sans-papiers movement began with the occupation of the St. Bernard Church in Paris in 1996, when a group of residents of France who were the victims of increasingly restrictive immigration laws publicly announced their status as sans-papiers and their intention to challenge the laws that had excluded them from documentation and the rights that flowed from it.

The movement has challenged the categories through which immigrants are named and therefore are marginalized within the French Republic. By organizing themselves the sans-papiers helped transform the broader discourse surrounding illegal immigrants in France. The sans-papiers movement was in fact a loose collective of an extremely varied and diverse set of organizations which gathered together African, Caribbean, Chinese and Eastern European immigrants, organized in some cases according to their places of origin, and in others according to where they lived in France. These groups used a variety of strategies to make themselves heard within French society (Simeant 1998). In June 1997, for instance, a group within the broader movement called the Artistes Sans Frontières organized what they called a *parrainage Républicain* – a Republican god-parenting ceremony. The Socialist mayor of the town of Pantin, outside Paris, had agreed to allow the ceremony to take place in the town hall, and his assistant was present for the ceremony. One by one, ten sans-papiers presented themselves, each time accompanied by two French citizens. The mayor asked these two citizens to confirm that they wished to become the godparents of the sans-papiers. All three then signed a document which looked like a French identity card, and which was given to the sans-papiers to be carried as an unofficial document to help them in their dealings with state officials. By creating these documents, the sans-papiers movement asserted the connections between citizens and those without papers, and made a claim for the rights of those immigrants who suffered daily exclusion from the society in which they lived. The ceremony combined Republican symbols with performances by the various artists in the group, who sang Haitian and African music as a way of thanking those who had come to support them.

The demands of the sans-papiers movement were phrased in a language of Republican rights which argued that those who had immigrated to France had the right to a humane, consistent and logical process for gaining temporary residency papers and ultimately the right to live permanently in France. They attacked the labyrinthine processes through which the French administration essentially kept many foreigners in a constant cycle of illegality, even after they had spent many years in France. And they demanded that under certain conditions – for instance, when a person had family born in France – the right to residency be granted. Yet the political strategy of the *collectif des sans-papiers* also included a stream of highly visible demonstrations in which the origins of the demonstrators – Chinese, Malian, or Haitian, and others – were put forward through music, dress and banners written in various foreign languages. In asserting cultural particularities in the pursuit of universalist principles of Republican equality, the sans-papiers were on some level challenging cemented assumptions about the meaning of the Republic and of assimilation in the French context. For many French intellectuals and administrators, the expression of ethnic particularisms is seen as fundamentally incompatible with the 'Republican model of assimilation' in which new arrivals are to integrate themselves into the functioning of secular state institutions that grant them equal treatment as individuals.

The goal of avoiding the creation of 'ghettos' that for many officials is the inevitable result of the 'Anglo-Saxon model' of immigration, in which the particularity of an ethnic group as such is respected, has motivated a range of government policies on schooling and housing on the national and local level. Local administrations, for instance, have constantly acted to avoid the consolidation of certain groups of immigrants within certain housing developments. The political and rhetorical strategies of the sans-papiers movement therefore braided together approaches that were often assumed in French political life to be incommensurable. By creating both a recognizable cultural movement and articulating specific demands through claims towards universal rights, the sans-papiers productively used the space of possibility between a universalist language of rights and the evocation of cultural difference. The sans-papiers actively crafted a response to a question that had preoccupied many activists and scholars of the French anti-racist movements of the 1980s as they sought to confront the rise of racism in France, most powerfully symbolized by the electoral victories of Le Pen's Front National: what was the most effective strategy against racism – was it the claim of a right to cultural difference within France, or the invocation of universalist values of tolerance? The sans-papiers spoke of universalism in foreign languages, presenting themselves as 'foreign' cultures at home in France, and so articulated the issue not as one about the 'assimilation' of outsiders but rather as the problem of a Republic which was violating the rights of men and women who lived within it, who had constructed it and were a part of its past, present and future. Their movement contributed to the broader political changes brought about by the new Socialist government elected in the Spring of 1997, which developed new, liberalized laws on immigration and regularized many sans-papiers. The group *Artistes Sans Frontières* successfully lobbied for the creation of an 'artistic visa' which made it possible for foreign performers to come into France, something which had become more and more difficult for many from Africa and Latin America.

In the summer of 1998, in the midst of the euphoria surrounding France's World Cup victory, won by a team that symbolized the multicultural mix of France – with players from Guadeloupe (Thuram) and Algeria (Zidane) scoring the winning goals in the final games – it seemed possible that the Republic might achieve tolerance and co-existence among the different groups that now make up its population. The 'multicoloured' nature of the French team, and the fact that the youth of the banlieue saw themselves reflected in the team, was noted by observers. Many repeated the idea that in winning the World Cup, the French team had issued a powerful blow against Le Pen's Front National and its restricted vision of France. One commentator wrote: 'Through the World Cup, the French are discovering, in the faces of their team, what they have become, a République métissée, and that it works, that we can love one another and we can win' (Castro 1998). The writer Leila Sebbar published a 'letter to my father', who was a North African immigrant to France. He had experienced the victory, she wrote, 'As if you yourself had created today's favorite team, master artisan of the World Cup team, the work of your own life, so that la France métissée would win. Young, lively, against the ghosts that surround her. She won. You won' (Sebbar 1998). The stunning about-turn of Charles Pasqua, the architect of the very immigration laws which during the 1980s had created many of the sans-papiers in the first place, symbolized to many how deeply the victory might promise new possibilities and solutions. A few days after watching Thuram and Zidane bring the nation to victory, Pasqua declared that those sans-papiers whose situation had still not been resolved should be given papers immediately.

The power of political symbols, in this case the French national team's success, should not be underestimated in determining the course of the Republic. It was, after all, through symbolic and ritual means that many of the leaders of the French Revolution hoped to transform the souls of the French people and create a virtuous Republic. The first 'Festival of the Federation', on which the 1989 commemorations of the Revolution were based, expressed a dream of unity that continues to hold a certain promise. In their 1994 song, 'Citoyen 120', the group Zap Mama call on the 'citizens of the entire world' to wake up to the realities of those who are excluded and isolated. They punctuate their song with a chorus, 'and you will wake up from this nightmare . . .', which expresses hope for a solution for the 'Citoyen 120' whose citizenship seems so precarious (Zap Mama 1994). As Zap Mama suggest, the terms of citizenship provide a vocabulary both for a struggle for liberation and a locus of division, both the space of community and the isolation of the anonymous, numbered and unrealized citizen. Their powerful song invites reflection on citizenship's dangers and its possibilities. In crafting a future for the idea of citizenship, today's France must engage with its complicated colonial history, which carries both the cause – and, I would argue, the solution – to the end-of-the-century crisis surrounding the meanings of citizenship and national identity. To confront the present crisis is to enter into a dialogue with a contradictory past out of which the possibilities of citizenship were born.

References

Amselle, Jean-Loup (1996) *Vers un multiculturalisme français*, Paris: Aubier.

Balibar, Etienne (1991) 'The citizen-subject', in Eduardo Cadava (ed.) *Who Comes After the Subject?*, London: Routledge, 33–57.

Brubaker, Rogers (1992) *Citizenship and Nationhood in France and Germany*, Cambridge, MA: Harvard University Press.

Castro, Roland (1998) 'Allez la France Mondiale', *Liberation*, 10 July, 7.

Conklin, Alice (1997) *A Mission to Civilize: The Republican Idea of Empire in France and West Africa, 1895–1930*, Stanford, CA, Stanford University Press.

—— (1998) 'Colonialism and human rights, a contradiction in terms? The case of France and West Africa, 1895–1914', *American Historical Review*, 103(2), 419–42.

Coronil, Fernando (1997) *The Magical State: Nature, Money and Modernity in Venezuela*, Chicago, IL: University of Chicago Press.

Dubois, Laurent (1998a) 'A colony of citizens: revolution and slave emancipation in the French Caribbean, 1789–1802', PhD dissertation, University of Michigan.

—— (1998b) *Les Esclaves de la République: L'Histoire Oubliée de la Première Émancipation*, Paris: Calmann-Lévy.

Kaplan, Steven (1995) *Farewell, Revolution: Disputed Legacies, France 1789/1989*, 2 vols, Ithaca, NY: Cornell University Press.

Leruth, Michael Frank (1995) 'The spectacle of the state in postmodern France: the 'controlled madness' of Jean-Paul Goude's Parade for the bicentennial of the French Revolution', PhD dissertation, Pennsylvania State University.

Maspero, François (1994) *Roissy Express: A Journey Through the Paris Suburbs*, London: Verso.

Mehta, Uday (1990) 'Liberal strategies of exclusion', *Politics and Society*, 18(4), 427–54.

Noiriel, Gérard (1988) *Le Creuset Français: Histoire de L'Immigration, XIX–XX ème siècle*, Paris: Gallimard.

Sebbar, Leila (1998) 'Lettre à mon père', *Liberation*, 14 July, 12.

Simeant, Johanna (1998) *La Cause des Sans-Papiers*, Paris: Presses de Sciences Politiques.

Trouillot, Michel Rolph (1995) *Silencing the Past: Power and the Production of History*, CA: Stanford University Press, 114–53.

Wilder, G. (1999) 'Practicing citizenship in imperial Paris', in Comaroff, J.L. and Comaroff, J. (eds) *Civil Society and Political Imagination in Africa*, Chicago: University of Chicago Press.

Zap Mama (1994) *Sabysmla*, New York: Warner Brothers.

PART 12

New histories, new empires – and the 'colonial present'

Chapter 29

Anthony Pagden

IMPERIALISM, LIBERALISM AND THE QUEST FOR PERPETUAL PEACE

In a long series of works, Anthony Pagden has been among the most important contributors to our thinking about the intellectual history of empires – not just the place of colonialism in the history of political theory (though he is among the most distinguished scholars of that subject) but also in broader ways. Here he combines that expertise with provocative thinking about the present 'revival' of ideas of empire, especially in relation to American power, and its possible futures.

Stephen Howe

FOR AT LEAST TWO GENERATIONS, 'empire' and 'imperialism' have been dirty words. Already by 1959, when neither the French nor the British Empire had yet quite ceased to exist, Raymond Aron dismissed imperialism as a 'name given by rivals, or spectators, to the diplomacy of a great power' – something, that is, that only others did or had. By the 1970s, a consensus had emerged in liberal circles in the West that all empires – or at least those of European or North American origin – had only ever been systems of power that constituted a denial by one people of the rights (above all, the right to self-determination) of countless others. They had never benefited anyone but their rulers; all of those who had lived under imperial rule would much rather not have and finally they had all risen up and driven out their conquerors.

Very recently this picture has begun to change. Now that empires are no more (the last serious imperial outpost, Hong Kong, vanished in 1997), a more nuanced account of their long histories is beginning to be written. It has become harder to avoid the conclusion that some empires were much weaker than was commonly claimed; that at least some of the colonized collaborated willingly, for at least some of the time, with their colonizers; that minorities often fared better under empires than under nation-states; and that empires were often more successful than nation-states at managing the murderous consequences of religious differences. Ever since 9/11 and the war in Afghanistan, a few intrepid voices have even been heard to declare that some empires might in fact have been forces for good. Books both for and against – with such titles as *The Sorrows of Empire*, *America's Inadvertent Empire*, *Resurrecting Empire*, and *The Obligation of Empire* – now appear almost daily. As these titles suggest, the current revival of interest in empire is not unrelated to the behavior of the current US administration in international affairs, and to the widespread assumption that the United States has become a new imperial power. Even so, most Americans continue to feel uncomfortable with the designation, which (forgetting Hawaii, the Philippines, and Puerto Rico) they have long regarded as a European evil. Yet ever since the mid-1990s, the rhetoric of US international relations has become increasingly imperial. 'If we have to use force, it is because we are America,' declared Madeleine Albright in 1998, taking care not to pronounce the word 'empire.' 'We are the indispensable nation, We stand tall, We see further into the future.'[1] No British pro-consul could have put it better.

But for all the talk about a new American, is the United States today really, in Niall Ferguson's words, 'the empire that does not dare to speak its name – an empire in denial?'[2]

This would appear to suggest that the United States behaves like and pursues the recognized objectives of an empire while being unprepared to commit itself ideologically to imperialism, or to take the necessary measures to ensure that those objectives constitute a long-term success. Is that really so?

Before these questions can be answered, we need to answer a rather more fundamental one – namely, what is an empire? The word has been used to describe societies as diverse as Mesoamerican tribute-distribution systems (the so-called Aztec and Inca empires), tribal conquest states (the Mongol and Ottoman empires), European composite for perpetual monarchies (the Hapsburg and Austro- Hungarian empires), and even networks of economic and political clientage (the current relation of the First to the Third World) – not to mention the British Empire, which combined features of all of these. Faced with such diversity, simple definitions will clearly be of little use. It is, of course, possible to define the word so narrowly as to exclude all but the most obvious European (and a few Asian) megastates. On the other hand, defining it so widely as to include any kind of extensive international power runs the risk of rending the concept indeterminate.

So let me begin by saying that an empire is an extensive state in which one ethnic or tribal group, by one means or another, rules over several others – roughly what the first-century Roman historian Tacitus meant when he spoke of the Roman world as an 'immense body of empire' ('immensum imperii corpus').[3] As such, empires have always been more frequent, more extensive political and social forms than tribal territories or nations have ever been. Ever since antiquity, large areas of Asia were ruled by imperial states of one kind or another, and so too were substantial areas of Africa. Vishanagar, Assyria, Elam, Urartu, Benin, Maori New Zealand – all were, in this sense, empires. All empires inevitably involve the exercise of imperium, or sovereign authority, usually acquired by force. Few empires have survived for long without suppressing opposition, and probably all were initially created to supply the metropolis with goods it could not otherwise acquire. In 1918, the great Austrian economist Joseph Schumpeter described territorial expansion as 'the purely instinctual inclination towards war and conquest' and relegated it to an earlier atavistic period of human history that he believed was now past.[4] He would have to wait another half century for the final dismemberment of the world's last significant colonial outposts. But he could see that in the new global economies that he projected for the world in the wake of the Great War, conquest would no longer be possible and that without conquest there could be no empire.

But Schumpeter's view is only part of the picture. War and conquest would have achieved very little if that is all there had been. To survive for long, all empires have had to win over their conquered populations. The Romans learned this very early in their history.[5] 'An empire,' declared the historian Livy at the end of the first century BC, 'remains powerful so long as its subjects rejoice in it.' Rome had a lot to offer its conquered populations – architecture, baths, the ability to bring fresh water from distant hills, or to heat marble-lined rooms in villas in the wilds of Northumberland. The historian Tacitus acidly commented that in adopting baths, porticos, and banquets, all the unwitting Britons had done was to describe as 'humanity' what was in reality 'an aspect of their slavery.' Ultimately, however, Rome's greatest attraction was citizenship – a concept that, in its recognizably modern form, the Romans invented and that, ever since the early days of the Republic, had been the main ideological prop of the Roman world. Of course, not all Rome's subject peoples wished for such things; but if a substantial number had not, its empire could not have survived as long as it did.

All the later European empires did the best they could to follow at least part of the example Rome had set them. The Spanish and the French both attempted to create something resembling a single society governed by a single body of law. Similarly, the British in India could never have succeeded in seizing control of the former Mughal Empire without the active and sometimes enthusiastic assistance of the emperors' former subjects. Without Indian bureaucrats, Indian judges, and, above all, Indian soldiers, the British Raj would have remained a private trading company. At the Battle of Plassey in 1757, which marked the beginning of the East India Company's political ascendancy over the Mughal Empire, twice as many Indians as Europeans fought on the British side.[6]

It was this process of absorption – and with it the ambition to create a single community that would embrace, as the Roman Empire had, both the mother country and the indigenous inhabitants of its colonies – that allowed Edmund Burke to speak of the victims of the brutal regime of Warren Hastings, governor of Bengal, as 'our distressed fellow-citizens in India.'[7] Empire was a sacred trust, 'given,' as Burke insisted, 'by an incomprehensible dispensation of Divine providence into our hands.' To abuse it, as Hastings had, was not just morally offensive; more significantly for Burke, it threatened the very existence not only of the 'British constitution,' but of 'the civilization of Europe.'[8]

Yet the idea of empire based upon universal citizenship created a paradox. If all the inhabitants of the empire were indeed fellow citizens, then a new kind of society, universal and cosmopolitan, would have had to come into being to accommodate them. With hindsight it was possible to argue, as Edward Gibbon did, that in the second century, when 'the Roman Empire comprehended the fairest part of the earth and the most civilized portion of mankind,' a new kind of society had indeed arisen.[9] But in the eighteenth century, things did not look quite so harmonious. Instead of one world community, the European overseas powers had created what the French philosopher and economist the Marquis de Mirabeau described in 1758 as 'a new and monstrous system' that vainly attempted to combine three distinct types of political association (or, as he called them, esprits): domination, commerce, and settlement. The inevitable conflict that had arisen between these had thrown all the European powers into crisis. In Mirabeau's view, the only way forward was to abandon both settlement and conquest – especially conquest – in favor of commerce.

He was not alone. For those like Mirabeau and his near-contemporary Adam Smith, what in the eighteenth century was called 'the commercial society' seemed to provide a means to create a new, more ecumenical form of empire that now would benefit all its members. For, in theory at least, commerce created a relationship between peoples that did not involve dependency of any kind and that, most importantly, avoided any use of force. In these new commercialized societies, the various peoples of the world would swap new technologies and basic scientific and cultural skills as readily as they would swap foodstuffs. These would not be empires of conquest, but 'empires of liberty.'[10]

But this vision never materialized because, as Smith fully recognized, the European empires were not, nor had ever been, merely means to economic ends; they were also matters of international prestige.[11] Smith knew that without colonies Britain would be nothing more than a small European state. The disparity in size between the mother country and the rest of the empire remained a constant worry. Furthermore, as David Hume pointed out, the 'sweet commerce' in which Montesquieu and others had placed such trust was, at best, an uncertain panacea for the ills of mankind: in reality, even the most highly commercialized states tended to 'look upon their neighbours with a suspicious eye, to consider all trading states as their rivals, and to suppose that it is impossible for any of them to flourish, but at their expence.'[12]

Hume's skepticism proved all too accurate. It was in the long run more profitable, as both the British and the Dutch discovered in Asia, to exercise direct control over the sources of supply through conquest than it was to trade with them. But the Enlightenment vision of the future transvaluation of empire was finally swept aside not so much by the actual practice of the 'empires of liberty' as by Napoleon's attempt to build quite a different kind of empire within Europe itself.

Initially the very brevity and bloodiness of the Napoleonic ambition to transform Europe into a series of satellite kingdoms seemed to the liberals who had suffered from it – Alexis de Tocqueville and Benjamin Constant in particular – to have rendered all such projects unrepeatable. In 1813, with Napoleon apparently out of the way, Constant felt able to declare that, at last, 'pleasure and utility' had 'opposed irony to every real or feigned enthusiasm' of the kind that had always been the driving force behind all modes of imperialism. Napoleon and, above all, Napoleon's fall, had shown that post-revolutionary politics were to be conducted not in the name of 'conquest and usurpation,' but in accordance with public opinion. And public opinion, Constant confidently predicted, would have nothing to do with empire. 'The force that a people needs to keep all others in subjection,' he wrote, is today, more than ever, a privilege that cannot last. The nation that aimed at such an empire would place itself in a more dangerous position than the weakest of tribes. It would become the object of universal horror. Every opinion, every desire, every hatred, would threaten it, and sooner or later those hatreds, those opinions, and those desires would explode and engulf it.'[13]

Like Smith, Constant also believed that commerce, or 'civilized calculation,' as he called it, would come to control all future relationships between peoples. Nearly a century later, Schumpeter expressed, in characteristically unquestioning terms, the same conviction. 'It may be stated as beyond controversy,' he declared, 'that where free trade prevails no class has an interest in forcible expansion as such.'[14]

Ironically, in view of the similarity of these claims, what separated Schumpeter from Constant in time was a phase of imperial expansion that was more atavistic, more 'enthusiastic' even than the one Constant hoped he had seen the last of. For what in fact followed Napoleon's final defeat was not a return to the Enlightenment *status quo ante*, but the emergence of modern nationalism. After the Congress of Vienna, the newly self-conscious European states and, subsequently, the new nations of Europe – Belgium (founded in 1831), Italy (1861), and Germany (1876) – all began to compete with one another for the status and economic gains that empire was thought to bestow. Public opinion, far from turning an ironical eye on the imperialistic pretensions of the new European nations, embraced them with enthusiasm. National prestige was, for instance, the main grounds on which Tocqueville supported the French invasion of Algeria in 1830.

The new imperialism turned out to be very different from the kind of empire of liberty for which Burke and Smith and Mirabeau had argued. No 'sacred trust' was involved here – only, in Joseph Conrad's famous phrase, 'the taking away [of the earth] from those who have a different complexion or slightly flatter noses than ourselves.' In the new nationalist calculus, the more of this earth you could take away, the greater you became. By 1899, imperialism had indeed become, as Curzon remarked, 'the faith of a nation.'[15]

There was something else that was new about the new imperialism. With the exception of the Spanish, the earlier European powers had been only marginally concerned with changing the lives, beliefs, and customs of the peoples whose lands they had occupied. Missionaries – Catholic, Anglican, Lutheran, Calvinist – were present in British and French America, and even in British, French, and Dutch Asia, but their activities were always of secondary political importance and generally looked upon by the civilian authorities as something of a nuisance. In the nineteenth century, however, Africa and even India became the testing grounds for a new missionary zeal. Driven partly by Christian ideals, partly by a belief in the overwhelming superiority of European culture, the new imperialists sought to make of the world one world – Christian, liberal, and, ultimately (since none of the virtues peddled by the missionaries could be sustained in any other kind of society), commercial and industrial. In this vision of empire, the 'natives,' Rudyard Kipling's 'new-caught sullen peoples, half devil and half child,' had not merely to be ruled, they had to be ruled for their own good – however much they might resent it at first – and had to be made to recognize that one way of life was the inevitable goal of all mankind. This was empire as tutelage.

Ironically, and fatally for the imperial powers as it turned out, it also implied that one day all the subjects of all the European empires would become self-governing. 'By good government,' Lord Macaulay had declared as early as 1833, 'we may educate our subjects into a capacity for better government; that having become instructed in European knowledge they may, in some future age, demand European institutions.' He did not know when this would come about, but he was certain that when it did, 'it will be the proudest day in English history.'[16] In practice, self-determination would be postponed into the remote future. But Macaulay was forced to acknowledge that, theoretically at least, it could not be postponed indefinitely. Nationalist imperialism, however, brought to the fore a question that had remained unanswered for a long time: in the modern world what, precisely, was the nature of empire? Ever since 1648, the modern nation-state has been one in which imperium has been regarded as indivisible. The monarchs of Europe had spent centuries wresting authority from nobles, bishops, towns, guilds, military orders, and any number of quasi-independent, quasi-sovereign bodies. Indivisibility had been one of the shibboleths of pre-revolutionary Europe, and one which the French Revolution had gone on to place at the center of the conception of the modern state. The modern person is a rights-bearing individual, but – as the 1791 *Déclaration des droits de l'homme et du citoyen* had made clear – he or she is so only by virtue of being a citizen of a single indivisible state.[17]

Such a strong notion of sovereignty could apply, however, only within Europe. In the world beyond, things were very different. It had been impossible for any empire to thrive without sharing power with either local settler elites or with local inhabitants. As Henry Maine, a renowned jurist, historian, and legal member of the viceroy's council in India, had declared in 1887, 'Sovereignty has always been regarded as divisible in international law.'[18] Failure to cede this point had, after all, been the prime cause of the American Revolution and, after 1810, of the revolt of the Spanish colonies in South America – and had almost driven the French settlers of Saint-Domingue, Guadeloupe, and Martinique into the waiting arms of the British.

Nowhere was the question of divided sovereignty so acute as in the British Empire, which by the early nineteenth century had become larger and more widespread, and consequently more varied, than any of its rivals or predecessors. 'I know of no example of it either in ancient or modern history,' wrote Disraeli in 1878. 'No Caesar or Charlemagne ever presided over a dominion so peculiar.' If such a conglomerate was to survive at all, it could insist on no single constitutional identity. It was this feature of the empire that led the historian Sir Robert Seeley in 1883 to make his famous remark that it seemed as if England had 'conquered and peopled half the world in a fit of absence of mind.'[19]

Nothing, it seems, could be further removed from the present position of the United States. Is then the United States really an empire? I think if we look at the history of the European empires, the answer must be no. It is often assumed that because America possesses the military capability to become an empire, any overseas interest it does have must necessarily be imperial.[20] But if military muscle had been all that was required to make an empire, neither Rome nor Britain – to name only two – would have been one. Contrary to the popular image, most empires were, in fact, for most of their histories, fragile structures, always dependent on their subject peoples for survival. Universal citizenship was not created out of generosity. It was created out of need. 'What else proved fatal to Sparta and Athens in spite of their power in arms,' the emperor Claudius asked the Roman Senate when it attempted to deny citizenship to the Gauls in Italy, 'but their policy of holding the conquered aloof as alien-born?'[21]

This is not to say that the United States has not resorted to some of the strategies of past empires. Today, for instance, Iraq and Afghanistan look remarkably like British protectorates. Whatever the administration may claim publicly about the autonomy of the current Iraqi and Afghan leadership, the United States in fact shares sovereignty with the civilian governments of both places, since it retains control over the countries' armed forces. What, however, the United States is not committed to is the view that empire – the exercise of imperium – is the best, or even a possible, way to achieve this.

In a number of crucial respects, the United States is, indeed, very unimperial. Despite allusions to the Pax Americana, twenty-first-century America bears not the slightest resemblance to ancient Rome. Unlike all previous European empires, it has no significant overseas settler populations in any of its formal dependencies and no obvious desire to acquire any. It does not conceive its hegemony beyond its borders as constituting a form of citizenship. It exercises no direct rule anywhere outside these areas; and it has always attempted to extricate itself as swiftly as possible from anything that looks as if it were about to develop into even indirect rule.

Cecil Rhodes once said that he would colonize the stars if he could. It is hard to image any prominent American policymaker, even Paul Wolfowitz, even secretly, harboring such desires. As Viscount James Bryce, one of the most astute observers of the Americas both North and South, said of the (North) Americans, 'they have none of the earth-hunger which burns in the great nations of Europe.'[22] The one feature the United States does share with many past empires is the desire to impose its political values on the rest of the world. Like the 'liberal' empires of nineteenth-century Britain and France, the United States is broadly committed to the liberal-democratic view that democracy is the highest possible form of government and should therefore be exported. This is the American mission to which Madeleine Albright alluded, and it has existed in one form or another ever since the creation of the republic.

In addressing the need to 'contain' Communist China, Harry Truman – comparing America to Achaemenid Persia, Macedonian Greece, Antonine Rome, and Victorian Britain – claimed that the only way to save the world from totalitarianism was for the 'whole world [to] adopt the American system.' By this he meant, roughly, what George W. Bush means by freedom – democratic institutions and free trade. Truman, knowingly or unknowingly, took the phrase 'American system' from Alexander Hamilton, who firmly believed that the new republic should one day be able to 'concur in erecting one great American system superior to the control of all transatlantic force or influence and able to dictate the terms of the connections between the old world and the new.'[23] 'For the American system,' Truman continued, could only survive 'by becoming a world system.'[24] What for Hamilton was to be a feature of international relations, for Truman was to be nothing less than a world culture.

But even making the rest of the world adopt the American system did not mean, as it had for all the other empires Truman cited, ruling the rest of the world. For Truman assumed, as has every American administration since, that the world's 'others' no longer needed to be led and cajoled until one day they finally demanded their own democratic institutions. American values, as Bush put it in 2002, are not only 'right and true for every person in every society'– they are self-evidently so.[25] All humanity is capable of recognizing that democracy, or 'freedom,' will always be in its own best interest. All that has ever prevented some peoples from grasping this simple truth is fanaticism, the misguided claims of (certain) religions, and the actions of malevolent, self-interested leaders. Rather than empire, the United States' objective, then, is to eliminate these internal obstacles, to establish the conditions necessary for democracy, and then to retreat.

There can be little doubt that this assumption has been the cause, in Iraq as much as in El Salvador, of the failure to establish regimes that are democratic in more than name. Humanity is not, as Iraq and Afghanistan have demonstrated, destined to find democracy more enticing than any other alternative. You may not need to be an American to embrace 'American values' – but you certainly need to be much closer to American beliefs and cultural expectations than most of the populations of the Middle East currently are. Tocqueville made a similar point about Algeria. It would have been impossible to make Algeria into a modern nation without 'civilizing' the Arabs, he argued, a task that would be impossible to achieve unless Algeria was made into not a 'colony,' but 'an extension of France itself on the far side of the Mediterranean.'[26] The French government chose to ignore him and made it into a colony nonetheless. But such an arrangement has never been an option for the United States. If only because the United States is the one modern nation in which no division of sovereignty is, at least conceptually, possible. The federal government shares sovereignty with the individual states of which the union is composed, but it could not contemplate, as former empires all had to, sharing sovereignty with the members of other nations. Only very briefly has the mainland United States ever been considered an empire rather than a nation. As each new US territory was settled or conquered it became, within a very short space of time, a new state within the Union. This implied that any territories the United States might acquire overseas had, such as Hawaii, to be incorporated fully into the nation – or returned to its native inhabitants. No American administration has been willing to tolerate any kind of colonialism for very long. Even so resolute an imperialist as Teddy Roosevelt could not imagine turning Cuba or the Philippines into colonies.[27] The United States does possess a number of dependent territories – Guam, the Virgin Islands, Samoa, etc. – but these are too few and too small to constitute an overseas colonial empire. The major exception to this rule is Puerto Rico. The existence of a vigorous debate over the status of this 'commonwealth' – a term which itself suggests that Puerto Rico is an independent republic – and the fact that the status quo strikes everyone, even those who support its continuation, as an anomaly, largely proves the rule.[28]

Those advocating a more forceful US imperial policy overlook that if America is in denial, it is in it for a very good reason. To become a true empire, as even the British were at the end of the nineteenth century, the United States would have to change radically the nature of its political culture. It is a liberal democracy (as most of the Western world now conceives it) – and liberal democracy and liberal empire (as Mill conceived it) are incompatible.[29] The form of empire championed by Mill existed to enforce the virtues and advantages that accompanied free or liberal government in places that otherwise would be, in Mill's language, 'barbarous.' The time might indeed come when the inhabitants of such places would demand European institutions – but as Mill and even Macaulay knew, when that happened, the empire would be at an end. By contrast, the United States makes no claim to be holding Iraq and Afghanistan in trust until such time as their peoples are able to govern themselves in a suitable – that is Western – manner. It seeks, however imperfectly, to confer free democratic institutions directly on those places, and then to depart, leaving the hapless natives to fabricate as best they can the social and political infrastructure without which no democratic process can survive for long.

In the end, perhaps, what Smith, Constant, and Schumpeter prophesized has come to pass: commerce has finally replaced conquest. True, it is commerce stripped of all its eighteenth-century attributes of benevolence, but it is commerce nonetheless. The long-term political objectives of the United States, which have varied little from administration to administration, have been to sustain and, where necessary, to create a world of democracies bound inexorably together by international trade. And the political forms best suited to international commerce are federations (such as the European Union) and trading partnerships (the OECD or NAFTA), not empires.

In *Paradise and Power: America and Europe in the New World Order*, Robert Kagan boasts that whereas the 'old' Europeans had moved beyond:

> power into a self-contained world of laws and rules and transnational negotiation and cooperation . . . a post-historical paradise of peace and relative prosperity, the realization of Immanuel Kant's 'perpetual peace,' the United States remains mired in history, exercising power in an anarchic Hobbesian world where international rules are unreliable, and where true security and the defense

and promotion of a liberal order still depend on the possession and use of military might.[30]

It is difficult to know just what Kagan takes the words 'Kant' and 'Hobbes' to stand for. But on any reasoned understanding of the writings of Thomas Hobbes and Immanuel Kant, he would seem to have inverted the objectives of the Europeans and the Americans. For it is the Europeans (or at least the majority of them) who – by attempting to isolate the European Union as far as possible from all forms of external conflict that are considered to pose no immediate domestic threat – are the true Hobbesians. And in most respects the objectives of Kant's conception of a 'universal cosmopolitan existence' – which would constitute the 'matrix within which all the original capacities of the human race may develop'[31] – is, *mutatis mutandis*, what the current US government claims to be attempting to achieve.

Kant argued that the peoples of the world would never be at peace so long as the existing world powers – what he called 'universal monarchies' – were locked into internecine competition with one another. They had, he said, to be persuaded to join a league for their own mutual protection. To make this possible, however, it was not enough to rely on international trade agreements or peace treaties, because in the long run the parties to such agreements would honor them only if they perceived them to be in their interests. A true world federation could only come about once all the states of the world shared a common political order, what Kant called 'representative republicanism.' Only then would they all have the same interests, and only then would those interests be to promote mutual prosperity and to avoid warfare. The reason he believed this to be so was that such societies were the only ones in which human beings were treated as ends not means; the only ones, therefore, in which human beings could be fully autonomous; and the only ones, consequently, in which no people would ever go to war to satisfy the greed or ambition of their rulers.

With due allowance for the huge differences between the late eighteenth century and the early twenty-first, and between what Kant understood by representative republics and what is meant today by liberal democracies, the United States' vision for the world is roughly similar: a union of democracies, certainly not equal in size or power, but all committed to the common goal of greater prosperity and peace through free trade. The members of this union have the right to defend themselves against aggressors and, in the pursuit of defense, they are also entitled to do their best to cajole so-called rogue states into mending their ways sufficiently to be admitted into the union. This is what Kant called the 'cosmopolitan right.'[32]

We may assume that Truman had such an arrangement in mind when he said that the American system could only survive by becoming a world system. For like the 'American system,' Kant's 'cosmopolitan right' was intended to provide precisely the kind of harmonious environment in which it was possible to pursue what Kant valued most highly, namely, the interdependence of all human societies. This indisputably 'liberal order' still depended 'on the possession and use of military might,' but there would be no permanent, clearly identifiable, perpetual enemy – only dissidents, 'rogue' states, and the perverse malice of the excluded. Kant was also not, as Kagan seems to imply, some kind of high-minded idealist, in contrast to Hobbes, the indefatigably realist. He was in fact very suspicious of high-mindedness of any kind. 'This rational idea of a peaceful, even if not friendly, thorough-going community of all the nations on the earth,' he wrote, 'is not a philanthropic (ethical), principle, but a principle having to do with rights.'[33] It was based quite as firmly upon a calculation of reasonable self-interest as was Hobbes's suggestion for exiting from the 'war of all against all.'[34]

Kant, however, was also aware that bringing human beings to understand just what is in their own self-interest would always be a long and arduous task. In order to recognize that autonomy is the highest human good, humans have to disentangle themselves from the 'leading strings' by which the 'guardians' – priests, lawyers, and rulers – have made them 'domesticated animals.' Only he who could 'throw off the ball and chain of his perpetual immaturity' would be properly 'enlightened,' and only the enlightened could create the kind of state in which true autonomy would be possible.[35] Because of this, the cosmopolitan right still lay for most at some considerable distance in the future.

It still does – few states today fulfil Kant's criteria. And of course Kant never addressed the problem of how the transition from one or another kind of despotism to 'representative republicanism' was to be achieved (although he seems to have thought that the French Revolution, at least in its early phases, offered one kind of model). Kant's project for perpetual peace has often been taken to be some kind of moral blueprint for the United Nations. But in my view, it is far closer to the final objective of the modern global state system in which the United States is undoubtedly, for the moment at least, the key player. It is also, precisely because it is a project for some future time, a far better guide to the overall ideological objectives of the United States than anything that now goes under the name of 'empire.'

Notes

1   Quoted in Emmanuel Todd, *Après l'empire: essai sur la décomposition du système américain* (Paris: Gallimard, 2002) 22. Ironically – or perhaps not – she was justifying a missile attack on Iraq.

2   Niall Ferguson, *Empire: The Rise and Demise of the British World Order and the Lessons for Global Power* (New York: Basic Books, 2003) 317; Ferguson, *Colossus: The Price of America's Empire* (New York: Penguin Press, 2004) 3–7.

3   See P.A. Blunt, 'Laus imperii,' in Peter Garnsey and C.R. Whittaker (eds) *Imperialism in the Ancient World* (Cambridge: Cambridge University Press, 1978) 159–91.

4   Joseph Schumpeter, *Imperialism and Social Classes*, trans. Heinz Norden (New York: A.M. Kelley, 1951) 7.

5   This has been described most recently and with great brilliance by Clifford Ando, *Imperial Ideology and Provincial Loyalty in the Roman Empire* (Berkeley: University of California Press, 2000).

6   Linda Colley, *Captives: Britain, Empire and the World, 1600–1850* (London: Jonathan Cape, 2002) 259.

7   'Speech on the Nabob of Arcot's Debts,' quoted in Uday Singh Mehta, *Liberalism and Empire: A Study in Nineteenth-Century British Liberal Thought* (Chicago: University of Chicago Press, 1999) 157.

8   Edmund Burke, *On Empire, Liberty, and Reform: Speeches and Letters*, ed. David Bromwich (New Haven, CT: Yale University Press, 2000) 15–16.

9   Edward Gibbon, *Decline and Fall of the Roman Empire*, ch. 3.

10   See Anthony Pagden, *Lords of All the World: Ideologies of Empire in Spain, Britain and France* c. *1500–c. 1800* (New Haven, CT: Yale University Press, 1995) 178–87.

11   Adam Smith, 'Thoughts on the State of the Contest with America,' in Ernest Campbell Mossner and Ian Simpson Ross (eds), *Correspondence of Adam Smith*, vol. 6 (Oxford: Clarendon Press, 1977) 383.

12   David Hume, 'On the Jealousy of Trade,' in Eugene F. Miller (ed.) *Essays, Moral, Political, and Literary* (Indianapolis: Liberty Classics, 1985) 28.

13   Benjamin Constant, 'The Spirit of Conquest and Usurpation and their Relation to European Civilization' in *Political Writings* (ed.) and trans. Biancamaria Fontana (Cambridge: Cambridge University Press, 1988) 79.

14   Schumpeter, *Imperialism and Social Classes*, 99.

15   Quoted in Harold Nicolson, *Curzon: The Last Phase, 1919–1925: A Study in Post-War Diplomacy* (New York: Houghton Mifflin Company, 1934) 13.

16   Quoted in Thomas R. Metcalf, *Ideologies of the Raj* (Cambridge: Cambridge University Press, 1994) 34.

17   See Anthony Pagden, 'Human Rights, Natural Rights and Europe's Imperial Legacy,' *Political Theory*, 2003, 31, 171–99.

18   Quoted in Edward Keene, *Beyond the Anarchical Society: Grotius, Colonialism and Order in World Politics* (Cambridge: Cambridge University Press, 2002) 63.

19   Sir John Robert Seeley, *The Expansion of England* (London: Macmillan, 1883) 12.

20   This, for instance, is the argument behind Robert D. Kaplan's *Warrior Politics: Why Leadership Demands a Pagan Ethos* (New York: Random House, 2002) and in a very different and more measured tone, Chalmers A. Johnson's, *The Sorrows of Empire: Militarism, Secrecy, and the End of the Republic* (New York: Metropolitan Books, 2004) – although Kaplan approves and Johnson disapproves.

21   Tacitus, Annals II, 23–4.

22   Quoted by Arthur Schlesinger, Jr. in 'The Making of a Mess,' *The New York Review of Books*, September 2004, 51(14), 41.

23   Federalist 11 in *The Federalist Papers*, Isaac Kramnick (ed.) (Harmondsworth: Penguin, 1987) 133–4.

24   Quoted in Ferguson, *Colossus*, 80.

25   Quoted in Rashid Khalidi, *Resurrecting Empire: Western Footprints and America's Perilous Path in the Middle East* (Boston: Beacon Press, 2004) 3.

26   'Rapport fait par M. Tocqueville sur le projet de la loi relative aux credits extraordinaires demandés pour l'Algérie,' in Seloua Luste Boulbina (ed.) *Tocqueville sur l'Algérie*, 1847 (Paris: Flammarion, 2003) 228.

27   Frank Ninkovich, *The United States and Imperialism* (Malden, MA: Blackwell Publishers, 2001) 75.

28   See Christina Duffy Burnett and Burke Marshall (eds) *Foreign in a Domestic Sense: Puerto Rico, American Expansion, and the Constitution* (Durham, NC: Duke University Press, 2001).

29   On this term, see Michael Mann, *Incoherent Empire* (London: Verso, 2003) 11.

30   Robert Kagan, *Paradise and Power: America and Europe in the New World Order* (London: Atlantic Books, 2003) 3.

31   Immanuel Kant, 'Idea for a Universal History with a Cosmopolitan Purpose,' in Hans Reiss (ed.), *Political Writings* (Cambridge: Cambridge University Press, 1991) 51.

32   Immanuel Kant, *The Metaphysics of Morals*, trans. Mary Gregor (Cambridge: Cambridge University Press, 1991) 156.

33   Kant, *The Metaphysics of Morals*, 158; Anthony Pagden, 'Stoicism, Cosmopolitanism and the Legacy of European Imperialism,' *Constellations*, 2000, 7, 3–22.

34   Immanuel Kant, 'Perpetual Peace: A Philosophical Sketch,' in Reiss (ed.) *Political Writings*, 112.

35   Immanuel Kant, 'An Answer to the Question: "What is Enlightenment?"' in Reiss (ed.) *Political Writings*, 54–5.

Chapter 30

Partha Chatterjee

EMPIRE AFTER GLOBALISATION

Partha Chatterjee, another notable alumnus of the Subaltern Studies school, has also been a central figure in rethinking the history both of colonialism and of anticolonial nationalism. He is also a frequent and powerful commentator on current affairs, in India and beyond. In this essay, he finds striking connections between the nineteenth-century British takeover of Awadh and the 'imperial' politics of the twenty-first century – and reflects on the whole range of forms of thought about empires, past and present.

Stephen Howe

IN THIS CHAPTER, I WILL TRY TO answer two questions. One, is the US imperial project today an expected outcome of the process of globalisation that has taken place in the world in the last two decades? Two, is this empire compatible with democracy? The two questions are closely connected.

But we can only answer these questions in the shadow of Michael Hardt and Antonio Negri's analysis of *Empire*.[1] That ingenious and influential book has proposed a way of looking at the new global order as necessarily imperial and, at the same time, necessarily democratic. Let us review that proposal before we move into our discussion.

Hardt and Negri speak of two logics of sovereignty within the modern political imagination. One is the transcendent sovereignty of the nation state, demarcated over territory, located either in a sovereign monarchical power (à la Hobbes) or a sovereign people (à la Rousseau). Its logic is exclusive, defining itself as identical to the people that constitutes a particular nation state as distinct from other nation states. Its dynamic is frequently expansionist, leading to territorial acquisitions and rule over other peoples that are known in modern world history as imperialism. The second logic is that of the immanent sovereignty of the democratic republic, located, they argue, in the constituent power of the multitude (as distinct from the people) working through a network of self-governing institutions embodying multiple mechanisms of powers and counter-powers. The logic of immanent sovereignty is inclusive rather than exclusive. Even when territorialised, it sees its domain as marked by open frontiers. Its dynamic tendency is towards a constantly productive expansiveness rather the expansionist conquest of other lands and peoples. Germinating in the republican ideals of the US constitution, the logic of immanent sovereignty now points towards the global democratic network of Empire.[2]

It is necessary to point out that even in their description of the historical evolution of the US as an immanent Empire, Hardt and Negri acknowledge that there were closed and exclusive boundaries. First of all, it was possible to conceive of the expansive open frontier only by erasing the presence there of native Americans who could not be imagined as being part of the supposedly inclusive category of the constituent multitude. That was the first inflexible border. Second, there were the African-Americans who were, as Hardt and Negri point out, counted as unequal parts of the state population for purposes of calculating the state's share of seats in the house of representatives but, of course, not given the rights of citizens until the late 20th century. The latter became possible not by the operation of an open frontier expanding outwards but rather by the gradual loosening of an internal border through a pedagogical, and indeed redemptive, project of civilising, i.e. making citizens.[3] Hence, even in the paradigmatic case of the US as an immanent Empire, there was always a notion of an outside that could not be wishfully imagined as an ever-receptive open space that would simply yield to the expansive thrust of civilisation. This outside consisted of practices (or cultures) that were resistant to the expansion of Empire and thus had to be conquered and colonised. As with all historical empires, there are only two ways in which the civilising imperial force can operate: a pedagogy of violence and a pedagogy of culture.

From this perspective, one has to see the US myth of the melting pot as not one of hybridisation at all, as Hardt and Negri would have it, but rather as a pedagogical project of homogenisation into a new, internally hierarchised, and perhaps frequently changing, normative American culture. In this respect, the US empire is no different from other empires of the modern era for whom contact with colonised peoples meant a constant danger of corruption: an exposure to alien ways that could travel back and destroy the internal moral coherence of national life. Hence, the pedagogical aspect of civilising has only worked in one direction in the modern era – educating the colonised into the status of modern citizens; never the other way, as in many ancient empires, of conquerors allowing themselves to be civilised by their subjects. It is hard to see any evidence that the US empire is an exception to this modern rule.

Hardt and Negri also make the argument that since the new Empire is immanent and inclusive, and its sovereignty de-territorialised and without a centre, the forms of anti-imperialist politics that had proved so effective in the days of national liberation and decolonisation have become obsolete. Anti-imperialist nationalism, grounded in the transcendent reification of the sovereign people as actualised in the nation state, can now only stand in the way of the global multitude poised to liberate itself in the ever-inclusive, hybrid and intrinsically democratic networks of Empire.[4] Most readers have found this to be perhaps the least persuasive argument in *Empire*. But the point that needs to be made here is that although the transcendent and territorialised idea of sovereignty located in an actual people-nation is a predominant performative mode in most third-world nationalisms, the immanent idea of a constituent power giving to itself the appropriate machineries of self-government is never entirely absent. Indeed, just as the 'people' can be invoked to legitimise exclusive, and often utterly repressive, national identities held in place by nation state structures, so can it be invoked to critique, destabilise and sometimes to overthrow those structures. One might even say that the relative lack of stable institutionalisation of modern state structures in postcolonial countries – a matter of persistent regret in the political development literature – is actually a sign of the vital presence of this immanent notion of a constituent power that has still not been subdued into the banal routine of everyday governmentality. Think of an entire generation of Bengalis who went, from the 1930s to the 1970s, imagining themselves first as part of an anti-colonial Indian nationalism, then as part of a religion-based Pakistani nationalism, and finally as a language-based Bangladeshi nationalism, re-inventing itself every time as a new territorial nation state and yet, surely, remaining, in some enduring sense, the same constituent power giving itself the institutions of self-rule. If immanence and transcendence are two modes of sovereign power in the modern world, it is hard to see in what way the US constitution has a monopoly over them.

If Hardt and Negri's claim of a self-identity between the new globalised networks of production, exchange and cultural flows and the new immanent, de-territorialised and centreless Empire is false, then there is no obvious reason why the globalisation of the recent period should have led to what is now widely seen as a US imperialism. In other words, it is still reasonable for me to ask my first question. Further, if the global Empire has not made anti-imperialist national resistance entirely redundant, it is also reasonable for us to ask the second question: is Empire consistent with democracy, both at home and abroad?

Let me attempt to answer the two questions

The fact that several features of what is called globalisation today are not unprecedented in the history of the modern world has been remarked upon by many commentators.[5] It has been pointed out that there was a significant phase of globalisation at the end of the 19th century leading up to the First World War. Large amounts of capital were exported from Europe to many parts of the world, especially to North and South America and to the British and French colonies. In fact, scholars have argued that the rate of export of capital at the end of the 20th century was actually lower than that at the end of the 19th. Capital exports were disrupted by First World War and did not pick up again until the last two decades of the 20th century. The historical pattern of international trade is similar to that of capital exports. Trade expanded through all of the 19th century until the First World War and then contracted in the middle of the 20th century. It began to grow again from around 1975. As far as migration is concerned, as distinct from mere travel, more people migrated to and settled down in other countries in the 19th century than did at the end of the 20th. Of course, in the matter of communications, needless to say, the volume, range, density and speed of global communication today are far superior to those in the 19th century. Nevertheless, it is beyond doubt that the period from the 1880s to the First World War saw a major process of globalisation comparable to that at the end of the 20th century. In fact, much of the celebration over globalisation in the 1990s was the result of a comparison with the situation in the middle of the 19th century rather than with that at the end of the 19th.

The latter half of the 19th century was also the high noon of imperialism. Britain was the predominant world power, but its hegemony was challenged when France, Germany, Russia, the US and Japan began their scramble to acquire colonies in the last remaining territories of the world in Africa, central Asia and the Pacific. The idea of empire was popular in western democracies and politicians such as Joseph Chamberlain in Britain and Theodore Roosevelt in the US made their careers by championing an expansionist, morally aggressive, imperial cause. Their arguments were a combination of strategic geopolitics and progressive social engineering. Joseph Chamberlain, for instance, on a visit to Egypt in 1889, reminded British officials there that their ancestors 'had not been ashamed to peg out claims for posterity, thereby creating that foreign trade without which the population of Great Britain would starve'. Some years later, defending Frederick Lugard's policy of keeping Uganda under British control, he said:

> Make it the interest of the Arab slave trader to give up the slave trade, and you will see the end of that traffic. Construct your railway and thereby increase the means of traffic and you will take away three-fourths, if not the whole, of the temptation to carry on the slave trade.[6]

The fiercely competitive scramble for colonies by the big powers was a major condition for the outbreak of First World War.

Colonialism of this kind came to an end in most of the world in the two decades following the Second World War. There was, on the one hand, rising popular support in colonised countries for the anti-colonial movements. When the French and the Dutch re-occupied their colonies in Southeast Asia after the defeat of Japan in the Second World War, they were met by armed popular resistance. The Dutch soon gave up Indonesia. In Indochina, the French withdrew in the mid-1950s but, of course, the region was soon engulfed in another kind of conflict. The nationalist armed resistance became victorious in Algeria in the early 1960s.

In the British colonies, the transfer of power to nationalist governments was generally more peaceful and constitutionally tidy. It is said that this was because the liberal democratic tradition of politics in Britain ultimately made it impossible for it to sustain the anomaly of a despotic colonial empire and to resist the moral claim to national self-government by the colonised people. By acquiescing in a process of decolonisation, it was asserted, British liberal democracy redeemed itself. The claim has been recently celebrated once more by Niall Ferguson in his Empire, intended as a manual of historical instruction for aspiring American imperialists.[7]

Of course, alongside the question of the moral incompatibility of democracy and empire, another argument had also come to dominate discussions on colonialism in the middle of the 20th century. This was the utilitarian argument, often attributed to the so-called Manchester school of economic thinking, which claimed that the economic benefits derived from colonies were far outweighed by the costs of holding them in subjection. By giving up the responsibility of governing its overseas colonies, a country such as Britain could secure the same benefits at a much lower cost by negotiating suitable economic agreements with the newly independent countries. However, not every section of ruling opinion in Britain took such a bland cost-benefit view of something so sublime and noble as the British imperial tradition. Conservative governments in the 1950s were hardly keen to give up the African colonies, and when Nasser nationalised the Suez Canal in 1956, Britain and France decided to intervene with military force. It was American pressure that finally compelled them to pull back. By then, it had become clear that the future of British industry and trade were wholly dependent on the protective cover extended by the US dollar. The decolonisation of Africa in the 1960s effectively meant the end of Britain as an imperial power. The cost-benefit argument won out, leaving the moral reputation of liberal democracy largely in the clear.[8]

The UN, as it emerged in the decades following the Second World War, was testimony to the historical process of decolonisation and the universal recognition of the right of self-determination of nations. It was living proof of the universal incompatibility of democracy and empire.

The declared American position in the 20th century was explicitly against the idea of colonial empires. The imperialist fantasies of Theodore Roosevelt at the beginning of the century soon turned into the stuff of cartoons and comic strips. Rather, it was an American president, Woodrow Wilson, who enshrined the principle of self-determination of nations within the framework of the League of Nations. After the Second World War, US involvement in supporting or toppling governments in other parts of the world was justified almost entirely by the logic and rhetoric of the Cold War, not those of colonialism. If there were allegations of US imperialism, they were seen to be qualitatively different from old-fashioned colonial exploitation: this was a neo-imperialism without colonies.

In fact, it could be said that through the twentieth century, the process of economic and strategic control over foreign territories and productive resources was transformed from the old forms of conquest and occupation to the new ones of informal power exercised through diplomatic influence, economic incentives and treaty obligations. A debate that was always part of the 19th-century discourse of imperialism – direct rule or informal control – was decisively resolved in favour of the latter option.

Has globalisation at the end of the 20th century changed the conditions of that choice? The celebratory literature on globalisation in the 1990s argued that the removal of trade barriers imposed by national governments, greater mobility of people and the cultural impact of global information flows would make for conditions in which there would be a general desire all over the world for democratic forms of government and greater democratic values in social life. Free markets were expected to promote 'free societies'. It was assumed, therefore, as an extension of the fundamental liberal idea, that in spite of differences in economic and military power, there would be respect for the autonomy of governments and peoples around the world precisely because everyone was committed to the free and unrestricted flow of capital, goods, peoples and ideas. Colonies and empires were clearly antithetical to this liberal ideal of the globalised world.

However, there was a second line of argument that was also an important part of the globalisation literature of the 1990s. This argument insisted that because of the new global conditions, it was not only possible, but also necessary for the international community to use its power to protect human rights and promote democratic values in countries under despotic and authoritarian rule. There could be no absolute protection afforded by the principle of national sovereignty to tyrannical regimes. Of course, the international community had to act through a legitimate international body such as the UN. Since this would imply a democratic consensus among the nations of the world (or at least a large number of them), international humanitarian intervention of this kind to protect human rights or prevent violence and oppression would not be imperial or colonial.

The two lines of argument, both advanced within the discourse of liberal globalisation, implied a contradiction. At one extreme, one could argue that democratic norms in international affairs meant that national sovereignty was inviolable except when there was a clear international consensus in favour of humanitarian intervention; anything less would be akin to imperialist meddling. At the other extreme, the argument might be that globalisation had made national sovereignty an outdated concept. The requirements of peace-keeping now made it necessary for there to be something like an Empire without a sovereign metropolitan centre: a virtual Empire representing an immanent global sovereignty. There would be no more wars, only police action. This is the argument presented eloquently, if unpersuasively, by Hardt and Negri.

What was not much discussed in the 1990s was the possibility of conflicts of interest emerging between the major economic and military powers precisely because those national interests were now perceived to be global in their scope. The era of globalisation has seen the undermining of national sovereignty in crucial areas of foreign trade, property and contract laws, and technologies of governance. There is overwhelming pressure towards uniformity of regulations and procedures in these areas, overseen, needless to say, by the major economic powers through new international economic institutions. Can one presume a convergence of interests and a consensus of views among those powers? Or could there be competition and conflict in a situation where international interventions of various kinds on the lesser powers are both common and legitimate? One significant line of potential conflict has already emerged: that between the dollar and the euro-economic regions. A second zone of potential conflict is over the control of strategic resources such as oil. A third may be emerging over the spectacular surge of the Chinese economy that could soon make it a potential global rival of the western powers. These were the kinds of competitive metropolitan interests that had led to imperialist annexations and conflicts in the 19th century. Are we seeing a similar attempt now to stake out territories of exclusive control and spheres of influence? Is this the hidden significance of the differences among the major powers over the Anglo-American occupation of Iraq? Can this be the reason why the US political establishment has veered from the multilateral, globalising, neo-liberalism of the Clinton period to the unilateral, ultra-nationalist, neo-conservatism of the Bush regime?[9]

If there is a more material substratum of conflicts of interest in the globalised world at the beginning of the 21st century, then it becomes possible to talk of the cynical deployment of moral arguments to justify imperialist actions that are actually guided by other motivations. This is a familiar aspect of 19th-century imperial history. It was in the context of an increasingly assertive parliamentary and public opinion, demanding accountability in the activities of the government in foreign affairs, especially those that required the expenditure of public money and troops, that the foreign and colonial policies of European imperial powers became suffused with a public rhetoric of high morality and civilising virtues. And it was as an integral part of the same process that a 'realist' theory of *raison d'etre* emerged in the field of foreign affairs, as a specialist discourse used by diplomats and policy-makers, that would seek to insulate a domain of hard-headed pursuit of national self-interest, backed by military and economic power, from the mushy, even if elevated, sentimentalism of the public rhetoric of moral virtue. This was the origin of ideological 'spin' in foreign and colonial affairs – a specific set of techniques for the production of democratic consent in favour of realist and largely secretive decisions made in the pursuit of the so-called national interest by a small group of policy-makers. Looking at the history of this imperialist rhetoric in the 19th century, one cannot but be struck by the remarkable continuity in the arguments being employed today to justify military action in Iraq. Let me introduce what I think is the basic form of the moral argument. I will then describe a case of imperialist annexation in India in the middle of the 19th century to show the similarity in ideological rhetoric, even in their minor details.

I think the roots of the most persistent moral argument for empire in the modern world go all the way back to John Locke, regarded by many as the founding father of the liberal conception of rights. I am not thinking here of the uses made of Locke's argument about man mixing his labour with what he finds in nature and making that his rightful property. James Tully has shown how this argument was used in both colonial and republican America to justify the wholesale expropriation of the native inhabitants and the colonisation of the land by European settlers.[10] However, this is not an idea that is likely to carry much persuasive power in the world after decolonisation. So we will let that pass and consider instead another, much less noticed, argument from Locke.

All men are naturally in a state of perfect freedom, Locke said. They were also in a natural state of equality. Nonetheless, there were some who were not capable of being free men. Such persons could never be let loose to the disposure of their own will, because they knew no bounds to it, had not understanding, its proper guide, but were under the tuition and government of others, all the time their own understanding was incapable of that charge. Under this category of persons who were incapable of being free men Locke included lunatics and idiots, children, innocents and madmen.[11] I don't know the exact difference between lunatics and madmen; perhaps a specialist in 17th-century English lunacy could help us sort that out.

This little section in the Second Treatise has been seldom commented on, because in the context of constitutional rights, it seems such an obvious, almost trivial, qualification. If one looks at the ideological history of empire, however, one discovers that this contained a potent argument for the moral justification of imperial rule. People who were morally handicapped (i.e. lunatics and idiots), or in a state of moral infancy, deserved a benevolent despot who would protect and look after them, because they were incapable of acting on behalf of themselves. Thus, John Stuart Mill declared:

> Liberty, as a principle, has no application to any state of things anterior to the time when mankind have become capable of being improved by free and equal discussion. Until then, there is nothing for them but implicit obedience to an Akbar or a Charlemagne, if they are so fortunate as to find one.[12]

Some of the readers of this chapter will share with me my utter dismay when, as an innocent undergraduate in Calcutta, I discovered that the author of the stirring declamation on the emancipation of women had, almost at the same time, emphatically announced that Indians were culturally unfit for representative government. It was divine providence, said Mill, that they had escaped their own home-grown barbarous despotisms and come under the enlightened absolutism of the British. 'Such is the ideal rule of a free people over a barbarous or semi-barbarous one.' The British must rule Indians (or Africans or indeed the Irish) until such time as they were mature enough to rule themselves.[13] I will not multiply the instances when this argument was employed to justify imperial domination in the 19th century. Uday Singh Mehta has usefully compiled a large catalogue in his book *Liberalism and Empire*.[14] These were arguments about empire as a moral paternalism.

This framework, I believe, continues to serve as the basic structure of justification for the new imperial interventions of the 21st century. It is used, as it was a hundred and fifty years ago, to persuade democratic opinion in the metropolitan countries – the political representatives, the press and those sections of the public that care about foreign affairs. Now, as then, executive decision-makers often find it exasperating that vital matters of foreign policy, defence and national security have to be discussed and defended before an uninformed and unpredictable public and their representatives. Hence, the moral and political justification of imperial policy is explicitly seen as an ideological cloak – 'spin', in today's language – made necessary by the demands of democratic politics, in order to conceal from the public the calculations of *realpolitik*.

Come to think of it, the two arguments about the relation between democracy and empire are as old as the history of democracy. The choice was always between two forms of control – a pedagogy of violence based on the demonstration of superior force and the right of conquest, and a pedagogy of culture based on exchange and economic benefit. Thucydides tells us of the debate in Athens between Cleon and Diodotus over what to do with the Mitylenians. The latter had shown signs of rebellion and the Athenians, in a fit of anger, had decided to put to death the entire adult male population of Mitylene and to make slaves of the women and children. But a few days later, there were appeals to reconsider this unusually harsh judgment. When the Athenian assembly seemed inclined to lessen the punishment, Cleon, 'the most violent man at Athens, and at that time by far the most powerful with the commons', berated the Athenians with the following words:

> I have often before now been convinced that a democracy is incapable of empire, and never more so than by your present change of mind in the matter of Mitylene. Fears or plots being unknown to you in your daily relations with each other, you feel just the same with regard to your allies, and never reflect that the mistakes into which you may be led by listening to their appeals, or by giving way to your own compassion, are full of danger to yourselves, and bring you no thanks for your weakness from your allies; entirely forgetting that your empire is a despotism and your subjects disaffected conspirators, whose obedience is ensured not by your suicidal concessions, but by the superiority given you by your own strength and not their loyalty.

Cleon maintained that the Mitylenians must be given an exemplary punishment to demonstrate to one and all that the penalty of rebellion was death. Diodotus, on the other hand, argued that 'the question before us as sensible men is not their (the Mitylenians') guilt, but our interests. Though I prove them ever so guilty, I shall not, therefore, advise their death, unless it be expedient; nor though they should have claims to indulgence, shall I recommend it, unless it be clearly for the good of the country . . . we are not in a court of justice, but in a political assembly; and the question is not justice, but how to make the Mitylenians useful to Athens.' He claimed that Athens would gain little by killing and enslaving an entire city; rather, there were many more profitable ways of holding a dependency.[15]

Similar arguments were repeated in the middle of the 19th century when the Indian kingdom of Awadh (the British called it Oude or Oudh) was sought to be annexed by the English East India Company. It was the last instance in which the strategy of direct occupation and annexation was exercised by the British in India. It is instructive to revisit the debates carried out at the time in British imperial circles in the context of the recent debates over the military occupation of Iraq.

Awadh at the end of the 18th century was a kingdom comprising the greater part of the Gangetic plains, roughly equal in size to and possibly greater in population than Great Britain. It had emerged as an independent principality through the 18th century with the decline of the Mughal empire. In the second half of the century, the British power had risen in Bengal in the east of India and expanded to the frontiers of Awadh in the north. The ruling Nawabs of Awadh were forced into various treaties with the British that allowed the East India Company special privileges in matters of trade and recruitment of soldiers to its army, but the sovereignty of Awadh was protected. In 1775, when the Nawab died, the British claimed new privileges. 'Assuming, with calculated cynicism,' as the British writer Michael Edwardes described the move, 'that the death of the Nawab cancelled the agreements entered into with him, the Calcutta Council (of the East Indian Company) insisted on negotiating a fresh treaty with his successor. By it, the Nawab became a puppet in the hands of the governor-general, and the state of Oudh a dependency of the East India Company.'[16] From this time, a British Resident was appointed to the court of Awadh to represent the supervisory authority of the Company. Awadh also became a substantial supplier of raw cotton, textiles, indigo and opium to British Bengal.[17]

In the early decades of the 19th century, Awadh was practically governed by a dual authority. The Nawab's administration was crippled by the constant interference of the British Resident. Most historians agree that under this 'system of meddling', the Nawab and his ministers were left with little initiative or responsibility: 'a corrupt administration was guaranteed by the presence of the Company's troops.'[18] It was later alleged that the Awadh rulers stopped ruling and retired into a life of wine, women and poetry. However, a modern historian writes: 'Indolence was the only appropriate response to the situation in which the princes of Oudh were placed: in which they could not be overthrown but could not act effectively in either the old way or the new.'[19]

It is necessary to point out here that there were at least two views within the British colonial establishment at this time on how best to pursue its imperial interests. One view thought it prudent not to interfere in the internal affairs of the subsidiary Indian allies, because that was both the letter and the spirit of the treaties that the British had signed with them, and also because constant interference tended to sour relations without bringing any permanent benefits. Lord Moira (later Lord Hastings), governor-general in 1813, reminded John Baillie, a particularly pushy and arrogant Resident in Awadh, that:

> The Resident should consider himself as the ambassador from the British government to an acknowledged sovereign; a respectful urbanity and a strict fulfilment of established ceremonials should thence be preserved by the Resident towards His Excellency.[20]

But the policy of non-interference also made the British presence in these dependencies utterly anomalous. British officers complained that the Company's troops were being asked to protect a corrupt and oppressive native administration; indeed, the British power was becoming an accomplice in the perpetration of countless crimes and immoralities. This view of the imperial mission was voiced with great fervour from the 1820s by a new liberal and evangelical movement.

The liberals had two main items on their agenda for the Indian Empire: the spread of English education among Indians and the opening of India to Christian missionaries. Originating in the so-called Clapham sect, formed around the radical abolitionist William Wilberforce, the liberals had powerful proponents within the Company establishment in officials such as Charles Grant, Thomas Macaulay and Charles Trevelyan. In their minds, the duties of evangelical Christianity were wonderfully married, in a blissful ménage à trois, to thriving commerce as well as to progressive social reform. As Grant put it:

> In considering the affairs of the world as under the control of the Supreme Disposer, and those distant territories . . . providentially put into our hands . . . is it not necessary to conclude that they were given to us, not merely that we might draw an annual profit from them, but that we might diffuse among their inhabitants, long sunk in darkness, vice and misery, the light and benign influence of the truth, the blessings of well-regulated society, the improvements and comforts of active industry? . . . In every progressive step of this work, we shall also serve the original design with which we visited India, that design still so important to this country – the extension of our commerce.[21]

The liberal programme achieved momentum in the period 1828–1835, when Lord William Bentinck was governor-general. Unlike other 19th-century imperialist heroes, Bentinck is not famous for any major military campaigns. Rather, he led the British power in India into an ambitious project of social reform by law and administration, most notably in the abolition of suttee.[22] By then, the liberal cause in India had been taken over by the Mills – father and son – who promoted a Benthamite utilitarian project of 'improving' India to a higher state of civilisation. At its core, therefore, the liberal vision was informed by a universalist idea of civilisation. As a recent historian has summed it up: 'Contemporary European, especially British, culture alone represented civilisation. No other cultures had any intrinsic validity. There was no such thing as "Western" civilisation; there existed only "civilisation".'[23] The evangelical tone was particularly prominent among the non-official British population of India – among merchants, missionaries and newspaper editors. In 1850, for instance, the *Delhi Gazette* put the following challenge to the government:

> What we contend for is, that our countrymen should either govern Oudh or abandon its rulers to their fate. As it is, we are powerless for good and unwilling accomplices in evil. We do infinite and perpetual wrong, because some of our nation in times past made treaties which it is immoral to observe.[24]

A little more than a year after the annexation – in May 1857 – all of northern India broke out in the most widespread and violent revolt in the history of British India. Awadh was at the centre of the revolt, locally led by one of the wives of the deposed king, various landlords and chiefs and a mysterious Islamic preacher.[25] For ten months, Lucknow, and much of the countryside around it, was in the hands of the rebels. Henry Lawrence, who had advised against annexation and was appointed to succeed Outram in Lucknow, died during a rebel attack on the besieged residency. Later, critics in the British Indian establishment would attribute the so-called Indian mutiny to the evangelical zeal of the liberals.[26] The second half of the 19th century in India was mostly dominated by a conservative colonial ideology that shied away from social intervention and preferred to rule through local chiefs and power brokers, anticipating the form of indirect rule that would become the theory of British colonialism in Africa.[27]

When imperialism became a matter of popular enthusiasm in Britain after the extension of the suffrage in the 1870s, it was Egypt and Africa that emerged as the new focus of attention.[28] Many of the strategic and moral arguments justifying the imperial project that would be used to mobilise democratic opinion had already been played out decades before in India.[29]

What is remarkable is how many of the same arguments, including the evangelical fervour, the axiomatic assumption of the mantle of civilisation, the fig-leaf of legalism, the intelligence reports, the forgeries and subterfuges and the hard-headed calculations of national interest, remain exactly the same at the beginning of the 21st century. Are we then in a new cycle of the age of empire? What is clear is that the formula 'democracy at home, despotism abroad' is perfectly applicable today in the context of realist discourses of national interest, that the liberal evangelical creed of taking democracy and human rights to backward cultures is still a potent ideological drive, and hence, that the instrumental use of that ideological rhetoric for realist imperialist ends is entirely available, as we have seen in Iraq. Eight months after the 'liberation' of Iraq, Lt. Col. Nathan Sassaman, a battalion commander in the US occupying forces, was reported as saying: 'With a heavy dose of fear and violence, and a lot of money for projects, I think we can convince these people that we are here to help them.'[30]

The question is: will the people of the occupied countries agree to the renewed state of colonial tutelage? The conditions in which this choice might be made have changed dramatically in the course of the 20th century. As I argued in the opening section of this chapter, the idea of popular sovereignty, whether transcendent and territorial or immanent and constitutive, is now virtually universal in the whole world. And despite the efforts of many recent critics to write its obituary, the nation continues to be the dominant political form in which this sovereignty is imagined by most people. The territorial definitions of the nation state may be contested, its internal structures of governance may be bitterly criticised and resented and, needless to say, could stray far from the standards of constitutional democracy. But even when the existing institutions of the nation state are pulverised into rubble by imperialist interventions, as in the continuing wars in Afghanistan since the 1980s and the wars and sanctions in Iraq since the 1990s, the immanent consciousness of popular sovereignty steadfastly rejects the claims of imperial benevolence and to uphold the axiomatic, even if imagined, legitimacy of national self-rule. This is a condition that was established in world history by the success of the anti-colonial movements in the 20th century and does not appear to have been supplanted by anything else.

The new question that arises is: what resources can democratic politics in the western countries mobilise to prevent a relapse into the 19th-century world of secret diplomacy and imperialist warfare cloaked by the hypocritical rhetoric of civilisation and moral virtue? It is a question about the intrinsic quality of western democracy as it actually exists today. It is a question that, ironically, is being asked by those people to whom the west professes to give lessons in democracy. The students are now shouting: 'Teacher, learn your own lessons first.' Whether the teachers will listen remains to be seen. That indeed may be the encounter that will define the history of the 21st century.

Notes

1   Michael Hardt and Antonio Negri, *Empire*, Harvard University Press, Cambridge, MA: 2000.
2   *Empire*, 160–82.
3   See in this connection the interesting discussion by Talal Asad of the effectiveness in the US political context of Martin Luther King's religious discourse of civil rights and the relative lack of success of Malcolm X's secular discourse of human rights. Talal Asad, *Formations of the Secular: Christianity, Islam, Modernity* (Stanford University Press, Stanford, 2003) 128–58.
4   *Empire*, 114–36.
5   I have culled the following facts from standard readings on globalisation, most usefully from Saskia Sassen, *Losing Control? Sovereignty in an Age of Globalisation* (University Press, New York: Columbia, 1996).
6   *Dictionary of National Biography, 1912–1921*, H.W.C. Davis and J.R.H. Weaver (eds) (Oxford University Press, London, 1927) 102–18.
7   Niall Ferguson, *Empire: The Rise and Demise of the British World Order and the Lessons for Global Power* (Basic Books, New York, 2002).
8   Wm Roger Louis and Ronald Robinson, 'The Imperialism of Decolonisation', *Journal of Imperial and Commonwealth History*, 22(3), 462–511.
9   David Harvey has hinted at this possibility in his recent book *The New Imperialism* (Oxford University Press, Oxford, 2003).
10   James Tully, *Strange Multiplicity: Constitutionalism in an Age of Diversity* (Cambridge University Press, Cambridge, 1995).
11   John Locke, *Two Treatises of Government*, Peter Laslett (ed.) (Cambridge University Press, Cambridge, 1988) 308.
12   John Stuart Mill, 'On Liberty' in A.D. Lindsay (ed.) *Utilitarianism, Liberty, Representative Government* (Dent, London, 1964) 73.
13   Chapter 18 of *Considerations on Representative Government* is entitled, 'Of the Government of Dependencies by a Free State', ibid, 376–93.
14   Uday Singh Mehta, *Liberalism and Empire: A Study in 19th-century British Liberal Thought* (University of Chicago Press, Chicago, 1999).
15   Thucydides, *History of the Peloponnesian War*, trans. Richard Crawley and J.M. Dent (London, 1993) 141–9.
16   Michael Edwardes, *The Orchid House: Splendours and Miseries of the Kingdom of Oudh, 1827–1857* (Cassell, London, 1960) 13.
17   P.J. Marshall, 'Economic and Political Expansion: The Case of Oudh', *Modern Asian Studies*, (1975), 9(4), 465–82.
18   Edwardes, *The Orchid House*, 21.
19   Thomas R. Metcalf, *Land, Landlords, and the British Raj: Northern India in the 19th century* (University of California Press, Berkeley, 1979) 40.
20   John Pemble, *The Raj, the Indian Mutiny and the Kingdom of Oudh 1801–1859* (Harvester Press, Sussex, 1977) 9.
21   Cited in Pemble, *The Raj*, 63.
22   Cited in Eric Stokes, *The English Utilitarians and India* (Clarendon Press, Oxford, 1959) 34.
23   For a study, see John Rosselli, *Lord William Bentinck: The Making of a Liberal Imperialist 1774–1839* (Thompson Press, Delhi, 1974).
24   Thomas R. Metcalfe, *Ideologies of the Raj: The New Cambridge History of India*, III 4, (Cambridge University Press, Cambridge, 1995) 34.
25   For a history, see Rudrangshu Mukherjee, *The Revolt in Awadh 1857–1858: A Study of Popular Resistance* (Oxford University Press, Delhi, 1984).
26   For a discussion, see Thomas R. Metcalf, *The Aftermath of Revolt: India 1857–1870* (Princeton University Press, Princeton, 1964).
27   See Mahmood Mamdani, *Citizen and Subject: Contemporary Africa and the Legacy of Late Colonialism* (Princeton University Press, Princeton, 1996).

28   See, for an interesting collection of essays, J.M. MacKenzie and Patrick Dunae (eds) *Imperialism and Popular Culture* (Manchester University Press, Manchester, 1984).

29   See, for instance, A.P. Thornton, *The Imperial Idea and Its Enemies: A Study in British Power* (Macmillan, London, 1959) and E.J. Hobsbawm, *The Age of Empire 1875–1914* (Weidenfeld and Nicolson, London, 1987).

30   Dexter Filkins, 'Tough New Tactics by US Tighten Grip on Iraq Towns', *The New York Times* (New York, December 7, 2003).

Index